VIETNAM WAR ALMANAC

VIETNAM WAR ALMANAC

HARRY G. SUMMERS, JR.
Colonel of Infantry

Facts On File Publications
New York, New York • Oxford, England

VIETNAM WAR ALMANAC

Library of Congress Cataloging in Publication Data

Summers, Harry G.
    The Vietnam war almanac.

    Includes index.
    Bibliography: p.
    1. Vietnamese Conflict, 1961-1975.   I. Title.
DS557.7.S94   1985   959.704'3   83-14054

ISBN 0-8160-1017-X (hc.)
ISBN 0-8160-1813-8 (pbk.)

Printed in the United States of America

10 9 8 7 6 5 4 3

In Honor of
General
FRED C. WEYAND
United States Army

Who brought the Armed Forces of the United States out of Vietnam—and out of the Vietnam war—in good military order, true to their oath to the Constitution and faithful to their commitment to the American people.

CONTENTS

PART I

THE SETTING

PART II

PART III

ACKNOWLEDGMENTS

This almanac was designed to accomplish one central purpose—to show the complexity and diversity of America's quarter-century involvement in Vietnam. From the arrival of the first American military mission to the Associated States of Indochina on September 17, 1950 until the last American military forces were heli-lifted from the roof of the U.S. embassy in Saigon on April 30, 1975, almost 3.5 million American soldiers, sailors, airmen, Marines and Coast Guardsmen served in Southeast Asia. And the war had a profound effect upon the way all Americans think of themselves and their nation, whether they actually served in Vietnam or not.

To accurately chronicle such a complex war would have been impossible without enormous help. The advice and support of those responsible for compiling the official military histories of the war—Dr. Jeffrey Greenhut and others at the Army's Center of Military History; Admiral John D. H. Kane, Jr., Director of Naval History, Dr. Richard H. Cohn, Chief of Air Force History, and Dr. Wayne W. Thompson in that office; Brigadier General Edwin H. Simmons, Director of Marine Corps History; and Vice Admiral B. L. Stabile, Vice Commandant of the Coast Guard—were invaluable.

An accurate portrayal of the Vietnam war requires the widest possible horizons, for even among those who served there, time and space circumscribed their vision. Those who served in the Mekong Delta in 1964 have an entirely different view of the "reality" of Vietnam than those who served in the A Shau Valley in 1968. Thus I owe a debt of thanks to my Army, Navy, Air Force, Marine and State Department students here at the Army War College whose diversified experiences in the Vietnam war made its totality more understandable. This understanding was enhanced by such fellow Army War College faculty members as Army Colonels Donald Lunday and Ralph Allen, Navy Captain Jack R. (Buzz) Greenwood, Air Force Colonel Edward B. White and Marine Colonels Donnal E. Hiltbrunner and Brian D. Moore as well as Visiting Professor John P. Lovell of Indiana University. Thanks also go to Colonel Rod Paschall, Director of the Army Military History Institute, and Michael J. Winey, Curator, for their assistance. Special thanks go to Miss Rita Rummel for spending her evenings and weekends preparing the many drafts of the manuscript.

Assistance was also received from Major Karen Laski, Office of the Secretary of the Army, in obtaining data on women in the military and from William Jayne of the Veterans Administration and Richard Kolb of the Vietnam Veterans Leadership Program, who provided detailed statistics on Vietnam war veterans. Also helpful were many Vietnam veterans groups, including the division associations of the Americal Division, the First Cavalry Division, First Infantry Division, Ninth Infantry Division, 25th Infantry Division and 101st Air Assault Division. Major Earl Tilford of the Air War College was most helpful in obtaining Air Force photographs; the information on the Viet Cong and the North Vietnamese provided by Professor Douglas Pike of the Center for IndoChina Studies at the University of California at Berkeley was invaluable, and Peter Braestrup, Editor of the *Wilson Quarterly,* and Robert V. Kane, Publisher of Presidio Press, also provided help and encouragement.

I especially want to thank retired Army Captain Shelby Stanton, an infantry and Special Forces veteran of Vietnam invalided for wounds, whose *Vietnam Order of Battle, The Rise and Fall of an American Army* and *Green Berets at War* were indispensable sources of factual information. His detailed review of the manuscript as well as the maps and photographs he so graciously provided added a major dimension to this work.

A final word of thanks to Mr. James Warren, Associate Editor of Facts On File Publications, who provided the initial inspiration for this work; to Joseph Reilly, Chief Copy Editor, for his assistance in making this almanac more readable as well as providing background material on non-military personalities; to Eleanora Schoenebaum, Editor, for supplying historical insights on the Vietnam era; and to my wife, Eloise, and our two sons, Captain Harry Glenn Summers, III, United States Army Reserve, and Captain David Cosgrove Summers, United States Army.

In expressing my thanks to those who provided comments and advice, I must add that the conclusions and such errors as this book contains are solely my responsibility.

H.G.S.
Carlisle Barracks, Pennsylvania
August 31, 1985

A NOTE TO THE READER

Statistics on various aspects of the Vietnam war have been compiled by many U.S. government agencies, the four U.S. armed services and numerous individual scholars. Even today, more than 10 years after the conclusion of the American military involvement in Southeast Asia, there remains disagreement on how to accurately measure such sensitive and controversial data as casualty figures, veterans affected by post-traumatic stress disorder and Agent Orange, minority participation in combat units and the like. In putting together the VIETNAM WAR ALMANAC, the statistics used were those which, given the information available as the book was being written, seemed most balanced and objective.

Entries in the book are alphabetized letter by letter to the end of the entry title without regard for punctuation. Thus NAVY CROSS comes before NAVY, U.S. and 196TH LIGHT INFANTRY BRIGADE comes before 173RD AIRBORNE BRIGADE. The field forces and the corps tactical zones are alphabetized as follows: I as *i*, II as *two*, III as *three* and IV as *four*.

Part I

the setting

MISPERCEPTIONS: THE ROOTS OF A TRAGEDY

ONE OF THE GREAT TRAGEDIES OF the Vietnam war is that although American armed forces defeated the North Vietnamese and Viet Cong in every major battle, the United States still suffered the greatest defeat in its history. A clue to how this could happen was provided by Sun Tzu, the famous Chinese strategist, over 2,500 years ago. "If you know . . . not the enemy," he wrote, "for every victory gained, you will suffer a defeat."[1]

The sad truth is that before the U.S. involvement began, Americans knew almost nothing about Vietnam. Although it had been discovered earlier, East Asia, including Southeast Asia, only fully entered Western consciousness in the 19th century as colonial empires began to blossom there. As a result, when the United States began to become concerned with Vietnamese affairs in the closing days of World War II, its maps did not even show the existence of a country called Vietnam. It was hidden under the label "French Indochina." The name "Indochina" itself was confusing, since it suggested that the area was simply an appendage of China. This misperception held at the very highest reaches. For example, at the Yalta Conference in early 1945, when the Allied powers were deciding the makeup of the postwar world, President Franklin D. Roosevelt asked General Chiang Kai-shek, China's leader, "Do you want Indo-China?" With full knowledge of Vietnamese history and tradition, Chiang replied: "We don't want it. They are not Chinese. They would not assimilate into the Chinese people."[2] The United States took 30 years and a bitter and divisive war to discover what Chiang Kai-shek then knew only too well.

The fact that Vietnam was part of the French colonial empire also obscured America's understanding. The French did not encourage foreign "meddling" in their affairs and there were few outside accounts of conditions in Vietnam. While scholarly literature on Vietnamese history, culture and tradition existed, it was almost entirely in French. It was not until 1958, well after the United States became involved, that the first English-language history of Vietnam, Joseph Buttinger's *The Smaller Dragon*, was published in the United States. As a result, there was an almost complete lack of knowledge—not only among the American people but in academia and government as well—about the geography, the history and the culture of Vietnam. As Sun Tzu had predicted, Americans would pay dearly for their ignorance.

Not only ignorance but America's essentially European cultural orientation as well played a part in its misunderstandings. Perhaps because Vietnam was located almost exactly halfway around the world from the United States in what to most was an obscure part of Asia, Americans tended to think of it as a "small country." But it is only a small country in the sense that Germany, with which the United States fought two World Wars, is a small country. In fact, Vietnam—North and South Vietnam combined—with a total land area of some 127,207 square miles, is only slightly smaller than the 137,836 square miles that

1. Sun Tzu, *The Art of War,* edited by James Clavell (New York: Delacorte Press, 1983), p. 18.

2. Clyde Edwin Pettit, *The Experts* (Secaucus, N.J.: Lyle Stuart, 1975), p. 13.

1

2 VIETNAM WAR ALMANAC

ASIAN COLONIAL EMPIRES

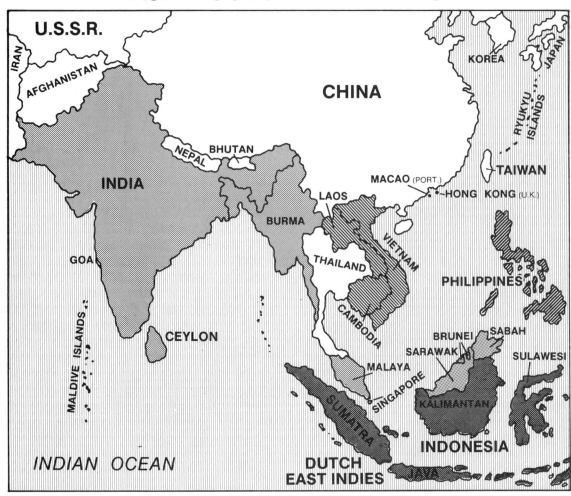

Independent countries, formerly dependencies of:

 UNITED KINGDOM   NETHERLANDS

FRANCE   SPAIN (U.S. after 1898)

comprise East and West Germany. Vietnam's coastline alone stretches for some 1,400 miles, longer than the coastline of California and roughly the Atlantic Coast distance between Boston and Miami. Nor is Vietnam a small country in terms of population. According to the latest Census Bureau figures, with a 1982 population estimated at 53,036,000 it now ranks 13th in the world, just behind West Germany but ahead of Italy, the United Kingdom and France.

Another misperception was that Vietnam was a "new" country. The French occupation and the general ignorance in America of Asian history combined to obscure the fact that Vietnam was one of the world's oldest nations. Its legendary past stretched back to the third millennium BC and its recorded history to 111 BC, a half century before the Roman legions landed on Great Britain's shores. While under Chinese domination for most of its early history, it won its independence in 946 AD, and except for a brief period of Chinese control from 1406 to 1426, Vietnam was an independent nation until the French conquest in the middle of the 19th century.

These and other misperceptions about Vietnam, rooted as they were in a lack of knowledge and understanding, proved in the end to be fatal. To discover why, this section of the book will detail the physical and historical realities of Vietnam and then analyze the significance of these realities in shaping American military and political operations.

THE PHYSICAL
REALITIES

I N TODAY'S WORLD, THE STUDY OF geography is considered somewhat quaint and old-fashioned. The idea has grown, even within the military, where "terrain" has been a concern, that modern technology has rendered geography unimportant. But the physical setting of a nation has enormous and far reaching consequences on the evolution of its culture, the pattern of its settlements and the development of its economy. This was particularly true in the case of South Vietnam.

South Vietnam, with an area of about 66,200 square miles, occupied the lower eastern extremity of the Southeast Asian peninsula. Lying entirely below the Tropic of Cancer, the area has a hot and humid climate. The monthly mean temperature is about 80°F, and the annual rainfall is consistently heavy. The monsoons, blowing generally from the south in the summer and from the north in the winter, profoundly influence the temperature and rainfall. The strength and direction of the wind, as well as the amount and timing of the rainfall, however, vary considerably from place to place.

In geographic terms, South Vietnam comprised three major regions: the Mekong Delta, the southern portions of the Chaîne Annamitique and the coastal enclaves. The Mekong Delta occupied the southern two-fifths of the country; its fertile alluvial plains, favored by heavy rainfall,

made it one of the great rice-growing areas of the world. The Chaîne Annamitique, with several high plateaus, dominated the area northward from the Mekong Delta to what during the war was called the Demilitarized Zone, or DMZ, between North and South Vietnam and extended into North Vietnam. The coastal enclaves consisted of fertile, narrow, coastal strips between the eastern slopes of the Chaîne Annamitique and the South China Sea.

The Mekong Delta was formed by the 2,800-mile-long Mekong River, one of the 12 great rivers of the world. From its source in the high plateau of Tibet, it flows through Tibet and China to the northern border of Laos. There it separates Burma from Laos and, farther downstream, Laos from Thailand. Flowing through Cambodia, it divides into several branches and begins to form a delta, the broad base of which is in Vietnam. In what was South Vietnam, the delta proper, approximately 26,000 square miles in area, forms a low, level and very fertile plain, nowhere more than 10 feet above sea level. In the mid-1960s, more than 9,000 square miles of delta land were under rice cultivation. So much sediment is brought to the sea that the coastline to the south has been advancing as much as 250 feet per year. Drainage is effected chiefly by tidal action, which differs greatly from place to place. The southernmost tip of the delta, the Ca Mau Peninsula, is covered with dense jungles and the shoreline with mangrove swamps.

The next major region, the Chaîne Annamitique, includes the southernmost spur of mountains originating in Tibet and China. The peaks of the Chaîne Annamitique range in height from about 5,000 feet to 8,521 feet. In South Vietnam they extended southeastward from the DMZ for some 750 miles—almost the entire length of the country. Terminating about 50 miles north of Saigon, this mountain chain formed the western border of South Vietnam, separating it from first Laos and then Cambodia. Irregular in height and form, the Chaîne Annamitique breaks off into numerous spurs, which divided South Vietnam's coastal strip into a series of enclaves and rendered north-south communication difficult.

In the middle of South Vietnam, the Chaîne Annamitique forms a plateau area, the Central

GEOGRAPHIC REGIONS

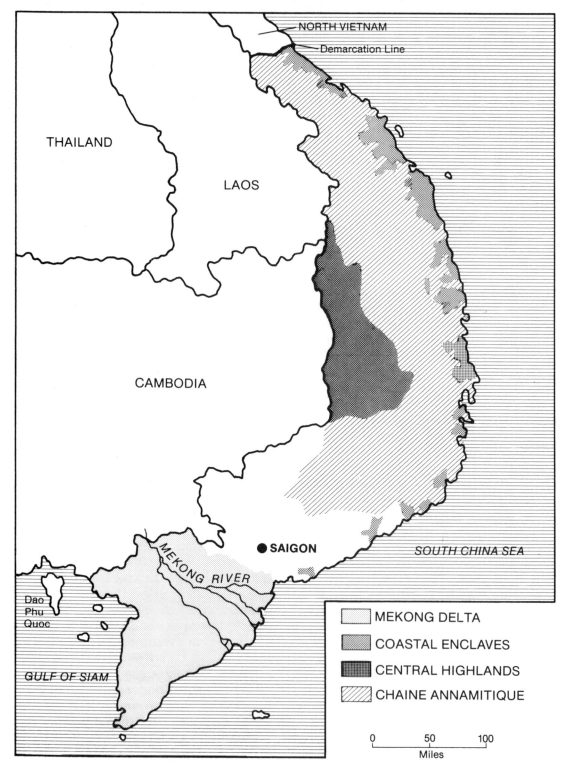

NORTH VIETNAM

Demarcation Line

THAILAND

LAOS

CAMBODIA

● SAIGON

SOUTH CHINA SEA

MEKONG RIVER

Dao
Phu
Quoc

GULF OF SIAM

MEKONG DELTA

COASTAL ENCLAVES

CENTRAL HIGHLANDS

CHAINE ANNAMITIQUE

0   50   100
Miles

Highlands, about 100 miles wide and 200 miles in length. A sparsely settled region covering approximately 20,000 square miles, the Central Highlands consists of two distinct parts. The northern part extends some 175 miles north from the vicinity of Ban Me Thuot. Irregular in shape, it varies in elevation from about 600 feet to 1,600 feet, with a few peaks rising much higher. This area of approximately 5,400 square miles is covered mainly with bamboo and tropical broadleaf forests interspersed with farms and rubber plantations. The southern portion of the Central Highlands, much of it over 3,000 feet above sea level, includes about 4,000 square miles of land suitable for growing coffee, tea, tobacco and certain vegetables. The forest growth is predominantly of broadleaf evergreens at higher elevations and bamboo on the lower slopes.

The third major region is a series of coastal enclaves, which in South Vietnam extended along the sea from the Mekong Delta northward to the DMZ. These enclaves are formed by the east-west spurs of the Chaîne Annamitique, which in some places lies nearly 40 miles inland from the South China Sea and in other places reaches to the shore of the sea. The result is occasional stretches of quite fertile low-lying land suitable for wetland rice cultivation. They begin about 100 miles north of the upper reaches of the Mekong Delta and continue along the entire coast. In South Vietnam the enclaves were most predominant along the central coastline, where it was possible to grow two rice crops a year.

Physical Realities and the Evolution of Culture

The physical realities of Vietnam described above had a major—some would say determining—influence on the evolution of Vietnamese culture. The north-south mountain ridges of the Chaîne Annamitique had the effect of turning Vietnam into a cultural peninsula. They blocked the eastward flow of Indian culture and encouraged the southward flow of Chinese culture, as the mountains protected and channeled the Vietnamese prehistoric migration from the southern part of China. Because of this mountain barrier,

Vietnam, alone among the nations of Southeast Asia, was primarily influenced by Chinese rather than Indian culture.

As a result, Chinese culture shaped Vietnamese language, writing, religion and political institutions. Like Chinese, the Vietnamese language is tonal—i.e., the meaning of words is changed by inflection, giving Vietnamese a sing-song character quite unlike Western languages. Vietnamese was written in Chinese characters, or ideographs, until the 17th century, when it was transcribed into the Roman alphabet by a French priest, Alexandre de Rhodes, who added a series of diacritical marks to the alphabet to indicate the five tones that characterize the Vietnamese language. A further tie with Chinese culture was through Mahayana Buddhism, which Vietnam shared with China, Korea and Japan. Preceding the Buddhist influence, however, and heavily influencing Vietnamese political institutions were Chinese Confucian political philosophies. As early as the first century, the Vietnamese had a sophisticated governmental structure and a civil service system based on the Chinese model, in which Mandarins (government officials) were selected through countrywide examinations.

The impact of Vietnam's physical realities on the development of its culture is apparent when the Vietnamese people are compared with the Burmese, Thai and Lao people, who, like the Vietnamese, originally migrated to the Southeast Asia peninsula from South China, pushing the original inhabitants, of Khmer, Australoid and Indonesian stock, before them into what is now Cambodia. In the first century Hindu princes from India had established kingdoms among these original inhabitants of Southeast Asia, and as the Burmese, Thai and Lao people migrated southward, they were heavily influenced by this Indian culture, which is especially apparent in their art, religions, and written languages. Hinayana rather than Mahayana Buddhism is their dominant religion, a form closer to Hindu roots. Their religious texts were written in the Pali script, which remains the basis of the written languages of Burma, Cambodia, Laos and Thailand.

This cultural heritage shaped the fundamental philosophies and attitudes of the Vietnamese people, just as Greek and Roman philosophies, the

Judeo-Christian ethic, the Magna Carta and the evolution of democratic systems in Great Britain and later in the United States shaped American political philosophies and attitudes. These differing cultural roots resulted in profound differences between the political philosophies and attitudes of the Vietnamese and those of Americans. For example, rather than the American notions of the loyal opposition and the peaceful transition of political power, the Vietnamese inherited from the Chinese the concept of the "mandate of heaven," under which a ruler governed by divine right and his subjects had an obligation to support and obey him. However, if the ruler lost the mandate of heaven, as evidenced by natural disorders or by political anarchy and chaos, the people also had a duty and a responsibility to change the mandate and install a new ruler. In fact, the very word for revolution in Vietnamese, *cach minh*, translates literally as "change the mandate." With such a traditional political and cultural philosophy, the communist models of the "dictatorship of the proletariat" and their hierarchical government structure of "democratic centralism" as well as the autocratic models of Ngo Dien Diem and others were closer attuned to Vietnamese historical values than were concepts of Western democracy. It can thus be argued that by ignoring these cultural and political realities and promoting its own model for the Republic of Vietnam (South Vietnam), the United States weakened and undermined the very government it was attempting to strengthen and support.

Physical Realities and Socioeconomic Development

Just as the Chaîne Annamitique influenced the evolution of Vietnamese culture, so the low-lying fertile plains along the coast influenced Vietnamese settlement patterns and economic development. Originally settling in the Red River Delta in North Vietnam (which still contains the bulk of the North Vietnamese population), the Vietnamese people moved gradually southward, establishing settlements in the fertile enclaves they found along the coast. It was not until the mid-18th century (about the time Americans were first pushing westward across the Appalachians into the Ohio Valley) that the Vietnamese reached their present limits on the southwestern edge of the Mekong Delta.

A comparison of the maps showing land utilization, ethnic distribution and population distribution indicates the profound effect of Vietnamese physical realities. It is apparent from these maps that the Vietnamese people settled primarily in the coastal enclaves and the Mekong Delta, where rice cultivation was possible, leaving the inland area to Vietnam's "indians," the Montagnard tribes (*see* entry on MONTAGNARDS in Part III) that are the remnants of the area's original inhabitants. It is also apparent that the coastal enclaves and the Mekong Delta contained the bulk of the population of South Vietnam.

Physical Realities and the Conduct of the War

One of the reasons the Vietnam war was difficult for most Americans to understand was that they unconsciously saw Vietnam as a microcosm of contemporary America. But given the physical realities of Vietnam, the war there would have been much more understandable if Vietnam had been compared not to the United States in the 20th century but to America as it existed in the 1750s during the French and Indian wars. At the time American settlers lived mostly on a narrow strip between the Atlantic and the foothills of the Appalachians. To the west were a series of outposts—Fort Pitt at the confluence of the Monongahela and the Allegheny, for instance, some 250 miles west of New York—built to protect settlements from attack by the French and their Indian allies.

Superimpose South Vietnam on the map and note that its coastline extends about the distance from Pittsburgh (Fort Pitt) to Savannah. Like early American settlers, the majority of the Vietnamese also lived in a narrow strip along the coast. In place of the Appalachians are the mountains of the Chaîne Annamitique. Beginning in the late 1950s, North Vietnamese military forces (like the French and Indians who threatened from Canada to the north and from the

CULTURAL INFLUENCES

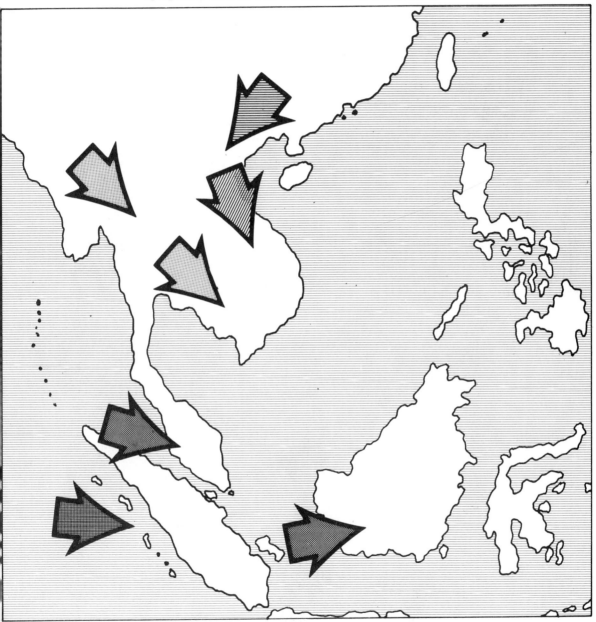

INDIAN CULTURE	**CHINESE CULTURE**	**ISLAMIC CULTURE**
Hinduism	Confucianism	Islamic Religion
Himayana Buddhism	Taoism	Jawi Script
Pali Script	Mayayana Buddhism	*To Indonesia,*
	Chinese Script	*South Philippines, Malaya*

LAND UTILIZATION

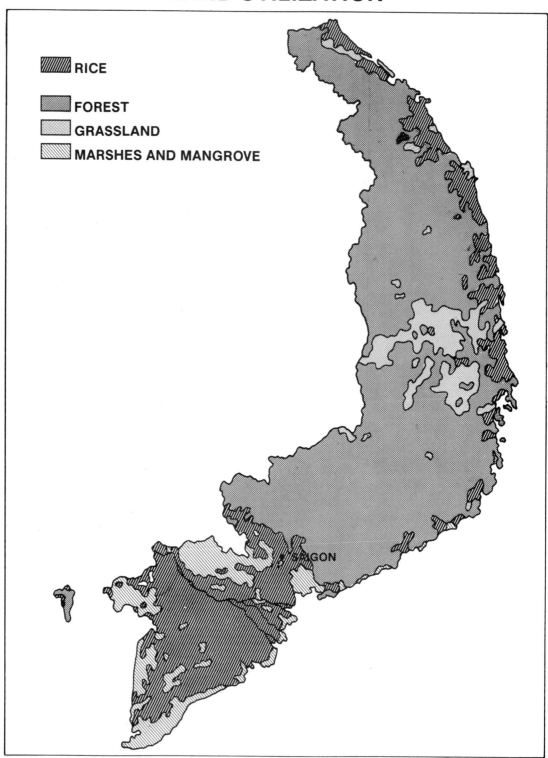

RICE

FOREST

GRASSLAND

MARSHES AND MANGROVE

SAIGON

Appalachians to the west) were poised to attack south from the DMZ and out of the west from the so-called Ho Chi Minh Trail (*see* entry on HO CHI MINH TRAIL in Part III) in supposedly neutral Laos and Cambodia. Given these socioeconomic realities, the proposals by some critics of American military strategy that U.S. forces be used to protect coastal enclaves (*see* entry on ENCLAVES in Part III) were more reasonable than they appeared to be at the time. The same realities also make more logical the ill-fated decision of the South Vietnamese government in the spring of 1975 to abandon the Central Highlands and concentrate its forces to protect the population centers (*see* entry on CENTRAL HIGHLANDS in Part III).

And in purely military terms, these physical realities gave the North Vietnamese the advantage of interior lines. To understand this important concept, visualize a long bow, with the Ho Chi Minh Trail representing the bow string and South Vietnam's north–south road nets representing the bow itself. By moving in a relatively straight line, North Vietnamese forces could move quickly to threaten almost any point in South Vietnam. By comparison, the South Vietnamese forces moving along the curvature of the bow were at an inherent disadvantage. These physical realities, however, were to a large degree canceled out by modern American military technology. By using their military airlift capabilities and taking advantage of the mobility afforded by helicopters, American forces could react more rapidly than could the North Vietnamese. But this advantage ended when U.S. forces withdrew in 1973. North Vietnam's use of interior lines played a major part in its successful 1975 campaign.

Earlier it was noted that even though American military doctrine traditionally emphasized terrain, i.e., physical realities, as one of the fundamentals of the military planning process, a fascination with modern technology during the Vietnam era caused this fundamental to be ignored. Use of air mobility to overcome the North Vietnamese advantage of interior lines did indeed give U.S. forces the ability to ignore terrain. But terrain cannot always be so safely ignored. A case in point was America's concern over possible Chinese intervention in the Vietnam war.

During the Korean war, when American forces approached China's northern border with North Korea in the fall of 1950, the United States was severely shaken by an unexpected and massive Chinese intervention. The "lesson" was drawn that the Chinese could be expected to react in a similar manner if their southern border with North Vietnam was threatened by an American invasion of that country. Missing from that analysis was the profound difference in the physical realities of the two borders. China's border with Korea is on the edge of a relatively flat and open area that has served as a traditional invasion route into the North China plain. From this direction China had been conquered time and again by such invaders as the Huns, the Mongols and the Manchus. It was to block this invasion route that the Chinese built the Great Wall over 2,000 years ago. China's southern border with Vietnam, on the other hand, has a natural "Great Wall," the mountains of South China, which severely restrict movement. Unlike the North China plain, where the majority of China's population is concentrated, the South China area adjacent to Vietnam is an autonomous region sparsely populated by non-Chinese tribes. Never in its long history has China been threatened by an invasion from this area. America's failure to appreciate these physical realities severely inhibited its political decisions as well as their supporting military strategies.

Suggestions for further reading: The most complete description of Vietnam's physical environment can be found in area handbooks prepared for the U.S. Army by researchers at the American University in Washington, D.C. The most recent editions are *Area Handbook for South Vietnam,* by Harvey H. Smith et al (Washington, D.C.: U.S. Government Printing Office, 1967) and *Area Handbook for North Vietnam,* by Harvey H. Smith et al (Washington, D.C.: U.S. Government Printing Office, 1967).

Particularly recommended for an understanding of Vietnamese cultural development is *The Vietnamese and Their Revolution,* by John T. McAlister and Paul Mus (New York: Harper & Row, 1970). Mus' *Viêt-Nam: Sociologie d'une guerre* (Paris: Editions du Seuil, 1950) is the landmark work in this area, and many of his insights are contained in the English-language work cited above. The opening chapters of Stanley Karnow's *Vietnam: A History* (New York: Viking, 1983) also contain accounts of Vietnamese cultural development, as does the first volume in the Boston Publishing Company's Vietnam series, Edward Doyle and Samuel Lipsman's *Setting the Stage*, The Vietnam Experience (Boston, 1981). See also *The Birth of Vietnam* by Keith Weller Taylor (Berkeley: University of California Press, 1983) and *Fire in the Lake*, by Frances FitzGerald (Boston: Atlantic-Little Brown, 1972).

HISTORICAL REALITIES

NOT ONLY DID THE UNITED STATES ignore the realities of Chinese border terrain on the conduct of the Vietnam war, it also ignored the history of Chinese-Vietnamese relations. This led the United States from the very beginning to see the North Vietnamese as military proxies of China. As early as the 1954 Geneva Conference, when the two Vietnams first came into being, the U.S. government operated under the fallacy that any extension of the area under North Vietnamese control would mean a dangerous enlargement of the area of China's effective power. Throughout the entire Vietnam war, the Chinese threat continued to be a dominant theme in the official justification of U.S. involvement.

Such a misunderstanding was the result of a gross lack of appreciation for Vietnamese history. This lack of appreciation, as noted earlier, derived from the fact that American impressions of East Asia had been formed in the 19th century, when East Asia first entered Western consciousness. Sinitic civilization, which centered on China but also included Korea and Vietnam, was then in one of its periodic declines. What was therefore not apparent was the ebb and flow of Chinese power that had shaped and determined East Asian history. Chinese civilization began in the North China plain, but it was only during the third century BC that the first great Chinese empire, the Han dynasty, which ruled from 207 BC until 220 AD, expanded into present-day China and into Korea and Vietnam. After a 400-year interregnum, another great empire, the T'ang dynasty, rose in 618 and again expanded Chinese power throughout East Asia. In 907 it, too, fell and China again disintegrated into contending states. Three hundred years later the invading Mongols established the Yuan dynasty, which again reunited China, only to be replaced in 1368 by the Ming dynasty, rulers of yet another great Chinese empire. The Ming dynasty was overthrown by the invading Manchus, who conquered China in 1644 and established the Ch'ing dynasty, which in its decline was "discovered" by the West in the mid-19th Century. Against this backdrop Vietnamese history developed.

The first historical records pertaining to the people in the Red River Delta were written by the Chinese after China's expansion southward from the North China plain in the third century BC. Still earlier Chinese accounts mention a Viet (Yüeh in Chinese) kingdom that existed about 500 BC south of the Yangtze River. This kingdom fell in 333 BC and its inhabitants, one of the many tribal peoples in southern China at the time, moved farther south. There emerged a number of small, competing states, which after 207 BC were united as the Kingdom of Nam ("Southern") Viet under a Chinese general. Nam Viet controlled the areas west of the present site of Canton and through the Red River Delta down to the coastal plain south of Hué.

In 111 BC the armies of the Chinese Han dynasty (202 BC–220 AD) overthrew the Kingdom of Nam Viet, marking the end of the legendary period of Vietnamese history. Nam Viet became Giao Chi, the southernmost Chinese province. An armed revolt in 39 AD led by two sisters, Trung Trac and Trung Nhi, briefly threw off the Chinese yoke. Defeated by the Chinese after a four-year joint rule, the Trung sisters drowned themselves rather than submit to foreign domination. In so doing, they became symbols of Vietnamese patriotism. For example, after South Vietnam gained independence, the South Vietnamese government named one of Saigon's main thoroughfares in their honor. Chinese domination survived the collapse of the Han dynasty in 220 AD and the ensuing period of confusion during which several anti-Chinese revolts were attempted by the Vietnamese. In 679 the Chinese

ETHNIC GROUPS

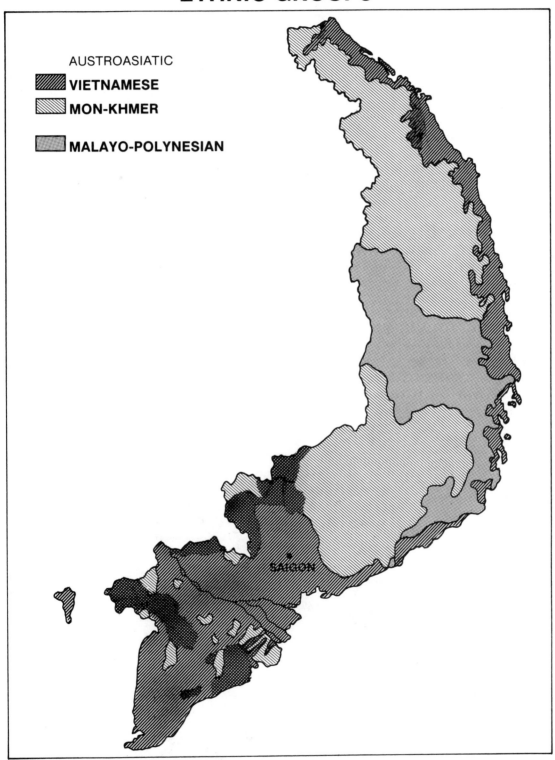

AUSTROASIATIC

VIETNAMESE

MON-KHMER

MALAYO-POLYNESIAN

SAIGON

POPULATION

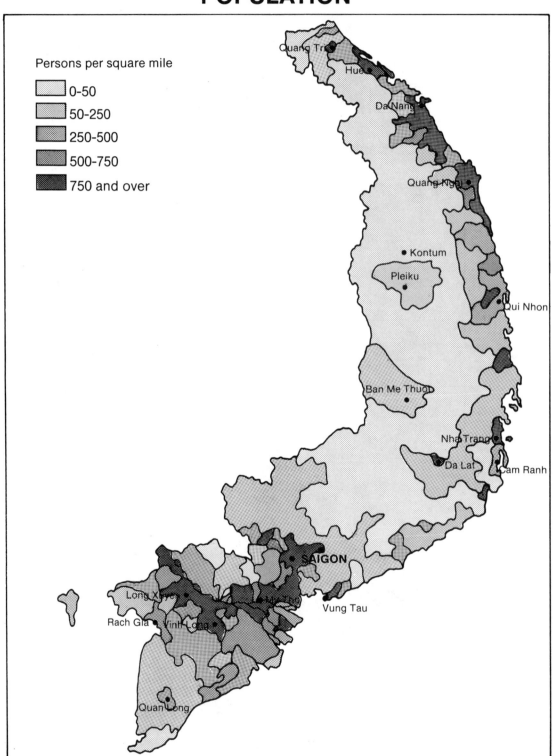

Persons per square mile

- 0-50
- 50-250
- 250-500
- 500-750
- 750 and over

Quang Tri
Hue
Da Nang
Quang Ngai
Kontum
Pleiku
Qui Nhon
Ban Me Thuot
Nha Trang
Da Lat
Cam Ranh
SAIGON
Long Xuyen
My Tho
Vung Tau
Rach Gia
Vinh Long
Quan Long

T'ang dynasty (618–907) made the province of Giao Chi a protectorate-general and renamed it Annam ("Pacified South"), a term still resented by the Vietnamese. Annam thrived; the population increased and culture was enriched under Buddhist influence, first introduced by a Chinese monk around 188 AD.

As the T'ang dynasty declined and finally disintegrated, the Vietnamese saw the chance they had long awaited. In 938 a Vietnamese General, Ngo Quyen, led a revolt, and in the Battle of Bach Dang his forces drove the occupying Chinese forces from the Red River Delta. He founded the short-lived Ngo dynasty. Chinese attempts to retake the Red River valley were repelled, and by 946 the first independent state of Vietnam had become a historical reality. With the exception of a 20-year interlude of Chinese reoccupation early in the 15th century, Vietnam remained independent for the next 900 years.

During the latter part of the 10th century, there were no less than a dozen autonomous local leaders in the Red River valley. One of them, Dinh Bo Linh, defeated his rivals in 968 and called his new state Dai Co Viet ("Great Viet State").

Aware of the superior power that China, even in one of its periods of disintegration, could bring against him, Dinh Bo Linh sent an embassy to the Chinese court requesting confirmation of his authority over Dai Co Viet. Vietnam thus became one of the subordinate suzerain states of the Imperial Chinese Empire, a relationship that was to continue until almost the beginning of the 20th century. In return for subscribing to the myth that the Vietnamese ruler served only at the pleasure of the Chinese emperor, a subservience acknowledged by periodic tributes, Vietnam received Chinese guarantees of political support and noninterference in domestic affairs.

While peace with China was thus maintained, relations with the Kingdom of Champa (192–1471) to the south were another matter. Under the influence of India and composed of non-Mongoloid peoples, Champa was not only a political threat but a cultural and ethnic threat as well. As a result, the two kingdoms were in frequent conflict.

The Dinh dynasty did not outlast its first emperor, who died in 980. It was succeeded by the Ly dynasty, established in 1009. The first of the great Vietnamese dynasties, the Ly rulers adopted the Confucian Chinese model, which gave the government the form it retained until the French conquest. The Ly dynasty created not only an efficient government but an efficient army as well. As a result, the Vietnamese not only repelled a Chinese invasion in 1076 but also held the aggressive Kingdom of Cambodia at bay and seized territory from the Kingdom of Champa, which then controlled territories corresponding roughly to the present coastal enclaves and Central Highlands. It was after one of the victories over Champa in 1069 that Thanh-Tong, the third Ly emperor and one of the greatest Vietnamese sovereigns, renamed the country Dai-Viet ("Greater Viet"). The country kept this name until 1802, when Emperor Gia Long changed it to Viet Nam. It was during the Ly dynasty that the Vietnamese version of America's western expansion—the expansionist policy of *nam-tien* ("the march to the south")—began in earnest, a policy that continued for the next 700 years until the southern tip of the Indochinese peninsula was wrested from Cambodia in 1780.

In 1225 the throne was seized by the Tran dynasty. It held power for 175 years of repeated military crises, including prolonged conflict with the Kingdom of Champa. Under Vietnamese General Tran Hung Dao, three invasions by the Mongol armies of Kublai Khan—in 1257, 1284 and 1287—were repelled, but following a pattern set 400 years earlier, the Tran monarch sent a mission to Kublai Khan after the Vietnamese victory and reestablished peace by making Vietnam a suzerain state of the Mongol Yuan dynasty.

In 1400 an ambitious regent, Ho Qui Ly, took advantage of economic and social crises following the devastation of the continuing wars with Champa to usurp the throne, thereby giving the Chinese Ming dynasty (1368–1662) the occasion to intervene on the pretext of restoring the Vietnamese Tran dynasty. Within a year of the Chinese invasion in 1406, Dai-Viet was again a province of China. The Ming were harsh overlords and their oppression sparked a Vietnamese national resistance movement led by Le Loi, an aristocratic landowner. Employing guerrilla tactics, he waged a 10-year fight against the Chinese, defeating them in 1427. Shortly after the Chinese left the country, he ascended the throne under the name of Le Thai To and founded the Le dynasty, which lasted for 360 years.

During the early years of this dynasty, Vietnam continued to develop, particularly under the leadership of Emperor Le Thanh-Tong. Tribute continued to be paid to the Chinese emperor and, as a result, relations with the Chinese were peaceful. At the same time, war was vigorously pursued against the Kingdom of Champa; when it was finally conquered in 1471, the majority of Champa territory was annexed. The remaining territory became a vassal state in tribute to Dai-Viet and was gradually absorbed into the Vietnamese state.

The historical precedent for the partition of Vietnam in 1954 dates back to about the time the first English colonies were established in America. In 1497, the powerful Le emperor, Le Thanh-Tong, died and the country fell into a period of decline. The throne was usurped in 1527 by a Vietnamese General, Mac Dang Dung, who attempted to form his own dynasty. This usurpation was short-lived, however, for in 1592 the nascent Mac dynasty was overthrown by the Trinh family, which ostensibly restored the Le dynasty by placing a Trinh puppet on the throne.

In the meantime, another family, the Nguyen, also claimed to have restored the Le dynasty and to that end had created a government-in-exile south of the 17th parallel (which after 1954 became the Demilitarized Zone between North and South Vietnam). As they waged war against each other, both the Trinh in the north, who controlled the Le emperors at this time, and the Nguyen in the south, who ruled as independent autocrats, claimed support of the Le emperor, the symbol of national unity, as justification for the legitimacy of their respective regimes. In 1673, after a half century of bloody and inconclusive fighting, the two sides concluded a truce, which for the first time divided Vietnam at the 17th parallel into two separate entities.

The 100 years of peace that followed brought a great cultural resurgence, especially to the north, where the Vietnamese civilization was well established. In the south, under the Nguyen, Vietnamese expansion was vigorously pursued. The remaining coastal territories of the Champa were gradually absorbed, and in the 17th and 18th centuries, a series of short but decisive wars were waged with the Cambodians, who then occupied the Mekong Delta and most of the south-central portion of the Indochinese peninsula. The acquisition of the vastly fertile Mekong Delta represented a gain of major proportion for the land-hungry Vietnamese. By the end of the 18th century, Vietnamese control extended to the limits of contemporary southern Vietnam.

After being divided into two nations for some 150 years, roughly the period from the landing of the Pilgrims at Plymouth Rock until the American Revolution, Vietnam was reunited in the late 1700s. Three brothers of a Nguyen family in the village of Tay Son in central Vietnam led an uprising against the ruling Nguyen (to whom they were not related) that gained widespread public support. By 1778 the oldest of the brothers, Nhac, had driven the Nguyen lords out of the south and proclaimed himself Emperor over southern Dai-Viet. The youngest brother, Hue, led an attack on the Trinh in the north, defeating them in 1786. In 1788, after abolishing the decrepit Le dynasty and repelling a Chinese invasion attempt, Hue extended his power to the south at the expense of his brother and made himself Emperor of a reunited Vietnam.

But Hue's rule was fated to be brief. Early in the Tay Son rebellion, Nguyen Anh, the last descendant of the southern Nguyen lords, escaped annihilation with the aid of a French missionary, Pigneau de Béhaine, Bishop of Adran, who had hopes of placing a Christian prince on the throne of Annam. After he failed in his attempt to gain official French government assistance and support, Pigneau privately organized a small force of Frenchmen to help Nguyen Anh. The bloody struggle that followed ended with the defeat of the last King of Tay Son in 1802 and the installation of Nguyen Anh as the Emperor Gia Long—Gia Long being the contraction of Gia Dinh (which later became Saigon) and Thanh Long (later Hanoi). With the founding of the Nguyen dynasty at Hué, the reunified country was renamed Vietnam ("the Viet of the South"). In 1803 the Emperor's authority was formally recognized by the Chinese Ch'ing dynasty, to

COMPARISON BETWEEN U.S. AND SOUTH VIETNAM

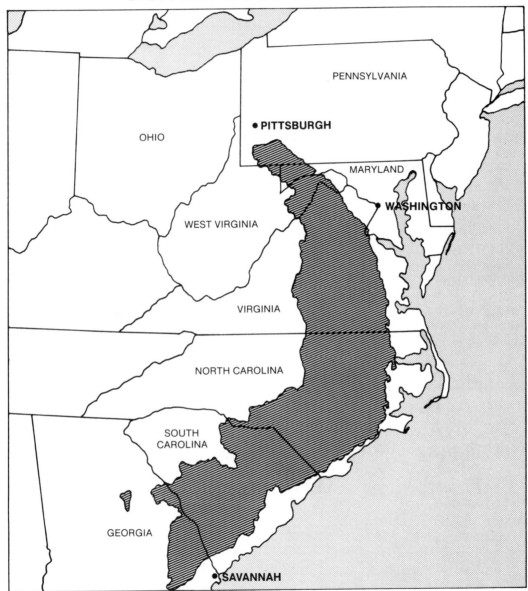

which Gia Long agreed to pay tribute biannually. The Nguyen dynasty lasted until the abdication of Bao Dai at the end of World War II.

Historical Realities and the Conduct of the War

As the above discussion makes clear, American notions that North Vietnam was a military proxy for China were absurd. While Vietnam had recognized Chinese suzerainty, it had fiercely protected its independence. A modern version of this relationship obtained during the Vietnam war, or Second Indochina War, for China's support of North Vietnamese efforts was purely a marriage of convenience. In historical terms, the "natural" state of Vietnamese-Chinese relations was best revealed in February 1979, four years after the end of the Vietnam war, when China launched an armed attack all along the Sino-Vietnamese border. While the fighting has stopped, hostility continues to this day (*see* entry on CHINA in Part III).

Suggestions for further reading: A concise history of the historical development of Vietnam is contained in the *Area Handbooks* (cited earlier). A more recent work, Stanley Karnow's *Vietnam: A History* (New York: Viking Press, 1983) also gives an excellent overview of this period, as does the first volume of the Boston Publishing Company's Vietnam series, Edward Doyle and Samuel Lipsman's *Setting the Stage*, The Vietnam Experience (Boston, 1981).

The landmark work, however, is Joseph Buttinger's *The Smaller Dragon: A Political History of Vietnam* (New York: Praeger, 1958), which contains voluminous notes on additional sources. An abridged version appears in Buttinger's *Vietnam: A Political History* (New York: Praeger, 1968).

THE FRENCH OCCUPATION: TONKIN, ANNAM AND COCHIN CHINA

WHILE EMPEROR GIA LONG RE-united the country, his acceptance of French help to gain power was a fatal step. He had unwittingly opened the way for the French conquest of Vietnam.

Although as early as the 14th century Western travelers, such as Marco Polo, had visited East Asia, it was not until the 1500s that contacts began in earnest when Portuguese, Dutch, English and French traders began to establish commercial footholds in the area. By the middle of the 19th century, these sporadic contacts had led to the establishment of European colonial empires that spread from India to Indochina and finally to China itself. Great Britain established colonial empires in India, Burma and Malaysia and the Dutch established a colonial empire, known as the Dutch East Indies, in Indonesia. China itself came under attack from Great Britain in the so-called Opium Wars from 1839 to 1842.

Not to be outdone, France decided to establish its own colonial empire on the Southeast Asian peninsula. Using the pretext of protecting its missionaries, France's conquest began in September 1857 with the decision to capture Da Nang. The city fell in 1858 and the French thereafter turned their attention to the south. Inflicting heavy losses on the Vietnamese, they took Saigon by July 1861. In June 1862 the Vietnamese court at Hué ceded Saigon and the adjacent area to France and agreed to pay a war indemnity. They also promised not to cede territory to any other power without French permission. The western part of the southern delta, which was virtually cut off from the rest of Vietnam, was annexed by France in 1867, thus completing the territorial formation of what later became the French colony of Cochin China.

The French next turned their attention to the Red River Delta in North Vietnam and in 1883 an expeditionary force brought this area under French control. French protectorates were established over northern Vietnam (Tonkin) and central Vietnam (Annam); all of southern Vietnam (Cochin China) had been in French hands since its conquest in 1867. Now, with the end of what was left of the country's independence, the name "Vietnam" was officially eliminated. In Annam the Emperor and his officials were left in charge of internal affairs except for customs and public works, but they functioned under the eye of the French, who had the right to station troops in the area. The protectorate over Tonkin made few concessions to the appearance of autonomy and French resident officers in the larger towns directly controlled their administration.

These developments did not go unchallenged. The Chinese denied the validity of treaties made between the Vietnamese and the French without Chinese approval, but a Chinese force sent in to expel the invaders was defeated by the French and in 1885 China formally recognized the French Protectorate over Tonkin and Annam. The French found the Vietnamese more difficult to cope with. Beginning in 1885, under the 12-year-old Emperor

HO CHI MINH TRAIL

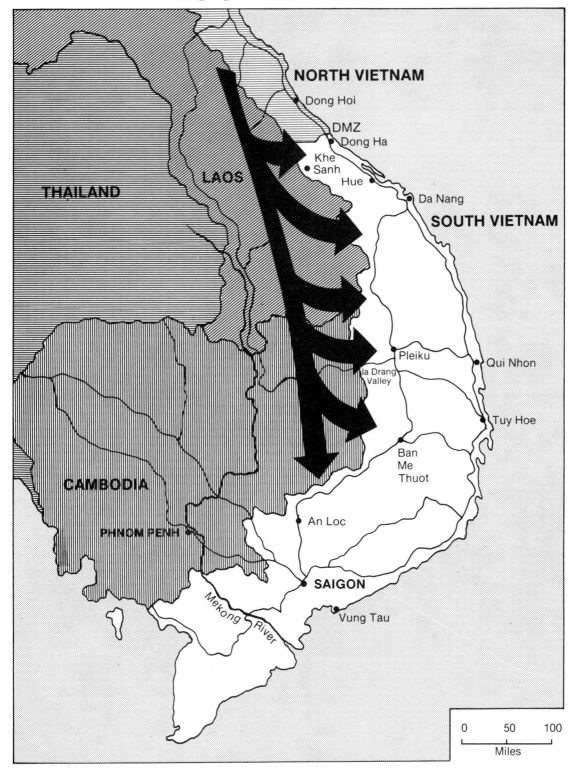

FOURTEENTH CENTURY VIETNAM

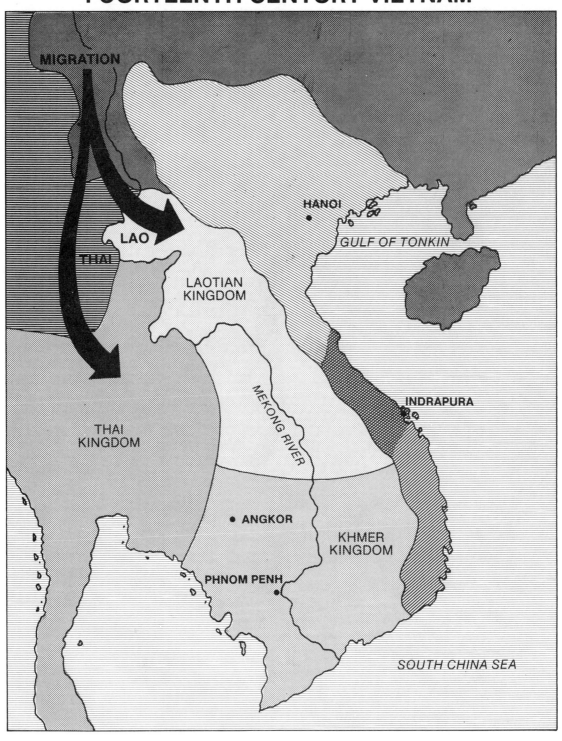

Ham Nghi, a general uprising broke out against the French. It failed and Ham Nghi was exiled in 1888. Active armed resistance continued into the early 20th century but was unsuccessful, largely because the movements were localized and made no systematic attempts to arouse popular nationalist sentiments.

The final phase of French consolidation was marked by the formation of an Indochinese Union in 1887. Consisting of Tonkin, Annam, Cochin China and Cambodia (a French protectorate since 1863), the Union was administered under a French governor-general, who was responsible directly to the Ministry of Colonies in Paris. In 1893 Laos, following annexation by France, was also added to the Union.

French influence permeated nearly all walks of Vietnamese society. As a direct consequence, aspiring Vietnamese turned to Western-type, rather than Chinese-type, schooling, traditionally the most important means for the attainment of power and wealth. This shift exposed educated Vietnamese to liberal and radical political ideals of the West, stimulating them to question the capability of their Confucian-oriented social order to withstand new challenges from the West.

Throughout East Asia attempts were made to turn back this Western invasion. These movements gained impetus after Japan's victory over Russia in 1905 and acquired further strength during World War I, when President Woodrow Wilson's concept of self-determination gained a widespread following. In China, and in Vietnam as well, "Mr. Science" and "Mr. Technology" were advanced as the models to be used in reversing the Western tide. But when President Wilson's ideas were disregarded by the framers of the 1919 Treaty of Versailles, many Chinese and Vietnamese seeking change turned to the model of the successful 1917 Russian Revolution. Among those attracted by this new Marxist-Leninist model was Ho Chi Minh (see entry on HO CHI MINH in Part III).

Within Vietnam numerous anti-French secret societies sprang up and in 1930 an uprising was staged at Yen Bay, northwest of Hanoi. Severely repressed by the French, this nationalist movement was forced underground and came under the control of the Indo-Chinese Communist Party. Some nationalists, including Ngo Dinh Diem (see entry on NGO DINH DIEM in Part III) believed that Emperor Bao Dai, who had returned to Vietnam in 1932 after being educated in France, offered a more peaceful solution to Vietnam's problems. It soon became obvious, however, that the French had no intention of granting real power to Bao Dai or his government and these "legitimate" attempts to gain power withered away.

World War II was to break the French hold on Vietnam. After the fall of France in June 1940, the Vichy government acceded to Japanese demands in Southeast Asia, which ultimately led to Japanese control over all of the French Indochina peninsula. In August 1940 the Vichy authorities agreed to accept Japan's "preeminent" position in the Far East and to grant the Japanese certain transit facilities in Tonkin in return for recognition of French sovereignty over Indochina. Under this accord the French colonial administration structure was kept intact, and the French community maintained its privileged position with little change to indicate to the population the eclipse of French power in Indochina. This arrangement gave the Japanese the benefit of the services of the French officials and freed Japanese personnel for duties elsewhere. There were clashes between Japanese and French forces along the northern border of Tonkin, and Japanese aircraft bombed the port of Haiphong. But after the Vichy government had agreed, in September 1940, to the stationing of Japanese troops on the northern side of the Red River, the French troops offered no further military opposition and continued their traditional garrison duties.

Japan's position was further consolidated in July 1941, when the French and Japanese governments signed a military agreement providing for the "common defense of French Indochina," under which Japan was permitted to station troops in southern Indochina. The agreement also enabled Japan to control virtually all airfields in the south and important port facilities and railroads elsewhere. Immediately after Japan's attack on Pearl Harbor, the French made another agreement reaffirming the existing Franco-Japanese pledge of cooperation, and this uneasy relationship continued until the Japanese coup d'état in March 1945. In the meantime, a Vietnamese resistance movement began against both the Japanese and the French. This resistance was aided by the Office of Strategic Services (OSS), which made contact with Ho Chi Minh, one of the guerrilla leaders, in early 1945 (see entry on CIA [CENTRAL INTELLIGENCE AGENCY] and HO CHI MINH in Part III).

In September 1944 the Tokyo government, alarmed over growing indications of anti-Japanese activities in Vietnam, decided to displace the French and grant independence to the Vietnamese. Initially, this plan was to be executed on April 25, 1945, but the reoccupation of the Philippine Islands by U.S. forces in October and the growing awareness that Japan was losing the war advanced the date of the Japanese coup to March 9, 1945.

At the instigation of the Japanese, Emperor Bao Dai proclaimed the independence of Vietnam under Japanese "protection." He formed a new government at Hué, proclaimed a political amnesty and attempted to create a Vietnamese administration to replace the ousted French administration. Meanwhile, in Hanoi, the Viet Minh, portraying themselves as a strong nationalist movement that enjoyed the support of the soon to be victorious Allies, announced the formation of a Committee for the Liberation of the Vietnamese People, with Ho Chi Minh as President.

Bao Dai, apparently convinced that a united and independent nation offered the only possibility of preventing the return of French control, decided to abdicate. Recognizing only the nationalist character of the Viet Minh movement and assuming that it had Allied support, he abdicated in its favor on August 25, 1945 and handed over his imperial seal and other symbols of office to Ho Chi Minh, becoming a high counselor to the new government. To the overwhelming majority of the people this clearly meant that Ho Chi Minh had won "the mandate" and that therefore he had the legitimate right to rule.

On September 2 Ho Chi Minh formally proclaimed the independence of Vietnam and the establishment of the Democratic Republic of Vietnam. To facilitate gaining international recognition of the new government's legitimacy, communist domination of the government was carefully concealed and emphasis placed on the "democratic," Vietnamese character of the regime

The French Occupation and the American Conduct of the Vietnam War

The almost 100 years of French occupation of Vietnam and the partition of the nation into three parts had a profound effect on Vietnamese attitudes. This period of occupation strengthened the Vietnamese people's awareness of themselves as a distinct and homogeneous people and strengthened Vietnamese xenophobia. But it also exacerbated regional differences. Much has been made of the force of Vietnamese nationalism as a potent factor in the Vietnam war. But this nationalism had been shaped by historical realities. As noted earlier, before the French occupation Vietnam had been reunited for only about 70 years after its 150-year division under the Trinh and Nguyen dynasties, and then it was again divided for some 70 years by the French partition of the country into Tonkin, Annam and Cochin China. While united by a common language and common heritage, there were significant regional differences. As recently as 1981, American visitors to Vietnam found that southern animosity toward northerners remained strong, even among former Viet Cong. Critics of the Vietnam war have argued that the north–south partition of Vietnam was "unnatural," but it was not unnatural in light of Vietnamese history.

Suggestions for further reading: A concise history of the French colonial period is contained in the *Area Handbooks* (cited earlier). A more recent work, Stanley Karnow's *Vietnam: A History* (New York: Viking Press, 1983) also gives an excellent overview of this period as does the first volume of the Boston Publishing Company's Vietnam series, Edward Doyle and Samuel Lipsman's *Setting the Stage*, The Vietnam Experience (Boston, 1981).

The landmark work, however, remains the first volume of Joseph Buttinger's *Vietnam: A Dragon Embattled* (New York: Praeger, 1967), which not only provides a thorough analysis but also contains voluminous notes on additional sources. An abridged version appears in Buttinger's *Vietnam: A Political History* (New York: Praeger, 1968).

FRENCH INDOCHINA

Other works include John Cady's *The Roots of French Imperialism in Indochina* (Ithaca: Cornell University Press, 1954); David G. Marr's *Vietnamese Anticolonialism 1885–1925* (Berkeley: University of California Press, 1971) and *Vietnamese Tradition on Trial* (Berkeley: University of California Press, 1981); and Ngo Vinh Long's *Before the Revolution: The Vietnamese Peasants under the French* (Cambridge: MIT Press, 1973).

THE FIRST INDOCHINA WAR

AFTER WORLD WAR II THE VIETnamese expected the Allies to support their claims to independence. China, which had traditionally seen itself as Vietnam's "protector," opposed the return of France to Indochina. As an anticolonialist nation, the United States in principle favored the formation of a provisional international trusteeship for Vietnam. As a result, the question of whether France would be allowed to repossess its "colonies" was deliberately kept ambiguous at the Potsdam Conference of July 1945. The Allies agreed that the British were to accept the surrender of the Japanese south of the 16th parallel, and the Chinese would perform a similar duty north of the 16th. Ten days after the first British troops arrived in Saigon on September 12, 1945, the British, concerned about preserving their own Asia colonial empire, permitted French troops to come ashore. Almost immediately the Vietnamese rose up in defense of their newly won freedom. The British not only assisted the French but also rearmed Japanese troops to help put down the resistance. By the end of November, all strategic points within Cochin China had been taken. But resistance in the south did not cease; guerrilla forces were organized and continued to clash with French units.

In the meantime, the Chinese forces occupying the north during the fall of 1945 found that the Viet Minh regime was willing to cooperate. The Indo-Chinese Communist Party had ostensibly been dissolved in November 1945, and elections were held in January 1946 for a national assembly, which formed a nationalist coalition government headed by Ho Chi Minh. But like the British in the south, the Chinese were concerned with their own interests, not those of the Vietnamese. In February 1946 a Franco-Chinese agreement allowed the return of the French to Indochina in exchange for various concessions, including France's surrender of its extraterritorial rights in China. Because the United States, too, was concerned with its own interests—primarily shoring up France to resist Soviet pressure in Europe—it acquiesced in France's return to its Indochinese empire. Faced with the loss of outside support, the Viet Minh were forced to reconsider their policy toward the French.

In March 1946 the French government and Ho Chi Minh signed an agreement by which the Democratic Republic of Vietnam was recognized as a "free state" within the Indochinese Federation (yet to be created) and the French Union. The new state, which was not precisely defined in the agreement, was interpreted by the Vietnamese as consisting of Tonkin, Annam and Cochin China (in Vietnamese, "Bac-bo," "Trung-bo" and "Nam-bo"). Vietnam was to have its own national assembly, manage its own finances and maintain its own army. The French, however, did not appear to imply recognition of any single government to rule the three regions, and details of the new state's relationship to France remained to be decided.

As a result of this agreement, French forces were permitted to land in the north. Bao Dai, who had been acting as high counselor to Ho Chi Minh, was sent on a "goodwill" mission to China, where he remained in exile, thus eliminating the possibility that he might provide a rallying point for groups not completely aligned with the Viet Minh.

Differences between the French government and the Democratic Republic of Vietnam immediately developed over the question of defining the "free state." A delegation of Vietnamese representatives, headed by Ho Chi Minh, traveled to Paris to settle the differences. Although initially derailed in early June 1946, when a Republic of Cochin China was established in the south under the support of separatist French elements, the Paris conference concluded in September 1946 when Ho Chi Minh signed an agreement designed to facilitate the resumption of French economic and cultural activities in return for French promises to introduce a more liberal regime. This agreement did not include recognition of Vietnamese unity or independence and was opposed by many within Ho Chi Minh's regime. French actions to enforce customs controls in October 1946 aroused further hostility. In November 1946 shooting broke out in Haiphong, and subsequent bombardment of the city by the French reportedly killed more than 6,000 Vietnamese.

The French demands that followed were so completely unacceptable to the Democratic Republic of Vietnam that it decided to go to war rather than to accept them. On December 19, 1946, with the support of the majority of the Vietnamese people, the Viet Minh launched their first attack on the French in what came to be known as the First Indochina War, a war that was to last for the next eight years.

In the early months of 1947, the French military forces reestablished their control over the principal towns in Tonkin and Annam and cleared the road between Haiphong and Hanoi. This forced the Viet Minh to resort to the guerrilla tactics that became the chief characteristic of the war. Ho Chi Minh's armed forces made use of the jungle to neutralize French mechanized mobility and firepower. By selecting their objectives and retiring when they met superior strength, they presented a problem with which the French could not cope. After three years of fighting, the Viet Minh controlled large areas throughout the country, while the French controlled only the large cities.

During this period two Vietnamese "governments" emerged, both competing for popular support. First was Ho Chi Minh's "Democratic Republic" of Vietnam (DRV). The other was what became the "Republic" of Vietnam (RVN). Early in the struggle the French sought to encourage the Vietnamese anti-Communist nationalists to take a stand against the Viet Minh and to cooperate with them, but the effort failed as the nationalists claimed the French would not clarify their policy with respect to future Vietnamese unity and independence. It was not until June 1949 that France finally approved limited independence for "the State of Vietnam" within the French Union. Bao Dai assumed the role of chief of state, but the principal nationalists, including Ngo Dinh Diem, failed to unite behind him, since they claimed that the French did not offer real independence. Although the new government was permitted internal autonomy and an army of its own, strong safeguards to protect French nationals and economic interests were maintained, and the foreign policy of the new state was coordinated with that of France.

After the communists defeated the nationalists in China in late 1949, China became the first state to recognize the DRV in North Vietnam as the legitimate government of all Vietnam. Soviet-bloc countries quickly followed suit. In early 1950, after North Vietnam began to receive assistance from China, offensive action was initiated against French Union forces, which were composed of French and Vietnamese soldiers. In the meantime, Ho Chi Minh rid his coalition government of moderates and nationalists whom he had accepted earlier, and showed himself to be completely communist. In March 1951 the Indo-Chinese Communist Party, which had been dissolved in 1945, was revived as the Workers Party, or Lac Dong.

In February 1950 Great Britain and the United States recognized the State of Vietnam headed by the former Emperor Bao Dai as the legitimate government. When France concluded agreements with Laos and Cambodia similar to that which it had with Vietnam, the three countries became the Associated States of Indochina and were accorded diplomatic recognition by more than 30 other nations. In May 1950 the United States announced a decision to give aid to Bao Dai through France, and a U.S. economic mission arrived in Saigon. In September 1951 American and Vietnamese representatives signed an agreement that provided for direct U.S. economic assistance. In 1951 the advance of the communist forces was temporarily halted with the aid of American equipment, but in 1952 the communists started a new offensive in several areas. Vigorous counterattacks brought no decisive results, and a military stalemate followed.

While the military battle was raging, steps were

being taken to bring a negotiated end to the First Indochina War. France's ability to continue the war was weakening, and Ho Chi Minh, under apparent Sino-Soviet pressure, had let it be known that he was ready to discuss peace. In February 1954 the Big Four powers (France, Great Britain, the Soviet Union and the United States) agreed that a conference should be held to seek a solution for the Indochina War and Korea (*see* entry on GENEVA CONFERENCES in Part III).

On April 28, 1954, two days after the opening of the conference at Geneva, a Franco-Vietnamese declaration, proclaiming Vietnam to be unequivocally sovereign and independent, was made public. It was only after May 8, however, that the conference began focusing its attention primarily on Indochina. The immediate cause was the decisive French defeat at Dien Bien Phu (*see* entry on DIEN BIEN PHU in Part III) by Viet Minh forces on May 7 and the resultant public pressure in France for a rapid conclusion of the war. The Indochinese phase of the conference was attended, under the cochairmanship of Great Britain and the Soviet Union, by representatives of the United States, France, the United Kingdom, the Soviet Union, China, the State of Vietnam, the Democratic Republic of Vietnam, Cambodia and Laos.

Final negotiations for an armistice were conducted directly between the French High Command and the Viet Minh People's Army High Command. The First Indochina War came to an end when the two high commands signed a truce agreement covering the territory of both North and South Vietnam on July 20. Separate truce agreements were also concluded for Cambodia and Laos, respectively.

The First Indochina War and the American Conduct of the Vietnam War

Although over a decade would elapse between the end of the First Indochina War and the massive commitment of ground combat forces by the United States to support its South Vietnamese ally during the Second Indochina War, this period had a profound effect on American conduct of the war.

First, from a strategic point of view, Vietnam became important to the United States not because of itself but because of larger global strategic interests. As already noted, the United States acquiesced in France's return to Indochina after World War II because of its concern for French stability in Europe and French support against the growing Soviet threat there. Further, as the war in Vietnam began to escalate, the United States increased its involvement because it saw the Viet Minh struggle as part of a worldwide attempt by "monolithic world communism" orchestrated by Moscow to extend its influence by force of arms, a misperception reinforced by the North Korean attack on South Korea in June 1950. As a direct consequence of that attack, on September 17, 1950 the United States established the Military Assistance Advisory Group-Indochina to provide military aid through the French to Laos, Vietnam and Cambodia. Many Vietnamese nationalists consequently identified the United States with their French colonial oppressors, a viewpoint that North Vietnamese propaganda was to exploit throughout the Second Indochina War—the Vietnam war.

Perhaps even more damaging was that the United States assumed the paternalistic attitudes of its French ally, seeing Vietnam not as an equal sovereign state but as a dependency that had to be nurtured and protected.

Suggestions for further reading: A concise history of the French colonial period is contained in the *Area Handbooks* (cited earlier). A more recent work, Stanley Karnow's *Vietnam: A History* (New York: Viking Press, 1983) also gives an excellent overview of this period, as does Edward Doyle, Samuel Lipsman and Stephen Weiss's *The Vietnam Experience: Passing the Torch* (Boston: Boston Publishing Co., 1981).

The landmark work, however, remains the second volume of Joseph Buttinger's *Vietnam: A Dragon Embattled* (New York: Praeger, 1967), which not only provides a thorough analysis but also contains voluminous notes on additional sources. An abridged version appears in Buttinger's *Vietnam: A Political History* (New York: Praeger, 1968).

Other works include Bernard Fall's *Street Without Joy: Insurgency in Vietnam, 1946-1963* (Harrisburg, Pa.: Stackpole Books, 1961) and his earlier *The Viet Minh Regime* (Ithaca, N.Y.: Cornell University

Press, 1956); and Edgar O'Ballance's *The Indochina War 1945–1954: A Study in Guerrilla Warfare* (London: Faber & Faber, 1964).

THE REPUBLIC OF VIETNAM

ALTHOUGH THE REPUBLIC OF VIETnam came into being as a result of the armistice that ended the First Indochina War and the agreements reached at the Geneva Conference, it is important to note that it was not a party to those agreements.

The Geneva Conference agreement for Vietnam fixed a provisional military demarcation line, later known as the Demilitarized Zone (DMZ), roughly along the 17th parallel. North of the 17th parallel the agreement provided for the total evacuation of the military forces of France and the State of Vietnam, and south of the 17th it allowed the evacuation of the Viet Minh forces (*see* entry on DMZ [DEMILITARIZED ZONE] in Part III). For a period of 300 days freedom of movement was to be allowed for all persons wishing to move from one sector to the other, and in the months that followed some 900,000 refugees, mainly Roman Catholics, fled to the south. In addition to the agreement, a Final Declaration of the Geneva Conference, dated July 21, called for general elections to be held throughout North and South Vietnam in July 1956 under the supervision of the International Control Commission, with preliminary discussions concerning the elections to begin in July 1955 (*see* entry on ELECTIONS in Part III).

The State of Vietnam, which did not sign the agreements, vainly protested the manner in which the truce was arranged, as well as its terms, particularly those relating to the partitioning of the country. It demanded that the whole country be placed under the control of the United Nations until conditions warranted the holding of free general elections. It also objected to the Final Declaration, protesting that the French High Command arrogated to itself, without prior consultation with the State of Vietnam, the right to fix the date for elections.

While the government of Ho Chi Minh, seated at Hanoi, moved steadily to achieve its program of communization north of the 17th parallel, France transferred the remnants of its administration and military control to the State of Vietnam, with its capital at Saigon. Shortly before the end of the Geneva Conference, Bao Dai, as chief of state, had called on Ngo Dinh Diem to form a new government. Ngo Dinh Diem became Prime Minister of the new government, which was formed on July 7, 1954, but almost immediately he was confronted with the overwhelming problem of bringing order and stability to a country near social and economic collapse.

The first tasks of the new regime were to devise a workable political structure, revive the national economy and resettle the refugees from the communist north. Moreover, the authorities were confronted with a series of conspiracies. The government itself was overtly challenged by such armed politico-religious dissidents as the Cao Dai and the Hoa Hao sects, and a group of racketeer gangsters called the Binh Xuyen. By early October 1955 Prime Minister Ngo Dinh Diem had effectively extended his authority in South Vietnam by suppressing the dissident religious sects, executing the leader of the Hoa Hao and crushing the Binh Xuyen by force. Meanwhile, Diem took steps to improve the efficiency and reliability of the government's armed forces, aided in part by economic and military assistance from the United States, which began channeling its military aid directly to the Vietnamese government beginning in January 1955.

Feeling politically secure, Diem called a national referendum on October 23, 1955 to decide whether the country should become a republic under his leadership as chief of state and President or whether Bao Dai should continue as chief of state. The Prime Minister reportedly won 98 percent of the votes, and on October 26 he proclaimed South Vietnam the Republic of Vietnam and became its first President. A constitution, written at his direction and bearing American and French precedents, was adopted in July 1956 and promulgated on October 26, 1956. Diem used these elections as yet another reason to renounce the nationwide elections prescribed by the Geneva agreement.

It is interesting to note that the failure to hold elections to reunify Vietnam was not seriously challenged at the time by the United States, the Soviet Union or China. Like the State of Vietnam, the United States had not concurred with the terms of the truce agreement or the Final Declaration (which was not signed by any of the parties). As far as elections were concerned, the U.S. position was that the matter "should be left to the Vietnamese themselves." Further, neither the Soviet Union nor China, which had signed the truce agreements, pressed for countrywide elections. A factor in their decision may well have been the precedent such an election would establish, for of the three divided nations of the world, Germany, Korea and Vietnam, only in Vietnam did the communist side contain the bulk of the population. In early 1957 the Soviet Union even went so far as to propose that both North and South Vietnam be admitted to the United Nations "as two separate states," a move blocked by the United States, which did not want to "legitimize" communist aggression.

Since North Vietnam could not achieve total control of the country through political measures, it resorted to other means. Despite the cease-fire agreement, a well-organized Viet Minh underground network was deliberately left behind in the south, especially in the jungle regions in the southern Mekong Delta and along the Cambodian and Laotian border regions where French Union forces had not been able to establish effective control. In January 1959 North Vietnam's Central Executive Committee made the decision to activate these forces and begin an armed struggle in order to seize power in the south. The Second Indochina War had begun.

The Republic of Vietnam and the American Conduct of the Vietnam War

Because of its global policy of containment of communist expansion, the United States trans-ferred the support it had been giving the French in their war against the Viet Minh to the newly formed Republic of Vietnam. The U.S. Military Assistance Advisory Group-Vietnam was formed in November 1955 to replace the Military Assistance Advisory Group-Indochina and massive amounts of U.S. economic and military aid were provided to the Republic of Vietnam.

Such support not only had the complete backing of Congress, it also had the overwhelming approval of the American people. For example, in July 1959 the *New York Times* (later to become an outspoken critic of the Vietnam war) editorialized, "With American help [the Republic of Vietnam] has been made less vulnerable from a military point of view. . . . A five-year miracle . . . has been carried out. Vietnam . . . is becoming stronger. . . . There is reason, to date, to salute President Ngo Dinh Diem."

By 1959 the setting for American involvement in the Second Indochina War was complete.

Suggestions for further reading: A concise history of the formation of the Republic of Vietnam is contained in the *Area Handbooks* (cited earlier). A more recent work, Stanley Karnow's *Vietnam: A History* (New York: Viking Press, 1983) also gives an excellent overview of this period, as does the second volume of the Boston Publishing Company's Vietnam series, Edward Doyle, Samuel Lipsman and Stephen Weiss's *Passing the Torch*, The Vietnam Experience (Boston, 1981).

The landmark work, however, remains the second volume of Joseph Buttinger's *Vietnam: A Dragon Embattled* (New York: Praeger, 1967), which not only provides a thorough analysis but also contains voluminous notes on additional sources. An abridged version appears in Buttinger's *Vietnam: A Political History* (New York: Praeger, 1968).

Other works include Bernard Fall's *The Two Vietnams: A Political and Military Analysis* (New York: Praeger, 1967) and Joseph Buttinger's *Vietnam: The Unforgettable Tragedy* (New York: Horizon, 1977).

Part II

the vietnam war: chronology 1959-1975

1959*

January — The Vietnam war begins when North Vietnam's Central Executive Committee issues Resolution 15, changing its strategy toward South Vietnam from "political struggle" to "armed struggle."

4 April — In an address at Gettysburg College, President Eisenhower makes his first commitment to maintain South Vietnam as a separate national state.

22 April — Christian A. Herter replaces John Foster Dulles as Secretary of State.

May — North Vietnam organizes Group 559 to begin enlargement of the Ho Chi Minh Trail.

1 July — General Lyman Lemnitzer replaces General Maxwell Taylor as Chief of Staff, U.S. Army.

8 July — First American servicemen (Major Dale Buis and Master Sergeant Chester Ovnard) killed by Viet Cong attack on Bien Hoa billets.

July — North Vietnam organizes Logistical Group 759 to oversee movement of men and supplies from North Vietnam to the south.

1 December — Thomas S. Gates, Jr. replaces Neil H. McElroy as Secretary of Defense.

31 December — Approximately 760 U.S. military personnel now in Vietnam. South Vietnamese Armed Forces (SVNAF) now total 243,000 personnel.

1960

January — General David M. Shoup succeeds General Randolph McC Pate as Commandant of the Marine Corps.

April — North Vietnam imposes universal military conscription and begins infiltration of cadres into South Vietnam.

September — North Vietnamese leadership calls for intensified struggle in the south and formation of a "broad national united front."

Lieutenant General Lionel McGarr replaces Lieutenant General Samuel Williams as Commander, MAAG-Vietnam (U.S. Military Assistance Advisory Group-Vietnam). Williams had served since November 1955.

1 October General George Decker replaces General Lyman Lemnitzer as Chief of Staff, U.S. Army.

October General Lyman Lemnitzer replaces General Nathan Twining as Chairman, Joint Chiefs of Staff.

November John F. Kennedy defeats Richard M. Nixon in election for President of the United States.

20 December Formation of National Liberation Front announced in Hanoi.

31 December Approximately 900 U.S. military personnel now in Vietnam. SVNAF strength remains at 243,000.

1961

21 January John F. Kennedy succeeds Dwight D. Eisenhower as President.

Dean Rusk succeeds Christian A. Herter as Secretary of State.

Robert S. McNamara succeeds Thomas S. Gates, Jr. as Secretary of Defense.

McGeorge Bundy succeeds Gordon Gray as National Security Adviser.

25 January In his first presidential news conference, President Kennedy supports the idea of a neutral Laos.

28 January President Kennedy approves a Vietnam counterinsurgency plan that calls for government reform and military restructuring as the basis for expanded U.S. assistance.

23 March In a television news conference, President Kennedy warns of communist expansion in Laos and says that a cease-fire must precede the start of negotiations to establish a neutral and independent nation.

March Republic of Vietnam Campaign Medal with "1960 Device" authorized by the government of South Vietnam for members of the U.S. armed forces who served in Vietnam for a minimum of six months.

April Frederick Nolting replaces Elbridge Durbrow as U.S. Ambassador to Vietnam. Durbrow had served since 1957.

Bay of Pigs invasion of Cuba fails.

9–15 May Vice President Lyndon Johnson visits Southeast Asia and recommends a "strong program of action" in Vietnam.

Geneva Conference on Laos begins.

9 June President Ngo Dinh Diem requests U.S. troops for training the South Vietnamese Army.

June General Curtis LeMay replaces General Thomas White as Chief of Staff of the U.S. Air Force.

1 July	General Maxwell Taylor becomes military adviser to the President.
25 July	President Kennedy calls for $3.25 billion to meet commitments in the wake of the Berlin crisis and asks Congress for the power to increase the size of the armed forces by 217,000.
August	Admiral George Anderson replaces Admiral Arleigh Burke as Chief of Naval Operations.
1 October	South Vietnam requests a bilateral defense treaty with the United States.
3 November	After a trip to Vietnam General Maxwell Taylor reports to President Kennedy that prompt U.S. military, economic and political action can lead to victory without a U.S. takeover of the war. He privately recommends sending 8,000 U.S. combat troops to Vietnam.
4 December	Armed Forces Expeditionary Medal authorized by Presidential Executive Order 10977 for award to U.S. military personnel participating in "operations of assistance for a friendly foreign nation". Personnel in Vietnam after July 1, 1958 and Laos after April 19, 1961 qualify.
15 December	President Kennedy renews the U.S. commitment to preserve the independence of Vietnam and pledges American assistance to its defense effort.
31 December	3,205 U.S. military personnel are now in Vietnam. SVNAF strength remains at 243,000.

1962

6 February	MACV (U.S. Military Assistance Command Vietnam) formed, with headquarters in Saigon under command of General Paul Harkins. Major buildup of American advisers and support personnel begins.
14 February	President Kennedy warns that U.S. military advisers in Vietnam will return fire if fired upon.
15 March	Vietnam Advisory Campaign begins.
22 March	The United States begins its first involvement in the Vietnam strategic hamlet (rural pacification) program.
15 May	President Kennedy sends 5,000 Marines and 50 jet fighters to Thailand in response to communist expansion in Laos.
23 July	Geneva Accords on Laos signed at second Geneva Conference.
1 October	General Earle Wheeler replaces General George Decker as Chief of Staff, U.S. Army. General Maxwell Taylor replaces General Lyman Lemnitzer as Chairman, Joint Chiefs of Staff.
October	Cuban missile crisis. U.S. Air Force deploys Second Air Division to Vietnam.
31 December	11,300 U.S. military personnel now in Vietnam. SVNAF strength remains at 243,000.

1963

January	First major defeat of the South Vietnamese Army—Army of the Republic of Vietnam (ARVN) —by Viet Cong units at Battle of Ap Bac.
24 February	A U.S. Senate panel reports that annual American aid to South Vietnam totals $400 million and that 12,000 Americans are stationed there "on dangerous assignment."
May–August	Buddhists stage demonstrations, revolts, self-immolations.
21 August	South Vietnamese government forces under Ngo Dinh Diem attack Buddhist pagodas.
22 August	Henry Cabot Lodge replaces Frederick Nolting as U.S. Ambassador to Vietnam.
24 August	Ambassador Henry Cabot Lodge receives a State Department cable stating that the United States can no longer tolerate Ngo Dinh Nhu's influence in President Ngo Dinh Diem's regime.
August	Admiral David McDonald replaces Admiral George Anderson as Chief of Naval Operations.
1 November	Military coup topples government of South Vietnamese President Ngo Dinh Diem.
2 November	Diem and his brother Ngo Dinh Nhu assassinated.
22 November	President Kennedy assassinated. Vice President Lyndon Johnson assumes presidency.
31 December	16,300 U.S. military personnel now in Vietnam. SVNAF strength remains at 243,000.

1964

January	Lieutenant General William Westmoreland appointed Deputy Commander MACV (U.S. Military Assistance Command Vietnam).
	General Wallace Greene replaces General David Shoup as Commandant of the Marine Corps.
7 February	President Johnson orders the withdrawal of American dependents from South Vietnam.
April	North Vietnam begins infiltration of regular army units into South Vietnam.
May	MAAG-Vietnam (U.S. Military Assistance Advisory Group-Vietnam) disbanded.
30 June	Admiral Ulysses S. Grant Sharp replaces Admiral Harry D. Felt as CINCPAC (Commander-in-Chief, Pacific Command).
	New operational terminology adopted by MACV, including "search and destroy," "clearing operations," "securing operations."
June	General William Westmoreland replaces General Paul Harkins as MACV Commander.

General Earle Wheeler replaces General Maxwell Taylor as Chairman, Joint Chiefs of Staff.

General Maxwell Taylor replaces Henry Cabot Lodge as U.S. Ambassador to Vietnam.

3 July General Harold Johnson replaces General Earle Wheeler as Chief of Staff, U.S. Army.

July U.S. Navy stages Operation DeSoto to observe junk traffic off North Vietnam and to conduct electronic surveillance.

2 August U.S. destroyer *Maddox* reports attack by North Vietnamese patrol boats in Tonkin Gulf.

4 August U.S. destroyer *Turner Joy* reports attack by North Vietnamese patrol boats.

7 August U.S. Congress passes Tonkin Gulf Resolution.

30 October Viet Cong attack Bien Hoa Air Base. Six U.S. B-57 bombers destroyed, five American service personnel killed.

October China explodes its first atomic bomb.

Nikita Khrushchev ousted as Premier of Soviet Union. Leonid Brezhnev, Alexsei Kosygin assume leadership.

U.S. Fifth Special Forces Group deploys to Vietnam from Fort Bragg, North Carolina, to oversee Special Forces operations in Vietnam.

2 November President Johnson defeats Senator Barry Goldwater in presidential election.

24 December Viet Cong terrorists bomb U.S. billets in Saigon; Two American servicemen killed.

U.S. Air Force begins Operation Barrel Roll to strike targets in northern Laos in support of Royal Lao and Meo forces.

31 December 23,300 U.S. military personnel now in Vietnam. SVNAF strength increases to 514,000.

1965

7 February Viet Cong attack American military installations in South Vietnam.

February U.S. Air Force conducts Operation Flaming Dart, a tactical air reprisal against targets in the southern panhandle of North Vietnam for attacks on U.S. bases in South Vietnam.

General John McConnell replaces General Curtis LeMay as Chief of Staff, U.S. Air Force.

2 March U.S. Air Force begins Operation Rolling Thunder to strike targets in North Vietnam and interdict flow of supplies to the south.

8 March Vietnam Defense Campaign begins.

8-9 March First American combat troops land in Vietnam; U.S. Third Marine Regiment, Third Marine

Division deployed to Vietnam from Okinawa to defend Da Nang airfield.

March U.S. Ninth Marine Expeditionary Brigade headquarters established at Da Nang.

U.S. First Marine Aircraft Wing deployed from Japan and Okinawa to Vietnam to support U.S. Marine operations in I Corps.

6 April President Johnson authorizes use of U.S. ground combat troops for offensive operations in South Vietnam.

7 April President Johnson in Johns Hopkins University speech offers North Vietnam developmental aid in exchange for peace.

8 April North Vietnamese Prime Minister Pham Van Dong rejects President Johnson's offer.

15 April Students for Democratic Society sponsor antiwar rally in Washington, D.C.

26 April Secretary of Defense Robert McNamara states that the Vietnam war effort costs the United States about $1.5 billion a year.

April U.S. First Logistical Command formed at Long Binh near Saigon to control logistics buildup in Vietnam.

U.S. Air Force begins Operation Steel Tiger in Laos to strike targets in the panhandle next to North Vietnamese border to interdict troop and supply movements.

May U.S. 173rd Airborne Brigade

deploys to Vietnam from Okinawa for combat operations in III Corps.

U.S. III Marine Amphibious Force headquarters established at Da Nang to control Marine combat operations in I Corps, replacing Ninth Marine Expeditionary Brigade.

Headquarters U.S. Third Marine Division deployed to Vietnam from Okinawa for combat operations in I Corps.

U.S. Fourth Marine Regiment, Third Marine Division deployed to Vietnam from Okinawa for combat operations in I Corps.

U.S. Navy begins Operation Market Time to detect and intercept surface traffic in South Vietnam coastal waters and to seize or destroy enemy craft.

8 June The State Department reports that President Johnson has authorized the use of U.S. troops in direct combat if the South Vietnamese Army requests assistance.

June Australia deploys First Battalion Royal Australian Regiment to Vietnam for combat operations in III Corps.

Arc Light campaign begun by U.S. Air Force, using B-52 strategic bombers to strike enemy targets in South Vietnam.

3 July Vietnam Service Medal authorized by Presidential Executive Order 11231 for award to members of U.S. armed forces serving in Vietnam.

8 July	Henry Cabot Lodge reappointed U.S. Ambassador to South Vietnam to succeed Maxwell Taylor.
July	USARV (U.S. Army Vietnam) headquarters formed at Long Binh near Saigon to support Army operations in Vietnam.
	U.S. Second Brigade, First Infantry Division deploys to Vietnam from Fort Riley, Kansas for combat operations in III Corps.
	U.S. First Brigade, 101st Airborne Division deploys to Vietnam from Fort Campbell, Kentucky for combat operations in II Corps.
	U.S. Navy establishes Coastal Surveillance Force, Task Force 115, for operations in II Corps.
	New Zealand deploys field artillery battery to Vietnam for combat operations in III Corps.
18–21 August	Operation Starlight, U.S. Marine four-day operation, against *Viet Cong* First Regiment south of Chu Lai in Quang Ngai Province, I Corps. 700 known enemy casualties.
August	U.S. Seventh Marine Regiment, First Marine Division deployed to Vietnam from Camp Pendleton, California for combat operations in I Corps.
September	U.S. I Field Force Vietnam headquarters formed at Nha Trang to coordinate Army combat operations in the Central Highlands.
	U.S. 1st Cavalry Division (Airmobile) deploys to Vietnam from

Fort Benning, Georgia for combat operations in II Corps.

U.S. 18th Engineer Brigade deployed to Vietnam from Fort Bragg, North Carolina to provide engineer support for U.S. forces in Vietnam.

15–16 October	Protests against U.S. policy in Vietnam are held in some 40 cities.
23 October	Operation Silver Bayonet begun by U.S. First Cavalry Division (Airmobile) and ARVN in Pleiku Province, II Corps.
October	Entire U.S. First Infantry Division deploys to Vietnam from Fort Riley, Kansas to join Second Brigade for combat operations in III Corps.
	U.S. Navy establishes a support activity at Da Nang to support U.S. naval operations in Vietnam.
	South Korea—Republic of Korea (ROK)—deploys ROK Capital Division to Vietnam for combat operations in II Corps.
	South Korea deploys ROK Marine Brigade to Vietnam for combat operations in II Corps.
14–16 November	In first major engagement of the war between regular U.S. and NVA forces, U.S. Third Brigade, First Cavalry Division (Airmobile) defeats NVA 32nd, 33rd and 66th Regiments in the Ia Drang valley, II Corps.
20 November	Operation Silver Bayonet ends; 1,771 known North Vietnamese

casualties, including those in Ia Drang battle.

November   U.S. Air Force Third Tactical Fighter Wing deploys to Bien Hoa for combat operations in III Corps.

U.S. Air Force 12th Tactical Fighter Wing deploys to Cam Ranh Bay for combat operations in II Corps.

25 December   President Johnson suspends bombing of North Vietnam (Rolling Thunder) to induce North Vietnam to negotiate.

Vietnamese Counteroffensive Campaign begins.

31 December   184,300 U.S. military personnel now in Vietnam. 636 U.S. military personnel killed in action to date.

22,420 Free World Military Forces personnel now in Vietnam. SVNAF strength remains at 514,000.

December   U.S. Third Brigade, 25th Infantry Division deployed to Vietnam from Hawaii for combat operations in II Corps.

U.S. Navy establishes River Task Force, Task Force 116, for naval operations in II Corps.

Operation Tiger Hound begun by U.S. Air Force to strike targets in the southern panhandle of Laos next to South Vietnamese border to interdict troop and supply movements.

Arc Light campaign extended to Laos.

1966

19 January   Operation Van Buren begins. First Brigade, 101st Airborne Division, ROK Second Marine Brigade and ARVN, 47th Regiment conduct operations in Phu Yen Province, II Corps.

President Johnson asks Congress for an additional $12.8 billion for the war in Vietnam.

24 January   Operation Masher/White Wing/ Thang Phong II begins, with U.S. First Cavalry Division (Airmobile), ARVN and ROK forces in Binh Dinh Province, II Corps; in first large unit operation across corps boundaries, U.S. Marines from I Corps cross into Binh Dinh and link up with First Cavalry Division.

31 January   Bombing of North Vietnam (Rolling Thunder) resumes.

January   U.S. First Marine Division deployed from Camp Pendleton, California to Vietnam for combat operations in I Corps.

4 February   Senate Foreign Relations Committee begins televised hearings on the war.

6-8 February   At the Honolulu Conference, Johnson announces renewed emphasis on "The Other War," the attempt to provide the South Vietnamese rural population with local security and economic and social programs to win their active support.

21 February   Operation Van Buren ends; 679 known enemy casualties.

February   U.S. Air Force 460th Tactical Reconnaissance Wing deployed for combat operations in Vietnam.

U.S. First Marine Regiment. First Marine Division deployed to Vietnam from Camp Pendleton, California for combat operations in I Corps.

1 March   The Senate rejects an amendment repealing the Tonkin Gulf Resolution.

4–8 March   Operation Utah conducted by U.S. Marine Corps/ARVN units in vicinity of Quang Ngai city, I Corps, against NVA and VC main force units; 632 known enemy casualties.

6 March   Operation Masher/White Wing/ Thang Phong II ends; 2,389 known enemy casualties.

20–24 March   Operation Texas conducted by U.S. Marine Corps/ARVN/ South Vietnamese Marine Corps reaction force to retake An Hoa outpost in Quang Ngai Province, I Corps; 623 known enemy casualties.

March   U.S. Air Force 366th Tactical Fighter Wing deployed to Vietnam for service in I Corps.

U.S. Air Force 14th and 315th Air Commando Wings deployed for combat operations in Vietnam.

U.S. II Field Force Vietnam deploys to Vietnam from Fort Hood, Texas to coordinate Army combat operations in III Corps and IV Corps.

1 April   Walt Rostow replaces McGeorge Bundy as National Security Adviser.

April   U.S. 25th Infantry Division deploys to Vietnam from Hawaii for operations in III Corps.

U.S. First Signal Brigade deployed to Vietnam from Fort Gordon, Georgia to provide signal support for U.S. forces in Vietnam.

U.S. 44th Medical Brigade deployed to Vietnam from Fort Sam Houston, Texas to provide medical support for U.S. forces in Vietnam.

Headquarters U.S. Naval Forces Vietnam formed to coordinate naval activities in Vietnam.

U.S. Seventh Air Force Headquarters organized at Tan Son Nhut to coordinate U.S. Air Force activities in Vietnam.

U.S. Air Force 35th Tactical Fighter Wing deployed to Vietnam for service in II Corps.

U.S. Fifth Marine Regiment, First Marine Division deployed to Vietnam from Camp Pendleton, California for combat operations in I Corps.

Australia deploys First Australian Task Force, including Second Battalion, Royal Australian Regiment, to Vietnam to control Australian combat operations in III Corps.

U.S. Navy begins Operation Game Warden to interdict North

Vietnamese and Viet Cong bases and lines of communication in inland waterways in III and IV Corps.

U.S. Air Force Arc Light campaign extended to North Vietnam.

1 May   The U.S. forces shell communist targets in Cambodia.

10 May   Operation Paul Revere/Than Phone 14 begun with Third Brigade, U.S. 25th Infantry Division and ARVN forces border screening, area control operation in Pleiku Province, II Corps.

May   U.S. First Aviation Brigade organized in Vietnam to provide Army aviation support for U.S. forces throughout Vietnam.

U.S. Naval Support Activities Saigon formed to coordinate naval activities in Saigon area.

2 June   Operation El Paso II begun by U.S. First and ARVN Fifth Divisions against VC Ninth Division in Binh Long Province, III Corps.

2–21 June   Operation Hawthorne/Dan Tang 61 conducted by U.S. First Brigade, 101st Airborne Division and ARVN units in Kontum Province, III Corps; 53 known enemy casualties.

29 June   President Johnson orders the bombing of oil installations at Haiphong and Hanoi.

June   U.S. Third Naval Mobile Construction Brigade (Seabees) formed at Da Nang to support U.S. Navy and Marine operations in I Corps.

First Battalion, Royal Australian Regiment returns to Australia.

1 July   Vietnam Counteroffensive Campaign Phase II commences.

4 July   Operation Macon, security operation for An Hoa industrial complex in Quang Nam Province, I Corps, begun by U.S. Marine Corps.

7 July   Operation Hastings/Deckhouse II begun by U.S. Marine Corps/ARVN/South Vietnamese Marine Corps forces in Quang Tri Province, I Corps, against NVA 324B Division in area of DMZ.

13 July   Operation El Paso II ends; 855 known enemy casualties.

30 July   Operation Paul Revere/Than Phong 14 ends; 546 known enemy casualties.

1–25 August   Operation Paul Revere II conducted by U.S. First Cavalry Division (Airmobile) and ARVN in Pleiku Province, II Corps; 809 known enemy casualties.

3 August   Operation Hastings/Deckhouse II ends; 882 known enemy casualties.

Operation Prairie, a continuing U.S. Third Marine Division operation in Con Thien/Gio Linh areas of the DMZ, I Corps, to keep track of the NVA 324B Division.

6–12 August   Operation Colorado/Lien Ket 52, conducted by U.S. Marine Corps/ARVN in Quang Nam/Quang Tin Provinces, I Corps; 674 known enemy casualties.

26 August Operation Byrd economy-of-force operation begun by U.S. First Cavalry Division in Binh Thuan Province, II Corps; usually one or two battalions involved.

August U.S. Fourth Infantry Division deploys to Vietnam from Fort Carson, Colorado for operations in II Corps.

U.S. 196th Light Infantry Brigade deploys to Vietnam from Fort Devins, Massachusetts for operations in III Corps.

Philippines deploys Philippine Civic Action Group (PHILCAG) to Vietnam for operations in III Corps.

14 September Operation Attleboro initiated by U.S. 196th Light Infantry Brigade in War Zone C (Tay Ninh Province, III Corps); no significant contact until October 19, when sizable base area is uncovered. By early November U.S. First Infantry Division; Third Brigade, Fourth Infantry Division; 173rd Airborne Brigade; and several ARVN battalions are involved.

23 September Operation Maeng Ho 6 begun by ROK Capital Division in Binh Dinh Province, II Corps.

The U.S. military command in Vietnam announces that it is using defoliants to destroy communist cover.

September U.S. 11th Armored Cavalry Regiment deploys to Vietnam from Fort Meade, Maryland for combat operations in III Corps.

U.S. 18th Military Police Brigade deployed to Vietnam from Fort Meade, Maryland to provide military police support for U.S. forces in Vietnam.

ROK Ninth Infantry Division deployed to Vietnam for combat operations in II Corps.

2–24 October Operation Irving conducted by U.S. First Cavalry Division (Airmobile), ARVN and ROK units against NVA 610th Division in Binh Dinh Province, II Corps; 681 known enemy casualties.

18 October Operation Paul Revere IV begins; continuing operation near the Cambodian border of Pleiku Province, II Corps conducted primarily by newly arrived U.S. Fourth Infantry Division along with elements of U.S. 25th Infantry Division and First Cavalry Division (Airmobile).

25 October Operation Thayer II begun by U.S. First Cavalry Division (Airmobile) in Binh Dinh Province (II Corps) in the rich northern coastal plain and the valleys to the west.

26 October President Johnson visits U.S. troops in Vietnam.

27 October Operation Macon ends; 507 known enemy casualties.

October U.S. Air Force 834th Air Division deployed to Vietnam.

U.S. Air Force 483rd Tactical Airlift Wing deployed for combat operations in Vietnam.

U.S. Navy begins Operation Sea Dragon to interdict enemy supply vessels in coastal waters off North Vietnam.

9 November   Operation Maeng Ho 6 ends; 6,161 known enemy casualties.

24 November   Operation Attleboro ends; 1,106 known enemy casualties in largest U.S. operation to date.

30 November   Operation Fairfax initiated by three battalions—one each from U.S. First, Fourth and 25th Infantry Divisions—in and around Saigon (III Corps); taken over by U.S. 199th Light Infantry Brigade in January 1967. Emphasis is on joint U.S./ARVN operations. Upon withdrawal of 199th, area of operations is taken over by ARVN Fifth Ranger Group.

November   U.S. 199th Light Infantry Brigade deployed to Vietnam from Fort Benning, Georgia for operations in III Corps.

30 December   Operation Paul Revere IV ends; 977 known enemy casualties.

31 December   385,300 U.S. military personnel now in Vietnam. 6,644 U.S. military killed in action to date.

52,500 Free World Military Forces personnel now in Vietnam. SVNAF strength increases to 735,900 personnel. 47,712 SVNAF killed in action to date.

December   U.S. Ninth Infantry Division deployed to Vietnam from Fort Lewis, Washington for operations in III Corps.

U.S. Air Force 31st Tactical Fighter Wing deployed to Vietnam for combat operations in II Corps.

1967

1 January   Operation Sam Houston begun; a continuation of U.S. Fourth and 25th Infantry Divisions border surveillance operations in Pleiku and Kontum Provinces, II Corps.

6 January   Operation Palm Beach begun by U.S. Ninth Infantry Division in Dinh Tuong Province, IV Corps.

8–26 January   Operation Cedar Falls conducted jointly by U.S. First and 25th Infantry Divisions, 173rd Airborne Brigade and 11th Armored Cavalry Regiment and ARVN units against VC headquarters in the Iron Triangle, III Corps; 720 known enemy casualties.

31 January   Operation Prairie ends; 1,397 known enemy casualties.

January   U.S. Navy forms Mekong Delta Mobile Riverine Force, Task Force 117, to support U.S. Ninth Infantry Division combat operations in IV Corps.

1 February   Operation Prairie II begun; continuation of U.S. Third Marine Division operations in the area of the DMZ Zone, I Corps.

11 February   Operation Pershing begun by U.S. First Cavalry Division (Airmobile) in Binh Dinh Province against elements of NVA 610th Division and VC units;

followed by Pershing II in the same area when major elements of First Cavalry Division move to I Corps.

12 February Operation Thayer II ends; 1,757 known enemy casualties.

13 February Operation Enterprize begun by U.S. Ninth Infantry Division combined with ARVN and Regional and Popular Forces in Long An Province, III Corps.

22 February Operation Junction City, largest operation in Vietnam to date, begun by 22 U.S. battalions and four ARVN battalions, including elements of the U.S. First, Fourth and 25th Infantry Divisions, 196th Light Infantry Brigade, 11th Armored Cavalry Regiment and 173rd Airborne Brigade, in Tay Ninh and bordering provinces, III Corps.

7 March Operation Oh Jac Kyo I, largest South Korean operation to date, initiated to link up two ROK division areas of operations along the central coastal area, II Corps.

11 March Operation Enterprize ends; 2,107 known enemy casualties.

18 March Operation Prairie II ends; 693 known enemy casualties.

5 April Operation Sam Houston ends; 733 known enemy casualties.

Operation Francis Marion begun by U.S. Fourth Infantry Division operation in western highlands of Pleiku Province, II Corps.

15 April 100,000 antiwar protestors rally in New York; 20,000 in San Francisco.

18 April Operation Oh Jac Kyo I ends; 831 known enemy casualties.

21 April Operation Union begun by First Marine Division against NVA forces in Quang Nam and Quang Tin Provinces, I Corps.

April U.S. 26th Marine Regiment, Fifth Marine Division attached to First Marine Division for combat operations in I Corps.

Australia deploys Seventh Battalion, Royal Australian Regiment to Vietnam to join First Australian Tactical Force for combat operations in III Corps.

1 May Ellsworth Bunker replaces Henry Cabot Lodge as U.S. Ambassador to South Vietnam.

9 May Robert Komer appointed deputy to the MACV Commander for CORDS (Civil Operations and Revolutionary Development Support).

14 May Operation Kole Kole begun by U.S. 25th Infantry Division in Hau Nghia Province, III Corps.

Operation Junction City ends; 2,728 known enemy casualties.

17 May Operation Union ends; 865 known casualties.

Sixteen Senators critical of administration policy in Vietnam warn Hanoi, in a letter drafted by Senator Frank Church, that they oppose unilateral U.S. withdrawal.

19 May	U.S. planes bomb a power plant in Hanoi.
25 May	Operation Union II begun by U.S. First Marine Division against NVA forces in Quang Nam and Quang Tin Provinces, I Corps.
31 May	Operation Palm Beach ends; 570 known enemy casualties.
1 June	Vietnam Counteroffensive Phase III Campaign begun.
5 June	Operation Union II ends; 701 known enemy casualties.
2–14 July	Operation Buffalo, continuing U.S. Third Marine Division operation in the DMZ, I Corps, begun; 1,281 known enemy casualties.
7 July	Congress's Joint Economic Committee issues a report stating that the Vietnam war created "havoc" in the U.S. economy during 1966 and predicting that the war will cost $4 to $6 billion more in 1967 than the $20.3 billion requested by President Johnson.
16 July	Operation Kingfisher, continuing U.S. Third Marine Division operation in the DMZ, I Corps, begun.
20 August	U.S. 20th Engineer Brigade deployed to Vietnam from Fort Bragg, North Carolina to provide engineer support for U.S. forces in Vietnam.
August	Admiral Thomas Moorer replaces Admiral David McDonald as Chief of Naval Operations.

3 September	Nguyen Van Thieu elected President of South Vietnam.
4–15 September	Operation Swift conducted by U.S. First Marine Division in Quang Nam and Quang Tin Provinces, I Corps; 517 known enemy casualties.
5 September	Operation Dragon Fire begun by elements of ROK Second Marine Brigade in Quang Ngai Province, I Corps.
27 September	Operation Shenandoah II begun by U.S. First Infantry Division in Binh Duong Province and extended to include Loc Ninh area of Binh Long Province, III Corps, after enemy attacks on the district town.
29 September	In a speech at San Antonio, Texas, President Johnson modifies the U.S. position on Vietnam negotiations, saying that the United States is willing to stop all bombing if the halt will promptly lead to negotiations.
September	U.S. Americal Division (23rd Infantry Division) formed in Vietnam for combat operations in I Corps; division includes previously separate 196th Light Infantry Brigade already in country and soon-to-arrive 11th and 198th Light Infantry Brigades. Thailand deploys "Queen's Cobras" Regiment to Vietnam for combat operations in III Corps. Base at Khe Sanh established as a potential launch point for ground operations to cut the Ho Chi Minh Trail.

12 October	Operation Francis Marion ends; 1,203 known enemy casualties.
	Operation MacArthur begun by U.S. Fourth Infantry Division as one of continuing operations in the western highlands, II Corps.
21 October	"March on the Pentagon" by estimated 50,000 antiwar demonstrators.
30 October	Operation Dragon Fire ends; 541 known enemy casualties.
31 October	Operation Kingfisher ends; 1,117 known enemy casualties.
October	U.S. 198th Infantry Brigade deployed to Vietnam from Fort Hood, Texas to join American Division for combat operations in I Corps.
	Operation Neutralize ends.
	U.S. public opinion on war shifts, as for the first time, more Americans oppose than support the war.
1 November	Operation Scotland begun by U.S. Third Marine Division in westernmost part of Quang Tri Province, I Corps; action centered on the Khe Sanh area.
	Operation Kentucky begun by U.S. Third Marine Division as one of continuing operations in Con Thien area of DMZ, I Corps.
11 November	Operation Wheeler/Wallowa begun by American Division (two brigades) in Quang Nam and Quang Tin Provinces, I Corps.

19 November	Operation Shenandoah II ends; 956 known enemy casualties.
7 December	Operation Kole Kole ends; 645 known enemy casualties.
8 December	Operation Yellowstone begun by U.S. 25th Infantry Division in War Zone C (Tay Ninh Province, III Corps).
14 December	Operation Fairfax ends; 1,043 known enemy casualties.
17 December	Operation Uniontown begun by U.S. 199th Light Infantry Brigade in Bien Hoa Province, III Corps.
	Operation Maeng Ho 9 begun by ROK Capital Division operation in Binh Dinh Province, II Corps.
19 December	Operation Muscatine begun by American Division (one brigade) in Quang Ngai Province, I Corps.
December	U.S. 11th Light Infantry brigade deployed to Vietnam from Hawaii to join American Division for combat operations in I Corps.
	U.S. 101st Airborne Division (Airmobile) deployed to Vietnam from Fort Campbell, Kentucky to join its First Brigade elements already in country for combat operations in II Corps.
	Australia deploys Third Battalion, Royal Australian Regiment to join First Australian Task Force for combat operations in III Corps.

New Zealand deploys infantry company to Vietnam for combat operations in III Corps.

485,600 U.S. military personnel now in Vietnam. 16,021 U.S. military killed in action to date.

At end of year, 59,300 Free World Military Forces personnel in Vietnam; SVNAF strength increases to 798,000; 60,428 SVNAF killed in action to date.

1968

3 January Minnesota Senator Eugene McCarthy announces his candidacy for the Democratic presidential nomination.

19 January Operation Pershing ends; 5,401 known enemy casualties.

Operation McLain begun by U.S. 173rd Airborne Brigade as reconnaissance-in-force operation in support of pacification in Binh Thuan Province, II Corps.

20 January Operation Byrd ends; 849 known enemy casualties.

21 January Khe Sanh besieged by North Vietnamese Army. Operation Niagara begun by U.S. Air Force to support U.S. Marines in combat operations at Khe Sanh.

22 January Operation Pershing II begun; continuation of U.S. First Cavalry Division (Airmobile) operations in Binh Dinh Province, II Corps, after major division forces deployed to I Corps.

Operation Jeb Stuart begun by U.S. First Cavalry Division (Airmobile) initial operation in northern I Corps following Pershing operations in II Corps.

30 January During the Tet holiday Viet Cong and North Vietnamese mount major offensives in three-fourths of the 44 provincial capitals of South Vietnam. U.S. and ARVN forces launch Tet Counteroffensive.

Operation Maeng Ho 9 ends; 749 known enemy casualties.

31 January Attack on U.S. embassy in Saigon repulsed.

Hué captured by Viet Cong and North Vietnamese; Battle of Hué begins as ARVN and U.S. Marine elements counterattack to expel enemy from city.

General Leonard F. Chapman replaces General Wallace M. Greene as Commandant of the Marine Corps.

January U.S. Navy begins Operation Clearwater to interdict enemy bases and lines of communication on inland waterways in I Corps.

1 February Richard M. Nixon announces his candidacy for the presidency.

1–25 February Viet Cong and North Vietnamese massacre 2,800 civilians in Hué.

5–17 February Operation Tran Hung Dao conducted by ARVN in Saigon area, III Corps, with six South Vietnamese Marine Corps, four ranger and five airborne battalions during the Tet Offensive; 953 known enemy casualties.

10–17 February All-time high weekly rate of U.S. casualties—543 killed in action, 2,547 wounded in action.

16 February Operation Maeng Ho 10 begun by ROK Capital Division in Binh Dinh Province, II Corps.

17 February Operation Tran Hung Dao II begun; continuation of Operation Tran Hung Dao in Saigon area, III Corps, with slightly reduced forces.

20 February The Senate Foreign Relations Committee begins hearings on the events leading to the passage of the Tonkin Gulf Resolution.

24 February Operation Yellowstone ends; 1,254 known enemy casualties.

25 February Battle of Hué ends with recapture of city by U.S./South Vietnamese forces; 5,113 known enemy casualties.

27 February U.S. military leaders request 206,000 additional troops for Vietnam and for security in other parts of the world.

29 February Operation Pershing II ends; 614 known enemy casualties.

Operation Napoleon/Saline begun as part of U.S. Marine Corps operations along the Cua Viet River to keep this supply line of communications open to the port facility in the Dong Ha area of Quang Tri Province (I Corps).

February U.S. Third Brigade, 82nd Airborne Division deployed to Vietnam from Fort Bragg, North Carolina for combat operations in II Corps.

U.S. 27th Marine Regiment, Fifth Marine Division deployed to Vietnam to join U.S. First Marine Division for combat operations in I Corps.

1 March Operation Maeng Ho 10 ends; 664 known enemy casualties.

Operation Truong Cong Dinh begun by ARVN units and elements of U.S. Ninth Infantry Division in Dinh Tuong and Kien Tuong Provinces, IV Corps; combined with Operation Duong Cua Dan on May 21.

Clark Clifford replaces Robert MacNamara as Secretary of Defense.

8 March Operation Uniontown ends; 922 known enemy casualties.

Operation Tran Hung Dao II ends; 953 known enemy casualties.

11 March Operation Saratoga ends; 3,862 known enemy casualties.

Operation Quyet Thang, largest operation to date, initiated in Saigon area and five surrounding provinces, III Corps by elements of U.S. First, Ninth and 25th Divisions and ARVN Fifth and 25th Divisions, airborne battalions and South Vietnamese Marine Corps Task Forces—a total of 22 U.S. and 11 ARVN battalions.

12 March In the New Hampshire Democratic primary, Eugene Mc-Carthy wins a surprising 42% of the vote against Johnson's 48%.

16 March New York Senator Robert Kennedy announces his candidacy for the Democratic presidential nomination.

17 March Operation Duong Cua Dan begun as part of operations by Ninth Infantry Division to provide security for engineers working on Route 4, IV Corps; combined with Operation Truong Cong Dinh on May 21.

25–26 March The Senior Advisory Group on Vietnam meets to discuss proposed troop increases and recommends de-escalation.

30 March Operation Cochise Green begun by 173rd Airborne Brigade in Binh Dinh Province, II Corps.

31 March President Johnson announces de-escalation of the war, states he will not run for reelection.

Operation Scotland ends; 1,561 known enemy casualties.

Operation Jeb Stuart ends; 3,268 known enemy casualties.

March My Lai massacre of Vietnamese civilians by members of U.S. First Battalion, 20th Infantry, American Division.

U.S. Navy Operation Sea Dragon terminated.

Operation Niagara ends.

U.S. 27th Marine Regiment, Fifth Marine Division departs Vietnam.

1 April Operation Carentan II begun by U.S. 101st Airborne Division and Third Brigade, 82nd Airborne Division in conjunction with the ARVN First Division operations along lowlands of Quang Tri and Thua Thien Provinces, I Corps.

1–15 April Operation Pegasus/Lam Son 207 conducted by U.S. First Cavalry Division (Airmobile) with U.S. Marine and ARVN airborne battalions to relieve siege of Khe Sanh. I Corps; 17 U.S. and four ARVN battalions involved; 1,044 known enemy casualties.

2 April Vietnam Counteroffensive Phase IV Campaign begun.

7 April Operation Quyet Thang ends; 2,658 known enemy casualties.

8 April Operation Toan Thang, largest operation to date, begun; combined III ARVN Corps and II Field Force offensive to destroy Viet Cong and North Vietnamese Army forces within the Capital Military District, III Corps; 42 U.S. and 37 South Vietnamese battalions involved.

Operation Burlington Trail, combat sweep operation, begun by U.S. 198th Infantry Brigade, American Division in Quang Tin Province along the Quang Nam Province border, I Corps.

15 April Operation Scotland II begun as a continuation of U.S. Marine Corps operations around Khe Sanh upon termination of Operation Pegasus, I Corps.

19 April Operation Delaware/Lam Son 216 begun by U.S. First Cavalry

Division (Airmobile), 101st Airborne Division and elements of 196th Light Infantry Brigade, plus ARVN First Division and ARVN Airborne Task Force Bravo in A Shua Valley to pre-empt enemy preparations for attack on Hué area, I Corps.

26 April 200,000 people in New York City demonstrate against the war.

27 April Vice President Hubert Humphrey announces he will run for the presidency.

3 May President Johnson announces that the United States and North Vietnam have agreed to begin formal peace talks in Paris.

4 May Operation Allen Brook begun by U.S. Marine Corps units west of Hoi An City in southern Quang Nam Province, I Corps.

12 May Vietnam peace talks begin in Paris.

17 May Operation Carentan II ends; 2,100 known enemy casualties.

Operation Delaware/Lam Son 216 ends; 869 known enemy casualties.

Operation Jeb Stuart III begun as a continuation of U.S. First Cavalry Division (Airmobile) operations along the border of Quang Tri and Thua Thien Provinces, I Corps.

Operation Nevada Eagle begun as a continuation of U.S. 101st Airborne Division operations in Central Thua Thien Province, I Corps.

18 May Operation Mameluke Thrust begun by U.S. First Marine Division in central Quang Nam Province, I Corps.

6 June Robert Kennedy, the victim of an assassination, dies.

10 June Operation Muscatine ends; 1,129 known enemy casualties.

June Australia deploys Fourth Battalion, Royal Australian Regiment to Vietnam to replace Second Battalion, Royal Australian Regiment and to conduct combat operations in III Corps.

1 July Vietnam Counteroffensive Phase V Campaign commences.

U.S. First Brigade, Fifth Infantry Division (Mechanized) deploys to Vietnam from Fort Carson, Colorado for combat operations in I Corps.

General Creighton Abrams replaces General William Westmoreland as Commander, MACV (U.S. Military Assistance Command Vietnam).

3 July General William Westmoreland replaces General Harold Johnson as Chief of Staff, U.S. Army.

17 July Operation Quyet Chien begun as part of ARVN Seventh, Ninth and 21st Infantry Divisions operations in IV Corps.

30 July Operation Duong Cua Dan ends; 1,251 known enemy casualties.

31 July Admiral John McCain replaces Admiral U.S. Grant Sharp as CINCPAC.

15 August	U.S. XXIV Corps established to coordinate U.S. Army combat operations in I Corps.
24 August	Operation Allen Brook ends; 1,017 known enemy casualties.
	Operation Tien Bo begun as part of ARVN 23rd Division operations in Quang Due Province, II Corps.
28 August	Antiwar protests and riots in Chicago at site of Democratic Party's national convention.
9 September	Operation Tien Bo ends; 1,091 known enemy casualties.
23 October	Operation Mameluke Thrust ends; 2,728 known enemy casualties.
24 October	Operation Henderson Hill begun as part of U.S. Fifth Marine Regiment search-and-clear operations in Quang Nam Province, I Corps.
31 October	President Johnson announces complete halt to bombing of North Vietnam; U.S. Air Force Operation Rolling Thunder ends.
2 November	Vietnam Counteroffensive Phase VI Campaign begins.
3 November	Operation Jeb Stuart III ends; 2,114 known enemy casualties.
5 November	Richard Nixon defeats Hubert Humphrey in election for President of United States.
11 November	Operation Wheeler/Wallowa ends; 10,000 known enemy casualties.
	Operation Burlington Trail ends 1,931 known enemy casualties.
November	Operation Commando Hunt conducted by U.S. Air Force to interdict enemy supply lines and test effectiveness of sensor systems along 1,700-mile length of Ho Chi Minh Trail.
1 December	Operation Speedy Express begun as part of U.S. Ninth Infantry Division operations throughout IV Corps.
6 December	Operation Taylor Common begun as part of U.S. First Marine Division operations in Quang Nam Province, I Corps.
	Operation Henderson Hill ends 700 known enemy casualties.
9 December	Operation Napoleon/Saline ends; 3,495 known enemy casualties.
31 December	536,100 U.S. military personnel now in Vietnam. 30,610 U.S military killed in action to date
	65,600 Free World Military Forces personnel now in Vietnam. SVNAF strength increases to 820,000. 88,343 SVNAF killed in action to date.

1969

1 January	Operation Quyet Thang, multidivision operation involving ARVN Seventh, Ninth and 21st Infantry Divisions in IV Corps Tactical Zone, begun.

Operation Rice Farmer begun as part of operations conducted throughout Mekong Delta by elements of U.S. Ninth Infantry Division and ARVN Fifth Regiment together with appropriate supporting forces, IV Corps.

22 January Richard Nixon replaces Lyndon Johnson as President.

William Rogers replaces Dean Rusk as Secretary of State.

Melvin Laird replaces Clark Clifford as Secretary of Defense.

Henry Kissinger replaces Walt Rostow as National Security Adviser.

Operation Dewey Canyon begun by U.S. Ninth Marine Regiment (Reinforced) north of A Shau Valley, I Corps.

31 January Operation MacArthur ends; 5,731 known enemy casualties.

Operation McLain ends; 1,042 known enemy casualties.

Operation Cochise Green ends; 929 known enemy casualties.

23 February Tet 1969 Counteroffensive Campaign begins.

24 February Operation Quyet Thang 22 begun by ARVN Second Division in Quang Ngai Province, I Corps.

27 February Operation Quang Nam begun by ARVN First Ranger Group in Quang Ngai Province, I Corps.

28 February Operation Kentucky ends; 3,921 known enemy casualties.

Operation Scotland II ends; 3,311 known enemy casualties.

Operation Mameluke Thrust ends; 2,728 known enemy casualties.

1 March Operation Oklahoma Hills begun as part of U.S. Seventh and 26th Marine Regiments' operations southwest of Da Nang in Quang Nam Province, I Corps.

Operation Wayne Grey begun as part of U.S. Fourth Infantry Division operations in Kontum Province, II Corps.

4 March Operation Quyet Chun ends; 15,953 known enemy casualties.

10 March Operation Quyet Thang 22 ends; 7,777 known enemy casualties.

18 March Operation Dewey Canyon ends; 1,335 known enemy casualties.

Operation Menu, secret bombing of Cambodia, begun by U.S. Air Force. B-52 bombing of eastern Cambodia to depth of five miles beyond the Vietnam border.

20–31 March Operation Quyet Thang 25 conducted by ARVN Fourth Regiment in Quang Ngai Province, I Corps; 592 known enemy casualties.

26 March Women Strike for Peace pickets Washington, D.C. in the first large anti-war demonstration since Nixon's inauguration.

March "Vietnamization" of the war announced by Secretary of Defense Melvin Laird.

14 April	Operation Wayne Grey ends; 608 known enemy casualties.
15 April	Operation Washington Green begun. U.S. 173rd Airborne Brigade conducts a pacification operation in the An Lao Valley of Binh Dinh Province, II Corps.
16 April	Cambodia reestablishes diplomatic relations with United States after four-year break.
18 April	Operation Dan Thang 69 begun by ARVN 22nd Division in Binh Dinh Province, II Corps.
22 April	Operation Lam Son 277 begun by ARVN Second Regiment in Quang Tri Province, I Corps.
	Operation Putnam Tiger begun as part of operations by U.S. Fourth Infantry Division in Kontum and Pleiku Provinces, II Corps.
30 April	U.S. military personnel in Vietnam peak at 543,400.
1 May	Operation Virginia Ridge begun by U.S. Ninth Marine Regiment, Third Marine Division in northern Quang Tri Province along the DMZ, II Corps.
10 May	Operation Apache Snow begun by U.S. Ninth Marine Regiment, Third Marine Division and elements of 101st Airborne Division (Airmobile) in western Thua Thien Province, I Corps.
14 May	President Nixon proposes an eight-point peace plan for Vietnam; it provides for mutual troop withdrawal.
15 May	Operation Dan Quyen 38-A begun by ARVN 42nd Regiment and ARVN 22nd Ranger Group in Ben Het-Dak To area, II Corps.
16 May	Operation Lamar Plain begun by elements of U.S. American and 101st Airborne Divisions southwest of Tam Ky in Quang Tin Province, I Corps.
29 May	Operation Oklahoma Hills ends; 596 known enemy casualties.
31 May	Operation Taylor Common ends; 1,299 known enemy casualties.
	Operation Speedy Express ends; 10,899 known enemy casualties.
May	Battle of "Hamburger Hill" (Ap Bia) involves elements of U.S. 101st Airborne Division (Airmobile).
7 June	Operation Apache Snow ends; 977 known enemy casualties.
	Operation Dan Quyen 38-A ends; 945 known enemy casualties.
8 June	President Nixon announces withdrawal of 25,000 troops from Vietnam.
9 June	Vietnam Summer-Fall 1969 Campaign commences.
20 June	Operation Quang Nam ends; 688 known enemy casualties.
	Operation Lam Son 277 ends; 541 known enemy casualties.
16 July	Operation Virginia Ridge ends; 560 known enemy casualties.

21 July	Operation Idaho Canyon begins. Operations by U.S. Third Marine Regiment in Quang Tri Province, I Corps.
25 July	"Nixon Doctrine" announced.
13 August	Operation Lamar Plain ends; 524 known enemy casualties.
25 August	Operation Lien Ket 414 begun by ARVN Fourth Regiment in Quang Ngai Province, I Corps.
26 August	Operation Lien Ket 531 begun by ARVN Fifth Regiment in Quang Tin Province, I Corps.
27 August	U.S. Ninth Infantry Division (less Third Brigade) withdraws from Vietnam.
31 August	Operation Rice Farmer ends; 1,860 known enemy casualties.
August	General John Ryan replaces General John McConnell as Chief of Staff, U.S. Air Force.
3 September	Ho Chi Minh dies in Hanoi.
22 September	Operation Putnam Tiger ends; 563 known enemy casualties.
25 September	Operation Idaho Canyon ends; 565 known enemy casualties.
29 September	Operation Quyet Thang 21/38 begun as part of ARVN 32nd Regiment operations in An Xuyen Province, IV Corps.
1 October	President Nixon allows draft deferments for graduate students.
15 October	National Moratorium antiwar demonstrations attract huge crowds in Washington, D.C. and other cities.
1 November	Vietnam Winter–Spring 1970 Campaign commences.
	Operation Dan Tien 33D begun by ARVN 23rd Division in Quang Duc Province, II Corps.
12 November	Operation Dan Tien 40 begun by ARVN 23rd Division in Quang Duc Province, II Corps.
15 November	Antiwar demonstrations in Washington, D.C. sponsored by New Mobilization Committee to End the War in Vietnam ("New Mobe") draw some 250,000 demonstrators, largest such rally to date; follows three-day "March against Death."
16 November	My Lai massacre revealed.
30 November	U.S. Third Marine Division withdraws from Vietnam.
1 December	The first draft lottery since 1942 is held at Selective Service System headquarters.
7 December	Operation Randolph Glenn begun by U.S. 101st Airborne Division (Airmobile) in coordination with ARVN First Infantry Division to provide shield of security on periphery of populated lowlands of Thua Thien Province, I Corps.
11 December	U.S. Third Brigade, 82nd Airborne Division withdrawn from Vietnam.
13 December	Philippine Civic Action Group departs Vietnam.

28 December   Operation Dan Tien 33D ends; 746 known enemy casualties.

Operation Dan Tien 40 ends; 1,012 known enemy casualties.

31 December   Operation Quyet Thang ends; 37,874 known enemy casualties.

Operation Dan Thang 69 ends; 507 known enemy casualties.

Operation Lien Ket 414 ends; 710 known enemy casualties.

Operation Lien Ket 531 ends; 542 known enemy casualties.

Operation Quyet Thang 21/38 ends; 721 known enemy casualties.

U.S. military personnel strength in Vietnam declines to 475,200. 40,024 U.S. military personnel killed in action to date.

Free World Military Force personnel in Vietnam now 70,300. SVNAF strength increases to 897,000. 110,176 SVNAF killed in action to date.

1970

20 February   Henry Kissinger begins secret peace talks in Paris.

February   Operation Good Luck begun by U.S. Air Force in Laos to strike North Vietnamese and Pathet Lao forces in Plaine Des Jarres.

16–22 March   The New Mobilization Committee to End the War in Vietnam ("New Mobe") sponsors a national "antidraft week."

18 March   Prince Norodom Sihanouk of Cambodia overthrown by General Lon Nol.

31 March   Operation Randolph Glen ends; 670 known enemy casualties.

March   U.S. 26th Marine Regiment Fifth Marine Division departs Vietnam.

1 April   Operation Texas Star begun by U.S. 101st Airborne Division (Airmobile) in the western portion of Quang Tri and Thua Thien Provinces, I Corps.

2 April   Massachusetts Governor Francis Sargent signs bill challenging legality of Vietnam war.

4 April   The largest Washington, D.C. prowar demonstration since America's involvement in Vietnam.

15 April   U.S. First Infantry Division withdraws from Vietnam.

29 April   Operations in Cambodia begun. 13 major ground operation (two of which involve U.S. ground campaign units) to clear North Vietnamese sanctuaries within 19 miles of the South Vietnamese border.

30 April   President Nixon announces Cambodian "incursion."

April   Operation Patio begun by U.S. Air Force to strike targets in Cambodia in support of U.S. ground operations.

1 May   Sanctuary Counteroffensive Campaign commences.

4 May   Four students killed at Kent State University in Ohio by National Guardsmen during antiwar protest.

9 May   President Nixon meets with students protesting Cambodian "incursion."

May   U.S. Air Force Operation Patio ends.

Operation Freedom Deal begun by U.S. Air Force to strike targets in Cambodia in support of Cambodian army.

U.S. Air Force Operation Menu ends.

30 June   Allied ground operations in Cambodia end; 10,000 known enemy casualties.

1 July   Vietnam Counteroffensive Phase VII Campaign commences.

July   Admiral Thomas Moorer replaces General Earle Wheeler as Chairman, Joint Chiefs of Staff.

Admiral Elmo Zumwalt replaces Admiral Thomas Moorer as Chief of Naval Operations.

5 September   Operation Texas Star ends; 1,782 known enemy casualties.

Operation Jefferson Glenn begun by U.S. 101st Airborne Division (Airmobile) in coordination with ARVN First Infantry Division in Thua Thien Province, I Corps.

9 October   Khmer Republic proclaimed in Cambodia.

11 October   U.S. Third Brigade, Ninth Infantry Division withdraws from Vietnam.

21 November   U.S. raid on Son Tay prison camp in North Vietnam.

7 December   U.S. Fourth Infantry Division withdraws from Vietnam.

U.S. First Logistical Command withdraws from Vietnam.

8 December   U.S. 25th Infantry Division (less Second Brigade) withdraws from Vietnam.

14 December   U.S. 44th Medical Brigade withdraws from Vietnam.

22 December   U.S. Congress prohibits U.S. combat forces or advisers in Cambodia and Laos.

31 December   U.S. military personnel strength in Vietnam declines to 334,600. 44,245 U.S. military killed in action to date.

Free World Military Forces personnel in Vietnam decline to 67,700. SVNAF strength increases to 968,000. 133,522 SVNAF killed in action to date.

1971

1 January   Operation Washington Green ends; 1,957 known enemy casualties.

30 January   Operation Dewey Canyon II

begun by U.S. First Brigade, Fifth Infantry Division (Mechanized) in vicinity of Khe Sanh, I Corps, to secure launch site for Operation Lam Son 719.

7 February Operation Dewey Canyon II ends; U.S. units continue to provide support for ARVN operations in Laos.

8 February Operation Lam Son 719 begun by ARVN with operations in Laos along Route 9 adjacent to two northern provinces of South Vietnam; U.S. forces furnish aviation, airlift and firepower support.

3 March U.S. Fifth Special Forces Group withdraws from Vietnam.

5 March U.S. 11th Armored Cavalry Regiment, less Second Squadron, withdraws from Vietnam.

29 March Lt. William L. Calley, Jr. found guilty of premeditated murder at My Lai by U.S. Army court-martial at Fort Benning, Georgia.

6 April Operation Lam Son 719 ends; 19,360 known enemy casualties.

14 April U.S. III Marine Amphibious Force withdraws from Vietnam.

20 April Demonstrators in Washington, D.C. and San Francisco urge Congress to end war in Indochina.

29 April U.S. First Cavalry Division (Airmobile), less Third Brigade, withdraws from Vietnam.

30 April I Field Force Vietnam disestablished.

U.S. Second Brigade, 25th Infantry Division returns to Hawaii.

Reverend Philip Berrigan and seven others are indicted for plotting to kidnap Henry Kissinger and blow up heating tunnels in government buildings.

April U.S. First Marine Division withdraws from Vietnam.

2 May II Field Force Vietnam disestablished.

3–5 May Peoples Coalition for Peace and Justice holds antiwar protests in Washington, D.C.

13 June *New York Times* begins publication of *Pentagon Papers*.

30 June The Supreme Court rules that articles based on classified Pentagon material may be published by newspapers.

1 July Consolidation I Campaign commences.

9 July U.S. troops relinquish total responsibility for defense of the area just below the DMZ to South Vietnamese troops.

25 August U.S. 173rd Airborne Brigade withdraws from Vietnam.

27 August U.S. First Brigade, Fifth Infantry Division (Mechanized) withdraws from Vietnam.

31 August Royal Thai Army, less Second Brigade, withdraws from Vietnam.

August United States ends 20-year opposition to China presence in United Nations.

20 September U.S. 18th and 20th Engineer Brigades withdraw from Vietnam.

8 October Operation Jefferson Glenn ends; last major operation in which U.S. ground forces participate; 2,026 known enemy casualties.

12 November President Nixon announces that U.S. ground forces in Vietnam are now in defensive role; offensive activities now undertaken entirely by the South Vietnamese.

29 November U.S. Americal Division, including 11th Infantry Brigade and 198th Infantry Brigade, disbanded.

1 December Consolidation II Campaign commences.

26 December U.S. Air Force bombing of North Vietnam resumed.

31 December U.S. military strength declines to 156,800. 45,626 U.S. military killed in action to date.

Free World Military Forces personnel decline to 53,900. SVNAF strength increases to 1,046,250 personnel. 156,260 SVNAF killed in action to date.

1972

16 January Religious leaders from 46 Protestant, Catholic and Jewish denominations, meeting in Kansas City, Missouri to discuss Vietnam ask the administration to withdraw all American troops and refuse aid to the Indochinese governments.

January General Robert Cushman replaces General Leonard Chapman as Commandant of the Marine Corps.

21 February U.S. strategy in Pacific changes dramatically as President Nixon arrives in Peking for talks with People's Republic of China.

February ROK Marine Brigade withdraws from Vietnam.

10 March U.S. 101st Airborne Division (Airmobile) withdraws from Vietnam.

12 March Australian First Task Force withdraws from Vietnam.

23 March The U.S. delegation to the Paris peace talks announces an indefinite suspension of the conference until North Vietnamese and National Liberation Front representatives enter into "serious discussions" on concrete issues determined beforehand.

30 March Vietnam Cease-Fire Campaign commences.

North Vietnamese launch Eastertide Offensive.

March U.S. Air Force Operation Commando Hunt ends.

Lon Nol named President of Cambodia.

Royal Thai Army Second Brigade withdraws from Vietnam.

6 April U.S. Second Squadron, 11th

	Armored Cavalry departs Vietnam.
7 April	NVA begins siege of provincial capital at An Loc, III Corps.
15 April	U.S. Air Force resumes bombing of Hanoi and Haiphong after four-year lull.
15–20 April	Hundreds of antiwar demonstrators arrested in incidents across the country as the escalation of the bombing in Indochina provokes a new wave of protests.
27 April	The Paris peace talks resume after a one-month break.
1 May	Provincial capital of Quang Tri, I Corps, falls to North Vietamese attack.
4 May	The United States and South Vietnam call an indefinite halt to the Paris peace talks after the 149th session.
8 May	North Vietnamese ports mined by U.S. Navy.
15 May	U.S. Army Vietnam headquarters disestablished.
May	Operation Linebacker I, tactical air support of ARVN forces to repulse NVA Eastertide Offensive, begun by U.S. Air Force.
18 June	Siege of An Loc ends as NVA forces withdraw in defeat.
26 June	U.S. Third Brigade, First Cavalry Division (Airmobile) withdraws from Vietnam.
29 June	U.S. 196th Infantry Brigade, the last U.S. Army combat brigade in Vietnam, withdraws.
30 June	U.S. XXIV Corps disestablished.
June	General Fred Weyand replaces General Creighton Abrams as Commander, U.S. Military Assistance Command Vietnam (MACV).
	New Zealand forces withdraw from Vietnam.
1 July	General Bruce Palmer, Jr. becomes Acting Chief of Staff, U.S. Army, replacing General William Westmoreland.
13 July	The Paris peace talks resume after a 10-week suspension.
23 August	U.S. Third Battalion, 21st Infantry, the last U.S. ground combat battalion, withdraws from Vietnam.
15 September	Provincial capital of Quang Tri recaptured by South Vietnamese forces.
26–27 September	Henry Kissinger holds more private talks with North Vietnamese representatives in Paris.
September	Admiral Noel Gayler replaces Admiral John S. McCain, Jr. as CINCPAC (Commander-in-Chief, Pacific Command).
16 October	General Creighton Abrams assumes office as Chief of Staff, U.S. Army.
17 October	Peace talks begin in Laos.
19–20 October	Henry Kissinger and other U.S. officials hold meetings with South Vietnamese President Nguyen Van Thieu in Saigon.
October	U.S. Air Force Operation Linebacker I ends.

7 November President Nixon defeats Senator George McGovern and is re-elected President of United States.

U.S. First Signal Brigade departs Vietnam.

11 November U.S. logistical base at Long Binh turned over to South Vietnamese, marking end to direct U.S. Army participation in the war.

20–21 November Henry Kissinger and Le Duc Tho hold more private discussions to work out a final Indochina peace agreement.

4 December Henry Kissinger and Le Duc Tho resume private Indochina peace talks near Paris after a nine-day recess.

13 December Paris peace talks deadlock.

18–29 December Operation Linebacker II, so-called "Christmas Bombing" of Hanoi and Haiphong, conducted by U.S. Air Force.

31 December U.S. military strength declines to 24,200. 45,926 U.S. military personnel killed in action to date.

Free World Military Forces personnel decline to 35,500. SVNAF strength increases to 1,048,000. 195,847 SVNAF killed in action to date.

1973

8–12 January Henry Kissinger and Le Duc Tho hold more secret peace talks.

15 January President Nixon announces halt to all U.S. offensive action against North Vietnam.

27 January Peace pact signed in Paris by U.S., South Vietnamese, Viet Cong and North Vietnamese.

End of U.S. military draft announced by Secretary of Defense Melvin Laird.

28 January Vietnam Cease-Fire Campaign ends.

30 January Elliot L. Richardson replaces Melvin Laird as Secretary of Defense.

21 February Peace agreement signed in Laos; U.S. bombing ends and cease-fire begins.

16 March ROK Capital and Ninth Infantry Divisions withdraw from Vietnam.

28 March Cut-off date for award of Vietnam Service Medal and Republic of Vietnam Campaign Medal.

U.S. First Aviation Brigade departs Vietnam.

29 March MACV (U.S. Military Assistance Command Vietnam) headquarters disestablished.

U.S. 18th Military Police Brigade departs Vietnam.

The withdrawal of all American troops from South Vietnam and release of 590 U.S. war prisoners held by the communists are completed.

March U.S. Navy Operations Market

Time, Game Warden and Clearwater discontinued.

22 May Henry Kissinger and Le Duc Tho end their talks on implementation of the Vietnam truce agreement.

13 June A new accord aimed at strengthening the January 27 cease-fire agreement in South Vietnam is signed in Paris by the United States, North Vietnam, South Vietnam and the National Liberation Front.

24 June Graham Martin replaces Ellsworth Bunker as U.S. Ambassador to South Vietnam.

1 July U.S. Congress votes to end all bombing in Cambodia after August 15.

2 July James Schlesinger replaces Elliot Richardson as Secretary of Defense.

14 August U.S. Air Force Operations Arc Light and Freedom Deal end, as United States officially ceases bombing in Cambodia and thus all direct U.S. military action in Cambodia-Laos-Vietnam ceases.

22 September Henry Kissinger replaces William Rogers as Secretary of State and continues as National Security Adviser.

September General George Brown replaces General John Ryan as Chief of Staff, U.S. Air Force.

7 November U.S. Congress overrides presidential veto of War Powers Act.

31 December Size of U.S. military contingent in Vietnam limited to 50. 46,163

U.S. military killed in action to date.

No Free World Military Forces personnel remain in Vietnam. SVNAF estimated strength is 1,110,000. 223,748 SVNAF killed in action to date.

1974

July General David Jones replaces General George Brown as Chief of Staff, U.S. Air Force.

General George Brown replaces Admiral Thomas R. Moorer as Chairman, Joint Chiefs of Staff.

Admiral James Holloway replaces Admiral Elmo Zumwald as Chief of Naval Operations.

9 August Richard Nixon resigns as President; Vice President Gerald R. Ford becomes President of the United States.

20 August U.S. Congress cuts aid to South Vietnam from $1 billion to $700 million.

4 September General Creighton Abrams, Chief of Staff, U.S. Army dies in office.

16 September President Ford signs a proclamation offering clemency to Vietnam war-era draft evaders and military deserters.

3 October General Fred Weyand appointed Chief of Staff, U.S. Army.

13 December North Vietnamese attack South

Vietnamese positions in Phuoc Long Province, II Corps.

31 December U.S. military strength in Vietnam limited to 50 personnel. SVNAF statistics not available.

1975

6 January Phuoc Long Province falls to North Vietnamese attack.

8 January North Vietnamese Politburo orders major offensive to "liberate" South Vietnam by NVA cross-border invasion.

10 March Ban Me Thuot, II Corps, falls to NVA attack.

14 March President Nguyen Van Thieu orders withdrawal of ARVN forces from Central Highlands, II Corps.

19 March Quang Tri Province, I Corps, falls to North Vietnamese attack.

26 March City of Hué falls to NVA attack.

30 March City of Da Nang falls to NVA attack.

1 April Cambodian President Lon Nol abdicates.

Cities of Qui Nhon, Tuy Hoa and Nha Trang are abandoned

by the South Vietnamese, yielding entire northern half of country to North Vietnamese.

8–20 April Battle of Xuan Loc rages, as ARVN 18th Infantry Division attempts to hold off attack by three NVA divisions.

11–13 April U.S. Navy conducts Operation Eagle Pull to evacuate U.S. embassy staff from Phnom Penh, Cambodia.

12 April South Vietnamese President Nguyen Van Thieu resigns.

14 April American airlift of homeless children to the United States from South Vietnam ends. A total of about 14,000 children arrived.

17 April Cambodia falls as Khmer Rouge troops capture Phnom Penh and government forces surrender.

29 April NVA begins attack on Saigon.

Corporal Charles McMahon, Jr., USMC and Lance Corporal Darwin Judge, USMC are last U.S. military personnel killed in action in Vietnam, struck by shrapnel from NVA rocket.

29–30 April U.S. Navy conducts Operation Frequent Wind to evacuate all U.S. personnel and selected South Vietnamese from Vietnam.

NVA captures Saigon.

30 April Vietnam war ends.

Part III

the vietnam war: A to Z

A

ABRAMS, CREIGHTON WILLIAMS, JR. (1914–1974)

Born in Springfield, Massachusetts on September 16, 1914, Abrams graduated from the U.S. Military Academy in 1936. He won fame in World War II as one of the Army's foremost tank commanders. A Division and Corps Commander in the early 1960s, he served as the Deputy Chief of Staff for Operations and Vice Chief of Staff of the Army before becoming deputy to General William Westmoreland in the MACV (U.S. Military Assistance Command Vietnam) in 1967.

When General Westmoreland was appointed Chief of Staff of the Army in July 1968, General Abrams assumed command of the MACV. He had the difficult task of implementing the so-called Vietnamization policies instituted by the Nixon Administration. They required the gradual reduction of American forces in Vietnam while keeping North Vietnamese forces at bay. The Cambodian "incursion" in 1970 was part of his plan to take pressure off the withdrawal.

In 1972 General Abrams again succeeded General Westmoreland as Chief of Staff of the Army. Among his major contributions were the plans and strategies for the post-Vietnam Army and his revitalization of the Army following its withdrawal from Vietnam. General Abrams died in office on September 4, 1974.

See also CAMBODIA, VIETNAMIZATION.

Suggestions for further reading: *The 25-Year War: America's Military Role in Vietnam,* by Bruce Palmer, Jr. (Lexington: University of Kentucky Press, 1984).

General Creighton W. Abrams. (Courtesy U.S. Army.)

ACE

In aerial warfare, downing five enemy aircraft qualifies a fighter pilot for the unofficial designation "ace." Since in Vietnam the primary U.S. fighter aircraft, the F-4 Phantom, a twin-engine supersonic fighter, required a weapons system/radar-intercept officer as well as the pilot, both got credit for the downing of an enemy aircraft.

As a result, for the first time ever aviators rated as navigators rather than pilots became air aces. U.S. Air Force Captain Charles D. DeBellevue, a weapons system officer, was the leading air ace, with six North Vietnamese MIG kills, five of them with Air Force F-4 pilot Captain Richard S.

Ritchie, who also qualified as an ace. The only other Air Force ace was another rated navigator, Captain Jeffrey S. Feinstein. Although U.S. Navy aviators shot down some 57 enemy MIGs over North Vietnam, the only Navy aces were F-4 pilot Lieutenant Randy Cunningham and his radar-intercept officer, Lieutenant (junior grade) William Driscoll, who shot down three North Vietnamese MIG-17s in one day. A total of 193 North Vietnamese aircraft were lost in air-to-air combat; the United States lost 89 aircraft, the majority early in the war.

Suggestions for further reading: *Aces and Aerial Victories—The United States Air Force in Southeast Asia, 1965-1973*, edited by James N. Eastman, Jr., Walter Hanak and Lawrence J. Paszek (Washington, D.C.: U.S. Government Printing Office, 1976); *The Tale of Two Bridges and The Battle for the Skies over North Vietnam*, edited by A. J. C. Lavalle (Washington, D.C.: U.S. Government Printing Office, 1976); *Air Warfare in the Missile Age*, by Lon O. Nordeen, Jr. (Washington, D.C.: Smithsonian Institution Press, 1985).

AD HOC TASK FORCE ON VIETNAM

In late February 1968 following the Tet Offensive, President Johnson convened the Ad Hoc Task Force on Vietnam to examine a request from General William C. Westmoreland and the Joint Chiefs of Staff for more than 200,000 troops. The purpose of the request was to increase troop levels in Vietnam and to strengthen U.S. security in other parts of the world. The task force was chaired by incoming Secretary of State Clark Clifford, and at Clifford's request, it debated the need for these troops and the nature of the entire U.S. role in Vietnam. Those members in favor of the request included General Earle Wheeler, Chairman of the Joint Chiefs of Staff, Walt W. Rostow, Special Assistant to the President, and General Maxwell Taylor. Among those opposed to the request were Deputy Undersecretary of Defense Paul Nitze, Undersecretary of State Nicholas Katzenbach and Assistant Secretary of

Defense for International Security Affairs Paul Warnke. Clifford remained neutral, attempting to use the debate to formulate his own position. The task force on March 7 recommended immediate deployment of 23,000 troops to Vietnam and approval of reserve callups, larger draft calls and extended tours of duty to provide additional troops. However, on March 31, the President, following consultation with a group of senior statesmen, announced a de-escalation of the U.S. war effort.

See also CLIFFORD, CLARK; JOHNSON, LYNDON; SENIOR ADVISORY GROUP; TET OFFENSIVE.

ADVISERS

See ADVISORY EFFORT, MAAG-VIETNAM (U.S. MILITARY ASSISTANCE ADVISORY GROUP-VIETNAM), MACV (U.S. MILITARY ASSISTANCE COMMAND VIETNAM)

ADVISORY EFFORT

After World War II the practice of sending U.S. advisers to assist allied armed forces became regularized. When in 1948 the newly formed government of South Korea, known officially as the Republic of Korea (ROK), asked the United States for help in setting up its armed forces, the Korean Military Advisory Group (KMAG) was formed there. When war broke out in 1950, KMAG was subordinated to the U.S. Eighth Army, the field army headquarters responsible for the prosecution of the war, and at the request of ROK President Syngman Rhee, ROK combat forces were also placed under Eighth Army operational control. At the height of the war, some 2,000 KMAG advisers were attached to these ROK units.

At the same time President Harry S Truman ordered American troops into Korea on June 27, 1950, he directed "acceleration in the furnishing of military assistance to the forces of France and the Associated States in Indo-China [i.e., Cambodia, Laos and Vietnam] and the dispatch of a military mission to provide close working relations with those forces." This "military mission" was the U.S. Military Assistance Advisory Group (MAAG) Indochina, which was established in Saigon on September 17, 1950. After the formation of South Vietnam, known officially as the Republic of Vietnam (RVN) by the Geneva Accords in 1954, the title was changed to the MAAG-Vietnam. Advisory teams were first assigned to South Vietnam's Joint General Staff, Defense Ministry, Army, Navy and Air Force, then to military schools, training centers and Army divisions as well. Their mission included combat arms training for the South Vietnamese Armed Forces (SVNAF) and, as MAAG strength increased, province and regimental advisers were assigned to South Vietnamese units in the field. There were some 900 military advisers in Indochina when President Dwight D. Eisenhower left office in 1961. By 1963, under President John F. Kennedy, the figure had risen to 16,300.

In February 1962 a new headquarters, the U.S. Military Assistance Command Vietnam, which became known as the MACV, was formed in Saigon. Subordinate to the Commander-in-Chief of the Pacific Command in Honolulu, the MACV absorbed the MAAG-Vietnam in 1964. When the buildup of U.S. combat forces began in 1965, the advisory effort was not subordinated to a field army headquarters, as in the Korean war. Instead the MACV took command of U.S. ground combat operations while continuing its concentration on internal South Vietnamese issues, thereby making the external enemy—the North Vietnamese Army—a secondary concern.

Further, the MACV deliberately chose not to request operational control of SVNAF units. They remained under command of the SVNAF Joint General Staff throughout the war. With no command authority but with the authority to request and coordinate U.S. fire support and facilitate military aid, U.S. advisers were attached to all provinces and districts and within SVNAF to the battalion level.

In addition to these military advisers, CORDS (Civil Operations and Revolutionary Development Support) also had large numbers of advisers in the field. At its peak strength, around the end of 1969, CORDS had about 6,500 military personnel and 1,100 Foreign Service officers, Agency for International Development personnel, U.S. Infor-

A. U.S. Marine shows two South Vietnamese soldiers how to use a flamethrower. (Courtesy U.S. Army.)

mation Agency personnel and other U.S. government civilians assigned to it.

The effect of this enormous advisory effort was exactly the opposite from what had been intended. Instead of building an independent, self-reliant armed force (as had eventually been the case with ROK forces), the MACV produced a force dependent on U.S. advice and support. In 1975, with this advice and support no longer available, the SVNAF crumbled in the face of North Vietnam's cross-border blitzkrieg.

See also AUSTRALIA; CORDS (CIVILIAN OPERATIONS AND REVOLUTIONARY DEVELOPMENT SUPPORT); FARM GATE; MAAG-VIETNAM (U.S. MILITARY ASSISTANCE ADVISORY GROUP-VIETNAM); MACV (U.S. MILITARY ASSISTANCE COMMAND VIETNAM); MARINE CORPS, U.S.; NAVY, U.S.; SVNAF (SOUTH VIETNAMESE ARMED FORCES). For MACV Field Advisory Group, *see* MACV.

Suggestions for further reading: *Bureaucracy Does Its Thing: Institutional Constraints on US-GVN Performance,* by Robert W. Komer (Santa Monica: RAND, 1972); *The Fall of South Vietnam: Statements by Vietnamese Military and Civilian Leaders,* by Stephen T. Hosmer et al (Santa Monica: RAND, 1978); *Strategy and Tactics,* by Hoang Ngoc Long (Washington, D.C.: U.S. Government Printing Office, 1980); *On Strategy: A Critical Analysis of the Vietnam War,* by Harry G. Summers, Jr. (Novato, Calif.: Presidio Press, 1982); *The 25-Year War: America's Military Role in Vietnam,* by Bruce Palmer, Jr. (Louisville: University of Kentucky Press, 1984); *The RVNAF,* by Dong Van Khuyen (Washington, D.C.: U.S. Government Printing Office, 1980); *The U.S. Advisor,* by Cao Van Vien et al (Washington, D.C.: U.S. Government Printing Office, 1980); *The Development and Training of the South Vietnamese Army 1950-1972,* by James Lawton Collins, Jr. (Washington, D.C.: U.S. Government Printing Office, 1975); *The United States Army in Vietnam, Advice and Support: The Early Years 1941-1960,* by Ronald H. Spector (Washington, D.C.: U.S. Government Printing Office, 1984); *The United States Navy and the Vietnam Conflict: The Setting of the Stage to 1959,* by Edwin B. Hooper, Dean C. Allard and Oscar P. Fitzgerald (Washington, D.C.: U.S. Government Printing Office, 1976); *The United States Air Force: The Advisory Years to 1965,* by Robert F. Futrell (Washington, D.C.: U.S. Government Printing Office, 1981); *U.S. Marines in Vietnam: The Advisory and Combat Assistance Era, 1954-1964,* by Robert C. Whitlow (Washington, D.C.: U.S. Government Printing Office, 1977); *The Vietnam Experience: Passing the Torch,* by Edward Doyal, Samuel Lipsman and Stephen Weiss (Boston: Boston Publishing Co., 1981). One of the best accounts of early advisory efforts in Vietnam is David Halberstam's novel *One Very Hot Day* (New York: Warner Books, 1984).

AEROMEDICAL EVACUATION

Aerial evacuation of casualties was one of the major advances in medical treatment during the Vietnam war. In World War II, when no tactical aircraft were made available to fly American casualties from the battlefield, 4.5 percent of wounded U.S. soldiers died after finally reaching a medical facility. In the Korean war, where about one of every seven U.S. casualties was evacuated by helicopter, the rate dropped to 2.5 percent.

In Vietnam the rate dropped further, to under 1 percent, thanks to evacuation of the majority of U.S. casualties from the battlefield by air ambulance helicopters, evacuation of seriously wounded to in-country hospitals by tactical airlift fixed-wing aircraft and evacuation out of country by the U.S. Military Airlift Command's aeromedical evacuation aircraft.

See also DUSTOFF, 834TH AIR DIVISION, MILITARY AIRLIFT COMMAND.

AGENT ORANGE

One of the terrible legacies of the Vietnam war is what many veterans believe to be their contamination with Agent Orange. Used as a herbicide and sprayed by the U.S. Air Force from C-123 aircraft in a defoliation operation called Ranch Hand from 1962 to 1970, this chemical contained minute amounts (approximately 2.0 parts per million) of a poisonous substance called 2, 3, 7, 8-tetrachloridibenzo-para-dioxin (TCDD), a type of dioxin, which has been claimed to result in various health problems.

According to a Veterans' Administration study, the major herbicides sprayed in Vietnam were assigned code names corresponding to the color of identification bands painted on the herbicide storage drums. During the initial stages of light herbicide use in Vietnam, from 1962 through 1964, the most commonly used herbicides were Purple and Pink.

During this period of Operation Ranch Hand, approximately 145,000 gallons of Purple and 123,000 gallons of Pink were sprayed in South Vietnam. After 1964 the most widely used herbicides were Orange, White and Blue, which rapidly replaced Purple and Pink. The approximate annual and total volumes of Orange, White and Blue sprayed in Vietnam from August 1965 through February 1971 are shown below.

Heavily sprayed areas included inland forests near the DMZ; inland forests at the junction of the borders of Cambodia, Laos and South Vietnam; inland forests north and northwest of Saigon; mangrove forests on the southernmost peninsula of Vietnam; and mangrove forests along major inland shipping channels southeast of Saigon. Crop destruction missions were concentrated in northern and eastern central areas of South Vietnam (*see* maps).

Most of the herbicides used in Vietnam were sprayed by fixed-wing aircraft, although a substantial number of missions were also carried out by helicopter, particularly after mid-1970. Only small amounts of herbicides were sprayed by ground sources such as river boats, trucks and personnel wearing back-pack sprayers.

The aerial spraying of herbicides rapidly declined in 1970 after reports were released concerning the toxicity of the dioxin contaminant in Agent Orange. The last spraying of herbicides by airplane in Vietnam occurred in January 1971. After that, sprayings were carried out by helicopter or on the ground; these operations were terminated by the end of 1971.

The primary use of herbicide was to kill vegetation and thereby deny cover to enemy forces. By making ambushes more difficult, Agent Orange undoubtedly saved American lives. Often confused with pesticides that were sprayed directly over U.S. installations by Air Force planes to control malaria-carrying mosquitoes, Agent Orange was not normally sprayed directly on troops. But soldiers did come in contact with it as they moved through jungle areas that had been defoliated.

Beginning in the late 1970s, Vietnam veterans began to cite dioxin as the cause of health problems ranging from skin rashes to cancer to birth defects in their children. Although dioxin has proven extremely poisonous in laboratory animals, considerable controversy still exists over its effect on humans. While not admitting any liability, chemical companies that manufactured the herbicide have agreed to establish a $180 million fund to be distributed to eligible veterans by a "special master" appointed by the U.S. District Court in Brooklyn, New York. The agreement

Application of Herbicides in the Vietnam War, by Year

Millions of Gallons

Year	1962– July 1965	Aug-Dec 1965	1966	1967	1968	1969	1970	1971	Total
Orange	NA[a]	.37	1.64	3.17	2.22	3.25	.57	.00	11.22
White	NA[a]	0	.53	1.33	2.13	1.02	.22	.01	5.24
Blue	NA[a]	0	.02	.38	.28	.26	.18	.00	1.12
Total	1.27	.37	2.19	4.88	4.63	4.53	.97	.01	18.85

[a] Not Available.

Source: Veterans Administration, *Review of Literature on Herbicides, Including Phenoxy Herbicides and Associated Dioxins*, Vol. 1 (Washington, D. C.: U.S. Government Printing Office, October 1981).

A U.S. Air Force plane spraying Agent Orange defoliant. (Courtesy Air War College)

was made in response to a class action suit by veterans. According to the terms of the settlement, a claimant "who dies or becomes totally disabled from an illness (not caused by trauma such as auto accident or gunshot wound) anytime during the period from the Vietnam war to December 31, 1994" and who meets the exposure standard will be eligible.

A team from the Centers for Disease Control, U.S. Public Health Service, has set out to correlate areas defoliated by Agent Orange with U.S. troop locations at the time the defoliant was used so as to determine precisely who meets such exposure standards.

Since the late 1970s the Veterans Administration has provided free medical tests to veterans citing health problems that they believe may be related to Agent Orange.

Suggestions for further reading: "The Veterans' Ordeal," a review article of Fred A. Wilcox's *Waiting for an Army to Die: Tragedy of Agent Orange* (New York: Random House, 1983), by C. D. B. Bryant, *The New Republic*, June 27, 1983, pp. 26–33; *Operation Ranch Hand: The United States Air Force and Herbicides in Southeast Asia, 1961–1971*, by William

A. Buckingham (Washington, D.C.: U.S. Government Printing Office, 1982); *Tactical and Matériel Innovations*, by John H. Hay, Jr. (Washington, D.C.: U.S. Government Printing Office, 1974); *Review of Literature on Herbicides, Including Phenoxy Herbicides and Associated Dioxins*, 4 vols., Veterans Administration (Washington, D.C.: U.S. Government Printing Office, 1984). For background on dioxin, see *Scientific Yearbook 1985*, edited by Bryan Bunch (New York: Facts On File Publications, 1985).

AIR AMERICA

The cover name for aircraft operated by the CIA in Southeast Asia. Growing out of the air support provided by the ostensibly Chinese Nationalist Civil Air Transport as early as 1954, Air America was established by the CIA in 1959. It provided clandestine air support for CIA operations throughout Indochina, including support for local tribesmen in Laos.

See also CIA (CENTRAL INTELLIGENCE AGENCY); LAOS; NEUTRALITY.

Suggestions for further reading: *Air America*, by

Christopher Robbins (New York: G. P. Putnam's Sons, 1979); *The Vietnam Experience: Thunder from Above* and *Rain of Fire*, by John Morrocco (Boston: Boston Publishing Company, 1984 and 1985).

AIRBORNE FORCES

Airborne forces—that is, soldiers who either parachuted into battle or were landed by gliders—came into their own in World War II. Widely used in that war, they became an integral part of many of the world's armies.

Although several U.S. airborne units were deployed to Vietnam—the 101st Airborne Division; the Third Brigade, the 82nd Airborne Division and the 173rd Airborne Brigade—airborne operations as such played little part in the Vietnam war. While elements of the 173rd Airborne Brigade made a combat parachute jump during Operation Junction City on February 22, 1967, in most of their combat operations these units were as light infantry carried into battle by helicopter rather than by parachute.

The U.S. Marine divisional reconnaissance battalions had airborne-qualified personnel, and one reconnaissance company made a combat jump near Chu Lai on June 14, 1966.

The U.S. Military Assistance Command Vietnam Studies and Observation Group (MACV-SOG) and the Vietnamese Strategic Technical Directorate had an airborne element that dropped commandos into remote areas of Vietnam, Laos and Cambodia. The Australian Special Air Service (SAS) also had an airborne capability, and its Third

A South Vietnamese Army airborne insignia.

Members of the U.S. 101st Airborne Division parachute into Dong Ba Tinh, South Vietnam in July 1965. (Courtesy U.S. Army.)

SAS Squadron made a parachute assault in Phuoc Tuy Province in December 1966.

The South Vietnamese Army had several airborne battalions, which were combined into an Airborne Division in 1968. Headquartered in Saigon, these parachute troops were used as a "fire brigade" throughout Vietnam to reinforce beleaguered units, to hold the line at critical areas, and to act as an offensive shock unit. Some of these battalions conducted combat parachute assaults from 1962 through 1966, when helicopters were provided to them, although South Vietnamese paratroopers jumped in the Pleiku area to open a road as late as May 4, 1972.

The U.S. Army Special Forces raised six airborne-qualified mobile strike force battalions, composed of Chinese Nung as well as Jarai, Sedang and Rhade Montagnards. Led by Army Special Forces paratroopers, these battalions conducted four combat jumps inside South Vietnam during 1967 and 1968 to establish Special Forces camps in Viet Cong-dominated territory.

Neither the North Vietnamese Army nor the Viet Cong possessed an airborne capability.

Suggestions for further reading: An account of combat operations of U.S. airborne units is contained in Shelby L. Stanton's *The Rise and Fall of an American Army* and *The Green Berets at War* (Novato, Calif: Presidio Press, 1985); the 173rd Airborne Brigade's combat jump is further discussed in Bernard Williams Rogers' *Cedar Falls-Junction City: A Turning Point* (Washington, D.C.: U.S. Department of the Army Vietnam Studies, 1974).

AIR CAVALRY

The traditional role for cavalry on the battlefield was to reconnoiter enemy positions and to provide a screen behind which the infantry and artillery could prepare their main battle positions. While usually not a decisive force in itself, in the U.S. Army horse-mounted cavalry played a major role in operations against Indians on the Western plains. During World War II the horse was replaced by light mechanized vehicles, but cavalry functions remained essentially unchanged.

During the Vietnam war there were both armored cavalry units with tanks and armored personnel carriers and air cavalry units using helicopters and helicopter gunships. Air cavalry units included the Seventh Squadron, First Cavalry; Troop F, Fourth Cavalry; Troop F, Eighth Cavalry, the First Squadron, Ninth Cavalry; Troop H, 10th Cavalry; Troop C, 16th Cavalry; Troop F, Ninth Cavalry; the Second and Third Squadrons, 17th Cavalry; and independent Troops D, H and K of the 17th Cavalry.

See also AIRMOBILE OPERATIONS, FIRST CAVALRY DIVISION, 101ST AIRBORNE DIVISION.

Suggestions for further reading: Chapter 11, "Cavalry," *Vietnam Order of Battle*, by Shelby L. Stanton (Washington, D.C.: U.S. News Books, 1981); *Vietnam Studies: Airmobility, 1961-1971*, by John J. Tolson (Washington, D.C.: U.S. Government Printing Office, 1973).

AIRCRAFT CARRIERS

U.S. Navy aircraft carriers played a major role in the Vietnam war. They were on station in August 1964 during the Gulf of Tonkin Incident, which precipitated American combat involvement in Vietnam, and they were on station in April 1975 during Operation Frequent Wind, which evacuated the last Americans from Vietnam.

Operating from what was called Dixie Station and Yankee Station off the coast of Vietnam in the South China Sea, the Seventh Fleet's Task Force 77 was formed around these carriers. Attack carrier striking forces launched interdiction operations over North and South Vietnam, Laos and Cambodia and provided close air support for Army and Marine ground operations.

Aircraft carriers were not permanently stationed off Vietnam but were rotated in and out of the combat zone. During the course of the war, 19 aircraft carriers served separate combat deployments on station in the South China Sea, some as many as nine times. They included the *America* (CVA 66), *Bon Homme Richard* (CVA 31), *Constellation* (CVA 64), *Coral Sea* (CVA 43), *Enterprise* (CVAN 65), *Forrestal* (CVA 59), *Franklin D. Roosevelt* (CVA 42), *Hancock* (CVA 19), *Hornet* (CVS 12), *Independence* (CVA 62), *Intrepid* (CVS 11), *Kitty Hawk* (CVA 63),

Midway (CVA 41), *Oriskany* (CVA 34), *Ranger* (CVA 61), *Saratoga* (CVA 60), *Shangri-La* (CVS 38), *Ticonderoga* (CVA 14), and *Yorktown* (CVS 10).

Generally two or three carriers operated in Task Force 77, but after August 1966 the number increased to three or four. On each ship a carrier wing controlled 70 to 100 aircraft usually grouped into two fighter and three attack squadrons and other detachments. These aircraft included the A-4 Skyhawk, propeller-driven A-1 Skyraider, A-7 Corsair II and A-6 Intruder for strike operations. The F-4 Phantom II flew strike as well as fighter-escort missions, as did the F-8 crusader.

See also FIGHTERS AND FIGHTER-BOMBERS; LINE-BACKER OPERATIONS; NAVY, U.S.; ROLLING THUNDER; STEEL TIGER; TIGER HOUND.

Suggestions for further reading: *A Short History of the United States Navy and the Southeast Asian Conflict 1950–1975*, by Edward J. Marolda and G. Wesley Pryce, III (Washington, D.C.: Naval Historical Center, 1984); *The Naval Air War in Vietnam: 1965–1975*, by Peter Mersky and Norman Polmar (Annapolis: Nautical and Aviation Publishing Co. of America, 1981).

AIR CUSHION VEHICLES

A unique means of mobility employed during the Vietnam war, air-cushioned hovercraft (PACV) and airboats were used on a limited basis to patrol South Vietnam's extensive marshlands. In May 1966 the U.S. Navy began experimenting with PACVs, and the Army Special Forces started using airboats to patrol the Mekong Delta, which was subject to extensive flooding after the rainy season. While the Viet Cong could reach most areas by sampan, conventional allied boats were useless during periods when the water level dropped to the point that grasses fouled propellers. During these periods, airboats and PACVs successfully provided mobility for South Vietnamese troops, since the water was still too deep for foot soldiers.

The Navy was dissatisfied with PACVs because they were considered too noisy and too mechanically sophisticated to maintain in the riverine war, but the Army Special Forces welcomed their service in the Delta. After unsatisfactory service around Da Nang, the Navy pulled its craft back to the United States in 1968 for reevaluation. The Army used the PACVs in a special Ninth Infantry Division unit, the 39th Cavalry Platoon, from May 1968 until September 1970. The Army Special Forces and the Ninth Infantry Division used airboats with considerable success from 1966 until their departure from Vietman, although the airboats proved both expensive to operate and logistically difficult to support.

See also RIVER PATROL FORCE.

Suggestions for further reading: *A Short History of the United States Navy and the Southeast Asian Conflict 1950–1975*, by Edward J. Marolda and G. Wesley Pryce, III (Washington, D.C.: Naval Historical Center, 1984); *Tactical and Matériel Innovations*, by John H. Hay, Jr. (Washington D.C.: U.S. Government Printing Office, 1974). Airboats are extensively described in Shelby L. Stanton's *The Green Berets at War* (Novato, Calif.: Presidio Press, 1985).

AIR DEFENSE

Air defense for U.S. forces in Vietnam was provided primarily by the Air Force, which maintained air control over Vietnam and thus prevented North Vietnamese use of air power to support their combat operations in the south. It was not until April 28, 1975, two days before the fall of South Vietnam, that Saigon was bombed by four captured U.S. A-37 jet fighters.

As a second line of defense, in February 1965 the U.S. Marine Corps deployed Hawk Missile units to Da Nang and in September 1965 the U.S. Army deployed the 97th Artillery Group to Vietnam. Consisting of two battalions armed with Hawk missiles, one battalion—the Sixth Battalion, 56th Artillery—was initially stationed at Tan Son Nhut Air Base near Saigon and later moved north to Chu Lai. The other battalion—the Sixth Battalion, 71st Artillery—was first stationed at Qui Nhon and later relocated to Cam Ranh Bay. These units were withdrawn from Vietnam in October 1968. In addition, several other air defense artillery battalions that normally would have been part of the Army's air defense cover-

This is the notorious "shoot-down" series of postage stamps issued by Hanoi as part of its air defense campaign.

U.S. Army air defense Hawk missiles. (Courtesy U.S. Army Military History Institute)

age—the Fifth Battalion, Second Artillery; the First Battalion, 44th Artillery; and the Fourth Battalion, 60th Artillery—were deployed to Vietnam. These latter units, armed with 40-mm M-42 "duster" antiaircraft guns and augmented by several separate batteries equipped with quad M-55 mounted .50-caliber machine guns, were not used for air defense coverage but for direct support of ground combat operations.

In South Vietnam, North Vietnamese and Viet Cong air defense was provided primarily by rifles and machine guns. In the closing days of the war, the Soviet SA-7 man-portable antiaircraft missile was introduced and by 1974 some Soviet SA-2 medium-range surface-to-air missiles (SAMs) were deployed to South Vietnam.

North Vietnam, on the other hand, had one of the most effective air defense systems in history. The system included a mix of MIG-17 and later MIG-21 fighter aircraft and SA-2 surface-to-air missiles as well as thousands of other weapons, ranging from 12.7-mm to 100-mm guns. The guns forced attacking aircraft to fly high, where they were more vulnerable to the SAMs and the MIGs. Conversely, flying low to avoid the SAMs and MIGs increased their vulnerability to antiaircraft fire. Aircrews flying combat operations over the north likened the experience to flying into a wall of steel.

See also SAMs (SURFACE-TO-AIR MISSILES).

Suggestions for further reading: *The Battle for the Skies over North Vietnam, 1964–1972,* by Paul Burbage, et al, USAF Southeast Asia Monograph Series (Washington, D.C.: U.S. Government Printing Office, 1976); *The Vietnam Experience: Thunder from Above* and *Rain of Fire,* by John Morrocco (Boston: Boston Publishing, 1984 and 1985); *Air War over Southeast Asia,* 3 vols. (Carrollton, Tex.: Squadron/Signal Publications); *Aces and Aerial Victories—The United States Air Force in Southeast Asia, 1965–1973,* edited by James N. Eastman, Jr., Walter Hanak and Lawrence J. Paszek (Washington, D.C.: U.S. Government Printing Office, 1976).

AIR FORCE CROSS

With the U.S. Army's Distinguished Service Cross and the Navy Cross, the Air Force Cross is the nation's second highest award for bravery. The Air Force Cross is awarded in the name of the

President of the United States by the Air Force for extraordinary heroism, not justifying the award of a Medal of Honor, while engaged in an action against the enemy. The act or acts of heroism have to be so notable and have involved risk of life so extraordinary as to set the individual apart from his comrades. Subsequent awards are denoted by an oak leaf worn on the ribbon.

See also DISTINGUISHED SERVICE CROSS, NAVY CROSS.

The Air Force Cross.

AIR FORCE, NORTH VIETNAMESE

See AIR DEFENSE, FIGHTERS AND FIGHTER-BOMBERS.

AIR FORCE, REPUBLIC OF VIETNAM (VNAF)

See FIGHTERS AND FIGHTER-BOMBERS, SVNAF (SOUTH VIETNAMESE ARMED FORCES).

AIR FORCE, SOUTH VIETNAMESE

See FIGHTERS AND FIGHTER-BOMBERS, SVNAF (SOUTH VIETNAMESE ARMED FORCES).

AIR FORCE, U.S.

Air power was a major part of the U.S. military presence in Southeast Asia, and the U.S. Air Force played a key role in the war effort there.

Air Force operations fell into four major categories in Southeast Asia. First was the air war in South Vietnam, which involved close air support of ground operations, interdiction of enemy supply lines, tactical—intratheater (within Southeast Asia)—airlift, coordination of B-52 Arc Light strikes by the Strategic Air Command and coordination of intertheater (between Vietnam and countries outside of Southeast Asia, including the United States) airlift by the Military Air Command.

The second category was the air war over North Vietnam, which included the Rolling Thunder campaigns beginning in 1965 and the Linebacker campaigns in 1972. The third and fourth categories involved interdiction of the Ho Chi Minh Trail in southern Laos from 1965 to 1973 and air support for the Royal Laotian Army in northern Laos from December 1963 to February 1973.

In addition to these major categories, Air Force operations included support of government forces in Cambodia from March 1969 to August 1973, the Ranch Hand Operation to defoliate enemy base areas, search-and-rescue operations and an advisory effort in support of the South Vietnamese Air Force.

During the Vietnam war, command and control of air operations was extremely complicated. Except for the Strategic Air Command's B-52 bomber operations, the Seventh Air Force Commander was in charge of Air Force activity throughout Southeast Asia. For air operations over South Vietnam and for air operations against the southern portions of the Ho Chi Minh Trail just north of the DMZ through southern Laos and Cambodia, the Seventh Air Force Commander took his orders from the MACV Commander. Outside these areas (i.e., air operations over northern Laos and over North Vietnam except for the area just north of the DMZ), the Seventh Air Force Commander took his orders from the Commander-in-Chief of the Pacific Air Force (CINCPACAF) in Honolulu. Both CINCPACAF and the MACV Commander reported to the Commander-in-Chief of the Pacific Command (CINCPAC), also in Honolulu, who allocated air missions between the Air Force and the Navy.

Of the 47,244 Americans killed in action, 1,737 were Air Force personnel, as were 939 of the 153,329 Americans wounded in action severely enough to require hospitalization and 2,518 of the 150,375 Americans lightly wounded in action. Air Force casualties included 1,099 fixed-wing and 88 helicopter pilots and aircrew members killed in action. As of February 1985, 941 Air Force personnel were still missing in action and unaccounted for. Aircraft losses, both from combat and other operational causes, totaled 2,257 planes. Twelve Medals of Honor were awarded to Air Force personnel for bravery in Vietnam and three Air Force aviators were designated as aces for downing North Vietnamese MIG aircraft over North Vietnam.

See also ACE, AGENT ORANGE, ARC LIGHT, COMMAND AND CONTROL, LAOS, LINEBACKER OPERATIONS, MENU OPERATION, MILITARY AIRLIFT COMMAND, NIAGARA OPERATION, POW/MIA, ROLLING THUNDER OPERATION, SVNAF (SOUTH VIETNAMESE ARMED FORCES), SEVENTH AIR FORCE, STRATEGIC AIR COMMAND, TACTICAL AIR COMMAND.

Suggestions for further reading: *The U.S. Air Force in Southeast Asia 1961–1973,* edited by Carl Berger (Washington, D.C.: U.S. Government Printing Office, 1977); *The Vietnam Experience. Thunder from Above* and *Rain of Fire,* by John Morrocco (Boston: Boston Publishing Co., 1984 and 1985).

Seal of the United States Air Force.

AIR MEDAL

First authorized in World War II, the Air Medal is awarded in the name of the President of the United States to recognize single acts of merit or heroism or for meritorious service while participating in aerial flight. Awards (denoted by a "V" worn on the ribbon) are given for acts of heroism in connection with military operations against an armed enemy that were of a lesser degree than required for award of the Distinguished Flying Cross. Awards are also made for single acts of control of combat operations. After the first award, a numeral worn on the ribbon indicates the number of subsequent awards.

AIRMOBILE OPERATIONS

One of the major battlefield innovations of the Vietnam war was the extensive use of airmobile operations. Beginning in the early 1950s, the U.S. Army began to develop the concept of using helicopters both to transport soldiers to the battlefield and to provide battlefield fire support. By the early 1960s, this concept was tested by the 11th Air Assault Division at Fort Benning, Georgia. The rapidly deteriorating situation in Vietnam caused the Army to convert this test division into a regular unit—renaming it the First Cavalry Division (Airmobile) in 1965—which was soon thereafter deployed to Vietnam. Later the 101st Airborne Division was also converted to an airmobile division and it remains the only airmobile division in the U.S. Army. Airmobile operations, however, were not confined to these specially designated units. While these units had helicopters assigned, other Army and Marine infantry units were able to conduct periodic airmobile assaults by using helicopter units that were attached to them from independent aviation units.

Airmobile operations enabled U.S. forces to frustrate Viet Cong and North Vietnamese ambush tactics and were successful in keeping the North Vietnamese and Viet Cong off balance. In a conventional infantry assault, troops move into position while artillery softens up the enemy; they then launch an assault to seize the enemy position. In airmobile operations, artillery, jet fighters and helicopter gunships rake an area with fire while infantry units close into the battle area in transport helicopters. Moments before they land, the supporting fire is lifted and the soldiers embark from their helicopters with guns blazing. This tactic was highly successful and allowed U.S. combat forces to counter the enemy tactic of ambushing road-bound reinforcements and supply convoys.

Suggestions for further reading: *Airmobility 1961–1971*, by John J. Tolson (Washington, D.C.:

The Air Medal.

meritorious achievement, involving superior airmanship, that were of a lesser degree than required for award of the Distinguished Flying Cross but were nevertheless accomplished with distinction beyond that normally expected.

Further, awards for meritorious service are provided for sustained distinction in the performance of duties involving regular and frequent participation in aerial flight for a period of a least six months. Such awards are primarily intended to recognize those whose duties required them to participate in aerial flight on a regular and frequent basis. In addition to aircrews, they include those in the attack elements of units involved in air-land assaults against an armed enemy and those directly involved in airborne command and

A U.S. Army airmobile operation underway. (Courtesy U.S. Army Military History Institute.)

U.S. Government Printing Office, 1973): *Tactical and Matériel Innovations,* by John H. Hay, Jr. (Washington, D.C.: U.S. Government Printing Office, 1974). For selected airmobile battlefield operations, see *The Rise and Fall of an American Army,* by Shelby L. Stanton (Novato, Calif.: Presidio Press, 1985).

AK-47 RIFLE

The Soviet AK-47 assault rifle (the Avtomat Kalashnikova 1947, named for its Soviet inventor, Mikhail Timofeyevich Kalashnikov, who copied it in 1947 from a 1944 German assault rifle) became, with the Chinese copy, the T-56, the standard infantry weapon of the Viet Cong (VC) and the North Vietnamese Army (NVA). This rifle was vastly superior to the South Vietnamese weapons, which were World War II-vintage American arms of a heavier and less automatic nature. The AK-47 rifle provided NVA and VC forces with a battlefield firepower superiority over the South

The AK-47 assault rifle was the preferred weapon of the North Vietnamese and the Viet Cong. (Courtesy U.S. Army Military History Institute.)

Vietnamese Army until 1968, when the South Vietnamese began receiving large quantities of M-16s for their own use.

Using a 7.62 mm bullet, the AK-47 could be fired either single shot or on full automatic. Easy to maintain and simple to operate, the AK-47 was an extremely effective battlefield weapon.

See also M-16 RIFLE.

AMBASSADOR TO THE REPUBLIC OF VIETNAM, U.S.

See AMBASSADOR TO SOUTH VIETNAM, U.S.

AMBASSADOR TO SOUTH VIETNAM, U.S.

Ambassadors of the United States have authority over all U.S. government personnel—except those under military commands—within their country of assignment. In July 1964 President Johnson directed that in Vietnam the U.S. Ambassador's "overall responsibility includes the whole military effort in South Vietnam and authorizes the degree of command and control that [the Ambassador may] consider appropriate."

From the first U.S. military deaths in 1959 until the end of the Vietnam war in 1975, the post of U.S. Ambassador to South Vietnam changed hands six times: Elbridge Durbrow (1957-61), Frederick J. Nolting (1961-63), Henry Cabot Lodge (1963-64), Maxwell D. Taylor (1964-65), Lodge again (1965-67), Ellsworth Bunker (1967-73) and Graham Martin (1973-75).

See also BUNKER, ELLSWORTH; COMMAND AND CONTROL; LODGE, HENRY CABOT; MARTIN, GRAHAM; NOLTING, FREDERICK J.; TAYLOR, MAXWELL D.

AMERICAL INFANTRY DIVISION

The American Division was formed on the battlefield in World War II, deriving its name from the phrase "Americans in New Caledonia," an island in the South Pacific that it defended from Japanese attack. In October 1942 the Americal Division became the first U.S. Army unit of World War II to go on the offensive, taking part in the attack on Guadualcanal.

During the Vietnam war it became necessary in February 1967 to reinforce Marine units operating in I Corps in Vietnam's northernmost provinces. Army brigades from the First Cavalry, Fourth Infantry and 101st Airborne Divisions along with the 196th Brigade served initially under a combat headquarters called Task Force Oregon until September 1967, when the Americal Division, as in World War II, was activated on the battlefield, releasing the divisional brigades to return to their parent units and in their place bringing together three previously independent units—the 11th, 196th and the 198th Light Infantry Brigades. The Americal Division (officially designated the 23rd Infantry Division) consisted of 11 battalions of light infantry (the Second and Third Battalions, First Infantry; the Fourth Battalion, Third Infantry; the First Battalion, Sixth Infantry; the First Battalion, 20th Infantry; the Third and Fourth Battalions, 21st Infantry; the Fourth Battalion, 31st Infantry; the First and Fifth Battalions, 46th Infantry; and the First Battalion, 52nd Infantry). Its other combat elements included one armored cavalry squadron (the First Squadron, First Cavalry, which had been and is again part of the First Armored Division), two armored reconnaissance troops (Troop E, First Cavalry and Troop F, 17th Cavalry) and an air reconnaissance troop (Troop F, Eighth Cavalry); and six battalions of artillery—three with 105-mm howitzers (the Sixth Battalion, 11th Artillery; the First Battalion, 14th Artillery; and the Third Battalion, 82nd Artillery), two battalions with 155-mm howitzers (the Third Battalion, 16th Artillery and the First Battalion, 82nd Artillery); and the Third Battalion, 18th Artillery with 8-inch howitzers and 175-mm guns. The division also had its own aviation group, with three battalions of assault helicopters and gunships and two companies of assault support helicopters. In effect, the division's air mobility was equal to that of the designated airmobile divisions (the First Cavalry and the 101st Airborne).

The Americal Division fought continuously in the three southern provinces of I Corps; but as in World War II, elements of the division were dispatched to other areas, fighting at the side of U.S. Marine units along the DMZ and in other northern provinces in the I Corps area. Unlike most of the Army units in Vietnam, which battled Viet Cong guerrillas, the Americal Division's combat operations were primarily against North Vietnamese regulars. The American Division less the 196th Infantry Brigade was deactivated in December 1971. The 196th Brigade remained in Vietnam until June 1971 and was the last U.S. combat brigade to depart Vietnam.

The Americal Division was awarded the Cross of Gallantry with Palm by the South Vietnamese government in recognition of its combat service. Soldiers of the division won 11 Medals of Honor for bravery on the battlefield. While overall casualty figures are difficult to obtain because the Americal Division was a composite unit, the 11th Light Infantry Brigade suffered some 5,400 soldiers killed or wounded in Vietnam, the 196th Light Infantry Brigade suffered 6,610 soldiers killed or wounded and the 198th Light Infantry Brigade suffered some 5,555 killed or wounded. The 17,565 casualties suffered by these three brigades alone were more than four times as high as the 4,209 casualties the entire Americal Division suffered in World War II.

Although the Americal Division is no longer on active duty, there is an Americal Division Veterans Association that publishes a periodic newsletter. Further information can be obtained from Mr. William L. Dunphy, 247 Willow Street, West Roxbury, Massachusetts 02132. The association also maintains a museum at Fort Devens, Massachusetts.

See also I CORPS TACTICAL ZONE, 196TH INFANTRY BRIGADE, XXIV CORPS.

Suggestions for further reading: *Vietnam Studies: War in the Northern Provinces 1966–1968*, by Willard Pierson (Washington, D.C.: U.S. Government Printing Office, 1975) and *Vietnam Order of Battle*, by Shelby L. Stanton (Washington, D.C.: U.S. News & World Report Books, 1981). An account of the division's combat operations, including selected small unit actions, is contained in Shelby L. Stanton's *The Rise and Fall of an American Army* (Novato, Calif.: Presidio Press, 1985).

AMPHIBIOUS FORCES

The Seventh Fleet's amphibious task force (Task Force 76) was organized into a number of amphibious ready groups (ARG) and special landing forces (SLF).

An ARG usually consisted of three or four ships: an attack transport (APA) or an attack

U.S. Marines landing at Da Nang in the spring of 1965. (Courtesy U.S. Marine Corps.)

cargo ship (AKA) or both; a dock landing ship (LSD) or landing platform dock (LPD) and a tank landing ship (LST). An SLF was a 2,000-man unit composed of a Marine helicopter squadron of about 25 aircraft and a Marine battalion landing team—an infantry battalion reinforced with artillery, armor and other support elements.

Landed by helicopter, by boat or by 41-tracked landing vehicles, the amphibious task force was supported by carrier air cover, naval gunfire and other fleet elements. From 1965 to 1969 Task Force 76 conducted numerous amphibious assaults, especially in I Corps in support of III Marine Amphibious Force operations.

In May 1972, during the North Vietnamese Army (NVA) Eastertide offensive, it landed South Vietnamese Army units behind enemy lines in I Corps to interdict enemy supply lines. In April 1975 Task Force 76 elements designated the Refugee Assistance Group (Task Group 76.8) assisted in the evacuation of Phnom Penh, Cambodia (Operation Eagle Pull) and the evacuation of Saigon (Operation Frequent Wind). The task force had landed the first U.S. ground combat troops in Vietnam in 1965. Ten years later, on April 30, 1975, it took the last Americans out.

See also EAGLE PULL OPERATION; EASTERTIDE OFFENSIVE; FREQUENT WIND OPERATION; NAVY, U.S.; II MARINE AMPHIBIOUS FORCE.

Suggestions for further reading: *A Short History of the United States Navy and the Southeast Asian Conflict 1950–1975,* by Edward J. Marolda and G. Wesley Pryce, III (Washington, D.C.: Naval Historical Center, 1984); "Marine Corps Operations in Vietnam, 1965–66, 1967, 1968, 1969–72," by Edwin H. Simmons, and "Amphibious Doctrine in Vietnam," by Peter L. Hilgartner, in *The Marines in Vietnam 1954–1973* (Washington, D.C.: U.S. Government Printing Office, 1974).

AN LOC, BATTLE OF

The capital of Binh Long Province, located 65 air miles north of Saigon, An Loc was the site of one of the major battles of the North Vietnamese Eastertide Offensive in 1972.

Striking from their Cambodian base areas on April 5, 1972, the Fifth Division—composed of Viet Cong (VC) and regular North Vietnamese Army (NVA) units supported by NVA tank and artillery regiments—overran the town of Loc Ninh (which became the capital of the Provisional Revolutionary Government of South Vietnam [PRG]), some 15 miles to the north of An Loc, and then moved to seize An Loc.

Meanwhile, South Vietnamese President Thieu moved the South Vietnamese Army Fifth Division into An Loc with orders to hold at all costs. Soon thereafter the NVA Ninth Division—also composed of VC and NVA units—moved from its Cambodian base area and joined in the attack, shelling An Loc with tank and artillery fire. To prevent reinforcement of the South Vietnamese units, the NVA Seventh Division barred the road south of An Loc.

The main assault began on April 13 and continued for 95 straight days. Although driven back, the South Vietnamese continued to hold. Massive bombing by U.S. Air Force B-52s supported their defense and helped break up enemy concentrations. The North Vietnamese and Viet Cong lifted the siege on July 11, 1972 and withdrew to their base areas in Cambodia.

See also EASTERTIDE OFFENSIVE.

Suggestions for further reading: *The Vietnam Experience: South Vietnam on Trial,* by David Fulghum and Terrence Maitland (Boston: Boston Publishing Co., 1984); *Battles and Campaigns in Vietnam 1954–1984,* by Tom Carhart (New York: Crown Publishers, 1984).

ANNAM

A name first applied to Vietnam by the Chinese in the seventh century. Composed of the Chinese character "an [安]" (a pictograph of a woman under a roof, hence "contented" or "pacified") and "nam [南]" (south), the name implied that the Vietnamese had reconciled themselves to Chinese rule and it was therefore deeply resented by them.

The name was revived in the mid-nineteenth century by the French, who used it as the title of their protectorate over central Vietnam. The

Vietnamese people and their language were thus frequently referred to as "Annamese."

See also Part I, THE SETTING.

ANTIWAR MOVEMENT

One of the salient features of the Vietnam war was the size and intensity of the American antiwar movement. There had been dissent against every other American war, but the opposition had usually been peripheral. A complex movement, opposition to the Vietnam war sprang from a variety of sources, including students, academics, members of the clergy, pacifists, social activists, civil rights advocates, government officials, the media, members of Congress, writers, intellectuals, artists and entertainers, as well as radicals from the new left and black power movements. Eventually, it included almost every segment of American society.

Early dissent came from foreign policy specialists who viewed Southeast Asia as an area of negligible strategic interest and who saw U.S. involvement there as a dangerous diversion from America's primary interests in Europe. Some State Department officials advised against supporting what they believed to be an authoritarian regime in South Vietnam that lacked popular support. President Eisenhower's personal representative to South Vietnam, General J. Lawton Collins, urged the President to withdraw support of President Ngo Dinh Diem because of his failure to carry out reforms. Chester Bowles, during his brief tenure as Undersecretary of State in the Kennedy Administration, unsuccessfully advanced a policy of neutralization for Vietnam similar to that being sought for Laos. Bowles' successor, George Ball, was for several years the only high ranking administration dissenter against military involvement in Vietnam. Yet this dissent stayed largely within the confines of the foreign policy elite. (*See* BALL, GEORGE W.; COLLINS, J. LAWTON; KENNAN, GEORGE F.)

Eventually, several high-level officials of the Johnson Administration, as well as some senior members of previous administrations, turned against the war and worked toward achieving a peaceful solution. After leaving government service, some of them spoke at antiwar rallies. (*See* CLIFFORD, CLARK; GOLDBERG, ARTHUR; HARRIMAN, AVERELL; HILSMAN, ROGER; HOOPES, DAVID; NITZE, PAUL H.; SENIOR ADVISORY GROUP; WARNKE, PAUL C. *See also* BUNDY, McGEORGE; JOHNSON, LYNDON B.; McNAMARA, ROBERT S.; McNAUGHTON, JOHN T.)

There was little dissent among the nation's political leaders during the early years of the war. The Tonkin Gulf Resolution sailed through Congress in 1964, introduced by the man who would become the most visible and persistent critic of the war in Congress, J. William Fulbright, and opposed by only Wayne Morse and Ernest Gruening. Two years later Fulbright, who bitterly regretted his action, conducted televised hearings during which top administration officials were forced to defend American involvement in Vietnam against foreign policy critics. It was the first time questions and doubts about the war were raised in a public hearing. However, a subsequent attempt to repeal the Tonkin Gulf Resolution was defeated. (*See* TONKIN GULF RESOLUTION.)

Although doubts about the growing U.S. entanglement in the war had by then affected several Senators, only a small minority had spoken out against it—Frank Church, John Sherman Cooper, George McGovern and Gaylord Nelson, as well as Fulbright, Gruening and Morse. Following Johnson's escalation of the conflict in 1965 and early 1966, the list grew steadily to include many prominent members of Congress, both Democrats and Republicans. Two Democratic Senators—Eugene McCarthy and Robert Kennedy, a one-time vocal supporter of the war—declared themselves "peace" candidates for the presidency in 1968, contributing to Johnson's decision not to seek re-election. Yet it would be long into the Nixon Administration before Congress seriously attempted to use the power of the purse to legislate an end to, or even a curtailment of, the war. Many Senators and Representatives who opposed the war simply would not vote to cut off funding for it while U.S. troops were still in Vietnam. (*See* CHURCH, FRANK; COOPER, JOHN SHERMAN; FULBRIGHT, J. WILLIAM; GRAVEL, MIKE; GRUENING, ERNEST; HATFIELD, MARK O.; JAVITS, JACOB K.; KENNEDY, ROBERT F.; MANSFIELD, MIKE; McCARTHY, EUGENE J.; McGOVERN, GEORGE S.; SYMINGTON, STUART.)

The media, like Congress, endorsed U.S. policy in Vietnam in the early years. In 1962 American newspapers, including the *New York Times* and the *Washington Post*, backed the U.S. commitment. A year later, however, stories in the *Times* and, through the wire services, in other newspapers conflicted with some of the optimistic reports issued by the administration. When President Johnson escalated the war in 1965, *Times* columnist James Reston questioned the administration's candor and syndicated columnist Walter Lippmann, once a supporter of President Johnson, began attacking the administration's policy as well as its honesty. Press coverage grew more critical thereafter, but it was not until the Tet Offensive in early 1968—after the public had registered its disapproval of the war—that the *Washington Post* and *Time* and *Life*, which President Johnson had regarded as his strongest allies in the war effort, began to call for a change in policy. Even the *Wall Street Journal* predicted that the United States might have to accept a solution short of victory. (*See* HALBERSTAM, DAVID; LIPPMANN, WALTER; MEDIA; SALISBURY, HARRISON, E.)

The networks too accepted the administration's line on the war and ignored most protest activities at the outset. However, nightly news clips from Vietnam, combined with press accounts, showed that the war was more difficult, the enemy more tenacious and the chances for victory more remote than the administration had declared. Television magnified the length of the war, which Americans had been led to believe would end quickly. In 1967 the fighting was described as a "stalemate" and American forces as "bogged down." Following Tet, Walter Cronkite reported that the United States might have to accept a stalemate. The defection of Cronkite was a serious blow to the President, who had always considered him the voice of the average citizen. (*See* CRONKITE, WALTER; MEDIA; TELEVISION.)

Early opposition to the war among private citizens came from pacifists, like Dave Dellinger and A. J. Muste, who had opposed previous wars and violence in general, and social activists, such as Daniel Berrigan and William Sloane Coffin, who were also opposed to violence and concerned about diversion of funds from programs to alleviate poverty. Benjamin Spock, the noted pediatrician, gravitated toward the antiwar movement from his involvement with the antinuclear movement. Many of the early opponents of the war spoke at colleges and universities, where they found enthusiastic audiences. (*See* BERRIGAN, DANIEL; COFFIN, WILLIAM SLOANE; SPOCK, BENJAMIN.)

The sixties was a decade marked by student activism and social protest and there was a feeling alive on campuses that the system could be changed, that protest could be successful. Students found the war immoral and unjust for a variety of reasons, and the attractiveness of activism contributed to their commitment. They heard arguments that the United States was acting like a colonial power, that it was seeking to impose an American solution on a foreign people, that it was waging a war with excessive cruelty, that it was interfering in what was essentially a civil war and violating international agreements, among other charges. But self-interest was also a motivating factor in student protests. Even though the Johnson Administration had granted college students deferment from the draft, they still faced the threat of the draft upon graduation. (*See* DRAFT.)

Some of the inspiration for student activism in the antiwar movement sprang from participation in civil rights demonstrations. In early 1965 a coalition of civil rights and antiwar groups, coordinated by Students for a Democratic Society, brought 20,000 people to Washington to protest the war. James Bevel, a member of the Southern Christian Leadership Conference and an associate of Martin Luther King, Jr., called for an alliance between the antiwar and civil rights movements. Yet when Martin Luther King, Jr. openly identified with the antiwar movement, he was criticized by other prominent civil rights leaders, including Roy Wilkins of the NAACP and Whitney Young of the Urban League, who wished to keep the civil rights struggle separate from foreign policy issues. For King, whose opposition to the war had initially sprung from concerns that it was taking attention and funds away from efforts to eradicate poverty and inequality in America, the antiwar movement came to represent a broadening of his commitment to nonviolence on an

Antiwar demonstrators assemble opposite the Lincoln Memorial on October 21, 1967. (Courtesy AP/Wide World Photos.)

international scale. (*See* BEVEL, JAMES L.; KING, MARTIN LUTHER, JR.)

Beginning about 1965 numerous organizations and peace coalitions were formed to protest the war and some existing organizations began directing their energies to the same purpose: the Spring Mobilization Against the War, Women's Strike for Peace, Clergy and Laity Concerned about Vietnam, Committee for a Sane Nuclear Policy, or SANE, and the Vietnam Day Committee. Despite their common opposition to the war, there was often disagreement among and within these groups over the proper tactics to be used. Some advocated peaceful means of protest: teach-ins, marches, support of peace candidates, etc. Others pursued more militant tactics, such as attempts to disrupt troop trains. There were exhortations to resist the draft, draft card burnings, attempts to destroy Selective Service files and advice to servicemen to disobey unlawful orders.

By 1967 the movement had attracted a sector intent on confrontation with what it perceived as a corrupt political and social system. Rather than change the system, this element sought to make a mockery of it and included some who wanted to overthrow it. Their actions culminated in the bloody riots during the Democratic National Convention in August 1968. That riot combined with mass arrests at the Pentagon in October 1967, student takeovers of university buildings and other protests left the impression that the country was being torn apart. (*See* CHICAGO SEVEN; DEMOCRATIC NATIONAL CONVENTION, 1968; HAYDEN, THOMAS E.; HOFFMAN, ABBIE; RUBIN, JERRY.)

Such activities no doubt hardened people's attitudes toward continued support of the war—a poll in 1967 showed that 75% of Americans thought the movement was hurting the country. Yet, the antiwar movement in the mid-1960s

Demonstrators approach lines of U.S. marshals and military police in front of the Pentagon during an antiwar rally on October 21, 1967.

stirred concern among people who had never given much thought to America's involvement in a war in Vietnam, and it tended to offset the administration's efforts to play down the nation's escalating commitment there.

Motives in the antiwar movement ranged from moral, religious and ethical commitment to peace, the political vision of a different kind of America, the conviction that the war was ill-chosen, badly planned and too costly and radical political hopes that the war might help overthrow the present system to self-interest, indifference or unwillingness to fight in or to pay for the war. No one group had any exclusive claim on any one motivation.

The single most potent factor in ending the war was the American public. President Johnson's efforts to keep the war as low key as possible led to a lack of understanding of the objectives, the costs and the duration of the conflict, resulting in a credibility gap between the government and the

people. Slowly, as the casualties rose, the costs increased and the dates for victory came and went, the American political center turned against the war. In 1967, for the first time a majority of Americans believed that military involvement in the war had been a mistake, although many objected to the lack of a winning strategy and constraints on the military—a feeling that has persisted into the 1980s. (*See* PUBLIC OPINION.) While the North Vietnamese later conceded it to be a devastating defeat, the Tet Offensive suggested that even with half a million American troops and sustained bombing of North Vietnam, the enemy was very much alive. The strategy pursued by the administration was not working.

After Tet, the public, joined by Congress and the media, would continue to press for an end to U.S. involvement, although the President was still able to rally a majority of Americans behind military escalation during periods of crisis. The withdrawal of public support for the war forced Lyndon Johnson to de-escalate and drove him from office. It also contributed to the defeat of his heir apparent, Hubert Humphrey, by Richard Nixon, who claimed to have a secret plan to end the war. (*See* HUMPHREY, HUBERT H.)

Ten months after Nixon's inauguration in January 1969, the first Moratorium Against the War brought out huge crowds of Americans in several cities. The demonstrations were somber, in marked contrast to the upheaval in Chicago the summer before. In November the largest antiwar protest to date was staged in Washington, D.C. Thereafter, demonstrations moved beyond campuses into communities and attracted an increasing number of ordinary citizens, people who were unaccustomed to protest. (*See* BROWN, SAM; MORATORIUM AGAINST THE WAR.)

The first Moratorium drew a message of support from Hanoi, which would direct similar messages at the peace movement in the future. There would also be publicized trips to North Vietnam by antiwar activists seeking to gain the release of American prisoners of war or to see first-hand the war's effects. Their statements were often exploited by Hanoi for propaganda, and they appeared to many Americans to be cooperating with the enemy.

The Cambodian incursion in 1970 touched off a storm of protest at colleges and universities. Four students were killed in a confrontation with National Guardsmen at Kent State University in Ohio, which in turn led to hundreds of college shutdowns. The incursion also evoked strong criticism from the press, as well as from educators, business leaders and other vocal elements of the population. Although Congress rejected a measure to bar U.S. ground incursions into Cambodia, it banned the introduction of American ground troops into Laos or Thailand, and momentum was gaining for further curbs on the President's war-making powers. (*See* CAMBODIA, COOPER-CHURCH AMENDMENT, KENT STATE INCIDENT.)

The mass protests against the war, coupled with the revelation in the *New York Times* in 1969 that U.S. planes were bombing Cambodia, created a siege mentality within the White House. As in the Johnson years, there was concern that domestic protest of foreign policy decisions would hurt

U.S. prestige abroad, and Nixon and his chief foreign policy adviser, Henry Kissinger, felt it necessary to adopt illegal or extralegal tactics to deter their more radical and resolute foes. Federal agencies gathered data and kept files on antiwar groups and eventually on private citizens critical of the administration's Vietnam policy.

Contributing to this siege mentality, in 1971 the *New York Times* published a top secret study of U.S. military involvement in Southeast Asia, called the *Pentagon Papers*, that had been stolen from the Defense Department by Daniel Ellsberg, a civilian defense analyst. A short time later, a unit was created within the White House to "plug" leaks of information to the press. The illegal activities of this unit, including an attempt to obtain derogatory information about Ellsberg, eventually resulted in the Watergate scandal, which forced President Nixon to resign. The *Pentagon Papers* seemed to confirm long-held suspicions that the government had misinformed the public about the Vietnam war. (*See* ELLSBERG, DANIEL; PENTAGON PAPERS.)

Pressure to repatriate all American troops continued to mount in 1971. Congress rejected a bill by Senators McGovern and Hatfield that called for a withdrawal of all combat troops by the end of the year. A similar bill by Senator Mansfield was also defeated, but other end-the-war measures were introduced. Protests against the war, including a huge rally in Washington, D.C., in the spring, continued across the country. Thus far peace negotiations had failed to make any substantial progress.

In response to a North Vietnamese offensive in the spring of 1972, Nixon ordered bombing of the Hanoi-Haiphong area and mining of Haiphong harbor, again unleashing denunciations from the press and setting off more protests. He repeated the tactic in December, when peace talks with the North Vietnamese broke down. Dubbed the "Christmas Bombing," the raids sparked yet another burst of criticism from news commentators. In January 1973 a formal cease-fire was signed and the last U.S. troops left Vietnam at the end of March.

By steadily withdrawing U.S. forces from Vietnam, President Nixon managed to take some of the force out of antiwar protests, and the public in general approved of his handling of the war. Nevertheless, because of continued demand at home for an end to the war, the United States was compelled to make a major concession to the North Vietnamese: North Vietnamese troops were allowed to remain in place in South Vietnam. In return the North Vietnamese dropped their demand for the ouster of South Vietnamese President Nguyen Van Thieu. At the end of 1973 the President signed a bill that barred the use of funds for U.S. military operations in or over Vietnam, Laos or Cambodia. Two years later South Vietnam fell. (*See* CASE-CHURCH AMENDMENT; KISSINGER, HENRY A.; NIXON, RICHARD M.; PARIS ACCORDS; VIETNAMIZATION.)

Extremists aside, the majority of the antiwar movement were decent and honorable Americans genuinely concerned with a war that had never been adequately explained or justified and that, therefore, in conscience they could not support.

The Vietnam war and the antiwar movement in the United States left both activists and the "silent majority" drained and suspicious of their government. The sixties generation that had both fought and protested the war had begun the decade in the full promise of justice and a new age of opportunity. They left it embittered and exhausted. In the wake of countless books, films and documentaries on the period, however, by the 1980s the Vietnam generation had begun to reevaluate the events and emotions of those years, postwar events in Southeast Asia and the value and effect of the peace movement.

Suggestions for further reading: *American Catholics and Vietnam,* edited by Thomas E. Quigley (Grand Rapids: Eerdman's 1968); *War, Presidents, and Public Opinion,* by John E. Mueller (New York: John Wiley, 1973); *The War at Home: Vietnam and the American People 1964-1968,* by Thomas Powers (New York: Grossman, 1973; reissued Boston: G. K. Hall, 1984); *Soldiers in Revolt,* by David Cortright (Garden City, N.Y.: Doubleday, 1975); *Chance and Circumstance: The Draft, the War and the Vietnam Generation,* by Lawrence Baskir and William A. Straus (New York: Random House, 1978); "Fallibility and the Fourth Estate," by Richard Reeves, *Esquire,* (February 1978: 8+); *With Clumsy Grace: The American Catholic Left 1961-1975,* by Charles A. Meconis (New York: Seabury-Continuum, 1979); *Why We Were in Vietnam,* by Norman Podhoretz (New York: Simon & Schuster, 1982); *Choice of Conscience: Vietnam Era Military and Draft Resisters in Canada,* by David S. Surrey (New York: Praeger, 1982); Chapter 11, "Homefront USA," in *Vietnam Anthology and Guide to a Television History,* by Steve Cohen (New York: Knopf, 1983); *The Vietnam Experience: A Nation Divided. The War at Home, 1945-1972,* by Clark Dougan and Samuel Lipsman (Boston: Boston Publishing Co., 1984); *Who Spoke Up? American Protest Against the War in Vietnam 1963-1975,* by Nancy Zaroulis and Gerald Sullivan (New York: Doubleday, 1984); "Reflections on the Vietnam Antiwar Movement and on the Curious Calm at the War's End," by John Mueller, in *Vietnam As History,* edited by Peter Braestrup (Washington, D.C.: University Press of America, 1984); *Long Time Passing: Vietnam and the Haunted Generation,* by Myra MacPherson (Garden City, N.Y.: Doubleday, 1984); *Vietnam Reconsidered: Lessons from a War,* edited by Harrison E. Salisbury (New York: Harper & Row, 1984); *Touched with Fire: The Future of the Vietnam Generation,* by John Wheeler (New York: Franklin Watts, 1984); *Vietnam: A History,* by Stanley Karnow (New York: Viking, 1983); *The Powers That Be,* by David Halberstam (New York: Alfred A. Knopf, 1979).

AP BIA

See HAMBURGER HILL.

APCs

See ARMORED PERSONNEL CARRIERS (APCs).

ARC LIGHT

Arc Light was the code name for the use of B-52 bombing missions to support ground tactical operations, to interdict enemy supply lines in Vietnam, Laos and Cambodia and later to strike targets in North Vietnam.

In 1964 the Air Force began to train strategic bomber aircrews in the delivery of conventional (i.e., non-nuclear) bombs, and the B-52F was modified to carry 24 750-pound bombs in addition to the 27 normally carried in its bomb bays. Later, B-52Ds were modified to carry 108 500-pound bombs.

Deployed to Andersen Air Force Base in Guam and later to bases in Okinawa and U-Tapao, Thailand, B-52s were ordered into action for the first time in June 1965. Within months such bombing raids became a daily occurrence. Releasing their bombs from 30,000 feet, the B-52s could be neither seen nor heard from the ground. The damage they inflicted, however, was awesome.

Used for the first time in close support of troops during the Battle of the Ia Drang Valley in November 1965, B-52s were instrumental in breaking up enemy concentrations besieging Khe Sanh in 1968 and An Loc in 1972. Between June 1965 and August 1973, 126,615 B-52 combat sorties were flown over Southeast Asia. Altogether, the Air Force lost 29 B-52s—17 from hostile fire over North Vietnam and 12 from operational causes.

See also NIAGARA OPERATION, STRATEGIC AIR COMMAND.

Suggestions for further reading: *The Vietnam Experience: Thunder from Above* and *Rain of Fire*, by John Morrocco (Boston: Boston Publishing Co., 1984 and 1985); *The United Air Force in Southeast Asia*, edited by Carl Berger (Washington, D.C.: U.S. Government Printing Office, 1977).

ARMED STRUGGLE

"Armed struggle" was an integral part of the basic North Vietnamese strategy of *dau tranh*. Normally translated as "struggle" or "struggle movement," this strategy consists of two elements: *dau tranh vu trang*, or "armed struggle," and *dau tranh chinh tri*, or "political struggle."

According to an analysis by Douglas Pike, Director of the East Asia Institute, University of California at Berkeley, "armed struggle" involved not only traditional military activity, including the use of North Vietnamese regular forces in concert with Viet Cong guerrilla forces against U.S. and South Vietnamese forces, but also kidnappings, assassinations and similar acts. Although "armed struggle" and "political struggle" were inexorably linked, the North Vietnamese shifted their emphasis on these two elements several times during the course of the war. Within the North Vietnamese high command, General Vo Nguyen Giap was the primary proponent of armed struggle, for he believed that victory was best achieved through direct military action. This strategy was followed from 1965 until the Tet Offensive in 1968, in which the communists sustained very heavy losses. It was again emphasized during the disastrous Eastertide Offensive of 1972 and during the Final Offensive in 1975.

See also EASTERTIDE OFFENSIVE; FINAL OFFENSIVE; POLITICAL STRUGGLE; STRATEGY, NORTH VIETNAMESE; TET OFFENSIVE.

Suggestions for further reading: *Viet Cong: The Organization and Techniques of the National Liberation Front of South Vietnam*, by Douglas Pike (Cambridge, Mass.: MIT Press, 1966); *History of the Vietnamese Communist Party* (Stanford: Hoover Institution, 1978).

ARMOR

Although the Vietnam war was normally thought of as a jungle war fought by infantry at close quarters, extensive use was made of armor—i.e., tanks and armored personnel carriers—by the U.S. Army and the South Vietnamese Army (ARVN, for Army of the Republic of Vietnam) and, in the later stages of the war, by the North Vietnamese Army (NVA) as well.

The U.S. Army deployed three tank battalions to Vietnam—the Second Battalion, 34th Armor to III Corps; the First Battalion, 69th Armor to II Corps; and the First Battalion, 77th Armor to I Corps. Company D, 16th Armor—with M-56 "scorpion" self-propelled 90-mm antitank guns—supported the 173rd Airborne Brigade. In addition, the 11th Armored Cavalry Regiment, five armored cavalry squadrons and several independent armored cavalry troops—equipped with tanks and armored personnel carriers modified to serve as fighting vehicles—as well as 10 battalions of mechanized infantry mounted in armored personnel carriers were also sent to Vietnam.

With each of its two divisions the U.S. Marine Corps deployed a tank battalion equipped with M-48A3 Patton tanks, an antitank battalion equipped with ONTOS self-propelled guns (each with six 106-mm recoilless rifles) and an amphibious tractor battalion. The Australian task force had an armored cavalry squadron.

Originally equipped with some armored cars and armored personnel carriers, by 1974 ARVN forces had, in each of the four corps tactical zones, an armored brigade consisting of four or five armored cavalry units and (except in IV Corps) a tank battalion.

North Vietnamese armor made its first appearance in February 1968, when 13 PT-76 amphibious tanks took part in the assault on the Special Forces camp outside Khe Sanh, the northernmost U.S. Marine installation in South Vietnam. During their Eastertide Offensive of 1972, the North Vietnamese used armor extensively, including T-54 Soviet tanks, in the battles of An Quang Tri and An Loc.

After being beaten back with heavy losses by ARVN defenders, the NVA, with Soviet help, rebuilt their armor capability to the point where on the eve of their Final Offensive they had some 700 tanks, almost double the 352 tanks available to the ARVN. This superiority in armor played a major role in the success of their 1975 blitzkrieg.

See also U.S. Army and Marine divisional listings, AIR CAVALRY, ARMORED PERSONNEL CARRIERS, 11TH ARMORED CAVALRY REGIMENT.

Suggestions for further reading: *Mounted Combat in Vietnam,* by Donn A. Starry (Washington, D.C.: U.S. Government Printing Office, 1979); *Vietnam Order of Battle,* by Shelby L. Stanton (Washington, D.C.: U.S. News & World Report Books, 1981); *Vietnam Tracks: Armor in Battle 1945–75,* by Simon Dunstan (Novato, Calif.: Presidio Press, 1982); *Tactical and Matériel Innovations,* by John H. Hay, Jr. (Washington, D.C.: U.S. Government Printing Office, 1974).

ARMORED PERSONNEL CARRIERS (APCs)

Armored Personnel Carriers (APCs) were widely used by U.S. and allied forces in Vietnam. The M113 APCs were the mainstay of armored cavalry formations of both the U.S. Army and the South Vietnamese Army. There were a number of variations, such as standard troop carriers, command post carriers, porta-bridge carriers, escort machine gun carriers, mortar carriers and

U.S. M-48 battle tanks in action northwest of Saigon. (Courtesy U.S. Army.)

A modified M-113 armored personnel carrier of the 11th Armored Cavalry Regiment. (Courtesy U.S. Army.)

flamethrower carriers. With the addition of gun shields, hatch armor and heavy and medium machine guns, the standard APCs were used as assault vehicles. Despite initial command concerns over their ability to traverse tropical terrain, the APCs proved a valuable addition to allied mobility and shock power on the battlefield.

See also ARMOR.

ARMY, NORTH VIETNAMESE

See NVA (NORTH VIETNAMESE ARMY).

ARMY, SOUTH VIETNAMESE

See SVNAF (SOUTH VIETNAMESE ARMED FORCES).

ARMY, U.S.

Since the war in Vietnam was primarily a ground war, the U.S. Army furnished the majority of the American combat units and thereby suffered the majority of the casualties. An Army general (the Commander of the U.S. Military Assistance Command Vietnam [COMUSMACV]) was in overall command in Vietnam itself, and in three of the four corps tactical zones, Army forces were the dominant military presence.

During the war the U.S. Army deployed seven infantry divisions, four independent infantry brigades and an armored cavalry regiment to Vietnam. These combat forces comprised 81 infantry battalions, three tank battalions, 12 cavalry squadrons, 70 artillery and air defense artillery battalions, and 142 aviation companies and air cavalry troops. Among other decorations and awards, 155 Medals of Honor were awarded to U.S. Army soldiers for conspicuous bravery in action in Vietnam. Of the 47,244 Americans killed in action, 30,868 were Army soldiers, as were 96,811 of the 153,329 Americans wounded in action severely enough to require hospitalization and 104,725 of the 150,375 Americans lightly wounded in action. As of

February 1985, 767 Army personnel were still missing in action and unaccounted for.

See also BATTALION; BRIGADE; CHIEF OF STAFF, U.S. ARMY; CORPS; DIVISION; REGIMENT; listings for specific units.

Suggestions for further reading: *Vietnam Order of Battle,* by Shelby L. Stanton (Washington, D.C.: U.S. News & World Report Books, 1981).

ARTILLERY

Artillery, the "king of battle," has always played a major role in American combat operations. In Vietnam the U.S. Army deployed some 65 battalions of artillery, including 32 battalions (with three batteries of six howitzers each) of 105-mm towed artillery, two battalions of self-propelled 105-mm howitzers, seven battalions of 155-mm towed artillery, five battalions of 155-mm self-propelled howitzers, five battalions of mixed 155-mm and 8-inch howitzers, 12 battalions of mixed 175-mm guns and 8-inch howitzers and two aerial rocket artillery battalions. Those artillery battalions that were not part of infantry divisions were organized into five artillery groups. The 41st and 52nd Artillery Groups provided fire support for I Field Force Vietnam, the 23rd and 54th Artillery Groups provided fire support for II Field Force Vietnam and the 108th Artillery Group supported XXIV Corps.

The U.S. Marine Corps deployed the First Field Artillery Group to Vietnam; it consisted of the 11th and 12th Marine Artillery Regiments, with 10 battalions and five separate batteries of artillery. In addition, the U.S. Navy provided naval gunfire support for the Marine Corps from ships of the Seventh Fleet. In 1967 alone the Navy fired over a half million rounds in support of ground combat operations.

In addition to American artillery, New Zealand provided an artillery battery, Australia an artillery battalion, the Philippines an artillery battalion, Thailand a three-battalion artillery brigade and South Korea six battalions of 105-mm and two battalions of 155-mm howitzers. By 1972 South Vietnamese Army artillery had increased to 44 battalions of 105-mm howitzers, 15 battalions of

A 105-mm howitzer crew in action near Qui Nhon. (Courtesy Shelby L. Stanton.)

A self-propelled U.S. Army M-107 175-mm gun. This gun had a crew of five and a maximum range of 32,600 meters. (Courtesy Army News Features.)

155-mm howitzers and five battalions of 175-mm guns.

In the early days of the war, North Vietnamese Army (NVA) fire support was limited primarily to mortars and rockets. Along the DMZ, however, NVA artillery played a significant role. In the latter days of the war, the North Vietnamese Army began to deploy its artillery in South Vietnam. The 1972 Eastertide Offensive was supported by NVA medium and heavy artillery, and the NVA's Final Offensive in 1975 was supported by some 400 pieces of artillery, including 76-mm, 85-mm, 100-mm, 122-mm and 130-mm guns and howitzers as well as rockets and 82-mm and 120-mm mortars. As a result, in their attack in the Central Highlands in 1975, for example, the North Vietnamese had a two-to-one superiority in heavy artillery over the South Vietnamese defenders.

See also U.S. Army and Marine divisional listings; AUSTRALIA; KOREA, SOUTH; MORTARS; NAVAL GUNFIRE SUPPORT; NEW ZEALAND; PHILIPPINES; ROCKETS; THAILAND.

Suggestions for further reading: *Field Artillery*

1954–1973, by David Ewing Ott (Washington, D.C.: U.S. Government Printing Office, 1975); *Vietnam Order of Battle,* by Shelby L. Stanton (Washington, D.C.: U.S. News & World Report Books, 1981).

ARVN (ARMY OF THE REPUBLIC OF VIETNAM)

See SVNAF (SOUTH VIETNAMESE ARMED FORCES).

ASEAN (ASSOCIATION OF SOUTHEAST ASIAN NATIONS)

A political and economic association formed in 1965 to promote cooperation among Indonesia, Malaysia, the Philippines, Singapore and Thailand. During the Vietnam war ASEAN deliberately avoided military cooperation; since the fall of South Vietnam, however, this association has increased its emphasis on security matters.

A SHAU VALLEY

Located in southwestern Thua Tien Province in western I Corps near the Laotian border, the A Shau Valley was a rugged, remote and relatively uninhabited area. U.S. Special Forces organized the local inhabitants into a CIDG (Civilian Irregular Defense Group) camp in April 1963 to block North Vietnamese Army (NVA) infiltration from Laos, but this camp was overrun in March 1966 and the area abandoned to the North Vietnamese. It soon became an NVA base area and a terminus for soldiers and war materials shipped south from North Vietnam along the nearby Ho Chi Minh Trail in Laos.

Several U.S. and South Vietnamese military operations were conducted in the A Shau Valley in 1968 and 1969 to dislodge the NVA. The most publicized was the battle for Ap Bia Mountain in May 1969, better known as the battle for "Hamburger Hill." Such operations were usually suc-

THE A SHAU VALLEY

cessful in pushing NVA forces out of the A Shau across the border into Laos, but as soon as U.S. and South Vietnamese forces withdrew, the NVA moved back into the area.

See also HAMBURGER HILL; *see* map at I CORPS TACTICAL ZONE.

Suggestions for further reading: For accounts of combat operations in the A Shau Valley, see *The War in the Northern Provinces,* by Willard Pearson (Washington, D.C.: U.S. Government Printing Office, 1975); *The Rise and Fall of an American Army,* by Shelby L. Stanton (Novato, Calif.: Presidio Press, 1985).

ATROCITIES

While atrocities occurred during the war in Vietnam, it is important to note that for American forces such actions were aberrations in direct violation of U.S. military law and specific MACV directives. For the Viet Cong and the North Vietnamese Army, however, atrocities were a deliberate, sanctioned tactic.

Ironically, the perception has been precisely the

reverse. The terrible slaughter by American forces run amok at My Lai has been seen as the norm, while the coldly calculated use of terror by the VC and NVA—at Hué in 1968, for example—has been forgotten.

The Vietnamese communist tactic of "political struggle" included the use of terror to isolate the people from their government. From the very beginning of their campaign to overthrow the South Vietnamese government, selected assassination of government officials was official policy. From 1958 to 1966, for example, some 61,000 South Vietnamese government officials were murdered, and such political assassinations continued throughout the war. It was not until 1967 that the Phoenix program was launched to eliminate the Viet Cong political infrastructure.

Ordinary civilians were also not immune. In December 1967 the Montagnard village of Dak Son was raided by the Viet Cong. Using flamethrowers, they razed the village and burned 252 of the villagers to death as an object lesson to other villages to cooperate. When VC and NVA forces overran the city of Hué in 1965, some 2,800 civilians were massacred and buried in makeshift graves. After the war, as Stanley Karnow relates in his *Vietnam: A History,* "The Communists proceeded to shunt four hundred thousand South Vietnamese civil servants and army officers as well as doctors, lawyers, teachers, journalists, and other intellectuals into 're-education' centers—and the concentration camps still hold between fifty and a hundred thousand people." According to refugee reports, these prisoners have been subject to the same brutal treatment accorded American prisoners of war. As former American POWs have vividly testified, torture was a normal procedure officially approved by the North Vietnamese government.

Contrary to the antiwar movement's charges of a "war crimes industry," atrocities by American forces were the exception, and those accused of such offenses were brought to trial. From 1965 to 1973, 201 Army personnel and 77 Marines were court-martialed for serious crimes against Vietnamese civilians. The My Lai Incident was the most serious of such incidents.

See also MORALITY, MY LAI INCIDENT, PHOENIX PROGRAM, POLITICAL STRUGGLE, POW/MIA, RHEAULT AFFAIR.

Suggestions for further reading: *America in Vietnam,* by Guenter Lewy (New York: Oxford University Press, 1978); *Vietnam: A History,* by Stanley Karnow (New York: Viking, 1983); *POW,* by John G. Hubbell (New York: Reader's Digest, 1976); *The Viet Cong Strategy of Terror,* by Douglas Pike (Saigon: U.S. Information Agency, 1970); *These Gallant Men on Trial in Vietnam,* by John Stevens Berry (Novato, Calif.: Presidio Press, 1984); *Law at War: Vietnam 1964–1973,* by George S. Prugh (Washington, D.C.: U.S. Government Printing Office, 1975).

ATTRITION

Attrition was the primary U.S. military strategy during the Vietnam war. One of the traditional methods of warfare, attrition aims at wearing down the enemy by killing or disabling so many of its soldiers that its armed forces are destroyed and its will to resist is broken. Sometimes labeled "the American way of war," this method plays to America's matériel and technological strengths, and it was just such massive use of American firepower that broke the resistance of Germany and Japan in World War II and of North Korea and China during the Korean war.

As John E. Mueller has pointed out, this strategy, when applied to Vietnam, was based on a logical historical premise. What was not considered, however, was the unprecedented price North Vietnam was willing to pay for eventual victory. In comparison with the 47,244 Americans killed in action in Vietnam, communist losses ranged between 600,000 and 1 million. Using the lower figure, the communists lost some 3 percent of their prewar population in battle deaths, compared with the 1.4 percent Japanese battle deaths in World War II and the less than two-tenths of 1 percent Chinese/North Korean battle deaths in the Korean war.

Given this North Vietnamese willingness to accept such enormous casualties (the equivalent in population terms of some 6 to 7 million American battle deaths), it is obvious in retrospect that

U.S. military strategy was based on the false premise that attrition alone would break the enemy's will to resist.

See also BODY COUNT; CASUALTIES; SEARCH-AND-DESTROY; STRATEGY, U.S.

Suggestions for further reading: "The Search For the 'Breaking Point' in Vietnam: The Statistics of a Deadly Quarrel," by John E. Mueller, *International Studies Quarterly*, vol. 4, no. 4, December 1980, pp. 497–519.

AUSTRALIA

Australian assistance to South Vietnam began in 1962, when a team of jungle warfare specialists was sent to assist South Vietnamese Army training. In 1964 an aviation detachment and an engineer civic action team were deployed.

In May 1965, with the deployment of the First Battalion, Royal Australian Regiment (RAR),

Australia began to take an active part in ground combat operations. With the formation of the First Australian Task Force in 1966, the Australians established their own base camp in III Corps near Ba Ria, Phuoc Tuy Province. The task force was augmented in March 1967 by a Special Air Service (SAS) squadron of commandos and in October 1967 by an additional infantry battalion, a medium tank squadron and a helicopter squadron as well as a signal, engineer and other support forces and a field hospital. It is interesting to note that soldiers of the Australian Army, like American soldiers, served a one-year Vietnam tour, but the Australians rotated entire units rather than individuals. For example, the First Battalion RAR was replaced by the Fifth Battalion RAR. In the course of the war, nine battalions of the RAR rotated through Vietnam.

In addition to ground forces, Australia also provided a squadron of B-57 Canberra bombers, which operated with U.S. Air Force units, as well as a guided missile destroyer, *Hobart*, which joined

Two Australian soldiers on patrol. (Courtesy U.S. Army Military History Institute.).

U.S. Navy forces in patrolling Vietnamese waters. A highly respected fighting body, by 1969 Australian forces in Vietnam totaled some 7,672 personnel. From this peak strength, the Australian government (like its U.S. counterpart, under pressure from antiwar protesters) began to reduce its forces in Vietnam, and by December 1971, all had returned to Australia, except a small contingent, the Australian Army Assistance Group Vietnam, which continued to assist South Vietnamese Army training until its withdrawal in January 1973.

During its Vietnam service, Australian forces in Vietnam suffered 386 killed in action and 2,193 wounded in action.

See also FREE WORLD MILITARY FORCES, NEW ZEALAND, III CORPS TACTICAL ZONE.

Suggestions for further reading: *Allied Participation in Vietnam,* by Stanley Robert Larsen and James Lawton Collins, Jr. (Washington, D.C.: U.S. Government Printing Office, 1975); *Vietnam Order of Battle,* by Shelby L. Stanton (Washington, D.C.: U.S. News & World Report Books, 1983); *Australia's Vietnam,* edited by Peter King (Boston: George Allen & Unwin, 1983).

BALL, GEORGE W(ILDMAN) (1909–)

Ball was born on December 21, 1909 and graduated from Northwestern University Law School in 1933. He practiced law in Chicago and held several government positions, including Director of the U.S. Strategic Bombing Survey, a post he assumed in 1944. During the Kennedy Administration, Ball became Undersecretary of State, the second-ranking post in the State Department, in November 1961. He was a key adviser to the President on Vietnam war policy, although much of his advice was not followed.

Ball strongly opposed the recommendations of presidential advisers General Maxwell Taylor and Walt Rostow in late 1961 to introduce U.S. combat forces into Vietnam. Ball also opposed the regime of South Vietnamese President Ngo Dinh Diem—in August 1963 he urged that American support be withdrawn from Diem in order to force either a change of policy or a coup. The latter occurred in November.

Ball continued to oppose American involvement in Vietnam during the Johnson Administration, arguing against the spring 1965 decision to increase troop strength and launch regular bombing attacks against North Vietnam. His rationale in opposing bombing of the north, expressed in a January 1966 memorandum to Johnson, was that it would most likely strengthen the north's resolve, not weaken it.

Convinced that he could not change Administration policy, Ball resigned in September 1966. In March 1968 he served as a member of the Senior Advisory Group convened to assess U.S. policy in Vietnam. A majority of the group favored the course that Ball had long advanced—disengagement from the war. On March 31 Johnson announced a de-escalation of the war.

In *Diplomacy for a Crowded World,* Ball wrote, "The . . . lesson [of Vietnam] is that America must never commit its power and authority in defense of a country of only marginal strategic interests when that country lacks a broadly based government, or the will to create one."

See also ANTIWAR MOVEMENT; JOHNSON, LYNDON B; KENNEDY, JOHN F; SENIOR ADVISORY GROUP.

Suggestions for further reading: *The Best and the Brightest,* by David Halberstam (New York: Random House, 1973); *Diplomacy for a Crowded World,* by George W. Ball (Boston: Atlantic-Little, Brown, 1976).

BAN ME THUOT

A town in Darlac Province in the Central Highlands, Ban Me Thuot was headquarters for the South Vietnamese 23rd Division and, at times during the U.S. involvement, a brigade of the U.S. Fourth Infantry Division. This town was fated to become the initial target of the North Vietnamese Final Offensive. Attacked on March 10, 1975 by three North Vietnamese Army divisions supported by tanks and heavy artillery, it fell on March 12, 1975.

See also FINAL OFFENSIVE, II CORPS TACTICAL ZONE.

Suggestions for further reading: *Vietnam from Cease Fire to Capitulation*, by William E. LeGro (Washington, D.C.: U.S. Government Printing Office, 1981).

BAO DAI (1913–   )

Born Nguyen Vinh Thuy on October 22, 1913, Bao Dai was the son of Emperor Khai Kinh. Educated in France, he was crowned Emperor in 1925 and took the name Bao Dai ("Keeper of Greatness"). He set out to modernize Vietnam, but he was merely a figurehead under the French and under the Japanese for a brief period in 1945. After the Japanese surrendered and the Viet Minh seized power, he abdicated but served in a symbolic advisory role until he became dissatisfied and fled to Hong Kong in 1946. At the request of the French, who had regained power, Bao Dai in 1949 agreed to return to Vietnam and was reinstalled as Emperor. Pursuing a life of pleasure, he reigned until 1955, when he was deposed by Ngo Dinh Diem in a referendum held while he was out of the country.

See also Part I, THE SETTING; DIEM, NGO DINH.

Suggestions for further reading: *Vietnam: A History*, by Stanley Karnow (New York: Viking, 1983); *Setting the Stage*, by Edward Doyle et al (Boston: Boston Publishing Co., 1981).

BARREL ROLL OPERATIONS

The code name for U.S. air operations over northern Laos in support of the Royal Lao Government, Barrel Roll was conducted by U.S. Navy aircraft flying off carriers in the South China Sea and by U.S. Air Force aircraft flying from bases in Thailand. The operations began in December 1964 and ended on February 21, 1973, with the signing of a peace agreement between the Royal Lao government and the Pathet Lao.

See also LAOS.

Suggestions for further reading: *Air Power in Three Wars*, by William W. Momyer (Washington, D.C.: U.S. Government Printing Office, 1978); *The United States Air Force in Southeast Asia*, edited by Carl Berger (Washington, D.C.: U.S. Government Printing Office, 1977); *The Vietnam Experience: Thunder from Above*, by John Morrocco (Boston: Boston Publishing Co., 1984); *Battles and Campaigns in Vietnam 1954–1984*, by Tom Carhart (Greenwich: Bison Books, 1984); *Without Honor: Defeat in Vietnam and Cambodia*, by Arnold R. Isaacs (Baltimore: John Hopkins Press, 1983).

BASE CAMPS, U.S.

One of the major differences between the Vietnam war and other wars was that the logistical base areas—the main support bases for combat operations—were located in-country. In World War II, U.S. troops staged for the invasion of Europe from base camps in England, and in the Korean war, the major U.S. support activities were located in Japan. In the Vietnam war, however, these facilities were constructed in-country during the course of America's involvement. Initially U.S. forces were served only by a seaport at Saigon; by the end of the war 10 additional major ports had been constructed. These included Da Nang and Chu Lai in I Corps; Qui Nhon, Vung Ro, Nha Trang, Cam Ranh and Phan Rang in II Corps; Vung Tau and additional facilities at Saigon in III Corps; and Dong Tam and Can Tho in IV Corps.

In addition to the existing airfield at Tan Son Nhut near Saigon, seven other jet-capable airfields were constructed, including Da Nang and Chu Lai in I Corps; Phu Cat, Tuy Hoa, Cam Ranh and Phan Rang in II Corps; and Bien Hoa in III

A U.S. Army base camp at Cu Chi in July 1966. (Courtesy U.S. Army.)

Corps. Aside from these jet-capable fields, many additional airfields were constructed throughout the country.

Some 27 major base camps were constructed throughout Vietnam. The logistical base at Long Binh near Saigon, for example, had a capability to house some 50,000 soldiers. Unlike in other wars in which the United States was involved, base camps were also constructed in forward areas to house combat troops. While this provided some relief from field living conditions, it tied enormous numbers of troops down in base camp security and severely limited tactical mobility.

Suggestions for further reading: *Base Development in South Vietnam 1965-1970,* by Carroll H. Dunn (Washington, D.C.: U.S. Government Printing Office, 1972); *U.S. Army Engineers 1965-1970,* by Robert R. Ploger (Washington, D.C.: U.S. Government Printing Office, 1974); *Southeast Asia, Building the Bases: The History of Construction in Southeast Asia,* by Naval Facilities Engineering Command (Washington, D.C.: U.S. Government Printing Office, 1975); *Tactical and Matériel Innovations,* by John H. Hay, Jr. (Washington, D.C.: U.S. Government Printing Office, 1974).

BATTALION

A battalion is one of the basic organizational elements of the U.S. Army and U.S. Marine Corps. Normally commanded by a lieutenant colonel, it consists of two or more companies. The size of a battalion varies according to its type. For example, in the U.S. Army an infantry battalion consists of some 900 officers and men, yet an artillery battalion has only about 500. These figures, however, are somewhat deceiving since in Vietnam battalion front-line strength (i.e., the number of soldiers actually deployed against the enemy) was often considerably lower (sometimes by more than 50 percent) than "authorized" battalion strength. Thus, while on paper North Vietnamese Army and Viet Cong infantry battalions comprised only 300 to 500 soldiers, in actuality their combat strength often equaled and sometimes exceeded that of U.S. battalions.

While the numbering system for Marine Corps infantry battalions is relatively straightforward (i.e., the First Battalion, Fifth Marines is subordinate to the Fifth Marine Regiment), in the U.S. Army the situation is confusing. Traditionally,

Army combat elements were organized into regiments, each of which contained three battalions. After the Korean war, however, the regimental headquarters were eliminated in all but separate armored cavalry units, but for historical purposes, the battalion designations remained unchanged. Where at one time the First Battalion, Second Infantry could be assumed to be part of the Second Infantry Regiment, in Vietnam this was no longer the case, since the regimental headquarters had been replaced by brigade headquarters. Thus the First Battalion, Second Infantry was under the operational control of the First Brigade, First Infantry Division for much of its Vietnam service; while the Second Battalion, Second Infantry was under the operational control of the Third Brigade, First Infantry Division. Because these assignments were not fixed as they were in the regimental system, these two battalions often operated under other brigade control-headquarters during specific combat operations.

See also BRIGADE, ORGANIZATION FOR COMBAT, REGIMENT.

Suggestions for further reading: *Vietnam Order of Battle*, by Shelby L. Stanton (Washington, D.C.: U.S. News & World Report Books, 1981).

BATTERY

In the U.S. Army and U.S. Marine Corps, "battery" is the designation for a company-sized unit of artillery. Commanded by a captain, it is composed of just over 100 officers and men and is equipped with a varying number of guns or howitzers. It is normally part of an artillery battalion. A number of separate specialized artillery batteries were deployed to Vietnam. These included target acquisition batteries, search light batteries, .50-caliber machine gun batteries as well as several separate howitzer batteries.

See also ORGANIZATION FOR COMBAT.

Suggestions for further reading: *Vietnam Order of Battle*, by Shelby L. Stanton (Washington, D.C.: U.S. News & World Report Books, 1981).

BEEHIVE AMMUNITION

A special U.S. artillery shell for howitzers, aerial rockets and recoilless rifles. The beehive projectile was designed for direct fire against a massed infantry attack. Unlike the normal solid artillery round, it produced a massive blast which was similar to that of a shotgun. The projectile contained some 8,500 tiny steel arrows, or flechettes. First used in December 1966, it proved devastating against Viet Cong and North Vietnamese ground attacks on U.S. fire bases.

Suggestions for further reading: *The Vietnam Experience: Tools of War*, by Edgar C. Doleman, Jr. (Boston, MA: Boston Publishing Company, 1984).

BEN SUC OPERATION

A fortified Viet Cong village in the so-called Iron Triangle north of Saigon in III Corps, Ben Suc gained notoriety in the United States from a series of articles and a later book by *New Yorker* magazine correspondent Jonathan Schell that highlighted what appeared to be an unwarranted disruption of village life and focused on the lack of postsettlement facilities due to graft and corruption among local officials.

In January 1967 the U.S. Army's II Field Force Vietnam launched Operation Cedar Falls to eliminate Viet Cong strongholds in the Iron Triangle. One of the primary targets was the village of Ben Suc. Headquarters for four Viet Cong rear-service transport companies, Ben Suc had been under Viet Cong control since 1964. After an assault by the First Battalion, 26th Infantry, First Infantry Division (under the command of then Lieutenant Colonel Alexander M. Haig), the village was secured, and 5,987 civilians, 247 water buffalo, 225 oxen, 158 oxcarts and 60 tons of rice were air-evacuated to resettlement areas. The village was then razed and abandoned.

See also TUNNEL WARFARE.

Suggestions for further reading: *The Village of Ben Suc*, by Jonathan Schell (New York: Knopf, 1967); *Cedar Falls-Junction City: A Turning Point*, by Bernard William Rogers (Washington, D.C.: U.S. Government Printing Office, 1974); *America in Vietnam*, by Guenter Lewy (New York: Oxford University Press, 1978). For an account of the key role Ben Suc played in Viet Cong operations, see

The Tunnels of Cu Chi, by Tom Mangold and John Penycate (New York: Random House, 1985).

BERRIGAN, DANIEL (1921-   )

Born in Virginia, Minn. on May 9, 1921, Berrigan entered a Jesuit seminary and, after studying philosophy and theology at Woodstock College in Maryland and West College in Massachusetts, was ordained in 1952. Over the next two years Berrigan served as an auxiliary military chaplain in Germany. Influenced by French worker-priests, he was attracted to social activism and became a staunch critic of the Catholic Church's views on social consciousness and of American political and social institutions. After returning to the United States, he taught at Le Moyne College in Syracuse, where he gathered a dedicated group of followers committed to pacifism and civil rights.

Starting in 1964, Berrigan fasted, protested and spoke out against the Vietnam war. In 1965 he helped form the interdenominational Clergy and Laymen Concerned about Vietnam. In October 1967 Daniel Berrigan's brother, Father Philip Berrigan, poured blood on Selective Service files housed in the Baltimore Customs House. While awaiting sentencing for this action, he persuaded Daniel to join him in a second protest. On May 17, 1968 the two priests and seven other Catholics walked into the draft board office in Catonsville, Maryland and set fire to the draft cards with homemade napalm. The Catonsville Nine were tried in October for conspiracy and destruction of government property and found guilty.

Daniel Berrigan was sentenced to three years in prison, but before the start of his prison term, he went underground. He was apprehended in 1970 and served 18 months in a federal prison. In 1972 he was named an unindicted co-conspirator in connection with the federal government's unsuccessful prosecution of Philip Berrigan on charges of conspiracy to kidnap Henry Kissinger and blow up the heating systems of federal buildings in Washington, D.C. The Berrigans later became active in the antinuclear movement.

See also ANTIWAR MOVEMENT.

BERRIGAN, PHILIP

See BERRIGAN, DANIEL.

BEVEL, JAMES L(UTHER) (1936-   )

Bevel was born in October 1936 in Itta Bena, Mississippi. He became a Baptist minister in 1959 and shortly thereafter joined the civil rights movement. He was closely associated with Martin Luther King, Jr. during the most important civil rights struggles of the mid-1960s.

Bevel also became a strong opponent of the Vietnam war during the mid-1960s. In 1965 he urged the formation of an "international peace army," in which civil rights groups would share tactics and organizers with the antiwar movement. He reportedly persuaded King in early 1967 to come out openly in support of the antiwar movement. This stand drew the criticism of several black leaders, including Roy Wilkins and Whitney Young. In January 1967 he became a leader of the Spring Mobilization Committee to End the War in Vietnam and helped organize the large antiwar demonstrations of April 15 in New York and San Francisco. In New York 125,000 people participated, including King. Bevel later returned to the civil rights movement.

See also KING, MARTIN LUTHER, JR.

BIEN HOA

Capital of the province of Bien Hoa, the city of Bien Hoa is located some 20 miles northeast of Saigon. Headquarters for the South Vietnamese Army III Corps, it was also the site of a U.S. corps-level headquarters, II Field Force Vietnam. The U.S. Air Force Third Tactical Fighter Wing flew combat missions from the major jet-capable airfield located there, and Long Binh, a major U.S. Army supply complex and headquarters, was constructed on its outskirts.

See also LONG BINH, II FIELD FORCE VIETNAM; *see* map at III CORPS TACTICAL ZONE.

BINH, NGUYEN THI (1927–   )

Ostensibly the Foreign Minister of the Provisional Revolutionary Government of South Vietnam (i.e., the Viet Cong), Madam Binh was much in the news during the Paris peace talks in the early 1970s. As with other Viet Cong leaders, however, Madame Binh fell into obscurity after the North Vietnamese conquest of the south. At last report she was serving in Vietnam's Ministry of Education.

BINH XUYEN

See Part I, THE SETTING.

BLACKS IN THE U.S. MILITARY

Ironically, the Vietnam war was the first war in which black American servicemen and women participated on an equal basis with whites, and initially they paid a high price for that long-sought goal. Although black service personnel made up 10.6% of the total U.S. force in Vietnam, compared with the 13.5 percent proportion of military-age blacks in the general population, a disproportionate number of black servicemen initially served in front-line combat units. As a result, they at first suffered a higher percentage of combat fatalities than whites. In 1965–66 black soldiers constituted over 20 percent of the U.S. battlefield deaths. The Army and Marine Corps took specific personnel actions to overcome this problem, such as re-assigning black servicemen to other than front-line jobs so as to equalize battlefield exposure, and by 1967 the proportion had declined to just over 13 percent. It continued to decrease and in 1972 black soldiers suffered 7.6 percent of U.S. battlefield deaths. Taking the war as a whole, black battlefield fatalities were almost exactly in proportion to the percentage of black Americans in the general population—of the total 47,244 U.S. service personnel killed in action, 5,711 were black, or 12.1 percent. Overall, for the Army, Navy, Air Force and Marine Corps, black servicemen suffered 12.5 percent of the deaths in Vietnam, 1 percent less than their proportion of the total U.S. population.

Suggestions for further reading: *Blacks in the Military*, by Martin Binkin et al (Washington, D.C.: Brookings Institution, 1982), was the source of the above statistical data. Further information is contained in Lawrence M. Basker and William A. Strauss' *Chance and Circumstance: The Draft, the War, and the Vietnam Generation* (New York: Knopf, 1978). For black combat experiences, see Wallace Terry's *Bloods: An Oral History of the Vietnam War by Black Veterans* (New York: Random House, 1984) and Stanley Goff and Robert Sandfors' *Brothers: Black Soldiers in the Nam* (Novato, Calif.: Presidio Press, 1982); *Black Eagle: General Daniel "Chappie" James, Jr., USAF*, by James R. McGovern (Tuscaloosa: University of Alabama Press, 1985). See also *Blacks in the American Armed Forces 1776–1983: A Bibliography* (Westport, Conn.: Greenwood Press, 1985).

BOAT PEOPLE

Part of the terrible aftermath of the Vietnam war has been the exodus of more than a million refugees fleeing from communist oppression. While some have fled overland into Thailand, the majority have attempted to escape in small boats across the South China Sea to Indonesia or the Philippines or across the Gulf of Siam to Thailand or Malaysia. It is estimated that some 200,000 have died from exposure, drowning or attacks by pirates while making this perilous voyage.

See also REEDUCATION CAMPS, REFUGEES.

Suggestions for further reading: *Vietnam: A History*, by Stanley Karnow (New York: Viking, 1983); "Agony of the Boat People," in *Newsweek*, July 2, 1979. For an account of the nightmare endured by boat people, see "The Women's Center," in *To Bear Any Burden: The Vietnam War and Its Aftermath in the Words of Americans and Southeast Asians*, by Al Santoli (New York: Dutton, 1985).

BODY COUNT

An outgrowth of Secretary of Defense Robert

S. McNamara's attempts to quantify the war in Vietnam, "body count" involved the tabulation of enemy soldiers killed on the battlefield, which was reported to Washington, D.C. and disseminated to the media. Because success soon became measured in these terms, this practice led to inflated reports and a widening credibility gap between the military and the American public. In addition, measuring success in such grisly terms further eroded American public support for the war.

Ironically, these numbers proved more accurate than at first believed. In an interview in 1969, North Vietnamese General Vo Nguyen Giap admitted that the North Vietnamese had lost over 500,000 soldiers killed on the battlefield, which was roughly the number that body counts had indicated.

Suggestions for further reading: "The Search for the 'Breaking Point' in Vietnam: The Statistics of a Deadly Quarrel," by John E. Mueller, *International Studies Quarterly*, vol. 24, no. 4, December 1980, pp. 497–519.

BOLO

Code name for a U.S. Air Force "fighter sweep" against the North Vietnamese MIG-21s over the Hanoi area on January 2, 1967. In the largest aerial battle of the war to that time, F-4s from Colonel Robin Olds' Eighth Tactical Fighter Wing, flying out of Ubon Air Base in Thailand, shot down seven MIGs in 12 minutes without the loss of a single aircraft.

Suggestions for further reading: *The United States Air Force in Southeast Asia 1961–1973*, edited by Carl Berger (Washington, D.C.: U.S. Government Printing Office, 1977); *Airpower in Three Wars*, by William W. Momyer (Washington, D.C.: U.S. Government Printing Office, 1978).

BOMBER AIRCRAFT

While the majority of bombing missions in Vietnam were flown by fighter-bomber aircraft, several types of bomber aircraft also participated

in the Vietnam war. In 1962 U.S. Air Force "air commandos" deployed World War II–vintage A-26 light bombers in support of South Vietnamese military operations. Assigned to the Second Air Division (later Seventh Air Force) in Saigon, these propeller-driven aircraft were replaced by B-57 jet bombers in February 1965. Built by Martin in the 1950s from a British design, the B-57 "Canberra" jet bomber had a two-man crew and carried six 750-pound bombs. Also used in Vietnam by the Royal Australian Air Force, it was used by the U.S. Air Force, primarily to interdict enemy supply routes. Both the A-26 and B-57 bombers were withdrawn from Southeast Asia in 1969.

The primary bomber used in the Vietnam war was the Strategic Air Force's B-52 Stratofortress jet bomber (see illustration). First flown in 1952, it was designed as a nuclear delivery aircraft. With a crew of six (including a tail gunner), the aircraft had a range of more than 7,500 miles unrefueled. During the Vietnam war the B-52 was modified to carry conventional (nonnuclear) bombs and was used in support of ground operations in the south as well as in raids over North Vietnam.

See also ARC LIGHT, FIGHTERS AND FIGHTER-BOMBERS, LINEBACKER OPERATIONS, STRATEGIC AIR COMMAND.

Suggestions for further reading: *Air War over Southeast Asia*, 3 vols., by Lou Drendel (Carrollton, Tex.: Squadron/Signal Publications, 1984); *B-52 Stratofortress in Action* (Carrollton, Tex.: Squadron/

A B-52 bomber on a mission. (Courtesy Air War College.)

Signal Publications); *The United States Air Force in Southeast Asia, 1961–1973,* edited by Carl Berger (Washington, D.C.: U.S. Government Printing Office, 1977).

BOMBING

During the course of the war in Southeast Asia, bomb tonnage by U.S. Air Force bombers and fighter-bombers alone (not counting the considerable tonnage dropped by Navy and Marine Corps fighter-bombers and by South Vietnamese aircraft) totaled some 6,162,000 tons. This was almost triple the 2.150 million tons dropped during World War II and far exceeded the 0.454 million tons dropped during the Korean war.

These tonnages are somewhat misleading, however, since the most of the bombs were dropped on uninhabited jungle areas along the Ho Chi Minh Trail in an unsuccessful attempt to block enemy infiltration. Contrary to the wildly exaggerated reports of "carpet bombing" of Hanoi heard during the war, the North Vietnamese now freely admit that nonmilitary targets in the city itself were never specifically targeted.

Suggestions for further reading: *The United States Air Force in Southeast Asia, 1961–1973,* edited by Carl Berger (Washington, D.C.: U.S. Government Printing Office, 1977): *Vietnam: A History,* by Stanley Karnow (New York: Viking, 1983).

BOOBY TRAPS

Booby traps were widely used during the war in Vietnam. They ranged from such primitive devices as *pungi* stakes (*see* illustration), consisting of sharpened bamboo stakes upon which a victim could be impaled, to more sophisticated devices, such as grenades, mines and specially rigged aerial bombs. Many were "command detonated" (i.e., set off by an electrical charge when soldiers were in the target area), which made them particularly deadly. The relative simplicity of such devices led to their widespread use by the North Vietnamese and Viet Cong. Booby traps, some improvised and

some imported from China and the USSR, accounted for some 11 percent of American deaths and 17 percent of American wounds in Vietnam, as compared with 3 to 4 percent of American deaths and wounds in World War II and the Korean war.

See also CASUALTIES.

Suggestions for further reading: *The Vietnam War: The Illustrated History of the Conflict in Southeast Asia,* edited by Ray Bonds (New York: Crown Publishers, 1983); *The Vietnam Experience: Tools of War,* by Edgar C. Doleman, Jr. (Boston: Boston Publishing Company, 1983).

BRIGADE

In the U.S. Army, a brigade is one of the basic organizational elements. Because its current usage is somewhat confusing, some historical background is necessary to understand its place within the organizational hierarchy.

Prior to World War II the Army was organized into so-called square divisions. Each division consisted of two brigades commanded by brigadier generals. Each brigade, in turn, consisted of two regiments. In the early 1940s, the Army adopted the so-called triangular division, which eliminated the brigades and reduced the number of regiments from four to three. In the infantry divisions, these regiments were fixed at three battalions each (the First, Second and Third Battalions, Second Infantry), but in the armored divisions the equivalent headquarters was a combat command. These combat commands, unlike the regiments, had no fixed number of battalions but were tailored to fit their operational mission by assigning varying numbers of armored infantry and tank battalions. In 1962, after experimenting with the so-called pentomic division of five battle groups, the Army was again reorganized, using the World War II armored divisions as a guide.

This "new" structure, which continued throughout the Vietnam war, consisted of a division organized into three brigades, each commanded by a colonel. Infantry and armor battalions organic to the division were attached to these brigades, but the number could vary according to the brigade's mission.

In addition to these brigades assigned to a division, a number of separate infantry brigades were also organized. Normally commanded by a brigadier general, five separate infantry brigades were deployed to Vietnam. Three of these—the 11th, 196th and 198th Infantry Brigades—were later combined to form the Americal (23rd) Infantry Division. The 173rd Airborne Brigade and the 199th Infantry Brigade remained as separate entities and normally operated directly under corps (field force) control. In addition to these combat brigades, a number of combat support (such as aviation units that directly supplied combat units) and combat service support brigades (i.e., those that provided supplies, material and maintenance, medical and other rear-area support) were also deployed to Vietnam. They included the First Aviation Brigade, the 18th and 20th Engineer Brigades, the 18th Military Police Brigade, the First Signal Brigade and the 44th Medical Brigade.

See also DIVISION, ORGANIZATION FOR COMBAT, REGIMENT.

Suggestions for further reading: *Vietnam Order of Battle*, by Shelby L. Stanton (Washington, D.C.,: U.S. News & World Report Books, 1981).

BRONZE STAR MEDAL

First authorized in World War II, the Bronze Star Medal is awarded in the name of the President of the United States for heroic or meritorious achievement or service in connection with military operations against an armed enemy not involving participation in aerial flight. Awards are made for acts of heroism, denoted by a "V" on the ribbon, performed under circumstances as described, which were of lesser degree than required for the award of the Silver Star. Awards were also made to recognize single combat zone acts of merit or meritorious service. Subsequent awards were denoted by an oak leaf (a star for the Navy and Marine Corps) worn on the ribbon.

BROWN, GEORGE S(CRATCHLEY) (1918–1978)

Born August 17, 1918 in Montclair, New Jersey,

Brown graduated from the U.S. Military Academy in 1941. He served with the U.S. Eighth Air Force in Europe in World War II and won the Distinguished Service Cross for heroism during the low-level bombing raid against the oil refineries at Ploesti, Romania in August 1943. During the Korean war he served as Director for Operations for the Fifth Air Force.

In July 1973 President Nixon named General Brown Air Force Chief of Staff. Senate hearings on Brown's appointment raised the issue of his role in the secret bombing of Cambodia in 1969 and 1970, when Brown was in command of the Seventh Air Force in Vietnam. He explained that the bombing missions had been kept secret for security reasons on orders from higher authority. Brown was confirmed and a year later was appointed Chairman of the Joint Chiefs of Staff.

Brown took an active role in the Ford Administration's final attempts to save South Vietnam in March 1975. The Administration advocated sending military aid to South Vietnam in response to

The Bronze Star.

the North Vietnamese Final Offensive but was constrained by recent congressional legislation, notably the War Powers Act of 1973, limiting the President's authority to act abroad. Brown linked the collapse of Saigon's forces before the North Vietnamese offensive to congressional cutbacks in military aid. He stressed that aircraft, tanks and armored personnel carriers lost in battle had not been replaced by the United States.

Terminally ill, Brown retired from active duty in 1978 and died on December 5.

See also CAMBODIA.

BROWN, SAM(UEL) (WINFRED) (1943–)

Brown was born in Council Bluffs, Iowa on July 27, 1943. He received a B.A. in 1965 from the University of Redlands and an M.A. in government in 1966 from Rutgers University. He entered Harvard Theological Seminary in the autumn of 1966 and became increasingly active in the growing student movement against the war in Vietnam.

In 1968 Brown joined Senator Eugene McCarthy's presidential campaign as coordinator of student volunteers. For the New Hampshire primary, Brown brought in hundreds of college students, who rang doorbells and canvassed voters throughout the state. The student volunteer effort received a large amount of the credit for McCarthy's impressive showing in the primary.

In 1969 he helped found and became coordinator of the Vietnam Moratorium Committee (VMC), an umbrella organization of antiwar activists. Endorsed by almost 500 college student body presidents and editors of campus newspapers, the committee took out a full-page ad in *The New York Times* of September 21 to announce a nationwide "moratorium" against the war to be held on October 15. The VMC won the support of politicians, civic, religious and labor leaders and many community organizations. Protests took place across the country on a large scale and revealed that opposition to the war extended far beyond the ranks of college students.

Immediately afterward, Brown announced a two-day moratorium for November 13 and 14 and endorsed the antiwar rally planned for November 15 in Washington, D.C. by the New Mobilization Committee to End the War in Vietnam, a more radical antiwar group. Together the November actions were the largest demonstrations against the war up to that time.

The Vietnam Moratorium Committee disbanded in April 1970 with Brown citing financial pressures and the end of "the need for which we came together."

See also MORATORIUM AGAINST THE WAR.

BUDDHISTS

Vietnam is a predominantly Buddhist nation. Although 70 to 80 percent of the population is nominally Buddhist, only a small part are active participants. Practicing the Mahayana form imported from China, rather than the Indian-influenced Hinayana form practiced in the rest of Southeast Asia, the Buddhist clergy normally played no large role in Vietnamese society. In 1963, however, opposition to the dominant power of Roman Catholics surrounding President Ngo Dinh Diem led to increased politicization of Buddhist monks. Government suppression of the monks led to rioting in South Vietnamese cities and angered the Kennedy Administration. Under the leadership of Thich Tri Quang, Buddhists

A Buddhist pagoda in Bao Loc, South Vietnam. (Courtesy Shelby L. Stanton.)

began a series of demonstrations leading to the immolations of several Buddhist monks in Saigon in June 1963. These incidents evoked world-wide criticism of the Diem government and contributed to its downfall in November. In 1966 Buddhists revolted in Hué and Da Nang over Prime Minister Nguyen Cao Ky's failure to hold elections and his dismissal of General Nguyen Chanh Thi, who was aligned with Thich Tri Quang. After an unsuccessful attempt to put down the uprising by force, Ky reached a settlement with the Buddhist leaders. One of the first acts of the North Vietnamese after their conquest of Saigon was to place Thich Tri Quang under house arrest.

See also DIEM, NGO DINH; KY, NGUYEN CAO.

Suggestions for further reading: *Vietnam: A History,* by Stanley Karnow (New York: Viking, 1983).

BULLDOZERS

See ROME PLOWS.

BUNDY, McGEORGE (1919–   )

Born March 30, 1919 in Boston, Bundy graduated first in his class from Yale University in 1940. During World War II he served in the U.S. Army and participated in the planning of the invasions of Sicily and France. A brilliant scholar, in 1953 he became Dean of Arts and Sciences at Harvard while teaching government there.

In January 1961 President Kennedy appointed him Special Assistant to the President for National Security Affairs, a post he held until February 1966. Bundy became one of the chief architects of U.S. policy in Southeast Asia. When the Kennedy Administration was considering withdrawal of support for South Vietnamese President Ngo Dinh Diem in 1963, Bundy advised that the United States should not thwart any coup that seemed potentially successful but should have the "option of judging and warning on any plan with poor prospects of success." In effect, this was the policy Kennedy followed.

Although there is some controversy surrounding the exact nature of Bundy's recommendations for changes in the Johnson Administration's Vietnam policies in late 1964, following a trip to Vietnam in February 1965, he recommended that the United States adopt an extensive air campaign, varying the intensity of the bombing raids with the rate of communist troop infiltration into the south. The bombing campaign was adopted under the name of Operation Rolling Thunder and begun in March. Bundy was convinced that a major U.S. commitment was necessary to keep South Vietnam afloat and to demonstrate U.S. resolve to halt communist expansion. During the remainder of his tenure at the White House, Bundy reviewed targets for the Rolling Thunder raids and became a leading spokesman for the administration's position on Vietnam.

Bundy considered himself a pragmatist and was therefore anxious to base American policy on detailed assessments of specific situations rather than ideological abstractions. Consequently, much of his counsel was directed at advising the President of all possible policy options and in keeping choices open until a major decision was unavoidable.

See also BUNDY, WILLIAM; JOHNSON, LYNDON B.; KENNEDY, JOHN F.; ROLLING THUNDER OPERATION; SENIOR ADVISORY GROUP.

Suggestions for further reading: *The Best and the Brightest,* by David Halberstam (New York: Random House, 1972); *The Irony of Vietnam: The System Worked,* by Leslie Gelb and Richard Betts (Washington, D.C.: Brookings Institution, 1979).

BUNDY, WILLIAM (1917–   )

Born September 24, 1917 in Washington, D.C., William Bundy graduated from Yale in 1939 and, after service in the U.S. Army in World War II, from Harvard Law School in 1947. He joined the CIA in 1950. Like his brother, McGeorge, William Bundy played a key role in formulating U.S. policy in Indochina. In 1961 Bundy, serving as Deputy Assistant Secretary of Defense for International Security Affairs, was one of a group of government officials asked to analyze South

Vietnam's request for a bilateral defense treaty and expanded military aid. Bundy recommended an early and aggressive program to arrest communist expansion in that country.

In February 1964 he was appointed Assistant Secretary of State for Far Eastern Affairs. In May 1964 he drafted a resolution that, if passed, would have given the President the right to use American military power to support any Southeast Asian nation threatened by communist aggression without congressional approval. In the fall of 1964 Johnson ordered the National Security Council Working Group, headed by Bundy and John McNaughton, to review operations and make recommendations for the future course of the war. The recommendations of the group led eventually to the bombing of North Vietnam, called Operation Rolling Thunder.

In May 1966 Bundy submitted a memorandum to Secretary of State Dean Rusk that would serve as a guideline for U.S. policy in Vietnam until 1969. The paper argued that bombing was a viable means of bringing North Vietnam to the bargaining table, and that the United States should cease bombing operations only if the North Vietnamese agreed to limit infiltration of troops into the south and to halt Viet Cong operations there. In the spring of 1967 Bundy opposed continued escalation of the conflict, claiming that to escalate would have an adverse effect on our allies and would have limited impact upon Hanoi.

William Bundy left government service in 1969.

See also BUNDY, McGEORGE; JOHNSON, LYNDON B.; ROLLING THUNDER OPERATION.

Suggestions for further reading: *The Best and the Brightest,* by David Halberstam (New York: Random House, 1972).

BUNKER, ELLSWORTH (1894–1984)

Born in Yonkers, New York on May 11, 1894, Ellsworth Bunker was educated at Yale. He left the family sugar business in 1951 to accept the post of Ambassador to Argentina, the first in a long series of diplomatic positions he would hold. In April 1967 Bunker succeeded Henry Cabot Lodge as Ambassador to South Vietnam.

Throughout his tenure in South Vietnam, Bunker was a wholehearted supporter of U.S. policy in Vietnam and the rest of Southeast Asia. He backed the 1970 incursion into Cambodia by South Vietnamese and American troops, believing that destruction of North Vietnamese bases in that country would give the South Vietnamese Armed Forces more time to develop at a point when U.S. troop strength, under President Nixon's "Vietnamization" policy, was diminishing.

Bunker was reportedly involved in the controversial October 1971 South Vietnamese presidential elections, in which Vice President Nguyen Cao Ky and General Duong Can Minh withdrew their candidacies, claiming U.S. interference. President Nguyen Van Thieu ran unopposed and was reelected.

Ellsworth Bunker resigned his post in March 1973 and, after returning to Washington, D.C., became ambassador-at-large. He died on September 27, 1984.

CALLEY, WILLIAM L., JR. (1943–   )

Born on June 8, 1943 in Miami, Florida, William

L. Calley, Jr. was a platoon leader in the First Battalion, 20th Infantry, Americal Division. He was court-martialed for and found guilty of the murder of Vietnamese civilians at My Lai in

March 1968. He was initially sentenced to life imprisonment at hard labor, dismissal from the U.S. Army and forfeiture of his pay and allowances pending the outcome of an automatic review of the case by another command. After a lengthy review process in both military and civilian courts, his sentence was reduced to 10 years. After serving one-third of his term, he was released on parole in 1974 and given a dishonorable discharge. Other officers and enlisted men were investigated and tried for their roles in the massacre, but Caley was the only one found guilty.

See also MY LAI MASSACRE.

CAMBODIA

An ancient civilization ethnically and culturally distinct from the Vietnamese, the territory of Cambodia (now known as Kampuchea) had been gradually eroded for a thousand years as the Vietnamese pushed southward from their beginnings in the Red River Delta. Saved from extinction by the French intervention in the mid-19th century, it remained a protectorate until 1954. After the withdrawal of the French, its ruler, Prince Norodom Sihanouk, attempted to preserve its neutrality. By the mid-1960s, however, North Vietnamese and Viet Cong units had established base areas in eastern Cambodia and were using the port of Sihanoukville (Kompong Som) to move war supplies into position. With the tacit agreement of Prince Sihanouk, President Nixon ordered the so-called "secret" bombing of these Cambodian base areas on March 18, 1969 to take pressure off the ongoing U.S. troop withdrawal from Vietnam and to put pressure on the North Vietnamese to enter serious negotiations. The bombing was also designed to close off the flow of war supplies from North Vietnam entering through the Cambodian port of Sihanoukville. Code-named Operation Menu, this bombing would continue until ended by Congress on August 15, 1973.

Although elaborate measures were taken to keep the bombings secret, lest their revelation fuel antiwar protests, the *New York Times* published a story about the bombings in May. The news infuriated Nixon and national security adviser Henry Kissinger. The telephones of several journalists and government officials were wire-tapped. When the bombings were officially acknowledged in 1973, they stirred the demand in Congress for President Nixon's impeachment.

The bombing of the Cambodian base areas and Cambodian attempts to constrain North Vietnamese expansion led to unrest within Cambodia and on March 18, 1970, Prince Sihanouk, who was not in Cambodia at the time, was deposed by General Lon Nol.

Seeking to forestall North Vietnamese attacks on then withdrawing U.S. forces, President Nixon ordered a limited "incursion" into Cambodia on April 29, 1970. Conducted by elements of the U.S. Army's II Field Force and South Vietnamese Army's III and IV Corps, the operation continued until June 30, 1970. News of the incursion set off a wave of antiwar demonstrations, including one at Kent State University that resulted in the killing of four students.

CAMBODIA

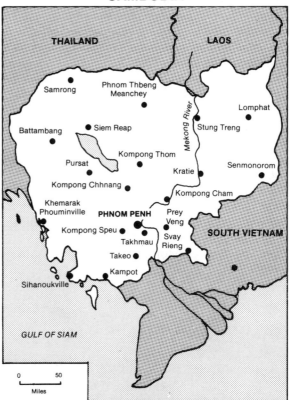

The U.S. permanent military presence in Cambodia was limited to a small joint armed forces contingent called Military Equipment Delivery Team, Cambodia. It was organized in Saigon on January 30, 1971 and moved to Phnom Penh on October 9. The organization was responsible for supervising military deliveries to the Khmer Republic, and was closed down in April 1975 as the capital fell.

The Lon Nol government came under increasing attack from Cambodian Khmer Rouge insurgents and on April 12, 1975, in what was called Operation Eagle Pull, all U.S. personnel were withdrawn. On April 17, 1975 the capital of Phnom Penh fell to the Khmer Rouge. A holocaust ensued with an estimated two million Cambodians executed or starved to death. This bloodbath was ended in December 1978, when Vietnam invaded and subsequently occupied Cambodia, but a guerrilla war continues against the Vietnamese occupation.

See also EAGLE PULL OPERATION; FANK TRAINING COMMAND; KENT STATE; KHMER ROUGE; MENU OPERATION; NEUTRALITY; NIXON RICHARD M.; SIHANOUK, NORODOM; VIETNAMIZATION.

Suggestions for further reading: *Cambodia: Year Zero,* by François Ponchaud, translated by Nancy Amphoux (New York: Holt, Rinehart & Winston, 1978); *Sideshow: Kissinger, Nixon, and the Destruction of Cambodia,* by William Shawcross (New York: Simon & Schuster, 1979); *The Cambodian Incursion,* by Tran Dinh Tho (Washington, D.C.: Indochina Monograph, U.S. Army Center of Military History, 1979); *The Khmer Republic at War and the Final Collapse,* by Sak Sutsakhan (Washington, D.C.: Indochina Monograph, U.S. Army Center of Military History, 1980); *Without Honor: Defeat in Vietnam and Cambodia,* by Arnold R. Isaacs (Baltimore: Johns Hopkins Press, 1983); "Vietnam's Vietnam," by Stephen Morris, in *The Atlantic,* January 1985.

CAMPAIGN MEDALS, U.S.

Beginning with the Civil War, what traditionally has been called a campaign medal (but officially called a service medal) has been awarded to members of the U.S. armed forces to recognize their wartime service. The Vietnam Service Medal was authorized to recognize service in Vietnam during the period July 3, 1965 through March 28, 1973 and for those holders of the Armed Forces Expeditionary Medal for service after July 7, 1958. The medal was awarded for one or more days service in Vietnam itself or aboard a Navy vessel directly supporting military operations or as a crew member in aerial flights into air space above Vietnam directly supporting military operations.

A Service Star (commonly called a battle star) is worn on the ribbon of a service medal to denote each separate campaign in which the serviceman or woman participated (*see* CAMPAIGNS, U.S. MILITARY).

The Armed Forces Expeditionary Medal was authorized to recognize the service of those who served in Vietnam prior to 1965 or served during

Vietnam Service Medal.

the evacuation of Vietnam in 1975 (*see* EXPEDITIONARY MEDAL).

In addition to the Vietnam Service Medal, the National Defense Service Medal was also authorized for all members of the U.S. armed forces who served during the Vietnam war period, and the South Vietnamese government authorized the Republic of Vietnam Campaign Medal for award to all U.S. servicemen and women who actually served in Vietnam.

See also NATIONAL DEFENSE SERVICE MEDAL, VIETNAM SERVICE AWARDS.

CAMPAIGN PLAN

A campaign plan is an agreed upon set of general guidelines for the conduct of future military operations. The initial campaign plan for U.S. forces in Vietnam was prepared by General William C. Westmoreland, Commander of the U.S. Military Assistance Command, Vietnam (MACV), in 1965. As approved by the Secretary of Defense, it consisted of three general phases: Phase One—commit those American and allied forces necessary "to halt the losing trend" by the end of 1965; Phase Two—"during the first half of 1966," take the offensive with American and allied forces in "high priority areas" to destroy enemy forces and reinstitute pacification programs; and Phase Three—if the enemy persisted, he might be defeated and his forces and base areas destroyed during a period of a year to a year and a half following Phase Two.

MACV also published annual campaign plans setting forth specific guidelines and goals for allied forces in planning their operations. These were prefixed by an AB designator in series, such as AB-141, etc. As with the initial campaign plan, they were submitted to the Commander-in-Chief of the Pacific Command (CINCPAC) in Honolulu and then to the Joint Chiefs of Staff in Washington, D.C. for ultimate approval by the Secretary of Defense in the name of the President.

Suggestions for further reading: *A Soldier Reports*, by William C. Westmoreland (Garden City: Doubleday, 1966); *The Unmaking of a President: Lyndon Johnson and Vietnam*, by Herbert Y. Schandler (Princeton: Princeton University Press, 1977); *The 25-Year War: America's Military Role in Vietnam*, by Bruce Palmer, Jr. (Lexington: University of Kentucky Press, 1984).

CAMPAIGNS, U.S. MILITARY

The U.S. military categorizes each war in which it has been involved in terms of a series of campaigns, defined as a connected series of military operations forming a distinct phase of a war. For units involved in these operations, a streamer embroidered with the name of the particular campaign is displayed with the unit's colors (its official flag) and those individuals who participated are authorized to wear a bronze "battle star" on their campaign ribbon. Seventeen campaigns were authorized for the Vietnam war:

Campaign	Inclusive Dates
Vietnam Advisory	March 15, 1962–March 7, 1965
Vietnam Defense	March 8, 1965–December 24, 1965
Vietnam Counteroffensive	December 25, 1965–June 30, 1966
Vietnam Counteroffensive Phase II	July 1, 1966–May 31, 1967
Vietnam Counteroffensive Phase III	July 1, 1965–January 29, 1968
Tet Counteroffensive	January 30, 1968–April 1, 1968
Vietnam Counteroffensive Phase IV	April 2, 1968–June 30, 1968
Vietnam Counteroffensive Phase V	July 1, 1968–November 1, 1968
Vietnam Counteroffensive Phase VI	November 2, 1968–February 22, 1969
Tet '69 Counteroffensive	February 28, 1969–June 8, 1969
Vietnam Summer–Fall 1969	June 9, 1969–October 31, 1969
Vietnam Winter–Spring 1970	November 1, 1969–April 30, 1970
Sanctuary Counteroffensive	May 1, 1970–June 30, 1970

Vietnam Counteroffensive Phase VII	July 1, 1970–June 30, 1971
Consolidation I	July 1, 1971– November 30, 1971
Consolidation II	December 1, 1971– March 29, 1972
Vietnam Cease-Fire	March 30, 1972– January 28, 1973

See also CAMPAIGN MEDALS.

CAM RANH BAY

A protected natural harbor located in Khanh Hoa Province south of the city of Nha Trang in II Corps, Cam Ranh Bay was developed into one of the largest seaports in South Vietnam. Beginning in May 1965, the U.S. Army's First Logistical Command established a support command at Cam Ranh to provide logistic support for the 72,000 U.S. and allied troops in the southern half of II Corps. These terminals and supply depots were turned over to South Vietnam in June 1972 as was a jet-capable airfield with a 10,000-foot runway, which was constructed there to serve as base for the U.S. Air Force's 12th Tactical Fighter Wing and 483rd Tactical Air Wing.

Security for the area was provided by South Korea's Ninth Infantry (White Horse) Division, whose 30th Infantry Regiment was headquartered at Cam Ranh Bay. A key logistical base during the Vietnam war, Cam Ranh Bay fell to the North Vietnamese in April 1975. It is now being used by the Soviet navy.

Suggestions for further reading: *Base Development, 1965–1970,* by Carroll H. Dunn (Washington, D.C.: U.S. Government Printing Office, 1972); *U.S. Army Engineers, 1965–1970,* by Robert R. Ploger (Washington, D.C.: U.S. Government Printing Office, 1974); *Vietnam: A History,* by Stanley Karnow (New York: Viking, 1983); *Vietnam Order of Battle,* by Shelby L. Stanton (Washington, D.C.: U.S. News & World Report Books, 1981).

CANADA

Although not directly involved in the war, Canada was involved in the International Control Commission set up by the Geneva Conference in 1954. Unlike India and Poland, which supported North Vietnam, Canada attempted to remain impartial. However, it provided economic assistance to South Vietnam. The International Control Commission was superseded by the International Commission of Control and Supervision (ICCS) as a result of the Paris Accords of 1973. Canada and Poland remained members but India was replaced by Indonesia. When it became apparent that the North Vietnamese had no intention of living up to the accords, Canada withdrew on July 31, 1973 and was replaced by Iran. Canada's role as a haven for Americans evading the Vietnam war is perhaps better known. It has been estimated that there were some 30,000 Americans living in exile in Canada during the war. Less known is that during the war approximately 50,000 Canadians reportedly either enlisted in or were drafted into the U.S. military and some 30,000 served in Vietnam.

See also ICCS (INTERNATIONAL COMMISSION OF CONTROL AND SUPERVISION).

Suggestions for further reading: *Chance and Circumstance: The Draft, the War and the Vietnam Generation,* by Lawrence M. Baskir and William A. Strauss (New York: Knopf, 1978); *Without Honor: Defeat in Vietnam and Cambodia,* by Arnold R. Isaacs (Baltimore: John Hopkins Press, 1983); *Sixty Days to Peace,* by Walter Scott Dillard (Washington, D.C.: U.S. Government Printing Office, 1982); "The Loneliness and Pain of Canadian Veterans of the Vietnam War," by Doug Clark, in the *Toronto Globe and Mail,* July 9, 1984.

CATONSVILLE NINE

See BERRIGAN, DANIEL

CAO DAI

A Vietnamese religious sect with headquarters in the city of Tay Ninh, 60 miles northwest of Saigon, Cao Dai drew its doctrine heavily from the teachings of Buddhism, Taoism, Confucianism and Christianity. Tightly controlled, it administered its own territory and maintained its own army until 1955, when it was brought under control by South Vietnamese President Ngo Dinh Diem. It remained, however, a potent religious force.

The Army Special Forces utilized these tough religious warriors as mercenaries for its CIDG (Civilian Irregular Defense Group) program, in which they fought well to oust the Viet Cong from several sacred pagodas that were located on strategic mountain tops.

Suggestions for further reading: *Vietnam: A History,* by Stanley Karnow (New York: Viking, 1983); *Passing the Torch,* by Edward Doyle et al (Boston: Boston Publishing Co., 1981).

CAP (USMC COMBINED ACTION PLATOON)

A major difference between the U.S. Army and the U.S. Marine Corps in Vietnam involved the use of military forces to support pacification—i.e., how to best provide local security for South Vietnamese hamlets so as to facilitate the reassertion of government control and thus permanently drive out Viet Cong insurgents.

U.S. Army combat operations in Vietnam began against regular North Vietnamese Army (NVA) regimental-sized units in the sparsely settled Central Highlands with the battle of the Ia Drang in November 1965. Marine Corps combat operations began against Viet Cong insurgents in the heavily populated Da Nang coastal area in March 1965. From these early experiences the Army advocated search-and-destroy operations against larger organized Viet Cong main forces and NVA regular units. The Marines emphasized an "ink-blot" strategy to gradually enlarge their coastal enclaves through "clear-and-hold" operations.

The organization developed by the Marine Corps for such operations was called the combined action platoon, initiated informally in 1965 by the Third Battalion, Fourth Marines in the Phu Bai area. Ad hoc combined action platoons had been created successfully by assigning a Marine Corps squad, with a Navy corpsman attached, to a Popular Force (South Vietnamese local home-guard) platoon. This concept was formalized in January 1966 with the creation of combined action companies, each containing several combined action platoons.

Both the Army and Marine approaches rested on the premise that eventually security would be turned over to local South Vietnamese authorities (since the whole purpose of being in Vietnam was to strengthen the government).

When pacification began to take hold by 1966, the NVA sent their regular divisions south across the DMZ, forcing the Third Marine Division to be taken off pacification duties and deployed north to meet this threat. In a September 1967 article in the North Vietnamese newspaper *Quang Doi Nhan Dan,* General Vo Nguyen Giap acknowledged that the purpose of the DMZ battles was to pull American forces away from the pacification effort, but this tactic failed and by the end of 1968 there were 102 combined action companies organized into four combined action group (CAG) headquarters—First CAG at Chu Lai, Second CAG at Da Nang, Third CAG at Phu Bai and Fourth CAG at Quang Tri. As U.S. forces withdrew from Vietnam, the CAG program contracted. The Fourth CAG at Quang Tri was disbanded in July 1970, and by the end of August the First CAG at Chu Lai and the Third CAG at Phu Bai were also disbanded. By September 1970 the Second CAG was down to six companies and 38 platoons, and on May 7, 1971 all were deactivated as the last of the Marines departed Vietnam.

See also CLEAR-AND-HOLD, CORDS (CIVILIAN OPERATIONS AND REVOLUTIONARY DEVELOPMENT SUPPORT), COUNTERINSURGENCY, HEARTS AND MINDS, PACIFICATION, SEARCH-AND-DESTROY.

Suggestions for further reading: *The Village,* by Francis J. West, Jr. (New York: Harper & Row, 1972); "Marine Corps Operations in Vietnam, 1965–66, 1967, 1968, 1969–72," by Edwin H. Simmons, in *The Marines in Vietnam, 1954–1973* (Washington, D.C.: U.S. Government Printing Office, 1974); *The War in the Northern Provinces, 1966–1968,* by Willard Pearson (Washington, D.C.: U.S. Government Printing Office, 1975); *U.S. Marines in Vietnam: The Advisory and Combat Assistance Era 1954–1964,* by Robert H. Whitlow (Washington, D.C.: U.S. Government Printing Office, 1976); *U.S. Marines in Vietnam: The Landing*

A Caribou C-7 aircraft. (Courtesy U.S. Army Military History Institute.)

and the Buildup, 1965, by Jack Shulimson and Charles M. Johnson (Washington, D.C.: U.S. Government Printing Office, 1978); *U.S. Marines in Vietnam: An Expanding War 1966,* by Jack Shulimson (Washington, D.C.: U.S. Government Printing Office, 1982). For a fictionalized account of U.S. Marine Corps operations in Vietnam, see Marine Corps Vietnam veteran James Webb's *Fields of Fire* (Englewood Cliffs, N.J.: Prentice-Hall, 1978).

CARIBOU AIRCRAFT

Developed by the de Haviland Aircraft Corporation in Canada, the Caribou C-7 aircraft was a twin-propellor-driven 32-passenger aircraft that could take off from remarkably short crude airstrips and had a rear unloading door that facilitated rapid cargo handling. Adopted by the U.S. Army in the early 1960s, it was deployed to Vietnam shortly thereafter. By 1966 the Army was operating six Caribou companies in Vietnam. Because of a long-standing disagreement between the Army and the Air Force over fixed-wing aircraft, control of the C-7 was transferred to the Air Force in January 1967.

Suggestions for further reading: *Airmobility 1961–1971,* by John J. Tolson (Washington, D.C.: U.S. Government Printing Office, 1973).

CASE-CHURCH AMENDMENT

On June 14, 1973 the Senate passed an amendment, sponsored by Senators Frank Church and Clifford Case, to a State Department funding bill banning the use of any past or future appropriations for U.S. combat activities in any part of Indochina without the specific authorization of Congress. On June 30 Congress approved a compromise with President Nixon on the funding of U.S. combat activities in Indochina that allowed bombing raids in Cambodia to continue until August 15. Thereafter funding for military action in any part of Indochina would be subject to congressional approval.

On December 17 President Nixon signed a foreign aid authorization bill that contained a ban on the use of any funds for U.S. military operations in or over Vietnam, Laos or Cambodia.

CASUALTIES

Except for the United States, casualty figures for the war in Vietnam are inexact, and even for the United States the figures vary depending upon the source. Total casualty figures include the numbers of servicemen killed in action, those who died from accidents or disease and those wounded in action. According to 1983 Veterans Administration figures, 47,244 Americans were killed in action in Vietnam. Accidents and disease accounted for another 10,446 deaths. Those hospitalized for wounds totaled 153,329, while an additional 150,375 Americans received wounds not severe enough to require hospitalization.

The ratio of Americans killed in action to those who died from other causes during the Vietnam war is revealing. In World War I significantly more servicemen died of disease than died on the battlefield. These figures reversed in World War II, and in the Korean war there were approximately three Americans killed in action for every two who died from other causes. In Vietnam, because of improved combat medical care, the ratio of battle to nonbattle deaths increased to almost five to one.

Also revealing was the cause of U.S. battlefield casualties. As the accompanying table illustrates, in World War II and Korea "fragments" (i.e., shrapnel from artillery, rockets and mortars) were the primary cause of U.S. Army deaths and wounds. While they remained the primary cause of wounds in Vietnam, rapid-fire infantry weapons, such as the AK-47 rifle, changed the primary cause of death in Vietnam to small-arms fire. Although exaggerated claims have been made that such guerrilla weapons as booby traps and *pungi* stakes caused the majority of Vietnam war casualties, they represented the causes of only 11 percent of those killed and 17 percent of those wounded in action.

While the overall 1,078,162 U.S. casualties (i.e., those killed in action, those who died from other

South Vietnamese Army soldiers carrying the wounded to a UH-1D Medevac helicopter. (Courtesy U.S. Army.)

causes and those wounded in action severe enough to require hospitalization) in World War II compared to the 214,074 casualties in Vietnam would make it appear that the latter war was less severe, statistics for the infantry divisions actually involved in the fighting tell another story. In almost all cases at the fighting level, casualties in Vietnam exceeded those in World War II (*see* listings for specific Army and Marine infantry divisions).

In addition to American casualties, South Korea suffered some 4,407 servicemen killed in action; Australia and New Zealand lost 469; and Thailand suffered 351 battle deaths. The armed forces of South Vietnam, however, suffered the majority of allied casualties in Vietnam. Not including the Final Offensive, for which statistics are not available, South Vietnam had 223,748 service members killed in action and some 570,600 wounded in action. While figures for the North Vietnamese and Viet Cong are not available,

General Vo Nguyen Giap admitted in 1969 that they had lost 500,000 men from 1964 to 1969 alone, and it has been estimated that the total was some 666,000 killed in action.

Further estimates are that some 300,000 South Vietnamese civilians also died in the war. Additionally, North Vietnamese civilian deaths from American bombing totaled some 65,000 people. These statistics on civilian casualties are a matter of considerable controversy and the true totals will probably never be known.

See also BOOBY TRAPS, DUSTOFF.

Suggestions for further reading: *America in Vietnam,* by Guenter Lewy (New York: Oxford University Press, 1978); *Medical Support of the U.S. Army in Vietnam 1965–1970,* by Spurgeon Neel (Washington, D.C.: U.S. Government Printing Office, 1973); *Data on Vietnam-era Veterans* (Washington, D.C.: Office of Information Management and Statistics, Veterans Administration, September 1983).

Table 1
Number of Deaths in Three Wars: World War II, Korea and Vietnam

	Battle Deaths	Other (Accidents Disease etc.)
WW I	53,513	63,195
WW II	292,131	115,185
Korea	33,629	20,617
Vietnam	47,244	10,446

Table 2
Percent of Deaths and Wounds According to Agent, U.S. Army, in Three Wars: World War II, Korea and Vietnam

Agent	Deaths			Wounds		
	World War II	Korea	Vietnam [1]	World War II	Korea	Vietnam [1]
Small arms	32	33	51	20	27	16
Fragments	53	59	36	62	61	65
Booby traps, mines	3	4	11	4	4	15
Punji stakes	—	—	—	—	—	2
Other	12	4	2	14	8	2

[1] January 1965–June 1970.

Source: *Statistical Data on Army Troops Wounded in Vietnam, January 1965–June 1970,* Medical Statistics Agency, Office of the Surgeon General, U.S. Army.

Table 3
Number of Casualties Incurred by U.S. Military Personnel in Connection
with the Conflict in Vietnam
(Cumulative from January 1, 1961 through September 30, 1980*)

	Army	Navy[a]	Marine Corps	Air Force	Total
A. CASUALTIES FROM ACTIONS BY HOSTILE FORCES					
1. Killed	25,341	1,097	11,494	504	38,436
2. Wounded or injured					
a. Died of wounds	3,521	146	1,454	48	5,169
b. Nonfatal wounds					
Hosp. care required	96,811	4,180	51,399	939	153,329
Hosp. care not required	104,725	5,898	37,234	2,518	150,375
3. Missing					
a. Died while missing	1,961	295	107	1,161	3,524
b. Return to control	54	5	2	34	95
c. Current missing[c]	—	1	1	11	13
4. Captured or Interned					
a. Died while captured or interned	45	36	10	24	115
b. Returned to control	134	145	38	333	650
c. Current captured or interned[c]	—	—	—	1	1
5. Deaths					
a. From aircraft accidents/incidents					
Fixed Wing	98	278	179	1,099	1,654
Helicopter	2,404	75	449	88	3,016
b. From ground action	28,366	1,221	12,437	550	42,574
TOTAL DEATHS[b]	30,868	1,574	13,065	1,737	47,244
B. CASUALTIES NOT THE RESULT OF ACTIONS BY HOSTILE FORCES					
6. Current Missing[c]	—	—	—	—	—
7. Deaths					
a. From aircraft accidents/incidents					
Fixed Wing	286	221	51	295	853
Helicopter	1,946	62	245	19	2,272
b. From ground action	5,017	626	1,389	289	7,321
TOTAL DEATHS	7,249	909	1,685	603	10,446

*Data after September 30, 1980 are not available.
[a]Navy figures include a small number of Coast Guard casualties.
[b]Sum of 1, 2a, 3a and 4a.
[c]Technical status at time of cease-fire.
   Have not been released to U.S. control and are currently unaccounted for.
Note: Includes casualties incurred in the Mayaguez incident.
Source: Department of Defense, OASD (Comptroller), Directorate for Information Operations and Control.
Source: *Data on Vietnam Era Veterans*, Office of Information Management and Statistics, Veterans Administration, Washington, D.C., September 1983.

CATHOLICS

Catholicism was introduced into Vietnam by European missionaries in the 16th century. Flourishing during the period of French occupation, it became an important force in South Vietnam both because of the 700,000 Catholic refugees who fled from the north in 1954 (*see* Part I, THE SETTING) and because of the leadership of President Ngo Dinh Diem, a Catholic. After his assassination in 1963, Catholic influence declined but remained an important force in South Vietnam.

See also BUDDHISTS; DIEM, NGO DINH.

Suggestions for further reading: *Vietnam: A History,* by Stanley Karnow (New York: Viking, 1983).

CAVALRY

See AIR CAVALRY, ARMOR.

CEASE-FIRE

During the war in Vietnam, there were many cease-fires on the battlefield. For example, President Johnson initiated some 16 bombing pauses and 70 peace initiatives in attempts to placate American public opinion and to induce the North Vietnamese to cease their aggressions.

These cease-fires grew out of a faulty perception of the nature of military power. Theorists saw such power as "diplomatic signaling devices" rather than instruments of force to compel the adversary to do as the United States willed. As a result, the enemy was encouraged, instead of discouraged, in its aggression. The North Vietnamese and Viet Cong violated cease-fire agreements whenever it suited their purpose, the most flagrant example being the Tet Offensive of 1968. This same pattern persisted after the cease-fire implemented by the Paris Accords of 1973.

See also TET OFFENSIVE, PARIS ACCORDS.

Suggestions for further reading: "Vietnam and the American Theory of Limited War," by Stephen Peter Rosen, in *International Security,* vol. 7, no. 2, fall 1982.

CENSORSHIP

Unlike during World War II, censorship was not instituted during the Vietnam war. According to a 1985 study by Peter Braestrup, such censorship was considered in 1965 at the Defense Department's request, but it was ruled out at the urging of U.S. officials in Saigon for the following reasons: (1) it was impractical, given the freedom of reporters in Saigon to travel to Hong Kong or elsewhere to file stories without censorship; (2) there was no censorship in the United States and there could not be without a declaration of war; (3) the South Vietnamese, hosts to the U.S. forces, would have to have a hand in censorship, and they had already set some unpopular precedents with their own press; (4) it was impossible to censor television film because of a lack of technical facilities; and (5) it was difficult to suddenly impose censorship during a war that had long been covered without it.

In the absence of any formal censorship, U.S. officials and reporters worked out a set of ground rules to govern combat reporting. Among other things these rules banned casualty reports and unit identification related to specific action except in general terms, such as "light," "moderate" or "heavy" (overall casualty summaries would be reported weekly); troop movements or deployments until released by MACV (U.S. Military Assistance Command Vietnam); and identification of units participating in battles.

With respect to combat photography and television, it was emphasized that visual close-ups of identification of wounded or dead and interview of wounded (without prior approval of a medical officer) should be avoided, out of respect for the feelings of the next of kin or the wounded person's right of privacy.

From 1964 to 1968 there were relatively few violations of the ground rules by newsmen in Vietnam. Barry Zorthian, a former U.S. Mission spokesman in Saigon, observed in March 1984 that:

> In the four years (1964-68) that I was in Vietnam with some 2,000 correspondents accredited . . . we had only four or five cases of security violations . . . of tactical military information. Our leverage was the lifting of credentials and that was done in only

four or five cases and at least two or three of these were simply unintentional errors on the part of the correspondent. There was only once or twice that [ground rules] were deliberately challenged, and the correspondent's credentials were immediately lifted.

See also MEDIA, PENTAGON PAPERS, TELEVISION.

Suggestions for further reading: A useful discussion of battlefield censorship in a historical context can be found in Peter Braestrup's "Background Paper" in *Battle Lines: Report of the Twentieth Century Fund Task Force on the Military and the Media* (New York: Priority Press, 1985). The pros and cons of battlefield censorship are discussed in *Vietnam: 10 Years Later* (Fort Benjamin Harrison, Indiana: Defense Information School, 1984).

CENTRAL HIGHLANDS

The term "Central Highlands" was used to describe a highland area in the western part of II Corps stretching roughly from Ban Me Thuot in Darlac Province north to Kontum Province and the southern border of I Corps. An area of approximately 5,400 square miles, it was sparsely populated, primarily by Montagnard tribesmen.

Recognized early by North Vietnamese Army (NVA) strategists as the key to the conquest of Vietnam, an NVA attempt to cut Vietnam in two in 1965 with an attack from Cambodian sanctuaries across the Central Highlands to the sea was foiled by the U.S. First Cavalry Division in the Battle of the Ia Drang.

In 1975 they repeated this same strategy with a three-division attack on Ban Me Thuot on March 10, 1975. In the face of this attack, South Vietnamese President Nguyen Van Thieu made the decision on March 14, 1975 to withdraw his overextended forces from the highlands to coastal enclaves. Under increasing NVA pressure, this withdrawal turned into a rout. By March 31, 1975 the NVA 320th Division reached Tuy Hoa on the coast of the South China Sea. South Vietnam had been cut in two, and a month later Saigon fell to the NVA.

See also FINAL OFFENSIVE; IA DRANG, BATTLE OF. *See* map at II CORPS TACTICAL ZONE.

Suggestions for further reading: *Vietnam from*

Ceasefire to Capitulation, by William E. LeGro (Washington, D.C.: U.S. Government Printing Office, 1981).

CENTRAL HIGHLANDS WITHDRAWAL

See FINAL OFFENSIVE.

CENTRAL INTELLIGENCE AGENCY

See CIA.

CENTRAL OFFICE FOR SOUTH VIETNAM

See COSVN (CENTRAL OFFICE FOR SOUTH VIETNAM).

CHAIRMAN, JOINT CHIEFS OF STAFF

By law the Chairman of the Joint Chiefs of Staff is the senior officer of the U.S. armed services. A statutory adviser to the National Security Council, he presides over the Joint Chiefs of Staff. Contrary to popular opinion, he does not command the armed forces but only transmits the commands of the President and the Secretary of Defense. From the time of the first military deaths in 1959 until the end of the Vietnam war in 1975, this position was held by six different men: Air Force General Nathan F. Twining (1957–60), Army General Lyman L. Lemnitzer (1960–61), Army General Maxwell D. Taylor (1961–64), Army General Earle G. Wheeler (1964–70), Admiral Thomas H. Moorer (1970–74), and Air Force General George S. Brown (1974–78).

See also BROWN, GEORGE S.; COMMAND AND CON-

TROL; JOINT CHIEFS OF STAFF; MOORER, THOMAS H.; TAYLOR, MAXWELL D.; WHEELER, EARLE G.

Suggestions for further reading: *U.S. Defense Planning: A Critique,* by John M. Collins (Boulder: Westview Press, 1982).

CHICAGO SEVEN

The defendants in the famous conspiracy trial arising out of the bloody events attending the Democratic National Convention in August 1968. The defendants included Abbie Hoffman and Jerry Rubin, both of the Youth International Party, or "Yippies"; Rennie Davis and Tom Hayden, both former SDS leaders (Students for a Democratic Society); Dave Dellinger, the national cochairman of the Mobilization Against the War; Lee Weiner and John Froines, both young academics; and Bobby Seale, a leader of the Black Panthers. The group came to be called the "conspiracy." On March 19, 1969, they were indicted on charges of conspiracy and crossing state lines with intent to riot. The trial began in September 1969 and lasted until February 1970 under the jurisdiction of Judge Julius Hoffman.

During the first weeks of this trial, Seale made repeated courtroom outbursts, for which he was gagged and bound to a chair. His case was separated out as a mistrial, and he was sentenced to four years for contempt of court.

The rest of the trial of the then "Chicago Seven" was conducted in a circus-like atmosphere, the defendants released daily to make speaking engagements, the antics of Rubin and Hoffman infuriating Judge Hoffman. Twelve years in prison for 125 contempt citations were imposed on the defendants and their lawyers, William Kunstler and Leonard Weinglass. Dozens of witnesses testified for the defense, resulting in 22,000 pages of proceedings. In the end all the defendants were found guilty and sentenced to five years in prison. On appeal in 1972, however, they were all acquitted of the conspiracy charges because of improper rulings and behavior by Judge Hoffman. Hoffman was severely reprimanded by the appeals court for his "deprecatory and often antagonistic attitude toward the

defense." In December 1973 all but a few of the contempt charges were also dropped.

See also DELLINGER, DAVID; DEMOCRATIC NATIONAL CONVENTION, 1968; HAYDEN, THOMAS E.; HOFFMAN, ABBIE; RUBIN, JERRY.

CHIEF OF NAVAL OPERATIONS, U.S. NAVY

The Chief of Naval Operations is the senior military officer of the Department of the Navy and, unlike his other service counterparts, exercises command over the operating forces of the U.S. Navy. From the time of the first U.S. military deaths in 1959 until the Vietnam war ended in 1975, this position was held by six different men. In 1959 Admiral Arleigh A. Burke was Chief of Naval Operations. He was replaced in August 1961 by Admiral George W. Anderson, who was replaced, in turn, by Admiral David L. McDonald in August 1963. His successor, Admiral Thomas H. Moorer, had served as Commander-in-Chief of the Pacific Fleet from 1964 to 1965, in charge of U.S. Navy operations off Vietnam. When Admiral Moorer was appointed Chairman of the Joint Chiefs of Staff in July 1970, he was replaced by Admiral Elmo R. Zumwalt, who had served as Commander of U.S. Naval Forces Vietnam from 1968 to 1970. In July 1974 Admiral Zumwalt was replaced by Admiral James L. Holloway who served as Chief of Naval Operations until after the end of the war in Vietnam.

See also COMMAND AND CONTROL; JOINT CHIEFS OF STAFF; MOORER, THOMAS H.; NAVY, U.S.; ZUMWALT, ELMO K.

Suggestions for further reading. *U.S. Defense Planning: A Critique,* by John M. Collins (Boulder: Westview Press, 1982).

CHIEF OF STAFF, U.S. AIR FORCE

By law the Chief of Staff is the senior officer of the U.S. Air Force. From the first U.S. military deaths in 1959 until the end of the Vietnam war in

1975, the position of Air Force Chief of Staff was held by six different men. In 1959 General Thomas D. White was Air Force Chief of Staff. He was replaced in June 1961 by General Curtis E. LeMay, who was replaced by General John P. McConnell in February 1965. McConnell's successor, General John D. Ryan, had served as Commander-in-Chief of Pacific Air Forces from 1967 to 1968, the controller of strategic air operations over Vietnam. In July 1973 General Ryan was succeeded by General George S. Brown, who had served as Deputy Commander of the MACV (U.S. Military Assistance Command Vietnam) and as Commander of the Seventh Air Force in Vietnam from 1968 to 1970. When General Brown was appointed Chairman of the Joint Chiefs of Staff in July 1974, he was replaced by General David C. Jones, who had served in Vietnam in 1969 as the Operations Officer and Vice Commander of the Seventh Air Force.

See also AIR FORCE, U.S.; BROWN, GEORGE S.; COMMAND AND CONTROL; JOINT CHIEFS OF STAFF.

Suggestions for further reading: *U.S. Defense Planning: A Critique,* by John M. Collins (Boulder: Westview Press, 1982).

CHIEF OF STAFF, U.S. ARMY

By law the Chief of Staff is the senior officer of the U.S. Army. The position of Army Chief of Staff changed hands seven times from the time of the first U.S. military deaths in 1959 until the end of the Vietnam war in 1975. In January 1959 General Maxwell D. Taylor was Army Chief of Staff, but shortly thereafter, in July 1959, he was replaced by General Lyman L. Lemnitzer. On October 1, 1960, when General Lemnitzer was appointed Chairman of the Joint Chiefs of Staff, he was succeeded by General George H. Decker, who was replaced by General Earle G. Wheeler on October 1, 1962. When General Wheeler was appointed Chairman of the Joint Chiefs of Staff in July 1964, General Harold K. Johnson was appointed Army Chief of Staff and continued in that position until July 1968, when he was replaced by General William C. Westmoreland. In October 1972 General Creighton W. Abrams suc-

ceeded General Westmoreland. When General Abrams died in office in September 1974, he was replaced by his deputy, General Fred C. Weyand. It is noteworthy that each of these last three Army Chiefs of Staff—Generals Westmoreland, Abrams and Weyand—served previously as Commander of the U.S. Military Assistance Command Vietnam (COMUSMACV), that is, as field commanders for the Vietnam war.

By comparison with these seven Army Chiefs of Staff, General Van Tien Dung served as Chief of Staff of the North Vietnamese Army from 1953 until 1980, and he personally planned and led the Final Offensive in 1975.

See also ABRAMS, CREIGHTON W.; COMMAND AND CONTROL; DECKER, GEORGE H.; JOHNSON, HAROLD K.; JOINT CHIEFS OF STAFF; TAYLOR, MAXWELL D.; WESTMORELAND, WILLIAM C.; WEYAND, FRED C.; WHEELER, EARLE G.

Suggestions for further reading: *U.S. Defense Planning: A Critique,* by John M. Collins (Boulder: Westview Press, 1982).

CHIEU HOI

Literally "open arms," *Chieu Hoi* was an amnesty program instituted in early 1963 by South Vietnamese President Ngo Dinh Diem to subvert the morale of Viet Cong forces. The number of amnesty seekers reached an all-time high during 1969, when in the aftermath of the Viet Cong's disastrous Tet Offensive the previous year, 47,087 Viet Cong soldiers chose to side with South Vietnam. From 1963 to 1973 the program resulted in 159,741 Viet Cong deserters, who brought with them 10,699 individual weapons and 545 crew-served weapons (i.e., machine guns and mortars).

Suggestions for further reading: *Pacification,* Tran Dinh Tho (Washington, D.C.: Indochina Monograph, U.S. Army Center of Military History, 1980).

CHINA

Although Vietnam and China had a long and

acrimonious history dating back almost 2,000 years (*see* Part I, THE SETTING), the official American view in 1954, as espoused by Secretary of State John Foster Dulles, and for several years thereafter was that North Vietnam was a proxy for communist China and that any extension of North Vietnam's control in Vietnam would mean a dangerous enlargement of the area of China's effective control. The United States had succumbed to the mythology of Marxist-Leninist ideology that communism was a monolithic world force which transcended nationalism and thus made the past history of Sino-Vietnamese enmity irrelevant. There were some facts to back up this belief. The Viet Minh had received substantial aid from China in their fight against the French. Throughout the Vietnam War, China provided massive military aid to North Vietnam. As early as 1962, for example, China supplied some 90,000 rifles and machine guns to the North Vietnamese for use in their guerrilla war in the south. The Chinese even provided labor battalions to repair North Vietnam's supply routes into southern China.

This support was not motivated so much by ideology, however, as by China's desire to weaken American power in Asia. But growing Chinese conflicts with the Soviet Union caused China to reconsider its position toward the United States. This shift resulted in a cooling of relations between Vietnam and China, especially after President Richard M. Nixon's "opening" to China in 1971 and his visit there in 1972. Relations deteriorated rapidly after the end of the Vietnam war, and in February 1979 China and Vietnam went to war, ostensibly over boundary disputes but in reality over Chinese attempts to curb Vietnamese expansion in Southeast Asia. Since that time, China has continued to attempt to limit this expansion by such acts as providing aid and military assistance to Cambodian rebels fighting Vietnamese invaders and keeping military pressure on Vietnam's northern border.

One of the major ironies of the Vietnam war is that China, by supporting the "winner," emerged from the war as one of the great strategic losers. Rather than strengthening its southern borders by driving the United States out of Indochina, it has found its southern flank jeopardized by a hostile Vietnam. To make matters worse, Vietnam is now closely allied with the Soviet Union, China's most dangerous enemy.

Another irony is that although the United States initially became involved in Vietnam to check communist Chinese expansion, it now finds itself sharing a mutual interest with China in containing communist Vietnamese expansion in Southeast Asia.

See also COALITION WARFARE.

Suggestions for further reading: *Vietnam and China 1938-1954*, by King C. Chen (Princeton: Princeton University Press, 1969); *Vietnam: A History*, by Stanley Karnow (New York: Viking, 1983).

CHINA, REPUBLIC OF

See TAIWAN.

CHINOOK HELICOPTER

The CH-47 Chinook helicopter was widely used during the Vietnam war. With twin engines and rotor blades fore and aft, it was developed for the transportation of cargo, equipment and troops. It could carry up to 33 passengers and by use of external slings could transport light artillery and other loads. Normally its maximum range was 150 to 200 miles with a speed of about 110 to 120 knots.

Suggestions for further reading: *Airmobility, 1961-1971*, by John J. Tolson (Washington, D.C.: U.S. Government Printing Office, 1973).

CHOMSKY, NOAM A(VRAM) (1928-)

Born in Philadelphia, Pennsylvania on December 7, 1928, Chomsky received his bachelor's degree from the University of Pennsylvania in 1949, an M.A. in linguistics in 1951 and a Ph.D. in 1955. He immediately joined the faculty of linguistics at the

Massachusetts Institute of Technology. In the late 1950s and through the 1960s, Chomsky became the leading theoretician in linguistics.

As early as 1965 he emerged as one of the most articulate university critics of the Vietnam war, and his essay "The Responsibility of Intellectuals," which appeared in 1967, made him an international figure. In his book *American Power and the New Mandarins*, published in 1969, Chomsky indicted intellectuals who served as ideologues for the ends of government and big business, calling them the "new mandarins." In the same year Chomsky was one of 24 professors who publicly announced their support for the October 15 nationwide Moratorium Against the War in Vietnam. In 1971 he participated in the formation of an antiwar Labor-University Alliance with students, professors and trade union leaders. The alliance condemned the "widening of the war into Laos" and accused the Nixon Administration of obfuscating its real purpose—the military conquest of Vietnam. In the same year Chomsky, with David Dellinger of the "Chicago Seven" and Daniel Ellsberg, issued a statement calling for the release of the antiwar activist Berrigan brothers and all other political prisoners.

See also BERRIGAN, DANIEL.

CHRISTMAS BOMBING

A derogatory phrase for the bombing of Hanoi in December 1972, the "Christmas Bombing" was part of Operation Linebacker II.

See also LINEBACKER OPERATIONS.

CHU LAI

Located on the coast of the South China sea in Quang Tin Province, I Corps, Chu Lai was not even a town until the U.S. Marines constructed a major base there. When Marine Lieutenant General Victor H. Krulak selected the site for an airfield, a naval officer accompanying him remarked that the place looked good but was not marked on the maps. Krulak replied that the name was Chu Lai but later explained: "I had simply given him the Mandarin Chinese characters for my name." A major port and jet-capable airfield were constructed there. It was headquarters for the South Vietnamese Army's Second Division, and at one time or another elements of the U.S. Marines' First Division, South Korea's Second Marine Brigade and the U.S. Army's Americal Division were also stationed there. Chu Lai fell to the North Vietnamese during the Final Offensive.

See map at I CORPS TACTICAL ZONE.

Suggestions for further reading: *U.S. Marines in Vietnam: The Landing and the Buildup, 1965,* by Jack Shulimson and Charles H. Johnson (Washington, D.C.: U.S. Government Printing Office, 1978).

CHURCH, FRANK (FORRESTER) (1924–1984)

Born in Boise, Idaho on July 25, 1924, Church, who graduated from Stanford University Law School in 1950, practiced law in his native city of Boise until elected to the U.S. Senate in 1956. As a member of the Foreign Relations Committee, Church was critical of U.S. military involvement in South Vietnam and in 1963 opposed aiding the regime of Ngo Dinh Diem. In June 1965 he called for direct negotiations with the National Liberation Front, free elections in South Vietnam and a scaling down of the U.S. war effort. Nevertheless, during 1965 and 1966 he voted for supplemental arms appropriations bills necessary for sustaining the war effort. In May 1967 Church drafted a letter signed by 16 antiwar Senators warning the North Vietnamese that "our objective is the settlement of the war at the conference table, not the repudiation of American commitments already made to South Vietnam or the unilateral withdrawl of American forces from that embattled country."

In the spring of 1970 Church and Republican Senator John Sherman Cooper introduced an amendment to a foreign military sales bill barring funds for future military operations in Cambodia. After a seven-week filibuster, the Senate passed the amendment in late June by the vote of 58 to 37. The House, however, rejected the measure. A scaled-down version was passed in December as part of a defense appropriations bill. The rider prevented the introduction of ground troops into Laos or Thailand. The adoption of the Cooper-Church Amendment represented the first limitation ever voted on the President's power as Commander-in-Chief during a war situation.

In 1973 Congress passed a bill, sponsored by Church and Republican Senator Clifford Case, authorizing a cutoff of funds for all U.S. combat operations in Indochina.

Church was defeated in his bid for reelection in 1980. He died of cancer on April 7, 1984.

See also CASE-CHURCH AMENDMENT; COOPER-CHURCH AMENDMENT; COOPER, JOHN SHERMAN.

CIA (CENTRAL INTELLIGENCE AGENCY)

In the closing days of World War II, the CIA's predecessor agency, the Office of Strategic Services (OSS), parachuted a team into Vietnam to assist in the war effort against Japan. Ho Chi Minh, then one of several Vietnamese political figures struggling for power, became particularly friendly with an American agent, Major Archimedes L. A. Patti. He asked Patti to help him draft a declaration of independence patterned on that of the United States (from that evidence, Patti remains convinced that the United States missed an opportunity to ally itself with Ho Chi Minh). It would appear, however, that instead of the United States using Ho Chi Minh, it was Ho Chi Minh who used the United States. He played on his friendship with Patti to convince his political competitors that he and he alone had won the confidence and support of the United States, an act that assisted in his seizure of power when the Japanese surrendered in September 1945.

Among other CIA personnel who played a major role in the war between North and South Vietnam were Air Force Major General Edward G. Lansdale, who had assisted Philippine President Ramón Magsaysay in his struggle against communist insurgents, and William Colby, who became CIA Director. Colby later supervised Phoenix Program in South Vietnam, which was instituted to root out the Viet Cong infrastructure.

See also COLBY, WILLIAM; LANSDALE, EDWARD G.; PHOENIX PROGRAM; RHEAULT AFFAIR.

Suggestions for further reading: *Vietnam: A History*, by Stanley Karnow (New York: Viking, 1983); *Why Vietnam? Prelude to America's Albatross*, by Archimedes L. A. Patti (Berkeley: University of California Press, 1980); *In the Midst of Wars: An American's Mission to Southeast Asia*, by Edward Geary Lansdale (New York: Harper & Row, 1972); *Honorable Men: My Life in the CIA*, by William Colby and Peter Forbath (New York: Simon & Schuster, 1978).

CIDG (CIVILIAN IRREGULAR DEFENSE GROUP)

THE CIDG was a program conceived by the CIA office of MAAG-Vietnam during late 1961. The purpose was to arm and train various hill tribes and other factions so that they could protect their own villages against the Viet Cong. Starting in February 1962, the U.S. Army Special Forces became active in developing the first CIDG forces from Montagnard tribesmen in the Central Highlands, and on July 1, 1963 the Special Forces completely took over the CIDG effort from the CIA.

The CIDG program expanded rapidly after the involvement of Army Special Forces, which organized CIDG companies at a number of camps. However, Army Special Forces served only as advisers. The CIDG was commanded by the Luc Luong Dac Biet (LLDB), or South Vietnamese Special Forces. CIDG camps were situated to defend remote villages and hinder the infiltration of North Vietnamese forces into South Vietnam along the border. However, the CIDG forces always remained basically local security units; they were not trained or equipped to perform regular infantry duty. They were hired on a contractual basis, and their only official military connection was their exemption from the draft. CIDG troops were usually outclassed by the main force Viet Cong and North Vietnamese in combat, and allied commanders who understood their lim-

Aerial shot of the CIDG camp at Trai Bi. (Courtesy Shelby L. Stanton.)

itations employed them only for screening and patrolling.

In order to afford their isolated camps more protection, the Army Special Forces developed CIDG reaction Mike Force companies in all four corps tactical zones by 1966. These CIDG units received much more training, and were actually led—not advised—by the Army Special Forces. In March 1968 the Mike Forces were expanded, modernized, and relabeled Mobile Strike Force Commands. These were battalion- and brigade-sized infantry units capable of reinforcing threatened camps and engaging the Viet Cong and North Vietnamese in open combat.

At its height the CIDG program mustered the equivalent of four infantry divisions. As part of the "Vietnamization" program, most CIDG camp units were converted into South Vietnamese Army border ranger battalions by the end of 1970. The mobile strike forces were composed of different races. Upon disbandment the Cambodians became part of the Khmer Republic Army, the Chinese Nungs were hired by MACV-SOG (Military Assistance Command Vietnam-Studies and Observation Group) and the Vietnamese were used as replacements in South Vietnamese airborne and ranger battalions. In early 1971 the LLDB was integrated into the South Vietnamese Strategic Technical Directorate, which performed special missions.

See also AIRBORNE FORCES, MONTAGNARDS, SPE-

CIAL FORCES, STUDIES AND OBSERVATION GROUP, VIETNAMIZATION.

Suggestions for further reading: *U.S. Army Special Forces, 1961–1971,* by Francis J. Kelly (Washington, D.C.: U.S. Government Printing Office, 1973); *The Green Berets at War,* by Shelby L. Stanton (Novato, Calif.: Presidio Press, 1985); *Inside the Green Berets: The First Thirty Years,* by Charles M. Simpson, III (Novato, Calif.: Presidio Press, 1983).

CINCPAC (COMMANDER-IN-CHIEF PACIFIC COMMAND)

See (PACOM) PACIFIC COMMAND.

CIVIL WAR

A civil war, briefly defined, is a war between opposing groups of citizens of the same nation. The question of whether the Vietnam conflict was a civil war remains controversial today, more than 10 years after the fall of Saigon. The North Vietnamese, of course, always envisioned themselves as fighting a civil war. Indeed, the core assumption undergirding their cause was that the South Vietnamese government was an illegitimate puppet regime supported not by the allegiance of the people, but by the power of the United States. Any action taken by the North Vietnamese armed forces or the Viet Cong against that government was therefore justified. The South Vietnamese and American position, not surprisingly, was that North Vietnam was engaged in overt aggression against the sovereign state of South Vietnam.

Vietnam had a long history of internal divisions and was divided again by the 1954 Geneva Accords, which ended the war between the French and the Viet Minh. The communist government of the Democratic Republic of Vietnam (North Vietnam) controlled the area north of the 17th parallel, and the Republic of Vietnam (South Vietnam) controlled the area south of that line. Just as with East and West Germany and North and South Korea, which were also divided by "temporary" demarcation lines, the two Vietnams were internationally recognized as separate entities.

In 1957 the United Nations Security Council voted 8 to 1 and the General Assembly 49 to 9 to admit South Vietnam, but the move was vetoed by the Soviet Union. In turn, the Soviet Union suggested that both North and South Vietnam be admitted to the United Nations as "two separate states," but this was vetoed by the United States. By 1963 (two years before the major U.S. ground combat involvement) 60 nations had recognized the sovereignty of South Vietnam and 30 recognized North Vietnam.

The North Vietnamese now freely admit that the National Liberation Front in South Vietnam was never the independent entity it claimed to be, but was organized and directed by Hanoi to control the guerrilla movement in the south. After 1968 the Hanoi-directed guerrilla war in the south became moribund, and the war ended not by a civil uprising but by the North Vietnamese Army's cross-border blitzkrieg in 1975.

See also ELECTIONS, GENEVA CONFERENCES, NATIONAL LIBERATION FRONT.

Suggestions for further reading: *Vietnam: A History*, by Stanley Karnow (New York: Viking, 1983); *An International History of the Vietnam War: Revolution Versus Containment 1955–61*, by R. B. Smith (New York: St. Martin's Press, 1983).

CLAYMORE MINES

An antipersonnel land mine that could be command-detonated (i.e., detonated by a soldier some distance away by closing an electrical circuit) and that propelled projectiles in a fan-shaped pattern to a lethal range of some 50 meters, or about 54 yards. U.S. and allied forces used a standard-issue claymore mine. The Viet Cong and the North Vietnamese often used locally constructed mines filled with pieces of steel-connecting rods. Round in shape rather than rectangular, as were U.S.-made claymores, these homemade devices were often lethal to several hundred yards.

See also BOOBY TRAPS.

CLEAR-AND-HOLD

A basic tactic of pacification, clear-and-hold operations involved driving enemy units out of a populated area so that pacification efforts could proceed. While U.S. Army infantry units were often involved in clearing operations, the long-term effort necessary to hold an area—i.e., to eliminate local guerrilla units and uproot the enemy's political infrastructure—was normally conducted by South Vietnamese Army or Regional Forces. In I Corps the U.S. Marine Corps used a different approach. While Marine infantry units were also used to clear an area, Marine combined action platoons were used to hold these areas.

See also CAP (USMC COMBAT ACTION PLATOON); PACIFICATION; SEARCH-AND-DESTROY.

Suggestions for further reading: *Report on the War in Vietnam*, by U. S. G. Sharpe and William C. Westmoreland (Washington, D.C.: U.S. Government Printing Office, 1968).

CLEAR-AND-SECURE

See CLEAR-AND-HOLD.

A claymore mine with a pull-release device. (Courtesy Shelby L. Stanton.)

CLIFFORD, CLARK (McADAMS) (1906-   )

Born on December 25, 1906 in Fort Scott, Kansas, Clifford received a law degree from Washington University in 1928. Commissioned in the U.S. Naval Reserve in 1944, he became President Truman's naval aide in 1946 and within months his special counsel. He was a major force in molding the containment policy and the Truman Doctrine, both aimed at halting Soviet expansionism.

Clifford again became a presidential adviser during the Kennedy and Johnson Administrations. In 1965 he visited Southeast Asia as Chairman of the Foreign Intelligence Advisory Board. The optimism of U.S. military and South Vietnamese officials convinced him that U.S. policy was correct, and he held that conviction until he returned from a tour of America's allies in 1967. Clifford was disturbed that these countries—Australia, New Zealand, the Philippines—refused to increase their troop commitments and seemed less troubled by communist aggression in Southeast Asia than the United States. He began to wonder whether the U.S. concern about the danger to the stability of the region was justified.

Clifford's doubts were not widely publicized and he was named Secretary of Defense in January 1968. A month later he was appointed Chairman of the President's Ad Hoc Task Force on Vietnam, which was convened to study a request by the Joint Chiefs of Staff and General William C. Westmoreland for more than 200,000 additional troops. The purpose of the troop request, which was made following the Tet Offensive, was twofold: to augment U.S. forces in Vietnam and to strengthen U.S. security in other parts of the world. In transmitting the task force's recommendations to the President, Clifford made known his serious reservations about the Vietnam war, based on his inability to find out how many more troops would be needed, when the South Vietnamese would be able to take over or how long the war would continue.

In late March, Clifford assembled a group of senior statesmen to assess U.S. policy in Vietnam. The consensus of the group, which met with President Johnson on March 26, was to find a way to disengage from the war. Shortly thereafter Clifford proposed an alternative draft to a presidential speech on Vietnam which said the United States would stop all bombing north of the 20th parallel. President Johnson accepted the peace draft and delivered it over nationwide television on March 31. His address included the announcement that he would not seek another term as President. Clifford then aligned with W. Averell Harriman and Cyrus T. Vance, U.S. representatives to the Paris peace talks, in urging the President to order a total bombing halt to speed the negotiations with North Vietnam. In October, Johnson yielded to this position.

Clifford returned to his legal practice in January 1969.

See also AD HOC TASK FORCE ON VIETNAM; JOHNSON, LYNDON B.; SENIOR ADVISORY GROUP; TET OFFENSIVE.

Suggestions for further reading: *The Limits of Intervention,* by Townsend Hoopes (New York: David McKay, 1970); *The Best and the Brightest,* by David Halberstam (New York: Random House, 1972); *The Ten Thousand Day War: Vietnam*

Clark Clifford. (Courtesy U.S. Army Military History Institute.)

1945-1975, by Michael Maclear (New York: St. Martin's Press, 1981); *Vietnam: A History,* by Stanley Karnow (New York: Viking, 1983).

CLOSE AIR SUPPORT

A term used to designate fire support by U.S. Air Force, Navy and Marine aircraft in support of ground combat operations, close air support involves bombing, strafing and firing aerial rockets. It began in World War I and played a major role in combat operations in World War II and the Korean war. In Vietnam it was conducted by fighters, fighter-bombers, bombers and fixed-wing gunships. Close and accurate aerial fire support was provided by tactical fighters and fighter-bombers, guided and controlled by forward air controllers, referred to as FACs, in light propeller-driven spotter planes attached to ground forces. In addition, beginning in November 1965 with the Battle of the Ia Drang, B-52 strategic bombers were also used in support of ground operations. Among the U.S. innovations of the Vietnam war was the use of fixed-wing gunships. Transport planes were outfitted with flares and rapid-firing miniguns. Known to soldiers as "Spooky" and "Puff, the Magic Dragon," these gunships could saturate an area with remarkably accurate fire.

Although not part of the close air support system, helicopter gunships and helicopter aerial artillery assigned to U.S. Army and Marine units also provided fire support to ground operations.

See also FAC, GUNSHIPS, HELICOPTERS, STRATEGIC AIR COMMAND, TACTICAL AIR COMMAND.

Suggestions for further reading: *The United States Air Force In Southeast Asia,* edited by Carl Berger (Washington, D.C.: U.S. Government Printing Office, 1977); *Airpower in Three Wars,* by William W. Momyer (Washington, D.C.: U.S. Government Printing Office, 1978).

COALITION WARFARE

One of the factors that complicates understanding of the Vietnam war has been the popular misperception that the war was a contest between the United States and Viet Cong guerrillas.

In fact, the war in Vietnam—more correctly, the Second Indochina War—was a coalition war with North Vietnam and the guerrillas in the south, controlled by Hanoi through the National Liberation Front, allied with the Soviet Union and China on one hand and South Vietnam allied with the United States, Australia, New Zealand, South Korea, the Philippines and Thailand on the other.

One of the peculiarities of coalition warfare is that the objectives of each of the coalition partners are not precisely the same, nor is the intensity of each one's involvement. These factors thus create points of vulnerability that an enemy can exploit. From the beginning, North Vietnam sought to break the community of interest between South Vietnam and its allies. Because the United States did not fully realize that it was involved in a coalition war, it tended to look to such models as the successful counterguerrilla efforts of the British in Malaya or President Ramón Magsaysay in the Philippines. Overlooked was the fact that in both cases the conflict was simply between the government-in-being and the guerrillas, whereas in Vietnam the United States had to work through the government of South Vietnam. Because it failed to make this critical distinction, the United States dominated its side of the war and in so doing undermined the confidence and self-reliance of its own coalition partner.

It was not until the early 1970s that President Nixon began to "Vietnamize" the battlefield and to exploit the differences between North Vietnam and its Soviet and Chinese allies. This tactic ultimately proved so successful that the United States was able to mine Haiphong harbor and bomb Hanoi without Chinese or Soviet interference. By this time, however, the alliance between the United States and its Vietnamese ally had been so undermined by North Vietnamese propaganda efforts, by general U.S. public weariness with the war and by the lack of clearcut goals and objectives, that Nixon could not translate his diplomatic successes into a war-winning strategy. Because public support for the war had been eroded, the United States was forced to pressure its South Vietnamese ally into accepting the ill-fated Paris Accords of 1973. After the Watergate scandal that forced Nixon from office, U.S. support for South Vietnam was futher eroded, and the North Vietnamese correctly surmised that the United States would not again intervene, even after the North Vietnamese flagrantly violated the Paris Accords with their 1975 cross-border blitzkrieg.

See also CHINA, CONGRESS OF THE UNITED STATES, FREE WORLD MILITARY FORCES, NATIONAL LIBERATION FRONT, SOVIET UNION.

Suggestions for further reading: *Vietnam: A History,* by Stanley Karnow (New York: Viking, 1983); *White House Years,* by Henry Kissinger (Boston: Little, Brown & Co., 1979); *On Strategy: A Critical Analysis of the Vietnam War,* by Harry G. Summers, Jr. (Novato, Calif.: Presidio Press, 1982).

COASTAL SURVEILLANCE FORCE

The Coastal Surveillance Force was a U.S. Navy task force (Task Force 115) organized in March 1965. Initially controlled by the Seventh Fleet, and after July 1965 by the Commander of U.S. Naval Forces Vietnam (COMNAVFORV), the Coastal Surveillance Force was intended to curtail the seaborne infiltration of communist arms and supplies.

The 1,200-mile South Vietnamese coast from the 17th parallel to the Cambodian border was divided into nine patrol sectors. Within these areas surface search operations were conducted by ships and craft of the U.S. Navy, the U.S. Coast Guard and the South Vietnamese Navy. Controlled by Task Force 115 from headquarters in Saigon, and after July 1967 in Cam Ranh Bay, the Coastal Surveillance Force executed Operation Market Time. This operation involved establishing three barriers to infiltration. Farthest out—100 to 150 miles offshore—was an air barrier set up with long-range patrol planes. Closer in was an outer-surface barrier of destroyer escorts, minesweepers, Coast Guard cutters and the like. The mainstays of the inshore barrier were some 84

Swift boats. Fifty-foot vessels capable of 23 knots, they were armed with 50-caliber machine guns and an 81-mm mortar.

See also COAST GUARD, U.S.; GAME WARDEN OPERATION; MARKET TIME OPERATIONS.

Suggestions for further reading: *A Short History of the United States Navy and the Southeast Asia Conflict 1950-1975,* by Edward J. Marolda and G. Wesley Price, III (Washington, D.C.: Naval Historical Center, 1984); *On Watch,* by Elmo R. Zumwalt, Jr. (New York: Quadrangle, 1976); *The Brown Water Navy: The River and Coastal War in Indo-China and Vietnam 1948-1972,* by Victor Croizat (Poole, U.K.: Blandford Press, 1984).

COAST GUARD, U.S.

The U.S. Coast Guard operates within the Department of Transportation. (In 1965 it was part of the Department of Treasury.) When directed by the President, the Coast Guard, or any of its elements, serves within the U.S. Navy. On April 30, 1965 it was announced that U.S. Coast Guard units would operate with the U.S. Navy in Vietnam. Coast Guard Squadron One was formed for deployment to Vietnam. In July 1965 seventeen 82-foot patrol boats arrived in Vietnam, and in February 1966 nine more arrived.

On July 30, 1965 Naval Task Force 115 (Operation Market Time) was formed and Coast Guard units became part of the coastal surveillance centers established at Da Nang, Qui Nhon, Nha Trang, Vung Tau and An Thoi. In April 1967 Coast Guard Squadron Three, consisting initially of five cutters, sailed for Southeast Asian waters. Coast Guard cutters patrolled the Vietnamese coast from the DMZ to the Cambodian border, operating from bases in Da Nang, Cat Lo and An Thoi.

Between January 1969 and August 1970 all 26 patrol boats were transferred to Coast Guard-trained South Vietnamese crews and between 1971 and 1972 the cutters were turned over to the South Vietnamese.

In addition to its activities at sea, the Coast Guard provided security officers for South Vietnamese ports and explosives-handling detachments to supervise offloading of ammunition, bombs and other dangerous cargo. The Coast Guard also supplied aids to navigation, merchant marine details and humanitarian aid to South Vietnamese civilians.

During the war 56 combatant vessels of the Coast Guard were responsible for the boarding of nearly 250,000 junks and sampans in an effort to stop infiltration, and they participated in nearly 6,000 naval gunfire support missions. U.S. Coast Guard helicopters deployed with the U.S. Air Force in Vietnam and flew combat search-and-rescue missions. Seven Coastguardsmen were killed in action and 53 were wounded in action during the war. As of February 1985, one Guardsman was still missing in action and unaccounted for.

See also MARKET TIME OPERATIONS; NAVY, U.S.

Suggestions for further reading: *The United States Coast Guard in South East Asia During the Vietnam Conflict*, by Eugene Tulich (Washington, D.C.: U.S. Coast Guard Historical Monograph Program, 1975).

COBRA HELICOPTER

The AH-1G Cobra helicopter was a very powerful U.S. Army attack helicopter that used rockets, miniguns and grenade launchers to provide close and accurate fire support for infantry units. In Vietnam the Cobra helicopter was first used in large quantities during 1968.

COFFIN, WILLIAM SLOANE, JR. (1924–)

Born in New York City on June 1, 1924, Coffin entered Yale, but his studies were interrupted by four years as an officer in the U.S. Army. He returned to Yale in 1947 and later spent a year at the Union Theological Seminary. There Coffin became a follower of Reinhold Niebuhr, whose doctrine of "Christian realism" justified and encouraged political activism. From 1950 to 1953 he worked overseas for the CIA, specializing in

Russian affairs. After completing theological studies at Yale, Coffin was ordained a Presbyterian minister in 1956 and two years later was appointed Chaplain of Yale University. During the early 1960s he was involved in civil rights activities, for which he was arrested three times, and served as a training adviser to the Peace Corps.

Beginning in 1965 Coffin was strongly critical of American conduct in Vietnam. In January 1966 Coffin became acting Executive Secretary of the National Emergency Committee of Clergy Concerned about Vietnam.

By the fall of 1967 Coffin was counseling active resistance to the war and was one of the original signers of the September 1967 statement "A Call to Resist Illegitimate Authority," which supported draft resistance and the refusal of servicemen to obey orders to participate in the war. On October 16 Coffin was the main speaker at ceremonies at the Arlington Street Church in Boston, during which draft-eligible men burned or gave up their draft cards. Four days later Coffin

An AH-1G Cobra helicopter. (Courtesy of U.S. Army.)

was part of a delegation that turned over these and other draft cards to Justice Department officials in Washington, D.C.

For these and other acts Coffin, Benjamin Spock, Marcus Raskin, co-director of the Institute of Policy Studies, and two others were indicted on January 5, 1968 for conspiring to "counsel, aid and abet" young men to "refuse and evade service in the armed services. . . ." After a widely publicized trial all but Raskin were convicted on one conspiracy count, and on July 11 they were sentenced to fines and two-year prison terms. The convictions were overturned a year later. Coffin and another defendant were ordered retried, but the charges were dismissed at the request of the Justice Department. Coffin announced his resignation as Yale University Chaplain in February 1975, effective the next year.

See also SPOCK, BENJAMIN.

COLBY, WILLIAM E(GAN) (1920–)

Born on January 4, 1920 in St. Paul, Minnesota, William E. Colby graduated from Princeton University in 1940. Commissioned in the U.S. Army in 1941, he was detailed to the Office of Strategic Services (OSS) in 1943 and worked with the French underground. After World War II, Colby earned a law degree from Columbia University Law School, and when the Korean war broke out in June 1950, he joined the CIA.

Posted to South Vietnam in 1959 as First Secretary of the U.S. embassy and CIA station chief in Saigon, he was involved in the strategic hamlet program and the recruitment of Montagnard tribesmen by U.S. Special Forces. In 1962 he returned to Washington, D.C. to become head of the CIA's Far East Division. In that post he presided over the CIA's programs throughout Southeast Asia, including Air America operations and direction of a force of Laotian tribesmen against the communists in Laos, a U.S.-organized counterterror program in Vietnam and the joint U.S.-South Vietnamese Phoenix Program in Vietnam.

In 1968 he returned to Vietnam and on November 6 succeeded Robert Komer as Deputy

to the Commander of the U.S. Military Assistance Command Vietnam (COMUSMACV) responsible for CORDS (Civil Operations and Rural Development Support). He also coordinated the Phoenix Program, which was aimed at eliminating the Viet Cong infrastructure. Critics of the program charged that American officials condoned and participated in the torture of political prisoners and that during a period of 2½ years more than 20,000 suspected communists had been killed. In 1970 and 1971 Colby was called before congressional committees to testify about the program. He pointed out that many of the dead had been killed in battle but refused to state categorically that there had been no assassinations. Although the program was considered a failure at that time, North Vietnamese officials and former members of the Viet Cong have since acknowledged that it had a devastating effect on their war effort.

In June 1971 Colby resigned his post because of the serious illness of his daughter. He became Executive Director-Comptroller of the CIA in 1972 and Director of the CIA in 1973. He retired from the agency in 1976.

See also AIR AMERICA; CIA (CENTRAL INTELLIGENCE AGENCY); CORDS (CIVIL OPERATIONS AND RURAL DEVELOPMENT SUPPORT); KOMER, ROBERT W.; PHOENIX PROGRAM.

Suggestions for further reading: *Honorable Men: My Life in the CIA,* by William Colby and Peter Forbath (New York: Simon & Schuster, 1978).

COLLINS, J(OSEPH) LAWTON (1896–)

"Lightning Joe" Collins was born on May 1, 1896 in New Orleans, Louisiana. A graduate of the U.S. Military Academy, Collins saw combat in both world wars. From 1948 to 1953 he served as Army Chief of Staff.

Following the partition of Vietnam in 1954, Collins became prominently involved in the policy debate over U.S. support of Ngo Dinh Diem, the South Vietnamese President. Collins initially urged the Eisenhower Administration to withdraw support for Diem, whom Collins believed was incapable of successfully leading South Vietnam. After Eisenhower pledged to support Diem, however, Collins was sent to Vietnam as the President's personal representative to aid the South Vietnamese government in establishing a military training program and agrarian reforms.

It was Diem's refusal to carry out these reforms that led Collins, again, to advise Eisenhower to withdraw U.S. support. The State Department recommended a compromise, in which Diem would be retained as the titular head of state, while real power would be in the hands of the Dai Viet party. Collins accepted this plan, but before it could be implemented, Diem's forces crushed the opposition sects that had plagued him for so long. This ironically led to a reversal of U.S. policy to full support of Diem. Collins, who had come to symbolize American opposition to Diem, was soon replaced. He returned to Washington in May 1955.

COMBAT ACTION RIBBON

During World War II and the Korean war, U.S. Army combat infantrymen who bore the brunt of the fighting were recognized by award of the Combat Infantryman Badge. Marine Corps infantry personnel had no similar award, however. In 1969 the Secretary of the Navy authorized a Combat Action Ribbon for award to members of the Navy, Marine Corps and Coast Guard (when operating under the control of the Navy) who actively participate in ground or surface combat. The individual must have participated in a bona fide ground or surface combat firefight or action during which he was under enemy fire, and his performance while under fire must have been satisfactory. Those eligible include personnel involved in riverine and coastal operations, assaults, patrols, sweeps, ambushes, convoys, amphibious landings and similar activities who have participated in firefights; personnel assigned to areas subjected to sustained mortar and artillery attacks who actively participated in retaliatory or offensive actions; personnel in clandestine or special operations, such as UDT, reconnaissance or SEAL teams, when the risk of enemy fire was great and was expected to be encoun-

tered; and personnel aboard a ship when the safety of the ship and the crew were endangered by enemy attack, such as a ship hit by a mine or a ship engaged by shore, surface, air or subsurface elements.

See also COMBAT INFANTRYMAN BADGE.

COMBAT INFANTRYMAN BADGE

One of the most prized U.S. Army awards, since it evidences front-line combat service, the Combat Infantryman's Badge (CIB) was first authorized in World War II to distinguish those Army infantrymen actively engaged in ground combat. During the Vietnam war eligibility for the award of the CIB was extended to include those, regardless of branch of service, assigned as advisers to South Vietnamese infantry, ranger and infantry-type civil guard and self-defense corps units who served under fire with such units.

See also COMBAT ACTION RIBBON, COMBAT MEDICAL BADGE.

The Combat Infantryman's Badge.

COMBAT MEDICAL BADGE

The equivalent of the Combat Infantryman's Badge for Medical Corps personnel, the Combat Medical Badge was first authorized in World War II to distinguish those U.S. Army Medical Department personnel (and Navy Medical Department and Air Force Medical Service personnel attached to the Army) who performed medical duties in direct support of an infantry unit engaged in active ground combat. During the Vietnam war eligibility for award of the Combat Medical Badge was extended to include those medical personnel serving with Special Forces detachments and South Vietnamese units engaged in actual ground combat.

See also COMBAT ACTION RIBBON, COMBAT INFANTRYMAN BADGE.

The Combat Medical Badge.

COMMAND AND CONTROL

One of the fundamental principles of war is unity of command, which states that "for every objective, there should be unity of effort under one responsible commander." This principle was explicitly followed by the North Vietnamese, for under the leadership of Ho Chi Minh, General Vo Nguyen Giap was a member of the ruling Politburo, the Minister of Defense and the Commander-in-Chief of the Armed Forces. This unity of command gave the North Vietnamese an enormous advantage.

Although the Commander of the U.S. Military Assistance Command Vietnam (COMUSMACV) had been commonly perceived as the counterpart of General Giap, in fact there was no comparison. On the U.S. side, four Presidents—Kennedy, Johnson, Nixon and Ford—served as Commanders-in-Chief of U.S. armed forces during the years of major American military involvement. They were assisted by three national security advisers—McGeorge Bundy, Walt Rostow and Henry Kissinger. Command of the war was executed by five Secretaries of Defense—Robert McNamara, Clark Clifford, Melvin Laird, Elliot Richardson and James

Schlesinger—who were advised by five chairmen of the Joint Chiefs of Staff—Generals Lemnitzer, Taylor and Wheeler, Admiral Moorer and General Brown. Strategic direction of the war was exercised by four Commanders-in-Chief of the Pacific Command in Honolulu—Admirals Felt, Sharp, McCain and Gayler. None of these 21 individuals at any one time exercised the kind of direct command and control over forces that General Giap had throughout the war. None of them conducted their business from Southeast Asia.

As if this diffusion of authority and lack of continuity were not damaging enough, COMUSMACV's authority within Vietnam was severely limited. The air war over North Vietnam and Laos as well as naval operations outside of Vietnamese coastal waters were not under his command; nor were Marine Corps air units within Vietnam until late in the war. In Korea all combat operations were directed by a single commander. In Vietnam COMUSMACV did not exercise command over the South Vietnamese armed forces or the armed forces of such allies as Australia, New Zealand, South Korea and Thailand.

In addition, command of the MACV was held by four different men during the war: General Paul D. Harkins, General William C. Westemoreland, General Creighton W. Abrams and General Fred C. Weyand.

See also CHAIRMAN OF THE JOINT CHIEFS OF STAFF, NATIONAL SECURITY ADVISER, PACOM (PACIFIC COMMAND), PRESIDENT OF THE UNITED STATES, SECRETARY OF DEFENSE.

Suggestions for further reading: *The 25-Year War: America's Military Role in Vietnam,* by Bruce Palmer, Jr. (Lexington: University of Kentucky Press, 1984); *On Strategy: A Critical Analysis of the Vietnam War,* by Harry G. Summers, Jr. (Novato, Calif.: Presidio Press, 1982).

COMMANDANT, U.S. MARINE CORPS

By law the Commandant is the senior officer of the Marine Corps. The position of Commandant was held by five different men during the Vietnam war. At the time of the first U.S. military deaths in January 1959, General Randolph McC. Pate was Commandant of the Marine Corps. He was replaced in January 1960 by General David M. Shoup, who was replaced by General Wallace M. Greene in January 1964. Greene was succeeded by General Leonard F. Chapman in January 1968. In January 1972 General Robert E. Cushman, who had commanded the III Marine Amphibious Force in Vietnam from 1967 to 1969, was appointed Commandant and served in that position until after the end of the war.

See also COMMAND AND CONTROL; CUSHMAN, ROBERT E.; JOINT CHIEFS OF STAFF; MARINE CORPS, U.S.

COMMANDO HUNT

Code name for air operations to interdict North Vietnamese infiltration routes through Laos into South Vietnam, Commando Hunt involved a series of air operations by U.S. Air Force, Navy and Marine Corps aircraft. Beginning in 1968, the campaign terminated in January 1973. While infiltration was slowed by this campaign, it was not seriously disrupted.

See also HO CHI MINH TRAIL.

Suggestions for further reading: *Airpower in Three Wars,* by William W. Momyer (Washington, D.C.: U.S. Government Printing Office, 1978); *The United States Air Force in Southeast Asia,* edited by Carl Berger (Washington, D.C.: U.S. Government Printing Office, 1977); *The Vietnam Experience: Thunder from Above,* by John Morrocco (Boston: Boston Publishing Co., 1984); *Battles and Campaigns in Vietnam 1954–1984,* by Tom Carhart (Greenwich: Bison Books, 1984).

COMMENDATION MEDAL

First authorized in World War II, the Commendation Medal is normally awarded in the name of the Secretary of the U.S. Army, Navy or Air Force for meritorious achievement or meritorious service in peacetime. During the Vietnam war the Army Commendation Medal, Navy Commenda-

tion Medal, Air Force Commendation Medal, Coast Guard Commendation Medal and after 1967 Joint Service Commendation Medal awarded in the name of the Secretary of Defense were also awarded for acts of valor performed under circumstances which were of lesser degree than those required for award of the Bronze Star Medal. Awards for valor are denoted by a "V" device on the ribbon and subsequent awards are denoted by an oak leaf (a star for the Navy, Marine Corps and Coast Guard) also worn on the ribbon.

COMMUNICATIONS

Because of the technically complex mode of warfare conducted by the United States in Vietnam, its armed forces depended on very sophisticated communications-electronics apparatus. Communications ranged from portable radios to tropospheric radio relay and cable telephone exchanges. This was essential to control widely scattered units and fast moving, flexible airmobile operations. The North Vietnamese used manpacked radios, but Viet Cong local forces relied on such primitive devices as drums and gongs tied to jungle vines. On the battlefield, leaders of all sides used radios, arm and hand signals, flares, whistles and vocal orders to control their troops.

See also FIRST SIGNAL BRIGADE.

COMNAVFORV (COMMANDER U.S. NAVAL FORCES VIETNAM)

See NAVAL FORCES VIETNAM.

COMPANY

In the U.S. Army and Marine Corps (and in most other military organizations), a company is the basic organizational element. Commanded by a captain, it consists of two or more platoons. In the artillery a company-sized unit is termed a battery; in the cavalry it is called a troop. Normally part of a battalion, the personnel strength of a company varies widely in accordance with its mission. Companies that are permanently part of a battalion have letter designations; separate (independent) companies have number designations.

See also ORGANIZATION FOR COMBAT.

COMUSMACV (COMMANDER U.S. MILITARY ASSISTANCE COMMAND VIETNAM)

See MACV (U.S. MILITARY ASSISTANCE COMMAND VIETNAM).

CONGRESSIONAL MEDAL OF HONOR

See MEDAL OF HONOR.

CONGRESS OF THE UNITED STATES

Under the Constitution of the United States, the power to declare war and to raise and maintain armed forces is specifically restricted to the Congress. While President Johnson never requested an outright declaration of war, Congress provided initial approval of American involvement in Vietnam by passing the Gulf of Tonkin Resolution in 1964. Although many members spoke out against the war, Congress continued to vote the necessary funds to raise, train, arm and transport armed forces to Vietnam and to furnish them with all the materials and support services needed to conduct a war—in effect, giving the equivalent of a declaration of war.

As public support for the war began to erode starting in 1968, so did congressional support. In 1970 attempts were made to limit support for U.S. operations in Cambodia and in August 1973 all U.S. bombings in support of Cambodian government forces came to an end. Military assistance to South Vietnam was also cut in 1974 and 1975. Both Cambodia and South Vietnam fell in 1975.

A more long-lasting effect of the war in Vietnam was the passage of the War Powers Act over presidential veto in November 1973.

See also ANTIWAR MOVEMENT; CASE-CHURCH AMENDMENT; CHURCH, FRANK; COOPER, JOHN SHERMAN; COOPER-CHURCH AMENDMENT; FULBRIGHT, J. WILLIAM; GOLDWATER, BARRY; GRAVEL, MIKE; GRUENING, ERNEST; HATFIELD, MARK; JAVITS, JACOB; KENNEDY, ROBERT F.; McCARTHY, EUGENE; McGOVERN, GEORGE; MORSE, WAYNE; STENNIS, JOHN; SYMINGTON, STUART; TONKIN GULF RESOLUTION; TOWER, JOHN; WAR POWERS ACT.

Suggestions for further reading: *White House Years,* by Henry Kissinger (Boston: Little, Brown & Co., 1979); *Our Own Worst Enemy,* by I. M. Destler, Leslie H. Gelb and Anthony Lake (New York: Simon & Schuster, 1984); *Foreign Policy by Congress,* by Thomas M. Franck and Edward Weisband (New York: Oxford University Press, 1980).

CONTAINMENT

First advanced by George F. Kennan in 1947, the containment theory held that the way to deal with the communist threat was not to attack it head on but to contain its expansion. Used by President Truman in 1950 as the basis for his decision not to attack China after its intervention in the Korean war, and by President Eisenhower in 1956 for his decision to abandon U.S. rhetorical support for "rollback or liberation" during the Hungarian uprising, the theory of containment, as interpreted by successive administrations dating back to President Truman, undergirded U.S. involvement in Vietnam. In line with that policy, a ground invasion of North Vietnam was specifically ruled out. While there was a sound national policy rationale for this decision, the fact remains that this rejection of the strategic offensive to carry the war to the enemy in favor of the strategic defensive to contain North Vietnamese

A protected convoy traveling on a highway in the Central Highlands. (Courtesy U.S. Army.)

expansion was a major limiting factor in the prosecution of the war.

See also KENNAN, GEORGE; STRATEGIC DEFENSIVE; STRATEGIC OFFENSIVE; STRATEGY, U.S.

Suggestions for further reading: *On Strategy: A Critical Analysis of the Vietnam War,* by Harry G. Summers, Jr. (Novato, Calif.: Presidio Press, 1982).

CONVOYS, U.S. MILITARY

U.S. military truck convoys were essential to the safe delivery of supplies, munitions and food to forward areas from South Vietnam's ports. While aircraft delivered emergency resupply and high-priority items, trucks were required to sustain the massive resupply requirements of allied divisions. Convoys were usually escorted by gun jeeps and armored vehicles, with helicopters flying overhead. Convoys were very successful, and an entire set of new convoy tactics was developed over the course of the war. While many convoy battles were relatively minor, some were of considerable magnitude, especially along the highways in the Central Highlands and west of Saigon.

See also FIRST LOGISTICAL COMMAND.

COOPER-CHURCH AMENDMENT

In 1970 Senators John Sherman Cooper and Frank Church proposed an amendment to the foreign military sales portion of a Defense Department appropriations bill that would limit presidential authority to conduct military operations in Cambodia. The amendment prohibited the use of funds, without specific congressional authorization after June 30, 1970, for keeping U.S. troops in Cambodia, for the support of U.S. personnel who furnished military instruction or combat support for Cambodian forces, for implementing any contract or agreement to provide such instruction or support or for conducting air activity in direct support of Cambodian forces. The bill, which was introduced partly in reaction to the Cambodian "incursion," passed in the Senate by a vote of 58 to 37 but was defeated in the House by a vote of 237 to 153. A modified version of the Cooper-Church Amendment barring the introduction of U.S. ground troops in Laos or Thailand was passed by Congress on December 29 as part of a $66.6 billion defense appropriations bill for 1971.

See also, CAMBODIA; CHURCH FRANK; COOPER, JOHN SHERMAN.

COOPER, JOHN SHERMAN (1901–)

Cooper was born in Somerset, Kentucky on August 23, 1901. Following graduation from Yale University and Harvard Law School, he won election to the Kentucky state legislature. He became a local judge in 1928 and a district judge in the 1930s. He was ambassador to India in the Eisenhower Administration and won his first full Senate term in 1960. During the Truman, Eisenhower and Kennedy Administrations, Cooper established himself as a liberal Republican with an interest in foreign affairs.

Cooper was one of the Senate's early critics of the Vietnam war. Starting in January 1966 he began to criticize the bombing of North Vietnam, and at the time of the Tet Offensive in February 1968, he warned against an escalation of the conflict. Cooper teamed with Senator Frank Church in May 1970 to introduce an amendment to an appropriations bill prohibiting the President from spending any funds for U.S. troops fighting in Cambodia after July 1 without congressional approval. The ban also applied to support of advisers or troops from other countries aiding Cambodia or for air combat operations in Cambodia. The measure barred the introduction of U.S. ground troops into Thailand and Laos and forbade the spending of funds for Free World Forces used to provide military support for the Laotian or Cambodian governments. The stipulation, however, did not restrict the use of funds for action to safeguard the withdrawal of U.S. troops. The Senate passed the measure, but the House deleted the Cooper-Church Amendment from its appropriations bill. A modified version of the amendment restricting the powers of the President in the Vietnam war passed both houses of Congress in December.

Cooper abstained in 1972 in the vote on the Church-Case Amendment that provided for a cutoff of funds for all U.S. combat operations in Indochina subject to an agreement for the release of American prisoners of war. Instead he supported a Nixon-sponsored bill that tied this proposal to an internationally supervised cease-fire. The Senator explained his opposition to the origi-

nal amendment was based on fear that it would undercut Nixon's bargaining position in the upcoming peace talks.

Cooper retired from the Senate at the end of his term in 1973.

See also CHURCH, FRANK.

CORDS (CIVIL OPERATIONS AND REVOLUTIONARY DEVELOPMENT SUPPORT)

A U.S. program instituted under the supervision of Robert W. Komer in 1967, CORDS gathered together under a single command personnel and resources from the military services, the State Department, the Agency for International Development, the U.S. Information Agency and the CIA. It deployed unified civil-military advisory teams in all of South Vietnam's 250 districts and 44 provinces. CORDS revitalized South Vietnam's Regional and Popular Forces and encouraged its *Phung Huang* program to coordinate efforts of the Vietnamese agencies in neutralizing the Viet Cong infrastructure. A remarkable improvement over previous attempts at pacification, this approach eventually led to the virtual elimination of the Viet Cong threat to South Vietnam. The reaction of the communists was a deemphasis of the guerrilla war in favor of a conventional war, culminating in the 1975 North Vietnamese cross-border blitzkrieg, which ended the war.

See also KOMER, ROBERT W.; PACIFICATION; PHOENIX PROGRAM.

Suggestions for further reading: *Bureaucracy Does Its Thing: Institutional Constraints on U.S.-GVN Performance in Vietnam,* by R. W. Komer (Santa Monica: RAND, 1972); *Pacification,* by Tran Dinh Tho (Washington, D.C.: Indochina Monograph, U.S. Army Center of Military History, 1980); *Reorganizing for Pacification Support,* by Thomas Scoville (Washington, D.C.: U.S. Government Printing Office, 1982).

CORPS

In the military the term "corps" has both a

general and a specific meaning. In its general sense, it means a body of men and women who share similar functions, such as the Marine Corps, the Medical Corps or the Signal Corps. In its specific sense, the word designates an organizational unit comprised of two or more divisions. A corps, normally commanded by a lieutenant general, is designed primarily for control of combat operations. The corps commander issues operational orders to his subordinate division commanders and influences combat action by reinforcing with corps-level combat forces, such as artillery groups and armored cavalry regiments. A corps usually does not include logistical or support units.

In Vietnam the United States deployed four corps-level headquarters: I Field Force Vietnam, II Field Force Vietnam, III Marine Amphibious Force and XXIV Corps (*see* individual listings). The South Vietnamese also fielded a I, II, III and IV Corps. In 1974 the North Vietnamese organized their army into four corps for the Final Offensive on South Vietnam.

See also DIVISION; FIELD FORCES; I, II, III, IV CORPS TACTICAL ZONES; ORGANIZATION FOR COMBAT.

COSVN (CENTRAL OFFICE FOR SOUTH VIETNAM)

The North Vietnamese control headquarters for Viet Cong military forces, COSVN was the target of many American military operations. Located in a corner of Tay Ninh Province, III Corps, near the Cambodian border, it was the focus of Operation Junction City in 1967 and was the target of the Cambodian incursion in 1970. It eluded capture throughout the war.

More like what the U.S. military would term a forward command post, consisting of a few senior commanders and key staff officers, than the elaborate fixed U.S. and South Vietnamese headquarters, COSVN was extremely mobile, moving frequently to avoid being targeted.

See also CAMBODIA.

Suggestions for further reading: *Vietnam: A History,* by Stanley Karnow (New York: Viking, 1983).

COUNTERINSURGENCY

A tactic devised in the early 1960s as a counter to communist-proclaimed "wars of national liberation," counterinsurgency became the guiding doctrine of U.S. military forces. Pushed by President Kennedy under the direction of his special adviser, General Maxwell D. Taylor, it saw as a primary focus of war not the destruction of the enemy's armed forces but the winning of the allegiance of the people. As the U.S. Army's Vietnam-era doctrinal manual stated, "The fundamental purpose of U.S. military forces is to preserve, restore, or create an environment of order and stability within which the instrumentalities of government can function effectively under a code of laws." In Vietnam, however, the United States was faced with an adversary whose ultimate aim was the "destruction of the enemy's armed forces and his will to resist."

Counterinsurgency doctrine made some sense for South Vietnamese forces, who had to win the support of their own people, but it made little sense for U.S. forces, whose mission in Vietnam should have been to act as a coalition partner with the South Vietnamese forces rather than to "win the hearts and minds" of the South Vietnamese people. Because it failed to focus U.S. forces on what proved to be the decisive enemy—the regular armed forces of North Vietnam—counterinsurgency contributed to U.S. failure in Vietnam.

See also COALITION WARFARE; KENNEDY, JOHN F.; TAYLOR, MAXWELL D.

Suggestion for further reading: *The Counterinsurgency Era: U.S. Doctrine and Performance 1950 to Present,* by Douglas S. Blaufarb (New York: Free Press, 1977); *The Myth of the Guerrilla: Revolutionary Theory and Malpractice,* by J. Bower Bell (New York: Knopf, 1971); *Autopsy on People's War,* by Chalmers Johnson (Berkeley: University of California Press, 1973).

CRONKITE, WALTER (LELAND) (1916-   )

Born on November 4, 1916 in St. Joseph, Missouri, Cronkite attended the University of Texas

n Austin for two years while working as a reporter for the Scripps-Howard Bureau. During
World War II Cronkite was a correspondent for
United Press International. Joining the Columbia
Broadcasting System in 1950, he soon became one
of its most important network correspondents
and later its chief anchorman. On September 2,
1963 President Kennedy granted Cronkite an
exclusive interview in which he stated that the
success of the war in Southeast Asia would ultimately be determined by South Vietnamese will-
ngness to pursue the struggle.

In the mid-1960s Cronkite reflected network
variness about coverage of the Vietnam war that
vas critical of the Johnson Administration.
However, during the Tet Offensive in early 1968,
Cronkite visited Vietnam for the first time since
965, and shortly thereafter he reported on
nationwide television that the war was not
vorking and that the United States might have to
accept a stalemate. According to many observers,
he defection of Cronkite especially upset President
ohnson, who had regarded the anchorman as an
administration ally. David Halberstam in *The
Powers That Be* concludes that after Cronkite's
post-Tet report . . . [Johnson] realized he had lost
he center, that Walter both was the center and
reached the center, and thus his own consensus
was in serious jeopardy."

See also JOHNSON, LYNDON B.; TET OFFENSIVE.

Suggestions for further reading: *The Image
Empire,* by Erik Barnouw (New York: Oxford
University Press, 1970); *The Powers That Be,* by
David Halberstam (New York: Alfred H. Knopf,
1979).

CUSHMAN, ROBERT E.
(1914–1985)

Born in St. Paul, Minnesota on December 24,
1914, Cushman graduated from the U.S. Naval
Academy in 1935. After service in China prior to
World War II, Cushman won the Navy Cross for
Valor as commander of the Second Battalion,
Ninth Marine Regiment in the liberation of Guam
and was also decorated for bravery at Bougainville
and Iwo Jima.

In June 1967 Lieutenant General Cushman
became Commander of the III Marine Amphibious Force, in charge of the First and Third Marine
Divisions as well as several Army units engaged in
combat in I Corps. General Cushman was responsible for the defense of Khe Sanh, the counteroffensive in the wake of the Viet Cong Tet Offensive in 1968 and the retaking of the city of Hué,
which had been seized during the Tet Offensive.

After returning to the United States in 1969, he
became Deputy Director of the CIA and served in
that position until 1972, when he was appointed
Commandant of the Marine Corps. General
Cushman retired in 1975. He died on January 2,
1985.

See also HUÉ, BATTLE OF; KHE SANH, BATTLE OF; III
MARINE AMPHIBIOUS FORCE.

General Robert E. Cushman. (Courtesy U.S. Army Military History
Institute.)

DAK TO

See II CORPS TACTICAL ZONE.

DALAT

See II CORPS TACTICAL ZONE.

DA NANG

A city in Quang Nam Province in northern I Corps, Da Nang was the headquarters for South Vietnamese Army's I Corps and its Third Division. It was also the site of several major U.S. installations during the Vietnam war. A major port and a jet-capable airfield were constructed there. It served at one time or another as the headquarters for the U.S. III Marine Amphibious Force, the U.S. First and Third Marine Divisions and later the U.S. Army's XXIV Corps. It fell to the North Vietnamese Final Offensive in April 1975.

See map at II CORPS TACTICAL ZONE.

DANIEL BOONE

Daniel Boone was the code name for secret ground cross-border reconnaissance performed by U.S. Army Special Forces into Cambodia. MACV (U.S. Military Assistance Command) received permission to develop Operation Daniel Boone on June 27, 1966, but the first teams were

not used until May 1967, and they were confined to a small area. In October, Daniel Boone missions were extended to the entire border region. Later Daniel Boone was renamed Salem House and in the spring of 1971 received its final designation Thot Not (pronounced "Tot Note"). These missions, which were highly classified during the war and performed jointly by Special Forces and South Vietnamese long-range reconnaissance patrols and raiding forces under extremely dangerous conditions. The missions produced much of the intelligence used for the Cambodian incursion of 1970.

Suggestions for further reading: *The Green Beret at War,* by Shelby L. Stanton (Novato, Calif.: Presidio Press, 1985).

DECKER, GEORGE H(ENRY) (1902–1980)

Born February 16, 1902 in Catskill, New York, Decker graduated from LaFayette College in 1924 and received a commission in the U.S. Army. As Chief of Staff of the Sixth Army during World War II, he took part in the battle to liberate the Philippines. In October 1960 General Decker was appointed Army Chief of Staff. One of the few senior officers who resisted President John F. Kennedy's pressure to turn the military into a counterinsurgency force, General Decker was retired from active duty in October 1962. He died on February 6, 1980.

See also CHIEF OF STAFF, U.S. ARMY; COUNTERINSURGENCY.

Suggestions for further reading: *On Strategy: A Critical Analysis of the Vietnam War,* by Harry G.

Summers, Jr. (Novato, Calif.: Presidio Press, 1982).

DECLARATION OF WAR

Article I, Section 8 of the Constitution of the United States specifically reserves to Congress the power to declare war. The intent, as clearly indicated by Alexander Hamilton in *The Federalist,* was to make the military an instrument of the people rather than of the state. Although the President, under his authority as Commander-in-Chief under Article II, Section 2 of the Constitution, often committed American forces in response to immediate crises (Thomas Jefferson's response to the Barbary pirates in 1801, for example), any prolonged commitment of American forces to battle was usually accompanied by a declaration of war by Congress. Such a declaration focused attention on American objectives and set severe penalties for treason and giving aid and comfort to the enemy.

This changed in 1950, when President Truman committed American forces to combat in Korea without a declaration of war, using as justification the resolutions of the United Nations. With this precedent President Lyndon Johnson committed U.S. forces to combat in Vietnam without a declaration of war. At first (when even some critics agree that he could have had a declaration of war for the asking) he used as justification the Southeast Asia Resolution (better known as the Gulf of Tonkin Resolution) passed by the Congress on August 7, 1964. When support for that resolution flagged and congressional approval of a declaration of war was no longer possible, President Johnson fell back on his authority as Commander-in-Chief, as did his successor, President Nixon.

As a result of the ensuing controversy over who had the power to wage war, Congress passed the War Powers Act, over presidential veto, in 1973.

See also TONKIN GULF RESOLUTION, WAR POWERS ACT.

Suggestions for further reading: *On Strategy: A Critical Analysis of the Vietnam War,* by Harry G. Summers, Jr. (Novato, Calif.: Presidio Press, 1982); *The Federalist* (particularly essays #24 and #69), edited by James E. Cooke (Middletown, Conn.: Wesleyan University Press, 1961).

DECORATIONS, U.S.

U.S. military decorations include a series of medals awarded to individuals and units for bravery or especially meritorious acts. They are distinguished from service medals, which, as the name implies, are awarded to denote service during a specific time period or a particular campaign.

There are three decorations presented in the name of the President that are awarded for battlefield valor only—the MEDAL OF HONOR, the DISTINGUISHED SERVICE CROSS (NAVY CROSS for Navy, Marine and Coast Guard personnel; AIR FORCE CROSS for Air Force personnel) and the SILVER STAR MEDAL. Three others are awarded in the name of the President for lesser degrees of valor (and can also be awarded for exceptional meritorious service)—the DISTINGUISHED FLYING CROSS, the BRONZE STAR MEDAL and the AIR MEDAL. When the latter two are awarded for valor, a "V" device is worn on the ribbon. Finally, for yet lesser degrees of valor, the various COMMENDATION MEDALS are awarded in the name of the Secretary of Defense or the various service secretaries. Again, a "V" device is worn on the ribbon when the medal is awarded for valor. The PURPLE HEART MEDAL, although also classed as a decoration, is awarded exclusively for wounds received in combat.

Decorations for unit battlefield valor include the PRESIDENTIAL UNIT CITATION, the VALOROUS UNIT CITATION for Army units and UNIT COMMENDATIONS for the Air Force, Navy and Marines.

See also CAMPAIGN MEDALS: Individual award listings.

DEFENSE ATTACHE OFFICE

After the withdrawal of the MACV (U.S. Military Assistance Command in Vietnam) in January 1973, a Defense Attaché Office (DAO) was established in Saigon to assist the U.S. Ambassador and to coordinate military assistance to South Vietnam. Limited by the Paris Accords of 1973 to 50 U.S. Army, Navy, Air Force and Marine Corps personnel, it also contained a number of U.S. civilian employees. The DAO was headed initially by

Army Major General John Murray and from mid-1974 to April 1975 by Army Major General Homer D. Smith. It played a key role in the final evacuation of U.S. personnel from Saigon in April 1975.

See also FREQUENT WIND OPERATION, TAN SON NHUT.

Suggestions for further reading: *Vietnam from Cease-Fire to Capitulation*, by William E. LeGro (Washington, D.C.: U.S. Government Printing Office, 1981); *Peace with Honor?* by Stuart A. Herrington (Novato, Calif.: Presidio Press, 1984); *Last Flight from Saigon*, edited by A. J. C. Lavalle (Washington, D.C.: U.S. Government Printing Office, 1978).

DEFERMENTS

See DRAFT.

DEFOLIATION

See AGENT ORANGE.

DELAYED STRESS SYNDROME

See POST-TRAUMATIC STRESS DISORDER.

DELLINGER, DAVID (1915–   )

Born in Wakefield, Massachusetts on August 12, 1915, Dellinger graduated from Yale in 1936 and enrolled in Union Theological Seminary in 1939.

In the antiwar movement of the 1960s, Dellinger represented an older generation of radical pacifists—those who had been involved in labor and community organizing in the 1930s, had been conscientious objectors during World War II and had organized acts of civil disobedience on behalf of peace and civil rights throughout the 1940s and 1950s.

During the early stages of the Vietnam conflict, Dellinger favored an immediate withdrawal rather than negotiations. He also opposed the moratorium on militant action called by peace and civil rights leaders in 1964 to ensure a Democratic victory in the presidential election. When President Johnson ordered the bombing of North Vietnam, Dellinger helped organize a coalition of peace groups, the Assembly of Unrepresented People, that sponsored a series of acts of civil disobedience in Washington, D.C. in August 1965. Coinciding with the Vietnam Day Committee's attempt to block troop trains in the San Francisco Bay area, the arrests marked the first large-scale application of civil disobedience tactics to the antiwar movement.

In November 1966 Dellinger served as cochairman of the Spring Mobilization to End the War in Vietnam. The "Mobe" chose April 15, 1967 for demonstrations in New York and San Francisco. Over the next five months it organized churches, women's groups, universities, political clubs and peace groups in an attempt to show that active opposition to the war was not limited to a handful of radicals but included vast numbers of Americans. The marches in April were the largest demonstrations against government policy in American history up to that time.

Dellinger was involved in the demonstrations in Chicago during the Democratic Party's National Convention in August 1968. The violence of these events formed the basis for a five-month court trial in 1969, at which Dellinger and six others, who became known as the "Chicago Seven," were convicted by the federal government on charges of conspiracy to riot. The convictions were later overturned.

See also Chicago Seven; DEMOCRATIC NATIONAL CONVENTION, 1968; RUBIN, JERRY.

Suggestions for further reading: *Revolutionary Non-violence*, by David Dellinger (New York: Doubleday, 1971); *The War at Home: Vietnam and the American People*, by Thomas Powers (New York: Grossman, 1973).

DELTA

A term used to refer to the Mekong Delta area

in IV Corps, Delta was also the code name of the U.S. Army's Detachment B-52, Fifth Special Forces Group, a special Special Forces reconnaissance unit.

See also PART I, THE SETTING; LRRP (LONG RANGE RECONNAISSANCE PATROLS); FIFTH SPECIAL FORCES; IV CORPS TACTICAL ZONE.

DEMARCATION LINE

See DMZ.

DEMILITARIZED ZONE

See DMZ (DEMILITARIZED ZONE).

DEMOCRATIC NATIONAL CONVENTION, 1968

To show their continued opposition to the Vietnam war and to pressure the Democratic presidential candidate to repudiate the war policies of President Johnson, 10,000 demonstrators converged on Chicago to hold rallies and protests outside the Democratic National Convention from August 25 to 29, 1968. Much of the preliminary talk of "nude-ins," spiking the city water supply with LSD, or even burning the city to the ground by some of the demonstrations' organizers alarmed Chicago's politicians and police. The demonstrators were allowed to hold daily rallies in Lincoln Park, far from the convention site, but they were denied parade permits, and 12,000 police and 11,000 Army and National Guard troops armed with riot gear were mobilized.

While most of the demonstrators were peaceful, some had come intent on confrontation, and their ranks included government agent provocateurs. The radicals burned American flags, hurled rocks, bottles, and garbage and taunted an already edgy police into action. The result was a full-scale riot. The climax of the week came as the Democrats nominated Vice President Hubert H. Humphrey as their presidential candidate amid convention floor pandemonium. Americans watched as Senator Abraham Ribicoff rose before national television to condemn Mayor Richard Daley for his "Gestapo tactics." Meanwhile, cameras cut to the streets where police and demonstrators fought pitched battles, resulting in numerous injuries to both sides. The police used tear gas and wielded clubs on the crowds, which included innocent bystanders. In the end the demonstrators were never able to reach the Convention Hall to hold their protests. "Chicago" was a disaster for the Democratic Party and the most violent episode in the peace movement of the 1960s.

See also ANTIWAR MOVEMENT; CHICAGO SEVEN; HUMPHREY, HUBERT H.

DEROS

A U.S. Army acronym meaning "Date Eligible to Return from OverSeas." Unlike in World War II or the early days of the Korean war, when combat zone service was "for the duration," in the Vietnam war the tour of duty was fixed at 12 to 13 months, depending on the particular service. An outgrowth of this fixed DEROS was "short-timer's calendars," as soldiers marked off the days until their return to the States (the "world," in combat jargon). Such fixed tours, while designed to boost morale, ultimately had the opposite effect, as soldiers tended to develop "short-timers' attitudes" and in some cases evade dangerous services as their DEROS approached. In addition, the length of the tour contributed to a lack of unit integrity, since it was difficult to establish close relationships during a one-year tour.

DESERTION

Of the 7,575,000 American service personnel who served on active duty during the Vietnam war era, there were some 550,000 incidents of desertion (defined as unauthorized absence exceeding 30 days). Most eventually returned to duty, but some 100,000 service personnel received less-than-honorable discharges for desertion. More than two-thirds of these cases were unrelated to Vietnam service and involved family and other personal problems.

Of the 32,000 desertion cases related to Vietnam, some 7,000 involved failing to report for shipment there. Another 20,000 involved unauthorized absences after service in Vietnam. Of the 5,000 desertion cases in Vietnam, 1,000 involved absence without leave (AWOL) in non-combat zones and 2,000 involved AWOL in rest areas outside the country. In the combat zone there were only 24 cases of desertion to avoid hazardous duty. By comparison, 20,000 soldiers were court-martialed in World War II for desertion in combat and one was executed for that offense.

At the end of the war some 10,115 deserters were fugitives from the law. Some 7,115 took advantage of clemency programs initiated by President Ford in 1974–1975 and another 239 took advantage of a program ordered by President Carter in 1977. Some 2,761 Vietnam-era deserters remained at large at the end of the clemency period on October 4, 1977.

See also DRAFT.

Suggestions for further reading: *Chance and Circumstance: The Draft, the War, and the Vietnam Generation,* by Lawrence M. Baskir and William A. Strauss (New York: Knopf, 1978); *Long Time Passing: Vietnam and the Haunted Generation,* by Myra MacPherson (New York: Doubleday, 1984).

DIEM, NGO DINH (1901–1963)

Born in 1901 in Annam (central Vietnam) President Diem was active in Vietnamese politics during the French occupation, serving as Chief of Quang Tri Province in 1930–31 and later as Minister of Justice. An ardent nationalist, he was asked to become Ho Chi Minh's Minister of the Interior when the Viet Minh took control from the Japanese in 1945, but he declined the offer.

A devout Catholic, Diem lived for a while in a Maryknoll seminary in New Jersey and later in a Benedictine monastery in Belgium. Returning to Vietnam in 1954, he became Prime Minister under Bao Dai in the government of South Vietnam (officially, the Republic of Vietnam), which was formed after the partition of Vietnam prescribed by the Geneva Accords ending the war between the French and the Viet Minh (1946–54). Diem's early years in office were marked by a number of direct challenges to his authority by political sects in Saigon, including the Hoa Hoa, the Binh Xuyen and the Cao Dai. In April 1955 Diem faced a particularly strong challenge from the French-backed Binh Xuyen. Fighting broke out in the streets of Saigon, but by the end of May, Diem's forces managed to oust the rival factions from the city.

By the end of 1955, with American help (notably that of Colonel Edward Lansdale, a U.S. intelligence officer), Diem defeated Bao Dai in a presidential election, garnering a suspiciously high percentage of the vote (more than 95 percent in some precincts).

Over the next several years American aid to South Vietnam would increase considerably, as Diem attempted to consolidate his power and to check the growing influence of the communists in South Vietnam. His efforts to gain widespread support of the populace, however, were ineffective. He channeled "the bulk of U.S. aid," Stanley Karnow has written, "into South Vietnam's military and police machinery, leaving only a small fraction for economic development; and he was less interested in building an army to fight Vietcong guerrillas than in forming conventional units that would protect him against his rivals in Saigon." Diem's effectiveness as a leader was also limited by his desire to keep power within his own family. His brother Ngo Dinh Nhu ran a secret police force, and other family members exercised dictatorial control over various provinces in South Vietnam. Throughout his tenure as President, Diem ignored requests for internal political reform.

All of these factors would contribute to Diem's downfall, but his persecution of the Buddhists, by heightening the level of political turmoil, was the immediate catalyst.

The key incident involved the breakup of a

Buddhist celebration in Hué on May 8, 1963, in which eight children and one woman were killed. On June 11, after a number of Buddhist protests had been broken up by force, a Buddhist monk set himself on fire in protest against the government's persecution. But still Diem took no significant action toward punishing those responsible, despite a warning from the U.S. embassy that U.S. support could evaporate if repression of the Buddhists continued.

In late August, Nhu initiated another series of assaults on dissidents, particularly Buddhists, sparking widespread protest among the South Vietnamese. A complex series of communications concerning the increasingly volatile situation passed between Washington and Saigon after these attacks. The details remain obscure, but it is clear that at one point Henry Cabot Lodge, the U.S. Ambassador to South Vietnam, was instructed to tell a group of South Vietnamese military officers who had been conspiring to overthrow Diem that the United States would not stand in their way. After considerable planning and intrigue by the South Vietnamese generals, a coup took place on November 1, 1963. Diem and his brother Nhu were assassinated the following day after surrendering to the insurgent forces.

Some accounts of the coup do not directly implicate the United States in its planning or execution, but rather suggest that it happened with Washington's tacit consent. Lodge told Kennedy on November 6 "that the ground in which the coup seed grew into a robust plant was prepared by us, and that the coup would not have happened [as] it did without our preparation."

See also BUDDHISTS, CAO DAI; HARRIMAN, AVERELL; HILSMAN, ROGER; KENNEDY, JOHN F.; LANSDALE, EDWARD G.; LODGE, HENRY CABOT; NHU, NGO DINH.

Suggestions for further reading: *Roots of Involvement: The U.S. in Asia 1784–1971,* by Marvin Kalb and Elie Abel (New York: Norton, 1971); *Our Endless War,* by Tran Van Don (Novato, Calif.: Presidio Press, 1972); *Our Vietnam Nightmare,* by Marguerite Higgins (New York: Harper & Row, 1965); *The Best and the Brightest,* by David Halberstam (New York: Random House, 1972); *The Last Confucian,* by Denis Warner (New York: Macmil-

lan, 1963); *Vietnam: A History,* by Stanley Karnow (New York: Viking, 1983).

DIEN BIEN PHU

Site of the climactic battle that effectively ended the war between France and the Viet Minh (1946–1954), Dien Bien Phu was a small village on the border between Laos and North Vietnam. About 180 miles from the nearest French post, it was fortified by some 16,000 French troops, including soldiers of the French Foreign Legion and Vietnamese, Laotians and Cambodians fighting on the French side, to draw the Viet Minh into a set-piece battle in which it was supposed superior French firepower would destroy them.

But the French had underestimated their enemy. Viet Minh General Vo Nguyen Giap entrenched artillery in the surrounding mountains and massed five divisions totaling about 60,000 troops (including one division led by Brigadier General Van Tien Dung, who 21 years later would lead the final assault on Saigon).

The battle began with a massive Viet Minh artillery barrage on March 13, 1954 and was followed by an infantry assault. At the height of the battle, military support was requested from the United States, but domestic political considerations—lack of congressional support—diplomatic considerations, including lack of allied (particularly British) support and opposition to U.S. intervention within the Joint Chiefs of Staff, led by Army Chief of Staff General Matthew B. Ridgway, caused President Eisenhower to deny the request. Fighting continued to rage until May 7, 1954, when the French positions were finally overrun. The shock of the fall of Dien Bien Phu led France, already plagued by public opposition to the war, to agree to the independence of Vietnam at the Geneva Conference in 1954.

See also DUNG, VAN TIEN; GENEVA CONFERENCES; GIAP, VO NGUYEN; RIDGWAY, MATTHEW B.

Suggestions for further reading: *Hell in a Very Small Place: The Siege of Dien Bien Phu,* by Bernard Fall (Philadelphia: Lippincott, 1966); *Soldier: The Memoirs of Matthew B. Ridgway,* by Matthew B. Ridgway (New York: Harper & Bros., 1956); *The Battle of*

Dien Pien Phu, by Jules Roy translated by Robert Baldick (New York: Harper & Bros., 1965); *Dien Bien Phu,* by Vo Nguyen Giap (Hanoi: Foreign Language Publishing House, 1962); *The Sky Would Fall. Operation Vulture: The U.S. Bombing Mission in Indochina, 1954,* by John Prados (New York: Dial, 1983).

DISTINGUISHED FLYING CROSS

First authorized in 1926, the Distinguished Flying Cross is awarded in the name of the President of the United States for heroism or extraordinary achievement while participating in aerial flight. The performance of the act of heroism has to be evidenced by voluntary action above and beyond the call of duty. The extraordinary achievement has to have resulted in an accomplishment so exceptional and outstanding as to clearly set the individual apart from his comrades or from other persons in similar circumstances. Subsequent awards are denoted by an oak leaf for the U.S. Army and Air Force and by a star for the Navy and Marine Corps; they are worn on the ribbon.

The Distinguished Flying Cross.

DISTINGUISHED SERVICE CROSS

First authorized in World War I, the Distinguished Service Cross, with the Air Force Cross and the Navy Cross, is America's second highest award for bravery. It is awarded in the name of the President by the U.S. Army for extraordinary heroism, not justifying the award of a Medal of Honor, while engaged in an action against the enemy. The act or acts of heroism has to have been so notable and have involved risk of life so extraordinary as to set the individual apart from his comrades. Subsequent awards were denoted by an oak leaf worn on the ribbon.

See also AIR FORCE CROSS, NAVY CROSS.

DIVISION

In the U.S. Army and Marine Corps (and in most other military organizations as well), the division is the basic combined arms organization for waging warfare. Normally commanded by a major general in the United States, it consists of approximately 20,000 men organized into two or more brigades (or regiments) plus supporting artillery, engineer and other elements. During the Vietnam war seven Army divisions—the First Cavalry Division, First Infantry Division, Fourth Infantry Division, Ninth Infantry Division, Americal (23rd) Infantry Division, 25th Infantry Division and 101st Airborne Division—as well as

The Distinguished Service Cross.

21 numbered divisions—the First, Second, Third, Seventh, 10th, 101D, 304th, 304B, 308th, 308B, 312th, 316th, 320th, 320B, 324B, 325th, 330th 338th, 341st, 380th and 711th. In 1973 15 of these divisions were deployed in South Vietnam; others were in Laos or training in North Vietnam. With their supporting artillery regiments and armored brigades most were committed to battle in the NVA Final Offensive in 1975. In addition, two divisions—the Fifth and Ninth—although ostensibly Viet Cong divisions, were heavily reinforced by NVA personnel.

The term "division" is also used by the U.S. Air Force to designate a unit smaller than a numbered air force (e.g., Seventh Air Force) but larger than an air wing. In the early days of the Vietnam war, U.S. Air Force units in Vietnam were subordinate to the Second Air Division, but on April 1, 1966 this division was replaced by the Seventh Air Force. Later the 834th Air Division was formed by the Seventh Air Force as a control headquarters for tactical airlift.

See also NVA (NORTH VIETNAMESE ARMY), ORGANIZATION FOR COMBAT, SVNAF SOUTH VIETNAMESE ARMED FORCES), VIET CONG, listings for individual U.S. divisions.

Suggestions for further reading: *Vietnam Order of Battle,* by Shelby L. Stanton (Washington, D.C.: U.S. News & World Report Books, 1981); *Vietnam from Cease Fire to Capitulation,* by William E. LeGro (Washington, D.C.: U.S. Government Printing Office, 1981); *The United States Air Force in Southeast Asia 1961–1973,* edited by Carl Berger (Washington, D.C.: U.S. Government Printing Office, 1977).

divisional brigades from the Fifth Infantry Division and 82nd Airborne Division were deployed to Vietnam. The U.S. Marine Corps deployed the First and Third Marine Divisions as well as regiments from the Fifth Marine Division.

The South Vietnamese Armed Forces deployed 11 numbered divisions—the First, Second, Third, Fifth, Seventh, Ninth, 18th (formerly the 10th), 21st, 22nd, 23rd, and 25th Infantry Divisions—as well as an Airborne division and a Marine division. The Royal Thai Army fielded one expeditionary division in Vietnam, and South Korea deployed the Capital and Ninth Infantry Divisions in South Vietnam.

The North Vietnamese Army (NVA) deployed

DIXIE STATION

Designation of a staging area off the South Vietnamese coast southwest of Cam Ranh Bay in the South China Sea. Located at 11°N 110°E, it was used from 1965 to 1966 as a reference point for air operations by the U.S. Navy's Seventh Fleet Attack Carrier Striking Force (Task Force 77).

See also AIRCRAFT CARRIERS, YANKEE STATION.

Suggestions for further reading: *A Short History of the United States Navy and the Southeast Asian Conflict 1950–1975,* by Edward J. Marolda and G. Wesley Pryce, III (Washington, D.C.: Naval Historical Center, 1984).

DMZ (DEMILITARIZED ZONE)

The 1954 Geneva Conference established, as a temporary demarcation between North and South Vietnam, a boundary, usually thought of as the 17th parallel, that was actually a river, the Song Ben Hai, as far as the hamlet of Bo Ho Su, then a straight line running west to the Laotian border. Twenty-five miles south of the two great walls of Dong Hoi and Truong Duc, which were erected in the 17th century by the Nguyen Dynasty to hold back the invading Trinh emperors (see Part I, THE SETTING), the demarcation line was the center of a five-mile-wide buffer zone.

Because U.S. policy had prohibited ground or artillery attacks into this buffer zone—the so-called Demilitarized Zone, or DMZ—in 1966 the North Vietnamese Army (NVA) moved heavy artillery, rockets and first its 324B Division and later its 308th, 320th, 325C and 341st Divisions into the southern half of the buffer zone. From these positions the NVA launched artillery, rocket and ground attacks against U.S. and South Vietnamese Army positions south of the DMZ.

In October 1966 the U.S. Third Marine Division moved into this area to reinforce the South Vietnamese First Division. A series of fire support bases were constructed along Route 9, which ran generally parallel to the DMZ. From Khe Sanh on the west to the Rockpile, Ca Lu, Camp Carroll, Cam Lo and Gio Linh to Cua Viet on the east, these fire bases were able to provide artillery fire support for ground operations against NVA positions in the DMZ. The fire bases were frequently the scene of particularly fierce battles.

See also I CORPS TACTICAL ZONE; KHE SANH, BATTLE OF; NIAGARA OPERATION; QUANG TRI, BATTLE OF; THIRD MARINE DIVISION.

Suggestions for further reading: "Marine Corps Operations in Vietnam, 1965–66, 1967, 1968, 1969–72," by Edwin H. Simmons, and "Fire Support Base Development," by Robert V. Nicoli, in *The Marines in Vietnam 1954–1973* (Washington, D.C.: U.S. Government Printing Office, 1974).

DOGS, U.S. MILITARY

The U.S. military made extensive use of dogs for a variety of duties in Vietnam, including scouting, mine detecting, tracking, sentry duty, flushing out tunnels, and drug detecting.

Military dogs were used by all the services, but most dogs served either as Air Force sentinels guarding air bases or as scout dogs for the Army. Army dog training began at Fort Benning, Georgia, where the best dogs were chosen for combat duty in Vietnam. During their six-month training cycle, dogs learned to detect mines, booby traps, tunnel systems and weapon caches as well as humans. When the dogs arrived in Vietnam, they were taken to the USARV (U.S. Army Vietnam) Scout Dog headquarters in Bien Hoa for further training and acclimatizing.

The most common use of military dogs was in combat tracker teams. These were five-man teams that used dogs chosen for endurance, color, stability and good nature rather than ferocity, as in the case of sentry dogs. These teams could track

THE DMZ FRONT

An Air Force sentry on duty with his German Shepherd at the Ton Son Nhut air base. (Courtesy of U.S. Air Force.)

the enemy for miles, and performed duties ranging from ambush avoidance to detection of sampan movement at night. Dogs played a valuable role in Vietnam.

Suggestions for further reading: Although there are no books specifically dealing with the use of dogs in Vietnam, Ken Miller's novel, *Tiger the Lurp Dog* (New York: Little, Brown, 1983) tells their story in an authentic fashion.

DOMINO THEORY

A theory used by several U.S. Presidents as a rationale for U.S. presence and eventually military intervention in Southeast Asia, the domino theory argued that if the United States did not make a stand in South Vietnam, then the rest of the nations of Southeast Asia and beyond— Cambodia, Laos, Thailand, Malaysia, Burma, Indonesia, the Philippines—would accommodate to communist power and eventually—as with a stack of dominoes—topple one after the other.

In support of that theory, it is certainly true

that with American abandonment of South Vietnam in 1975, the Laotian and Cambodian "dominoes" fell in rapid succession. But the almost quarter century of U.S. involvement in South Vietnam did give other nations an opportunity to resist communist expansion and build their own defenses. The Indonesian "domino" fell toward the west in 1965, and in 1985 the Thailand "domino" continues to repel Vietnamese attacks on its eastern borders.

DON, TRAN VAN (1917–   )

Don was born in 1917 in Bordeaux, France, the son of a wealthy Vietnamese doctor and landowner in Long Xuyen in the Mekong Delta, which was part of the French colony of Cochinchina. He attended the University of Paris, and he was called to active duty as a cadet in the French Army when World War II began in 1939. Don received the Croix de Guerre at the Battle of the Loire, then was captured by the Nazis in the blitzkrieg that led to the fall of France in 1940. Released after France's surrender, he returned to Vietnam and in 1942 was promoted to Second Lieutenant in the French Army Reserves. A member of the Vietnamese National Army fighting the Viet Minh, General Don attended the French Army Command and Staff College in 1950. Upon his return to Vietnam, he was appointed Chief of Military Security and promoted to Major in 1952.

After South Vietnam was established in 1954, General Don was appointed Chief of Staff of the South Vietnamese Army and in October 1957 assigned command of I Corps. In December 1962 he returned to Saigon as Commander of the Army. He was instrumental in the coup that overthrew President Ngo Dinh Diem in 1963. Don was appointed Minister of National Defense in 1964 and continued to serve as Minister of Defense until the fall of Saigon in April 1975. He managed to escape the North Vietnamese Army blitzkrieg, remarkably similar to the one in which he was captured 35 years earlier, and now resides in the United States.

See also DIEM, NGO DINH.

Suggestions for further reading: *Our Endless*

War: Inside Vietnam, by Tran Van Don (Novato, Calif.: Presidio Press, 1978); *Vietnam: A History,* by Stanley Karnow (New York: Viking, 1983).

DONG, PHAM VAN (1906–)

Born on March 1, 1906 in Quang Nam Province in the French protectorate of Annam, Pham Van Dong was an early member of the communist party and at age 24 was imprisoned for seven years by the French for revolutionary activities. A close collaborator with Ho Chi Minh, he was active in the Viet Minh before and during their 1946–54 war with the French.

A leading member of the Lao Dong Workers Party (now the Communist Party of Vietnam) and Minister of Foreign Affairs and later Prime Minister of the North Vietnamese government during the 1959–1975 Vietnam war, Pham Van ·Dong was appointed Prime Minister of the Socialist Republic of Vietnam in July 1976.

Suggestions for further reading: *Vietnam: A History,* by Stanley Karnow (New York: Viking, 1983).

DRAFT

Congress, which under the Constitution of the United States has the sole authority to raise armies, first legislated involuntary conscription— a "draft"—to fill military ranks in the Civil War. Used again in World Wars I and II with great success, it was reinstituted in 1948 and continued in effect through both the Korean and Vietnam wars. In January 1973 it was suspended by President Nixon and today only a registration requirement remains.

During the Vietnam era slightly over 53 million Americans were of draft age. Half were women and not liable to the draft (although some 261,000 women served in the military and 7,500 served in Vietnam). Of the 26,800,000 men of draft age, 8,720,000 enlisted voluntarily, 2,215,000 were drafted and 15,980,000 never served. Of those who did not serve, some 15,410,000 were deferred, exempted or disqualified. Apparent draft dodgers numbered some 570,000, of whom 209,517 were actually accused of dodging by the government. Of those accused, 8,750 were convicted of draft evasion, but the majority of cases were dropped or pardoned under the 1974–75 clemency program by President Ford and the 1977 blanket pardon by President Carter.

These statistics obscure the fact that the Vietnam-era draft was a national disgrace. Those who benefited the most from American society— the affluent, the well-educated—were the least likely to serve. College deferment, which did not end until December 1971, was a major loophole. Thus a high school graduate was twice as likely to serve in the military as a college graduate. Although conscience played a role in some student's efforts to avoid a war that was never satisfactorally explained or justified, the loophole provided by college deferment was a key factor fueling the antiwar movement, for college activism fell off dramatically as soon as the draft ended.

See also ANTIWAR MOVEMENT, DESERTION.

Suggestions for further reading: *Chance and Circumstance: The Draft, the War, and the Vietnam Generation,* by Lawrence M. Baskir and William A. Strauss (New York: Knopf, 1978); *Long Time Passing: Vietnam and the Haunted Generation,* by Myra MacPherson (New York: Doubleday, 1984).

DRV (DEMOCRATIC REPUBLIC OF VIETNAM)

Although neither democratic nor a republic, the Democratic Republic of Vietnam (DRV) was proclaimed by Ho Chi Minh on January 14, 1950, in the midst of the war between the Viet Minh and the French (1946–54). Recognized by China, the Soviet Union and Yugoslavia, the DRV became the official designation of North Vietnam at the Geneva Conference of 1954. Shortly after its conquest of the Republic of Vietnam (RVN), i.e. South Vietnam, in 1975, the name of the entire country was changed to the Socialist Republic of Vietnam (SRV).

See also SRV (SOCIALIST REPUBLIC OF VIETNAM), VIET CONG.

DUAN, LE (1908–1986)

Born in 1908 in the province of Quang Tri in the French protectorate of Annam, central Vietnam, Le Duan was an early member of the Indochina Communist Party. In 1959 he was appointed Secretary-General of the Lao Dong (Worker's Party). After the death of Ho Chi Minh in 1969, Le Duan emerged as one of the leading members of the government of North Vietnam.

Suggestions for further reading: *Vietnam: A History*, by Stanley Karnow (New York: Viking, 1983).

DULLES, JOHN FOSTER (1888–1959)

Born on February 25, 1888 in Washington, D.C., Dulles graduated from Princeton University in 1908 and earned a law degree from George Washington University in 1911. During World War I he served as a major in the U.S. Army.

Dulles was appointed Secretary of State by President Eisenhower in 1953. In the spring of the following year the French sought U.S. intervention in Vietnam to relieve their beleaguered garrison at Dien Bien Phu. Although the aim of the French was to reach a favorable settlement in their war with the communist Viet Minh (1946–54), Dulles proposed using the deterrent of massive retaliation (i.e., use of nuclear weapons delivered by bombers and missiles) to defeat communism in Southeast Asia, which he viewed as an extension of the monolithic communism threatening other parts of the world. However, he failed to generate support from Congress or from U.S. allies—Britain and France—both of which feared his proposal would prevent a peaceful compromise.

At the Geneva Conference of 1954 Dulles opposed a negotiated settlement and on his order the United States did not sign the Geneva Accords, which divided Vietnam, leaving the communists in control of the north and a pro-Western government in control of the south. In a unilateral declaration the United States declared that "it would view any renewal of the aggression in violation of the . . . agreements with great concern and as seriously threatening international peace and security," thereby providing the basis for subsequent U.S. involvement in Vietnam. In the fall of 1954 Dulles announced that military and economic aid would be sent to South Vietnam, as well as advisors to help Diem solidify his position.

Terminally ill, Dulles resigned in April 1959 and died on May 24th.

See also EISENHOWER, DWIGHT D,; ELECTIONS; GENEVA CONFERENCES; SEATO (SOUTHEAST ASIA TREATY ORGANIZATION).

Suggestions for further reading: *The Devil and John Foster Dulles*, by Townsend Hoopes (Boston: Atlantic-Little, Brown, 1973); *The Best and the Brightest*, by David Halberstam (New York: Random House, 1972); *Vietnam: A History*, by Stanley Karnow (New York: Viking, 1983).

DUNG, VAN TIEN (1917–   )

Born in Ha Deng Province in Tonkin (North Vietnam) on May 1, 1917, Dung became an active communist revolutionary in 1936. He fought in the Viet Minh guerrilla movement against the French and the Japanese during World War II, and in 1954 he commanded the North Vietnamese Army's 320th Division in the siege of Dien Bien Phu, which ended the war between the Viet Minh and the French (1946–54).

A protégé of Senior General Vo Nguyen Giap, Dung was appointed Chief of Staff of the North Vietnamese Army in 1953 and promoted to Senior General in 1974. Named Commander of the Saigon Liberation Campaign Command on April 8, 1975, General Dung planned and led the North Vietnamese blitzkrieg that conquered South Vietnam in 1975. On February 7, 1980 he replaced General Giap as Minister of National Defense and at last report was also a member of the Socialist Republic of Vietnam Politboro and Deputy First Secretary of the Central Military Party Committee.

See also FINAL OFFENSIVE; GIAP, VO NGUYEN.

Suggestions for further reading: *Great Spring Victory* by Van Tien Dung (translated by Foreign

Broadcast Information Service) (FBIS Supplement 38, June 7, 1976; FBIS Supplement 42, July 7, 1976).

General Van Tien Dung.

DUSTOFF

Derived from the radio call-sign of medical evacuation helicopter pilot Major James L. Kelly, who was killed in action on July 1, 1964, "Dustoff" was the nickname for medical evacuation helicopters, one of the major medical innovations of the Vietnam war. The bravery and determination of these medical evacuation helicopter crews in landing almost anywhere they were needed regardless of enemy fire, poor visibility or dangerous weather conditions saved numerous American lives. Their courage won Dustoff crews the respect and admiration of all combat soldiers and marines.

First used in 1962 to support U.S. Army Special Forces operations at Nha Trang, Army evacuation helicopter units increased to a peak in 1968 of two medical companies (air ambulance) and 11 medical detachments (helicopter ambulance), a total of 116 air ambulances. Each of these helicopters could transport six to nine patients at a time. As a result, the more seriously wounded on the battlefield usually reached a hospital within one to two hours after they were injured. Of the wounded who reached medical facilities, about 97.5 percent survived.

See also 44TH MEDICAL BRIGADE.

Suggestions for further reading: *Medical Support of the U.S. Army in Vietnam 1965–1970* by Spurgeon Neel (Washington, D.C.: U.S. Government Printing Office, 1973).

EAGLE FLIGHT

A name given to a type of tactical operation that employed a heliborne assault force of squad or platoon size to reconnoiter likely enemy positions. Eagle Flights were also used as emergency reaction forces. Larger standby forces were normally on alert for reinforcement if contact was made with the enemy.

Eagle Flights were first used in the Mekong Delta in the fall of 1963, and their use spread throughout Vietnam. The first U.S. ground force to employ Eagle Flights was the Fifth Special Forces Group, which formed its initial Eagle Flight at Pleiku during October 1964.

EAGLE PULL OPERATION

Designation for the evacuation of U.S. embassy and military personnel from Phnom Penh, Cambodia on April 12, 1975. Helicopters of the U.S. Seventh Fleet evacuated 276 persons, including 159 Cambodians (mostly embassy employees and their families), 82 Americans, and 35 other non-Cambodians.

See also CAMBODIA, EXPEDITIONARY MEDAL.

Suggestions for further reading: *Without Honor: Defeat in Vietnam and Cambodia,* by Arnold R. Isaacs (Baltimore: Johns Hopkins Press, 1983).

EASTERTIDE OFFENSIVE

One of the major North Vietnamese miscalculations of the war was their so-called Eastertide Offensive, which began on March 30, 1972. It was an attempt to overrun South Vietnam by a massive cross-border attack using regular North Vietnamese Army (NVA) troops supported by tanks and artillery. With the majority of U.S. ground combat forces withdrawn from Vietnam, the NVA believed the South Vietnamese Armed Forces would be easy prey.

Committing almost their entire army to the offensive, the North Vietnamese launched a three-pronged attack. Four divisions attacked directly south across the DMZ from their bases in North Vietnam to seize the provincial capital of Quang Tri in I Corps. Another two divisions attacked east toward Quang Tri from bases in Laos. The second prong was a two-division attack in II Corps to seize Kontum in the Central Highlands while a third division attacked in the lowlands near the coast. The final prong was a three-division attack to seize the provincial capital of An Loc in III Corps.

After initial successes, especially against the newly formed South Vietnamese Third Division in I Corps, the North Vietnamese attack was stopped cold by the combination of defending South Vietnamese divisions and massive American firepower, including B-52 strikes to break up enemy concentrations. Estimates placed the NVA's casualties at more than 100,000 and at least one-half of its large-caliber artillery and tanks.

See also AN LOC, BATTLE OF; I CORPS TACTICAL ZONE; KONTUM; QUANG TRI, BATTLE OF; SVNAF (SOUTH VIETNAMESE ARMED FORCES).

Suggestions for further reading: *The Easter Offensive of 1972,* by Ngo Quang Truong (Washington, D.C.: U.S. Government Printing Office, 1980); *The Easter Offensive: Vietnam 1972* by G. H. Turley (Novato, Calif.: Presidio Press, 1985); *Battles and Campaigns in Vietnam 1954–1984,* by Tom Carhart (New York: Crown, 1984); *The Vietnam Experience: South Vietnam on Trial,* by David Fulghum and Terrence Maitland (Boston: Boston Publishing Company, 1984); *Airpower and the 1972 Spring Invasion,* edited by A. J. C. Lavalle (Washington, D.C.: U.S. Government Printing Office, 1976).

18TH ENGINEER BRIGADE

A veteran of four campaigns in Western Europe during World War II, the 18th Engineer Brigade deployed to Vietnam from Fort Bragg, North Carolina in September 1965. Charged with the responsibility of providing engineering efforts for I Field Force Vietnam in I and II Corps, the brigade

Insignia of the 18th Engineer Brigade.

at one time or another had operational control over the battalions of the 35th Engineer Group (Construction), 45th Engineer Group (Construction) and 937th Engineer Group (Combat). As U.S. force levels in Vietnam declined, the brigade departed Vietnam in September 1971.

See also BASE CAMPS, U.S.; I FIELD FORCE VIETNAM.

Suggestions for further reading: *Vietnam Order of Battle*, by Shelby Stanton (Washington, D.C.: U.S. News & World Report Books, 1981).

18TH MILITARY POLICE BRIGADE

Deployed to Vietnam in September 1966 from Fort Meade, Maryland, the 18th Military Police Brigade exercised command of military police activities throughout Vietnam. The brigade included the three military police (MP) battalions assigned to the 16th MP Group in I and II Corps and the four MP battalions assigned to the 89th

Insignia of the 18th Military Police Brigade.

MP Group in III and IV Corps. The brigade provided such services as convoy escort, highway and bridge security, refugee and detainee evacuation and traffic control.

See also CONVOYS, U.S. MILITARY.

Suggestions for further reading: *Vietnam Order of Battle*, by Shelby L. Stanton (Washington, D.C.: U.S. News & World Report Books, 1981).

834TH AIR DIVISION

Organized on October 25, 1966 at Tan Son Nhut Air Base in the suburbs of Saigon, the U.S. Air Force 834th Air Division was responsible to the Seventh Air Force for tactical airlift within South Vietnam.

Subordinate units included the 315th Special Operations Wing at Phan Rang (II Corps), with four squadrons of C-123 Provider aircraft, the 483rd Tactical Air Lift Wing at Cam Ranh Bay (II Corps), with six squadrons of C-7a Caribou aircraft; and the Second Aerial Port Group at Tan Son Nhut, with three in-country aerial port (administrative) squadrons and numerous detachments throughout the country.

Also under the 834th Air Division were the Common Service Airlift System (CSAS) and its Airlift Control Center (ALCC). The ALCC functioned countrywide through local airlift control elements, liaison officers, field mission commanders and mobile combat control teams. The ALCC also controlled the C-130 aircraft that were rotated on one- to two-week cycles into South Vietnam from the 315th Air Division at Tachikawa, Japan, including its 15 C-130 squadrons there as well as squadrons at its subordinate units: the 374th Troop Carrier Wing at Ching Chuan Kang Air Base in Taiwan and the 463rd Troop Carrier Wing at Clark Air Base in the Philippines. At the height of the war in February 1968, 96 C-130s were deployed to South Vietnam. The C-118s of the 903rd Aeromedical Evacuation Squadron also worked through the 834th Air Division to provide in-country medical evacuation.

In November 1970, as the United States withdrew its forces from Vietnam, the 834th Air Division was disestablished and its C-123 and C-7 aircraft were subsequently transferred to the South Vietnamese Air Force as part of the Vietnamization of the war.

See also CARIBOU AIRCRAFT, TACTICAL AIRLIFT.

Suggestions for further reading: *The United States Air Force in Southeast Asia 1961-1973,* edited by Carl Berger (Washington, D.C.: U.S. Government Printing Office, 1977); *The U.S. Air Force in Southeast Asia: Tactical Airlift,* by Ray L. Bowers (Washington, D.C.: U.S. Government Printing Office, 1983).

82ND AIRBORNE DIVISION, THIRD BRIGADE

Part of the illustrious 82nd Airborne Division that won fame (as an infantry division) on the battlefields of World War I and as an airborne division in World War II, the Third Brigade, 82nd Airborne Division was deployed to Vietnam in February 1968 as part of the emergency response to the Tet Offensive. It served in II Corps, protecting the ancient capital of Hué, and later in III Corps, guarding the approaches to Saigon.

The brigade consisted of the First and Second Battalions, 505th Airborne Infantry; the First Battalion, 508th Airborne Infantry; the Second Battalion, 321st Artillery; Troop B, First Squadron, 17th Cavalry; and other support elements.

During its combat service in Vietnam the Third Brigade suffered 184 soldiers killed in action and 1,009 wounded in action. In December 1969 it returned to its home base at Fort Bragg, North Carolina. The 82nd Airborne Division has an active veterans' association, and further information can be obtained from Mr. Robert L. Riggs, 82nd Airborne Division Association, 317 South Butler Avenue, Indianapolis, Indiana 46219.

Suggestions for further reading: *Vietnam Order of Battle,* by Shelby L. Stanton (Washington, D.C.: U.S. News & World Report Books, 1981). An account of battle actions of the brigade is contained in *The Rise and Fall of an American Army,* by Shelby L. Stanton (Novato, Calif.: Presidio Press, 1985).

Insignia of the 82nd Airborne Division, Third Brigade.

EISENHOWER, DWIGHT D(AVID) (1890-1969)

The 34th President of the United States, Eisenhower was born on October 14, 1890 at Denison, Texas. He graduated from the U.S. Military Academy in 1915 and won fame as the Supreme Allied Commander in Europe during World War II.

Elected President in 1952, he served two terms. During the siege of Dien Bien Phu in 1954, he refused to intervene militarily on behalf of the French in their war with the Viet Minh (1946-54). Lack of allied support, especially from Great Britain, lack of congressional support and the opposition of U.S. Army Chief of Staff General Matthew B. Ridgway played a major role in this decision. At the 1954 Geneva Conference, the United States supported what was to become the Republic of Vietnam (South Vietnam). After the conference the administration dispatched economic and military aid to the government of South Vietnam and military advisers to the newly formed South

Vietnamese Armed Forces. President Eisenhower returned to private life in 1961. He died on March 28, 1969.

See also DIEN BIEN PHU; DULLES, JOHN FOSTER; GENEVA CONFERENCES; RIDGWAY, MATTHEW B.

Suggestions for further reading: *Holding the Line: The Eisenhower Era, 1952–1961,* by Charles C. Alexander (Bloomington: Indiana University Press, 1975); *The White House Years,* by Dwight D. Eisenhower (Garden City, N.Y.: Doubleday, 1963–65) *Eisenhower: President and Elder Statesman,* by Stephen E. Ambrose (New York: Simon & Schuster, 1984).

ELECTIONS

A persistent point of controversy over the Vietnam war was the issue of elections to reunify Vietnam after the 1954 Geneva Conference. The antiwar movement claimed that U.S. support for South Vietnam was illegal because President Ngo Dinh Diem had violated the Geneva Accords by refusing to hold elections in the south.

The nine-nation conference in Geneva in 1954 produced six unilateral declarations, three signed cease-fire agreements and an unsigned Final Declaration. The most important of these documents was the Agreement on the Cessation of Hostilities in Vietnam, signed by France and North Vietnam, which ended the war between the French and the Viet Minh (1946–54).

The United States and South Vietnam specifically disassociated themselves from the Final Declaration which contained a purposely vague statement that "free general elections by secret ballot" would be held by July 1956 under the aegis of an International Commission of Supervision. There was a practical reason for the U.S.-South Vietnamese action. The population of North Vietnam exceeded that of South Vietnam by several million, so a "head count" alone would favor the north. Such a demographic difference was more than likely the reason the communist world never pressed the election issue, for in the other two divided nations of the world, East-West Germany and North-South Korea, the bulk of the population was not in the communist sector.

See also CIVIL WAR, GENEVA CONFERENCES.

Suggestions for further reading: *America in Vietnam,* by Guenter Lewy (New York: Oxford University Press, 1978); *Vietnam: A History,* by Stanley Karnow (New York: Viking, 1983); *An International History of the Vietnam War,* by R. B. Smith (New York: St. Martin's Press, 1983).

11TH ARMORED CAVALRY REGIMENT

First organized as a horse cavalry regiment in 1901, "the Blackhorse Regiment," as it was nicknamed, served in the Philippine Insurrection at the turn of the century and the Mexican Border Expedition in 1916. Mechanized for service in World War II, the 11th Armored Cavalry fought in the Normandy, northern France, Rhineland, Ardennes-Alsace and Central Europe campaigns.

The Blackhorse Regiment was ordered to Vietnam in September 1966. Consisting of three squadrons, each with three armored cavalry troops, a tank troop and a howitzer battery, the

Insignia of the 11th Armored Cavalry Regiment.

regiment was a formidable combat force. When it arrived in Vietnam, it had 51 tanks, 296 armored personnel carriers, 18 self-propelled 155-mm howitzers, nine flamethrower vehicles and 18 helicopters.

During its Vietnam service the regiment conducted combat operations in III Corps, especially in War Zone C. Attached to the First Cavalry Division, it participated in the Cambodian incursion in 1970. The 11th Armored Cavalry Regiment departed Vietnam in March 1971, leaving behind its Second Squadron, which rejoined the regiment a year later. During its combat service in Vietnam, the Blackhorse Regiment lost 635 troopers killed in action and suffered 5,521 wounded in action. Three of its troopers won the Medal of Honor for bravery on the battlefield.

Now guarding the frontier in West Germany, the 11th Armored Cavalry has an active veterans' association. Further information can be obtained from CSM Bill Sauires, The Blackhorse Association, Box C, Fort Knox, Kentucky 40121.

See also ARMOR, III CORPS TACTICAL ZONE, II FIELD FORCE VIETNAM.

Suggestions for further reading: *The Rise and Fall of an American Army,* by Shelby L. Stanton (Novato, Calif.: Presidio Press, 1985); *Vietnam Order of Battle,* by Shelby L. Stanton (Washington, D.C.: U.S. News & World Report Books, 1981).

11TH INFANTRY BRIGADE

See AMERICAL INFANTRY DIVISION.

ELLSBERG, DANIEL (1931–   )

Born on April 7, 1931 in Chicago, Ellsberg received a B.A. in economics from Harvard in 1952. After two years in the U.S. Marine Corps, he returned to Harvard, where he wrote his dissertation on strategic military planning. After working for the RAND Corp., he joined the Defense Department in 1964. Touring Vietnam in 1965, Ellsberg was a strong proponent of the Johnson Administration's Vietnam policy. Follow-

ing his return to the RAND Corp., Ellsberg participated in a massive study of U.S. involvement in Southeast Asia commissioned by Secretary of Defense Robert S. McNamara in 1967. The study convinced Ellsberg that the war was unjust, the result of several Presidents' unwillingness to bear responsibility for the loss of South Vietnam to the communists. In 1969, after urging immediate withdrawal from Vietnam in memos, position papers and magazine articles, he used his top secret clearance to obtain the Pentagon study and photocopied it. When prominent opponents of the war declined to use it, Ellsberg gave a copy of the study to the *New York Times,* which began publishing excerpts in June. On June 30 the Supreme Court ruled in favor of the *Times'* right to publish the documents.

Ellsberg was tried twice for theft of government property and espionage, but all charges were dropped in May 1973 when a second mistrial was declared because of government involvement in the burglary of the office of Ellsberg's former psychiatrist and the taping of Ellsberg's phone conversations.

After the war Ellsberg became active in the antinuclear movement.

See also PENTAGON PAPERS.

Suggestions for further reading: *Papers on the War,* by Daniel Ellsberg (New York: Pocket Books, 1972).

ENGINEERING, CIVIL

While all military forces use engineers to facilitate combat operations, the U.S. armed forces instituted a major engineering effort toward the goal of nation building in South Vietnam that has been largely ignored by students of the war. Army construction engineers and Navy Seabees built and upgraded roads, extended highways, constructed ports and buildings, and installed pipelines and railroads. This extensive enterprise was designed to modernize South Vietnam and stimulate its economy, only indirectly benefiting combat operations. Major firms, such as Pacific Architects and Engineers, Brown and Root, Philco-Ford, Vinnell Corporation, Morrison-Knudson and others, contributed a large share of the actual engineering construction and maintenance of power plants and other projects.

See also BASE CAMPS, U.S.; 18TH ENGINEER BRIGADE; SEABEES; 20TH ENGINEER BRIGADE.

U.S. Navy Seebees assembling a building at Phu Bai, South Vietnam. (Courtesy U.S. Navy.)

EXPEDITIONARY MEDAL

The Armed Forces Expeditionary Medal was authorized to recognize those service members who served in Indochina during the periods other than July 3, 1965 through May 28, 1973, for whom the Vietnam Service Medal (*see* CAMPAIGN MEDALS) was authorized. These periods include service in Laos from April 19, 1961 to October 7, 1962; in Cambodia, and in Thailand in support of operations in Cambodia, from March 29 to August 19, 1973 and during the evacuation of Cambodia from April 11 to April 13, 1975; and in Vietnam from July 1, 1958 to July 3, 1965 and during the evacuation of Vietnam from April 29 to April 30, 1975.

EXPLOSIVE ORDNANCE DISPOSAL

During the Vietnam war the Viet Cong (VC)

and the North Vietnamese Army (NVA) made extensive and ingenious use of automatic mechanical devices, mines and booby traps to destroy equipment and inflict casualties. Explosive ordnance disposal (EOD) experts in each of the U.S. armed services had the task of disarming these devices, under great pressure and time constraints.

Among their other deeds EOD personnel defused satchel charges set to explode the Long Binh ammunition depot during the Tet Offensive of 1968, disarmed bombs following aircraft crash landings and cut trip wires to booby traps that threatened to explode among U.S. military bulldozer crews. Many of the EOD deeds saved numerous civilian lives threatened by NVA and VC explosive devices, which were used to maim and terrorize the South Vietnamese population.

Explosive ordnance disposal experts at work in the field. (Courtesy U.S. Army.)

FAC (FORWARD AIR CONTROLLER)

In World War II and the Korean war a FAC (forward air controller) was used only to control air strikes in close proximity to friendly troops. Once beyond the "bomb line" (a designated point beyond which aircraft could bomb and strafe without checking with friendly ground forces—in effect, a "free fire zone"), aircrews assumed that anything moving was a legitimate target.

Because there were no fixed front lines in Vietnam, any village or town could be in a combat zone. To prevent indiscriminate attacks on civilian populations, a policy in 1961 established that all strike aircraft (i.e., fighters, fighter-bombers, bombers and gunships) were to be under control of a FAC who would clear combat strikes with local civilian officials. Because of a shortage of South Vietnamese Air Force personnel, U.S. Air Force FACs were deployed to Vietnam beginning in 1961. Working throughout South Vietnam's 44 provinces, they became a prime source of combat intelligence.

When major U.S. ground combat units were deployed to Vietnam in 1965, FACs were assigned to each combat battalion. Experienced fighter pilots who had served in fighter units for the first part of their Vietnam tour, they were in effect local air commanders and as such advised and assisted ground force commanders in determining air support requirements. Because the jungle terrain limited control of air strikes from the ground, these FACs would fly over the battlefield in 0-1 Bird Dogs, OV-2 Skymasters or twin-engine OV-10 Broncos (*see* illustration), light propeller-driven aircraft. In radio contact both with the ground commander and with U.S. Air Force

strike aircraft, the FACs would provide fighters with a description of the target and the location of friendly forces and would then mark the target with an air-to-ground smoke rocket. At all times the FAC was the final authority on whether strikes would continue. Their slow and low-flying planes were attractive targets for North Vietnamese and Viet Cong ground fire, and FACs took enormous risks to coordinate air support for the ground forces. Of the 12 Medals of Honor awarded to Air Force personnel for bravery in the Vietnam war, two went to forward air controllers.

See also CLOSE AIR SUPPORT, FREE FIRE ZONES.

Suggestions for further reading: *Airpower in Three Wars*, by William W. Momyer (Washington, D.C.: U.S. Government Printing Office, 1978).

FANK TRAINING COMMAND

The FANK (Forces Armées Nationale Khmer) Training Command was composed of U.S. Army Special Forces personnel, who trained Cambodian light infantry and marine fusilier battalions for the Khmer Republic.

When President Nixon authorized military aid for Cambodia commencing in April 1970, the Special Forces was assigned to provide the training for a new Khmer army. Three training sites were established at Long Hai, Dong Ba Thin and Chi Lang (later moved to Phuoc Tuy). When the Fifth Special Forces Group departed Vietnam, these trainers were retained and redesignated as the U.S. Army Individual Training Group on March 1, 1971. Australian and New Zealand jungle instructors were also assigned to the group, which was redesignated as the FANK Training Command in May 1972 and finally as the Field Training Com-

A Cambodian soldier wielding an AK-47. (Courtesy U.S. Army.)

mand on December 1, 1972. Before it closed down at the end of January 1973, the command and its predecessors had created an entirely new national army, having trained 86 Cambodian infantry and marine battalions.

Suggestions for further reading: *The Green Berets at War*, by Shelby L. Stanton (Novato, Calif: Presidio Press, 1985).

FARM GATE

Code name for the U.S. Air Force advisory effort in support of the South Vietnamese Air Force, which began in November 1961.

See also SVNAF (SOUTH VIETNAMESE ARMED FORCES).

Suggestions for further reading: *Airpower in Three Wars*, by William W. Momyer (Washington, D.C.: U.S. Government Printing Office, 1978); *The United States Air Force: The Advisory Years 1961 to 1965*, by Robert F. Futrell (Washington, D.C.: U.S. Government Printing Office, 1981).

FIELD FORCES

Field force was the designation used during most of the Vietnam war to classify U.S. military corps-level tactical control headquarters. When these units were deployed to Vietnam in 1966, the decision was made not to use U.S. corps designations (a decision later reversed when the U.S. XXIV Corps was formed in 1968). The rationale was that since the headquarters was to operate within an existing South Vietnamese corps zone, it would be confusing to introduce another corps designation within the same zone. Further, unlike a corps headquarters, which has only tactical functions, the field force organization was more flexible and could handle additional responsibilities, including supply, pacification and an advisory role.

See also I FIELD FORCE VIETNAM, II FIELD FORCE VIETNAM.

Suggestions for further reading: *Vietnam Order of Battle* by Shelby L. Stanton (Washington, D.C.: U.S. News and World Report Books, 1981); *Command and Control 1950-1969*, by George S. Eckhardt (Washington, D.C.: U.S. Government Printing Office, 1974).

FIFTH INFANTRY DIVISION, FIRST BRIGADE

Part of the U.S. Army's Fifth Infantry Division (Mechanized), the First Brigade deployed to Vietnam in March 1968. A heavily armored fighting force, it consisted of the First Battalion, 11th Infantry; the First Battalion, 61st Infantry (Mechanized); the First Battalion, 77th Armor; a 155-mm self-propelled artillery battalion—the Fifth Battalion, Fourth Artillery—an armored cavalry reconnaissance troop; and other support units.

Headquartered at Quang Tri in I Corps Tactical Zone, the brigade operated along the DMZ and in conjunction with U.S. Marine Corps combat forces. In January 1971 it seized attack positions in the western portion of the DMZ as a base for South Vietnam's operation Lam Son 719 to cut the Ho Chi Minh Trail in Laos.

During its combat operations in Vietnam, the brigade suffered 403 soldiers killed in action and 3,648 wounded in action. In August 1971 it returned to the United States and is now part of its parent division stationed at Fort Polk, Louisiana.

See also I CORPS TACTICAL ZONE; LAM SON 719; MARINE CORPS, U.S.

Suggestions for further reading: *Vietnam Order of Battle,* by Shelby L. Stanton (Washington, D.C.: U.S. News & World Report Books, 1981); *The Rise and Fall of an American Army,* by Shelby L. Stanton (Novato, Calif.: Presidio Press, 1985).

FIFTH MARINE DIVISION

To compensate for not calling up the Fourth Marine Division from the U.S. Marine Corps' Organized Reserve, Secretary of Defense Robert S. McNamara on March 1, 1966 authorized the reactivation of the Fifth Marine Division (which in World War II had fought at Iwo Jima) at Camp Pendleton, California. On April 1 the Fifth Division's First Battalion, 26th Marines was reactivated and on June 25, 1966 it deployed to the western Pacific. Shortly thereafter the division's other two infantry regiments, the 27th and 28th Marines, and its artillery regiment, the 13th Marines, were reactivated.

By April 1967 the entire regimental landing team (RLT 26) of the 26th Marines was in South Vietnam, and at the year's end it was assigned the defense of the combat base at Khe Sanh, for which action it was awarded the Presidential Unit Citation. In February 1968 RLT 27 deployed from Camp Pendleton to Vietnam and later joined RLT 26 in operations south of Da Nang. RLT 27 returned to Camp Pendleton in September 1968; it was followed in 1969 by RLT 26. The Fifth Marine Division was deactivated on November 26, 1969.

See also FIRST MARINE DIVISION; KHE SANH, BATTLE OF; THIRD MARINE DIVISION.

Suggestions for further reading: *Vietnam Order of Battle,* by Shelby L. Stanton (Washington, D.C.: U.S. News & World Report Books, 1981).

FIFTH SPECIAL FORCES GROUP

Although some of their "A-team" members had served in Vietnam earlier on six-month temporary duty tours, it was not until October 1964 that the U.S. Army's Fifth Special Forces Group deployed to Vietnam from Fort Bragg, North Carolina. Establishing its headquarters at Nha Trang, the group replaced the provisional organization created several years earlier.

The Fifth Special Forces Group was organized into four "companies" (properly redesignated battalions after the Vietnam war), each commanded by a lieutenant colonel. The companies were further organized into detachments. Each company included a C detachment to control operations and a number of B detachments. These B detachments controlled several A-teams, which were the actual operating elements commanding Special Forces camps, strike forces and reconnaissance teams.

The insignia of the Fifth Special Forces Group.

Company A was stationed at Bien Hoa with five B detachments and 23 A-teams scattered throughout III Corps. Company B was stationed in Pleiku with four B detachments and 34 A-teams throughout the Central Highlands in II Corps. Company C was stationed at Da Nang with two B detachments and nine A-teams along the Laotian border in I Corps. Company D was stationed in Can Tho with five B detachments and 20 A-teams scattered throughout the Mekong Delta in IV Corps. The group also advised the Vietnamese Special Forces and MACV (U.S. Military Assistance Command Vietnam) recondo training centers, fielded several mobile strike force commands, and raised the Delta, Sigma, Omega and Rapid Fire special reconnaissance projects. The Fifth Special Forces Group Special Operations Augmentation placed Special Forces personnel in MACV-SOG (Studies and Observation Group).

From 951 U.S. personnel directing some 19,000 Montagnard tribesmen and other ethnic groups organized into CIDG (Civilian Irregular Defense Group) camps in October 1964, the effort grew to the point where in October 1969 it involved 3,741 and 9,326 strike forces.

During its service in Vietnam the Fifth Special Forces Group was awarded the Presidential Unit Citation for battlefield bravery, the Meritorious Unit Citation for exceptional service and the Vietnamese Cross of Gallantry with Palm and Civil Actions Medal. Among other individual awards for valor were 13 Medals of Honor and 75 Distinguished Service Crosses won by personnel of the Fifth Special Forces for conspicuous bravery under enemy fire in Vietnam. This enemy fire cost the Fifth Special Forces Group 546 soldiers killed in action and 2,704 wounded in action.

Beginning in 1968, the Fifth Special Forces began a "Vietnamization" program to transform their indigenous units into Regional Forces and Popular Forces or into South Vietnamese Ranger battalions. Once this was accomplished, the Fifth Special Forces Group returned to Fort Bragg, North Carolina, in March 1971, where it remains stationed today.

See also CIDG (CIVILIAN IRREGULAR DEFENSE GROUP), SPECIAL FORCES, SOG (STUDIES AND OBSERVATION GROUP).

Suggestions for further reading: *Vietnam Order of Battle,* by Shelby L. Stanton (Washington, D.C.: U.S. News & World Report Books, 1981), which has the most detailed breakdown of Special Forces organization available; *U.S. Army Special Forces 1961–1971,* by Francis J. Kelly (Washington, D.C.: U.S. Government Printing Office, 1973); *Inside the Green Berets: The First Thirty Years,* by Charles M. Simpson, III (Novato, Calif.: Presidio Press, 1983). *The Green Berets at War,* by Shelby L. Stanton (Novato, Calif: Presidio Press, 1985).

FIGHTERS AND FIGHTER-BOMBERS

A variety of fighters and fighter-bombers were flow during the Vietnam war. They ranged from the propeller-driven A-1 Skyraider (nicknamed "Spad") to the most advanced supersonic aircraft, including the swept-wing F-111.

The workhorse for U.S. bombing strike missions over North Vietnam was the Air Force F-105 Thunderchief (nicknamed "Thud"), which flew 75 percent of the Air Force's Rolling Thunder missions. For the U.S. Navy and Marine Corps, a mainstay was the A-4 Skyhawk, which could carry a 5,000-pound bomb load. Even more lethal was the A-6 Intruder, which could carry 30 500-pound bombs.

The F-4 Phantom, used by the Air Force, Navy and Marine Corps, was the MIG-killer of the war. A twin-engine supersonic fighter, it downed an estimated 107 North Vietnamese aircraft. It was also used for close air support, as was the F-100 Super Sabre (nicknamed "Lead Sled") and the A-7 Corsair.

Air Force fighters and fighter-bombers operated out of bases at Bien Hoa, Cam Ranh Bay, Da Nang, Phan Rang, Phu Cat, Tan Son Nhut and Tuy Hoa in South Vietnam and from Korat, Takhli, Ubon and Udorn in Thailand. Navy fighters and fighter-bombers operated from attack carriers in the South China Sea, and Marine aircraft from the air bases at Chu Lai and Da Nang in the northern part of South Vietnam.

Although the French had trained some Vietnamese pilots during their war with the Viet Minh (1946–54), the South Vietnamese Air Force

A U.S. Air Force F-100 on a bombing attack on a Viet Cong base camp. (Courtesy Air War College.)

(VNAF) did not really begin to take shape until 1961, when the United States began an intensive pilot-training program and supplied the VNAF with propeller-driven T-28 trainers modified to be fighter-bombers and propeller-driven World War II-vintage B-26 bombers. By 1973 the VNAF had grown to 16 squadrons of fighters and fighter-bombers, including propeller-driven A-1 Skyraiders, F-5 Freedom Fighter jet fighters and A-37 Dragonfly jet fighter-bombers, which were used for interdiction of enemy supply lines and for close air support.

It was not until shortly after the Tonkin Gulf Incident in August 1964 that the North Vietnamese began to acquire fighter aircraft. China initially supplied a number of MIG 15 and MIG 17 subsonic jet aircraft and soon thereafter the Soviet Union followed suit. By June 1965 the North Vietnamese Air Force consisted of some 70 MIG 15 and MIG 17 jet fighters. In December 1965 the North Vietnamese began to receive supersonic MIG 21 jet fighters, which became their primary interceptor aircraft. At its peak strength in 1972 the North Vietnamese Air Force had an estimated 93 MIG 21s and some 113 MIG 15s, 17s and 19s. These aircraft were used exclusively for air defense and did not support ground combat operations.

See also ACE; AIR FORCE, U.S.; AIRCRAFT CARRIERS; BOMBER AIRCRAFT; BOMBING; CLOSE AIR SUPPORT; FIRST MARINE AIRCRAFT WING; NAVY, U.S.; OPERATIONS, U.S. MILITARY; SVNAF (SOUTH VIETNAMESE ARMED FORCES).

Suggestions for further reading: *The United States Air Force in Southeast Asia 1961–1973*, edited by Carl Berger (Washington, D.C.: U.S. Government Printing Office, 1977); *The Vietnam Experience: Thunder from Above* and *Rain of Fire*, by John Morrocco (Boston: Boston Publishing Co., 1984 and 1985); *THUD Ridge*, by Jack Broughton (New York: Lippincott, 1969); *Phantom over Vietnam: Fighter Pilot, USMC*, by John Triotti (Novato, Calif:

Presidio Press, 1984); *Airpower in Three Wars,* by William W. Momyer (Washington, D.C.: U.S. Government Printing Office, 1978); *The Vietnamese Air Force, 1951–1975: An Analysis of Its Role in Combat,* by William W. Momyer, Vol. 3, USAF Southeast Asia Monograph (Washington, D.C.: U.S. Government Printing Office, 1975); "Marine Aviation in Vietnam: 1962–1970," by Keith B. McCutcheon, in *The Marines in Vietnam 1954–1973* (Washington, D.C.: U.S. Marine Corps, 1974).

FINAL OFFENSIVE

Beginning in 1959, the North Vietnamese never lost focus of their ultimate objective—the capture of Saigon and the conquest of South Vietnam. Their attempts to accomplish this objective by a Hanoi-directed guerrilla war were thwarted by the intervention of American ground combat forces in 1965. Until 1968 the North Vietnamese continued to cling to illusions of a "great popular uprising," in which the people of South Vietnam would flock to their side, but these notions were shattered during their Tet Offensive of 1968, when the South Vietnamese failed to rally to the communist cause. Not only did the North Vietnamese not win popular support with the offensive, but their Viet Cong guerrilla forces, by coming out in the open, were virtually destroyed.

In 1972, believing South Vietnam to be fatally weakened by the withdrawal of American ground combat forces, the North Vietnamese committed almost their entire regular army, heavily reinforced by tanks and artillery, to the Eastertide Offensive, but they were beaten back with over 100,000 casualties by the determined stand of the South Vietnamese Armed Forces (SVNAF) aided by massive American fire support.

After these bloody reversals General Vo Nguyen Giap was eased out of power, and command was turned over to the Chief of Staff, Senior General Van Tien Dung. As he began planning in 1974, his first step was to assess the possibility of American reintervention. He concluded that the Watergate scandal had fatally weakened the American presidency to the point that it could not honor its commitments to South Vietnam to uphold the 1973 Paris Accords. Evidence of this weakening had appeared in 1973, when the U.S. Congress reduced American military aid to South Vietnam. Nevertheless General Dung decided to launch a limited-objective attack to see whether a deliberate violation of the peace agreement would provoke an American response.

With 20-plus divisions heavily reinforced by Soviet-supplied tanks and artillery organized into four corps, General Dung directed the North Vietnamese Army (NVA) 301st Corps to seize the lightly defended province of Phuoc Long, located due north of Saigon along the Cambodian border. Led by the tank-supported NVA Third and Seventh Divisions, the attack began on December 13, 1974. Using artillery preparations of up to 1,000 rounds, the NVA tanks drove back the South Vietnamese defenders, and on January 6, 1975 the NVA captured Phuoc Binh, capital of Phuoc Long Province, the first provincial capital in South Vietnam to fall since the cease-fire two years earlier.

When the United States did not react to this flagrant violation of the Paris Accords, General Dung knew the time was ripe for the Final Offensive. Repeating almost exactly the plan to cut South Vietnam in two with an attack across the Central Highlands that had been thwarted 10 years earlier by the U.S. First Cavalry Division in the battle of the Ia Drang, General Dung began the NVA Final Offensive with a three-division assault on Ban Me Thuot, a town in the Central Highlands just south of the Ia Drang Valley. Unwittingly South Vietnamese President Nguyen Van Thieu played right into General Dung's hands, for on March 14, 1975, he ordered the evacuation of the Central Highlands in order to concentrate his overextended army at the population centers located in enclaves along the seacoast. Under enemy pressure this evacuation soon turned into a rout.

In the meantime, General Dung had launched another prong of his attack by a blitzkrieg across the DMZ, striking due south along the coast. Defeating SVNAF forces in detail (i.e., one at a time), Dung's forces were soon closing in on the approaches to Saigon. After a determined stand by the SVNAF 18th Division at Xuan Loc destroyed three of his divisions, Dung overcame this resistance and invested the capital city of Saigon.

With the situation hopeless, U.S. Ambassador Graham Martin requested approval from Washington to order the evacuation of American personnel, and at 11:08 AM, April 29, 1975, in what was called Operation Frequent Wind, all Americans and a number of South Vietnamese were withdrawn by elements of the U.S. Seventh Fleet. By the morning of April 30, 1975, it was all over. As NVA tanks broke through the gates of the Presidential Palace in Saigon, the Vietnam war came to an end.

See also IA DRANG, BATTLE OF; FREQUENT WIND OPERATION; XUAN LOC, BATTLE OF; CENTRAL HIGHLANDS; MARTIN, GRAHAM; DUNG, TRAN VAN; TRA, TRAN VAN; EASTERTIDE OFFENSIVE; FOUR PARTY JOINT MILITARY TEAM.

Suggestions for further reading: *Vietnam from Ceasefire to Capitulation,* by William E. LeGro (Washington, D.C.: U.S. Government Printing Office, 1981); *Great Spring Victory,* by Van Tien Dung (Washington, D.C.: Foreign Broadcast Information Service [FBIS] Supplements 38 and 42, 1976); *Ending the 30 Years War* (Ket Thuc Cuoc Chien Tranh 30 Nam), by Tran Van Tra (Ho Chi Minh City: Literature Publishing House, 1982).

FIRE SUPPORT BASES, U.S.

Because there were no fixed front lines in Vietnam as in other wars, when U.S. combat operations were launched bases had to be established to provide artillery firepower for support of infantry

A CH-47 Chinook helicopter lowers a 105 mm howitzer into an ARVN fire support base. (Courtesy U.S. Army.)

attacks. Just as infantry units were often transported by helicopters into an attack, so artillery was often moved into position by Chinook helicopters. Hasty defense fortifications were rapidly constructed around fire support bases, and in dangerous areas infantry units were detached to provide additional security. Among the fiercest battles of the war were attempts by North Vietnamese Army or Viet Cong units to overrun such bases. In some cases the artillery was forced to lower its tubes and, using beehive ammunition, fire directly into the attacking enemy.

See also ARTILLERY, BEEHIVE AMMUNITION, CHINOOK HELICOPTER.

Suggestions for further reading: *Field Artillery— 1954–1973*, by David Ewing Ott (Washington, D.C.: U.S. Government Printing Office, 1975); *Tactical and Matériel Innovations,* by John H. Hay, Jr. (Washington, D.C.: U.S. Government Printing Office, 1974). For accounts of enemy attacks on fire bases, see *The Rise and Fall of an American Army,* by Shelby L. Stanton (Novato, Calif.: Presidio Press, 1985).

Insignia of the First Aviation Brigade.

FIRST AVIATION BRIGADE

Organized at Tan Son Nhut Air Base near Saigon on May 25, 1966, the First Aviation Brigade became one of the largest U.S. commands in Vietnam. With up to seven aviation groups, some 20 aviation battalions and four air cavalry squadrons under its control at one time or another, the First Aviation Brigade conducted tactical combat assaults, direct fire support, aerial reconnaissance, medical evacuation, troop lift and cargo hauling throughout the entire country.

Moved to Long Binh in December 1967, the brigade at its peak strength had some 641 fixed-wing aircraft, 441 Cobra attack helicopters, 311 Chinook cargo helicopters, 635 observation helicopters and 2,202 UH-1 Huey utility helicopters.

Returned to its former base at Tan Son Nhut in December 1972, the First Aviation Brigade was one of the last U.S. units to leave Vietnam, departing March 28, 1973. During its service in Vietnam four Medals of Honor were awarded to brigade personnel for bravery in action.

See also AIRMOBILE OPERATIONS, CARIBOU AIRCRAFT, CHINOOK HELICOPTER, HELICOPTERS, HUEY HELICOPTER.

Suggestions for further reading: *Vietnam Order of Battle,* by Shelby L. Stanton (Washington, D.C.: U.S. News & World Report Books, 1981); *Vietnam Studies: Airmobility 1961–1971,* by John J. Tolson (Washington, D.C.: U.S. Government Printing Office, 1973).

FIRST CAVALRY DIVISION

Organized in 1921, the First Cavalry Division brought together several famous horse cavalry regiments that had distinguished themselves during the Indian wars on the Western plains. During World War II, it was reorganized to fight on foot and deployed for combat in the southwest

Pacific. The first American unit to enter Manila, the division was selected by General MacArthur to be the first American division to land in Japan. As a result of these historic firsts, the division became known as the "First Team." When the Korean war broke out, the First Cavalry Division went into combat in July 1950 and three months later was the first division in Pyongyang, the capital of North Korea. Remaining in the Far East after the war, the division returned to Fort Benning, Georgia, in 1965, and in July of that year became the first air mobile division in the U.S. Army. The First Cavalry Division soon thereafter scored yet another historic first: the first Army division to be deployed to Vietnam, arriving there on September 11, 1965.

The division consisted of nine battalions of air mobile infantry—the First and Second Battalions, Fifth Cavalry; First, Second and Fifth Battalions, Seventh Cavalry; First and Second Battalions, Eighth Cavalry; and First and Second Battalions, 12th Cavalry. Other combat elements included an air reconnaissance unit, the First Squadron, Ninth Cavalry, and six battalions of artillery—four with 105-mm howitzers (the Second Battalion, 17th Artillery; Second Battalion, 19th Artillery; First Battalion, 21st Artillery and First Battalion, 77th Artillery), one battalion—the First Battalion, 30th Artillery—with 155-mm howitzers and a unique unit, the Second Battalion, 20th Artillery, a heliborne unit armed with aerial rockets. Another unique feature of the First Cavalry Division was its 11th Aviation Group, three aviation battalions consisting of some 11 companies of assault helicopters, assault support helicopters and gunships.

The First Cavalry Division was the only American division to have fought in all four corps tactical zones in South Vietnam. Initially deployed to II Corps, the division took part in the Battle of Ia Drang in November 1965, the first major meeting engagement between U.S. and North Vietnamese Army forces. In 1968 the division deployed to I Corps, where it took part in operations around Hué and relieved the embattled U.S. Marine base at Khe Sanh. In October 1968 the division again redeployed, this time to III Corps to blunt a threatened enemy attack on Saigon, and later conducted tactical operations in

both III and IV Corps and took part in the invasion of Cambodia in 1970.

The First Cavalry Division was the only U.S. Army division awarded the Presidential Unit Citation, receiving the award from President Johnson for its actions in the Battle of Ia Drang. In addition, it was awarded the Vietnamese Cross of Gallantry with Palm and the Vietnamese Civil Action Medal. Among other individual awards, troopers of the First Cavalry Division won 25 Medals of Honor, 120 Distinguished Service Crosses, 2,766 Silver Stars, 2,697 Distinguished Flying Crosses, 8,408 Bronze Stars for Valor, 2,910 Air Medals for Valor and 5,328 Army Commendation Medals for Valor. During the fighting in Vietnam the division suffered more than 30,000 soldiers killed or wounded in action, almost half again as many as the 4,055 casualties it suffered in World War II and the 16,498 casualties the division suffered in the Korean war combined.

The bulk of the First Cavalry Division departed Vietnam on April 29, 1970, leaving behind its Third Brigade, which did not depart Vietnam until

Insignia of the First Cavalry Division.

June 26, 1972. The division, now a mechanized rather than an air mobile division, is currently stationed at Fort Hood, Texas. The First Cavalry Division maintains a museum at Fort Hood and has an active Division Association that schedules periodic reunions for members and former members of the "First Team." Further information can be obtained from Colonel Robert F. Little, Jr., First Cavalry Division Association, Copperas Cove, Texas 76522.

See also AIR CAVALRY; AIRMOBILE OPERATIONS; CAMBODIA; HUÉ, BATTLE OF; I, II, III, IV CORPS TACTICAL ZONES: IA DRANG, BATTLE OF; KHE SANH, BATTLE OF.

Suggestions for further reading: *Airmobility, 1961-1971,* by John J. Tolson (Washington, D.C.: U.S. Government Printing Office, 1973); *The 1st Air Cavalry Division: Vietnam, August 1965 to December 1969* (Tokyo: Dia Nippon Printing Company, 1970) and *First Air Cavalry Division in Vietnam* (New York: W. M. Lads Publishing Company, 1967); and *Vietnam Order of Battle,* by Shelby L. Stanton (Washington, D.C.: U.S. News & World Report Books, 1981). An account of the division's combat operations, including selected small unit actions, is contained in Shelby L. Stanton's *The Rise and Fall of an American Army* (Novato, Calif: Presidio Press, 1985). See also *Year of the Horse—Vietnam: First Air Cavalry in the Highlands,* by Kenneth D. Mertel (New York: Exposition Press, 1968).

FIRST CORPS TACTICAL ZONE

See I CORPS TACTICAL ZONE.

FIRST FIELD FORCE VIETNAM

See I FIELD FORCE VIETNAM.

FIRST INFANTRY DIVISION

One of the most distinguished units in the U.S. Army, the First Infantry Division was organized in May 1917 and landed in France the following month as the first element of the American Expeditionary Force. Taking part in the battle at Cantigny and the Aisne-Marne, St. Mihiel, Meuse-Argonne and Montidier-Noyons offensives, it won the nickname the "Big Red One." In World War II it took part in the invasions of North Africa and Sicily and was one of the first units ashore at Omaha Beach during the Normandy invasion. It captured Aachen and helped stem the German counteroffensive in the Battle of the Bulge. Breaking through the Siegfried Line, it drove across Germany and into Czechoslovakia, where it met the advancing Russian forces.

The first Army infantry division to arrive in Vietnam, the Big Red One deployed to III Corps in October 1965. The division consisted of seven battalions of light infantry (First Battalion, Second Infantry; Second Battalion, 16th Infantry; First and Second Battalions, 18th Infantry; First Battalion, 26th Infantry; First and Second Battalions, 28th Infantry) and two battalions—Second Battalion, Second Infantry and First Battalion, 16th Infantry—of mechanized infantry. Other combat elements included an armored reconnaissance unit (First Squadron, Fourth Cavalry) and four battalions of artillery, three with 105-mm howitzers (First Battalion, Fifth Artillery; First Battalion, Seventh Artillery and Second Battalion, 33rd Artillery) and one with 155-mm howitzers (Eighth Battalion, Sixth Artillery).

The approaches to Saigon and the border regions between Vietnam and Cambodia in III Corps were the major battlefields for the First Infantry Division in Vietnam. It took part in Operation Junction City and the Tet Counteroffensive of 1968 and conducted extensive pacification operations in conjunction with South Vietnamese forces. The Big Red One returned to Fort Riley, Kansas in April 1970. With one brigade deployed to West Germany, the First Division (now a mechanized division) remains stationed at Fort Riley.

The First Infantry Division was awarded the Vietnamese Civil Action Medal and the Vietnamese Cross of Gallantry with Palm. Among other individual awards, Big Red One soldiers won 11 Medals of Honor, 67 Distinguished Service Crosses and 905 Silver Star Medals for bravery in

Vietnam. The division suffered 20,770 soldiers killed or wounded in action, more than the 20,659 casualties suffered in World War II and almost as many as the 22,320 casualties suffered in World War I.

The First Infantry Division maintains the Cantigny Museum at Wheaton, Illinois, which has exhibits and material on the division's Vietnam war experience. It also has its own war memorial located near the White House in Washington, D.C., which contains the names of Big Red One soldiers who fell on the battlefields of World War I, World War II and the Vietnam war. From the very beginning, the Society of the First Division kept close links with its Vietnam veterans. In addition to annual reunions, the division maintains a scholarship fund for the sons and daughters of its members who were killed in action in Vietnam. In 1985 the society's reunion will be dedicated to its Vietnam veterans. Further information can be obtained from Arthur L. Chaitt, Executive Director, Society of the First Division, 5 Montgomery Avenue, Philadelphia, Pennsylvania 19118.

See also III CORPS TACTICAL ZONE.

Suggestions for further reading: *Cedar Falls-Junction City: A Turning Point,* by Bernard W. Rogers (Washington, D.C.: U.S. Government Printing Office, 1974); *Vietnam Order of Battle,* by Shelby L. Stanton (Washington, D.C.: U.S. News & World Report Books, 1981). While there is no official history of the First Infantry Division in Vietnam, an account of its combat actions there is contained in *Charlie Company: What Vietnam Did to Us,* by Peter Goldman and Tony Fuller (New York: Morrow, 1983), a series of interviews with members of Company C, Second Battalion, 28th Infantry. Another source of the division's combat operations, including selected small unit actions, is Shelby L. Stanton's *The Rise and Fall of an American Army* (Novato, Calif.: Presidio Press, 1985).

FIRST LOGISTICAL COMMAND

Arriving from Fort Hood, Texas in March 1965, the First Logistical Command was responsible for all U.S. and allied support in Vietnam (except for I Corps, which was then a U.S. Navy responsibil-

ity). With subordinate U.S. Army support commands at Saigon to supply III and IV Corps at Cam Ranh Bay and to support II Corps at Qui Nhon (and after 1968 at Da Nang to support I Corps), the First Logistical Command supervised a number of depots, support groups, and ordnance ammunition, petroleum supply, maintenance and transportation battalions and separate companies, as well as mortuaries at Saigon and Da Nang. An enormous organization, the Saigon Support Command alone had an average of 33,000 personnel assigned to support some 235,000 U.S. and allied troops. Truck drivers who delivered ammunition and supplies to front-line units had a particularly hazardous task. Two medals of Honor were awarded to soldiers in First Logistical Command transportation units for conspicuous bravery in action.

Consolidated with USARV (U.S. Army Vietnam) in June 1970 as part of the U.S. force reduction, the First Logistical Command departed Vietnam in May 1972. It is currently stationed at Fort Bragg, North Carolina.

Suggestions for further reading: *Vietnam Order of Battle,* by Shelby L. Stanton (Washington, D.C.: U.S. News & World Report Books, 1981); *Logistic Support,* by Joseph M. Heiser, Jr. (Washington, D.C.: U.S. Government Printing Office, 1974).

FIRST MARINE AIRCRAFT WING

At its peak strength, the First Marine Aircraft Wing (First MAW) had six Marine Air Groups (MAG) under its command, each group containing approximately 75 aircraft, for a total of 225 helicopters and 250 fixed-wing aircraft. Three MAGs—MAG 16, 36 and 39—equipped with helicopters were based at Da Nang, Chu Lai, Quang Tri and Phu Bai. MAG 11 at Da Nang flew F-4 and A-6 fighter-bombers. MAG 12 at Chu Lai was an A-4 and A-6 attack squadron, and MAG 13 at Chu Lai flew A-4s.

Although the U.S. Marine UH-34 Helicopter Squadron had been sent to Soc Trang in IV Corps in April 1962, it was not until May 1965, when the U.S. buildup in Vietnam began in earnest, that the

First Marine Aircraft Wing (First MAW) head-quarters was established at Da Nang. Designated Deputy Commander of the III Marine Amphibi-ous Force (III MAF), the Commanding General of the First MAW was the Tactical Air Commander for III MAF.

Although in Vietnam the First MAW was rein-forced to support both the First and Third Marine Divisions, a Marine air wing normally supports a single Marine division and is kept directly under Marine Corps control. In Vietnam this Marine Corps concept clashed with Air Force doctrine, which called for a "single manager" for all air operations within a theater of war. The Air Force felt that control of the First MAW should be under the Commanding General of the Seventh Air Force, who was also the Deputy Commander of the MACV (U.S. Military Assistance Com-mand Vietnam) and controlled all other air opera-tions in Vietnam. Conflict on this issue came to a head during the Tet Offensive of 1968, and in March President Johnson made the decision that Marine Corps air operations would come under the single manager concept, i.e., the Commanding General of the Seventh Air Force. This included the helicopter support provided by the three MAG helicopter groups and the close air support provided by the three MAG fighter-bomber groups. It did not, however, apply to the consider-able number of sorties Marine fighter-bombers flew in support of Rolling Thunder operations over North Vietnam and Steel Tiger operations to interdict the Ho Chi Minh Trail in Laos, which were controlled by the Pacific Command in Honolulu. In addition, Marine ECM (electronic countermeasures) aircraft continued to support Navy carrier-launched air strikes against North Vietnam and Laos.

After five years of combat air operations in Vietnam, the First MAW left Vietnam on April 14, 1971. Two Marines assigned to the First MAW won the Medal of Honor for conspicuous bravery in Vietnam, in addition to other awards. In five years the First MAW lost 252 helicopters in com-bat and another 172 to operational causes (air crashes, mechanical malfunctions etc.); 173 fixed-wing aircraft were also lost, as were an additional 81 to operational causes.

When the North Vietnamese began their Eas-tertide Offensive in 1972, MAG 15 was ordered to move two F-4 squadrons to Da Nang in April for interdiction of enemy supply lines in I Corps and along the Laotian border. Mag 12 transferred two A-4 squadrons in May to Bien Hoa Air Base in III Corps for operations in II and III Corps. In the meantime, Seabees were opening an airfield at Nam Phong in northern Thailand, and in June 1972 MAG 15 was relocated from Da Nang to Nam Phong and began flying combat operations from Thailand against enemy positions in I Corps as well as in Laos and North Vietnam until January 1973.

See also FIGHTERS AND FIGHTER-BOMBERS, HELI-COPTERS, III MARINE AMPHIBIOUS FORCE.

Suggestions for further reading: *The Marines in Vietnam 1954–1973* (Washington, D.C.: History and Museums Division, U.S. Marine Corps, 1974); *U.S. Marines in Vietnam: The Advisory and Com-bat Assistance Era 1954–1964*, by Robert H. Whitlow (Washington, D.C.: U.S. Government Printing Office, 1976); *U.S. Marines in Vietnam: The Landing and the Buildup 1965*, by Jack Shulimson and Charles M. Johnson (Washington, D.C.: U.S. Government Printing Office, 1978); *U.S. Marines in Vietnam: An Expanding War 1966*, by Jack Shulim-son (Washington, D.C.: U.S. Government Print-ing Office, 1982).

FIRST MARINE DIVISION

The first division in U.S. Marine Corps history, the First Marine Division was organized on Feb-ruary 1, 1941. In World War II the division made amphibious assaults on Guadalcanal and Oki-nawa. During the Korean war, the division made an amphibious landing at Inchon and later took part in hard fighting around the Chosin Res-ervoir.

In March 1966 the First Marine Division joined its advance elements in Vietnam. Establishing a headquarters at Chu Lai, the division had its zone of operation originally in the two southern prov-inces of I Corps, Quang Tin and Quang Ngai. In addition to combat operations in these provinces, during the Tet Offensive of 1968, the First Marine Division assisted the South Vietnamese

Army forces in recapturing the city of Hué.

At its peak strength the First Marine Division consisted of four regiments of infantry: the First Marines, Fifth Marines, Seventh Marines and 27th Marines (attached from the Fifth Marine Division at Camp Pendleton, California). The division artillery, the 11th Marine Regiment, had six batallions of 105-mm, 155-mm and 8-inch howitzers. Other combat elements included the First Tank Battalion (with M-48 tanks), the First Antitank Battalion with multibarrel 106-mm recoilless rifle ONTOs, the First Amphibious Tractor Company, the First Reconnaissance Battalion and the First Force Reconnaissance Company.

After the departure of the Third Marine Division in late 1969, the First Marine Division, the only Marine division operating in South Vietnam, had the primary mission of providing a shield for the populated areas of Quang Nam Province. This meant keeping enemy forces at arm's length from the vital port and air base at Da Nang. As the U.S. force reduction continued, the First Marine Division was withdrawn from Vietnam in the spring of 1971. It is currently based at Camp Pendleton, California.

Twenty Marines of the First Marine Division marines won, in addition to other awards, the Medal of Honor for conspicuous bravery on the battlefield in Vietnam, as did two Navy medical corpsmen and one Navy chaplain attached to the division. The First Marine Division was twice awarded the Presidential Unit Citation for gallantry in action in Vietnam and received the Vietnamese Cross of Gallantry with Palm and the Vietnamese Civil Actions Award.

The division has an active veterans' association. Further information can be obtained from Sergeant Major George F. Meyer (USMC, Retired), First Marine Division Association, 1704 Florida Avenue, Woodbridge, Virginia 22191.

See also HUÉ, BATTLE OF; MARINE CORPS, U.S.; III MARINE AMPHIBIOUS FORCE.

Suggestions for further reading: *The 1st Marine Division and Its Regiments* (Washington, D.C.: History and Museums Division, U.S. Marine Corps); "Marine Corps Operations in Vietnam 1965–66, 1967, 1968, 1969–72," by Edwin H. Simmons, in *The Marines in Vietnam 1954–1973* (Washington, D.C.: U.S. Government Printing Office, 1974); *Semper Fidelis: The History of the United States Marine Corps*, by Allan Millett (New York: Macmillan, 1980); *Vietnam Order of Battle*, by Shelby L. Stanton (Washington, D.C.: U.S. News & World Report Books, 1981); *Battle of Hue, Tet 1968*, by Keith W. Noland (Novato, Calif: Presidio Press, 1983). An account of First Marine Division combat actions can be found in Shelby L. Stanton's *The Rise and Fall of an American Army* (Novato, Calif.: Presidio Press, 1985); *U.S. Marines in Vietnam: The Advisory and Combat Assistance Era 1954–1964*, by Robert H. Whitlow (Washington, D.C.: U.S. Government Printing Office, 1977); *U.S. Marines in Vietnam: The Landing and the Buildup 1965*, by Jack Shulimson and Charles M. Johnson (Washington, D.C.: U.S. Government Printing Office, 1978); *U.S. Marines in Vietnam: An Expanding War 1966*, by Jack Shulimson (Washington, D.C.: U.S. Government Printing Office, 1982). For a fictionalized account of Marine Corps operations in Vietnam, see Vietnam Marine Corps veteran James Webb's *Fields of Fire* (Englewood Cliffs: Prentice-Hall, 1978).

Insignia of the First Marine Division.

FIRST SIGNAL BRIGADE

Destined to become the largest combat signal unit ever formed, the First Signal Brigade arrived in Vietnam from Fort Gordon, Georgia in April 1966. With 200 sites in Vietnam and Thailand, it operated the most comprehensive military communications-electronics system in the history of warfare.

Subordinate to the brigade were four signal groups, each with a varying number of signal battalions and separate signal companies. The Second Signal Group provided communications support for II and IV Corps, the 12th Signal Group for I Corps, the 21st Signal Group for III Corps, and the 160th Signal Group for the headquarters complex in the Saigon area. In addition, the brigade assumed the combat theater signal functions of the U.S. Army Strategic Communications Command (STRATCOM).

Among the last U.S. Army units to leave Vietnam, it departed in November 1972.

Suggestions for further reading: *Vietnam Order of Battle,* by Shelby L. Stanton (Washington, D.C.: U.S. News Books, 1981); *Communications-Electronics 1962-1970,* by Thomas M. Rienzi (Washington, D.C.: U.S. Government Printing Office, 1972).

FLAMING DART OPERATION

Operational name for U.S. air strikes on North Vietnam just above the DMZ in reprisal for Viet Cong attacks on American installations at Pleiku and Qui Nhon. The beginning of a new air power strategy to increase pressure on North Vietnam to halt its aggression, the strikes were approved by President Lyndon B. Johnson in December 1964 and carried out in February 1965. Flaming Dart was superseded by Operation Rolling Thunder in March 1965.

see also ROLLING THUNDER OPERATION.

Suggestions for further reading: *Airpower in Three Wars* by William W. Momyer (Washington, D.C.: U.S. Government Printing Office, 1978).

FLIGHT

The lowest organizational unit in the U.S. Air Force. In Vietnam it consisted of approximately five aircraft and their crews and was commanded by a major. There were usually four flights in each squadron.

See also SQUADRON.

FORD, GERALD R(UDOLPH) (1913–   )

Ford was born on July 14, 1913 in Omaha, Nebraska. Graduating from the University of Michigan in 1935 and Yale Law School in 1941, he served as a U.S. Navy officer in World War II. He was elected to the U.S. House of Representatives in 1948 and served there until appointed Vice President by President Richard Nixon in October 1973. When President Nixon resigned from office on August 9, 1974, Ford became the 38th President of the United States.

In a sense, Ford's limited involvement as President with the Vietnam war mirrored the public's attitude toward that war in 1975. Shortly before leaving office, Nixon had signed into law a bill imposing a $1 billion ceiling on aid to South Vietnam. When the House of Representatives voted to trim the actual appropriation to $700 million, Ford reassured President Thieu in a letter that U.S. support would be "adequate." But as the communists drove toward Saigon in violation of the 1973 Paris Accords, Ford made no serious attempt to intervene, although the United States had promised it would do so if the North Vietnamese violated the accords. Two days before the fall of Saigon, Ford, in a speech he gave at Tulane University, conceded that America's war in Vietnam was over: "Today, Americans can regain the sense of pride that existed before Vietnam. But it cannot be achieved by refighting a war that is finished. . . . These events, tragic as they are, portend neither the end of the world nor of America's leadership in the world."

In 1976 Gerald Ford was defeated for reelection and returned to private life.

See also FINAL OFFENSIVE.

oint Military Team (FPJMT) came into existence on March 29, 1973. Like the FPJMC it was stationed in Saigon, and it had delegations from the United States, South Vietnam (officially, the Republic of Vietnam), North Vietnam (officially, the Democratic Republic of Vietnam) and the Viet Cong (officially, the Provisional Revolutionary Government of South Vietnam.

The main task for the U.S. delegation was to resolve the status of those Americans still missing in action (MIA). Lists were furnished to the North Vietnamese and Viet Cong, but they refused to cooperate. Stalled most of the time by communist intransigence, the FPJMT did manage to obtain the release of 23 bodies of U.S. MIA personnel in early 1974 after a year of negotiations.

In the course of their duties, the U.S. delegation provided weekly liaison flights in Hanoi, then the only open channel to the North Vietnamese. On one such trip on April 25, 1975, the U.S. delegation received North Vietnam's position on the withdrawal of U.S. personnel from Vietnam upon the fall of Saigon. Essentially the North Vietnamese position was that the U.S. Defense Attaché Office must go, the U.S. embassy could work out its own future and the U.S. delegation, the FPJMT, must stay. When Saigon fell five days later, both the U.S. delegation and the U.S. embassy were prepared to stay in Vietnam. At the last minute, however, they were ordered out by the White House.

On the direction of Ambassador Graham Martin, the three officers and three noncommissioned officers of the U.S. delegation organized and directed the evacuation of some 2,000 South Vietnamese refugees from the embassy compound and departed only when the evacuation was canceled on the morning of April 10, 1975.

See also FOUR PARTY JOINT MILITARY COMMISSION, FINAL OFFENSIVE, FREQUENT WIND OPERATION.

Suggestions for further reading: *Peace with Honor?* by Stuart A. Herrington (Novato, Calif.: Presidio Press, 1984).

FOURTH INFANTRY DIVISION

Its unit insignia and its nickname, the "Ivy Division," derived from the Roman numeral IV, the U.S. Fourth Infantry Division was organized in 1917 and fought in the Aisne-Marne, St. Mihiel and Meuse-Argonne campaigns in World War I. In World War II the Fourth Infantry Division took part in the D-Day invasion, fought in Normandy, liberated Paris and saw heavy action in the Battle of the Bulge.

In September 1966 the Ivy Division (less its Third Brigade) landed in Vietnam for combat operations in II Corps. The Third Brigade (consisting of the Second Battalion, 12th Infantry; Second and Third Battalions, 22nd Infantry; Second Battalion, 77th Artillery; and Second Battalion, 34th Armor) initially was attached to the 25th Infantry Division for operations in III Corps, while the Third Brigade, 25th Infantry Division (consisting of the First Battalion, 14th Infantry; First and Second Battalions, 35th Infantry; Second Battal-

The author's identification card as a member of the Four Party Joint Military Team.

Insignia of the Fourth Infantry Division.

ion, Ninth Artillery; and First Battalion, 69th Armor), which had been operating in II Corps since December 1965, was attached to the Fourth Infantry Division. In August 1967 the brigade headquarters returned to their parent divisions, leaving their battalions in place. In addition to the units enumerated above, the Fourth Infantry Division consisted of five additional battalions of light infantry (the First and Third Battalions, Eighth Infantry; First and Third Battalions, 12th Infantry; and First Battalion, 22nd Infantry) and one battalion—the Second Battalion, Eighth Infantry—of mechanized infantry. Other combat elements included an armored reconnaissance unit, the First Squadron, 10th Cavalry; and in addition to the artillery battalions already listed, two battalions—the Sixth Battalion, 29th Artillery and the Fourth Battalion, 42nd Artillery—of 105-mm howitzers and the Fifth Battalion, 16th Artillery with 155-mm howitzers.

The Central Highlands in II Corps and particularly the border regions between Vietnam and Cambodia were the major battlegrounds for the Fourth Infantry Division in Vietnam. To block infiltration from Cambodia, the Ivy Division attacked North Vietnamese sanctuaries there as part of the Cambodian incursion in 1970. Later that year the division was withdrawn from Vietnam and stationed at Fort Carson, Colorado,

where it remains today as a mechanized infantry division.

The Fourth Infantry Division was awarded the Vietnamese Civil Action Medal and the Vietnamese Cross of Gallantry with Palm. In addition, 11 of its soldiers won the Medal of Honor for bravery on the battlefield. During the fighting in Vietnam, the division suffered 16,844 soldiers killed or wounded in action. This amounted to one-third more than the casualties the division suffered in trench warfare in World War I and almost three-fourths of its 22,660 casualties in World War II.

The Fourth Infantry Division maintains a museum at Fort Carson, Colorado, which has exhibits and material on the division's Vietnam war experience. There is also an active division association, which schedules periodic reunions for members and former members of the Ivy Division. Further information can be obtained from the National Fourth Infantry (Ivy) Division Association's Vietnam war representative, Mr. Russell Armstrong, 206 Luzerne Street, Greensburg, Pennsylvania 15601.

See also CAMBODIA, II CORPS TACTICAL ZONES, 25TH INFANTRY DIVISION.

Suggestions for further reading: *Vietnam Order of Battle*, by Shelby L. Stanton (Washington, D.C.: U.S. News & World Report Books, 1981). Although there is no published history of the Fourth Infantry Division in Vietnam as such, an account of infantry combat there is contained in Ivy Division veteran Frederick Downs' *The Killing Zone: My Life in the Vietnam War* (New York: Norton, 1978). Another source of the division's combat operations, including selected small unit actions, is Shelby L. Stanton's *The Rise and Fall of an American Army* (Novato, Calif.: Presidio Press, 1985).

FRAGGING

A term first used in the Vietnam war, fragging involved the tossing of fragmentation hand grenades—hence the term "fragging"—by U.S. military personnel, usually into sleeping areas, to murder fellow soldiers. In combat units such incidents often involved attempts to rid the unit of leaders perceived to be incompetent and therefore a liability in battle. The use of such draconian means to dispose of incompetent leadership in order to increase chances of survival on the battlefield was not unknown in warfare; in the American Revolutionary War instances were recorded of incompetent officers being "hoisted" by canteens filled with gunpowder. In rear-echelon units, however, where the majority of such incidents occurred, fragging was often drug related.

Practically nonexistent in the first years of U.S. ground combat involvement, fragging first surfaced in the late 1960s as the rapid turnover of personnel weakened unit cohesion, as leadership declined in the face of repetitive Vietnam tours, as the sense of purpose evaporated with the gradual U.S. withdrawal from the war and as public disenchantment with an apparently inconclusive and unending war spread to the battle area.

Although fragging received much attention, the actual number of cases was comparatively small. In 1969 the U.S. Army reported 126 incidents, involving 76 officers or NCOs and resulting in 37 deaths. In 1971 there were 333 incidents, involving 158 officers or NCOs and resulting in 12 deaths. By 1972 most Army troops had been withdrawn from Vietnam. The rate of incidents per thousand soldiers ranged from 0.35 in 1969 to 1.75 in 1971.

Suggestions for further reading: *America in Vietnam*, by Guenter Lewy (New York: Oxford University Press, 1978).

FRANCE

See Part I, THE SETTING.

FREE FIRE ZONES

One of the most misunderstood aspects of the Vietnam war, the very term "free fire zone," with its connotation of indiscriminate use of firepower, provoked an emotional reaction among many Americans. The irony was that in World War II, for example, the entire continent of Europe was generally a free fire zone, as was

everything north of the front lines in the Korean war. In Vietnam an attempt was made to limit such indiscriminate use of firepower, and permission had to be received from Vietnamese province and district chiefs before artillery or air attacks could be made. Only uninhabited areas or areas totally under enemy control were approved by Vietnamese authorities as free fire zones.

In December 1965 the official designation of such areas was changed to specified strike zones (SSZ), to correct the connotation of indiscriminate use of firepower, but the damage was already done and the term "free fire zone" continued to be widely used throughout the war.

See also FAC (FORWARD AIR CONTROL).

Suggestions for further reading: *America in Vietnam*, by Guenter Lewy (New York: Oxford University Press, 1978).

FREE WORLD MILITARY FORCES

The designation of allied units deployed to Vietnam to support the South Vietnamese, Free World Military Forces included units from Australia, South Korea, Thailand, New Zealand and the Philippines and 30 advisers from Taiwan. Several other countries sent relief or commodity aid at varying times after 1964. All told, 39 nations besides the United States helped South Vietnam under the Free World assistance program. They included Japan, Pakistan, Iran, Israel, Turkey, Liberia, Tunisia, Belgium, Ireland, United Kingdom, Canada, Venezuela and Brazil.

Allied combat forces at their height in 1969 included 7,672 Australians, 48,869 Koreans, 11,568 Thais, 552 New Zealanders, 189 Filipinos (down from 1,576 in 1968), 29 Taiwanese and 10 Spaniards, organized into 31 infantry battalions. The 1969 total of some 68,889 Free World military personnel was significantly greater than the 39,000 U.N. soldiers sent by other nations to assist the United States and South Korea during the Korean war.

See also AUSTRALIA; KOREA, SOUTH; NEW ZEALAND; PHILIPPINES; TAIWAN; THAILAND.

Suggestions for further reading: *Allied Participa-*

An Australian soldier instructs a South Vietnamese soldier in the use of the M-79 grenade launcher at the Duc My Ranger Training Center. (Courtesy U.S. Army.)

tion in Vietnam, by Stanley R. Larsen and James L. Collins, Jr. (Washington, D.C.: U.S. Government Printing Office, 1975).

FREQUENT WIND OPERATION

Designation for the evacuation of U.S. embassy and military personnel and selected Vietnamese civilians from Saigon on April 29–30, 1975. Conducted by Task Force 76 of the U.S. Seventh Fleet, with the aircraft carriers *Enterprise* and *Coral Sea* of Task Force 77 providing air cover, the operation began at 11:08 AM local time on April 29, 1975. At the primary evacuation site, the Defense Attaché Office compound at Tan Son Nhut Air Base in the suburbs of Saigon, some 5,000 U.S. civilian and military personnel and South Vietnamese were evacuated by 9:00 PM. The evacuation continued at the embassy in downtown Saigon until 5:00 AM

on the morning of April 20. There, Ambassador Graham Martin and 2,100 American, South Vietnamese and other foreign nationals were rescued. Two hours later North Vietnamese tanks crashed through the gates of the nearby Presidential Palace and Saigon fell.

In addition to the formal evacuation, South Vietnamese Air Force aircraft loaded with aircrews and their families made for Task Force 76. Ships of the task force recovered 41 such aircraft, but another 54 were thrown over the side to make room for incoming U.S. evacuation helicopters. This aerial exodus was complemented by an outgoing tide of junks, sampans and small craft of all types as well as barges towed to sea by tugboats of the Military Sealift Command (MSC). Some 30,000 Vietnamese sailors, their families and other civilians were carried to safety by a flotilla of 26 South Vietnamese Navy and other vessels.

On May 2, 1975 Task Force 76 carrying 6,000 passengers; nine MSC transports, with 44,000

A U.S. Marine CH-53 Sea Stallion aboard the U.S.S. *Okinawa*, which was used as an evacuation ship during Operation Frequent Wind. (Courtesy Stuart Herrington, U.S. Army.)

refugees; and the South Vietnamese Navy flotilla—some 80,000 evacuees in all—set sail for reception centers in the Philippines and Guam.

See also BOAT PEOPLE, FINAL OFFENSIVE.

Suggestions for further reading: *A Short History of the United States Navy and the Southeast Asian Conflict 1950-1975,* by Edward J. Marolda and G. Wesley Pryce, III (Washington, D.C.: Naval Historical Center, 1984); *Without Honor: Defeat in Vietnam and Cambodia,* by Arnold R. Isaacs (Baltimore: Johns Hopkins Press, 1983); *Peace with Honor?* by Stuart A. Herrington (Novato, Calif.: Presidio Press, 1984); *Last Flight from Saigon,* edited by A.J.C. Lavalle (Washington, D.C.: U.S. Government Printing Office, 1978).

FULBRIGHT, J(AMES) WILLIAM (1905-   )

Born in Sumner, Missouri on April 9, 1905, Fulbright graduated from the University of Arkansas in 1925, attended Oxford University on a Rhodes scholarship and earned a law degree from George Washington University in 1931. Elected to the U.S. Senate from Arkansas in 1944, he became Chairman of the Foreign Affairs Committee in 1959.

During the Kennedy Administration, Fulbright

began an involvement in Vietnam affairs that would become his major preoccupation for the remainder of his Senate career. Although he expressed doubts about American aid to Vietnam as early as 1961, Fulbright, who was an enthusiastic supporter of Lyndon Johnson, initially backed the President's policy in Vietnam. At Johnson's request he introduced the Tonkin Gulf Resolution in the Senate on August 6, 1964, a move he came to regret. Despite growing doubts, he continued to express approval of the President's Vietnam policy even after Johnson ordered systematic bombing of the north in February 1965. Yet he publicly questioned the administration's belief that a defeat in Vietnam would lead to Chinese expansion in the area.

Fulbright voiced caustic criticisms of Vietnam policy during televised hearings of the Foreign Relations Committee in February 1966. During the hearings foreign policy critic George Kennan and retired General James Gavin questioned the strategic need for U.S. involvement in Southeast Asia and warned of a possible war with China, while top administration aides Maxwell Taylor and Dean Rusk insisted that the United States was engaged in a limited war which was necessary to halt Chinese expansion in the area. At Johns Hopkins University in April, Fulbright stated that America was in danger of succumbing to the "arrogance of power which has afflicted, weakened and in some cases destroyed great nations in the past."

During February 1968 Fulbright held closed hearings to determine if the United States had provoked the Tonkin Gulf Incident, if North Vietnamese vessels had actually attacked U.S. ships and if the administration had misled Congress into passing the Tonkin Gulf Resolution. Fulbright charged that the resolution was introduced under "a completely false idea of what had happened" and that his own support was "based upon information which was not true." Although he denounced the resolution, Fulbright did not attempt to have it repealed at the time because he felt some senators who opposed the war would nonetheless feel compelled to support the President on this issue.

After President Nixon took office in 1969, Fulbright applauded the President's announced intention to gradually withdraw all U.S. troops. However, after nationwide protests against the war in October 1969, he deplored Nixon's call for a moratorium on dissent and instead urged a "moratorium on killing." In December he characterized "Vietnamization" as another form of waging "a continuing war of stalemate and attrition."

Fulbright attacked the President's decision to invade Cambodia in 1970, and after the United States provided support for a South Vietnamese invasion of Laos in 1971, he held "end-the-war" hearings to consider legislation that would curb the President's war-making powers. In 1973 he backed the War Powers Act.

Fulbright lost the Democratic senatorial primary to Governor Dale Bumpers in 1974.

See also ANTIWAR MOVEMENT; JOHNSON, LYNDON B.; TONKIN GULF RESOLUTION; WAR POWERS ACT.

Suggestions for further reading: *The Arrogance of Power* and *The Crippled Giant*, by J. William Fulbright (New York: Random House, 1967 and 1972); *Fulbright: The Dissenter*, by Haynes Johnson and Bernard Gwertzman (Garden City, N.Y.: Doubleday & Co., 1968).

GAME WARDEN OPERATION

Designation for an operation established on December 18, 1965 by the U.S. Navy to control enemy transportation of arms and supplies on the rivers and inland waterways of South Vietnam. It was conducted by the River Patrol Force (Task Force 116) under the command of U.S. Naval Forces Vietnam.

See also RIVER PATROL FORCE (TASK FORCE 116).

Suggestions for further reading: *A Short History of the United States Navy and the Southeast Asian Conflict 1950–1975*, by Edward J. Marolda and G. Wesley Pryce, III (Washington, D.C.: Naval Historical Center, 1984).

GENEVA CONFERENCES

The first and second Geneva Conferences had a major impact on the Vietnam war. The first conference was held in 1954 to end the war in Indochina between the French and the Viet Minh (1946–54). The purpose of the second conference, in 1961–62, was to resolve the fate of Laos. The

outcome of neither conference was what it appeared to be.

By early 1954 the Viet Minh had almost beaten the French, and battlefield victory appeared at hand. Under pressure from both China and the Soviet Union, however, the communists agreed to meet with the French at Geneva to negotiate an end to the war. The conference began on April 26, 1954, cochaired by Great Britain and the Soviet Union, with representatives from the United States, France, China, the State of Vietnam (which was to become South Vietnam, officially the Republic of Vietnam [RVN]), the Democratic Republic of Vietnam (DRV) (which was to become North Vietnam), Cambodia and Laos.

On May 7, 1954 Dien Bien Phu fell to the Viet Minh, and France's will to continue the war, already weakened, collapsed entirely. Final negotiations for armistice were conducted in Geneva and a truce was signed by representatives of the French high command and the DRV on July 20, 1954, bringing hostilities in Indochina to a halt. (Since their victory in 1975 and their subsequent hostilities with their former Chinese allies, the North Vietnamese have complained that China pressured them into signing the 1954 agreement.)

The agreement fixed a provisional demarcation line roughly along the 17th parallel (which was to become the DMZ), pending countrywide elections to be held in July 1956. It also allowed the evacuation of French forces north of that line and Viet Minh forces south of it. Freedom of movement from either zone was allowed for 300 days, and restrictions were imposed on future military alliances. An International Control Commission (ICC) was formed with representatives from India, Canada and Poland to supervise implementation of the agreement, including the scheduled elections. In addition to the truce agreement, a separate "Final Declaration" on July 21, 1954 took note of the various elements of the agreement. This whole package came to be known as the Geneva Accords.

The armistice agreement was reached over the objection of South Vietnam, which did not sign it. The South Vietnamese also objected to the terms of the Final Agreement, which had been unilaterally agreed to by the French without prior consultation with South Vietnamese delegates to the conference. Likewise, the United States did not concur with either of these documents but pledged that it would refrain from use of force or the threat of force to disturb their provisions. However, it declared that it would look upon any renewed aggression in violation of the agreement "with grave concern." The statement was later invoked as a justification for U.S. involvement in Vietnam.

The 1954 Geneva Conference was, at best, a truce. While it ended the war between the French and the Viet Minh, by failing to deal with the primary issues involved (e.g., who would govern all of Vietnam), it almost guaranteed that a second Indochina war would follow. Within five years North and South Vietnam were openly at war.

Aimed at ending an ongoing civil war in Laos, the second Geneva Conference began in May 1961. Attended by 14 nations, the conference included the major powers (the United States, the Soviet Union, China, Great Britain and France), the member nations of the ICC (Canada, India and Poland) and the nations of mainland Southeast Asia (South Vietnam, North Vietnam, Cambodia, Laos, Thailand and Burma). In July 1962 the conference formally declared the neutrality of Laos

and created a neutral coalition government there under Prince Souvanna Phouma.

Believing Soviet guarantees of this "neutrality" (which the Soviets had neither the means nor the inclination to enforce), the U.S. government abandoned its focus on training the South Vietnamese to resist a cross-border Korean war-type invasion by an external enemy—and particularly to halt infiltration of communist guerrillas and supplies into South Vietnam along the Ho Chi Minh Trail through Laos, which had been constructed three years earlier—and concentrated instead on South Vietnam's internal problems. This change of orientation, reinforced by a fascination with new theories of counterinsurgency, was eventually to prove fatal.

See also DMZ (DEMILITARIZED ZONE); DULLES, JOHN FOSTER; ELECTIONS; HO CHI MINH TRAIL; LAOS; REFUGEES.

Suggestions for further reading: *The Devil and John Foster Dulles*, by Townsend Hoopes (Boston: Atlantic-Little, Brown, 1973); *Vietnam: A History*, by Stanley Karnow (New York: Viking, 1983); *Without Honor: Defeat in Vietnam and Cambodia*, by Arnold R. Isaacs (Baltimore: Johns Hopkins Press, 1983).

GIAP, VO NGUYEN (1912-   )

Born in 1912 in Quang Binh Province in the French protectorate of Annam (which was to become North Vietnam's southernmost province during the Vietnam war), Giap graduated from the French-run Lycée Albert Sarraut and University of Hanoi Law School in the mid 1930s. A high school history teacher, he was active in the communist underground. His anti-French sentiments were further hardened by the death of his wife in a French jail in 1941. Recruited by Ho Chi Minh in the early 1940s to help shape the Viet Minh movement, Giap organized his first military force in December 1944—a 34-man armed propaganda "brigade."

From this modest beginning, General Giap became the Viet Minh's foremost military commander during the war with the French (1946–54). In 1954 he won lasting fame by directing the Viet

Vo Nguyen Giap in 1975. (AP/Wide World Photos.)

Minh siege that overwhelmed the French garrison at Dien Bien Phu and effectively won Vietnam its independence. Giap became North Vietnam's Minister of Defense, a member of the ruling Politburo and Commander-in-Chief of the North Vietnamese Army (NVA).

A proponent of "armed struggle" rather than "political struggle" within the Poliburo, Giap favored attacking the American military head on during the Vietnam war. Military officers are often accused of "fighting the last war." Giap spent almost 10 years attempting to repeat his victory in the Battle of Dien Bien Phu, beginning with the Battle of Ia Drang in 1965, when NVA forces fought the U.S. First Cavalry Division in direct combat, and continuing with NVA and Viet Cong assaults on fortified U.S. fire bases, the siege of the U.S. 26th Marine Regiment at Khe Sanh in 1968 and the Tet Offensive that same year, in which frontal attacks were made on U.S. and South Vietnamese Army positions countrywide. These tactics were disastrous. Giap later admitted that such attacks had cost the lives of more than 500,000 NVA soldiers between 196· and 1969. The equivalent in terms of population to 7 million Americans killed, these losses ha· been to no appreciable gain. By late 1968 the Vie· Cong had been virtually destroyed and the NVA controlled no appreciable territory in the south.

In 1972 Giap convinced the Politburo tha· because the majority of U.S. ground comba· forces had been withdrawn, the time was ripe t· commit the entire NVA to combat in the south· Launching some 12 infantry divisions reinforce· by Soviet-supplied tanks and artillery in wha· became known as the Eastertide Offensive in March 1972, Giap had initial successes in I Corp· with the capture of the provincial capital o· Quang Tri. But in II and III Corps, his attacks were· stopped cold by a determined South Vietnamese· defense supported by massive American fir· power, including air strikes by U.S. B-52 bombers· Even in I Corps the NVA could not hold its gains· and by September 16, 1972 South Vietnamese· counterattacks had driven the attackers out o· Quang Tri. Estimates are that the NVA suffere· more than 100,000 casualties and lost more than· half of its tanks and heavy artillery.

Tarnished by these successive failures, Genera· Giap was eased from power in favor of his pro· tégé, NVA Chief of Staff Senior General Van· Tien Dung, who had commanded a division under· Giap at Dien Bien Phu. It was Dung, not Giap· who planned and commanded the Final Offensiv· that conquered South Vietnam in 1975. In 198C· General Giap was formally replaced as Minister o· Defense by General Dung and he now lives in· virtual retirement.

See also AN LOC, BATTLE OF; ARMED STRUGGLE· DIEN BIEN PHU; DUNG, VAN TIEN; EASTERTIDE· OFFENSIVE; FINAL OFFENSIVE; FIRE SUPPORT BASES· U.S.; IA DRANG, BATTLE OF; KHE SANH, BATTLE OF· POLITICAL STRUGGLE; QUANG TRI, BATTLE OF; TET· OFFENSIVE; VIET MINH.

Suggestions for further reading: *Dien Bien Phu* by Vo Nguyen Giap (Hanoi: Foreign Language· Publishing House, 1962); *Big Victory, Big Task*, by· Vo Nguyen Giap (New York: Praeger, 1967)· *Unforgettable Days* by Vo Nguyen Giap (Hanoi: Foreign Language Publishing House, 1978); *Vietnam A History*, by Stanley Karnow (New York: Viking· 1983).

GOLDBERG, ARTHUR J(OSEPH) (1908–   )

Born on August 8, 1908 in Chicago, Goldberg worked his through college and law school, practiced labor law and then served with the Office of Strategic Services during World War II. In 1948 he became general counsel for the United Steelworkers of America. After serving as President Kennedy's Secretary of Labor, Goldberg was appointed to the Supreme Court in August 1962.

Accepting President Johnson's assurances that he would have a direct hand in shaping American foreign policy and ending the Vietnam war, Goldberg accepted the post of Ambassador to the United Nations in July 1965.

The Vietnam war dominated Goldberg's U.N. tenure, and much of his work was directed toward finding a formula that would start negotiations between the United States and North Vietnam. Goldberg was unsuccessful in this task. The progressive escalation of the air war was Johnson's chief strategy for pressuring the North Vietnamese to negotiate. In turn, Hanoi maintained that the bombing of the north was the main stumbling block to the start of negotiations. Goldberg, who was not privy to the highest levels of administration decision making, often found himself out of step with or unaware of American military and political policy in Southeast Asia.

Nevertheless, he played an important role in the March 1968 reassessment of policy in Vietnam by the Senior Advisory Group, which recommended a bombing halt and de-escalation of the war. On March 31 Johnson announced the United States would de-escalate.

Goldberg resigned on April 25, 1968. Johnson accepted his departure in an unusually "chilly" letter that failed to praise him for his U.N. service. In 1969, Goldberg spoke at the October 15 Moratorium protest against the war.

See also ANTIWAR MOVEMENT; BUNDY, McGEORGE; JOHNSON, LYNDON B; SENIOR ADVISORY GROUP.

GOLD STAR

The U.S. Navy, Marine Corps and Coast Guard equivalent of the U.S. Army's Oak Leaf Cluster. A gold star is worn on medal ribbons to denote a subsequent award of the same decoration.

See also OAK LEAF CLUSTER.

GOLDWATER, BARRY M(ORSE) (1909–   )

Born on January 1, 1909 in Phoenix, Arizona, Goldwater left the University of Arizona after one year and became president of the family department store in 1937. He served with the Army Transport Command during World War II. In 1952 he won election to the U.S. Senate, and became the most effective spokesman of the Republican Party's conservative wing. Goldwater ran for President in 1964 but lost the election to Lyndon B. Johnson by a landslide. In 1968 he was reelected to the Senate.

Goldwater was one of the Senate's strongest advocates of America's Vietnam involvement. In 1972, for example, he attacked critics of the renewed bombing of North Vietnam after the North Vietnamese had started an offensive in the south. When raids against the port of Haiphong raised fears about Soviet involvement if Russian ships were hit, Goldwater said the raids were better than the "dilly-dally" bombing of supply lines that had gone on before.

Goldwater opposed all congressional efforts to legislate an end to the war, including the Cooper-Church Amendment to limit the President's authority to conduct military operations in Cambodia. At the same time he supported the Nixon Administration's attempts to end the war through negotiations. When a peace treaty was concluded in 1973, Goldwater, who was one of the strongest congressional supporters of the Saigon government, warned the South Vietnamese government not be an obstacle to the peace agreement. He continued to support military aid for South Vietnam after the peace treaty was signed. When the Senate Armed Services Committee debated the Ford Administration's request for additional military aid in April 1975, two weeks before the communists captured Saigon, Goldwater favored sending at least an additional $101 million. The committee rejected both this proposal and a $70 million proposal, which Goldwater opposed as inadequate.

GRAVEL, MIKE (1930–)

Born on May 13, 1930 in Springfield, Massachusetts, Gravel was a counterintelligence officer with the Army in Europe from 1951 to 1954. After graduating from Columbia University in 1956 with a B.A. in economics, he moved to Alaska and entered state politics. In 1968 he defeated Senator Ernest Gruening in the Democratic primary and went on to win the election.

Gravel gained national attention in spring 1971 when he placed portions of the *Pentagon Papers*, a top secret Defense Department study of U.S. involvement in Southeast Asia, into the Senate record. On June 29, the day after a federal grand jury indicted Daniel Ellsberg on charges of stealing the *Pentagon Papers*, Gravel called reporters to a late-night session of his Senate subcommittee and read aloud from a copy of the *Pentagon Papers* for three hours. In June 1972 the Supreme Court ruled 5 to 4 that Gravel could not be subpoenaed or indicted for reading the documents to the press.

Thereafter Gravel took an increasingly active role in opposing the Vietnam war, leading a three-month filibuster against extension of the draft and supporting attempts to cut off funding for the war.

In 1980 Gravel lost the Democratic senatorial primary.

See also ANTIWAR MOVEMENT; ELLSBERG, DANIEL; PENTAGON PAPERS.

GROUP

In the U.S. Army a group is a command structure controlling several battalion-sized elements and is subordinate to a brigade. Groups are used primarily by support and service commands that have a very large number of battalions under them. The Army Special Forces uses a fixed group structure as its highest ranking organizational component. Groups are usually commanded by colonels.

GRUENING, ERNEST H(ENRY) (1887–1974)

Born on February 6, 1887 in New York City, Gruening graduated from Harvard Medical School in 1912 but chose to become a journalist, editing several liberal publications in the 1920s and 1930s. Gruening was Governor of Alaska from 1939 to 1952 and became Alaska's first Senator in 1959.

Gruening was one of the earliest congressional critics of American involvement in Vietnam, voicing opposition in a March 1964 Senate speech entitled "The United States Should Get Out of Vietnam." In August 1964 he and Senator Wayne Morse cast the only votes against the Tonkin Gulf Resolution. He, Morse and Senator Gaylord Nelson consistently voted against the administration's requests for military appropriations for Southeast Asia, often forming the only opposition to such expenditures from 1965 to 1968.

Gruening stated repeatedly that the area was not essential to American security. Calling for negotiations with Hanoi, he and Morse assailed the bombing of North Vietnam in February 1965, and the following year Gruening was the only senator to support Morse's proposal to repeal the Tonkin Gulf Resolution. At the same time the Senate rejected, by a vote of 75 to 2, his amendment to prohibit sending draftees to Southeast Asia unless they volunteered for service there.

Gruening became one of the few Senators to associate himself with the early antiwar movement, and in April 1965 in Washington, D.C. he addressed the first large demonstration against the war.

Gruening, at age 81, lost the 1968 Democratic senatorial primary. He died on June 26, 1974.

See also ANTIWAR MOVEMENT; MORSE, WAYNE; TONKIN GULF RESOLUTION.

GUERRILLA WAR

Taking its name from the war waged by Spanish civilian forces against the French Army during the 1810–1812 Peninsular campaign in the Napoleonic war, guerrilla war involves the use of irregular forces to harass, interdict and wear down an opposing army by cutting communications, damaging roads, destroying bridges, raiding isolated outposts and other such measures. It is not intended to bring about total victory but to pave the way for regular forces and facilitate their combat operations. In World War II Ukrainian guerrilla forces, for example, operated in exactly this manner in support of Red Army operations against the Nazis, and similar actions were taken by the French underground in support of Allied operations on the western front.

Revolutionary war, on the other hand, involves seizure of power by insurgents operating on their own rather than in conjunction with regular forces. Although the Viet Cong were hailed as a revolutionary force (and many of them undoubtedly believed they were members of such a force), the North Vietnamese viewed them as an expendable guerrilla force whose purpose was to wear down the Americans and South Vietnamese. As a "revolutionary force" the Viet Cong lost, most decisively to the North Vietnamese, who cast them aside once victory was achieved. As a "guerrilla force," however, the Viet Cong were most successful in wearing down both U.S. and South Vietnamese forces.

See also NVA (NORTH VIETNAMESE ARMY), REVOLUTIONARY WAR, VIET CONG.

Suggestions for further reading: *On Strategy: A Critical Analysis of the Vietnam War* by Harry G. Summers, Jr. (Novato, Calif.: Presidio Press, 1982).

GULF OF TONKIN INCIDENT

See TONKIN GULF RESOLUTION.

GUNSHIPS

A major tactical innovation by American forces during the Vietnam war was the use of fixed-wing U.S. Air Force gunships to provide close air support for ground combat forces and to interdict enemy supply lines.

AH-1G Cobra gunships in action.

First deployed to Vietnam in December 1964, the original gunships were modified World War II-vintage twin-engine C-47 Gooneybird cargo planes. Redesignated the AC-47, with the more elegant name Dragonship, they were known to ground soldiers as "Puffs" (from the song "Puff, the Magic Dragon") or "Spookies." These AC-47s, and later modified AC-119 Flying Boxcars, were outfitted with three rapid-fire 7.62-mm gatling guns (i.e., multibarreled machine guns), each capable of firing 6,000 rounds per minute. They also carried a number of aerial parachute flares that could turn night into day.

In 1968 four-engine C-130 Hercules cargo planes were converted to gunships, AC-130s. In addition to two rapid-fire 7.62-mm and four 20-mm Vulcan gatling guns, they were equipped with 40-mm Bofers cannons as well as infrared sensors, radar, low-light television and laser designators to mark targets for accompanying fighters and fighter-bombers. Used not only for close support of ground troops but also to interdict the Ho Chi Minh Trail, the AC-130 became the best truck destroyer of the war.

Another innovation was the development of U.S. Army and Marine Corps helicopter gunships. In the early 1960s UH-1 Huey helicopter gunships were improvised by fitting UH-1s with machine guns and air-to-ground rocket pods. CH-47 Chinook helicopters were also fitted with armament pods, including quad 7.62-mm and 50-caliber machine guns and 20 mm-cannons. Beginning in 1967, this force of improvised gunships was augmented by specially designed AH-1 Cobra gunships. Typical armament included a bow-mounted multibarreled machine gun and 40-mm grenade launcher and 2.75-inch rocket pods. From 1966 to 1971, 3,952,000 helicopter attack sorties were launched over Vietnam, the majority in close support of ground operations.

See also CLOSE AIR SUPPORT, HELICOPTERS, HO CHI MINH TRAIL, TACTICAL AIR COMMAND.

Suggestions for further reading: For fixed-wing gunships, see *Airpower in Three Wars*, by William W. Momyer (Washington, D.C.: U.S. Government Printing Office, 1978; *The Vietnam Experience: Thunder from Above*, by John Morrocco (Boston: Boston Publishing Co., 1984); *The United States Air Force in Southeast Asia: Fixed Wing Gunships*, by Jack S. Ballard (Washington, D.C.: U.S. Government Printing Office, 1982). For helicopter gunships, see *Vietnam Order of Battle*, by Shelby L. Stanton (Washington, D.C.: U.S. News & World Report Books, 1981); *Airmobility, 1961–1971*, by John J. Tolson (Washington, D.C.: U.S. Government Printing Office, 1973).

HAIG, ALEXANDER (1924–)

Born on December 2, 1924 in Bala-Cynwyd, Pennsylvania, Haig graduated from the U.S. Military Academy in 1947 and received an MA in International Relations from Georgetown in 1961. In between his studies, Haig served in Japan, Korea and Vietnam and performed in various staff capacities at the Pentagon. In the mid-1960s he saw action in Vietnam as Commander of the First Battalion, 26th Infantry.

In late 1968 he was recommended to incoming National Security Adviser Henry Kissinger, who made Haig his military assistant at the National Security Council. Haig cemented his relationship with Kissinger by being a discreetly inconspicuous and competent staff man who solidly supported his superior on such controversial policies as the mining of Haiphong harbor and the bombing of Hanoi during the final phase of the Vietnam war. Haig's staff responsibilities evolved and expanded as Kissinger's prominence as a top presidential adviser grew. In June 1970, Haig was appointed Deputy Assistant to the President.

Haig was often used as a diplomatic trouble-shooter, particularly in Southeast Asia. As early as 1970 he began a series of visits to Vietnam to provide President Nixon with a first-hand assessment of the situation there. Then as negotiations for a peace settlement began to gain momentum during the summer of 1972, Haig became the major diplomatic courier between President Nixon and South Vietnamese President Nguyen Van Thieu. Between October 1972 and January 1973 Haig made over a dozen trips to South Vietnam acting in both a fact-finding capacity and in a persuasive role to keep President Thieu from sabotaging the Paris peace talks.

Haig continued his shuttle diplomacy during the winter of 1972. Fully aware of Nixon's belief that the prospect of the new and more dovish incoming Senate made a speedy settlement of the Vietnam conflict imperative, Haig took a tough line with President Thieu, who had refused to sign a draft agreement in October. Because Thieu also respected Haig's views as "a soldier and as someone completely familiar with communist treachery," Haig finally succeeded in securing South Vietnamese acquiescence to the January 27, 1973 cease-fire accord.

In December 1974 Haig assumed command of NATO forces and continued in that post into the Carter presidency.

See also KISSINGER, HENRY A.; NIXON, RICHARD M.; THIEU, NGUYEN VAN.

HAIPHONG

A city developed by the French as the port for Hanoi, Haiphong is located about 60 miles east of Hanoi on one of the lower tributaries of the Red River. Ten miles inland from the Gulf of Tonkin, it is served by a dredged channel and has docking facilities for oceangoing vessels. A rail line connects Haiphong to Hanoi.

During the Vietnam war Haiphong, with a population of about 180,000, was North Vietnam's most important port, where ships delivered much of Hanoi's war matériel. As U.S. air strikes damaged North Vietnam's rail links with China (and as China slowed down rail shipments from the Soviet Union to North Vietnam because of the widening Sino-Soviet split and because of its opening to the United States in 1971), the port became even more critical. Up to 85 percent of North Vietnam's war supplies were being received through Haiphong.

The U.S. Joint Chiefs of Staff had long advocated mining Haiphong harbor to cut this flow of supplies, but fear of provoking the Soviet Union, as well as certain U.S. allies whose ships used the harbor, prevented such a decision. On May 9, 1972, however, President Nixon ordered the isolation of North Vietnam from external support. Within hours U.S. planes from the aircraft carrier *Coral Sea* dropped magnetic-acoustic sea mines to close Haiphong harbor. Foreign ships were given three days to depart the area, after which time the mines self-armed. From May to December 1972 no large merchant vessels entered or left the harbor, and attempts to bring lighter cargo ashore were foiled by U.S. Navy surface and air strikes.

On February 5, 1973, as part of the Paris Accords' cease-fire agreement, the U.S. Seventh Fleet's Mine Countermeasures Force (Task Force 78) met with North Vietnamese officials in Haiphong and a joint effort was launched to sweep the area of mines. During a six-month operation 10 U.S. Navy ocean minesweepers were involved in clearing the harbor, and Navy instructors trained 40 North Vietnamese personnel in minesweeping operations. On July 26, 1973 the operation was completed and the port of Haiphong was once more open to ocean traffic.

See also LINEBACKER OPERATIONS; NAVY, U.S.

Suggestions for further reading: *A Short History of the United States Navy and the Southeast Asian Conflict,* by Edward J. Marolda and G. Wesley Pryce, III (Washington, D.C.: Naval Historical Center, 1984).

HAI VAN PASS

The Hai Van Pass was located in I Corps on the boundary between Thua Tien and Quang Nam Provinces. Running through the pass was Highway 1, the main north-south highway in Vietnam and the principal supply route from the ports of Chu Lai and Da Nang south of the pass to Hué, Quang Tri and the DMZ north of the pass.

Because of the lack of major port facilities north of the Hai Van Pass and because bad weather could prevent aerial resupply to forces in that area, the Hai Van Pass became what is known in the U.S. military as "key terrain" (defined as terrain whose possession gives the holder a distinct advantage). The North Vietnamese made repeated attempts to close that pass, and U.S. and South Vietnamese forces expended considerable effort to keep it open.

See map at I CORPS TACTICAL ZONE.

HALBERSTAM, DAVID (1934–   )

Born on April 10, 1934 in New York City, Halberstam graduated from Harvard in 1955. In 1960 he joined the *New York Times* and became its correspondent in Vietnam. At the time, the war was not going well for the South Vietnamese government. American correspondents who accurately reported this state of affairs were coming under increasing suspicion by the regime of Ngo Dinh Diem. With colleagues Malcolm Browne of the Associated Press and Neil Sheehan of United Press International, Halberstam began to report the deteriorating military situation in such areas as the Mekong Delta. These correspondents also reported that Diem's regime was indifferent to the needs of most of the population.

The incident that finally drew national attention to what columnist Joseph Alsop derisively called a group of "young crusaders" was a major battle at Ap Bac in January 1963, during which a South Vietnamese division was routed by the communists. Halberstam, Browne and Sheehan wrote critical stories of the battle, quoting U.S. adviser Lieutenant Colonel John Vann on the enemy's combat skill and the reluctance of the South Vietnamese troops to fight.

After writing the Ap Bac story Halberstam was subject to personal attacks. White House Press Secretary Pierre Salinger labeled press reports from Vietnam "emotional and inaccurate." In

October 1963 President Kennedy suggested to *New York Times* publisher Arthur Ochs Sulzberger that Halberstam should be reassigned because he was "too close to the story." Sulzberger refused to shift Halberstam, although the reporter left Vietnam in early 1964 to spend a year at the *Times'* New York bureau.

For his reporting in Vietnam, Halberstam shared a 1964 Pulitzer Prize with Browne. Halberstam later resigned from the *Times*. His book *The Best and the Brightest*, a best-selling indictment of American Vietnam policy, was published in 1972.

See also ANTIWAR MOVEMENT.

Suggestions for further reading: *The Making of a Quagmire* and *The Best and the Brightest*, by David Halberstam (New York: Random House, 1965 and 1972).

HAMBURGER HILL, BATTLE OF

A battle for a hill in the A Shau Valley, in I Corps, in May 1969 that received widespread unfavorable publicity in the United States. The battle of "Hamburger Hill" (a name evidently derived from the fact that the battle turned into a "meat grinder") was part of Operation Apache Snow, which was designed to keep pressure on North Vietnamese Army (NVA) units in the A Shau Valley to prevent them from mounting an attack on the coastal provinces. Apache Snow involved the Third Brigade, U.S. 101st Airborne Division (Airmobile), the U.S. Ninth Marine Regiment and the South Vietnamese Army Third Regiment, First Infantry Division.

After a heliborne assault along the Laotian border on May 10, 1969, the task force swept to the east. First contact with the enemy was made by the 101st Airborne Division's Company B, Third Battalion, 187th Infantry on May 11, 1969 on the slopes of Hill 937, known to the Vietnamese as Ap Bia Mountain. Entrenched in prepared defensive positions, the NVA 29th Regiment's Seventh and Eighth Battalions repulsed this initial contact and on May 14 beat back an attack by the entire Third Battalion, 187th Infantry. A particularly intense battle continued for the next 10 days.

On May 20, 1969 the Third Battalion, 187th Infantry was reinforced by the U.S. 101st Airborne Division's First Battalion, 506th Infantry and Second Battalion, 501st Infantry and an infantry battalion from the South Vietnamese Third Infantry Regiment. In the face of this four-battalion attack, the NVA retreated to sanctuary areas in Laos.

Since the operation was not intended to hold territory but to keep the NVA off balance, the mountain was abandoned soon thereafter and reoccupied by the NVA a month later. American public outrage over what appeared to be a senseless loss of American lives was exacerbated by publication in *Life* magazine of the pictures of the 241 U.S. soldiers killed in less than a week during the Hamburger Hill battle. In a reaction remarkably similar to restrictions imposed during the closing days of the Korean war, General Creighton Abrams, Commander of the U.S. Military Assistance Command Vietnam (COMUSMACV), was ordered to avoid such large-scale battles. From then on, U.S. emphasis was to be placed on "Vietnamization" rather than combat operations.

See also A SHAU VALLEY, 101ST AIRBORNE DIVISION.

Suggestions for further reading: *Vietnam: A History*, by Stanley Karnow (New York: Viking, 1983). An account of the battle is contained in *The Rise and Fall of an American Army*, by Shelby L. Stanton, (Novato, Calif.: Presidio Press, 1985).

HANOI

The capital of North Vietnam (now the capital of the Socialist Republic of Vietnam), Hanoi is located on the Red River in the heart of the fertile Red River Delta, about 75 miles inland from the South China Sea. One of Vietnam's oldest cities, it was the capital of the country from the 10th to the 17th century. During the French colonial period it became the capital of Indochina and took on a decidedly French appearance. Proclaimed the capital of the Democratic Republic of Vietnam by the Viet Minh after their defeat of the French in 1954, at the outbreak of the Vietnam war it was an important industrial center, with a population of some 693,000, and the hub of all rail and waterways network throughout the north.

Contrary to popular opinion, Hanoi itself was relatively undamaged during the Vietnam war. Although bombed intermittently during the war, most of the tonnage was dropped on military targets and especially the Paul Doumer Bridge across the Red River and the rail yards on the opposite side of the river from the city. Antiwar activists' claims of "carpet bombing," especially during the Christmas Bombing in 1972, appear to have been wildly exaggerated. Although selective film footage seemed to validate their charges, visitors to the city have remarked on the lack of visible bomb damage.

See also CHRISTMAS BOMBING.

Suggestions for further reading: *Vietnam: A History*, by Stanley Karnow (New York: Viking, 1983).

The single pedestal Pagoda illustrated on this stamp is the symbol of the city of Hanoi, much in the same way as the Statue of Liberty is the symbol of New York City.

Hanoi street scenes, shot after the war's end.

HARKINS, PAUL DONAL (1904–1984)

Born on May 15, 1904 in Boston, Massachusetts, Harkins graduated from the U.S. Military Academy in 1929. Commissioned in the cavalry, during World War II he served with General George S. Patton's Third Army and was Chief of Staff of the Eighth Army during the closing days of the Korean War.

On February 8, 1962 Harkins became the first Commander of the U.S. Military Assistance Command Vietnam (COMUSMACV). During the next two years he supervised the buildup of the U.S. support effort in Vietnam ordered by President Kennedy and set the structure that would continue throughout the war.

His opposition to the plotting that led to the overthrow and subsequent assassination of South Vietnamese President Ngo Dinh Diem in November 1963 put him at odds with U.S. Ambassador Henry Cabot Lodge. He was also criticized for requiring that optimistic reports be sent from Saigon to Washington, D.C., but such reporting had become traditional in Vietnam years before Harkins arrived. In July 1964 he was replaced by his deputy, General William C. Westmoreland, and retired from active duty that year. General Harkins died on August 21, 1984.

See also DIEM, NGO DINH; MACV (U.S. MILITARY ASSISTANCE COMMAND VIETNAM); LODGE, HENRY CABOT.

Suggestions for further reading: *Vietnam: A History*, by Stanley Karnow (New York: Viking, 1983); *The Best and the Brightest*, by David Halberstam (New York: Random House, 1972); *Command and Control 1950–1969*, by George S. Eckhardt (Washington, D.C.: U.S. Government Printing Office, 1974).

HARRIMAN, W(ILLIAM) AVERELL (1891–1986)

Harriman was born in New York City in 1891 and graduated from Yale in 1913. His long career of public service, begun in the late 1920s when President Roosevelt appointed him to a post in the National Recovery Administration, included serving as Ambassador to the Soviet Union.

Harriman played a key role in shaping U.S. policy in Southeast Asia during the Vietnam war. In 1962 he negotiated the agreement that generated the neutrality of Laos. In March 1963 President Kennedy appointed him Undersecretary of State for Political Affairs. As the American role in Vietnam expanded in the mid-1960s, Harriman maintained a skeptical attitude toward a purely military solution to the war there. During the spring and summer of 1963, he urged that the Administration separate the American effort from the fortunes of Ngo Dinh Diem's government in South Vietnam.

In August 1963, Harriman, Roger Hilsman and Michael Forrestal, an aide to National Security Adviser McGeorge Bundy, drafted a cable that would set the wheels in motion for a U.S. policy decision not to stand in the way of the coup to overthrow Diem, which was carried out on November 1 by South Vietnamese military officers. The cable, sent to Ambassador Henry Cabot Lodge, stated that Diem would have to institute reforms and rid himself of his brother Nhu, who bore responsibility for much of the repression in South Vietnam. The cable went on to say that if Diem refused to dispose of Nhu "we [the United States government] must face the possibility that Diem himself cannot be preserved."

In 1965 President Johnson appointed Harriman Ambassador at Large with the principal duty of handling Southeast Asian affairs. During 1965 and 1966 he traveled around the world seeking support for U.S. Vietnam policy while sounding out the possibilities for a negotiated settlement of the war. When preliminary peace talks opened in May 1968, Harriman went to Paris as chief U.S. negotiator, a post he would hold until succeeded by Henry Cabot Lodge in January 1969.

During the Nixon Administration Harriman pressed for a complete withdrawal of Americans from Vietnam on a fixed schedule. In 1971 he urged Congress to use the power of the purse to end the war.

See also ANTIWAR MOVEMENT; DIEM, NGO DINH; GENEVA CONFERENCES; HILSMAN, ROGER; LODGE, HENRY CABOT; NHU, NGO DINH.

Suggestions for further reading: *Special Envoy to*

Churchill and Stalin, by Averell Harriman (New York: 1975).

HATFIELD, MARK O(DUM) (1922–)

Hatfield was born in Dallas, Oregon on July 22, 1922. After earning his master's degree in political science from Stanford University in 1948, he taught political science at Willamette University. In 1959 Hatfield, a Republican, became Governor of Oregon and in 1966 he won a seat in the U.S. Senate on an antiwar platform.

During the Nixon Administration, Hatfield was one of the major doves in the Senate. In June 1970 he suggested that the Nixon-Agnew team might have to be replaced because it failed to deliver on its promise to end the war. In May 1970, when Nixon ordered American troops into Cambodia, Hatfield cosponsored with Democratic Senator George McGovern an amendment to an arms appropriations bill that provided for a cutoff of funds for the Vietnam war after December 31, 1971. The McGovern–Hatfield Amendment became a rallying cry for antiwar activitists, but the Senate defeated the amendment twice, once in 1970 and again in 1971. Hatfield also lobbied for the replacement of the draft with a voluntary army. His bill to end the draft never passed, but the Administration eventually ended the draft on its own initiative.

See also ANTIWAR MOVEMENT: McGOVERN, GEORGE.

HAYDEN, THOMAS E(MMETT) (1940–)

Hayden was born on December 12, 1940 in Royal Oaks, Michigan. After graduating from the University of Michigan in 1961, he worked with the Student Nonviolent Coordinating Committee and served as president of Students for a Democratic Society in 1962 and 1963.

He traveled to North Vietnam with other antiwar activists in 1965 and again in 1967, when three American prisoners of war were released as a gesture of good faith. Hayden participated in the student occupation of Columbia University in April 1968, and as project director of the National Mobilization Committee to End the War in Vietnam, he organized the antiwar demonstrations outside the Democratic National Convention in Chicago during August.

As a result of those demonstrations, on March 20, 1969 Hayden and seven others were indicted on charges of crossing state lines with intent to riot and conspiring to incite a riot. The trial was widely publicized as a test of the limits of dissent and became a cause célèbre for radicals. Hayden and four others were found guilty of crossing state lines with intent to riot and all the defendants and their lawyers received prison sentences for contempt of court. The convictions and the contempt sentences were eventually overturned.

Hayden spoke and wrote extensively about the war and about government repression of antiwar radicals. In January 1973 he married antiwar activist and actress Jane Fonda, and they directed the efforts of the Indochina Peace Campaign toward ending U.S. clandestine involvement in Vietnam and all U.S. aid to the Thieu government in South Vietnam.

HEARTS AND MINDS

A term used to describe the objectives of American counterinsurgency efforts in Vietnam. The "hearts and minds" concept was built on the false premise that the key to winning the war was to win the allegiance of the Vietnamese people (their "hearts and minds") by a combination of security operations and good works in the form of civil action programs.

Enormous amounts of time, effort and material were expended in these civil action programs, although they received comparatively little attention in the American media. They included myriad efforts by U.S. Army civil action teams, Navy Seabee technical assistance teams, Marine Corps combined action battalions and Seventh Air Force civil action medical teams, to name only a few.

While from a humanitarian point of view these programs aided the South Vietnamese people, from a military point of view they were irrelevant in the war against the North Vietnamese and Viet Cong, for in the end the key to the war was not the hearts and minds of the South Vietnamese people but the guns and bullets of the North Vietnamese Army. Their military forces, operating by the old rule that the purpose of an army was not good works but the destruction of the enemy's army, proved to be the decisive factor. As military analyst Stuart Herrington put it in *Silence Was a Weapon* (Novato, Calif.: Presidio Press, 1982), "Like us Hanoi had failed to win the 'hearts and minds' of the South Vietnamese peasantry. Unlike us, Hanoi's leaders were able to compensate for this failure by playing their trump card—they overwhelmed South Vietnam with a twenty-two division force."

Suggestions for further reading: "Civil Action" in *A Short History of the United States Navy and the Southeast Asian Conflict 1950–1975*, by Edward J. Marolda and G. Wesley Pryce, III (Washington, D.C.: Naval Historical Center, 1984); "Military Civil Action" in *The United States Air Force in Southeast Asia 1961–1973*, edited by Carl Berger (Washington, D.C.: U.S. Government Printing Office, 1977); *U.S. Marine Corps Civil Action Efforts in Vietnam March 1965–March 1966*, by Russel H. Stolfi (Washington, D.C.: Historical Branch, 1968); *U.S. Marine Corps Civil Affairs in I Corps Republic of Vietnam April 1966–April 1967*, by William D. Parker (Washington, D.C.: Historical Division, U.S. Marine Corps, 1970).

HELICOPTERS

Helicopters were the hallmark of U.S. military operations in the Vietnam war. Used by the U.S. Army, Navy, Air Force and Marines and by the South Vietnamese Air Force, helicopters fell into four general categories—utility helicopter (UH), cargo helicopter (CH), observation helicopter (OH) and assault helicopter (AH).

The UH-19 Chickasaw utility helicopter used early in the war was soon replaced by the UH-1 Huey. The workhorse of the Vietnam war, the Huey was used to transport troops and supplies and to evacuate the wounded; it was also modified to serve as a gunship.

One of the first helicopters to serve in Vietnam was the CH-21 Flying Banana cargo helicopter, deployed to Vietnam in July 1962. Although some CH-54 Flying Cranes were used in Vietnam, the standard cargo helicopter for the U.S. Army was the CH-47 Chinook. For the U.S. Navy and Marine Corps, the standard was the CH-46 Sea Knight and the larger CH-53 Sea Stallion.

Observation helicopters were also used for command and control—i.e., to oversee ground combat operations—for adjustment of artillery fire and for reconnaissance of enemy positions. They included the OH-13 Sioux and OH-23 Raven and after 1969 the newer OH-58 Kiowa and OH-6 Cayuse. Better known as the Loach (probably from a contraction of light-observation helicopters), the OH-6 was especially popular with air cavalry scouts.

Assault helicopter gunships in the early days of the war were modified Hueys and Chinooks, which carried a variety of add-on armaments, including rockets and machine guns. In 1967 they were augmented by the specially designed AH-1 Cobra gunship (*see* illustration). With a much narrower silhouette, to present a smaller target to the enemy, and a bow-mounted 40-mm grenade launcher and minigun (a multibarreled rapid-firing machine gun) and wingpods of machine

A U.S. Navy CH-53 Seahawk. (Courtesy Stuart Herrington, U.S. Army.)

A U.S. Navy UH-1B helicopter gunship. (Courtesy Bell Helicopters.)

guns and rockets, the Cobra was a formidable fighting aircraft.

The statistics on U.S. military use of helicopters in Vietnam are staggering. U.S. Army, Navy, Air Force and Marine Corps helicopters flew some 3,932,000 attack (gunship) sorties (a sortie is one combat flight by a military aircraft), 7,547,000 assault (troop landings in hostile areas) sorties, 3,548,000 cargo sorties and 21,098,000 command-and-control, artillery observation, battlefield reconnaissance, search-and-rescue and other sorties.

These 36,125,000 helicopter sorties were at a cost of 10 helicopters lost over North Vietnam, 2,066 lost over South Vietnam and 2,566 lost to nonhostile air crashes, resulting from accidents, mechanical malfunctions and other such causes. Five hundred sixty-four Army helicopter pilots were killed in action, as were 12 Navy, one Coast Guard, 74 Marine and 17 Air Force helicopter

pilots, together with 1,471 helicopter aircrew members. An additional 401 pilots and 994 aircrewmen died in helicopter air accidents and crashes caused by mechanical and other failures. The total 1,069 helicopter pilots who died from battle and nonbattle causes almost equaled the 1,084 fighter, fighter-bomber, bomber and other fixed-wing pilots who died in Vietnam.

See also AIR CAVALRY, AIRMOBILE OPERATIONS, CHINOOK HELICOPTER, GUNSHIPS, HUEY HELICOPTER.

Suggestions for further reading: *Vietnam Order of Battle,* by Shelby L. Stanton (Washington, D.C.: U.S. News & World Report Books, 1981); *Airmobility 1961–1971,* by John J. Tolson, (Washington, D.C.: U.S. Government Printing Office, 1973). *Chicken Hawk,* by Robert Mason (New York: Viking/Penguin, 1983), contains particularly vivid personal accounts of combat helicopter operations in Vietnam.

A U.S. Army CH-47a Chinook. (Courtesy U.S. Army.)

A U.S. Marine Corps CH-46 Sea Knight. (Courtesy U.S. Marine Corps.)

A U.S. Army CH-21c Shawnee carrying South Vietnamese troops into battle early in the war. (Courtesy U.S. Army.)

HIGHLANDS

See II CORPS TACTICAL ZONE.

HILSMAN, ROGER (1919–   )

Born on November 23, 1919 in Waco, Texas, Hilsman was a member of Merrill's Marauders and served with the Office of Strategic Services during World War II. He earned a PhD in international relations from Yale University in 1951 and taught international politics at Princeton University from 1953 to 1956.

In February 1961 President Kennedy appointed Hilsman Director of the State Department's Bureau of Intelligence and Research, which was responsible for analyzing current foreign developments and conducting research for long term planning. Hilsman became increasingly involved in the growing war in Vietnam and was one of the architects of the administration's Vietnam policy. In January 1962 he presented a plan, entitled "A Strategic Concept for South Vietnam," that defined the struggle against the communists as a political rather than a military one. He proposed policies to win the allegiance of the rural popula-

tion. One important aspect of his plan was the use of "strategic hamlets" to provide security for villagers and fortified areas that would allow the South Vietnamese government eventually to extend its control throughout the countryside. He recommended that the South Vietnamese adopt guerilla warfare tactics.

After returning from a December 1962 fact-finding mission to Vietnam with presidential aide Michael Forrestal, Hilsman expressed doubts about the conduct of the war and the viability of Ngo Dinh Diem's government. He and Forrestal concluded that only the Americans and those Vietnamese leaders with close ties to the Diem family supported Diem and his brother Ngo Dinh Nhu. They were skeptical about optimistic assessments of the war by many high ranking U.S. officials and foresaw a long and costly struggle. They also questioned the value of the strategic hamlet program as it was being implemented by Nhu, who seemed to have a poor grasp of his own people's needs. During meetings with the President's chief advisers in July 1963, Hilsman raised the possibility of a coup.

Following attacks on Buddhist dissidents by Nhu's secret police in August, Hilsman, Forrestal and Averell Harriman sent instructions to the new Ambassador to South Vietnam, Henry Cabot

Lodge, stating that Diem must be allowed to "rid himself of Nhu" but warned that if Diem refused "then we must face the possibility that Diem himself cannot be preserved." Lodge was also instructed to tell senior South Vietnamese generals that if Nhu remained the United States would "give them direct support in any interim . . . breakdown [of the] central government." A military coup was successfully carried out on November 1, 1963. A day later Diem and Nhu were killed by the insurgents.

In February 1964 Hilsman, who was at odds with President Johnson and Secretary of State Dean Rusk over Vietnam policy, resigned his State Department post. In 1967 his book *To Move a Nation* described the process of foreign policy formulation under President Kennedy and criticized the Johnson Administration's escalation of the war into a general ground and air conflict.

See also DIEM, NGO DINH; HARRIMAN, AVERELL; KENNEDY, JOHN F.; JOHNSON, LYNDON B.; LODGE, HENRY CABOT; NHU, NGO DINH; RUSK, DEAN; STRATEGIC HAMLETS.

Suggestions for further reading: *To Move a Nation: The Politics of Foreign Policy in the Administration of John F. Kennedy,* by Roger Hilsman (Garden City, N.Y.: Doubleday, 1967).

HOA HAO

A reformed Buddhist sect, the Hoa Hao was founded in 1939 by Huynh Phu So. Concentrated in the Mekong Delta, it grew to more than a million adherents. When Huynh Phu So was ambushed and killed by the Viet Minh in April 1947, the sect became strongly anticommunist. Their challenge to South Vietnamese President Ngo Dinh Diem in 1955 was put down with force, but they remained a potent and tightly organized political unit.

The Hoa Hao (pronounced "Wa-how") had been secretly recruited by the CIA since 1961, and its members were hired as part of the Army Special Forces CIDG (Civilian Irregular Defense Group) program. They served as crack anti-Viet Cong camp defenders in the Mekong Delta throughout the war.

Suggestions for further reading: *Passing the*

Torch by Edward Doyle et al (Boston: Boston Publishing Co., 1981); *The Green Berets at War*, by Shelby L. Stanton (Novato, Calif.: Presidio Press, 1985).

HO BO WOODS

See III CORPS TACTICAL ZONE.

HO CHI MINH (1890–1969)

Ho Chi Minh (literally, He Who Enlightens) was one of the many aliases of Nguyen Tat Thanh, born in 1890 in Nghe An Province in the protectorate of Annam (central Vietnam). Son of an impoverished mandarin, he left Vietnam in 1912 and ended up in France, where, under the alias Nguyen Ai Quoc ("Nguyen, the Patriot"), he became a founding member of the French communist party on December 30, 1920.

After later study in the Soviet Union, he was assigned as a Comintern agent in China in 1925, and five years later he founded the Indochina Communist Party in Hong Kong. Returning to Moscow in 1938, he was one of the few Comintern agents to survive the Stalinist purges underway there.

In May 1941 he returned to Vietnam, where he chaired the Eighth Plenum of the Indochina Communist Party and formed the Vietnam Doc Lap Dong Minh ("League for Vietnamese Independence"), better known as the Viet Minh. Taking a new alias, Ho Chi Minh, he traveled to China in 1942 to seek help from the Chinese Nationalist government for operations against the Japanese. Arrested as a communist agent, he remained in jail until 1943, when he was released by the Chinese to organize an anti-Japanese resistance movement in Vietnam.

Following Stalin's example (who earlier had downplayed communism in favor of Mother Russia to win public support for the "great patriotic war" against the Nazis), Ho Chi Minh proclaimed his anti-Japanese and anti-French Viet Minh as a nationalist rather than a communist movement and ostensibly dissolved the Indochina Communist Party in November 1945. Like Russia's "Uncle Joe," he became Vietnam's "Uncle Ho."

Earlier Ho had used his contacts with American OSS agents to convince his political opponents (including Emperor Bao Dai, who abdicated in Ho's favor) that he alone enjoyed the support of the United States, thereby enabling him to seize control of the Vietnamese nationalist movement. On September 2, 1945 Ho Chi Minh declared the independence of Vietnam from French colonial control. Through clever political maneuvering, he had gained almost total political power by the time the French returned to Vietnam in early 1946. Instead of confronting French power, Ho attempted to work out a compromise position for Vietnam within the French union, and he traveled to Paris for that purpose in May 1946. At first, agreement seemed possible but by September the talks had broken down. Three months later France and the Viet Minh were at war. The First Indochina War had begun.

Waging a guerrilla war against the French, Ho's fortunes ebbed and flowed. Nevertheless, on January 14, 1950 he proclaimed the Democratic Republic of Vietnam as the legitimate government of Vietnam, and this new "government" was promptly recognized by China, the Soviet Union and Yugoslavia. Hard fighting lay ahead, however, and it was another four years before an exhausted France finally agreed to peace talks in Geneva in April 1954. On May 7 Ho's military commander, General Vo Nguyen Giap, won a brilliant victory over the French at Dien Bien Phu, which forced them to give up the fight. A truce was signed on July 20, 1954, and the First Indochina War ended.

But the truce left Vietnam divided, and Laos and Cambodia became independent. Ho Chi Minh's Indochina Communist Party was still not a reality. Turning his attention to events at home, Ho again emulated Stalin by launching a campaign to eliminate the *kulaks*—"landlords"—in his land reform campaign of 1955. Thousands were murdered and thousands more sent to Vietnamese gulags. In Ho's own province a revolt broke out

Ho Chi Minh, left, talks with Prime Minister Pham Van Dong.

against these excesses in November 1956. Ho's troops ruthlessly stamped out the revolt, and 6,000 peasants were killed or imprisoned. Later he apologized for these excesses, and in recent years the North Vietnamese government claimed they had been pushed into such brutal measures by "Chinese advisers."

From 1956 to 1959 Ho Chi Minh continued to consolidate his power in the north. Although he had organized some 37 armed companies in the south, he discouraged them from armed attacks on the South Vietnamese government, believing that South Vietnam would collapse on its own. In 1959 all this changed. "Political struggle" was authorized for the Viet Cong, and assassinations of local village authorities and other government officials soared to over 4,000 a year. After a January 1959 Politburo decision to conquer South Vietnam by force, expansion of the Ho Chi Minh Trail began in May 1959, and in July aid was begun to the Pathet Lao guerrillas in Laos. In December 1960 a front organization—the National Liberation Front—was organized in the south. Ostensibly a nationalist coalition to oversee the Viet Cong, it took its orders directly from the North Vietnamese Politburo. The Second Indochina War had begun.

For the next 10 years Ho Chi Minh never waivered from his goal of an Indochina Communist Party. Suffering losses proportionately greater than the Japanese suffered in World War II, the North Vietnamese sent ever larger numbers of their soldiers to the south, especially after the disasters of the 1968 Tet Offensive had virtually eliminated their Viet Cong guerrillas.

When Ho Chi Minh died on September 2, 1969, victory was still far off. It would be almost six years until North Vietnamese tanks rolled into South Vietnam's Presidential Palace and Saigon became "Ho Chi Minh City." Although it took almost 50 years for Ho Chi Minh's Indochina Communist Party to become a reality, it was finally achieved with the domination of Laos in 1975 and the invasion of Cambodia on Christmas Day, 1978 and its subsequent occupation. Whether the prime motivation behind the Vietnamese conquest of Indochina was nationalism, Vietnamese chauvinism or communism is still a matter of considerable controversy.

A poster commemorating the 81st anniversary of Ho's birth.

With their November 1978 Friendship Pact with Vietnam, the Soviets' investment in Ho's education a half century earlier finally paid dividends—port facilities at Cam Ranh Bay, establishing a Soviet navy presence astride the trade routes in Southeast Asia, and a valuable Soviet ally on China's southern frontier.

See also CHINA, CIA (CENTRAL INTELLIGENCE AGENCY), SOVIET UNION, VIET MINH.

Suggestions for further reading: *Selected Works,* vols. 1–4, by Ho Chi Minh (Hanoi: Foreign Language Publishing House, 1966–67); *Prison Diary,* by Ho Chi Minh (Hanoi: Foreign Language Publishing House, 1966); *Ho Chi Minh: A Political Biography,* by Jean Lacouture, translated by Peter Wiles (New York: Random House, 1968); *Ho Chi Minh on Revolution,* edited by Bernard Fall (New York: Signet, 1968); *Ho,* by David Halberstam (New York: Random House, 1971); *Ho Chi Minh: A*

Biographical Introduction, by Charles Fenn (New York: Charles Scribner's Sons, 1973); *The Vietnam Experience: Setting the Stage* and *Passing the Torch,* by Edward Doyle et al (Boston: Boston Publishing Co., 1981); *Vietnam: A History,* by Stanley Karnow (New York: Viking, 1983).

HO CHI MINH CITY

After their conquest of South Vietnam, the North Vietnamese officially changed the name of Saigon to Ho Chi Minh City to honor their former leader, who had died six years earlier. Much as if Atlanta had been changed to "William Tecumseh Sherman City" in 1865, it is not surprising that the new name has not caught on among the South Vietnamese people.

See also SAIGON.

HO CHI MINH TRAIL

The so-called Ho Chi Minh Trail was North Vietnam's strategic key to the Vietnam war, for it gave the north a decisive logistic and tactical advantage. Logistics—arms, ammunition, gasoline, food and other supplies—are the sinews of war, and when North Vietnam decided in 1959 to conquer South Vietnam by force of arms, one of its first considerations was how to infiltrate soldiers and supplies into the south.

Although the North Vietnamese maintained the falsehood throughout the war that they had no soldiers in the south and that all fighting there was conducted by southern "revolutionaries," since their victory in 1975 they have openly admitted that they began to move soldiers and supplies to the south as early as 1959.

North Vietnamese Army (NVA) General Vo Bam revealed in a 1983 French television documentary that on May 19, 1959 he was ordered to begin construction of an infiltration route into the south. Taking advantage of existing mountain trails that ran south along the mountains of the Chaîne Annamitque through the Laotian panhandle and the eastern border regions of Cam-

bodia, General Bam and a 30,000-man work force expanded and improved these trails into a major road network. Spurs were also constructed off the main trail into base areas, such as the A Shau Valley in I Corps and the Ia Drang Valley in II Corps, and into War Zone C in III Corps. At the beginning of the project, it took six months to traverse the trail from North Vietnam to its final termini in the Mekong Delta west of Saigon. When the North Vietnamese launched their Final Offensive in 1975, the same trip took less than a week. The "trail" had become an expressway. As the commander of that offensive, NVA General Tran Tien Dung, described it:

> The strategic route east of the Truong Son Range [what we labeled the Ho Chi Minh Trail] was the result of the labor of more than 30,000 troops and shock youths. The length of this route, added to that of the other old and new strategic routes and routes used during various campaigns built during the last war, is more than 20,000 kms [12,500 miles]. The 8-meter [26.4 feet] wide route of more than 1,000 kms [625 miles], which we could see now, is our pride. With 5,000 kms [3,125 miles] of pipeline laid through deep rivers and streams and on the mountains more than 1,000 meters [3,300 feet] high, we were capable of providing enough fuel for various battlefronts. More than 10,000 transportation vehicles were put on the road. . . .

From the mid-1960s to 1970, this north-south supply line was complemented by a south-north supply line from the Cambodian port of Sihanoukville (Kompong Som). From oceangoing cargo ships supplies would be transported by truck through Cambodia to NVA base areas along the Cambodian-Laotian borders. This route was interdicted by the secret bombing of Cambodian base areas in 1969 (Operation Menu) and closed completely when Prince Sihanouk was deposed by Cambodian General Lon Nol in 1970. Another supplement to the Ho Chi Minh Trail was infiltration of troops and supplies by small boats—junks and sampans—from the South China Sea into the coastal inlets and inland waterways of South Vietnam. This infiltration, too, was drastically reduced by the U.S. Navy's Operation Market Time beginning in March 1965. As these alternative supply routes dried up, the Ho Chi Minh Trail became even more critical to North Vietnam's success.

The United States recognized the strategic

importance of the Ho Chi Minh Trail early on. Although the U.S. Air Force made no such claim, there were air power advocates who claimed that it could be closed by aerial assault alone. Beginning in March 1965 with Operation Rolling Thunder to interdict supply and transportation routes within North Vietnam and Operations Steel Tiger, Tiger Hound and Commando Hunt to interdict the Ho Chi Minh Trail in the southern panhandle of Laos, U.S. Air Force B-52 bombers and fixed-wing gunships and Air Force, Navy and Marine fighters and fighter-bombers struck these supply lines around the clock. Although the flow of men and supplies from North Vietnam was slowed and North Vietnam was forced to divert enormous assets into keeping the route repaired, air power was never able to close the Ho Chi Minh Trail completely.

As early as April 1967, the ground force commander, General William C. Westmoreland, requested authority to cut the trail by ground operations in Laos. His requests were not acted on, and in April 1968 he again requested authority to attack the trail complex but again to no avail.

The South Vietnamese Army attempted to cut the trail by a ground combat attack in February 1971 codenamed Lam Son 719. With U.S. air support it had some initial success, but the NVA reacted violently to this attempt to cut the lifeline to their forces in the south and the following month the South Vietnamese were forced to withdraw.

Apart from its logistical advantage, the Ho Chi Minh Trail also provided a tactical advantage—the advantage of "interior lines." According to military doctrine, interior lines, by virtue of location, permit a belligerent to move faster than its adversary to any given point on the battlefield. South Vietnam is shaped like a bow, with the coastal lowlands, where the majority of north-south transportation networks are located, representing the bow. The relatively straight Ho Chi Minh Trail represented the bow string. Using the Ho Chi Minh Trail and the spurs leading off into critical areas of South Vietnam, NVA forces could move more quickly than their South Vietnamese counterparts. From 1965 to 1973 U.S. intertheater airlift and helicopter mobility negated this advantage, but after the U.S. withdrawal the reali-

ties of geography came back into play. The NVA was able to concentrate its forces more rapidly than the South Vietnamese could react. According to NVA General Dung, "Because we concentrated the majority of our forces [by using the Ho Chi Minh Trail to bring combat forces into position] we achieved superiority over the enemy. . . . [During the opening battle of the Final Offensive] as for infantry, the ratio was 5.5 of our troops for each enemy soldier. As for tanks and armored vehicles, the ratio was 1.2 to 1. In heavy artillery, the ratio was 2.1 to 1."

The Ho Chi Minh Trail proved to be the road to victory.

See also COMMANDO HUNT; DUNG, VAN TIEN; FINAL OFFENSIVE; LAM SON 719; LAOS; MENU OPERATION; ROLLING THUNDER OPERATION; STEEL TIGER; TIGER HOUND; WESTMORELAND, WILLIAM C.

Suggestions for further reading: *On Strategy: A Critical Analysis of the Vietnam War*, by Harry G. Summers, Jr. (Novato, Calif.: Presidio Press, 1982). General Westmoreland's alternative strategy for cutting the Ho Chi Minh Trail is discussed in depth by his former deputy, General Bruce Palmer, Jr., in *The 25-Year War: America's Military Role in Vietnam*, by Bruce J. Palmer, Jr. (Louisville: University of Kentucky Press, 1984).

HOFFMAN, ABBIE (1936-)

Born on November 30, 1936 in Worcester, Massachusetts, Hoffman graduated from Brandeis University in 1959. He received an M.A. in psychology from the University of California, Berkeley, in 1960.

By 1967 Hoffman had become a spokesman for what he viewed as a growing "counterculture" of drugs, rock bands and sexual freedom. In October Hoffman and Jerry Rubin captured the attention of the media at an antiwar march in Washington, D.C., when they led a ceremony to "levitate" the Pentagon off its foundation. In 1967 Hoffman joined with Rubin and others to create the Yippies, or Youth International Party. In a book entitled *Revolution for the Hell of It* (1968), Hoffman defined the Yippies' concept of revolution as any-

Abbie Hoffman, a leader of the Youth International Party, or Yippies, being escorted by police after landing in Chicago's O'Hare Airport. Hoffman was arrested for failing to appear in court to answer charges of disorderly conduct and resisting arrest. (AP/Wide World Photos.)

thing that displayed irreverence for property and the Establishment.

During the summer of 1968 Hoffman and his fellow Yippies planned a massive "festival of life" in Chicago to contrast with what they called the "festival of death" at the Democratic National Convention. They came to Chicago along with thousands of other antiwar student activist and black power protestors from the National Mobilization Committee, Students for a Democratic Society and such groups as the Black Panthers. On August 26, at about the same time the Democratic National Convention was formally opened, the Yippies clashed with Chicago police, resulting in several injuries to demonstrators and police. The remaining days of the convention were full of similar disorders.

In March 1969 Hoffman was one of eight persons indicted by a federal grand jury in Chicago in connection with the 1968 disorders. After a tumultuous trial five of the original eight, including Hoffman, were convicted of conspiracy to riot. In November 1972 the verdicts were overturned by an appeals court.

See also ANTIWAR MOVEMENT; CHICAGO SEVEN;

DEMOCRATIC NATIONAL CONVENTION, 1968; RUBIN, JERRY.

HONOLULU CONFERENCES

A series of conferences held at the U.S. Navy's Pacific Command in Honolulu, Hawaii (the strategic command headquarters for the Vietnam war) to determine how the war would be fought, Honolulu conferences were held every year from 1962 to 1966. Normally in attendance were the U.S. Ambassador to South Vietnam, the Commander-in-Chief of the Pacific Command, the Commander of the U.S. Military Assistance Command Vietnam, as well as the Secretary of Defense, the Chairman of the Joint Chiefs of Staff and at times the Secretary of State. In 1966 President Johnson and South Vietnamese Premier Nguyen Cao Ky also attended the conference.

After 1964 the conferences were usually divided on the nature of the war and the appropriate military response. Clinging to the outmoded notions of counterinsurgency fostered earlier by the Kennedy Administration, the civilian conferees and the Chairman of the Joint Chiefs still believed the war to be an internal insurgency requiring American military response confined to South Vietnam. The military conferees charged with fighting the war were unable to convince them that because of the widespread infiltration of North Vietnamese Army (NVA) regulars, the war was more a conventional than an unconventional war and that the appropriate response was a strike at the source of the aggression. This argument was settled in the February 1966 conference. Despite his exhortation to Premier Ky and the American military commanders to win the war and give him "coonskins on the wall," President Johnson, concerned with rising public and congressional protests over military combat operations in Vietnam, directed the military to concentrate on "pacification" (i.e., resolving the internal affairs of South Vietnam) rather than waging war against the external enemy. With attention thus diverted from what was to prove the decisive enemy—the NVA—the course for eventual disaster was set.

Suggestions for further reading: *Vietnam: A His-*

ory, by Stanley Karnow (New York: Viking, 983); *A Soldier Reports*, by William C. Westmoreand (Garden City: Doubleday, 1976); *Airpower in Three Wars*, by William W. Momyer (Washington, D.C.: U.S. Government Printing Office, 1978); *Strategy for Defeat: Vietnam in Retrospect*, by U. S. G. Sharpe (Novato, Calif.: Presidio Press, 1978).

HOOPES, TOWNSEND (WALTER) (1922-   )

Hoopes was born on April 28, 1922 in Duluth, Minnesota. He graduated from Yale in 1944. During the Eisenhower and Kennedy Administrations he was a frequent consultant to the White House and State and Defense Departments.

In January 1965 President Johnson appointed Hoopes Deputy Assistant Secretary of Defense for International Security Affairs. By the end of 1965 Hoopes had become skeptical of achieving a military victory in a limited war, particularly through the intensive bombing of North Vietnam. In December he wrote his superior, John McNaughton, suggesting that the effect of the bombing had been "singularly inconclusive" and that any attempt to step up the operation would unify the communist world and draw increasing criticism from U.S. allies. Instead of escalation, Hoopes proposed that the United States limit its military objectives to the holding and pacification of certain defined cities and ports with the current level of U.S. and South Vietnamese combat forces.

Hoopes later sent a memorandum to Secretary of Defense Robert S. McNamara calling for a bombing halt and claiming that the military's argument—that bombing prevented countless American casualties—was false. McNamara did not answer the memorandum.

In October 1967 Hoopes became Undersecretary of the Air Force. In a personal letter to Clark Clifford, the incoming Secretary of Defense in February 1968, Hoopes called military victory in Vietnam a "dangerous illusion" and suggested a bombing halt and reduction in ground troops as a prelude to a negotiated settlement. A month later Hoopes reiterated his position in a report he prepared for a task force Clifford had formed to brief him on Vietnam. These reports, with others from such men as Paul Nitze and Paul Warnke helped convince Clifford that de-escalation was necessary. Clifford, in turn, was one of the advisors who eventually persuaded Johnson to announce a policy of de-escalation on March 31.

Hoopes left government service in 1969. He later became executive director of the American Association of Publishers.

See also AD HOC TASK FORCE ON VIETNAM; ANTIWAR MOVEMENT; CLIFFORD, CLARK.

Suggestions for further reading: *The Limits of Intervention*, by Townsend Hoopes (Boston: Little, Brown, 1969).

HUE, BATTLE OF

For centuries Hué had been the imperial capital of Vietnam. Halfway between Da Nang and the DMZ, Hué, with an official population in 1968 of 100,000 plus untold numbers of refugees, was South Vietnam's third largest city. Two-thirds of the population lived within the walls of the Old City, or Citadel. Rectangular in shape, the Citadel was encompassed by miles of massive walls, with multichannel moats outside them, except for the southeast wall, which bordered the Song Huong, or River of Perfume. Although flowing into the South China Sea some five miles to the east, the Perfume River was not suited for oceangoing shipping. South of the river and linked to the Citadel by the Nguyen Hoang Bridge was the more westernized New City.

Throughout the war, Hué had been treated almost as an open city, for the Viet Cong had regarded it with respect and it had remained remarkably free of war. The city had a considerable U.S. civilian presence, including Agency for International Development representatives and other State Department personnel, but no U.S. military garrison. Few U.S. soldiers or Marines, other than members of the MACV (U.S. Military Assistance Command Vietnam) had ever been in the city. Although the South Vietnamese Army (ARVN) First Division was headquartered in Hué, its troops were spread out along Highway 1,

U.S. Marines conduct a search-and-clear operation after a heavy fight at the old imperial capital of Hué. (Courtesy U.S. Marine Corps.)

which ran north from Hué to the DMZ. The only combat element in the city was the division's Black Panther reaction company.

Unknown to the South Vietnamese and their U.S. advisers, the North Vietnamese in early 1968 had infiltrated two regiments of their regular army into Hué. These soldiers came into the open in the early morning hours of January 31, 1968, when, as part of the countrywide Tet Offensive, the North Vietnamese Army (NVA) began its attack on Hué with a rocket and mortar barrage. The NVA Sixth Regiment, with two battalions of infantry, and the 12th Sapper Battalion pushed from the southwest toward the ARVN First Division headquarters. The Black Panthers briefly stopped the NVA 800th Battalion at the Hué airstrip, then fell back into the headquarters compound, where the division staff was defending against the NVA 802nd Battalion. By daylight the NVA Sixth Regiment held the entire Citadel, including the Imperial Palace, except the ARVN First Division headquarters. Meanwhile the NVA 806th Battalion had taken up blocking positions to prevent reinforcement from the north. South of the river in the New City, the NVA Fourth Regiment had twice assaulted the MACV compound, using the NVA 804th Battalion, but it was beaten off each time. Two Viet Cong battalions took the other government buildings in the New City. The NVA 810th Battalion was assigned to block reinforcement from the south.

North of the river the ARVN First Division Commander, Brigadier General Ngo Quang Truong, ordered his Third Regiment, reinforced with two Airborne battalions and an armored cavalry troop, to fight its way into the city. These reinforcements reached his headquarters late on January 31, and on the morning of February 1, Truong began his counterattack on a southern diagonal axis. With Truong fully occupied in the Citadel north of the river, the commanding general of South Vietnam's I Corps Tactical Zone, who was responsible for all of northern South Vietnam, asked U.S. forces to take complete charge of clearing Hué south of the Perfume River.

The initial U.S. military reaction to the attack had been mounted by company-sized elements of the First Marine Regiment, U.S. First Marine Division, which attempted to break through to the ARVN First Division headquarters on the morning of January 31. Forced to fall back to the MACV advisers' compound south of the river, the U.S. First Marine Regiment—consisting only of its First Battalion—was reinforced by the Second Battalion, Fifth Marine Regiment, U.S. First Marine Division, and on February 4 the Marines counterattacked to clear the New City. Fierce house-to-house fighting continued until February 9, when all enemy forces south of the river had been routed.

Meanwhile, on February 2, the U.S. Army First Air Cavalry Division's Third Brigade entered the battle. The Second Battalion, 12th Cavalry sealed off the city from the west and north, and it was soon joined by the First and Second Battalions, Seventh Cavalry and the First Battalion, 501st Infantry (attached to the Third Brigade from the U.S. Army 101st Airborne Division). For almost three weeks, these units would hold off the reinforcement of North Vietnamese troops in Hué by the NVA 24th, 29th and 99th Regiments. North of the river the ARVN First Division had been attempting to drive the enemy out of the Citadel. Meeting intense resistance, the division was reinforced on February 12 by two battalions of South Vietnamese Marines and the First Battalion, Fifth Marine Regiment, from the U.S

First Marine Division. Again house-to-house assaults were necessary to drive out the entrenched North Vietnamese forces. On February 24 the ARVN 1st Division attack reached the walls of the Citadel, where it linked up with elements of the U.S. Army's First Cavalry Division, which on February 21 had launched coordinated assaults on the city from their blocking positions to the west. Suffering some 5,000 soldiers killed in the city and 3,000 killed in the surrounding area, the remnant of the North Vietnamese Army assault force fled westward to sanctuaries in Laos, and on March 2, 1968 the battle for Hué was officially declared at an end.

Although the U.S. command had made efforts to limit damage to the city by relying on extremely accurate 8-inch howitzers and naval gunfire support provided by three cruisers and five destroyers laying offshore, the house-to-house fighting took its toll. Aside from this battle damage, the civilian population suffered terrible losses from the communist attackers. After the battle was over, it was discovered that North Vietnamese and Viet Cong communist death squads had systematically eliminated South Vietnamese government leaders and employees. Some 2,800 were found in mass graves, and at least 3,000 more were dead or missing.

Suggestions for further reading: *Battle of Hue: Tet 1968*, by Keith William Noland (Novato, Calif.: Presidio Press, 1983); "Marine Corps Operations in Vietnam, 1968," by Edwin H. Simmons, in *The Marines in Vietnam 1954–1973* (Washington, D.C.: U.S. Marine Corps, 1974); *The War in the Northern Provinces 1966–1968*, by Willard Pearson (Washington, D.C.: U.S. Government Printing Office, 1975); *Battles and Campaigns in Vietnam 1954–1984*, by Tom Carhart (New York: Crown Publishers, 1984).

HUEY HELICOPTER

Developed in several models (e.g., UH-1A, UH-1B), the UH-1 Huey was used by all U.S. military forces as a utility helicopter to transport troops and supplies, as an evacuation helicopter to evacuate wounded from the battlefield, as an assault helicopter to land combat forces in enemy territory and—when modified with machine gun and rocket armament packages—as an attack helicopter gunship. The UH-1 Huey was truly the workhorse of the Vietnam War.

See also AIR MOBILE OPERATIONS, DUSTOFF, GUNSHIPS, HELICOPTERS.

Suggestions for further reading: *Airmobility 1961–1971* by John J. Tolson (Washington, D.C.: U.S. Government Printing Office, 1973); *Huey*, by Lou Drendel (Carrollton, Tex.: Squadron/Signal Publications, 1982).

HUMANITARIAN SERVICE MEDAL

The Humanitarian Service Medal was authorized by the Department of Defense in 1975 to recognize meritorious direct participation in a significant military act or operation of a humanitarian nature. The Humanitarian Service Medal is authorized for those personnel who participated in the evacuation of refugees from Indochina from April 1 to December 20, 1975, the evacuation of Laos from April 1 to August 15, 1975, the evacuation of Cambodia on April 12, 1975, and the evacuation of Vietnam on April 29–30, 1975.

HUMPHREY, HUBERT H(ORATIO) (1911–1978)

Born on May 27, 1911 in Wallace, South Dakota, he earned a B.A. from the University of Minnesota in 1939 and an M.A. from Louisiana State University in 1940. Elected Senator in 1948, he became one of the Democratic Party's leading liberal spokesmen. In 1964 President Johnson chose Humphrey as his vice presidential running mate.

After the election Humphrey irritated the President by arguing against a hard-line policy in Vietnam, and he questioned the effectiveness of trying to bomb North Vietnam into negotiating. Angered by Humphrey's dissent, Johnson excluded him from foreign policy meetings for a year.

In February 1966 the President sent Humphrey on a tour of nine Asian nations, including South Vietnam. After his return, Humphrey outdid other administration officials in his optimism about the Vietnam war. His zeal alienated many of his former allies among liberals and intellectuals.

The war haunted Humphrey during his 1968 presidential campaign, following Johnson's withdrawal from the race. The assassination of Senator Robert Kennedy in June left Senator Eugene McCarthy with the allegiance of most of the party's antiwar wing by the time of the Chicago Democratic Convention in August. Although Humphrey won the nomination, bitter disputes inside the convention hall and clashes between police and young antiwar protesters outside the hall intensified rifts within the party and associated the Democrats with violence and chaos in the eyes of the public.

Plagued by his identification with an unpopular war, Humphrey presented a more conciliatory position on Vietnam in September, but he was unable to defeat Richard Nixon, who won by a narrow margin.

In 1970 Humphrey won the Senate seat vacated by Eugene McCarthy and was reelected in 1976. He died on January 13, 1978.

See also ANTIWAR MOVEMENT; JOHNSON, LYNDON.

Suggestions for further reading: *Almost to the Presidency: A Biography of Two American Politicians,* by Albert Eisele (Blue Earth, Minn.: Piper Co., 1972); *The Education of a Public Man: My Life and Politics,* by Hubert H. Humphrey (New York: Doubleday, 1976); *The Drugstore Liberal,* by Robert Sherrill and Cary Ernst (New York: Grossman Publishers, 1968).

HUNGARY

See ICCS.

IA DRANG, BATTLE OF

Although it was not apparent at the time, the Battle of the Ia Drang Valley between elements of the U.S. Army's First Air Cavalry Division and regiments of the North Vietnamese Army was especially significant. It not only marked the first major engagement between American and North Vietnamese troops, it also presaged the final campaign almost 10 years later that would lead to the total collapse of South Vietnam.

In 1964 the North Vietnamese Politburo had made the decision to commit regular army units to the war in the south. After a buildup in supposedly neutral Cambodia, the North Vietnamese intended to attack across the Central Highlands and drive to the sea, splitting South Vietnam in two and ultimately seizing the entire country. They executed this plan on October 19, 1965 with an attack on the U.S. Special Forces camp at Plei Me, but they did not foresee the reaction to this attack. General William Westmoreland made the decision to commit the U.S. Army First Air Cavalry Division, just arrived from the United States, to the relief of Plei Me. The division's helicopters enabled it to fly over enemy roadblocks, and its firepower was instrumental in breaking the Plei Me siege. On October 26, South Vietnamese relief forces were able to break through to the camp. With this success, General Westmoreland ordered the U.S. First Air Cavalry Division to switch from defensive to offensive operations and its reconnaissance units began to seek out the fleeing enemy.

Troops of the U.S. Army's First Cavalry Division charge forward firing on an enemy patrol in the Ia Drang Valley. (AP/Wide World Photos.)

Unknown to the Americans, the North Vietnamese Army's 2,000-man 66th Regiment, joined by the 700 survivors of the 33rd Regiment that had laid siege to Plei Me, was regrouping in the Ia Drang Valley to the southwest. On November 14, the 430 men of the U.S. First Battalion, Seventh Cavalry were ordered to make a helicopter assault into what appeared to be an unoccupied landing zone in the Ia Drang Valley. As soon as they landed they came in contact with elements of the North Vietnamese Army 66th Regiment. Fighting was intense and one U.S. platoon was cut off from the main body. Reinforced by air by elements of the U.S. Second Battalion, Seventh Cavalry and supported by intense artillery and air support, including strikes by B-52 bombers, the First Battalion was able to hold on in the face of heavy odds. On November 15 it was further reinforced by the Second Battalion, Fifth Cavalry, which had moved by air to a landing zone some two and a half miles to the southeast and had marched overland to the sound of guns. Thus reinforced, the First Battalion, Seventh Cavalry was finally able to reestablish contact with its isolated platoon. The North Vietnamese broke contact, with some troops fleeing back across the border into Cambodia and others fleeing eastward into the jungles of the Ia Drang Valley.

Ten years later the North Vietnamese would launch their Final Offensive to conquer South Vietnam just a few miles south of the Ia Drang Valley with their attack on Ban Me Thuot on March 10, 1975. They had tipped their hand to their long-range strategic objectives in 1965, but because the United States was so obsessed with the doctrines of counterinsurgency, it could not see that with the Battle of Ia Drang the entire nature of the war had changed. The North Vietnamese Army, not the Viet Cong, would prove to be the decisive military force in the war.

See also COUNTERINSURGENCY, FINAL OFFENSIVE, FIRST CALVALRY DIVISION. See map at II CORPS TACTICAL ZONE.

Suggestions for further reading: "Fight at Ia Drang, 14–16 November 1965," by John A. Cash, in Seven Firefights in Vietnam, by John Albright et al (Washington, D.C.: U.S. Government Printing Office, 1970); Airmobility 1961–1971, by John J. Tolson (Washington, D.C.: U.S. Government Printing Office, 1973); "The Bitter Triumph of Ia Drang," by Harry G. Summers, Jr., in American Heritage, February 1984.

ICCS (INTERNATIONAL COMMISSION OF CONTROL AND SUPERVISION)

Set up by the Paris Accords in 1973, the four-country ICCS (International Commission of Control and Supervision) was the successor agency to the three-country ICS (International Control Commission) established by the Geneva Conference of 1954. The ICC was composed of representatives from Canada, India and Poland, and when the ICCS was formed in 1973, these nations were asked to continue. Canada and Poland accepted, but India declined and was replaced by Indonesia. Hungary was added as a fourth member. When it became apparent that the North Vietnamese had no intention of living up to the accords, Canada withdrew and was replaced by Iran on July 31, 1973.

Headquartered at Tan Son Nhut Air Base near Saigon, the ICCS had no enforcement powers and could hardly be expected to settle quarrels over which both sides had been fighting and dying for more than two decades. The South Vietnamese public's cynical translation of ICCS was *Im cho coi sao*, which means "Wait quietly and see how things turn out." Characteristically, U.S. personnel working with the ICCS were more abrupt. They claimed ICCS stood for "I can't control shit."

See also CANADA, GENEVA CONFERENCES, TAN SON NHUT.

Suggestions for further reading: *Sixty Days to Peace*, by Walter Scott Dillard (Washington, D.C.: U.S. Government Printing Office, 1982); *Peace with Honor?* by Stuart A. Herrington (Novato, Calif.: Presidio Press, 1983).

I CORPS TACTICAL ZONE

With headquarters at Da Nang, South Vietnam's I (pronounced "eye") Corps was responsible for the defense of the northern portion of the country. Major assigned units included the South Vietnamese Army (ARVN) First, Second and Third Infantry Divisions, although both the ARVN Airborne Division and the South Vietnamese

Marine Division were also deployed there from time to time.

With North Vietnamese Army (NVA) divisions just across the DMZ to the north and NVA base areas fed by the Ho Chi Minh Trail in the southern portion of the Laotian panhandle to the west, I Corps was particularly vulnerable to NVA attack. The threat of such an attack induced U.S. Army Special Forces in the early 1960s to establish a number of CIDG (Civilian Irregular Defense Group) camps in I Corps to block enemy infiltration. It also led to the landing of the U.S. Ninth Marine Amphibious Brigade in Da Nang in March 1965. The first American ground combat force deployed to Vietnam, the brigade was replaced in May 1965 by the U.S. Third Marine Division, and a corps-level headquarters—the III Marine Amphibious Force—was established to provide combat assistance to I Corps and to control U.S. combat operations there. U.S. Marine and Air Force fighter wings were soon flying combat missions from the major jet-capable air bases constructed at Da Nang and Chu Lai. A Navy Seabee group improved and constructed

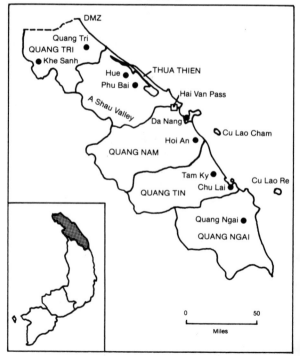

I CORPS

port facilities at these locations to supply the buildup. Reinforcements arrived in February 1966 with the U.S. First Marine Division, in August 1966 with South Korea's Second Marine Corps (Blue Dragon) Brigade and in April 1967 with a U.S. Army three-infantry brigade force. First designated Task Force Oregon, it became the American Division in September 1967.

In the aftermath of the North Vietnamese and Viet Cong 1968 Tet Offensive, MACV (U.S. Military Assistance Command Vietnam) in Saigon established an advance headquarters in I Corps and in August 1968 this became the U.S. Army XXIV Corps. Besides the American Division, at various times the U.S. Army's First Cavalry Division (Airmobile); 101st Airborne Division (Airmobile); First Brigade (Mechanized), Fifth Infantry Division; and Third Brigade, 82nd Airborne Division reinforced the III Marine Amphibious Force in I Corps. In addition to periodic sweeps, U.S. operations included continuing clashes along the DMZ; the defense and relief of Khe Sanh and the recapture of Hué in 1968; and battles in the A Shau Valley, including "Hamburger Hill," in 1968 and 1969.

When the U.S. withdrawal began, the Third Marine Division was the first to leave, departing Vietnam in November 1969. The First Marine Division and the III Marine Amphibious Force followed in April 1971. Next to go was the Army's First Brigade, Fifth Infantry Division in August 1971, the American Division (less the 196th Infantry Brigade) in November and the South Korean Second Marine Brigade in February 1972.

With virtually all U.S. combat units withdrawn, the NVA launched its Eastertide Offensive in March 1972. Sending four divisions south across the DMZ and another two divisions attacking east out of Laos, the North Vietnamese broke through the defense of the green ARVN Third Division and seized the provincial capital of Quang Tri. Supported by massive U.S. air strikes, ARVN forces counterattacked and by September 16, 1972 they had recaptured Quang Tri.

In the meantime the last of the U.S. ground troops—the Army's XXIV Corps and the 196th Infantry Brigade—had been withdrawn in June 1972. At the time of the January 1973 peace agreement, the North Vietnamese had 96,000

troops in I Corps, of which 87,000 were NVA regulars. They included the NVA 325th, 320B, 312th and 364th Divisions in northern I Corps and the NVA 324B, 711th and Second Divisions in southern I Corps. Reinforcing the First, Second and Third ARVN Divisions, the South Vietnamese deployed their strategic reserve—the Airborne Division and the Marine Division—to I Corps. But when the NVA Final Offensive began on March 8, 1975, the Airborne Division was suddenly recalled to shore up defenses elsewhere, leaving a gap in the South Vietnamese lines. As a result they were unable to hold I Corps. By nightfall on March 25, 1975, I Corps belonged to the NVA.

See also A SHAU VALLEY; CHU LAI; DA NANG; DMZ (DEMILITARIZED ZONE); EASTERTIDE OFFENSIVE; HAMBURGER HILL, BATTLE OF; HO CHI MINH TRAIL; HUE, BATTLE OF; KHE SANH, BATTLE OF; KOREA, SOUTH; QUANG TRI, BATTLE OF; III MARINE AMPHIBIOUS FORCE; XXIV CORPS.

Suggestions for further reading: *Vietnam Order of Battle*, by Shelby L. Stanton (Washington, D.C.: U.S. News Books, 1981); *Vietnam from Ceasefire to Capitulation*, by William E. LeGro (Washington, D.C.: U.S. Government Printing Office, 1981).

I FIELD FORCE VIETNAM

Organized at Fort Hood, Texas in early 1965 with cadres from III Corps, I (pronounced "eye") Field Force Vietnam (originally Task Force Alpha) arrived in Vietnam on August 1, 1965 to provide combat assistance to the South Vietnamese Army's II Corps and to control U.S. military operations in the Central Highlands. Headquartered at Nha Trang, it was redesignated I Field Force Vietnam, a corps-level headquarters, in March 1966.

Its assigned units included the 41st and 52nd Artillery Groups as well as various combat support and combat-service support battalions. Attached to I Field Force Vietnam at one time or another for specific combat operations were the U.S. First Cavalry Division (Airmobile); the Fourth Infantry Division; the Third Brigade, 25th Infantry Division; the First Brigade, 101st Airborne Division (Airmobile); and the 173rd Airborne Brigade.

As part of the U.S. military withdrawal, I Field Force Vietnam was disbanded on April 30, 1971.

During the course of the Vietnam war, command of I Field Force Vietnam changed five times:

Commanders	Assumed command
Lieutenant General Stanley R. Larsen	March 1966
Lieutenant General William R. Peers	March 1968
Lieutenant General Charles A. Corcoran	March 1969
Lieutenant General Arthur S. Collins, Jr.	March 1970
Major General Charles P. Brown	January 1971

See also CENTRAL HIGHLANDS, FIELD FORCES, II CORPS TACTICAL ZONE.

Suggestions for further reading: *Command and Control 1950-1969*, by George S. Eckhardt (Washington, D.C.: U.S. Government Printing Office, 1974); *Vietnam Order of Battle*, by Shelby L. Stanton (Washington, D.C.: U.S. News & World Report Books, 1981).

INDONESIA

See ICCS.

INFANTRY

The decisive force on every battlefield throughout history, the "queen of battle" played the dominant role in the Vietnam War. Although it was often carried into battle by helicopter in Vietnam, the infantry's essential mission was the same as it had been for centuries—"close with the enemy and destroy him by fire and maneuver."

Although popular opinion perceived the war as fought by elusive black pajama-clad guerrillas using hit-and-run tactics, the reality was that in most battles in Vietnam one side was entrenched in fortified positions. Both when North Vietnamese Army (NVA) and Viet Cong (VC) forces

assaulted U.S. fire bases and when U.S. forces assaulted NVA and VC positions, the fighting was intense. As the statistics for U.S. combat divisions indicate, the casualties were as high or higher than those in the Korean war or in World War II.

The most prized award in Vietnam for U.S. military personnel was the Combat Infantry Badge—Combat Action Ribbon for the Marine Corps—which honored the relatively few servicemen in Vietnam—primarily infantrymen—who fought the enemy face to face. During the course of the war, the U.S. Army deployed to Vietnam some 71 light infantry battalions, 10 mechanized infantry battalions, 14 ranger companies, and 33 combat tracker and scout-dog platoons. The U.S. Marine Corps deployed 24 battalions of infantry. Australia, Thailand, and South Korea provided an additional 33 infantry battalions for the allied cause.

At the time of the U.S. withdrawal in 1973, the South Vietnamese Army fielded some 124 infantry battalions and 55 ranger battalions. They were opposed by some 309 NVA infantry, sniper, security and reconnaissance battalions (which included remnants of VC units). When the North Vietnamese began their Field Offensive in March 1975 with an attack on South Vietnamese units at Ban Me Thuot, they had a five-to-one superiority in infantry. Once again, it was the decisive battlefield force.

See also CASUALTIES, COMBAT ACTION RIBBON, COMBAT INFANTRY BADGE, DIVISIONS.

Suggestions for further reading: *Vietnam Order of Battle*, by Shelby L. Stanton (Washington, D.C.: U.S. News & World Report Books, 1981); *Seven Firefights in Vietnam*, by John Albright, John A. Cash and Allan W. Sandstrum (Washington, D.C.: U.S. Government Printing Office, 1970; *The Rise and Fall of an American Army*, by Shelby L. Stanton (Novato, Calif.: Presidio Press, 1985); *The Grunts*, by Charles B. Anderson (Novato, Calif.: Presidio Press, 1976). The most comprehensive account of infantry battles in Vietnam is in *Infantry in Vietnam: Small Unit Actions in the Early Days 1965-1966* and *A Distant Challenge: The U.S. Infantryman in Vietnam 1967-1972*, edited by Albert N. Garland and the editors of *Infantry* magazine (Nashville: Battery Press, 1982, 1983). See also the series of books by S.L.A. Marshall listed in the Bibliography.

INFILTRATION

Although the North Vietnamese steadfastly insisted throughout the Vietnam war that they had no forces in South Vietnam, after the war they openly admitted that as early as May 1959 they had formed Group 559 to infiltrate cadres and weapons down the Ho Chi Minh Trail into South Vietnam. In July they formed Group 759 to send supplies south by sea. From the early 1960s until General Lon Nol seized power in 1970, the North Vietnamese used the port of Sihanoukville (Kompong Som) in Cambodia to bring in supplies that were moved by truck into their Cambodian and Laotian base areas. With some 20,000 personnel infiltrated into South Vietnam in the early years, by the mid-1960s this trickle had become a flood, and by the time of the cease-fire in January 1973, the North Vietnamese Army had infiltrated 123,000 combat troops into South Vietnam, not including thousands of political cadres and administrative and service personnel.

See also HO CHI MINH TRAIL.

Suggestions for further reading: *Vietnam: A History,* by Stanley Karnow (New York: Viking, 1983); *Vietnam from Ceasefire to Capitulation,* by William E. LeGro (Washington, D.C.: U.S. Government Printing Office, 1981).

IRAN

See ICCS.

IRON TRIANGLE

The nickname for a Viet Cong guerrilla base area less than 20 miles northwest of Saigon in III

American infantrymen on patrol in South Vietnam.

Corps, the "Iron Triangle" was the site of several major U.S. combat operations. Heavily forested and sparsely populated except for the village of Ben Suc, this 125-square mile area was laced with tunnels and fortifications. It served as the base for terrorist activities against Saigon and as a supply depot and staging area for raids against nearby population centers and transportation routes.

See also BEN SUC OPERATION, TUNNEL WARFARE. *See map at* WAR ZONES.

Suggestions for further reading: *Cedar Falls-Junction City: A Turning Point*, by Bernard William Rogers (Washington, D.C.: U.S. Government Printing Office, 1974).

JAPAN

Although not officially a participant in the war in Vietnam, Japan played an important part in the conflict there. Prior to 1965 logistical support for U.S. forces in Vietnam was provided by elements of the U.S. Army's Ninth Logistical Command on Okinawa. Then administered by the United States as the Ryukyus Command, Okinawa was also the home base for the Army's First Special Forces Group, which, prior to the activation of the Fifth Special Forces Group in 1964, rotated teams in and out of Vietnam and Laos. In addition it was the home base for the U.S. Army's 173rd Airborne Brigade and the U.S. Third Marine Division, both of which subsequently served in Vietnam. U.S. Navy facilities were also located there, as were elements of the U.S. Air Force's Strategic Air Command and tactical and airlift elements of the Pacific Air Force. Although the Ryukyu Islands, including Okinawa, reverted to Japanese sovereignty on May 15, 1972, the United States continued to operate bases there.

In Japan the U.S. Seventh Fleet was homeported at the naval base at Yokuska, near Yokohama. The U.S. Air Force's 315th Air Division, whose C-130 aircraft provided a major portion of tactical airlift within Vietnam, was located at Tachikawa and Yokota Air Force Bases near Tokyo. The U.S. Army maintained logistical bases at Fuji and Zama, and hospitals in Japan played a major role in casualty evacuation from Vietnam.

Japan also provided some $55 million in economic assistance to South Vietnam and sent two medical teams and considerable amounts of medical supplies to aid the civilian population.

Suggestions for further reading: *Vietnam Studies: Allied Participation in Vietnam*, by Stanley Robert Larsen and James Lawton Collins, Jr. (Washington, D.C.: U.S. Government Printing Office, 1975).

JAVITS, JACOB K(OPPEL) (1904–1986)

Javits was born in New York City on May 18, 1904. He received a law degree from New York University and was admitted to the bar in 1927. After serving in the Army during World War II, he won election to the House of Representatives in 1946 and was elected to the Senate in 1956.

During the Nixon Administration, Javits, who had compiled a liberal voting record in the 1960s, became increasingly critical of the war in Vietnam. In May 1969 he called Nixon's Vietnam policy "sterile" and asked the President to set a timetable for the withdrawal of U.S. troops. In 1970 he voted for the Cooper-Church Amendment to cut off funds for combat operations in Cambodia, and in 1971 he supported the McGovern-Hatfield end-the-war Amendment.

Javits introduced legislation in 1970 to limit the

war-making powers of the President. Finally passed by both houses of Congress on November 7, 1973 over President Nixon's veto, the War Powers Act limited to 60 days the President's ability to send U.S. troops into combat without congressional approval. In 1973 Javits wrote *Who Makes War: The President Versus Congress,* in which he outlined the rationale for the War Powers Act.

Javits was defeated in his bid to win the Republican senatorial nomination in 1980.

See also WAR POWERS ACT.

JOHNS HOPKINS SPEECH

In a speech at Johns Hopkins University on April 7, 1965, Baltimore, Maryland, President Johnson reiterated U.S. willingness to begin negotiations with North Vietnam without any preconditions. As bait he offered the possibility of American investment in a Mekong River development effort and pledged up to a billion dollars in U.S. aid.

Some scholars have maintained that Johnson's offer of aid, which was promptly turned down by the North Vietnamese, actually undercut support for the war in the United States because it amounted to a tacit recognition that Ho Chi Minh and the North Vietnamese were not "real" adversaries of the United States in the same sense as the Germans and Japanese were in World War II.

JOHNSON, HAROLD K(EITH) (1912–1983)

Born on February 22, 1912 in Bowesville, North Dakota, Johnson graduated from the U.S. Military Academy in 1933. As a battalion commander in the Philippine Scouts, he was captured by the Japanese in the fall of Bataan and took part in the infamous Bataan Death March. He spent the remainder of World War II as a prisoner of war. He was a regimental commander with the First Cavalry Division in the Korean war. His unit was among the first to make contact with Chinese forces when they intervened in the war in late 1950.

After serving as Commandant of the Army's Command and General Staff College in 1960, General Johnson served as Deputy Chief of Staff for Operations and Plans (and as Army Operations Deputy on the Joint Chiefs of Staff) from July 1963 until he was appointed Army Chief of Staff on July 6, 1964. Unlike Army Chief of Staff General George Marshall, who was a key participant in World War II decision making, General Johnson had little influence on the course of the Vietnam war. Because of changes in America's organization for combat after World War II, the Army Chief of Staff was rarely consulted on operational matters. During the height of the American buildup from June 1965 to June 1966, General Johnson saw the President privately twice.

General Johnson retired from active duty in July 1968. He died on September 24, 1983.

See also CHIEF OF STAFF, U.S. ARMY.

Suggestions for further reading: *The 25-Year War: America's Military Role in Vietnam,* by Bruce Palmer, Jr. (Louisville: University of Kentucky Press, 1984); *The Best and the Brightest,* by David Halberstam (New York: Random House, 1972); *Soldiers, Statesmen and Cold War Crises,* by Richard K. Betts (Boston: Harvard University Press, 1977); *Strategy for Tomorrow,* by Hanson W. Baldwin (New York: Harper & Row, 1970).

JOHNSON, LYNDON B(AINES) (1908–1973)

Born on August 27, 1908 at Stonewall, Texas, Johnson graduated from Southwest Texas State Teachers College in 1930. A Democrat, he was elected to the U.S. House of Representatives in 1938 and served four terms there. Elected to the U.S. Senate in 1948, he became Senate majority leader in 1953. Chosen to be John F. Kennedy's running mate, Johnson was elected Vice President in 1960. Upon Kennedy's assassination on November 22, 1963, Johnson assumed the presidency.

During the first several months of his presidency, Johnson sought to continue the Southeast Asian policy that President Kennedy had initiated. He retained Kennedy's top foreign policy advisers—

Robert McNamara, Dean Rusk, Maxwell Taylor, Walt Rostow and McGeorge Bundy—and remained committed to the "flexible response" doctrine, which called for the gradual application of force to halt communist aggression wherever and whenever it appeared.

As Commander-and-Chief of U.S. armed forces, Johnson was ultimately responsible for the step-by-step military escalation of the war, and for the "nation-building" policy in South Vietnam that went hand in hand with the military effort. Nation building was not so much an explicit, defined policy as much as a disparate collection of social and economic programs instituted by U.S. experts over time to, in Stanley Karnow's words, "reconstruct Vietnamese society along Western lines." These programs, based more upon American social science research and technology than upon a careful reading of Vietnamese history and culture, were bound to fail, and usually did.

Plans to increase U.S. military aid began in late 1963, when it became apparent that the South Vietnamese government was losing ground in its battle against the Viet Cong. The Gulf of Tonkin Incident of August 4, 1964 led Johnson to authorize retaliatory bombing of North Vietnam. On August 7, at Johnson's request, Congress passed the Tonkin Gulf Resolution, granting the President broad authority to use military force throughout Southeast Asia "to prevent further aggression."

In February 1965 communist guerrillas attacked the U.S. military installations at Pleiku and Qui Nhon; this, along with reports Johnson received claiming that the Viet Cong were expanding their control of the South Vietnamese countryside, prompted the President to order continuous bombing raids over the north by the end of February. Soon thereafter he authorized the landing of two combat-ready U.S. Marine battalions to protect the air base at Da Nang and on April 1 approved the use of U.S. ground troops for offensive actions. The gradual expansion of the U.S. forces would continue until early 1968, when some 500,000 American military personnel were in Vietnam.

A number of factors contributed to the step-by-step escalation of the war. Johnson, fearing the damaging effects a greatly escalated conflict might have on his domestic social programs, deliberately failed to mobilize the full support of the American people, choosing instead, in Norman Podhoretz's words, "to fight the war on the cheap." Throughout the war, too, Johnson feared that all-out escalation might prompt Chinese or Russian intervention. As the war dragged on, Johnson feared that a dramatic escalation would accelerate the defection of influential liberals and substantially increase the size of the antiwar movement. Another factor was the failure on the part of policy makers to appreciate the tenacity and will power of the communists, who were prepared to take—and, in fact, did take—astoundingly heavy losses.

Between 1965 and 1967, Johnson announced repeatedly that he favored negotiations with the North Vietnamese, and several bombing halts were called, ostensibly to facilitate the start of talks. Hanoi's leaders did not respond to the President's "peace feelers," in part because they insisted upon an unconditional halt to the bombing of the north, but also because they felt they could wear down the American will to carry on the war. In a September 1967 speech delivered at San Antonio, Johnson promised to halt the air war indefinitely if North Vietnam agreed promptly to begin peace negotiations and not to "take advantage of the cessation in bombing to resupply men and matériel to the South." Since there were already some 100,000 North Vietnamese troops in the south, Hanoi rejected the "San Antonio Formula."

Johnson reached the decision to de-escalate only after the Viet Cong's dramatic—yet militarily unsuccessful—Tet Offensive of February 1968, in which some 90 South Vietnamese cities were attacked by both Viet Cong and North Vietnamese Army forces. For Johnson the decision had been an agonizing one, brought about by a number of complex factors. Following Tet, General William C. Westmoreland and the Joint Chiefs of Staff asked for more than 200,000 additional troops, about half to be deployed to Vietnam and the rest to strengthen security in other parts of the world. Instead of granting the request, Johnson appointed his new Secretary of Defense, Clark Clifford, as head of a task force to study the proposal and examine its impact on the budget, public opinion and future prospects for negotiations with the North Vietnamese. Clifford's report, based upon extensive discussion with senior military and civilian Pentagon officials, called for mobilization of the reserves but only to meet contingency situations. It stated that "there is no reason to believe" that the additional troops requested for deployment to Vietnam would be able to do the job at hand. It also recommended that U.S. assistance be predicated upon the improved performance of the South Vietnamese government in cleaning up corruption. Paul Warnke's original draft of the document also mentioned that increasing troop strength at this stage would risk provoking "domestic crisis" because domestic programs would have to be curtailed to pay for such an increase.

On March 25, an informal group of "wise men" was assembled at the State Department, including Dean Acheson, George Ball, Matthew Ridgway and Henry Cabot Lodge. After listening to detailed briefings, the consensus was to de-escalate the war and begin negotiations with the North Vietnamese. Johnson would later admit that this informal group strongly influenced his decision to de-escalate, but there were other factors as well, notably the growing dissent in Congress over the war, the expansion of the antiwar movement and, indirectly, the Tet Offensive itself, which seemed to demonstrate to the American people, as well as to administration allies in the media, that not only was no end to the war in sight, but that the administration appeared to have no adequate plan to bring it to an end. Senator Eugene McCarthy's strong showing as a peace candidate in the March New Hampshire primary seemed to confirm the public's discontent with the war. Four days later Senator Robert Kennedy announced he too would run as an antiwar candidate.

On March 31 Johnson went before a nationwide television audience to announce a unilateral halt to air and naval bombardment of North Vietnam except for the area immediately north of the DMZ. He called on North Vietnam "to respond positively and favorably to this new step toward peace." At the close of the speech Johnson shocked the nation by announcing that he would not seek reelection. Three days later North

Vietnam agreed to open negotiations in Paris. Talks began that May.

Johnson returned to his home in Texas in 1969. He died on January 22, 1973, five days before the Paris Agreement on Ending the War and Restoring Peace in Vietnam was signed.

See also AD HOC TASK FORCE; ANTIWAR MOVEMENT; BUNDY, MCGEORGE; CLIFFORD, CLARK; CRONKITE WALTER; JOHNS HOPKINS SPEECH; KENNEDY, JOHN F.; KENNEDY, ROBERT F.; LUCE, HENRY R.; MCCARTHY, EUGENE J.; MCNAMARA, ROBERT S.; ROSTOW, WALT W.; RUSK, DEAN; SAN ANTONIO FORMULA; SENIOR ADVISORY GROUP; STRATEGY, U.S.; TAYLOR, MAXWELL D.

Suggestions for further reading: *The Vantage Point: Perspective of the Presidency 1963–1969*, by Lyndon Baines Johnson (New York: Popular Library, 1971); *Lyndon Johnson and the American Dream*, by Doris Kearns (New York: Harper & Row, 1976); *The Unmaking of a President: Lyndon Johnson and Vietnam*, by Herbert Y. Schandler (Princeton: Princeton University Press, 1977); *Why We Were in Vietnam*, by Norman Podhoretz (New York: Simon & Schuster, 1982); *Vietnam: A History*, by Stanley Karnow (New York: Viking, 1983).

JOINT CHIEFS OF STAFF

The Joint Chiefs of Staff (JCS) formally came into being after World War II as part of the reorganization of the U.S. defense establishment, which superimposed a Secretary of Defense between the President and his military advisers.

The JCS consists of five members: a chairman appointed on a rotating basis from the various armed forces, the Army Chief of Staff, the Chief of Naval Operations, the Air Force Chief of Staff and the Commandant of the Marine Corps. An advisory body, it has no command authority and only passes on the orders of the President and the Secretary of Defense to unified-command commanders in the field (in the case of Vietnam, the Commander-in-Chief of the Pacific Command in Honolulu).

During the Vietnam war 30 officers served on the JCS—six Chairmen, seven Army Chiefs of Staff, six Chiefs of Naval Operations, six Air

Force Chiefs of Staff and five Commandants of the Marine Corps. In addition to a lack of wartime continuity, the JCS system revealed major defects in America's ability to conduct combat operations in the field. In the aftermath of the war, Congress has been considering several proposals for JCS reorganization.

See also CHAIRMAN, JOINT CHIEFS OF STAFF; CHIEF OF NAVAL OPERATIONS, U.S. NAVY; CHIEF OF STAFF, U.S. AIR FORCE; CHIEF OF STAFF, U.S. ARMY; COMMANDANT, U.S. MARINE CORPS.

Suggestions for further reading: for critiques of JCS performance, see *Soldiers, Sailors and Cold War Crises,* by Richard K. Betts (Cambridge: Harvard University Press, 1977); *The 25-Year War: America's Military Role in Vietnam,* by Bruce Palmer, Jr. (Louisville: University of Kentucky Press, 1984); *The Joint Chiefs of Staff: The First Twenty-Five Years,* by Lawrence J. Korb (Bloomington: Indiana University Press, 1976).

JOINT GENERAL STAFF

The Joint General Staff (JGS) of the South Vietnamese Armed Forces (SVNAF), like the U.S. Joint Chiefs of Staff (JCS), was subordinate to South Vietnam's President and Minister of Defense. Unlike the JCS, however, the JGS had operational control over South Vietnam's armed forces. Headquartered in Saigon, it controlled the JGS reserve—the Airborne and Marine Divisions—and exercised command of the war through the Air Force and Navy Chiefs of Staff and the four SVNAF Corps Commanders.

The MACV (U.S. Military Assistance Command Vietnam) maintained liaison with JGS. In 1965 MACV Commander General William C. Westmoreland deliberately rejected recommendations that he exercise control over the SVNAF (as was the case with South Korean forces during the Korean war) in favor of a policy of "cooperation."

Suggestions for further reading: *Command and Control 1950-1969,* by George S. Eckhardt (Washington, D.C.: U.S. Government Printing Office, 1975); *A Soldier Reports,* by William C. Westmoreland (Garden City: Doubleday, 1976); *The RVNAF,* by Dong Van Khuyen (Washington, D.C.: U.S. Government Printing Office, 1980); *On Strategy: A Critical Analysis of the Vietnam War,* by Harry G. Summers, Jr. (Novato, Calif.: Presidio Press, 1982). See particularly *Our Endless War: Inside Vietnam,* by former South Vietnamese Minister of Defense Tran Van Don (Novato, Calif.: Presidio Press, 1978) and *The Final Collapse,* by former JGS Chairman General Cao Van Vien (Washington, D.C.: U.S. Government Printing Office, 1983).

KAMPUCHEA

See CAMBODIA.

KENNAN, GEORGE F(ROST) (1904–)

Born on February 16, 1904 in Milwaukee, Wisconsin, Kennan graduated from Princeton in 1925 and entered the Foreign Service the following year. He served with the first embassy to Moscow from 1933 to 1936, was stationed in Prague and Berlin during the opening years of World War II and was interned by the Nazis from December 1941 to May 1942.

In April 1947 Secretary of State George C. Marshall asked Kennan to head the State Department's newly created Policy Planning Staff and charged him with the responsibility for long range planning of U.S. actions in foreign policy. In a July 1947 issue of *Foreign Affairs* in an article entitled "The Sources of Soviet Conduct" and signed "Mr. X," Kennan foresaw the Soviet Union probing for weak links in the Western alliance. To meet this threat Kennan recommended "a long-term patient but firm and vigilant containment of Russian expansive tendencies through . . . the adroit and vigilant application of counterforce at a series of constantly shifting geographical and political points, corresponding to the shifts and maneuvers of Soviet policies."

Kennan's ambiguous use of the term "counterforce" prompted many in Washington to think the diplomat recommended military measures to contain Soviet expansion. In subsequent articles and speeches Kennan argued that he had never viewed containment in this manner. Reiterating that he did not see the USSR as a military threat, he maintained that he had attempted to justify the economic redevelopment of Western Europe and Japan to serve as buffer states against the Soviet Union. Despite his protestations, policymakers began viewing containment in terms of military force, and it became the foundation for U.S. foreign policy and its supporting military policy, including military intervention in Korea and later in Vietnam.

In the mid-1960s Kennan emerged as an important critic of American policy in Vietnam. In numerous articles and speeches and in testimony before several congressional committees, he argued that Vietnam was not vital to American strategic or diplomatic interests. He warned that precipitous escalation of the war in Vietnam would destroy the possibility of a negotiated settlement and force a reapprochement between the Soviet Union and China.

Kennan's analysis received its widest audience in nationally televised hearings of Senator J. William Fulbright's Foreign Relations Committee during February 1966. Kennan charged that because of the Johnson Administration's "preoccupation with Vietnam," Europe and the Soviet Union were not receiving proper diplomatic attention. He argued that the United States had no binding commitment to South Vietnam and questioned whether American credibility or prestige would be seriously damaged by a withdrawal. He advised a minimal military effort to maintain a U.S. presence in Vietnam until a peaceful settlement could be reached. Always a European-oriented diplomat, Kennan "emphatically" denied the applicability of the containment doctrine to Southeast Asia while urging its retention in Europe.

See also CONTAINMENT; DULLES, JOHN FOSTER; EISENHOWER, DWIGHT D.; FULBRIGHT, J. WILLIAM; JOHNSON, LYNDON B.; KENNEDY, JOHN F.; KISSINGER, HENRY A.; NIXON, RICHARD M.

Suggestions for further reading: *On Dealing with the Communist World*, by George F. Kennan (New York: Harper & Row, 1964); *Memoirs, 1950 to 1963*, by George F. Kennan (Boston: Little, Brown, 1967).

KENNEDY, JOHN F(ITZGERALD) (1917–1963)

Kennedy was born on May 29, 1917 in Brookline, Massachusetts. After graduation from Harvard University in 1940, he served as an officer in the U.S. Navy during World War II. Elected to the U.S. House of Representatives in 1946 and to the Senate in 1952, Kennedy in 1960 defeated Richard M. Nixon to become the 35th President of the United States.

Shunning the previous administration's reliance on nuclear deterrence, Kennedy sought a more flexible strategy in the Cold War, including an expanded military establishment with sufficient conventional, nuclear and counterinsurgency forces to oppose any level of communist aggression throughout the world. One of the areas threatened by communist aggression was Vietnam, which also seemed to Kennedy an ideal proving ground for the new emphasis on counterinsurgency. Consequently, Kennedy directed the armed services—the Army in particular—to develop counterinsurgency forces, and he appointed retired Army General Maxwell D. Taylor as his special military assistant to monitor counterinsurgency affairs. It was made known that future promotion of senior Army officers would depend on their proficiency in counterinsurgency operations. Army Chief of Staff General George

Decker, who opposed such emphasis, was replaced by the more amenable General Earle Wheeler.

Alarmed by reports that the military situation in South Vietnam was deteriorating, Kennedy sent Taylor on a two-week tour of Vietnam in the fall of 1961. Taylor recommended dispatching some 8,000 U.S. combat troops to Vietnam to indicate America's commitment to the government of President Ngo Dinh Diem. While he was concerned that a commitment of combat units might embroil the United States directly in the Vietnam war, Kennedy, who subscribed to both the containment doctrine and the domino theory, sought to avoid the loss of South Vietnam—and the rest of Southeast Asia—to the communists. So he opted for stepping up the level of military and economic aid and the number of military and civilian advisers, which had already increased by more than 1,000 since he took office and would eventually surpass 16,000 by the time of his assassination in 1963.

The die was cast for a faulty strategy in Vietnam that would ultimately prove disastrous. The prevailing wisdom was that a counterinsurgency effort combined with sufficient military aid would enable the South Vietnamese to prevail on the battlefield. In conjunction with the military effort, the United States would pressure the Diem government into opening up the political process to opposition groups and instituting various social reforms aimed at winning the allegiance of the people in the fight against the communists. The United States would supply additional economic aid and undertake civil action programs to improve the quality of life for the South Vietnamese, as part of an overall program to make South Vietnam a viable anchor of democracy in Southeast Asia. Through this social engineering, the United States was attempting to create its own notion of an acceptable form of government—a likeness of the American system.

With the resulting increased military presence came a greater involvement in the internal affairs of South Vietnam. However, Diem's continued refusal to institute various reforms recommended by U.S. advisers and his suppression of opposing political and religious factions eventually led the Kennedy Administration to give tacit approval to a coup that overthrew the Diem government on November 1, 1963.

Critics have charged that by meddling in the internal political affairs of South Vietnam, the Kennedy Administration unwittingly doomed any chance for South Vietnamese self-reliance, for the country became increasingly, and in the end fatally, dependent on the United States following the November 1963 coup.

Kennedy was assassinated on November 22, 1963.

See also BUNDY, McGEORGE; CONTAINMENT; COUNTERINSURGENCY; DECKER, GEORGE; DIEM, NGO DINH; HARRIMAN, AVERELL; HILSMAN, ROGER; JOHNSON, LYNDON B.; LODGE, HENRY CABOT; McNAMARA, ROBERT S.; ROSTOW, WALT W.; RUSK, DEAN; TAYLOR, MAXWELL D.

Suggestions for further reading: *Our Vietnam Nightmare*, by Marguerite Higgins (New York: Harper & Row, 1965); *A Thousand Days: John F. Kennedy in the White House*, by Arthur Schlesinger, Jr. (Boston: Houghton Mifflin, 1965); *The Best and the Brightest*, by David Halberstam (New York: Random House, 1972); *The Kennedy Imprisonment: A Meditation on Power*, by Gary Wills (Boston: Little, Brown, 1982); *Why We Were in Vietnam*, by Norman Podhoretz (New York: Simon & Schuster, 1982); *Kennedy in Vietnam*, by William J. Rust and the editors of U.S. News & World Report Books (New York: Charles Scribner's Sons, 1985).

KENNEDY, ROBERT F(RANCIS) (1925–68)

Robert Kennedy was born on November 20, 1925 in Brookline, Massachusetts. Following service in the U.S. Navy during World War II, he graduated from Harvard in 1948 and the University of Virginia Law School three years later.

After serving as chief counsel of the Senate Rackets Committee in the 1950s, Robert Kennedy became Attorney General after his brother, John, won the 1960 presidential election. He resigned in August 1964, nine months after John Kennedy's assassination, and was elected to the U.S. Senate from New York in November. An initial supporter of the Johnson Administration's Vietnam war policy, Kennedy became increasingly critical of the war effort following the President's resumption of the bombing of North Vietnam in early 1966. After Eugene J. McCarthy's surprisingly strong showing in the March 1968 New Hampshire primary, he declared his candidacy for the Democratic presidential nomination. Two weeks later Johnson announced he would not seek reelection. On June 4, after defeating Senator McCarthy in the California primary, Kennedy was shot and two days later he died.

Suggestions for further reading: *An American Melodrama,* by Lewis Chester, Godfrey Hodgson and Bruce Page (New York: Viking Press, 1969); *The Unfinished Odyssey of Robert Kennedy,* by David Halberstam (New York: Random House, 1968).

KENT STATE INCIDENT

In the aftermath of President Nixon's April 30, 1970 announcement that U.S. and South Vietnamese forces had been ordered to execute an "incursion" into Cambodia to destroy North Vietnamese base areas there, disturbances broke out on college campuses across the country.

At Kent State University in Ohio, student protesters torched the ROTC building on campus, and Ohio Governor James Rhodes called out the National Guard to restore order. On May 4, 1970, under harassment from the crowd, Guardsmen fired their rifles at the demonstrators, killing four.

The incident sparked hundreds of college shutdowns and protests, including a march on Washington, D.C. by 100,000 people. Later brought to trial, the Guardsmen were found not guilty.

See also ANTIWAR MOVEMENT.

Suggestions for further reading: *Vietnam: A History,* by Stanley Karnow (New York: Viking, 1983); *The Vietnam Experience: A Nation Divided,* by Clark Dougan and Samuel Lipsman (Boston: Boston Publishing Co., 1984).

KHE SANH, BATTLE OF

The North Vietnamese Army (NVA) assault on the U.S. Marine base at Khe Sanh in the predawn hours of January 21, 1968 signaled the beginning of one of the Vietnam war's most controversial battles.

National Guardsmen toss tear gas into a crowd of demonstrators at Kent State University. (AP/Wide World Photos.)

Empty 105 mm shell casings form a wall for this gun crew at Khe Sanh. (Courtesy U.S. Marine Corps.)

One of a series of combat bases and strong points that stretched from the mouth of the Cui Viet River on the coast of the South China Sea westward along Route 9 paralleling the DMZ, Khe Sanh was the westernmost anchor of this line. Close to North Vietnam's primary supply and infiltration route, the Ho Chi Minh Trail in nearby Laos, the critical importance of the old French outpost at Khe Sanh had long been acknowledged. U.S. involvement in the area began when Lang Vei, a small U.S. Army Special Forces camp, was established there in 1962. U.S. Marine units conducted patrols in the area in 1966, and beginning in the spring of 1967, a series of battles took place between the Marines and regular units of the North Vietnamese Army.

In the summer of 1967 General William C. Westmoreland made the decision to upgrade the Khe Sanh base as a potential launch point for an invasion into Laos to cut the Ho Chi Minh Trail. The U.S. Third Marine Division's 26th Marine Regiment, later reinforced with battalions from the Ninth and 13th Marine Regiments as well as the South Vietnamese 37th Ranger Battalion—a total of some 6,000 officers and men—were ordered to secure the base. While the decision to attack into Laos was pending in Washington, the North Vietnamese Army began to build up its forces in the Khe Sanh area and elements of the regular NVA 304th, 320th, 324B and 325C North Divisions were identified in the area. Some 15,000 to 20,000 North Vietnamese soldiers were believed to be near Khe Sanh itself, with several thousand more within striking distance.

The enemy buildup and the relative exposure of the Marine garrison raised fears in Washington that the North Vietnamese were about to execute another Dien Bien Phu. Since, by delivering the coup de grace to French public morale and political will to continue the war, the loss of Dien Bien Phu had led directly to the French defeat in Vietnam, President Johnson was especially concerned with preserving the Khe Sanh base. He went so far as to require a written guarantee from the Joint Chiefs of Staff that the Marines could hold Khe Sanh.

But on January 31, 1968, when the Viet Cong launched a countrywide attack on the cities of Vietnam during the Tet Offensive of 1968, the Battle of Khe Sanh took on a new light. Critics have charged that, far from trying to win another Dien Bien Phu, the North Vietnamese had actually used the attack there as a diversion to draw American forces away from the cities of South Vietnam. In conjunction with the Viet Cong attacks, the North Vietnamese continued to put pressure on Khe Sanh. On February 6 the Army Special Forces camp at Lang Vei was overrun by North Vietnamese Army regulars supported by artillery and nine Soviet PT-76 tanks, the communists' first use of tanks in South Vietnam. The Khe Sanh base itself was continually probed by enemy ground attacks and subjected to concentrated artillery fire. On February 23 alone, the base received 1,307 rounds of mortar, rocket and artillery fire. The staunch Marine defense, combined with massive American fire support, including Operation Niagara—massive air strikes by Air Force, Navy and Marine Corps fighters and fighter-bombers as well as bombing raids by B-52 bombers of the Strategic Air Command—continued to frustrate North Vietnamese efforts.

As the Tet Offensive ground to a close, General Westmoreland ordered the First U.S. Air Cavalry Division to relieve the Marine units at Khe Sanh. Reinforced by elements of the First Marine Division and the South Vietnamese Airborne Brigade, the relief operation began on April 1, and after hard fighting the siege of Khe Sanh was finally lifted on April 7, when the U.S. Army's Second Battalion, Seventh Cavalry linked up with the Marines. Ironically, after this intense American effort to defend the base, Khe Sanh was evacuated and abandoned in June 1968, since plans for ground interdiction of the Ho Chi Minh Trail failed to win approval in Washington.

In the battle for Khe Sanh, 205 American Marines lost their lives. While accurate North Vietnamese casualty figures are not available, 1,602 North Vietnamese bodies were left on the battlefield, and General Westmoreland estimated that the North Vietnamese lost between 10,000 and 15,000 men.

See also ARMOR; DIEN BIEN PHU; HO CHI MINH TRAIL; MARINE CORPS, U.S.; NIAGARA OPERATION; SPECIAL FORCES; TET OFFENSIVE. *See* maps at DMZ (DEMILITARIZED ZONE), I CORPS TACTICAL ZONE.

Suggestions for further reading: *The End of the Line: The Siege of Khe Sanh*, by Robert Pisor (New York: Norton, 1982); *Dispatches*, by Michael Herr (New York: Alfred A. Knopf, 1977); *The Battle for Khe Sanh*, by Moyers S. Shore, II (Washington, D.C.: Historical Branch, U.S. Marine Corps, 1969).

U.S. Marines in the trenches at Khe Sanh. (AP/Wide World Photos.)

KHMER ROUGE

Literally "Red Cambodians," Khmer Rouge is the name of the Cambodian Communist Party. Although originally organized and trained by the Vietnamese communists, it received little support from them as long as Cambodian chief of state Prince Norodon Sihanouk allowed North Vietnamese infiltration of supplies and equipment through the port of Sihanoukville (Kompong Som) and across Cambodia by truck to North Vietnamese Army (NVA) base areas along the Cambodian and Laotian borders with South Vietnam. When Sihanouk tacitly agreed to the secret U.S. bombing of these base areas in 1969 (Operation Menu)—and especially after Sihanouk was deposed in 1970 by General Lon Nol—the NVA stepped up its support to the Khmer Rouge. As the Khmer Rouge gained in power, however, it became increasingly estranged from the NVA. From 1970 to 1975 the Khmer Rouge waged an increasingly effective war against the Cambodian Army—Forces Armées Nationale Khmer (FANK)—and gradually pushed it into defensive positions in the cities. The communist Khmer's final offensive forced Lon Nol's army to capitulate.

The Khmer Rouge leader, Saloth Sar, who adopted the name "Pol Pot," had studied in Paris, where he developed pseudo-intellectual notions of an agrarian utopia. The personification of what Eric Hoffer called "the true believer" who will kill you for your own good, Pol Pot put his half-baked ideology into practice in Cambodia when the Khmer Rouge seized power in 1975. The Khmer atrocities, in Stanley Karnow's words, made "the Nazi holocaust seem tame by comparison." Proclaiming "Year Zero," the start of their "agrarian utopia," the Khmer Rouge emptied all the cities and towns and proceeded to exterminate as many as 2 million Cambodians—a quarter of the population.

The slaughter ended only when the NVA invaded Cambodia in December 1978 and seized control of most of the country. The Khmer Rouge retreated back to jungle hideaways, from where they began and continue to wage a guerilla war in conjunction with other Khmer resistance groups, including some controlled by Sihanouk, against the Vietnamese invaders.

See also CAMBODIA; FANK TRAINING COMMAND; MENU OPERATION; SIHANOUK, NORODON.

Suggestions for further reading: *Cambodia: Year Zero,* by François Ponchaud, translated by Nancy Amphoux (New York: Holt, Rinehart & Winston, 1978); *Sideshow: Kissinger, Nixon, and the Destruction of Cambodia,* by William Shawcross (New York: Simon & Schuster, 1979); *The Khmer Republic at War and the Final Collapse,* by Sak Sutsakhan (Washington, D.C.: Indochina Monograph, U.S. Army Center of Military History, 1980); *Without Honor: Defeat in Vietnam and Cambodia,* by Arnold R. Isaacs (Baltimore: Johns Hopkins Press, 1983); "Vietnam's Vietnam," by Stephen Morris in *The Atlantic,* January 1985.

KING, MARTIN LUTHER, JR. (1929–1968)

Born on January 15, 1929 in Atlanta, Georgia, King was ordained a Baptist minister in 1947. He received a B.A. from Morehouse College in 1948, a divinity degree from Crozer Theological Seminary in 1951 and a Ph.D. in theology from Boston University in 1955. He helped establish the Southern Christian Leadership Conference in 1957 to coordinate direct action protests in the South and was named its first president. In 1960 he helped organize the Student Nonviolent Coordinating Committee. Throughout the 1960s King was the major proponent of nonviolent direct action within the civil rights movement.

King began to speak out against American involvement in Vietnam in July 1965, and in 1967 he openly identified with the antiwar movement. He argued that the war diverted money and attention from domestic programs created to aid the black poor, but he was strongly criticized by most other prominent civil rights leaders for attempting to link the civil rights and antiwar movements. King's protests against the administration's Vietnam policy alienated President Johnson.

King's opposition to the Vietnam war began well before the antiwar movement became respectable or popular and represented for King a broadening of his commitment to nonviolence from the national to the international level. He was shot to death by a sniper on April 4, 1968.

See also ANTIWAR MOVEMENT.

Suggestions for further reading: *Where Do We Go from Here: Chaos or Community?* by Martin Luther King, Jr. (New York: Bantam, 1967); *King: A Critical Biography,* by David Lewis (New York: Praeger Publishers, 1970).

KISSINGER, HENRY A(LFRED) (1923-   )

Born on May 27, 1923 in Fürth, Germany, Kissinger came to the United States in 1938. After service in the U.S. Army in Europe during World War II, he attended Harvard University, receiving a PhD in 1954. A consultant to the Kennedy and Johnson Administrations in the areas of arms control and foreign policy, he was named Special Assistant to the President for National Security Affairs by President-elect Nixon in December 1968.

The major problem facing the Nixon White House was how to end U.S. involvement in the Vietnam war. Both Kissinger and Nixon ruled out a military victory, but they refused to consider a unilateral withdrawal because they felt such an act would be unworthy of a great power and would signal other nations that the United States could not be trusted to honor its commitments. In June 1969 they proposed a policy of "Vietnamization," which would gradually transfer the responsibility for conducting the war to the South Vietnamese and allow an American withdrawal. Kissinger, however, had little faith in Saigon's military capability and ultimately counted on a combination of personal diplomacy and periodic military escalations aimed at punishing and pressuring the North Vietnamese into resolving the conflict. Yet disengagement from Vietnam proved harder to achieve than Kissinger expected.

The central figure in negotiating a settlement of the war, Kissinger intermittently held secret talks with North Vietnamese diplomats in a suburb outside Paris beginning in August 1969. At these talks, which were in addition to the official negotiations being conducted in Paris, the North Vietnamese rejected his "two-track" formula, whereby the United States and the North Vietnamese would withdraw their military forces from South Vietnam and the South Vietnamese and the Viet Cong would negotiate a political settlement. Although he insisted on mutual withdrawal of troops until May 1972, the North Vietnamese continually refused to agree to remove their troops. On the other hand, the North Vietnamese insisted on the removal of South Vietnamese President Nguyen Van Thieu, whom the Uni-

ted States refused to abandon.

Kissinger's early diplomatic efforts, which made little progress toward a settlement, brought him much criticism from the antiwar movement. The outcry against Kissinger and the administration's Vietnam policy became most intense following the Cambodia "incursion" in the spring of 1970, which set off numerous campus demonstrations, some violent, and bitter press commentaries. Critics charged the administration with widening the war rather than ending it and Congress passed legislation prohibiting the use of U.S. troops in Laos or Thailand. Kissinger was particularly subject—and sensitive—to criticism from the left because of his standing as an academic, yet for the most part he remained popular with the public and with the media, which found his secret shuttle diplomacy especially newsworthy.

Pressure for an end to U.S. involvement in Vietnam mounted in 1971. While negotiations in Paris yielded no substantive progress, Kissinger and Nixon were pursuing an alternate route to a settlement of the Vietnam war as part of an overall strategy to exploit strained Sino-Soviet relations. Kissinger went to Peking in July 1971 to lay the groundwork for a historic visit there by Nixon in February 1972. After his trip to Peking the President traveled to Moscow in May 1972 for a summit with Soviet leader Leonid Brezhnev. In discussions with North Vietnam's two strongest allies, Nixon made resolution of the Vietnam conflict a high priority. That spring a major North Vietnamese offensive was stymied largely by U.S. bombing.

In the months leading up to the 1972 presidential election, Kissinger directed a major effort toward achieving a settlement of the war, conducting private talks with North Vietnam's chief negotiator, Le Duc Tho. Both sides moderated their previous positions somewhat and in October they worked out a peace agreement. Although President Thieu publicly repudiated the agreement, Kissinger declared, "Peace is at hand," to reassure North Vietnam of America's desire to achieve a peaceful solution. But he was unable to get Hanoi to agree to changes demanded by Saigon and further discussions deadlocked in December. President Nixon, with Kissinger's backing, ordered intense bombing of the Hanoi-Haiphong area to pressure the north into resuming negotiations, provoking another storm of condemnation from the press.

In January, Kissinger and Le Duc Tho settled on a peace agreement that was substantially the same as the October agreement. Nixon reassured Thieu of continued U.S. support and advised him to approve the settlement. A formal agreement was signed in Paris on January 27, 1973. Its terms included the withdrawal of U.S. military forces, a prisoner-of-war exchange and a cease-fire. North Vietnamese troops would be left in place and the Thieu government would remain in power.

In the spring of 1973, Kissinger was unable to convince Congress to allow a continuation of the bombing of Cambodia beyond August 15 to bring about a cease-fire there and to force North Vietnam to abide by the Paris Accords. In June he held talks with Le Duc Tho concerning the observance of the January agreement, but to little avail. Kissinger and some other analysts have blamed the failure of these talks and attempts to gain congressional approval for measures to prevent the collapse of the Saigon government on the Watergate scandal, which eventually caused Nixon to resign.

In September 1973 Kissinger was named Secretary of State by President Nixon, a post he would hold until the end of the Ford Administration. The following month he was awarded the Nobel Peace Prize with Le Duc Tho, who refused to accept it.

See also ANTIWAR MOVEMENT; CAMBODIA; CASE-CHURCH AMENDMENT; COALITION WAR; COOPER-CHURCH AMENDMENT; MENU OPERATION; NIXON, RICHARD M.; PARIS ACCORDS; PEACE TALKS; THIEU, NGUYEN VAN; THO, LE DUC.

Suggestions for further reading: *White House Years* and *Years of Upheaval*, by Henry Kissinger (Boston: Little, Brown, 1979 and 1982); *The Price of Power: Kissinger in the Nixon White House*, by Seymour Hersh (New York: Summit Books, 1983); *Vietnam: A History*, by Stanley Karnow (New York: Viking, 1983); *The 25-Year War: America's Military Role in Vietnam*, by Bruce Palmer, Jr. (Lexington: University of Kentucky Press, 1984); *Sideshow: Kissinger, Nixon and the Destruction of Cambodia*, by William Shawcross (New York: Simon & Schuster, 1979);

Diplomacy for a Crowded World, by George Ball (Boston: Atlantic-Little, Brown, 1976).

KIT CARSON SCOUTS

The Kit Carson Scouts were former Viet Cong who had agreed to live under the laws of the government of South Vietnam and to serve on the front line with the U.S. military forces. These scouts were very valuable, as they led U.S. units to numerous Viet Cong caches, camps and pathways.

KKK (KHMER KAMPUCHEA KRON)

The KKK in Vietnam were the Khmer Kampuchea Kron, an armed association of ethnic Cambodians who lived in the Delta region of South Vietnam and sought the return of two provinces to Cambodia. Although they initially opposed the government of South Vietnam, the U.S. Army Special Forces convinced them to fight the Viet Cong. Some CIDG (Civilian Irregular Defense Groups) camps in the Delta contained KKK soldiers, who were excellent fighters.

KOMER, ROBERT W(ILLIAM) (1922–)

Born on February 23, 1922 in Chicago, Illinois, Komer graduated from Harvard University in 1942. After service in the U.S. Army in World War II, he returned to Harvard to earn his master's degree in 1947 and then joined the CIA.

After service as a Middle East analyst for the CIA, Komer became a Middle East expert on the National Security Council. Named Special Assistant to President Johnson in March 1966, he was charged with revitalizing the effort against the insurgency movement in Vietnam. He convinced the administration that while the counterinsurgency effort should be under overall military authority, it should combine all U.S. resources under civilian control, and in May 1967 he was sent to Vietnam to put his theories into operation.

Named Deputy to the Commander of the MACV (U.S. Military Assistance Command Vietnam) with the rank of Ambassador, Komer organized the CORDS (Civil Operations and Rural Development Support) program, which was acknowledged as a major improvement in counterinsurgency operations.

Appointed Ambassador to Turkey in November 1968 by President Johnson, Komer left government service after President Nixon assumed office in 1969.

See also COLBY, WILLIAM E.; CORDS (CIVILIAN OPERATIONS AND RURAL DEVELOPMENT); PACIFICATION; PHOENIX PROGRAM.

Suggestions for further reading: *Bureaucracy Does Its Thing: Institutional Constraints on US-GVN Performance in Vietnam,* by Robert W. Komer (Santa Monica: RAND Corporation, 1972).

KONTUM

Provincial capital of Kontum Province, the town of Kontum was located in the northern portion of the Central Highlands in II Corps. Headquarters for several U.S. infantry brigades earlier in the war, in 1972 it was the site of a major battle during the North Vietnamese Army's (NVA) Eastertide Offensive.

With U.S. ground forces almost entirely withdrawn from Vietnam, the NVA launched a three-prong attack in the spring of 1972. One prong struck the town of Quang Tri in I Corps, another prong struck the town of An Loc in III Corps and a third prong was launched at Kontum. On April 12, 1972 the NVA's 320th Division struck South Vietnamese Army fire support bases on the high ground overlooking Dak To, 25 miles north of Kontum. The area, known as "Rocket Ridge," fell on April 20, 1972, and the NVA was then able to rain artillery on the two regiments of the South Vietnamese Army's (ARVN) 22nd Division in the valley below. On April 23 the NVA Second Division joined the 320th and on April 24 the two divisions, supported by tanks and heavy artillery, finally overwhelmed Dak To and its defenders. Stopping to regroup, the NVA gave the ARVN time to react. On April 28, 1972 the South Vietnamese 23rd Division moved into position at Kontum and began strengthening its defenses. Attacked by the NVA Second and 320th Divisions on May 16, 1972, the 23rd received heavy U.S. close air support, including strikes by B-52 bombers and by U.S. Army helicopters with TOW antitank missiles. By May 30, 1972, in the face of a strong ARVN counterattack, the NVA withdrew to its base areas in Laos.

Three years later, in March 1975, Kontum was abandoned by the ARVN as part of its withdrawal from the Central Highlands.

See also EASTERTIDE OFFENSIVE.

Suggestions for further reading: *Battles and Campaigns in Vietnam,* by Tom Carhart (New York: Crown Publishers, 1984); *South Vietnam on Trial,* by David Fulgham and Terrence Maitland (Boston: Boston Publishing Co., 1984).

KOREA, SOUTH

South Korea, officially, the Republic of Korea (ROK), furnished substantial combat forces to the South Vietnamese war effort. The South Koreans dispatched a liaison unit in August 1964, which was followed in February 1965 by what they termed a "dove" unit with engineer units and a mobile hospital. In September elements of the ROK Capital (Tiger) Division began arriving in Qui Nhon in II Corps and by April 1966 the entire division was in place. Meanwhile the ROK Marine Corps Second (Blue Dragon) Brigade landed in Vietnam in October 1965 and shortly thereafter established a base at Hui An in I Corps. The ROK Ninth (White Horse) Infantry Division followed in September and was based on Ninh Hoa, near Cam Ranh Bay, in II Corps.

The ROK Capital Division consisted of the Cavalry Regiment and the First and 26th Infantry Regiments; the 10th, 60th and 61st Field Artillery Battalions, with 105-mm howitzers and one battalion—the 628th Field Artillery Battalion— with 155-mm howitzers; and a reconnaissance company. The ROK Ninth Infantry Division consisted of the 28th, 29th and 30th Infantry Regiments; the 30th, 51st and 52nd Field Artillery Battalions, with 105-mm howitzers, and the 966th Field Artillery Battalions, with 155-mm

Soldiers of the ROK Tiger Division disembark from a U.S. Navy ship. (Courtesy U.S. Army.)

howitzers; and a reconnaissance company. The ROK Second Marine Corps Brigade consisted of four battalions of Marine Infantry.

The ROK divisions' primary area of responsibility was the central coastal area of II Corps from Phan Rang in Ninh Thuan Province to the north of Qui Nhon in Binh Dinh Province. Not only did they provide security and protection for the ports and logistical supply areas in this region, they also kept the several hundred miles of roads open between these depots and the U.S. air bases at Phu Cat to the north and Phan Rang to the south. In accomplishing these missions, 4,407 ROK soldiers and marines were killed in action.

Although the ROK Second Marine Corps Brigade returned to Korea in February 1972, the ROK Capital and Ninth Infantry Divisions were among the last units to leave Vietnam, departing on March 16, 1973.

See also FREE WORLD MILITARY FORCES, II CORPS TACTICAL ZONE.

Suggestions for further reading: *Allied Participation in Vietnam,* by Stanley Robert Larsen and James Lawton Collins, Jr. (Washington, D.C.: U.S. Government Printing Office, 1975); *Vietnam Order of Battle,* by Shelby L. Stanton (Washington, D.C.: U.S. News & World Report Books, 1981).

KY, NGUYEN CAO (1930–   )

Born September 8, 1930 in Son Tay, near Hanoi, in the French protectorate of Tonkin, Ky was drafted into the Vietnamese National Army (an army raised by the French to combat the Viet Minh insurrection) in 1950. After serving as an infantry Lieutenant, he volunteered for pilot training. After advanced training in France and Algeria, he graduated as a fully qualified pilot in 1954. Rising to the rank of lieutenant general in the newly formed South Vietnamese Air Force, he was one of the Young Turks who seized power in 1965 to end the near anarchy that had followed the assassination of President Ngo Dinh Diem two years earlier. Ky was elected by the Armed Forces Council to serve as Prime Minister. In 1966 Buddhists, among other political factions, demanded Ky's ouster, and protests, including immolations, took place in various cities, as they had under the Diem regime. The disturbances ended partly as a result of a government crackdown and partly because of a loss of support for the Buddhists among dissident elements of the

Nguyen Cao Ky (left). (Courtesy U.S. Army Military History Institute.)

military. Ky continued in the post of Prime Minister until the elections of 1967, when he became Vice-President of South Vietnam. He served in that position until 1971, when he chose not to run as an opposition candidate against President Nguyen Van Thieu. He reverted to the rank of Air Marshal in the air force. On April 29, 1975, during Operation Frequent Wind, he flew from Saigon to join the U.S. evacuation fleet.

Now a U.S. citizen, he resides in California.

See also BUDDHISTS; DIEM, NGO DINH; LODGE, HENRY CABOT; THIEU, NGUYEN VAN.

Suggestions for further reading: *Twenty Years and Twenty Days,* by Nguyen Cao Ky (New York: Stein & Day, 1976); *The Best and the Brightest,* by David Halberstam (New York: Random House, 1972); *Vietnam: A History,* by Stanley Karnow (New York: Viking, 1983).

LAIRD, MELVIN ROBERT (1922–)

Born on September 1, 1922 in Omaha, Nebraska, Laird graduated from Carleton College in 1942. Enlisting in the U.S. Navy in May 1942, he served aboard the destroyer *Maddox* (later of Tonkin Gulf fame), was twice wounded in action and was commissioned an officer. In 1952 Laird was elected to the U.S. House of Representatives and served there until appointed Secretary of Defense by President Nixon in January 1969.

As Secretary of Defense, Melvin Laird was instrumental in creating the "Vietnamization" program designed to improve the capabilities of South Vietnam's armed forces while withdrawing U.S. forces there.

Although initially concerned about the public's reaction to the Cambodian incursion in the spring of 1970, he backed the operation fully after President Nixon announced it, arguing that it was necessary for the safe withdrawal of American troops. By January 1973, with the Vietnamization programs in place and a cease-fire signed with the North Vietnamese, Secretary Laird chose not to serve in the second Nixon Administration and returned to private life.

See also CAMBODIA, VIETNAMIZATION.

Suggestions for further reading: *The Secretary of Defense,* by Douglas Kinnard (Louisville: Univer-

Melvin Laird (foreground, left). (Courtesy U.S. Army Military History Institute.)

sity of Kentucky Press, 1980); *Vietnam: A History,* by Stanley Karnow (New York: Viking, 1983).

LAM SON

Birthplace of Le Loi, a 15th century Vietnamese hero who led a 10-year fight to expel the Chinese from Vietnam, Lam Son was the code name prefix for many South Vietnamese Armed Forces ground combat operations (e.g., Lam Son 719, the 1971 South Vietnamese operation into Laos).

LAM SON 719

Code name for a South Vietnamese Armed Forces (SVNAF) attempt to raid the Ho Chi Minh Trail in the southern Laotian panhandle, Lam Son 719 began on February 8, 1971.

Earlier, elements of the U.S. 101st Airborne Division (Airmobile) and the First Brigade (Mechanized), Fifth Infantry Division plus artillery and aviation units had reoccupied the abandoned U.S. Marine base at Khe Sanh as an assault position for the SVNAF forces. Forbidden by Congress to cross into Laos, U.S. ground combat forces could only hold the door. Meanwhile a U.S. Navy task force (carrying the 31st Marine Amphibious Unit) conducted a drill off the North Vietnamese city of Vinh, and this threat of an amphibious invasion kept North Vietnamese Army (NVA) units from reinforcing in Laos. Air strikes by the U.S. Army and Air Force, however, would play a more direct role.

The objective of the SVNAF forces was not the permanent occupation of the area but instead a strategic raid—to drive westward from Khe Sanh astride a narrow rugged road, Route 9; cut the Ho Chi Minh Trail; seize Tchepone, some 25 miles away; then retire back into South Vietnam. Major SVNAF units, totaling some 16,000 soldiers, were the South Vietnamese Army (ARVN) First Infantry Division, First Armored Brigade, Airborne Division and a Ranger group, with the Vietnamese Marine Corps division in reserve.

Initially meeting little resistance, the SVNAF task force reached the halfway point on February 11, 1971. Meanwhile the weather had turned bad, limited close air support and helicopter resupply and made Route 9 into an almost impassable quagmire. The task force ground to a halt.

With its crucial supply lines threatened, the NVA reacted fiercely. Some 36,000 NVA regulars were committed, including the NVA LXX (70th) Corps, with the 304th, 308th and 320th Divisions plus the Second and 324th Divisions. All were heavily reinforced by PT-76 and T-54 Soviet-supplied tanks, 122-mm and 130-mm guns (which outranged all ARVN and U.S. artillery except a few 175-mm guns) and extensive air defense artillery weapons. They soon subjected the stalled SVNAF task force to heavy fire.

Supported by U.S. air strikes, including bombing runs by B-52 strategic bombers and assaults by Army helicopter gunships, and resupplied by U.S. Army helicopters, the task force held its positions. Disgusted with the operation's lack of progress, President Nguyen Van Thieu ordered a helicopter assault on Tchepone, and the abandoned village was seized on March 6, 1971. Its "objective" secured, the assault force was withdrawn on March 9, 1971.

But withdrawing the ground task force under North Vietnam pressure was another matter. Two weeks of hard combat were necessary for the task force to fight its way back to Vietnam.

Losses were heavy. The South Vietnamese suffered some 9,000 casualties, almost 50 percent of their force. U.S. forces incurred some 1,462 casualties. Aviation units lost 168 helicopters and another 618 were damaged. Fifty-five aircrewmen were killed in action, 178 were wounded and 34 were missing in action and four U.S. news photographers were killed when the helicopter in which they were riding was shot down by enemy ground fire. Although the NVA had emplaced 23-mm, 37-mm and 57-mm antiaircraft artillery (AAA) cannons, it was their 12.7-mm AAA machine gun (*see* illustration) that accounted for the majority of U.S. helicopter losses.

While some South Vietnamese units fought well, the failure of the operation had an adverse effect on morale. But a year later these same units would stop and turn back the NVA's 1972 Eastertide Offensive.

See also COOPER-CHURCH AMENDMENT, HO CHI MINH TRAIL. *See* map at LAOS.

Suggestions for further reading: *Lam Son 719*, by Nguyen Duy Hinh (Washington, D.C.: U.S. Government Printing Office, 1981). A most readable account of Lam Son 719 is contained in *South Vietnam on Trial*, by David Fulghum and Terrence Maitland (Boston: Boston Publishing Co., 1984).

LAND REFORM

Because 75 percent of the population in South Vietnam was engaged in farming, land reform was an early and effective communist organizing technique. In 1954, after the havoc of the war between the French and the Viet Minh (1946–54), about one-third of the rice-growing land in South Vietnam had been abandoned and irrigation and drainage had broken down. About 2.5 percent of the landowners held almost half of the arable land and 80 percent of the farmers owned no land at all. This was especially true in the Mekong Delta, South Vietnam's rice bowl.

Beginning in 1955 South Vietnam's President Diem issued a series of land reform decrees. Among other things, the decrees limited land holdings to no more than 100 hectares (247 acres), and any land in excess of that amount was purchased by the government for resale to landless farmers in five- to twelve-acre plots. Slow to start because of lack of South Vietnamese government funds, U.S. economic assistance aid permitted the government to purchase some 1.7 million acres in 1957. When North Vietnam began the Vietnam war in 1959, guerrilla activity and South Vietnamese government foot-dragging slowed the land reform program. In 1964 and again in 1965 land reform was pushed by the Saigon government, and the 750,000 acres of village communal land were included in the program. With American aid, President Nguyen Van Thieu also instituted extensive land reforms in the early 1970s, which author Arnold R. Isaacs has called "his administration's single most popular program, and his most important attempt to match the communists in offering social change to Vietnam's peasants."

Ironically, the communist use of land reform as an organizing technique had helped push the government of South Vietnam into instituting some imperfect but generally effective programs. But when the communists took over South Vietnam, they found they had helped create a monster, for the very land reforms they championed had turned the majority of farmers into entrepreneurs. When the new government—the Socialist Republic of Vietnam—tried to collectivize the farms (i.e., make the government the new landlord), the farmers strongly resisted. The Socialist Republic of Vietnam now has a food shortage as the disgruntled farmers sit on their hands.

Suggestions for further reading: *Area Handbook for South Vietnam,* by Harvey H. Smith et al (Washington, D.C.: U.S. Government Printing Office, 1967); *Without Honor: Defeat in Vietnam and Cambodia,* by Arnold R. Isaacs (Baltimore: John Hopkins Press, 1983); *Pacification,* by Tran Dinh Tho (Washington, D.C.: Center of Military History, 1980). See "Nguyen Van Hao's Missing Visa," by David Butler, *National Review* (March 23, 1984), for an account of the problems land reform has caused the current Socialist Republic of Vietnam government.

LANSDALE, EDWARD GEARY (1908-   )

After graduating from the University of California at Los Angeles, Lansdale worked for an advertising agency in San Francisco. He left advertising in 1941 to serve first in the Office of Strategic Services and then in the U.S. Army in the Pacific Theater during World War II. In 1947 he joined the newly formed Air Force.

President Eisenhower sent Lansdale to Vietnam in an advisory role in 1954. During the two years he was in Vietnam, Lansdale developed a number of programs designed to broaden the base of support for Ngo Dinh Diem, the President of South Vietnam. Lansdale helped the South Vietnamese government set up plans for the integration of northern refugees into the south and aided in the development of programs to train government administrators in provinces vacated by the Viet Minh.

Lansdale, who remains a controversial figure, was involved in many of the political imbroglios confronting the South Vietnamese and U.S. governments in the mid-1950s. In the autumn of 1954 he helped prevent a coup against Diem by disgruntled army officers and during the spring of 1955 he defended Diem against attempts to have him removed from power by J. Lawton Collins, whom Eisenhower had sent to Vietnam as his special representative, and the French. From 1965 to 1968 Lansdale served as a special assistant to the U.S. Ambassador in South Vietnam.

To some students and scholars of the war, Lansdale exemplified the best kind of American military adviser—interested not only in warfare but in helping the nation for which he fought. To others, he was a naive foreigner who did not understand the complexities of Vietnamese culture and whose well intentioned efforts seemed to result most often in strife and chaos. Graham Greene described him in this way in *The Quiet American*.

See also COLLINS, J. LAWTON; DIEM, NGO DINH.

Suggestions for further reading: *In the Midst of Wars: An American's Mission to Southeast Asia*, by Edward G. Lansdale (New York: Harper & Row, 1972).

LAOS

With 91,428 square miles of territory Laos is about the size of Great Britain, with an estimated 1983 population of 3,647,000—half ethnic Lao, half mountain tribesmen. Because of its location, Laos played a crucial role in the Vietnam war.

Laos was no stranger to Indochinese machinations. Made a French protectorate in 1893 as part of the Union of Indochina, it won its independence as a constitutional monarchy in July 1949. As a portent of things to come, however, North Vietnamese Army (NVA) General Vo Nguyen Giap in 1954 maneuvered his forces through Laos during the siege of Dien Bien Phu, just across the Laotian border in western Vietnam. Laos was soon to find that France was not the only nation with dreams of an Indochina Union. In July 1959 the North Vietnamese Politburo formed Group 959 to furnish weapons and supplies to communist guerrillas in Laos.

Officially the Neo Lao Hak Sat (Lao Liberation Front), the communist guerrillas were better known as the Pathet Lao. Soon they were threatening the survival of the Royal Lao government, and on January 19, 1961, when President Eisenhower was about to leave office, he told his successor, President Kennedy, that Laos was "the key to the entire area of Southeast Asia."

By May, however, the problem seemed to have

gone away. A conference was convened at Geneva to set up a coalition government and in July 1952 the neutrality of Laos was officially proclaimed. But this neutrality was a farce from the beginning. The North Vietnamese Army (VNA) maintained up to 80,000 soldiers in Laos (most in transport units in the southern panhandle), and starting in December 1963, the United States provided aerial support (Operation Barrel Roll) to the Royal Lao government.

There were two wars in Laos. One in the north between the Royal Lao government and the Pathet Lao government was essentially a stalemate. The other war was carried out along the Ho Chi Minh Trail, which the NVA had begun to build in 1959 to transport men and supplies into South Vietnam. With Operations Steel Tiger and Tiger Hound, from 1965 to 1973 the United States dropped 2,092,900 tons of bombs on Laos (almost exactly as much as were the 2.15 million

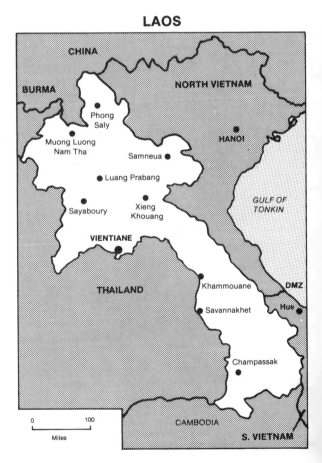

LAOS

ons dropped in all of World War II), most of it on
he Ho Chi Minh Trail. But supplies continued to
nove south. In March 1975 Laos (or, more
pecifically, the Ho Chi Minh Trail in Laos)
ecame the key to the conquest of South Vietnam
nd ultimately to the subjugation of Cambodia
nd Laos. Almost a quarter century later, Presi-
ent Eisenhower was proven correct.

Meanwhile, on October 17, 1972 peace talks
etween the Pathet Lao and the Royal Lao
overnment had begun in the Laotian capital of
'ientiane. A peace agreement, signed on Febru-
ry 21, 1973, called for all U.S. bombing to come to
halt. On April 5, 1975 a coalition government
vas formed, but the Pathet Lao continued to
dvance and on August 23 Vientiane fell. The
eople's Democracy of Laos was proclaimed.

See also AIR AMERICA, BARREL ROLL, CIA (CENTRAL
NTELLIGENCE AGENCY), GENEVA CONFERENCES,
O CHI MINH TRAIL, STEEL TIGER, TIGER HOUND.

Suggestions for further reading: *Without Honor:
Defeat in Vietnam and Cambodia,* by Arnold R. Isaacs
Baltimore: Johns Hopkins Press, 1983); *Vietnam:
A History,* by Stanley Karnow (New York: Viking,
983); *The Royal Lao Government and U.S. Army Advice
nd Support,* by Gudone Sananikone (Washington,
).C.: U.S. Government Printing Office, 1981);
*LA Military Operations and Activities in the Laotian
anhandle,* by Solitchay Vongsavanh (Washington,
).C.: U.S. Government Printing Office, 1981);
he Pathet Lao: Leadership and Organization, by Joseph
.asloff (Lexington, Mass: D.C. Heath, 1973); *The
nd of Nowhere: American Policy Toward Laos Since 1954
Boston: Beacon Press, 1973); "White Star in Laos:
A Study in Miscalculation," by J. Rod Pachall,
npublished manuscript (Carlisle, Pa.: U.S. Army
Military History Institute, 1985).

AVELLE, JOHN D(ANIEL), 1916–1979)

Born on September 9, 1916 in Cleveland, Ohio,
avelle graduated from John Carroll University in
938 and joined the Army Air Corps in 1939,
eceiving his pilot wings and a commission in June
940. A combat fighter pilot in the European
Theater of Operations during World War II, he
commanded a supply depot in Japan during the
Korean war. Lavelle was assigned as Vice Commander-in-Chief of the Pacific Air Force in
Honolulu in September 1970, and in that position
he controlled U.S. Air Force strikes against North
Vietnam. On July 29, 1971 he was appointed
Commander of the Seventh Air Force in Saigon
and concurrently Deputy Commander of the
MACV (U.S. Military Assistance Command Vietnam).

Earlier, on October 31, 1968, the United States
had suspended bombing operations over North
Vietnam. However, there was a tacit "understanding" that reconnaissance flights would continue. When these aircraft were fired upon, the
Seventh Air Force was authorized to strike North
Vietnamese air defense installations. This authorization allowed attacks on North Vietnamese air
defenses, known as "protective reaction strikes,"
as soon as their radar guidance systems locked in
on American aircraft. This was the background
for charges that between November 1971 and
March 1972 General Lavelle had ordered strikes
on North Vietnamese installations under the
guise of such protective reaction. Called before
the House and Senate Armed Services Committee
in the fall of 1972 to explain "secret bombings,"
General Lavelle intimated that they had been
encouraged by higher authority. Charged with
ordering some 28 missions involving 147 sorties
against unauthorized targets in violation of
existing guidelines, General Lavelle was relieved
of command, reduced in rank and retired from
active duty. He died on July 10, 1979.

Suggestions for further reading: *America in Vietnam,*
by Guenter Lewy (New York: Oxford University Press,
1978).

LAW (LIGHT ANTITANK WEAPON)

The M72 light antitank weapon (LAW) was the
standard high-explosive antitank rocket used by
the U.S. Army for all purposes in Vietnam,
especially to destroy enemy bunkers. The LAW
was used most extensively by South Vietnamese
Army foot soldiers, who had to face North
Vietnamese armor by themselves.

An American soldier using an M-72 antitank weapon. (Courtesy U.S. Army News Features.)

LE DUAN

See DUAN, LE.

LE DUC THO

See THO, LE DUC.

LINEBACKER OPERATIONS

Code name for two distinct air operations over Vietnam, Operation Linebacker I was a reaction to the North Vietnamese Eastertide Offensive, which began in March 1972. U.S. Air Force and Marine aircraft flying from bases in South Vietnam and Thailand and Navy aircraft flying from carriers in the South China Sea flew some 41,000 sorties over North Vietnam during this operation. Using B-52 strategic bombers as well as Navy mine-laying aircraft, North Vietnamese harbors were mined and closed to oceangoing traffic; U.S. bombings destroyed 10 MIG bases, six major power plants and all large oil storage facilities in North Vietnam. Some 75 U.S. aircraft were lost in this operation. In October 1972, in response to progress in the peace negotiations

then underway in Paris, Linebacker operations were cut back and limited to the area south of the 20th parallel.

By December 1972 these negotiations had broken down and on December 18 President Nixon ordered an all-out air campaign against the Hanoi area. Known as Operation Linebacker II, it involved strikes by Air Force fighter-bombers flying from bases in Thailand, Navy fighter-bombers flying from carriers in the South China Sea and the concentrated use of B-52 strategic bombers. During an intensive 11-day air campaign, 700 B-52 sorties were flown as well as 1,000 fighter-bomber sorties. The North Vietnamese fired more than 1,000 SAMs (surface-to-air missiles) at these attacking aircraft and also used their MIG fighter-interceptor squadrons. Eight of these MIGs were shot down, two by B-52 tailgunners. Twenty-six U.S. aircraft were lost, including 15 B-52s. Three aircraft were downed by MIGs; the rest, including the B-52s, were downed by SAMs.

American antiwar activists labeled Linebacker II the Christmas Bombing, and the charge was made that it involved the "carpet bombing"—i.e. the deliberate targeting of civilian areas with intensive bombing designed to "carpet" (completely cover) a city with bombs, as in Dresden during World War II—of Hanoi. According to author Stanley Karnow, who visited Hanoi in 1981, "American anti-war activists visiting the city during the attacks urged the mayor to claim a death toll of 10,000. He refused, saying that his government's credibility was at stake. The official North Vietnamese figure for fatalities . . . was 1,318 in Hanoi."

The result of Linebacker II was the return of the North Vietnamese to the negotiating table and the signing of the Paris Accords less than a month later.

See also, NIXON, RICHARD M.; ROLLING THUNDER OPERATION.

Suggestions for further reading: *Airpower in Three Wars,* by William W. Momyer (Washington, D.C.: U.S. Government Printing Office, 1978); *The United States Air Force in Southeast Asia 1961–1973,* edited by Carl Berger (Washington, D.C.: U.S. Government Printing Office, 1977); *The Vietnam Experience: Rain of Fire,* by John Morrocco (Boston: Boston Publishing Co., 1985); *Battles and Campaigns in Vietnam 1954–1984,* by Tom Carhart (New York: Crown Publishers, 1984); *Vietnam: A History,* by Stanley Karnow (New York: Viking, 1983); *Linebacker II: A View from the Rock,* by George B. Allison, USAF Southeast Asia Monograph Series, Vol. VI (Washington, D.C.: U.S. Government Printing Office, 1979).

LIPPMANN, WALTER (1889–1974)

Born on September 21, 1889 in New York City, Lippmann graduated from Harvard in 1910. Four years later he cofounded the *New Republic.* In 1931 Lippmann began his long association with the *New York Herald Tribune,* which carried his column "Today & Tomorrow." He became one of the most influential columnists in the country.

In 1947 Lippmann engaged in a major debate with George Kennan over Kennan's policy of containment. He condemned containment because he thought it would lead to unending intervention and allow the Soviet Union to maintain the initiative in the Cold War. Lippmann attacked the Eisenhower Administration's attempt to couch foreign policy in terms of a moral crusade and he asserted that national interest should be determined by geopolitical and economic factors, not abstract theories of right versus wrong.

Lippmann's views on Vietnam shifted over the years, beginning in 1950 when he cautioned against aiding the French in their "colonial war" with the Viet Minh. In 1952, however, he said that a communist takeover of Southeast Asia would be a "catastrophe." Yet he never considered Vietnam an area of vital U.S. interest and opposed intervention there without the full political and military support of America's allies.

In the 1960s he advised the Kennedy Administration and later the Johnson Administration to seek neutralization of Southeast Asia, as recommended by Charles de Gaulle, but his advice, although constantly sought, went unheeded. He initially supported President Johnson's handling of the Vietnam war and even defended his bombing of the north, starting in early 1965, as a necessary prelude to a negotiated settlement of the conflict. However, he became increasingly pessimistic during the spring as a result of the deployment of American troops and escalation of the fighting. Lippmann tried to persuade the administration to de-escalate, but finally broke with President Johnson and then became engaged in an increasingly hostile feud with the President and his advisers.

Lippmann, whose column began appearing in *Newsweek* in 1963, retired in 1968. He died on December 14, 1974.

See also ANTIWAR MOVEMENT; JOHNSON, LYNDON B.

Suggestions for further reading: *Walter Lippmann and the American Century,* by Ronald Steele (New York: Random House, 1980).

Lippmann retired in 1968. He died on December 14, 1974.

LOC NINH

A village in Binh Long Province in III Corps, some 80 miles due north of Saigon near the Cambodian border and one-time site of a U.S. Special Forces camp, Loc Ninh was overrun on April 5, 1972 by the North Vietnamese Army

(NVA) during its attempt to capture the provincial capital of An Loc farther to the south as part of the Eastertide Offensive.

Although unsuccessful in capturing An Loc, the NVA retained control of Loc Ninh. It was proclaimed as the capital of the Provisional Revolutionary Government of South Vietnam (PRGSVN), i.e., the Viet Cong, a fiction the North Vietnamese maintained until their capture of Saigon in April 1975. Shortly thereafter the PRGSVN disappeared from sight.

See also AN LOC, BATTLE OF; EASTERTIDE OFFENSIVE; PRG (PROVISIONAL REVOLUTIONARY GOVERNMENT).

LODGE, HENRY CABOT (1902–1985)

Born on July 5, 1902 in Nahant, Massachusetts, Lodge graduated from Harvard University in 1924. He was elected to the U.S. Senate in 1936, resigned his seat to serve with the U.S. Army in Europe during World War II and was reelected in 1946. Defeated for reelection in 1952 by John F. Kennedy, Lodge was appointed Ambassador to the United Nations in 1953 by President Eisenhower. He ran unsuccessfully as Richard M. Nixon's vice-presidential candidate in 1960, defeated again by Kennedy.

In June 1963 President Kennedy, seeking bipartisan support for his Vietnam policy, appointed Lodge to be U.S. Ambassador to South Vietnam. He arrived in Saigon on August 22, in the midst of a crisis precipitated by a government attack on Buddhists protesting against the Diem regime. The attack had been carried out by President Ngo Dinh Diem's brother, Ngo Dinh Nhu. Two days after his arrival Lodge was instructed by the State Department to tell Diem he must rid himself of Nhu and to inform South Vietnamese military leaders that the United States would support them "in any interim . . . breakdown [of the] central government." Lodge proposed stating the U.S. position only to the Generals, thus indicating American support for a coup. The plot dissolved mainly because the Generals could not achieve a favorable balance of power in the Saigon area. A

few days later the State Department canceled its earlier instructions and ordered Lodge to "work for the reform of the Diem regime." Lodge remained convinced that the war could not be won with Diem in power.

When South Vietnamese Generals asked about the U.S. stand on a change of government in early October, the Ambassador indirectly informed them that the United States would not thwart any proposed coup. Whether this was done before or after Lodge received an October 5 message from the President ordering him not to give active "covert encouragement to a coup" but to "identify and contact possible alternative leadership" is unclear.

As the coup took shape at the end of October, several of the President's advisers decided to make one last attempt to deal with Diem and asked Lodge to delay or call off the coup. He informed them that the matter was in Vietnamese hands. A successful coup took place on November 1.

In May 1964 Lodge resigned his post but at the request of President Johnson, he became a presidential "consultant" on Vietnam and helped shape the decisions to launch an air war on North Vietnam and to make major ground troop commitments to the struggle.

In July 1965 he began a second tour as Ambassador to South Vietnam. He regenerated the pacification program, which had been subordinated to the military campaign during the early Johnson Administration. During the spring of 1966 Lodge became involved in efforts to end the conflict between the government of Premier Nguyen Cao Ky and the Buddhists. Prompted by the regime's failure to set a definite date for elections and its dismissal of General Nguyen Chanh Thi, the Buddhists demanded the overthrow of Ky and the installation of a civilian government. By the end of March anti-government Buddhists and sympathetic elements of the South Vietnamese Army had gained control of Hué and Da Nang. When conciliatory efforts failed, Lodge concurred in Ky's decision to use force. The Buddhist uprising ended in June as a result of government suppression and a loss of support for the Buddhists among dissidents within the South Vietnamese military.

In April 1967 Lodge again resigned the ambassadorship.

In March 1968 Lodge was a member of the Senior Advisory Group convened to assess the course of the war following the Tet Offensive and the military's request for a large number of additional troops for Vietnam. Although dissatisfied with current policy he was still reluctant to vote for a dramatic change. The panel recommended a policy of de-escalation. Johnson announced this policy on March 31, 1968.

In January 1969 President Nixon appointed Lodge chief negotiator to the Paris peace conference. Frustrated by North Vietnamese intransigence, he asked to be relieved in October 1969. In July 1970 Lodge became the President's Special Envoy to the Vatican, a post he held until 1977. He died on February 27, 1985.

See also BUDDHISTS; DIEM, NGO DINH; HARRIMAN, AVERELL; HILSMAN, ROGER; JOHNSON, LYNDON B; KENNEDY, JOHN F; KY, NGUYEN CAO; PACIFICATION; SENIOR ADVISORY GROUP.

Suggestions for further reading: *Vietnam: A History,* by Stanley Karnow (New York: Viking, 1983); *The Best and the Brightest,* by David Halberstam (New York: Random House, 1972); *The Lodges of Massachusetts,* by Alden Hatch (New York: Hawthorn Books, 1973); *The Storm Has Many Eyes: A Personal Narrative,* by Henry Cabot Lodge (New York: Norton, 1973); *Henry Cabot Lodge,* by William J. Miller (New York: Heineman, 1967).

LONG BINH

A logistical complex constructed by the United States on the outskirts of the city of Bien Hoa in III Corps on the Bien Hoa-Saigon highway. Site of numerous ammunition depots, supply depots and other logistic installations, it also contained a replacement depot, where many incoming and outgoing soldiers were processed, and a stockade (a "confinement facility," in current bureaucratic jargon), known to soldiers as the Long Binh Jail— or "LBJ" for short.

Long Binh served as headquarters for U.S. Army Vietnam, the First Logistical Command and other such activities.

See map at III CORPS TACTICAL ZONE.

LRRP (LONG RANGE RECONNAISSANCE PATROLS)

One of the tactical innovations of the Vietnam war was the organization of long range reconnaissance patrol (LRRP—pronounced "Lurp") units. The LRRP concept was a reaction to the nature of the battlefield, which had no fixed front lines, and to the nature of the South Vietnamese terrain (*see* Part I, THE SETTING), most of which was covered with jungles and mountains that provided the enemy with base areas and supply routes (e.g., the Ho Chi Minh Trail), with the majority of the population clustered in the coastal enclaves.

Three general types of LRRP units emerged. First were the special reconnaissance units organized by the U.S. Army Special Forces. Detachment B-52 (Project DELTA) was organized in May 1964 and grew to a strength of 93 U.S. Special Forces and 1,208 Vietnamese and other ethnic group irregular military personnel. It was organized into 12 reconnaissance teams, whose mission was to collect intelligence on North Vietnamese and Viet Cong troop movements, assess bomb damage,

Henry Cabot Lodge with an unidentified American officer.
(Courtesy U.S. Army Military History Institute.)

coordinate artillery and air strikes and conduct special raids. It also had 12 "Roadrunner" teams to conduct reconnaissance over North Vietnamese and Viet Cong trail networks. Based at Nha Trang, it was under the control of the MACV (U.S. Military Assistance Command Vietnam) and was used throughout the entire country. In September 1966 it received the additional duty of training LRRP teams organized by regular U.S. infantry units. In August 1966, Detachment B-50 (Project OMEGA) was formed at Ban Me Thuot in II Corps with 127 U.S. Special Forces and 894 ethnic troops. Similar in organization to Project DELTA, it was placed under the operational control of I Field Force Vietnam. At the same time an identical unit, Detachment B-56 (Project SIGMA) was formed at Ho Ngoc Nau, near Saigon, and came under operational control of II Field Force Vietnam. OMEGA and SIGMA were absorbed into MACV-SOG in November 1967.

Special Forces also had other highly-classified intelligence collection units, such as Detachment B-57 (Project GAMMA), which conducted long range reconnaissance patrols into Cambodia. Another highly classified unit was MACV's Studies and Observation Group (SOG), which included U.S. Army Special Forces, U.S. Air Force Air Commando units, U.S. Navy SEALs and U.S. Marine Corps force reconnaissance personnel, who among other assignments also conducted cross-border long range reconnaissance patrols.

In addition to the U.S. Special Force's LRRP teams, regular units of U.S. and Allied forces also had LRRP organizations. The Australian Task Force, for example, deployed a Special Air Service (SAS) squadron to Vietnam in April 1966. Composed of highly trained commandoes, the SAS routinely conducted long range reconnaissance patrols throughout the Australian area of responsibility, Phuoc Tuy Province in III Corps (*see* illustration). Beginning in 1967 a number of separate LRRP companies were organized, including the only U.S. Army National Guard rifle company to serve in Vietnam, Indiana's Company D, 151st Infantry. Later converted to Companies C through I and K through P, 75th Infantry (Ranger), they were assigned to Army divisions and separate infantry brigades to give these units a LRRP capability.

The final category of LRRP units was those raised either informally or formally by U.S. combat units in the early days of the war before the specially trained units were available. Consisting usually of a platoon organized by a division's cavalry squadron, which had responsibility for reconnaissance, they were widely used to gather battlefield intelligence.

See also, DELTA, FIFTH SPECIAL FORCES, MONTAGNARDS, SPECIAL FORCES.

Suggestions for further reading: *Vietnam Order of Battle* (Washington, D.C.: U.S. News & World Report Books, 1981) and *Green Berets at War* (Novato, Calif.: Presidio Press, 1985), by Shelby L. Stanton; *U.S. Army Special Forces 1961–1971*, by Francis J. Kelly (Washington, D.C.: U.S. Government Printing Office, 1973); LRRP actions in Vietnam are vividly described in Kenneth E. Miller's novel *Tiger the Lurp Dog* (Boston: Little, Brown, 1983).

LUCE, HENRY R(OBINSON) (1898–1967)

A Presbyterian missionary's son, Luce was born in Tengchow, China on April 3, 1898. After growing up in China, he received a B.A. from Yale in 1920. Luce cofounded *Time* in 1927. He and his publishing concern prospered with the notable additions of *Fortune* in 1930 and *Life* in 1936. Luce's

An Australian Long Range Reconnaissance Patrol returning to camp. (Courtesy U.S. Army Military History Institute.)

close ties with Chinese Nationalist leader Chiang Kai-shek influenced his magazines' coverage of events in Asia. Luce retired as Editor-in-Chief in April 1964 but retained much of his authority over the magazine as editorial chairman. He was succeeded by Hedley Donovan.

The Luce magazines, particularly *Time*, encouraged American military involvement in Vietnam and discouraged negative reporting about the war by their correspondents in Saigon. Dispatches were checked with the State and Defense Departments as well as the White House and edited accordingly. In an April 1964 speech Luce termed Vietnam "troublesome" but added that it represented an "entanglement in the cause of human freedom." *Time* and *Life* covered the August 1964 Tonkin Gulf Incident as an unprovoked challenge to freedom of the seas and their reports were bolstered by confidential Defense Department information that seemed to justify the administration's response. A 1965 issue of *Time* described American troops as "lean, laconic and looking for a fight" and told its 2.9 million subscribers that "the Viet Cong's once-cocky hunters have become the cowering hunted." *Time* made Army Gen. Wil-

liam C. Westmoreland its "Man of the Year" for 1965.

Luce died on February 28, 1967. In late summer doubts about the war and qualifications about its progress began to appear in *Time*, doubts that had affected Donovan during a trip to Vietnam in April. Very slowly Donovan, like the American political center, had started to turn against the war. By early 1968 *Time* and *Life* were calling for a change in policy in Vietnam. President Johnson, who had long regarded *Time* as a principal ally, was incensed by this switch and later said "Hedley Donovan betrayed me." In a June 1969 issue *Life* printed the photos of some 240 American soldiers killed in less than a week at "Hamburger Hill."

See also ANTIWAR MOVEMENT; HAMBURGER HILL; JOHNSON, LYNDON B.; MEDIA; TONKIN GULF RESOLUTION.

Suggestions for further reading: *The Power and the Glory*, by David Halberstam (New York: Alfred A Knopf, 1979); *Luce*, by John Kobler (Garden City, N.Y.: Doubleday, 1968); *Luce and His Empire*, by W.A. Swanberg (New York: Charles Scribner's Sons, 1972); *Vietnam, A History*, by Stanley Karnow (New York: Viking, 1983).

M-14 RIFLE

Designed as a replacement for the World War II- and Korean war-vintage .30 caliber M-1 rifle and compatibility with the rifles of Western European allies, the M-14 was the standard U.S. infantry rifle at the beginning of the Vietnam war. Weighing 9.3 pounds and firing a 7.62 mm cartridge, it had a 20-round magazine and an effective range of 506 yards (460 meters). Too heavy and unwieldy for jungle warfare, beginning in 1966 it was replaced by the M-16 rifle.

See also: M-16 RIFLE.

Suggestions for further reading: *The Great Rifle*

Controversy, by Edward Clinton Ezell (Harrisburg: Stackpole, 1984); *The Vietnam Experience: Tools of War*, by Edgar C. Doleman, Jr. (Boston: Boston Publishing Company, 1984).

M-16 RIFLE

Becoming the standard U.S. infantry rifle in Vietnam in 1967, the M-16 rifle (also known as the Stoner, for its inventor, Eugene M. Stoner, and as the ArmaLite, for one of its original manufacturers) replaced the M-14. Almost two pounds lighter and five inches shorter than the

An American soldier with an M-14 on the lookout for Viet Cong. (Courtesy U.S. Army.)

A South Vietnamese soldier firing his M-16.

M-14, but with the same effective range of just over 500 yards, it fired the smaller, and lighter, 5.56-mm cartridge. The M-16 rifle could be fired fully automatic (i.e., like a machine gun) or one shot at a time.

Because they were rushed into mass production, early models were plagued by stoppages that caused some units to request reissue of the M-14. Technical investigation revealed a variety of causes in both weapon and ammunition design and in care and cleaning in the field. With these deficiencies corrected, the M-16 became a popular infantry rifle, able to hold its own against the Soviet-made AK-47 assault rifle.

Although M-16 rifles had been issued earlier to South Vietnamese (ARVN) airborne and marine forces, it was not until mid-1968 that the World War II-vintage 30-caliber M-7 rifles and Browning automatic rifles used by the majority of ARVN forces were replaced by the M-16 and the older weapons issued to village militia forces.

See also AK-47 RIFLE.

Suggestions for further reading: *The Great Rifle Controversy,* by Edward Clinton Ezell (Harrisburg: Stackpole, 1984). *The Vietnam Experience: Tools of War* by Edgar C. Doleman, Jr. (Boston: Boston Publishing Co, 1984).

M-79 GRENADE LAUNCHER

First used in combat in the Vietnam war, the U.S.-made M-79 grenade launcher was a break-open shotgun-type weapon that fired a 40-mm grenade cartridge. A qualified gunner could fire five to seven rounds per minute to an effective range of approximately 375 yards. As well as a projectile that exploded on impact (with a casualty radius of up about 5 yards), the M-79 also fired a buckshot projectile that could be used at close ranges.

Suggestions for Further Reading: *The Vietnam Experience: Tools of War* by Edgar C. Doleman, Jr, (Boston: Boston Publishing Co., 1984).

An American soldier reloads his M-79 40 mm grenade launcher during a fire fight with North Vietnamese troops, 1968. (Courtesy U.S. Army.)

MAAG-VIETNAM (U.S. MILITARY ASSISTANCE ADVISORY GROUP VIETNAM)

After the 1954 Geneva Accords, the French advisory group (Mission Militaire Française) that had been training the Vietnamese National Army was gradually withdrawn, and on October 26, 1955 South Vietnam became the independent republic of Vietnam (RVN).

The U.S. Military Assistance Advisory Group Vietnam (MAAG-Vietnam) was formed on November 1, 1955 to provide military assistance to the RVN. It replaced MAAG-Indochina, which had been providing military assistance to "the forces of France and the Associated States in Indochina" (i.e., Cambodia, Laos and Vietnam) in accordance with President Harry S Truman's order of June 27, 1950.

MAAG-Vietnam had U.S. Army, Navy, Air Force and Marine Corps elements that provided advice and assistance to the RVN Ministry of Defense, Joint General Staff and corps and division commanders as well as to training centers and province and district headquarters. In May 1964 MAAG-Vietnam was disbanded and its personnel and responsibilities absorbed by the U.S. Military Assistance Command Vietnam (MACV), which had been established in Vietnam two years earlier.

See also ADVISORY EFFORT; SVNAF (SOUTH VIETNAMESE ARMED FORCES).

Suggestions for further reading: *Vietnam Order of Battle*, by Shelby L. Stanton (Washington, D.C.: U.S. News & World Report Books, 1981); *The United States Army in Vietnam: Advice and Support: The Early Years 1941–1960*, by Ronald H. Spector (Washington, D.C.: U.S. Government Printing Office, 1983); *The U.S. Advisor*, by Cao Van Vien et al (Washington, D.C.: U.S. Government Printing Office, 1980); *The United States Navy and the Vietnam Conflict: The Setting of the Stage to 1959*, by Edwin B. Hooper, Dean C. Allard and Oscar P. Fitzgerald (Washington, D.C.: U.S. Government Printing Office, 1976); *The United States Air Force: The Advisory Years to 1965*, by Robert F. Futrell (Washington, D.C.: U.S. Government Printing Office, 1981); *U.S. Marines in Vietnam: The Advisory and Combat*

Assistance Era, 1954–1964, by Robert C. Whitlow (Washington, D.C.: U.S. Government Printing Office, 1977); *The Vietnam Experience: Passing the Torch*, by Edward Doyle, Samuel Lipsman and Stephen Weiss (Boston: Boston Publishing Co., 1981).

MAC

See MILITARY AIRLIFT COMMAND.

MACV (U.S. MILITARY ASSISTANCE COMMAND VIETNAM)

The MACV was established in Saigon on February 8, 1962 to control the buildup of advisers and support personnel ordered by President Kennedy. U.S. military personnel in Vietnam had increased from 900 when President Kennedy was elected in 1960 to 3,205 at the beginning of 1962, with thousands more on the way. MAAG-Vietnam (U.S. Military Assistance Advisory Group Vietnam), the existing headquarters, had been overwhelmed by the buildup, and for the first two years MACV concentrated on liaison with the South Vietnamese government and on controlling the logistics increase, leaving the advisory function to MAAG-Vietnam.

Because its first commander, Army General Paul D. Harkins, had been USARPAC (U.S. Army Pacific) Commander in Honolulu and because existing plans called for the Army component Commander in the Pacific Command (i.e., General Harkins) to command any land force contingencies, when MACV was formed, it was formed as a "subordinate unified command." This seemingly minor bureaucratic point would have enormous consequences as the war progressed.

The designation of MACV as a "subordinate unified command" meant strategic direction of the war came from Honolulu, not Saigon. It also meant that MACV was not the headquarters of an independent theater of war reporting directly to the Secretary of Defense and the President. Instead everything had to be approved first by the

Commander-in-Chief of the Pacific Command (CINCPAC) in Honolulu. Furthermore, the only command-and-control authority the MACV possessed was what CINCPAC was willing to delegate. The MACV never controlled the air war over North Vietnam and Laos, for example, or the war at sea beyond Vietnam's coastal waters.

As it evolved through the course of the war, the MACV had three major functions. First was a high-level advisory mission. Working as part of the U.S. Ambassador's country team, the MACV Commander was deeply involved in consultations with the South Vietnamese government and thus his attention tended to be dominated by the internal problems of South Vietnam. The MACV's fixed location in Saigon (and later in the suburbs of Tan Son Nhut) and natural bureaucratic inertia tended to keep the focus there even after the nature of the war changed in late 1965 from a guerrilla war against local insurgents to a conventional war against Viet Cong (VC) main force and North Vietnamese Army (NVA) units.

As a result, the second function—to serve as a field army headquarters controlling battlefield operations from mobile headquarters near the front (as with Patton's Third Army in Europe in World War II or Ridgway's Eighth Army in Korea)—never fully developed. The focus on what was to prove to be the decisive enemy—the NVA and its supply lines—remained secondary.

The third mission—assistance to the South Vietnamese Armed Forces (SVNAF)—was performed by the MACV's Field Advisory elements. The U.S. Army element alone rose to a peak of 9,430 in 1968, and with U.S. advisers assigned down to battalion level within SVNAF, U.S. assistance in the form of advice, coordination of artillery and air firepower as well as moral support was invaluable. This was a tough and demanding job, and five MACV advisers won the Medal of Honor for conspicuous battlefield bravery. From the U.S. Army element alone, 378 advisers were killed in action and 1,393 were wounded in action. If there is a criticism of this field advisory effort, it is that U.S. advisers were too good, for they inadvertently helped to create a dependency that was to prove fatal once U.S. support was withdrawn in March 1973, after the Paris Accords were signed.

During the course of the Vietnam war, command of the MACV changed four times:

Commanders	Assumed Command
General Paul D. Harkins	February 1962
General William C. Westmoreland	June 1964
General Creighton W. Abrams	July 1968
General Frederick C. Weyand	June 1972

The MACV insignia.

See also ADVISORY EFFORT; MAAG-VIETNAM (U.S. MILITARY ASSISTANCE ADVISORY GROUP VIETNAM); SVNAF (SOUTH VIETNAMESE ARMED FORCES).

Suggestions for further reading: *Vietnam Order of Battle*, by Shelby L. Stanton (Washington, D.C.: U.S. News Books, 1981); *Command and Control 1950–1969*, by George S. Eckhardt (Washington, D.C.: U.S. Government Printing Office, 1974).

The 25-Year War: America's Military Role in Vietnam, by Bruce Palmer, Jr. (Louisville: University of Kentucky Press, 1984); *The Pentagon and the Art of War,* by Edward N. Luttwak (New York: Simon & Schuster, 1985); *The U.S. Advisor,* by Cao Van Vien et al (Washington, D.C.: U.S. Government Printing Office, 1980); *The United States Army in Vietnam: Advice and Support: The Early Years 1941–1960,* by Ronald H. Spector (Washington, D.C.: U.S. Government Printing Office, 1983); *The United States Navy and the Vietnam Conflict: The Setting of the Stage to 1959,* by Edwin B. Hooper, Dean C. Allard and Oscar P. Fitzgerald (Washington, D.C.: U.S. Government Printing Office, 1976); *The United States Air Force: The Advisory Years to 1965,* by Robert F. Futrell (Washington, D.C.: U.S. Government Printing Office, 1981); *U.S. Marines in Vietnam: The Advisory and Combat Assistance Era, 1954–1964,* by Robert H. Whitlow (Washington, D.C.: U.S. Government Printing Office, 1977); *The Vietnam Experience: Passing the Torch,* by Edward Doyle, Samuel Lipsman and Stephen Weiss (Boston: Boston Publishing Co., 1981). For a fictionalized account of MACV field advisers, see *One Very Hot Day,* by David Halberstam (New York: Warner Books, 1984).

MANSFIELD, MIKE (MICHAEL) (JOSEPH) (1903–)

Mansfield, who was born on March 16, 1903 in New York City, grew up in Montana. From 1918 to 1922 he served in all three branches of the armed services. He obtained B.A. and M.A. degrees from Montana State University in 1933 and 1934 respectively.

Following his election to the Senate in 1952, Mansfield established a liberal voting record. Despite low seniority, he was appointed Democratic Party whip by Senate majority leader Lyndon B. Johnson and in 1961 he became majority leader.

Although he initially backed the Johnson Administration's Southeast Asian policy, Mansfield grew disillusioned with the war effort. In 1965 he counseled President Johnson against sending ground troops to Vietnam, but his advice was disregarded. Following a fact-finding trip to Vietnam in 1966, he privately tried to persuade Johnson that a military victory was impossible. When it appeared that the President preferred to settle the war on the battlefield, Mansfield publicly criticized the war.

During President Nixon's first term, Mansfield emerged as one of the leading Democratic critics of the Administration's Vietnam policy. He was particularly concerned with the Executive's assumption of war-making powers traditionally held by the Congress. In 1970 Mansfield enthusiastically supported the Cooper-Church and McGovern-Hatfield Amendments. The following year he introduced his own end-the-war amendment, which called for withdrawal of U.S. military forces within nine months after the bill's passage subject to the release of all American prisoners of war. It passed the Senate but failed in the House.

Mansfield decided to retire from the Senate following the 1976 election. In 1977 President Carter appointed him Ambassador to Japan.

MARINE CORPS, SOUTH VIETNAMESE

See SVNAF (SOUTH VIETNAMESE ARMED FORCES).

MARINE CORPS, U.S.

Since the war in Vietnam was primarily a ground war, the U.S. Marine Corps played a major role. Next to the U.S. Army, it furnished the majority of the American combat units involved and suffered the majority of the casualties. Instrumental in setting up the South Vietnamese Marine Corps in 1954 and in providing helicopter support for South Vietnamese troops in Vietnam beginning in 1962, U.S. Marine forces were predominant in I Corps from 1965 until 1970, and a Marine general commanded the corps-level headquarters there—the III Marine Amphibious Force (MAF).

In one of the many anomalies of the war, the Marine Corps, which was neither trained nor

A battle-hardened U.S. Marine on patrol. (Courtesy U.S. Army Military History Institute.)

two Marine divisions, two additional Marine regimental landing teams and a reinforced Marine air craft wing to Vietnam, plus a number of battalion-size Marine special landing forces afloat with the Seventh Fleet. These combat forces included some 24 battalions of infantry, two tank battalions, two antitank battalions, three amphibious tractor battalions, two reconnaissance battalions, 10 battalions of artillery, and 26 flying squadrons, with about 225 helicopters and 250 fighters and fighter-bombers. Present at the beginning, the Marine Corps was also present at the end. In 1975 Marine Corps elements took part in the final evacuation of Cambodia and South Vietnam and the rescue of the *Mayaguez*.

Among other decorations and awards, 57 Medals of Honor were awarded to U.S. Marines for conspicuous bravery in Vietnam. Of the 47,244 Americans killed in action, 13,065 were Marines, as were 51,399 of the 153,329 Americans wounded in action severely enough to require hospitalization and 37,234 of the 150,375 Americans lightly wounded in action.

See also FIRST MARINE AIRCRAFT WING, FIRST MARINE DIVISION, PACOM (PACIFIC COMMAND), III MARINE AMPHIBIOUS FORCE, THIRD MARINE DIVISION.

Suggestions for further reading: "Marine

equipped for sustained defensive operations, ended up defending against cross-border attacks by regular North Vietnamese Army (NVA) units (which historian Allan R. Millett compared to "World War I on the Western Front") while the Army's Ninth Infantry Division was being retrained for amphibious operations with the Mobile Riverine Force. This situation developed because in 1965 existing contingency plans in the Pacific Command in Honolulu called for a Marine rather than an Army landing in I Corps for "temporary" operations, since there was a shortage of ports in that area and the Marines were capable of being resupplied over the beach. When the temporary landing of the Ninth Marine Expeditionary Force in 1965 turned into the long-term commitment of the III MAF, such contingency plans—rather than battle field realities—dictated the commitment.

During the course of the war the Marine Corps deployed one corps-level combat headquarters,

Insignia of the U.S. Marine Corps.

Corps Operations in Vietnam 1965–66, 1967, 1968, 1969–72," by Edwin H. Simmons, in *The Marines in Vietnam* (Washington, D.C.: U.S. Government Printing Office, 1974); *Semper Fidelis: The History of the United States Marine Corps*, by Allan R. Millett (New York: Macmillan, 1980); *Strange War, Strange Strategy*, by Lewis W. Walt (New York: Funk & Wagnall, 1976); *First to Fight: An Inside View of the U.S. Marine Corps*, by Victory H. Krulak (Annapolis: U.S. Naval Institute Press, 1984); *Vietnam Order of Battle*, by Shelby L. Stanton (Washington, D.C.: U.S. News & World Report Books, 1981); *U.S. Marines in Vietnam: The Advisory and Combat Assistance Era 1954–1964*, by Robert H. Whitlow (Washington, D.C.: U.S. Government Printing Office, 1977); *U.S. Marines in Vietnam: The Landing and the Buildup 1965*, by Jack Shulimson and Charles M. Johnson (Washington, D.C.: U.S. Government Printing Office, 1978); *U.S. Marines in Vietnam: An Expanding War 1966*, by Jack Shulimson (Washington, D.C.: U.S. Government Printing Office, 1982). For a fictionalized account of Marine Corps operations in Vietnam, see Marine Corps Vietnam veteran James Webb's *Fields of Fire* (Englewood Cliffs, N.J.: Prentice-Hall, 1978).

MARINE CORPS, REPUBLIC OF VIETNAM (VNMC)

See SVNAF (SOUTH VIETNAMESE ARMED FORCES).

MARKET TIME OPERATIONS

Market Time was the designation for operations established on March 11, 1965 by the U.S. Navy and the South Vietnamese Navy to curtail the seaborne infiltration into the country of communist arms and supplies. Conducted by ships and aircraft of the U.S. Navy, U.S. Coast Guard and the South Vietnamese Navy, it was originally controlled by the Vietnam Patrol Force (Task Force 71) under the command of the U.S. Seventh Fleet. On July 31, 1965 command was transferred to the Commander of Naval Forces Vietnam. After July 31, 1965 the patrol group was designated Task Force 115.

See also COASTAL SURVEILLANCE FORCE.

Suggestions for further reading: *A Short History of the United States Navy and the Southeast Asian Conflict 1956–1975*, by Edward J. Marolda and G. Wesley Pryce, III (Washington, D.C.: Naval Historical Center, 1984).

MARTIN, GRAHAM A(NDERSON) (1912–   )

Born on September 22, 1912 in Mars Hill, North Carolina, Martin graduated from Wake Forest College in 1932. He worked briefly as a journalist, served in the Army Reserve and joined the Foreign Service in 1947. In July 1963 he was appointed Ambassador to Thailand; four years later, he returned to Washington as Special Assistant to the Secretary of State for Refugee and Migration Affairs, a post he remained at until 1969, when he was named Ambassador to Italy.

In June 1973 he replaced Ellsworth Bunker as Ambassador to South Vietnam. Though his appointment came after the signing of the Paris Accords, Martin's instructions were to demonstrate unswerving U.S. support for President Thieu and thereby restore Thieu's faith in the United States as an ally. Martin, who lost a stepson in combat in Vietnam, was a firm supporter of U.S. policy there.

In early 1975 hostilities between North and South Vietnam resumed. Although Martin had been advised for weeks by his military analysts of the rapidly deteriorating situation and the communist preparation for an attack on Saigon, he persisted in his belief that a political solution was possible. On April 18, 1975 Martin said in an interview, "There has been no advice from Washington for Thieu to step down." At the same time, however, the Ambassador was actively discouraging a military coup against Thieu, assuring Vice President Nguyen Cao Ky that Thieu would soon step down, and on April 21 Martin, with the help of French Ambassador Jean-Marie Mérillon, persuaded Thieu to resign.

In the final days before the fall of South Vietnam, Ambassador Martin was caught in a dilemma. He had to continue the support of the South Vietnamese government and therefore could not openly begin the evacuation of U.S. personnel, since such an evacuation would not only undermine the government but might also precipitate a panic and jeopardize the lives of Americans still in Vietnam. On the other hand, he had to reduce the U.S. presence in Vietnam to manageable levels to facilitate an evacuation if it became necessary. Relying on his subordinates to unobtrusively evacuate their personnel without alarming the South Vietnamese, Martin was only partially successful in that difficult endeavor. The Defense Attaché Office, for example, managed to remove the majority of its personnel prior to the final evacuation, but both the CIA and the U.S. Information Agency failed to take adequate measures and ended up abandoning many of their key South Vietnamese personnel. One of the last Americans to leave South Vietnam, Ambassador Martin departed Saigon on the morning of April 30, 1985, after President Ford had canceled further evacuation.

See also FINAL OFFENSIVE; THIEU, NGUYEN VAN.

Suggestions for further reading: *The Fall of Saigon,* by David Butler (New York: Simon & Schuster, 1985); *The Vietnam Experience: The Fall,* by Clark Dougan and David Fulghum (Boston: Boston Publishing Co., 1985); *Peace with Honor?* by Stuart A. Herrington (Novato, Calif.: Presidio Press, 1983); *Decent Interval,* by Frank Snepp (New York: Random House, 1977).

McCAIN, JOHN SIDNEY, JR. (1911–1981)

Born January 17, 1911 in Council Bluffs, Iowa, McCain graduated from the U.S. Naval Academy in 1931. The son of a distinguished Navy aviator, McCain commanded submarines in both the Atlantic and Pacific during World War II, winning the Silver Star Medal and the Bronze Star Medal with V device for heroism in action.

In July 1968 Admiral McCain succeeded Admiral U. S. Grant Sharp as CINCPAC (Commander-in-Chief of the Pacific Command). As such he was the theater commander during the Vietnam war, exercising command through CINCPACFL (Commander-in-Chief of the Pacific Fleet) and

Admiral John S. McCain, Jr.

CINCPACAF (Commander-in-Chief of the Pacific Air Force) over Navy operations outside South Vietnam's coastal waters and air operations over North Vietnam, Laos and, after 1970, Cambodia. He also exercised command over ground and air operations in Vietnam through COMUSMACV (Commander of the U.S. Military Assistance Command Vietnam), Army General Creighton Abrams.

McCain's task was made more difficult by the fact that his eldest son, Lieutenant Commander John S. McCain, III, had been a prisoner of war since October 1967 when he was shot down over Hanoi. Admiral McCain had the difficult task of drawing down U.S. military forces in the Pacific Command in accordance with President Nixon's Vietnamization program and devising a response to the North Vietnamese Eastertide Offensive, which began in March 1972, with limited military assets.

Successful in both of these endeavors, Admiral McCain completed his tour as CINCPAC in September 1972, at about the same time as the

Eastertide Offensive came to an end with the South Vietnamese Army's recapture of Quang Tri—a recapture effected in large part by the air and naval gunfire support provided by forces under Admiral McCain's command.

Within three months of McCain's retirement from active duty, the Linebacker II air operations over Hanoi conducted by his successor helped bring about the Paris Accords of 1973 and the release of his son (now a congressman from Arizona). Admiral McCain died on March 24, 1981.

See also EASTERTIDE OFFENSIVE, LINEBACKER OPERATIONS, PACOM (PACIFIC COMMAND).

McCARTHY, EUGENE J(OSEPH) (1916–   )

McCarthy was born in Watkins, Minnesota on March 29, 1916. Following graduation from St. John's University in 1935, he taught at high schools and colleges. He won election to the U.S. House of Representatives in 1948 and to the Senate in 1958.

Through his opposition to the Vietnam war, McCarthy exerted a profound impact on the course of American foreign policy. He was not an early dissenter, having voted for the Tonkin Gulf Resolution in August 1964 and avoided any public criticism of President Johnson's war policy until January 1966. At that time he joined 14 other Senators in sending a letter to the President calling for a continuation of the suspension of air strikes against North Vietnam begun in December.

In early 1967 McCarthy grew more vocal in his opposition and soon he became one of the foremost critics of Johnson's Vietnam policy. In 1967, after persistent urging by antiwar liberals, McCarthy announced that he was running for the Democratic presidential nomination to further the campaign for a negotiated settlement of the war. His candidacy attracted a legion of idealistic young volunteers, dubbed the "children's crusade."

As a result of McCarthy's strong showing in the New Hampshire primary, Senator Robert Kennedy declared his candidacy and several weeks later President Johnson announced that he would not seek reelection. McCarthy's campaign, however, was soon overshadowed by those of Kennedy and Vice President Hubert Humphrey. At the Democratic National Convention in Chicago in August 1968, McCarthy was defeated by Humphrey.

McCarthy unexpectedly resigned from the Foreign Relations Committee in 1969 and retired from the Senate in 1971.

See also ANTIWAR MOVEMENT; JOHNSON, LYNDON B.

Suggestions for further reading: *Almost to the Presidency: A Biography of Two American Politicians,* by Albert Eisele (Blue Earth, Minn.: Piper Co., 1972). *The Year of the People,* by Eugene McCarthy (New York: Doubleday, 1969).

McGOVERN, GEORGE S(TANLEY) (1922–   )

Born in Avon, South Dakota on July 19, 1922, McGovern attended Dakota Wesleyan University and served in the Army Air Corps during World War II. He received his doctorate at Northwestern University in 1953. McGovern was elected to the U.S. House of Representatives in 1956 and in 1962 he became South Dakota's first Democratic Senator in 26 years.

McGovern was an early, outspoken foe of the Vietnam war. He first criticized U.S. involvement in September 1963, although he voted for the Tonkin Gulf Resolution the following August. In January 1965 he proposed a negotiated solution, leading to gradual withdrawal of U.S. troops and the neutralization of Vietnam protected by a U.N. presence. After visiting Vietnam in November, he called for a bombing halt and recognition of the National Liberation Front.

When President Nixon announced his first troop withdrawals in 1969, McGovern labeled the action "tokenism." In October he spoke before the Vietnam Moratorium rally in Boston and the following month addressed a massive antiwar demonstration in Washington, D.C.

After the invasion of Cambodia by U.S. troops in April 1970, McGovern voted for the Cooper-Church Amendment to cut off funds for U.S.

operations in Cambodia. With Sen. Mark Hatfield he introduced an "end-the-war" amendment to a military appropriations bill that would have legislated the withdrawal of all U.S. combat troops from Southeast Asia by the end of 1971. The Senate rejected the amendment in 1970 and 1971.

In 1972 McGovern won the Democratic presidential nomination. His platform called for an immediate end to the Vietnam war. He was decisively defeated by President Nixon in the 1972 election.

In 1984 McGovern made an unsuccessful bid for the Democratic presidential nomination.

See also ANTIWAR MOVEMENT.

Suggestions for further reading: *McGovern: A Biography,* by Robert Sam Anson (New York: Holt, Rinehart & Winston, 1972).

McNAMARA, ROBERT S(TRANGE) (1916–   )

Born on June 9, 1916 in San Francisco, California, McNamara graduated from the University of California at Berkeley in 1937 and from Harvard School of Business Administration in 1939. During World War II, he set up a statistical control system for the U.S. Army Air Corps and rose to the rank of Lieutenant Colonel before returning to civilian life in April 1946.

Together with other Air Corps statistical control experts who came to be known as the "whiz kids," he joined the Ford Motor Company after the war and in 1960 was named its president.

In December 1960 he accepted the post of Secretary of Defense in the incoming Kennedy Administration and served in that office until March 1968. McNamara would shape U.S. policy in Vietnam—and the presentation of that policy to the American people—as much as any American with the exception of Presidents Johnson and Nixon. Early in the Administration's involvement in Vietnam, the Defense Department rather than the State Department assumed primary responsibility for policy making because President Kennedy had such confidence in McNamara's abilities.

In the spring of 1962, when the United States had several thousand advisers in Vietnam, McNamara stated the United States had no plans to introduce combat troops there. In the fall of 1963 McNamara and General Maxwell Taylor visited Saigon and then advised Kennedy that the U.S. military role in Vietnam could be completed by the end of 1965, although there might be a need for advisers for some time after that. Within a year, however, he became considerably more pessimistic about a quick end to the conflict. In March 1964, McNamara, responding to the success of the Viet Cong and to congressional criticism that U.S. advisers were being forced to use inferior equipment, said that U.S. forces in Vietnam had a "blank check" on arms, manpower and funds.

By 1964 U.S. aircraft were aiding the South Vietnamese in carrying out covert raids on North Vietnam's coastal installations, but communist forces nonetheless seemed to be gaining strength in the south. Plans were drawn up for possible direct U.S. intervention. On August 4, when two U.S. destroyers were allegedly attacked by North Vietnamese gunboats, air strikes against North Vietnam were ordered. McNamara presented evidence of the attack to Congress, which on August 7 approved the Tonkin Gulf Resolution granting the President broad power to "take all necessary measures to repel . . . further aggression" throughout Southeast Asia.

In February 1965, following attacks on U.S. bases in Vietnam, McNamara joined other members of the National Security Council in approving retaliatory air strikes; by the beginning of March systematic bombing of the north had begun. McNamara approved General William C. Westmoreland's request for 3,500 Marines to defend the American air base at Da Nang. After meeting with Westmoreland in July, McNamara approved the General's request that 185,000 troops be sent to Vietnam by the end of the year. McNamara also supported a call-up of the reserves and a tax increase to pay for the war. Johnson rejected both measures as politically unpalatable.

At McNamara's request Johnson initiated a bombing halt in December 1965. McNamara's rationale at the time was that the halt might induce North Vietnam to enter into peace negotia tions. If it failed to do so, then more intensive bombing could be justified. The pause proved unproductive, and bombing was renewed on January 31, 1966.

Bombing strategy was a continuing source of controversy between McNamara and the Joint Chiefs of Staff. The President, McNamara, Secretary of State Dean Rusk and National Security Adviser McGeorge Bundy retained the right to review all bombing targets in North Vietnam. McNamara and his staff charged that the Joint Chiefs often selected targets of dubious military significance. The Joint Chiefs argued that McNamara placed unnecessary restrictions on U.S. air power.

In October 1966 McNamara returned to Vietnam for the eighth time. Publicly his assessment was optimistic, but privately he had growing doubts about the situation. Communist victory had been prevented, but American casualties were high, and the Secretary was pessimistic about chances of bringing an end to the conflict in the near future. Nor was McNamara pleased with the pace of reform within the government of South Vietnam. By 1967 he had become openly skeptical about the effectiveness of bombing the north to cut down the infiltration of men and material to the south.

While concerned about the military conduct of the war, McNamara became increasingly interested in finding a way to end the conflict through a negotiated settlement. In the summer of 1967 he helped draft the San Antonio Formula, a peace proposal asking the North Vietnamese only to begin productive discussion in exchange for an end to U.S. bombing. The proposal was rejected by North Vietnam in October. A month later McNamara submitted a memorandum to Johnson recommending that the U.S. freeze its troop levels, cease the bombing of the north and turn over major responsibility for the ground war to the South Vietnamese. Johnson rejected these proposals outright.

Unlike in previous American wars in which the Secretary of War managed the logistical side of the war and left the operational side to the uniformed professionals, in the Vietnam war McNamara controlled both. A number of analysts of McNamara's role in the war have pointed out that his strong emphasis upon statistical indices of success and quantitative analysis in the decision making process, and his belief that a war should, in effect, be run like a corporation, led to grave misperceptions about the nature of the war in Vietnam.

See also JOHNSON, LYNDON B; KENNEDY, JOHN F.; TAYLOR, MAXWELL D.; WESTMORELAND, WILLIAM C.

Suggestions for further reading: *How Much is Enough: Shaping the Defense Program 1961–1969,* by Alain C. Enthoven and K. Wayne Smith (New York: Harper & Row, 1971); *The Best and the Brightest,* by David Halberstam (New York: Random House, 1972). The most telling indictment of McNamara's tenure is *The McNamara Strategy and the Vietnam War: Program Budgeting in the Pentagon 1960–1968,* by Gregory Palmer (Westport: Greenwood Press, 1978). See also *Vietnam: A History,* by Stanley Karnow (New York: Viking, 1983); *The Kennedy Imprisonment: A Meditation on Power,* by Garry Wills (New York: Pocket Books, 1983); "How We Lost," by Harry G. Summers, Jr., in *The New Republic,* April 29, 1985; *Pentagon Papers,* Gravel edition (Boston: Beacon Press, 1971).

McNAMARA'S WALL

Officially named Operation Die Marker, "McNamara's Wall" was a scheme to construct a 25-mile barrier along the northern border of South Vietnam to block North Vietnamese Army (NVA) infiltration across the DMZ. The idea of such a physical barrier was not new; the U.S. Marine Corps had already constructed a "fire break" about 660 yards wide and 8.2 miles long from Con Thien through Gio Linh to the sea. The McNamara's Wall, however, was a more ambitious project—it was to consist not only of normal barrier material, such as land mines and barbed wire, but also acoustic sensors and infrared intrusion detectors. Work began on the project in April 1967.

Slowed by enemy mortar, rocket and artillery fire, the project was preempted in 1968 by the U.S. force buildup in the area to relieve the siege of Khe Sanh. While the line was never completed, the portions that were constructed did provide some early warning of enemy movement in the DMZ area.

See also DMZ (DEMILITARIZED ZONE), NIAGARA OPERATION.

Suggestions for further reading: "Marine Operations in Vietnam, 1967," by Edwin H. Simmons, in *The Marines in Vietnam 1954–1973* (Washington, D.C.: U.S. Government Printing Office, 1974). A diagram of the proposed barrier is contained in *The War in the Northern Provinces 1966–1968*, by Willard Pearson (Washington, D.C.: U.S. Government Printing Office, 1975). *The Vietnam Experience: Tools of War*, by Edgar C. Doleman, Jr. (Boston: Boston Publishing Company, 1984).

McNAUGHTON, JOHN T(HEODORE) (1921–1967)

McNaughton was born on November 21, 1921 in Bicknell, Indiana. A Rhodes Scholar and a Harvard University Professor of Law, he joined the Defense Department in 1961. Two years later he served as a member of the diplomatic team that successfully negotiated a treaty with the Soviet Union barring above-ground testing of atomic weapons. McNaughton was named Assistant Secretary of Defense for International Security Affairs in June 1964. He maintained a close working and personal relationship with Secretary of Defense Robert S. McNamara and soon became McNamara's chief assistant in developing strategy in Vietnam.

A month after the Tonkin Gulf Incident in August 1964, McNaughton advised support of South Vietnam's rural pacification programs and its naval and air warfare against North Vietnam, and he proposed renewal of U.S. Navy patrols off the coast of North Vietnam. McNaughton said that if the North Vietnamese could be induced to attack again, the United States could legitimately enter the war and begin military actions that would eventually include bombing and mining North Vietnamese harbors. Such actions, he believed, would force the North Vietnamese to enter peace negotiations.

In early 1965 the United States, in response to communist attacks on its military installations in South Vietnam, began systematic bombing of the north. McNaughton argued in March that the bombing alone would not force Hanoi to abandon its aggression in the south. He recommended that three U.S. and two Korean divisions be sent to Da Nang and Pleiku. He cautioned that it might take "massive deployment" of U.S. troops to change the military situation, which at that time was favorable to the communists. His memo was one of the factors that induced Johnson in early April to employ Marine units in active combat operations against communist forces.

In July, McNaughton and McNamara, increasingly skeptical about the advantages of bombing the north, began planning, over the objections of the Joint Chiefs of Staff, for an extended bombing halt. A halt was initiated in December 1965. There was no satisfactory response from Hanoi, and the bombing was renewed on January 31, 1966.

McNaughton was one of several Defense Department officials who met with McNamara at weekly sessions to review a list of bombing sites in North Vietnam proposed by the Joint Chiefs of Staff. The military argued that the civilian planners imposed illogical and arbitrary restrictions on the bombing. McNaughton countered that many of the requested military targets were of no strategic value and endangered the lives of civilians. He suggested that the bombing could be more effective if concentrated on infiltration routes south of Hanoi.

In April 1966 McNaughton reversed his previous endorsement of the domino theory and suggested that the loss of South Vietnam would "not affect the present line of containment from Korea to the Philippines." By May 1967 he had become so alarmed by the growing public protest against the war that he wrote President Johnson to warn "of a feeling widely and strongly held that 'the Establishment' is out of its mind. The feeling is that we are trying to impose some U.S. image on distant people we cannot understand." He advised Johnson to refuse the military's request for an additional 80,000 U.S. troops for Vietnam but to continue with military, pacification and political programs in the south and press for increases in the productivity of South Vietnam's military forces.

In June 1967 McNaughton became Secretary of

the Navy. On July 19 he, his wife and younger son were killed in an airplane crash in North Carolina.

See also ANTIWAR MOVEMENT; JOHNSON, LYNDON B.; McNAMARA, ROBERT S.; TONKIN GULF RESOLUTION.

Suggestions for further reading: *Pentagon Papers*, Gravel edition (Boston: Beacon Press, 1971).

MEDAL OF HONOR

First authorized during the Civil War, the Medal of Honor (often erroneously called the Congressional Medal of Honor) is the highest American military award for battlefield bravery. It is awarded by the President in the name of Congress to those members of the armed forces who have distinguished themselves conspicuously by gallantry and intrepidity at the risk of their lives above and beyond the call of duty while engaged in an action against the enemy. The deed performed has to have been one of personal bravery or self-sacrifice so conspicuous as to clearly distinguish the individuals above their comrades and must have involved risk of life.

During World War II 434 Medals of Honor were awarded and 131 were won in the Korean war. Of the several million Americans who served in Vietnam, 239 were awarded the Medal of Honor—155 Army, 57 Marine Corps, 15 Navy and 12 Air Force personnel.

Suggestions for further reading: *America's Medal of Honor Recipients* (Golden Valley, Minn.: Highland Publishers, 1980) and *And Brave Men Too*, by Timothy S. Lowry (New York: Crown, 1985) include not only the names of Vietnam-era Medal of Honor winners but also the citations for their awards.

MEDIA

Vietnam was the most reported conflict in the history of warfare. In 1964, when the massive American buildup began, there were some 40 U.S. and foreign journalists in Saigon. By August 1966, there were 419 news media representatives,

including support personnel, nonresident newsmen and wives of newsmen, in South Vietnam from 22 nations. Although there were 179 Americans included in this total, only about 40 were in the field with U.S. troops at any given time.

The Vietnam war correspondents in the field shared the dangers confronting the front-line forces—*Esquire*'s Michael Herr and the *Washington Post*'s Peter Braestrup at the siege of Khe Sanh, the *New York Times*' Charles Mohr at the battle of Hué, where he won the Bronze Star Medal with "V" device for rescuing a wounded Marine under enemy fire; *CBS News* reported Dan Rather in battles in the Central Highlands; the *Associated Press*' Peter Arnett and George Esper; and the many others who risked their lives to witness and report the realities of the battlefield. Sixteen American journalists lost their lives while covering the war.

American journalists are among the 42 U.S. civilians still missing in action and unaccounted for in Indochina, including *NBC News* correspondent Welles Hangen and *Time* photographer Sean Flynn, both of whom disappeared while covering the war in Cambodia. There were others who did not measure up to such high standards, but they were few in number. As the *Washington Post*'s George Wilson once remarked to a critical Army audience, "We had our Calleys the same as you did," driving home the point that both unprofessional reporters and unprofessional military officers were the exception, not the rule.

A noteworthy phenomenon of the Vietnam war is that the most objective accounts and analyses of that conflict have so far come from the media rather than from academia. These include such works as Marvin Kalb and Elie Abel's *The Roots of Involvement* (New York: Norton, 1971), Keyes Beach's *Not Without the Americans* (Garden City: Doubleday, 1971), Peter Braestrup's *Big Story* (New Haven: Yale University Press, 1983), Don Oberdorfer's *Tet!* (New York: De Capo Press, 1984), David Halberstam's *The Best and the Brightest* (New York: Random House, 1972), Stanley Karnow's *Vietnam: A History* (New York: Viking, 1983) and Peter Scholl-Latour's *Death in the Rice Fields* (New York: St. Martin's Press, 1985), to name only a few. Another noteworthy phenomenon is the increasing number of Vietnam war combat veterans now with the media, such as former Navy F-4 pilot Brad Knickerbocker of the *Christian Science Monitor,* former Army rifleman Jack Smith of *ABC News,* former Seabee Lou Marano of the *Washington Times,* former combat photographer Donald Graham, publisher of the *Washington Post,* and former Navy Lieutenant Craig Whitney of the *New York Times.* Their first-hand combat experience should ensure the continued objectivity of media accounts of the war in Vietnam.

There have been a number of staunch critics of media coverage of the war in Vietnam. However, it now appears that many of the problems with the media during the Vietnam war were not really the fault of the war correspondents in the field but of the newspaper and magazine editors and radio and television producers back home. The war correspondents, by and large, accurately reported what they saw. The editors and producers, however, were not always able to keep their own political agendas and their awareness of shifts in American public opinion out of the editing process. One criticism leveled against the war correspondents—a criticism that could have been leveled at correspondents in earlier wars as well—is that they concentrated on American operations and virtually ignored those of our allies. This imbalance, it has been argued, created the false impression that the South Vietnamese—who suffered the overwhelming majority of allied casualties during the war—were not pulling their share of the load.

See also CENSORSHIP; CRONKITE, WALTER; HALBERSTAM, DAVID; LIPPMANN, WALTER; LUCE, HENRY R.; SALISBURY, HARRISON E.; TELEVISION.

Suggestions for further reading: The best overall account of media reporting in the Vietnam war is "The Vietnam War" by Peter Braestrup in *Battle Lines: Report of the Twentieth Century Fund Task Force on the Military and the Media* (New York: Priority Press, 1985). Another useful account is a roundtable discussion of some fourteen reporters, producers, professors, and military public affairs officers contained in *Vietnam: 10 Years Later* (Fort Benjamin Harrison: Defense Information School, 1984). A list of the foreign journalists who died or who are missing in action in Indochina from 1961 to 1975 is contained in the dedication to Peter Braestrup's *Big Story* (New Haven: Yale University Press, 1983). For a critical account of media reporting in Vietnam, see "How to Lose a War" by Robert Elegant in *Encounter,* August 1981. See also *The Powers That Be,* David Halberstam (New York: Alfred A. Knopf, 1979).

MEDICAL SUPPORT

Servicemen fighting in Vietnam received the best medical care in the history of warfare. For example, the ratio of deaths as a percentage of Americans wounded declined from 29.3 percent in World War II and 26.3 percent in the Korean war to 19.0 percent in Vietnam.

On the front lines initial medical care was provided by U.S. Army combat medical aidmen and by Navy corpsmen attached to the front-line Marine units. Following this initial treatment, wounded personnel were rapidly evacuated from the battlefield by so-called Dustoff helicopters. These helicopters brought the wounded into clearing hospitals at the base camps, and the more seriously wounded were again evacuated to mobile Army surgical hospitals, evacuation hospitals, field hospitals within Vietnam and, in the case of the Marines, the hospital ships *Repose* and *Sanctuary,* anchored offshore. Those requiring more intensive care were evacuated out of country by Air Force hospital planes to the United States or to hospitals in the Philippines, Okinawa or Japan.

During the war in Vietnam, 153,329 military personnel were hospitalized because of wounds received in action. An additional 150,375 lightly wounded personnel were treated by local medical facilities and were able to return to duty.

A major accomplishment of medical personnel in Vietnam was in preventive medicine to counter such tropical diseases as malaria, dengue fever, infectious hepatitis and diarrheal diseases. As a result, the average annual disease admission rate for Vietnam was approximately one-third of that for the Pacific Theater in World War II and more than 40 percent less than the rate for the Korean war.

See also AEROMEDICAL EVACUATION, COMBAT MEDICAL BADGE, DUSTOFF, 834TH AIR DIVISION, 44TH MEDICAL BRIGADE, MILITARY AIRLIFT COMMAND, SEVENTH FLEET.

Suggestions for further reading: *Vietnam Studies: Medical Support of the U.S. Army in Vietnam 1965–1970,* by Spurgeon Neel (Washington, D.C.: Department of the Army, 1973); a vivid account of care of Vietnam wounded is contained in *365 Days,* by Ronald J. Glasser (New York: Braziller, 1971).

MEKONG DELTA

The Mekong is one of Southeast Asia's major rivers. From its source in the mountains of Tibet, it flows 12,000 miles south to the South China Sea. At Phnom Penh, the capital of Cambodia, it splits in two. The southern branch, the Song ("River") Hau Giang flows directly through to the sea. The northern branch splits several times as it runs through the Mekong Delta to the sea.

Built up over centuries by the silt carried by the branches of the Mekong River, the Mekong Delta proper covers about 26,000 square miles. No more than 10 feet above sea level, the delta is extremely fertile, especially suited for wetland rice growing. On its southwestern portion, however, are mangrove swamps, including the U Minh Forest, long a Viet Cong base area.

See also LAND REFORM; MOBILE RIVERINE FORCE; PART I, THE SETTING; PLAIN OF REEDS; RIVER PATROL FORCE; U MINH FOREST. *See* map at IV CORPS TACTICAL ZONE.

MENU OPERATION

Code name for the bombing of Cambodia, Menu was launched on March 18, 1969 to destroy North Vietnamese base camps in the border areas used as staging and logistical bases for attacks into South Vietnam. First concentrated on these North Vietnamese Army (NVA) base camps and supply depots, it was extended in May 1970 to support Cambodian Army operations against the Khmer Rouge insurgents and the code name was changed to Freedom Deal. By the time these operations ended on August 14, 1973, B-52 bombers had flown some 16,527 sorties and dropped 383,851 tons of bombs.

Since Cambodia was ostensibly neutral, an intricate reporting system was established at the Pentagon to prevent disclosure of the bombing. Only the highest Administration officials—President Nixon, National Security Adviser Henry Kissinger, Secretary of Defense Melvin Laird—and selected Defense Department officials plus a few congressmen knew of the operation. When the *New York Times* revealed the bombing campaign in May, the administration became obsessed with plugging information leaks to the press. This in turn led to wiretaps of government officials and of

Members of the Ninth ARVN Division cross a rice paddy in Vinh Long Province in the Mekong Delta. (Courtesy U.S. Army.)

A strategic hamlet in Chuong Thien Province, part of the Mekong Delta. (Courtesy Shelby L. Stanton.)

journalists and later was a factor in the establishment of a White House unit to plug leaks—the "Plumbers." This unit's illegal acts eventually resulted in the Watergate scandal, which brought about Nixon's resignation in 1974.

See also CAMBODIA; FANK TRAINING COMMAND; KHMER ROUGE; NEUTRALITY; NIXON, RICHARD M.

Suggestions for further reading: *The United States Air Force in Southeast Asia 1961–1973*, edited by Carl Berger (Washington, D.C.: U.S. Government Printing Office, 1977); *Vietnam: A History*, by Stanley Karnow (New York: Viking, 1983). For a critical account of the bombing, see *Sideshow: Kissinger, Nixon and the Destruction of Cambodia*, by William Shawcross (New York: Simon & Schuster, 1979).

MERITORIOUS UNIT COMMENDATION

The Meritorious Unit Commendation is awarded to units for exceptionally meritorious conduct in the performance of outstanding services for at least six continuous months during the period of military operations against an armed enemy. The unit must have displayed such outstanding devotion and superior performance of exceptionally difficult tasks as to set it apart and above other units with similar missions.

The U.S. Army, Navy, Air Force, Marine Corps and Coast Guard awards have somewhat different criteria, and each award emblem is distinct. The Army award requires the highest standard of performance; the degree of achievement required is the same as that which would warrant award of the Legion of Merit to an individual. The Navy, Marine Corps and Coast Guard award of the Meritorious Unit Commendation can be made for combat or noncombat conditions and the character of service must be only comparable to that which would merit award of a Bronze Star Medal or a similar caliber noncombat award to an individual. The Air Force Outstanding Unit Award can also be awarded for combat or noncombat operations. These emblems can be worn permanently by those personnel assigned to the unit at the time of the award.

MIA (MISSING IN ACTION)

See POW/MIA.

MILITARY AIRLIFT COMMAND, U.S.

The Military Airlift Command (MAC) (formerly known as the Military Air Transport Service) is the U.S. Air Force's strategic airlift organization charged with airlifting U.S. forces worldwide. While the Tactical Air Command's intertheater airlift is placed under operational control of commanders in the field, MAC airlift is under centralized control.

In early 1965 MAC had 34 squadrons, consisting of C-124 Globemasters, C-133 Cargomasters, C-130 Hercules and C-135 Stratolifters. These were augmented by aircraft from the U.S. Air National Guard and Air Reserve. Slow and obsolete, these older aircraft were replaced when fleet modernization began with the arrival of the C-141 Starlifter in late 1965 and received another

Insignia of Military Airlift Command.

boost with the first deliveries of the C-5 Galaxy to South Vietnam in 1971.

The MAC's aerial resupply missions went from 53,198 tons of cargo and 175,539 passengers in 1965 to 141,113 tons of cargo and 347,627 passengers in 1967, when the MAC flew some 210 million miles. It not only moved individual replacements but also entire units, including the Third Brigade, 25th Infantry Division from Hawaii to Vietnam in 1965; the 101st Airborne Division from Fort Campbell, Kentucky to Vietnam in 1967; and an emergency lift of the Third Brigade, 82nd Airborne Division from Fort Bragg, North Carolina to Vietnam during the 1968 Tet Offensive. The move of the 101st Airborne Division alone involved 10,355 paratroopers and 5,118 tons of equipment, including 37 helicopters, and required 413 C-141 and C-133 flights between November 17 and December 29, 1967.

Another critically important MAC function was aeromedical evacuation. By 1968 the MAC had one aeromedical evacuation group; three aeromedical squadrons, including a reserve unit called to active duty, the 34th Aeromedical Evacuation Squadron from Kelly Air Force Base in Texas; and some five detachments. From a monthly average of 342 medical evacuees in 1964, the pace increased to a monthly average of 5,956 in 1968.

Aeromedical evacuation crews included some 409 flight nurses by 1969, and with evacuation centers at Clark Air Base in the Philippines and Yokota Air Base in Japan and at Guam, Wake Island and Hawaii, patients were rapidly evacuated from the war zone. The original fleet of C-135s was eventually replaced by C-141s, which could carry 60 litter patients or 100 ambulatory patients. The C-141s in turn began to be replaced by the newer C-9s in March 1972. C-151s alone flew some 6,000 missions between 1965 and December 1972.

From 1963 to 1973, the MAC evacuated 406,022 patients from Vietnam, including 168,832 battle casualties.

Suggestions for further reading: *The United States Air Force in Southeast Asia 1961–1973,* by Carl Berger (Washington, D.C.: U.S. Government Printing Office, 1977).

MILITARY POLICE

Military police were used by the armed forces of the United States, South Vietnam and other allies in Vietnam. Although military police were trained primarily for troop disciplinary and traffic control purposes, they were used for many regular combat duties, since the war in Vietnam was often "frontless." Military police guarded convoys against ambush as part of their traffic responsibilities and were equipped with armored jeeps and commando cars. During the Tet Offensive in 1968 the military police also participated in urban combat situations, as they were also trained to perform as infantry in emergency circumstances. Military police guarded vital facilities, such as the U.S. embassy, and served at stockades and drug rehabilitation centers. In comparison to other wars, the military police of the U.S. armed forces in the Vietnam conflict performed in a greatly expanded and crucial role.

See also 18TH MILITARY POLICE BRIGADE.

MILITARY REGIONS (MR)

The title adopted in July 1970 to designate the four geographical divisions in South Vietnam. They were synonymous with the previously designated corps tactical zones. Thus Military Region (MR) 1 was the same as I Corps, MR II the same as II Corps etc.

See also I, II, III, IV CORPS TACTICAL ZONES.

MILITARY SEALIFT COMMAND, U.S.

The U.S. Navy's Military Sealift Command (MSC) (formally known as the Military Sea Transportation Service [MSTS]) was the lifeline for U.S. forces in Vietnam. During the war 99 percent of the ammunition and fuel and 95 percent of the supplies, vehicles and construction resources came by sea.

With primary responsibility for the sea line of communication to Southeast Asia, the Navy oversaw the development of this 7,000-mile transoceanic supply route. By mid-1967 the MSC controlled a fleet of 527 reactivated World War II Reserve Fleet ships—including converted escort carriers that served as aircraft ferries—and chartered vessels under U.S. and foreign registry. In addition to older ships, they included newer roll-on/roll-off ships, such as the *Bienville*, and fuel tankers, such as the 190,000-bl capacity *Maumee*.

MSC also controlled as many as 16 troop transports in the Pacific during the buildup of forces in South Vietnam and carried over 40,000 U.S. and allied combat and support troops to Southeast Asia.

Cargo shuttling along the coast was handled by a fleet of 42 LSTs (landing ships, tank), and in-port lighterage was accomplished with some 19 tugs and 33 barges of the MSC-contracted Alaska Barge and Transport Company.

During the final days of the Vietnam war in 1975, a number of MSC tugs, barges and ships assisted in the evacuation of South Vietnam, which included an intracoastal sealift of 130,000 U.S. and South Vietnamese citizens from the northern part of South Vietnam to the Saigon area and subsequently the final evacuation of 44,000 refugees.

Suggestions for further reading: *A Short History of the United States Navy and the Southeast Asian Conflict 1950-1975,* by Edward J. Marolda and G. Wesley Pryce, III (Washington, D.C.: Naval Historical Center, 1984); *Mobility, Support, Endurance: A Story of Naval Operational Logistics in the Vietnam War, 1965-1968,* by Edwin B. Hooper (Washington, D.C.: Naval History Division, U.S. Government Printing Office, 1972); *Report on Airlift and Sealift to South Vietnam,* by 90th Congress, First Session, U.S. Senate Committee on Armed Services (Washington, D.C.: U.S. Government Printing Office, 1967); *Logistic Support in the Vietnam Era: A Report,* by the U.S. Joint Logistics Review Board (Washington, D.C.: Department of Defense, 1970).

MINH, DOUNG VAN (1916-   )

Born in 1916 in My Tao, Dinh Tuong Province, in the upper Mekong Delta, in the French colony

The S.S. *Oakland,* a ship of the Military Sealift Command, docked at Cam Ranh Bay. (Courtesy U.S. Army News Features.)

A Mobile Riverine Force patrol. (Courtesy U.S. Army Military History Institute.)

of Cochinchina, "Big Minh" (as he became known to the Americans) was a French-trained soldier who first came into prominence in 1956, when he was instrumental in subduing the Hoa Hao sect and executing its leader. He then challenged the government of South Vietnam and its President, Ngo Dinh Diem.

Suspicious of Minh's resulting popularity, President Diem appointed him "Special Adviser" and thus removed him from troop command. Disgruntled, Minh was one of the key figures in the plot to overthrow President Diem in November 1963, and reportedly the one who gave approval for Diem's assassination.

After taking control of the South Vietnamese government as head of the Military Revolutionary Council, Minh was deposed by a countercoup on January 30, 1964. Exiled abroad until 1968, he was seen by some as the leader of a "third force," between President Nguyen Van Thieu and his followers and the communists. He was a presidential candidate in the South Vietnamese election of 1971 but withdrew when it became obvious he had no chance to win.

In April 1975 Minh again came to the fore as the one most likely able to negotiate with the North Vietnamese Army (NVA) forces closing in on Saigon. Appointed President of South Vietnam on April 28, 1975 following Thieu's resignation, he was captured by the NVA two days later.

See also DIEM, NGO DINH; LODGE, HENRY CABOT; THIEU, NGUYEN VAN.

Suggestions for further reading; *Vietnam: A History,* by Stanley Karnow (New York: Viking, 1983); *Without Honor: Defeat in Vietnam and Cambodia,* by Arnold R. Isaacs (Baltimore: Johns Hopkins Press, 1983).

MOBILE RIVERINE FORCE

The Mobile Riverine Force was a U.S. Army-Navy Task Force involving the Ninth Infantry Division's Riverine Forces (essentially the Second Brigade, Ninth Infantry Division, which included the Third and Fourth Battalions, 47th Infantry; the Third Battalion, 60th Infantry; and a 105-mm howitzer artillery, the Third Battalion, 39th Artillery) and the Navy's Task Force 117 (*see* RIV-

ERINE ASSAULT FORCE) and SEAL teams. The force was often combined with units from the South Vietnamese Army Seventh and 21st Infantry Divisions, South Vietnamese Marine Corps units and South Vietnamese Navy vessels. With the capability to move afloat up to 150 miles in 24 hours and launch combat operations with its 5,000-man force within 30 minutes after anchoring, the riverine force was truly mobile.

Reviving a concept used during the American Civil War, when Union Army forces operated with Navy gunboats on the Ohio, Mississippi and other inland waterways, Army forces underwent special training, including combat operations in the Rung Sat in Vietnam and at the Coronado Naval Base in California. Starting with an anchorage at Vung Tau in III Corps, a base was eventually constructed at Dong Tam in the upper Mekong Delta five miles west of My Tho on the My Tho River in IV Corps.

In June 1967 the Mobile Riverine Force became operational. A series of operations (Coronado I through XI) were launched throughout the Mekong Delta and the Rung Sat Special Zone, concluding in July 1968. These were followed by Operation Giant Slingshot, from November 1968 to January 1969, the first phase of the Sealords campaign, which continued until April 1971, when the last of the Mobile Riverine Force was turned over to South Vietnamese forces as part of the "Vietnamization" program.

See also IV CORPS TACTICAL ZONE, MEKONG DELTA, NINTH INFANTRY DIVISION, RIVERINE ASSAULT FORCE, RUNG SAT, SEALORDS, VUNG TAU.

Suggestions for further reading: *Riverine Operations 1966-1969*, by William B. Fulton (Washington, D.C.: U.S. Government Printing Office, 1973); *A Short History of the United States Navy and the Southeast Asian Conflict 1950-1975*, by Edward J. Marolda and G. Wesley Pryce, III (Washington, D.C.: Naval Historical Center, 1984). For a vivid fictionalized account of riverine operations, see *The Lionheads*, by Ninth Infantry Division veteran Josiah Bunting (New York: Braziller, 1972).

MOBILIZATION

Despite repeated requests by the Joint Chiefs of Staff, there was never a general mobilization of America's reserve military forces during the Vietnam war. Part of President Johnson's reluctance to mobilize the reserves stemmed from the same consideration that led him not to attempt to rally the American people in support of the Vietnam war—he did not want the war to interfere with his domestic programs. But part of his reluctance was also based on the experience of President Kennedy's mobilization in 1961 for the Berlin crisis, in which reserve forces were called to active duty and never used, creating widespread public dissent against the call-up. When President Johnson asked the Joint Chiefs of Staff for specific missions for mobilized reserves, they were not able to provide such information. Lacking a strategy for the war, they also lacked a strategy for mobilization.

There was, however, limited mobilization of reserve forces. On January 25, 1968 President Johnson ordered a partial call-up of National Guard and reserve forces in response to the North Korean seizure of the Navy intelligence-gathering ship *Pueblo.* Twenty-eight units comprising 14,801 unit members were mobilized under the January order: six units with 593 Navy Reserve members; 14 units with 9,340 members of the Air National Guard; and eight units with 4,868 Air Reserve members. No Army National Guard, Army Reserve, Marine Corps Reserve or Coast Guard Reserve units or individuals were called. Although the January 25 mobilization was not ordered specifically for Vietnam, four of the Air National Guard units (tactical fighter squadrons) were deployed to South Vietnam in May 1968. All six of the activated Naval Reserve units were demobilized by the end of calendar year 1968, as were seven of the eight Air Reserve units. By December 1969 all of the units mobilized under the January 25 order were deactivated.

On April 11, 1968 President Johnson ordered another limited mobilization specifically for Vietnam, calling to active duty approximately 24,500 men in some 88 units from the reserve components of the Army, Navy and Air Force. The majority (22,786) were from the Army and included 76 Army National Guard and Army Reserve units, 43 of which were actually deployed to Vietnam. Army combat units included Company D (Ranger), 151st Infantry, from the Indiana Army National Guard; and two 155-mm howitzer self-propelled battalions; the Second Battalion, 138th Artillery, from the Kentucky National Guard; and the Third Battalion, 197th Artillery, from the New Hampshire National Guard. The rest of the units were engineer, signal, transportation, quartermaster, medical and other such support units.

Air Force reservists included Tactical Air Force Command AC-119 fixed-wing gunship crews, transport pilots and crewmen (who made some 1,294 trips into the war zone) as well as aeromedical evacuation nurses and other medical personnel. Two units of the Naval Reserve and 10 units of Air National Guard and Air Force Reserve were also called up.

Suggestions for further reading: *Mobilization of the Army National Guard and Army Reserve: Historical Perspective and the Vietnam War,* by John D. Stuckey and Joseph H. Pistorius (Carlisle Barracks, Pa.: Strategic Studies Institute, U.S. Army War College, 1984); *The Unmaking of a President: Lyndon Johnson and Vietnam,* by Herbert Y. Schandler (Princeton: Princeton University Press, 1977/1984); *The United States Air Force in Southeast Asia,* edited by Carl Berger (Washington, D.C.: U.S. Government Printing Office, 1977).

MOMYER, WILLIAM WALLACE (1916–)

Born on September 23, 1916 in Muskogee, Oklahoma, Momyer graduated from the University of Washington in 1937. Enlisting in the U.S. Army Air Corps in 1938, he received his pilot wings in 1939. During World War II he led the 33rd Fighter Group in action over North Africa and Italy, won the Distinguished Service Cross and three Silver Star Medals for bravery and shot down eight enemy aircraft.

In July 1966 General Momyer was assigned as Commander of the Seventh Air Force in Vietnam and concurrently Deputy Commander of the MACV (U.S. Military Assistance Command Vietnam). Among other air operations, he coordinated the devastating air response to the North Viet-

namese Tet Offensive in February 1968.

Returning from Vietnam in August 1968, he commanded the Tactical Air Command until he retired from active duty on October 1, 1973.

See also SEVENTH AIR FORCE.

Suggestions for further reading: *Airpower in Three Wars,* by William W. Momyer (Washington, D.C.: U.S. Government Printing Office, 1978).

MONTAGNARDS

Montagnard (literally "mountain people") is the French name for the aborigine tribes that inhabited the mountains of the Chaîne Annamitique. The Montagnards were divided into a number of different tribes. The Montagnards north of the DMZ were primarily of mongoloid extraction, which indicated that they, like the Vietnamese, had migrated to Indochina from China in prehistoric times. The Montagnards in South Vietnam were primarily of Austroasiatic and Malayo-Polynesian ethnic extraction, indicating that they had originally migrated to Indochina from the islands to the south (*see* ethnic map in Part I, THE SETTING).

Much like the relationship between the American Indians and the early American colonists, the Montagnards disliked and distrusted the Vietnamese, who in turn looked down on the Montagnards as *moi,* ("savages"). Seeking to turn this animosity into an advantage, U.S. Special Forces began in 1961 to organize the Montagnards into CIDG (Civilian Irregular Defense Group) camps in the interior and the western border areas in the Central Highlands in II Corps in order to block North Vietnamese infiltration into these areas. By 1964, 21 camps had been constructed with Hre, Rhade, Cham, Tuong, Mien, Jarai, Bahnar, Mnong, Sedang, Halang, Ragulai, Rongao, Bong, Nongao, Koho, Ma, Chil and Drung tribesmen.

While U.S. efforts to organize the Montagnards were generally successful, attempts to turn these camps over to South Vietnamese government control by such agencies as the LLDB (Lac Luong Dac Biet—South Vietnamese Special Forces) were less successful. Montagnard-Vietnamese bad feelings led to an uprising in September 1964, which was resolved only when the government of South

These Montagnards are moving to a new strategic hamlet in Pleiku Province. (Courtesy Shelby L. Stanton.)

Vietnam agreed to a set of demands for Montagnard autonomy. A month earlier Y Bham, a Rhade leader, had founded FULRO—Front Unifié pour la Libération des Races Opprimées ("Unified Front for the Liberation of Oppressed Peoples"), which not only instigated the 1964 revolt but also led revolts in 1965 that forced further concessions from the government. Although most of the camps involved in the revolt were permanently closed, with new camp openings the actual number of CIDG camps in II Corps increased from 21 to 62.

By 1971 South Vietnamese-Montagnard relations had improved to the point where as U.S. forces withdrew, 19 CIDG camps were converted to South Vietnamese Army (ARVN) ranger battalions and 15 were converted to Regional Force (RF) battalions; the remainder were closed or abandoned. These units fought well in the 1972 Eastertide Offensive but, like the regular ARVN units, were overwhelmed by the NVA Final Offensive in 1975.

Montagnard-Vietnamese hostility still exists and FULRO conducts a continuing guerrilla war against its new Vietnamese overlords.

See also FIFTH SPECIAL FORCES, SPECIAL FORCES, II CORPS.

Suggestions for further reading: *U.S. Army* *Special Forces 1961–1971*, by Francis J. Kelly (Washington, D.C.: U.S. Government Printing Office, 1973); *Pacification*, by Tran Dinh Tho (Washington, D.C.: Center of Military History, 1980); *The Green Berets at War*, by Shelby Stanton (Novato, Calif.: Presidio Press, 1985).

MOORER, THOMAS H(INMAN) (1912–   )

Born on February 9, 1912 in Mount Willing, Alabama, Moorer graduated from the U.S. Naval Academy in 1933. He was a Navy aviator stationed at Pearl Harbor when the Japanese attacked on December 7, 1941. He was shot down north of Australia in February 1942, only to have his rescue ship torpedoed.

On October 13, 1962 Moorer was appointed Commander-in-Chief of the Seventh Fleet in the western Pacific. On June 26, 1964, just before the Gulf of Tonkin Incident, which precipitated direct U.S. combat involvement in the Vietnam war, he was named Commander-in-Chief of the Pacific Fleet. Promoted to Commander-in-Chief of the Atlantic Command in March 1965, in August 1967 he became Chief of Naval Operations and in

July 1970 he was appointed Chairman of the Joint Chiefs of Staff.

As Chairman, Admiral Moorer played a major role in withdrawing U.S. forces from Vietnam and in the "Vietnamization" of the war. He also coordinated U.S. military responses to the 1972 North Vietnamese Army Eastertide Offensive as well as the mining of Haiphong harbor and the bombing of Hanoi in 1972, which led to the Paris Accords in 1973.

In July 1974, his tour complete, Admiral Moorer retired from active duty.

See also CHIEF OF NAVAL OPERATIONS, U.S. NAVY; CHAIRMAN, JOINT CHIEFS OF STAFF.

Suggestions for further reading: *White House Years* by Henry Kissinger (Boston: Little, Brown, 1979).

MORALITY

From a philosophical point of view, the concept of morality in war is derived from the fourth century writings of Saint Augustine as refined by Saint Thomas Aquinas in the thirteenth century. The theory of "just war" has two parts: *jus ad bellum* (the decision to go to war) and *jus in bello* (the conduct of war). It sets three requirements for the decision to go to war: the decision must be made by a proper authority, it must involve a just cause and it must have the right intentions. For the conduct of war, it also establishes three requirements: the means used must be in proportion to the ends to be achieved, discrimination must be used to avoid harming nonbelligerents and civilians and the means must be in accordance with the positive laws of war.

From a legal point of view, morality is first defined in terms of the positive laws of war—primarily the Hague Convention of 1907 and the Geneva Convention of 1949, which had to do with rules of engagement, treatment of prisoners of war and the like. In addition to these treaties, to which the United States is signatory, within the U.S. military the authority "to make rules for the government and regulation of the land and sea forces" is delegated by the Constitution to Congress. In 1949 Congress passed the Uniform Code of Military Justice (UCMJ), better known as the court-martial manual, which, as amended, governed conduct of U.S. military personnel in Vietnam.

The MACV (U.S. Military Assistance Command Vietnam) issued a series of directives establishing Rules of Engagement to prevent indiscriminate use of firepower and to protect innocent civilians. This was especially necessary because the North Vietnamese and Viet Cong regularly shielded their forces by placing them in civilian villages and, as a tactic, fired on American forces from populated villages and religious shrines in order to provoke return fire that would alienate the civilian population from the Americans.

U.S. military personnel received instruction in both the Laws of War and the UCMJ in their basic training. Upon arrival in Vietnam, they were issued wallet-sized cards with guidelines on treatment of prisoners of war and proper treatment of Vietnamese civilians. But being aware of the rules and obeying them was, for some, a different matter.

See also ATROCITIES, MY LAI.

Suggestions for further reading: *Law at War*, by George S. Prugh (Washington, D.C.: U.S. Government Printing Office, 1975); *A Soldier Reports*, by William C. Westmoreland (Garden City: Doubleday, 1976); *America in Vietnam*, by Guenter Lewy (New York: Oxford University Press, 1978); *The Conduct of Just and Limited War*, William V. O'Brien (New York: Praeger, 1981); *Just and Unjust Wars: A Moral Argument with Historical Illustrations*, by Michael Walzer (New York: Basic Books, 1977). See also "Vietnam and Just-War Tradition," by Mackubin T. Owens, *This World* (Winter 1984); *Just War Tradition and the Restraint of War*, by James Turner Johnson (Princeton: Princeton University Press, 1981).

MORATORIUM AGAINST THE VIETNAM WAR

In the summer of 1969 antiwar activist Sam Brown decided that moderate antiwar protests should be staged in communities to demonstrate that not only students but average citizens were against the war. The plan was endorsed by academics, politicians, clergymen and civil rights activists. It also attracted the acclaim of the North Vietnamese. The first Moratorium was held in a number of cities across the country on October 15th. Some 250,000 people gathered in Washington, D.C. and large crowds met in New York, Detroit, Boston and other cities to protest the war. The crowds were addressed by antiwar notables, such as Benjamin Spock and David Dellinger, as well as prominent former members of the Johnson Administration, including Arthur Goldberg and Averell Harriman. The gatherings were peaceful and displayed none of the violence that had characterized demonstrations during the Democratic National Convention in Chicago in 1968. On November 15 an even larger demonstration was mounted in Washington, D.C., with some 500,000 people attending.

See also ANTIWAR MOVEMENT; BROWN, SAM; DEMOCRATIC NATIONAL CONVENTION, 1968; GOLDBERG, ARTHUR; HARRIMAN, AVERELL.

MORSE, WAYNE (LYMAN) (1900–1974)

Morse, who was born in Madison, Wisconsin on October 20, 1900, graduated from the University of Wisconsin in 1923 and received a law degree from the University of Oregon in 1928. In 1942 he won the Oregon Republican primary for the U.S. Senate and the general election. Morse quickly established a reputation as a maverick liberal who frequently refused to modify strongly held views for the sake of legislative compromise. In 1952 he resigned from the Republican Party to become an independent and three years later he became a Democrat.

During the 1960s Morse was one of the earliest and best known opponents of American military involvement in Vietnam. In August 1964 he and Senator Ernest Gruening were the only congressional opponents of the Tonkin Gulf Resolution. Morse challenged the administration's account of North Vietnamese attacks on U.S. Navy vessels in the Tonkin Gulf, charging that the incident was as much the "doing" of the United States as of North Vietnam.

In May 1965 Morse denounced both the U.S. air raids on North Vietnam, which had begun the previous February, and the subsequent dispatch of American combat troops to South Vietnam. He asserted that the conflict in the south was a civil war rather than an invasion from the north and that the United States was intervening on behalf of a despotic South Vietnamese regime that had little popular support.

In February 1966 Morse condemned the administration for lawlessly pursuing hostilities without a congressional declaration of war. On March 1 the Senate defeated a Morse amendment to repeal the Tonkin Gulf Resolution, which President Johnson had repeatedly cited as the legal authorization for his Vietnam policies. Critics of the Senator contended that the amendment was an example of Morse's tendency to undercut his own cause by taking extreme positions regardless of political considerations. They noted that a number of Senators who had reservations about the war but who did not want to totally repudiate the President had been forced to vote with the administration.

Morse was defeated in his reelection bid in 1968. He died on July 20, 1974.

See also ANTIWAR MOVEMENT; GRUENING, ERNEST; JOHNSON, LYNDON B.; TONKIN GULF RESOLUTION.

MORTARS

Smaller than artillery and easier to move, mortars were used extensively by both sides during the Vietnam war. U.S. and South Vietnamese forces used the man-transportable 60-mm and 81-mm (*see* illustration) mortars and the larger 4.2-inch mortars.

North Vietnamese Army and Viet Cong forces used the Soviet- and Chinese-supplied 82-mm and 120-mm mortars as well as captured U.S. mortars. Although radar was used to spot enemy mortar positions by tracking the trajectory of the projectiles, a good operator could "hang" (i.e., have in the air) a number of rounds before the first one hit the target. He could then pack up his mortar and move before radar operators were even aware an attack was underway.

MY LAI INCIDENT

The My Lai Incident has been called, with some justification, the worst disgrace that the U.S. Army has suffered, in its more than 200-year history. It occurred on March 16, 1968 in the hamlet of My Lai in Son My village, Quang Ngai Province, in I Corps. On that day C Company, First Battalion, 20th Infantry, 11th Infantry Brigade, Americal Division conducted a heliborne assault to secure the area.

Although C Company had suffered some casualties from enemy mines, it had never been in actual combat with the enemy. First Platoon leader Lieutenant William L. Calley, Jr. moved his 25 men into the hamlet and began rounding up Vietnamese civilians—old men, women, children and babies—and herded them into a ditch. These

American soldiers using an 81 mm mortar in combat. (Courtesy U.S. Army Military History Institute.)

estimated 150 unarmed civilians were then gunned down. Throughout the day Calley's platoon and other members of C Company, under the command of Captain Ernest L. Medina, committed murder, rape, sodomy and other atrocities. These gross violations of standing orders, military law and human decency were not reported by Captain Medina and were not investigated by either the Battalion Commander, Lieutenant Colonel Frank Barker (subsequently killed in action), or by the Brigade Commander, Colonel Warren K. Henderson. The Division Commander, Major General Samuel H. Koster, likewise took no action to investigate what should have been obvious discrepancies in the battle reports of the unit.

First brought to light in a letter written by former combat infantryman Ron Ridenhour on March 29, 1969, the incident was immediately investigated by the Army. The Secretary of the Army convened a formal board of inquiry, headed by Lieutenant General William R. Peers, who had formerly commanded the Fourth Infantry Division in Vietnam from January 1967 to January 1968, to investigate the accusations. Eventually court-martial charges were prepared against 12 officers for dereliction of duty. As a result of these charges, the Americal Division Commander, Major General Koster, who was then serving as the Superintendent of the U.S. Military Academy, was reduced in rank to Brigadier General. His assistant, Brigadier General George Young, was censured. The 11th Infantry Brigade Commander, Colonel Henderson, was tried by a general court-martial and acquitted on December 17, 1971. The court-martial charges against the other officers were dismissed for lack of sufficient evidence.

Thirteen officers and enlisted men were charged with war crimes. The First Battalion intelligence officer, Captain Eugene M. Kotouc, and the C Company Commander, Captain Medina, were found not guilty. Three sergeants were also found not guilty and the charges against the remaining men were dismissed. Only Lieutenant Calley was found guilty of war crimes—specifically the murder of 22 unarmed civilians—and sentenced to life imprisonment.

Although the court-martial board was composed of combat infantry veterans, most of whom had served in front-line combat in Vietnam, the cry went up that Calley had been railroaded. Enormous public pressure was brought to bear on behalf of Calley, and even though the conviction was upheld by the Court of Military Appeals, the Secretary of the Army eventually reduced Calley's sentence to 10 years. On March 19, 1974 he was paroled.

Feeling about this incident ran high among combat infantry veterans of the Vietnam war. A common reaction was that those who actually committed the atrocities and the senior officers who covered up the whole affair deserved the harshest punishment for their gross dereliction of duty. This opinion, however, was not widely shared among those who had not served in combat.

On the left many believed that the My Lai atrocities vindicated their charges that the Vietnam war was illegal, immoral and unjust. Many on the right saw Calley as the victim of the antiwar movement in the United States. Falling in the crack between these two poles of opinion, the public generally supported Calley in spite of his conviction as a mass murderer. Such support for Calley compounded the tragedy, for it rendered a major disservice to the overwhelming majority of American combat soldiers who risked their lives to protect—not harm—the men, women and children of South Vietnam.

See also ATROCITIES; CALLEY, WILLIAM J., JR.

Suggestions for further reading: The most balanced and objective account of the My Lai massacre is the official report of the U.S. Army's board of inquiry, *The My Lai Inquiry,* by W. R. Peers (New York: Norton, 1979). Another generally balanced account is *The Court Martial of Lieutenant Calley,* by Richard Hammer (New York: Coward, McCann & Geoghegan, 1971). Less objective is *My Lai 4: A Report on the Massacre and Its Aftermath,* by Seymour M. Hersh (New York: Random House, 1970). Several books reflect the hysteria of the times and defend Calley's actions. They include *Lieutenant Calley: His Own Story,* as told to John Sack (New York: Viking, 1971), and *Destroy or Die: The True Story of My Lai,* by Martin Gershen (New Rochelle: Arlington House, 1971). See also *America in Vietnam,* by Guenter Lewy (New York: Oxford University Press, 1978).

NAPALM

An acronym derived from *na*phthenic and *palm*itic acids, whose salts are used in its manufacture, napalm is a jellied gasoline used in flamethrowers and bombs. It was used by both sides in the Vietnam war—by the United States and South Vietnam primarily in the form of aerial bombs. The North Vietnamese and Viet Cong used it in flamethrowers, as in their massacre of the Montagnard villagers at Dak Son.

Although fire has been used as a weapon since prehistoric times, napalm came into widespread use in World War II, especially in flamethrowers used to destroy entrenched Japanese positions in the Pacific war. It was used extensively in the form of aerial bombs in the Korean war against Chinese and North Korean entrenchments. A favorite of television war coverage because of its vivid and awful visual display, use of napalm touched a primordial nerve among many Americans and aroused considerable controversy, including demonstrations against chemical companies that manufactured napalm.

See also ATROCITIES.

NATIONAL DEFENSE SERVICE MEDAL

First authorized during the Korean war, the

National Defense Service Medal was authorized for all members of the United States armed forces who served on active duty during the Vietnam era between January 1, 1961 and August 14, 1974. An oak leaf worn on the ribbon denotes Vietnam-era service by personnel who had been awarded the National Defense Service Medal for service during the Korean-war era.

NATIONAL LIBERATION FRONT

The National Liberation Front (NLF) was appropriately named, for it was a classic communist-front organization. Formed in Hanoi in December 1960, the NLF was designed to disguise its communist control and thus draw support from noncommunist South Vietnamese disaffected with their government. Many noncommunist members of the NLF thought they were working for southern independence, and the antiwar movement in the United States championed the NLF as the true representative of the South Vietnamese people. The NLF stressed land reform, expulsion of foreigners, unfairness of South Vietnam's tax system and other issues.

After the war the North Vietnamese freely admitted that the NLF was their own creation, totally controlled and directed from Hanoi. Betrayed and disillusioned, many southern NLF leaders have been purged or imprisoned or have fled into exile.

See also VIET CONG.

Suggestions for further reading: *Vietnam: A History*, by Stanley Karnow (New York: Viking, 1983); *A Viet Cong Memoir*, by Truong Nhu Tang, with David Chanoff and Doan Dan Toai (New York: Harcourt Brace Jovanovich, 1985); *Fire in the Lake: The Vietnamese and the Americans in Vietnam*, by Frances FitzGerald (Boston: Little, Brown, 1972).

NATIONAL POLICE, SOUTH VIETNAMESE

The South Vietnamese National Police operated against the Viet Cong as part of their normal law-and-order functions. They were given support from the military and civil intelligence agencies of both the United States and South Vietnam. The police fought the Viet Cong with two main branches: the National Police Field Forces and the National Police Special Branch. Both of these police organizations were designed to apprehend or eliminate local Viet Cong.

See also PACIFICATION, PHOENIX PROGRAM.

NATIONAL SECURITY ADVISER

The National Security Adviser, officially the Assistant to the President for National Security Affairs, is a member of the Executive Office of the President. He is a statutory adviser to the National Security Council and heads its administrative staff, but his actual power stems from his personal relationship with the President. In January 1961 McGeorge Bundy replaced Gordon Gray, who had served as Special Assistant to President Eisenhower. Bundy served under both President Kennedy and President Johnson until he was replaced by Walt Rostow in April 1966. In January 1969, with the election of President Nixon, Henry A. Kissinger became Special Assistant to the President and served in that position (and concurrently, after September 1973, as Secretary of State) until November 1975. During Kissinger's tenure the title was changed from Special Assistant to Assistant to the President, which was thought to be more prestigious.

Beginning with the Kennedy Administration and peaking during the first Nixon Administration, the post of National Security Adviser, although not a cabinet post, actually began to have more real power than either that of the Secretary of Defense or the Secretary of State. The bureaucracies at the State and Defense Departments appeared as impediments to Presidents Kennedy and Nixon, who wished to make their own foreign policy, and the office of the National Security Adviser became a way to circumvent those cumbersome organizations. What was lost, however, was the detailed scrutiny and intricate coordination of U.S. foreign and defense policies that these departments traditionally were expected to provide.

Suggestions for further reading: *The Limits of Intervention,* by Townsend Hoopes (New York: David MacKay Co., 1969); *The Vietnam Trauma in American Foreign Policy 1945–75,* by Paul Kattenburg (New Brunswick, N.J.: Transaction Books, 1980).

NATIONAL SECURITY COUNCIL

The National Security Council (NSC) was established by the National Security Act of 1947 to advise the President on the integration of domestic, foreign and military policies relating to the national security. Normally composed of the President, the Vice President, the Secretary of State, the Secretary of Defense, during the Vietnam war it also included the Director of the Office of Emergency Planning, with the Director of the Central Intelligence Agency and the Joint Chiefs of Staff as statutory advisers.

President Kennedy disregarded this formal structure in favor of irregular meetings at the White House, and President Johnson followed the same pattern. As a result, according to former Defense Department official Townsend Hoopes, "the decisions and actions that marked out large-scale military entry into the Vietnam war . . . reflected the piecemeal consideration of interrelated issues . . . that . . . was the natural consequence of a fragmented NSC and a general inattention to long-range policy planning."

One of President Nixon's first acts on assuming office in 1969 was to resurrect the NSC. Under the direction of his NSC adviser, Henry Kissinger (and Kissinger's assistant, U.S. Army Colonel Alexander Haig, who rose to four-star General in that job), the NSC played a major role in the later stages of the Vietnam war.

See also NATIONAL SECURITY ADVISER.

Suggestion for further reading: *The Limits of Intervention,* by Townsend Hoopes (New York: David MacKay Co., 1969); *White House Years,* by Henry A. Kissinger (Boston: Little, Brown, 1979).

NAVAL FORCES VIETNAM

Although U.S. Navy advisers had been part of the MAAG (U.S. Military Assistance Advisory Group)-Indochina and the MAAG-Vietnam since the beginning of the advisory effort in 1950 and part of the MACV (U.S. Military Assistance

The U.S.S. *Gallup* on patrol in August 1967. (Courtesy U.S. Navy.)

Command Vietnam) since its organization in 1962, increasing naval operational demands created a need for a new control headquarters.

On April 1, 1966 the position of COMNAVFORV (Commander of Naval Forces Vietnam) was created to meet this need. Subordinate to COMUSMACV (Commander of the MACV), this new command assumed control of naval activities in II, III and IV Corps. Eventually these included the Coastal Surveillance Force (Task Force 115), River Patrol Force (Task Force 116) and the Riverine Assault Force (Task Force 117)—the Navy component of the Joint Army-Navy Mobile Riverine Force.

COMNAVFORV also controlled the Naval Advisory Group, the Seabees of the Third Naval Construction Brigade, the Military Sea Transportation Service Office Vietnam and other activities, including the Commander of Coast Guard Activities Vietnam. It is important to note, however, that naval activities outside of Vietnamese coastal waters remained under the control of CINCPAC in Honolulu, not MACV in Saigon.

On March 29, 1973, in accordance with the Paris Accords, COMNAVFORV was formally disbanded.

See also COASTAL SURVEILLANCE FORCE; NAVY, U.S.; RIVER PATROL FORCE; RIVERINE ASSAULT FORCE; SEALORDS; SEVENTH FLEET.

Suggestions for further reading: *A Short History of the United States Navy and the Southeast Asian Conflict 1950–1975,* by Edward J. Marolda and G. Wesley Pryce, III (Washington, D.C.: Naval Historical Center, 1984).

NAVAL GUNFIRE SUPPORT AND SHORE BOMBARDMENT

U.S. naval gunfire support and shore bombardment was carried out throughout Vietnam by the U.S. Navy Seventh Fleet's cruiser-destroyer group. Organized into Task Group 70.8, the ships were assigned from the fleet's cruiser-destroyer command, from carrier escort units and amphibious units, from the Navy-Coast Guard Coastal Surveillance Force and from the Royal Australian Navy. Ships and weapons included the battleship *New Jersey,* with 16-inch guns; cruisers, with 8-inch and 5-inch guns; destroyers, with 5-inch guns; and IFSs (inshore fire support ships) and LSMRs (landing ships, medium rocket), with 5-inch guns and the capability to fire 380 5-inch rockets per minute.

Naval gunfire support and shore bombardment operations began in May 1965 and ranged the entire coast of Vietnam, but most of the operations took place off I Corps. During the 1968 Tet Offensive, Task Group 70.8 had as many as 22 ships at a time on the gun line. Such naval gunfire support was invaluable to U.S. ground forces. The battleship *New Jersey,* for example, on station from September 1968 to March 1969, fired 3,615 16-inch shells and nearly 11,000 5-inch shells, mainly in support of U.S. Third Marine Division operations along the DMZ.

In May 1972, as part of Operation Linebacker I, a Seventh Fleet cruiser-destroyer group bombarded targets near Haiphong and along the North Vietnamese coast, firing over 111,000 rounds at the enemy. One destroyer was hit by a MIG bombing attack and 16 ships were hit by communist shore batteries, but none were sunk.

See also NAVY, U.S.; SEA DRAGON.

Suggestions for further reading: *A Short History of the United States Navy and the Southeast Asian Conflict 1950–1975,* by Edward J. Marolda and G. Wesley Pryce, III (Washington, D.C.: Naval Historical Center, 1984); "Marine Corps Operations in Vietnam, 1965–66, 1967, 1968, 1969–72," by Edwin H. Simmons in *The Marines in Vietnam 1954–1973* (Washington, D.C.: U.S. Government Printing Office, 1974); *Navy in Vietnam: A Record of the Royal Australian Navy in the Vietnam War 1965–1972,* by Denis Fairfax (Canberra: Australian Government Publishing Service, 1980).

NAVY CROSS

First authorized in World War I, the Navy Cross, with the Air Force Cross and the Distinguished Service Cross, is the nation's second highest award for bravery. It is awarded in the name of the President by the U.S. Navy and Marine Corps for extraordinary heroism, not justifying the award of a Medal of Honor, while engaged in an action against the enemy. The act or

The Navy Cross.

acts of heroism has to have been so notable and have involved risks of life so extraordinary as to set the individual apart from his comrades. Subsequent awards are denoted by a gold star worn on the ribbon.

See also AIR FORCE CROSS, DISTINGUISHED SERVICE CROSS.

NAVY, REPUBLIC OF VIETNAM (VNN)

See SVNAF (SOUTH VIETNAMESE ARMED FORCES).

NAVY, SOUTH VIETNAMESE

See SVNAF (SOUTH VIETNAMESE ARMED FORCES).

NAVY UNIT COMMENDATION

The Navy Unit Commendation is awarded by the Department of the Navy to U.S. Navy and Marine Corps units for heroism in action against an armed enemy or for extremely meritorious conduct in support of military operations. The character of service must have been comparable to that which would merit award of a Silver Star for heroism or a Legion of Merit for meritorious service to an individual. The award element, the same as that for the Presidential Unit Citation (Navy), can be worn by personnel assigned to the unit at the time of award.

See also VALOROUS UNIT AWARD

NAVY, U.S.

The U.S. Navy played a major part in the Vietnam War. It was there at the beginning in the Gulf of Tonkin in 1964 and it was there at the end for the evacuation of Saigon in 1975. The officer in strategic command of the war was a Navy admiral, the Commander-in-Chief of the Pacific Command (CINCPAC), and the Navy not only transported the majority of ground combat forces to Vietnam but also supported them at sea and in the air with naval gunfire and close air support.

During the war the Navy deployed attack carrier strike forces, composed mainly of carriers escorted by cruisers, destroyers and other vessels, to launch air strikes aimed at interdicting enemy supply lines in North Vietnam and Laos. The Navy supplied the battleship *New Jersey*, cruisers, destroyers and other vessels to provide naval gunfire support and shore bombardment, and Navy amphibious ships landed troops and equipment for assaults on enemy positions.

Using inland waterways, the Navy combined forces with the U.S. Army to strike at enemy positions, and it provided vessels for surveillance and interdiction of enemy infiltration in the coastal waters of Vietnam. It also launched commando strikes against North Vietnamese targets and its ships mined the harbor of Haiphong.

Among other decorations and awards, Navy

U.S. Navy swift boats and monitors were used extensively throughout the Vietnam war. (Courtesy U.S. Army Military History Institute.)

officers and men won 14 Medals of Honor for conspicuous bravery in action in Vietnam. Of the 47,244 Americans killed in action, 1,574 were Navy and Coast Guard personnel, as were 4,180 of the 153,329 Americans wounded in action severely enough to require hospitalization and 5,898 of the 150,375 Americans lightly wounded in action.

See also AIRCRAFT CARRIERS; AMPHIBIOUS FORCES; COASTAL SURVEILLANCE FORCE; MOBILE RIVERINE FORCE; NAVAL FORCES VIETNAM; NAVAL GUNFIRE SUPPORT; PACOM (PACIFIC COMMAND); RIVER PATROL FORCE; SEALS; SEVENTH FLEET.

Suggestions for further reading: *A Short History of the United States Navy and the Southeast Asian Conflict 1950–1975,* by Edward J. Marolda and G. Wesley Pryce, III (Washington, D.C.: Naval Historical Center, 1984).

NEUTRALITY

One of the most controversial issues of the Vietnam war concerned the matter of violation of the neutrality of Laos and Cambodia. In fact, neither country was neutral as defined by international law, specifically the Hague Convention of 1907, which states that "A neutral country has the obligation not to allow its territory to be used by a belligerent. If the neutral country is unwilling or unable to prevent this, the other belligerent has the right to take appropriate counteraction."

In July 1959, the North Vietnamese Politburo formed Group 959 to furnish weapons and supplies to communist guerrillas in Laos. Two months earlier the North Vietnamese Army had begun construction of an infiltration route through the panhandle of southern Laos and the eastern border regions of Cambodia in order to infiltrate soldiers and supplies into South Vietnam. Nicknamed the Ho Chi Minh Trail, this route was continually expanded until the end of the war in 1975. As a reaction to these North Vietnamese moves, a U.S. Special Forces training team was introduced into Laos in July 1959. Later known as the White Star Mobile Training Team, the approximately 100 members of this team not only provided training for the Laotian Army but also supplied assistance to Hmoung hill tribesmen and organized them into guerrilla bands to harass North Vietnamese traffic along the Ho Chi Minh Trail. By 1962 the Special Forces White Star Force had grown to some 500 men. They were withdrawn that year as a result of the Geneva Conference, which established the neutrality of Laos.

It soon became clear that the North Vietnamese were continuing their use of the Ho Chi Minh Trail to support their war in South Vietnam. Beginning with Operation Barrel Roll in December 1963 and continuing with Operations Steel Tiger and Tiger Hound in 1965, the United States conducted intensive bombing campaigns against these Laotian infiltration routes, campaigns that would continue until 1974. In addition CIA involvement in Laos, which dated back to World War II with the Office of Strategic Services, intensified in 1953, particularly with the Civil Air Transport Company (later called Air America), providing support for military operations against the communists in Laos. Neutrality in Laos existed in name only.

The same was true of "neutrality" in Cambodia. In the mid-1960s North Vietnamese base areas were established within Cambodia across the border from South Vietnam to rest, resupply and train North Vietnamese and Viet Cong troops. War supplies were landed at the port of Sihanoukville (later renamed Kompong Som) and trucked overland to these sanctuaries. Although limited U.S. tactical air and artillery strikes were authorized beginning in 1966 to respond to North Vietnamese fire from across the border and U.S. reconnaissance patrols were conducted to locate North Vietnamese base areas, it was not until March 1969 that (with the tacit approval of Cambodian leader Prince Norodom Sihanouk) the United States struck directly at these North Vietnamese base areas in Cambodia. Code-named Operation Menu, secret B-52 raids hit targets along the Cambodian-South Vietnamese border. With the overthrow of Prince Sihanouk in March 1970, the facade of Cambodian neutrality came to an end and Cambodian military forces began to take an active part in the war against North Vietnam. At the end of April, President Nixon announced an "incursion" into Cambodia to destroy North Vietnamese bases and a year later the United States helped to organize an operation into Laos by the South Vietnamese Armed forces.

See also AIR AMERICA, BARREL ROLL, CAMBODIA, HO CHI MINH TRAIL, LAOS, LRRP (LONG RANGE RECONNAISSANCE PATROL), MENU OPERATION, STEEL TIGER, TIGER HOUND.

Suggestions for further reading: *No More Vietnams*, by Richard Nixon (New York: Arbor House, 1985); *The Vietnam Experience: Thunder from Above* and *Rain of Fire*, by John Morrocco (Boston: Boston Publishing Co., 1984 and 1985); *Without Honor: Defeat in Vietnam and Cambodia*, by Arnold R. Isaacs (Baltimore: Johns Hopkins University Press, 1983); *On Strategy: A Critical Analysis of the Vietnam War*, by Harry G. Summers, Jr. (Novato, Calif: Presidio Press, 1982).

NEWPORT

Newport was the name of the U.S. Army terminal facility at Saigon built during 1966 and 1967 to relieve the congestion at the older Saigon

The Newport terminal facility at Saigon. (Courtesy U.S. Army.)

port. The Army transportation corps was in charge of the complex. Newport and the Newport Bridge were prime Viet Cong targets during several battles in 1968 but were successfully defended. Newport handled over 150,000 tons of cargo a month.

See also FIRST LOGISTICAL COMMAND.

NEW ZEALAND

New Zealand first contributed to the defense of South Vietnam on July 20, 1964, when an engineer platoon and surgical team arrived in Vietnam for use in local civic action projects. In July 1965 these teams were replaced by the Royal New Zealand Artillery's 161st Battery, with four 105-mm howitzers. V and W Companies of the Royal New Zealand Infantry Regiment arrived in Vietnam in 1967 along with a platoon from New Zealand's commando force, the Special Air Service.

These New Zealand forces were integrated with the forces of the Australian Task Force and operated with them in Phuoc Tuy Province in III Corps. In 1971 these forces were withdrawn from Vietnam.

See also AUSTRALIA, LRRP (LONG RANGE RECONNAISSANCE PATROL).

Suggestions for further reading: *Allied Partici-*

The Royal New Zealand Artillery firing a 105 mm howitzer.
(Courtesy U.S. Army Military History Institute.)

vation in Vietnam, by Stanley Robert Larsen and James Lawton Collins, Jr. (Washington, D.C.: U.S. Government Printing Office, 1975).

NGO DINH DIEM

See DIEM, NGO DINH.

NGO DINH NHU

See NHU, NGO DINH.

NGO DINH NHU, MADAME

See NHU, MADAME NGO DINH.

NGUYEN CAO KY

See KY, NGUYEN CAO.

NGUYEN VAN THIEU

See THIEU, NGUYEN VAN.

NHA TRANG

A port located on the coast of the South China Sea in Khanh Hoa Province in II Corps, Nha Trang was the headquarters for the U.S. Fifth Special Forces Group and I Field Force Vietnam.

See also FIFTH SPECIAL FORCES GROUP, I FIELD FORCE VIETNAM, II CORPS TACTICAL ZONE.

NHU, NGO DINH (1910–1963)

Younger brother of South Vietnamese President Ngo Dinh Diem, Nhu was born into a Catholic family. He attended the Ecole des Chartes in France. Nhu was Diem's chief political officer and head of the secret police. A master of intrigue and organization, he created a network of undercover groups to report on opponents of the Diem regime. With such information Diem and Nhu were able to thwart all attempts to remove them from power until 1963, when Nhu's brutal suppression of Buddhists demonstrating against the government led U.S. officials to demand his ouster and set in motion a military coup that took place on November 1. Diem and Nhu were killed by the insurgents the following day.

See also BUDDHISTS; DIEM, NGO DINH; HARRIMAN, AVERELL; HILSMAN, ROGER; LODGE, HENRY CABOT.

Suggestions for further reading: *Vietnam: A History*, by Stanley Karnow (New York: Viking, 1983); *Fire in the Lake: The Vietnamese and the Americans in Vietnam*, by Frances FitzGerald (Boston: Little, Brown, 1972).

NHU, MADAME NGO DINH (1924–   )

Born Tran Le Xuan in 1924 in Hanoi to a wealthy family that was active in the French colonial government, Madame Nhu was the wife of Ngo Dinh Nhu and acted as official hostess for her bachelor brother-in-law, President Ngo Dinh Diem, from 1955 to 1963. Particularly outspoken and vitriolic, her 1963 comment that Buddhist immolations were a "barbeque" helped turn American public opinion against President

Diem. After the assassination of President Diem and her husband on November 2, 1963, Madame Nhu went into exile in Rome.

See also BUDDHISTS; DIEM, NGO DINH; NHU, NGO DINH.

Suggestions for further reading: *Vietnam: A History*, by Stanley Karnow (New York: Viking, 1983).

NIAGARA OPERATION

A joint U.S. Air Force, Navy and Marine Corps air campaign in support of the besieged U.S. Marine fire base at Khe Sanh, Operation Niagara began on January 14, 1968. Using sensors installed along the DMZ as part of "McNamara's Wall" and reconnaissance flights to pinpoint targets, some 24,000 tactical fighter-bomber sorties and some 2,700 B-52 strategic bomber sorties were flown, averaging more than 300 strikes per day. A three-aircraft B-52 bomber flight was on target every 90 minutes, some bombing within 300 yards of friendly positions.

The operation dropped more than 110,000 tons of bombs, including some 76,000 tons by B-52s, before it ended on March 31, 1968. This air power played a major role in the successful defense of Khe Sanh.

See also KHE SANH, BATTLE OF; MCNAMARA'S WALL.

Suggestions for further reading: *The United States Air Force in Southeast Asia 1961-1973*, edited by Carl Berger (Washington, D.C.: U.S. Government Printing Office, 1977).

NINTH INFANTRY DIVISION

First organized during World War I, the Ninth Infantry Division was one of the first American divisions to see action during World War II. It assaulted the beaches of North Africa in November 1942 and took part in the campaigns in Algeria, Morocco and Tunisia. After helping to liberate Sicily, the division participated in the invasion of Normandy in 1944, landing at D+4 on Utah Beach and fighting its way across France, and was the first unit to penetrate the Siegfried Line and invade Germany. After the Battle of the Bulge, units of the Ninth Infantry Division were the first across the Rhine River at Remagen and later linked up with Russian soldiers driving from the east. As a result of its World War II exploits, the division won the nickname the "Old Reliables."

In December 1966 units of the Ninth Infantry Division were deployed to Vietnam and established a base of operations in III Corps. In January 1967 the division was the first American infantry unit to establish a base camp in IV Corps in the Mekong Delta. In Vietnam the Ninth Division consisted of five battalions of light infantry (the Sixth Battalion, 31st Infantry; the Second, Third and Fourth Battalions, 39th Infantry; and the Second Battalion, 60th Infantry), two battalions of mechanized infantry (the Second Battalion, 47th Infantry and the Fifth Battalion, 60th Infantry) and three battalions of riverine infantry (the Third and Fourth Battalions, 47th Infantry and the Third Battalion, 60th Infantry). Other combat elements included an armored reconnaissance unit—the Third Squadron, Fifth Cavalry—and four battalions of artillery—two with 105-mm howitzers (the Second Battalion, Fourth Artillery, and the First Battalion, 11th Artillery), one battalion with 155-mm howitzers (the First Battalion, 84th Artillery), and a unique unit with 105-mm howitzers equipped to fire from floating platforms in support of riverine operations (the Third Battalion, 34th Artillery).

The division fought in two corps tactical zones. While portions of the division conducted combat operations in III Corps, its Second Brigade (with Naval Task Force 117) formed the Mobile Riverine Force for operations in the Mekong Delta in IV Corps. Using boats, helicopters and air-cushioned hovercraft, the division added a new dimension to battlefield mobility. It took part in Operation Junction City in 1967 and helped to turn back the Viet Cong during Tet Offensive 1968. Units of the division were among the first combat elements to depart from Vietnam. Leaving behind its Third Brigade, the Ninth Infantry Division withdrew from Vietnam in 1968 and was inactivated in 1969. The Third Brigade continued to serve in earnest in August 1972, three months before U.S. presidential elections. Hanoi's Chief N~~ tiator Le Duc Tho and National Security Ad~~ Henry Kissinger held frequent private talk~ Paris suburb, and by October it appeared peace settlement was imminent. The ~~ States dropped its demand for the withdr~~ NVA forces from the south, and North V~ no longer insisted on the removal o~ Vietnamese President Nguyen Van Thie~ ever, after hearing the details, Preside~ denounced the settlement. Kissinger a~ Tho resumed negotiations but they~ December over the future of South ~ was a contest of wills, and Han~ believed that U.S. antiwar sentiment~ Nixon to capitulate.

When he resumed the bombing of the n~~ months earlier, Nixon had said, "We have the power to destroy [North Vietnam's] war-making capacity. The only question is whether we have the *will* to use that power. What distinguishes me from [President] Johnson is that I have that *will* in spades." A master of what the Chinese called "fight-fight-talk-talk," Nixon on December 17, 1972 ordered an intensive bombing of Hanoi,

President Nixon in Vietnam with the First Infantry Division.
(Courtesy U.S. Army Military History Institute.)

a~~~ President Nixon no doubt would have tried to honor those guarantees when the North Vietnamese tested the U.S. response with a multidivision attack on Phuoc Long Province in December 1974 (*see* FINAL OFFENSIVE). To do so, he would have had to overcome a congressional ban on U.S. military operations in Indochina that was then in effect.

But in December 1974 Nixon was no longer President. Undone by the Watergate scandal, he had left office four months before. Now it was the North Vietnamese who "had the will in spades," and by April 30, 1975 their conquest of South Vietnam was complete.

See also ANTIWAR MOVEMENT; CAMBODIA; CASE-CHURCH AMENDMENT; CHINA; COOPER-CHURCH AMENDMENT; EASTERTIDE OFFENSIVE; HAIPHONG; HANOI; KENT STATE; KISSINGER, HENRY A.; LAIRD, MELVIN; MENU OPERATION; PACIFICATION; PARIS ACCORDS; PEACE TALKS; PENTAGON PAPERS; SOVIET UNION; THIEU, NGUYEN VAN; WITHDRAWAL OF U.S. FORCES.

Suggestions for further reading: *No More Vietnams,* by Richard Nixon (New York: Arbor House, 1985); *RN: The Memoirs of Richard Nixon,* by Richard Nixon (New York: Grosset & Dunlop, 1978); *White House Years,* by Henry A. Kissinger (Boston: Little, Brown, 1979); *Why We Were in Vietnam,* by Norman Podhoretz (New York: Simon & Schuster, 1982). For a critical view of President

Nixon's foreign policy, see *The Illusion of Peace: Foreign Policy in the Nixon Years,* by Tad Szulc (New York: Viking, 1978). Also see *The Lost Peace: America's Search for a Negotiated Settlement of the Vietnam War,* by Allan E. Goodman (Stanford: Hoover Institution, 1978); *The Vietnam Trauma in American Foreign Policy 1945-75,* by Paul Kattenburg (New Brunswick, N.J.: Transaction Books, 1980); *Sideshow: Kissinger, Nixon and the Destruction of Cambodia,* by William Shawcross (New York: Simon & Schuster, 1979); *Vietnam: A History,* by Stanley Karnow (New York: Viking, 1983).

NOLTING, FREDERICK E(RNEST), JR. (1911–   )

Nolting was born on August 24, 1911 in Richmond, Virginia. After service in the U.S. Navy in World War II, he joined the State Department, specializing in European affairs. From 1957 to 1961 he served as Deputy Chief of the U.S. delegation to the North Atlantic Treaty Organization.

President Kennedy appointed Nolting Ambassador to South Vietnam on February 17, 1961. Nolting replaced Elbridge Durbrow, who had criticized the Diem regime in reports to Washington. Nolting was initially instructed to avoid antagonizing President Ngo Dinh Diem, his brother Ngo Dinh Nhu and Nhu's outspoken wife, Madame Nhu. (Durbrow had suggested that Ngo Dinh Nhu go into voluntary exile.) Believing that overt pressure would only stiffen Diem's opposition to reforms, Nolting tried to win his cooperation with assurances of unconditional U.S. support.

When in late 1961 a fact-finding mission to South Vietnam headed by Maxwell Taylor, Kennedy's military adviser, recommended that to prevent the collapse of the Saigon government, the United States press Diem for more reforms, increase its military aid and commit 8,000 U.S. ground troops, Kennedy rejected the request for combat troops and instructed Nolting to insist upon the reforms as a condition of increased aid. Diem agreed to carry out the reforms in exchange for a letter from Kennedy, made public on December 15, that promised increased U.S. military assistance. The number of U.S. advisers would rise from 2,000 at the end of 1961 to some 16,000 in November 1963.

But the reforms were never carried out. Nevertheless, Nolting continued to give the Diem government his unflinching support while actively discouraging negative reporting about the government by American reporters in Saigon. In the summer of 1963 Diem was warned sternly by Nolting's deputy, William Trueheart, about further hostile treatment of Buddhists monks. Nolting, upon returning from a vacation, managed to get Diem to promise in mid-August that such abuses would cease. A week later, government troops attacked Buddhist pagodas, beating monks and desecrating religious relics. On August 22, Henry Cabot Lodge arrived in Saigon to replace Nolting, who returned to Washington. Diem's failure to adhere to his promise to Nolting was a factor in the decision to withdraw U.S. support from his government, which was toppled by a military coup on November 1. Diem and Nhu were killed the next day. Nolting retired from government service in 1964.

See also DIEM, NGO DINH; KENNEDY, JOHN F.; HARRIMAN, AVERELL; HILSMAN, ROGER; LODGE, HENRY CABOT; NHU, MADAME NGO DINH; NHU, NGO DINH; TAYLOR, MAXWELL D.

Suggestions for further reading: *Fire in the Lake: The Vietnamese and the Americans in Vietnam,* by Frances FitzGerald (Boston: Little, Brown, 1972); *Vietnam: A History,* by Stanley Karnow (New York: Viking, 1983).

NORTH VIETNAM

See SRV (SOCIALIST REPUBLIC OF VIETNAM).

NORTH VIETNAMESE ARMY

See NVA (NORTH VIETNAMESE ARMY).

NUCLEAR WEAPONS

The use of strategic and tactical nuclear weapons

in Vietnam was ruled out by the U.S. government. Their use had been proposed and rejected at the time of the siege of Dien Bien Phu, in 1954. During the furor over the survivability of the besieged outpost at Khe Sanh in late 1967 and early 1968, General William C. Westmoreland put together a small working group to study the feasibility of using small tactical nuclear weapons at Khe Sanh, but when word of this reached the Pentagon he was told to disband the group.

During a trip to Hanoi in April 1975 in connection with POW/MIA issues, the author reminded a North Vietnamese Colonel that the United States had the military capability to totally destroy North Vietnam with nuclear weapons. The Colonel replied that the North Vietnamese had always known that, but they had also known that the Americans would never use such weapons. But if U.S. nuclear weapons did not deter North Vietnam, Soviet and Chinese nuclear weapons had a major deterrent effect on the United States and were one of the primary reasons why a ground invasion of North Vietnam was never seriously considered.

Suggestions for further reading: *A Soldier Reports,* by William C. Westmoreland (Garden City: Doubleday, 1976).

NVA (NORTH VIETNAMESE ARMY)

The North Vietnamese Army (NVA) went through a major transformation during the course of the Vietnam war. In 1964 it was a conscript army of about 250,000 organized into 15 divisions armed with World War II-vintage small arms, mortars and artillery. In addition, it had some 25,000 to 30,000 Viet Cong guerrillas operating in the south.

By 1974 the NVA had grown to some 570,000 regulars organized into 18 infantry divisions, two training divisions and 10 regiments of artillery, equipped with 800 122-mm and 175 130-mm guns; 122-mm and 152-mm howitzers; 82-mm, 100-mm, 107-mm, 120-mm and 160-mm mortars; and 107-mm, 122-mm and 140-mm recoilless rifles. The NVA also had four armored regiments with 900 T-34, T-54 and T-59 medium tanks as well as PT-76 and other light tanks. In addition to these infantry divisions, the NVA had 20 independent infantry regiments, 24 antiaircraft artillery regiments and 15 SAM (surface-to-air missile) regiments, each equipped with 18 SA-2 launchers.

In 1974 half of the NVA was deployed in South Vietnam and in Laotian and Cambodian border areas. In 1975 the remainder of the NVA moved south to launch the blitzkrieg that was to overwhelm South Vietnam.

See also FINAL OFFENSIVE.

Suggestions for further reading: *PAVN: People's Army of Vietnam* by Douglas Pike (Novato, CA: Presidio Press, 1986)

OAK LEAF CLUSTER

To denote subsequent awards of military decorations (except for the Air Medal, on which a metallic numeral is worn), a metallic oak leaf cluster is worn on the medal ribbon by U.S. Army and Air Force personnel. Subsequent awards for U.S. Navy, Marine Corps and Coast Guard personnel are denoted by a metallic gold star.

OKINAWA

See JAPAN.

101ST AIRBORNE DIVISION (AIRMOBILE)

Although first organized during World War I, the then 101st Infantry Division did not see action during that war. Reverting to a Wisconsin reserve unit, it derived both its unit insignia and its nickname, "Screaming Eagles," from the American eagle "Old Abe," which was carried into battle by the Eighth Wisconsin Infantry Regiment during the Civil War. The division was recalled to active duty in 1942 and became the 101st Airborne Division. Under the command of Major General Maxwell D. Taylor, the 101st Airborne Division took part in the invasion of Normandy on June 6, 1944 and the subsequent Market Garden airborne operation in the Netherlands. Later the division distinguished itself by its defense of Bastogne during the Battle of the Bulge and ended World War II with the capture of Hitler's mountain retreat at Berchtesgaden.

In July 1965 the First Brigade of the 101st Airborne Division was deployed to Vietnam. It fought as a separate brigade until 1967, when in the only division-sized airlift of the war the remainder of the division arrived in Vietnam. The division consisted of 10 battalions of airmobile infantry—the Third Battalion, 187th Infantry; the First and Second Battalions, 327th Infantry; First and Second Battalions, 501st Infantry; the First and Second Battalions, 502nd Infantry; and the First, Second and Third Battalions, 506th Infantry. Other combat elements of the division included an air reconnaissance unit, the Second Squadron, 17th Cavalry; and six battalions of artillery—three with 105-mm howitzers (the Second Battalion, 319th Artillery; the Second Battalion, 320th Artillery; and the First Battalion, 321st Artillery), two battalions with 155-mm howitzers (the Second Battalion, 11th Artillery and the First Battalion, 39th Artillery) and a unique unit, the Fourth Battalion, 77th Artillery, a heliborne unit armed with aerial rockets. Another unique feature of the 101st Airborne Division was its aviation group, which consisted of three aviation battalions of assault helicopters, assault support helicopters and gunships.

The majority of the 101st Airborne Division's

Insignia of the 101st Airborne Division.

tactical operations were in the Central Highlands in II Corps and in the A Shau Valley in I Corps. Among its major operations was the fight for Dong Ap Bia mountain—the Battle of "Hamburger Hill." In 1971 the division assisted South Vietnamese troops with their attempt to cut the infiltration routes in Laos in Operation Lam Son 719.

The 101st Airborne Division was awarded the Vietnam Civil Action Medal and the Vietnam Cross of Gallantry with Palm. Among other individual awards, troopers of the 101st Airborne Division won 17 Medals of Honor for bravery in Vietnam. The division suffered almost 20,000 soldiers killed or wounded in action in Vietnam, over twice as many as the 9,328 casualties it suffered in World War II.

The last Army division to leave Vietnam, in 1972 the 101st Airborne Division returned to Fort Campbell, Kentucky, where it remains as the Army's only airmobile division. The 101st Airborne Division (Airmobile) maintains the Don F.

Pratt Museum at Fort Campbell, which has exhibits and unpublished manuscripts on the division's Vietnam-war experience. There is also an active division association, which schedules periodic reunions for members and former members of the Screaming Eagles. Further information may be obtained from Mr. George Rosie, 101st Airborne Division Association, P.O. Box 101AB, Court Station, Kalamazoo, Michigan 49005.

See also AIR CAVALRY; HAMBURGER HILL; I CORPS TACTICAL ZONE; LAM SON 719; II CORPS TACTICAL ZONE.

Suggestions for further reading: *Vietnam Studies: Airmobility 1961–1971,* by John J. Tolson (Washington, D.C.: U.S. Government Printing Office, 1973); *Vietnam Studies: The War in the Northern Provinces 1966–1968,* by Willard Pearson (Washington, D.C.: U.S. Government Printing Office, 1975); *Vietnam Order of Battle,* by Shelby L. Stanton (Washington, D.C.: U.S. News and World Report Books, 1981). Although there is no published history of the 101st Airborne Division in Vietnam as such, a fictionalized account is contained in Screaming Eagles veteran John Del Vecchio's *The 13th Valley* (New York: Bantam, 1982). Another source for the division's combat operations, including selected small unit actions, is Shelby L. Stanton's *The Rise and Fall of an American Army* (Novato, Calif.: Presidio Press, 1985).

198TH INFANTRY BRIGADE

See AMERICAL DIVISION.

199TH LIGHT INFANTRY BRIGADE

Formed at Fort Benning, Georgia, the 199th Light Infantry Brigade arrived in Vietnam in December 1966. Charged with guarding the approaches to Saigon, it conducted combat operations in III Corps and saw particularly hard fighting during the North Vietnamese Army's Tet Offensive in 1968. Operating directly under the corps-level II Field Force Vietnam throughout

its service in Vietnam, the 199th Light Infantry Brigade returned to the United States in October 1970.

During combat service soldiers of the brigade won four Medals of Honor for battlefield bravery and suffered 657 soldiers killed in action and another 2,571 wounded in action.

See also II FIELD FORCE VIETNAM, III CORPS TACTICAL ZONE.

Suggestions for further reading: *Vietnam Order of Battle,* by Shelby L. Stanton (Washington, D.C.: U.S. News & World Report Books, 1981). Accounts of battle actions of the 199th Light Infantry Brigade are contained in *The Rise and Fall of an American Army,* by Shelby L. Stanton (Novato, Calif.: Presidio Press, 1985).

196TH LIGHT INFANTRY BRIGADE

Formed at Fort Devens, Massachusetts in 1965, the 196th Light Infantry Brigade was dispatched to Vietnam in August 1966. Operating as an independent brigade, it conducted combat operations in the vicinity of Tay Ninh, III Corps until November 1967, when it was sent north to I Corps to meet a North Vietnamese threat there. Part of Task Force Oregon, it was integrated into the Americal Division, which was organized to replace Task Force Oregon. When the Americal Division was disbanded in November 1971, the 196th Light Infantry Brigade again became an independent unit and provided security for U.S. logistical areas in I Corps until it withdrew from Vietnam in June 1972—the last U.S. combat brigade to depart Vietnam.

The brigade consisted of the Second Battalion, First Infantry; the Third Battalion, 21st Infantry; the Fourth Battalion, 31st Infantry; the Third Battalion, 82nd Artillery, with 105-mm howitzers; and Troop F, 17th Cavalry.

Because it was for a time part of the Americal Division, statistics for the brigade alone are not complete. What is available reveals that the 196th Light Infantry Brigade suffered 1,004 soldiers killed in action and another 5,591 wounded in action, a third more than the entire Americal Division had suffered in World War II.

See also AMERICAL DIVISION.

Suggestions for further reading: *Vietnam Order of Battle,* by Shelby L. Stanton (Washington, D.C.: U.S. News & World Report Books, 1981). Accounts of battle actions of the 196th Light Infantry Brigade are contained in *The Rise and Fall of an American Army,* by Shelby L. Stanton (Novato, Calif.: Presidio Press, 1985).

173RD AIRBORNE BRIGADE

Organized in 1963 as the PACOM (Pacific Command) quick-reaction force, the 173rd Airborne Brigade was stationed on Okinawa when it received orders for temporary duty in Vietnam. Arriving in Vietnam in May 1965, it was the first major U.S. Army ground combat unit committed to the war.

Combat elements of the 173rd Airborne Brigade consisted of the First, Second, Third and Fourth Battalions, 503rd Airborne Infantry; the Third Battalion, 319th Airborne Artillery, with 105-mm howitzers; Company D, 16th Armor and Troop E, 17th Cavalry; and the 335th Aviation Company.

Headquartered at Bien Hoa Air Base near Saigon in III Corps from May 1965 to October 1967, it conducted combat operations in the III Corps area, including a combat parachute jump in February 1967 into War Zone C. In November 1967 the 173rd Airborne Brigade moved to II Corps and fought a major battle at Dak To with North Vietnamese Army (NVA) forces, winning the Presidential Unit Citation for bravery in action. After more than six years on the battlefield, its "temporary duty" complete, the brigade was withdrawn from Vietnam in August 1971.

During combat service 12 troopers of the 173rd Airborne Brigade won the Medal of Honor for conspicuous bravery; 1,606 were killed in action and 8,435 were wounded in action. These 10,041 casualties were almost five times the losses of the 187th Airborne Infantry Regiment in the Korean war, four times the losses of the 11th Airborne Division in the Pacific during World War II and

Insignia of the 173rd Airborne Brigade.

even greater than the losses of either the 82nd or 101st Airborne Division in particularly hard fighting in Europe during that war.

Suggestions for further reading: *Vietnam Order of Battle,* by Shelby L. Stanton (Washington, D.C.: U.S. News & World Report Books, 1981). Accounts of battle actions of the 173rd Airborne Brigade are contained in *The Rise and Fall of an American Army,* by Shelby L. Stanton (Novato, Calif.: Presidio Press, 1985).

OPERATIONS, ALLIED MILITARY

Thousands of U.S. Army, U.S. Marine, South Vietnamese and allied military ground operations were conducted during the Vietnam war. Identified by code names (i.e., Silver Bayonet, Junction

City, Dewey Canyon), they ranged from small-unit actions to operations involving several divisions. Such major allied ground operations included:

ABILENE	KLAMATH FALLS
ALA MOANA	LAM SON 54
APACHE SNOW	LAM SON 207
ATLAS WEDGE	LAM SON 216
ATTLEBORO	LAM SON 246
BADGER TOOTH	LAM SON 719
BEAU CHARGER	LEXINGTON III
BINH TAY I	MAC ARTHUR
BIRMINGHAM	MALLET
BUFFALO	MALHEUR I and II
CEDAR FALLS	MARAUDER
COLORADO	MASHER/WHITE WING
COBURG	MASSACHUSETTS
CRAZY HORSE	STRIKER
CRIMP	MASTIFF
DAVY CROCKETT	MONTANA MAULER
DEFIANT STAND	MONTANA RAIDER
DELAWARE	NEVADA EAGLE
DEWEY CANYON I	NEW YORK
and II	PAUL REVERE I-IV
DOUBLE EAGLE	PEGASUS
EL PASO I and II	PERSHING
ENTERPRISE	PIRANHA
FAIRFAX	PRAIRIE
FRANCIS MARION	SAM HOUSTON
FREDERICK HILL	SCOTLAND II
GARFIELD	SEWARD
GIBRALTAR	SILVER BAYONET
GREELEY	SOMERSET PLAIN
HARVEST MOON	STARLITE
HASTINGS	TEXAS
HAWTHORNE	TEXAS STAR
HICKORY	THAYER
HIGHLAND	TOAN THANG
HOLLINGSWORTH	TRAN HUNG DAO
HUMP	UNION I and II
IRVING	UNIONTOWN
JEFFERSON GLENN	UTAH
JOHN PAUL JONES	WHEELER/WALLOWA
JUNCTION CITY	YELLOWSTONE

A chronology of these major actions is contained in Part II and descriptions of the actual battles are found in Shelby Stanton's *The Rise and Fall of An American Army: U.S. Ground Operations in Vietnam 1965–1973* (Novato, Calif.: Presidio Press, 1985).

Major U.S. Navy operations—Eagle Pull, Frequent Wind, Game Warden, Market Time, Sea Dragon and Sealords—are discussed under separate headings, as are major U.S. Air Force, Navy, and Marine air operations, such as Barrel Roll, Bolo, Commando Hunt, Flaming Dart, Linebacker, Menu, Ranch Hand, Rolling Thunder, Steel Tiger and Tiger Hound.

ORANGE, AGENT

See AGENT ORANGE.

OREGON TASK FORCE

See AMERICAL INFANTRY DIVISION.

ORGANIZATION FOR COMBAT

Within the U.S. Army the primary combat organization is the squad. Its size varies in accordance with its type but is normally about nine soldiers commanded by a staff sergeant. Two or more squads make up a platoon, commanded by a lieutenant, and two or more platoons comprise a company (a battery in the artillery, a troop in the cavalry), commanded by a captain. Two or more company-sized units make up a battalion (a squadron in the cavalry), commanded by a lieutenant colonel. Two or more battalions or squadrons comprise a brigade (a regiment in the cavalry, a group in the artillery), commanded by a colonel. In Vietnam separate brigades (i.e., those not part of a division) were commanded by a brigadier general. A division consists of two or more brigades, commanded by a major general. Two or more divisions make up a corps, commanded by a lieutenant general. In World War II and the Korean war two or more corps comprised a field army (e.g., the Third Army in World War II, the Eighth Army in the Korean war), commanded by a general, but in the Vietnam war the corps (also called a field force) were under the command of the MACV (U.S. Military Assistance Command Vietnam.

The U.S. Marine Corps organization is similar to that of the Army except that in the Army infantry battalions are organized into brigades; in the Marine Corps they are assigned to regiments. Additionally, in Vietnam a Marine corps-level headquarters, the III Marine Amphibious Force, was also organized.

The highest U.S. Air Force organization in Vietnam was the Seventh Air Force. Subordinate to this headquarters was the 834th Air Division, commanded by a major general, and numerous Air Force wings, normally commanded by an Air Force colonel. Each wing contained a number of squadrons, commanded by lieutenant colonels, and each squadron contained a number of aircraft. While Seventh Air Force was subordinate to the MACV, the Air Force units involved in the bombing of North Vietnam and Laos were under separate commands.

In Vietnam, U.S. Navy forces were under the Commander of U.S. Naval Forces Vietnam. The majority of Navy forces off Vietnam, however, were assigned to battle groups of the Seventh Fleet, under the command of the Pacific Fleet in Honolulu.

Vietnamese forces—South Vietnamese, North Vietnamese and Viet Cong—were organized along lines similar to those of the U.S. forces. Like the U.S. Marines, the Vietnamese had regiments rather than brigades. While the South Vietnamese had four corps under the command of their Joint General Staff, the North Vietnamese did not adopt a similar organization until 1974, when they, too, organized four corps-level control headquarters.

See also AIR FORCE, U.S.; ARMY, U.S.; COMMAND AND CONTROL; MARINE CORPS, U.S.; NAVY, U.S. listings for specific unit types.

Suggestions for further reading: *Vietnam Order of Battle* by Shelby L. Stanton (Washington, D.C. U.S. News & World Report Books, 1981).

PACIFICATION

Pacification was a primary objective of the U.S. war effort in Vietnam. It was officially defined by the MACV (U.S. Military Assistance Command Vietnam) in November 1967 as "the military, political, economic, and social process of establishing or re-establishing local government responsive to and involving the participation of the people. It includes the provision of sustained, credible territorial security, the destruction of the enemy's underground government, the assertion or reassertion of political control and involvement of the people in government, and the initiation of economic and social activity capable of self-sustenance and expansion. The economic element of pacification includes the opening of roads and waterways and the maintenance of lines of communication important to economic and military activity."

Pacification was designed to achieve three basic objectives: (1) to end the war and restore peace, (2) to develop democracy and (3) to reform society. During the war in Vietnam pacification went through many different phases. First was the strategic hamlets program of South Vietnamese President Ngo Dinh Diem, which began in 1961 and was abandoned after his assassination in 1963. The next program was the Revolutionary Development program, which began in 1966 after some fits and starts. Then there was the Accelerated Pacification campaign, which ran from November 1968 to January 1969 and included the Phoenix program, and from 1971 to the end of the war, there was the Community Defense and Development program.

Ideally, as the schematic of northern I Corps illustrates, reconnaissance forces from U.S. Special Forces CIDG (Civilian Irregular Defense Group) camps (later South Vietnamese Army [ARVN] ranger border defense battalions) would provide reconnaissance to warn of North Vietnamese attacks from their base areas along the Ho Chi Minh Trail in Laos through the mountains of the Chaîne Annamitique in the interior. U.S. and ARVN combat forces would conduct search-and-destroy operations in the hinterlands to prevent the movement of these enemy units into populated areas and, if possible, to annihilate them. Territorial Forces—South Vietnamese Regional Forces and Popular Forces, including U.S. Marine combat action platoons—would conduct clear-and-hold pacification operations in the densely populated coastal plains, where the majority of the people resided.

The whole pacification program was dependent on the provision of security against North Vietnamese Army and Viet Cong main force units, which had the ability to ruin any advances made through pacification. Even if they did not attack pacified areas directly, the threat of such attack drained off U.S. and ARVN combat units and other pacification assets, since such forces had to be withdrawn from scattered locations throughout the countryside and concentrated to avoid being defeated in detail—picked off one at a time by superior enemy forces.

Thus, the arguments often heard during the Vietnam war about whether it was best to "search and destroy," using conventional military tactics, or to "clear and hold," using counterinsurgency techniques, missed the point. Both were essential and each was dependent on the success of the other. Although after 1968 pacification had significant successes, especially after South Vietnam armed the local villagers and they began providing their own local security, the ultimate inability of the ARVN to hold off NVA attacks after the withdrawal of U.S. combat troops and finally the withdrawal of U.S. fire support, were to undo all the gains that had been made.

See also CAP (COMBINED ACTION PLATOON), CLEAR-AND-HOLD, PHOENIX PROGRAM, REVOLUTIONARY DEVELOPMENT, SEARCH-AND-DESTROY, STRATEGIC HAMLETS, TERRITORIAL FORCES.

Suggestions for further reading: *Pacification*, by Tran Dinh Tho (Washington, D.C.: Center for Military History, 1980). For post-Tet 1968 attitudes in the countryside, see *The Rational Peasant: The Political Economy of Rural Society in Vietnam*, by Samuel Popkin (Berkeley: University of California Press, 1979). For earlier views of pacification, see *Village in Vietnam*, by Gerald Hickey (New Haven: Yale University Press, 1964); *War Comes to Long An: Revolutionary Conflict in a Vietnamese Province*, by Jeffrey Race (Berkeley: University of California Press, 1971); *The Village*, by Francis J. West (New York: Harper & Row, 1972), *Reorganizing for Pacification Support* by Thomas W. Scoville (Washington, D.C.: U.S. Government Printing Office, 1982); *Fire in the Lake: The Vietnamese and the Americans in Vietnam*, by Frances FitzGerald (Boston: Little, Brown, 1972).

PACOM (PACIFIC COMMAND)

Located in Honolulu, Hawaii, PACOM (Pacific Command) was one of the several "unified commands" reporting directly to the Secretary of Defense through the Joint Chiefs of Staff. The successor to General MacArthur's General Headquarters Far East Command in Tokyo (the strategic "theater" headquarters for U.S. forces during the Korean war), PACOM's area of responsibility included not only Vietnam but the rest of Asia and the Pacific as well. Included in this headquarters was an Army component, U.S. Army Pacific (USARPAC); a Navy component, Pacific Fleet (PACFLT); and an Air Force component, Pacific Air Force (PACAF). PACOM was commanded by a Navy admiral.

Because it was removed from the war by some 5,000 miles, PACOM often based its decisions on a particularly rigid adherence to preset contingency plans, which more often than not were out of touch with the realities of the situation. For example, because existing contingency plans called for the Army component commander to assume command of any major PACOM land force contingent, in 1962 the Army component commander, General Paul D. Harkins, was named Commander of the newly formed MACV (U.S. Military Assistance Command Vietnam). That command was made a "subordinate unified command" reporting directly to CINCPAC (Commander-in-Chief of the Pacific Command) in Honolulu. This made some sense prior to the change in the nature of the war in 1964–65 and the resulting major commitment of U.S. ground combat forces; it was irrational after that time, since common sense dictated that the ground commander should also have been the theater commander. These command arrangements actually hampered conduct of the war, since MACV had no control over air operations over North Vietnam and Laos nor over naval operations off the coast of Vietnam and therefore had no control over the North Vietnamese lines of communications (i.e., its supply lines and infiltration routes). This proved to be a fatal flaw.

It was not as if PACOM did not know better. In November 1964, as the changing nature of the war became apparent, the State Department's Political Adviser to CINCPAC, Norman B. Hannah, pointed out that cutting these lines of communication by ground operations and establishing defensive positions along the DMZ and across Laos to prevent infiltration was the most appropriate role for U.S. military forces. The PACOM staff vetoed that role, not for strategic reasons, but because "it would get [U.S.] forces committed out of synchronization with SEATO contingency plan commitments which did not envision use of U.S. military forces in that manner." This led to the concentration of U.S. forces against the internal problems of South Vietnam rather than against the external North Vietnamese Army (NVA) threat, which in the end was decisive.

Finally, the units that were committed against the NVA were those least trained and equipped to do so. Again existing plans were the villain. Because of lack of existing ports in northern I Corps, contingency plans for "temporary" operations called for use of Marine forces, which could be supplied over the beach. Thus when the two U.S. Marine divisions and III Marine Amphibious Force were subsequently committed for sustained combat operations, they were stationed in accordance with those preexisting plans. This meant that the Marine Corps, trained and equipped as an amphibious assault force, found itself entrenched against regular North Vietnamese Army divisions attacking across the DMZ, while Army forces, organized for such defensive operations, were being retrained for Marine-type riverine operations in the Mekong Delta. While dividing up the world into "unified commands" facilitated administration in peacetime, the failure to establish a separate theater of war for Vietnam was a major strategic mistake.

During the Vietnam war the post of Commander-in-Chief of the Pacific Command changed hands four times. When the war began Admiral Harry D. Felt was CINCPAC. He was replaced in June 1964 by Admiral U.S. Grant Sharp, who was replaced in July 1968 by Admiral John S. McCain. In September 1972 Admiral McCain was replaced by Admiral Noel Gayler, who remained in command until after the war in Vietnam ended.

In comparison to this succession of four U.S. military theater commanders, North Vietnamese strategic military command was exercised by General Vo Nguyen Giap throughout the entire course of the war.

See also COMMAND AND CONTROL; MCCAIN, JOHN S.; SHARP, U.S. GRANT.

Suggestions for further reading: *Strategy for Defeat: Vietnam in Retrospect,* by U.S. Grant Sharp, (Novato, Calif.: Presidio Press, 1978); *Command and Control 1950–1969,* by George S. Eckhardt (Washington, D.C.: U.S. Government Printing Office, 1974); *A Soldier Reports,* by William C. Westmoreland (Garden City: Doubleday, 1976); "Vietnam, Now We Know," by Norman B. Hannah, in *All Quiet on the Eastern Front,* edited by Anthony T. Bouscaren (Old Greenwich, Conn.: Devin-Adair, 1977); *On Strategy: A Critical Analysis of the Vietnam War,* by Harry G. Summers, Jr. (Novato, Calif.: Presidio Press, 1982); *The 25-Year War: America's Military Role in Vietnam,* by Bruce Palmer, Jr. (Lexington: University of Kentucky Press, 1984).

PARACHUTES

Parachutes were used by the U.S. military in Vietnam primarily to air-drop supplies to forward troops when weather, terrain, enemy fire or a shortage of helicopters made other means of aerial delivery impossible. Parachuted supplies were often used by beleaguered Special Forces camps where the close proximity of North Vietnamese antiaircraft guns made normal helicopter resupply extremely hazardous. Only the United States used parachute delivery extensively, as other allies found the system too expensive and the North Vietnamese and Viet Cong had no control of the air. Parachutes were seldom used to drop troops.

See also AIRBORNE FORCES.

A typical supply air drop. (Courtesy Shelby L. Stanton.)

PARIS ACCORDS

The Paris Peace Accords, officially the Agreement on Ending the War and Restoring Peace in Vietnam, was signed in Paris on January 27, 1973 by the United States, the Republic of Vietnam (South Vietnam), the Democratic Republic of Vietnam (North Vietnam) and the Provisional Revolutionary Government of the Republic of South Vietnam (the Viet Cong).

As events would prove, these so-called peace accords were in reality only a temporary armed truce between North Vietnam and South Vietnam. In exchange for the return of American prisoners of war, the United States withdrew the few units of its remaining armed forces from Vietnam, but the North Vietnamese continued to maintain substantial numbers of their regular armed forces in the south.

Although the accords set up an International Commission of Control and Supervision (ICCS), the agreement was almost immediately violated by both sides and the ICCS proved to be impotent.

Like the Geneva Accords of 1954, the Paris Accords of 1973 were not an end to war in Vietnam but merely a prelude to its next phase.

See also FOUR PARTY JOINT MILITARY COMMISSION; FOUR PARTY JOINT MILITARY TEAM; ICCS.

Suggestions for further reading: the text of the Paris Accords can be found in both *The Lost Peace: America's Search for a Negotiated Settlement of the Vietnam War*, by Allan E. Goodman (Stanford: Hoover

The chief negotiators in Paris: Le Duc Tho of North Vietnam and Henry Kissinger of the United States. (AP/Wide World Photos.)

Institution Press, 1978) and *Sixty Days to Peace,* by Walter Scott Dillard (Washington, D.C.: U.S. Government Printing Office, 1982).

PATHET LAO

See LAOS.

PATHFINDERS

Pathfinders were specially trained, airborne-qualified U.S. infantrymen who were air-dropped or air-landed in small teams into hostile territory to determine the best approaches and landing sites for aircraft and helicopters and to set up and operate navigational aids for landing zones. Pathfinders were used extensively in Vietnam by the Army and Marine Corps because of the difficult jungle terrain, which often had to be cleared of trees, underbrush or booby traps prior to heli-borne insertion of troops. Nearly every aviation group in Vietnam had its own Pathfinder platoons or detachments used. The largest use of pathfinders was made by the Army's First Cavalry Division and the Fifth Special Forces Group. Pathfinders were often known as "Black Hats," as they wore black baseball caps.

PEACE TALKS

The Vietnam peace talks opened in Paris on May 13, 1968. Karl Von Clausewitz, the preeminent military theorist, said that war is a continuation of politics with the addition of other means. For the North Vietnamese, negotiations were a continuation of war with the addition of other means. For the United States, on the other hand, negotiations were seen as a bargaining process aimed at reaching a compromised settlement. As a

A pathfinder of 101st Airborne Division at work. (Courtesy Army News Features.)

result of this divergence between the two major parties, the effectiveness of the peace talks was limited. They were ultimately damaging to the United States because lack of progress eroded the American public's support of the war effort and repeatedly proved useful for North Vietnam, which used the many bombing halts, offered as inducements to negotiate, to refurbish its military forces.

From December 1965 to May 1968, the United States used more bombing halts as a means of signaling to North Vietnam its willingness to negotiate a diplomatic settlement of the war. But it was not until January 1969, when the North Vietnamese saw that the 1968 U.S. presidential election had not gone their way, that negotiations began in earnest by representatives of North Vietnam and the Viet Cong. These open negotiations were reinforced by secret talks. It was not until October 1972 after the North Vietnamese-Soviet-Chinese alliance began to weaken with the U.S. opening to China in 1972 and the summit meeting in Moscow that same year—combined with the failure of North Vietnam's Eastertide Offensive to achieve its objectives by military means—that a breakthrough was reached between the United States and North Vietnam. Both sides had moderated their positions: North Vietnam dropped its demand for a coalition in the south and the United States dropped its insistence on a withdrawal of North Vietnamese forces from South Vietnam. Complicated by the unwillingness of the South Vietnamese government to agree to what appeared to them to be a negotiated surrender, the talks broke down in December 1972.

The use of U.S. military force—specifically the Linebacker II bombing campaigns—finally led to the Paris Accords of January 1973.

See also KISSINGER, HENRY A; LODGE, HENRY CABOT; PART II, THE CHRONOLOGY; THO, LE DUC.

Suggestions for further reading: *The Lost Peace: America's Search for a Negotiated Settlement of the Vietnam War,* by Allan E. Goodman (Stanford: Hoover Institution Press, 1978); *Vietnam: A History,* by Stanley Karnow (New York: Viking, 1983); "The Vietnam Negotiations," in *Sentenced to Life,* by John P. Roche (New York: Macmillan, 1974).

PENTAGON PAPERS

Officially *The History of the U.S. Decision Making Process on Vietnam,* the so-called *Pentagon Papers* were a series of memoranda written at the direction of Secretary of Defense Robert S. McNamara to describe the history of U.S. involvement in Vietnam from 1954 to 1968. With an overall security classification of top secret, these memoranda were in the main self-serving attempts by those who had bungled the war to explain away their incompetence.

As Stanley Karnow in *Vietnam: A History* points out, the *Pentagon Papers* "convey the idea that plans drafted by bureaucrats all reflect official policy. In fact, Washington is always awash with proposals and projects, some incredible." The most damaging aspect was the publication of the appendices, which contained copies of documents from the Department of Defense, State Department, Central Intelligence Agency, Office of the Joint Chiefs of Staff and the White House that revealed classified sources and methods of intelligence collection.

The documents had been stolen by Daniel Ellsberg, a former "whiz kid" recruited by McNamara. Formerly a superhawk, Ellsberg had become an antiwar activist. After unsuccessfully offering the documents to prominent opponents of the war in the U.S. Senate, Ellsberg gave them to the *New York Times,* which began publishing them on June 13, 1971.

Although they had been written during the Johnson Administration and could have been used by President Nixon for his partisan political advantage, Nixon opposed publication both to protect the sources in the highly classified appendices and to prevent further erosion of public support for the war. On June 30 the Supreme Court ruled the *Times* had the right to publish the material.

From the public's perception, the *Pentagon Papers* provided evidence that they had been deliberately misled on the conduct of the war, thereby widening the credibility gap. The immediate effect of this publication from the government's point of view was to dry up allied intelligence sources, since other governments feared such open publication of their state secrets. The long-term effect was to severely hamper U.S. military operations, for there was a fear within the Defense Department that anything put on paper would be leaked to the press. Operational matters were either not reduced to writing or were kept so restricted that those who should have received them were denied access. As late as the disastrous raid into Iran in 1980, such caution inhibited the thorough review of operational plans that could have prevented that debacle.

The publication of the *Pentagon Papers*, along with previous suspected disclosures of information to the press led to the creation of a White House unit to plug leaks of information to journalists. The illegal activities of the unit, known as the "Plumbers," and their cover-up became known collectively as the Watergate scandal, which resulted in President Nixon's resignation in 1974.

See also ANTIWAR MOVEMENT; ELLSBERG, DANIEL; GRAVEL, MIKE; MENU OPERATION.

Suggestions for further reading: *Pentagon Papers*, Gravel edition, (Boston: Beacon Press, 1971); *Pentagon Papers, New York Times* edition, (Toronto: Bantam Books, 1970); *Vietnam: A History*, by Stanley Karnow (New York: Viking, 1983); "The Pentagon Papers," in *Sentenced To Life*, by John P. Roche (New York: Macmillan, 1974).

PEOPLES' WARS

The Chinese variety of Soviet "wars of national liberation," the concept of "peoples' wars" was derived from a 1920s Comintern propaganda theme that the world's "countryside" (i.e., the underdeveloped countries of the world) would surround and conquer the world's "cities" (the developed nations). It was further refined by Mao Tse-tung as a result of his successes in the Chinese civil war. Announced to the world in Chinese Marshal Lin Piao's "Long Live the Victory of People's War" in September 1965, it was seen at the time as the communist equivalent of *Mein Kampf* for world conquest.

What was missed by western analysts of revolutionary war was Lin Piao's emphasis on self-reliance. In words that were to apply almost directly to South Vietnam 10 years later, he wrote, "If one does not operate by one's own

effort . . . but leans wholly on foreign aid . . . no victory can be won, or be consolidated even if it is won."

See also COUNTERINSURGENCY, WARS OF NATIONAL LIBERATION.

Suggestions for further reading: *Essential Works of Chinese Communism*, edited by Winberg Chai (New York: Pica Press, 1970); *Autopsy on People's War*, by Chalmers Johnson (Berkeley: University of California Press, 1973).

PHAM VAN DONG

See DONG, PHAM VAN.

PHAN RANG

A port located on the coast of the South China Sea in Ninh Thuan Province in II Corps, Phan Rang was also the site of a major U.S. Air Force base. Periodically from 1966 to 1971, the 14th Air Commando Wing, 35th Tactical Fighter Wing and the 315th Tactical Airlift Wing were headquartered there.

Phan Rang fell to the North Vietnamese with the collapse of II Corps in March 1975.

See also II CORPS TACTICAL ZONE.

PHILIPPINES, THE

The Philippines assisted South Vietnam's war effort in two major ways. First, and perhaps more important, was the agreement by the Philippines to allow the United States to use Clark Air Force Base and the Naval facilities at Subic Bay and Cavite to support the war in Vietnam.

Second was the provision of assistance to South Vietnam by the Philippines. Assistance began informally as early as 1953. In July 1964 the Philippine Congress authorized the dispatch to Vietnam of a group of 34 physicians, surgeons, nurses and rural development workers, and four such groups served in turn between 1964 and 1966. In 1966 the Philippine Civic Action Group arrived in Vietnam and established a base camp in Tay Ninh in III

Filipino soldiers on patrol. (Courtesy U.S. Army Military History Institute.)

Corps. With approximately 1,500 personnel, the Philippine Civic Action Group conducted pacification operations in Tay Ninh, Binh Dong, Hau Ngia and Dinh Tuong Provinces. Because of political pressures at home, the Philippine Civic Action Group was withdrawn in January 1970, leaving behind a small contingent of medical and surgical teams much like those the Philippines had originally sent to Vietnam in 1964.

Suggestions for further reading: *Allied Participation in Vietnam,* by Stanley Robert Larsen and James Lawton Collins, Jr. (Washington, D.C.: U.S. Government Printing Office, 1975).

PHOENIX PROGRAM

The Phoenix Program (in Vietnamese the Phung Hoang, from a legendary bird endowed with magical powers remotely similar to the phoenix in Western mythology, was part of the Le Loi, or Accelerated Pacification, Program announced by South Vietnam's President Nguyen Van Thieu on July 1, 1968 in the wake of the North Vietnamese Army (NVA)-Viet Cong (VC) Tet Offensive earlier that year.

The groundwork for the program had been laid the year before when CORDS (Civil Operations and Revolutionary Development Support) Director Robert Komer had recommended a joint MACV (U.S. Military Assistance Command Vietnam) and CIA program, entitled ICEX (Intelligence Coordination and Exploitation) to combine the intelligence files and collection capabilities of the CIA and U.S. Military Intelligence with the South Vietnamese Central Intelligence Organization, Special Branch and National Police.

The goal of the program was to identify the estimated 70,000 members of the Viet Cong infrastructure (VCI)—the VC political leaders, proselyting and indoctrination cadre and other high ranking communist party members responsible for the tens of thousands of assassinations, terrorism bombings and like activity within South Vietnam. The program required that suspected VCI be identified by at least three separate sources. Once identified, their dossiers were divided into three categories: A for leaders, B for those in key positions and C for rank-and-file members. The last category was generally ignored and emphasis was placed on categories A and B.

Contrary to popular opinion, the program was not an assassination bureau. It was composed of a series of committees at the national, corps, province, district and village levels charged with bringing together all available intelligence and from that intelligence identifying VCI members. Once identified by the Phoenix committees, VCI names would be turned over to the South Vietnamese Army, the National Police, Amnesty Teams or the PRU (Provisional Reconnaissance Unit, a special police task force organized specifically for the purpose), which would take action to apprehend those identified.

According to congressional testimony by William Colby, a CIA official who was in charge of CORDS, from 1968 to 1971 some 17,000 VCI sought amnesty, 28,000 were captured and 20,000 were killed (the majority—some 85 percent—in military actions). The momentum of the program came to a standstill in 1972, when the North Vietnamese Army launched its Eastertide Offensive and pacification efforts had to be suspended to counter this attack.

Although plagued by South Vietnamese government inefficiency and corruption, the effectiveness of the Phoenix program was reflected at the time by the worldwide propaganda campaign North Vietnam mounted against it. In a remarkable display of chutzpah, the North Vietnamese, who had regularly used assassination as one of their tactics—executing an estimated 61,000 village officials and South Vietnamese civil servants from 1958 to 1966—denounced Phoenix as an assassination program. This theme was immediately echoed by American antiwar activists and led to congressional hearings on the program. But while assassinations no doubt occurred, assassination as an officially condoned tactic had been specifically prohibited in writing by Colby, one of the overseers of the Phoenix Program.

The effectiveness of the Phoenix Program was subsequently attested to by the Viet Cong themselves. In his 1981 visit to Hanoi, Stanley Karnow, author of *Vietnam: A History*, was told by three "top communist figures in Vietnam" that Phoenix had been "very dangerous," and one Viet Cong leader told him "We never feared a division of troops, but the infiltration of a couple of guys into our ranks created tremendous difficulties for us." Nguyen Co Thach, Vietnam's Foreign Minister after 1975, "admitted that the Phoenix effort 'wiped out many of our bases' in South Vietnam, compelling numbers of North Vietnamese and Viet Cong troops to retreat to sanctuaries in Cambodia."

See also COLBY, WILLIAM E.; PACIFICATION.

Suggestions for further reading: *Honorable Men: My Life in the CIA*, by William Colby (New York: Simon & Schuster, 1978); *Vietnam: A History*, by Stanley Karnow (New York: Viking, 1983); *Pacification*, by Tran Dinh Tho (Washington, D.C.: Center of Military History, 1980). For a first-hand account of the Phoenix program in action, see *Silence Was a Weapon: The Vietnam War in the Villages*, by Stuart A. Herrington (Novato, Calif.: Presidio Press, 1982).

PHOSPHOROUS

Phosphorous grenades and shells were used by all sides in the Vietnam war for both marking positions and causing casualties. Phosphorous munitions used chemicals that had a burning effect and were very lethal.

PLAIN OF REEDS

The Plain of Reeds was a flat, treeless, grassy basin in the northeastern part of the Mekong Delta, in the provinces of Kien Phong and Kien Tuong, that served as a Viet Cong base area.

See map at IV CORPS TACTICAL ZONE.

Suggestions for further reading: *Riverine Operations 1966-69*, by William B. Fulton (Washington, D.C.: U.S. Government Printing Office, 1973).

PLATOON

A platoon is a basic organizational element of a company-sized unit. Commanded by a lieutenant, with a noncommissioned officer second in command (a platoon sergeant), it consists of two or more squads.

See also ORGANIZATION FOR COMBAT.

PLEIKU

The provincial capital of Pleiku Province, II Corps in the Central Highlands, Pleiku was the location of the South Vietnamese Army's II Corps. From time to time between 1965 and 1970, the U.S. Third Brigade, 25th Infantry Division and brigades of the U.S. Fourth Infantry Division and the U.S. 173rd Airborne Brigade were also stationed there.

On orders from South Vietnam's President Nguyen Van Thieu in March 1975, the South Vietnamese Army withdrew from the Central Highlands, abandoning Pleiku to the North Vietnamese.

See also II CORPS TACTICAL ZONE.

POLAND

See ICCS.

POLITICAL STRUGGLE

During the Vietnam war the basic North Vietnamese strategy of *dau tranh,* normally translated as "struggle" or "struggle movement," consisted of two elements: *dau tranh vu trang,* or "armed struggle," and *dau tranh chinh tri,* or "political struggle."

According to Douglas Pike, Director of the East Asia Institute, University of California at Berkeley, political struggle involved three interrelated activities. The first, *dich ban,* or "action among the enemy," involved the manipulation of public perceptions in South Vietnam and abroad, particularly in the United States. The second element, *binh van,* or "action among the military," was essentially a proselyting effort to weaken or destroy the South Vietnamese government and the army by nonmilitary means. The third element, *dien van,* or "action among the people," involved the administration of "liberated areas" under communist control.

Although "armed struggle" and "political struggle" were inexorably linked, the North Vietnamese shifted their emphasis on these two elements of their strategy several times during the course of the war. Within the North Viet-namese high command, Politburo member Truong Chinh was the primary proponent of political struggle, for he believed (correctly, as it turned out) that victory was to be achieved chiefly through external actions among the enemy (*dich ban*). This strategy was of primary importance from 1959 until 1965, from 1969 to 1971 and from 1974 to 1975.

See also ARMED STRUGGLE; EASTERTIDE OFFENSIVE; STRATEGY, NORTH VIETNAM; TET OFFENSIVE.

Suggestions for further reading: *Viet Cong: The Organization and Techniques of the National Liberation Front of South Vietnam* (Cambridge: MIT Press, 1966) and *History of the Vietnamese Communist Party* (Stanford: Hoover Institution, 1978) by Douglas Pike.

POPULAR FORCES

See TERRITORIAL FORCES.

POST-TRAUMATIC STRESS DISORDER

Post-traumatic stress disorder is a relatively new term used to describe a delayed reaction to

A street scene in Pleiku. (Courtesy Shelby L. Stanton.)

traumatic combat experiences. Symptoms of the disorder, which the American Psychiatric Association recognized as a bona fide psychological malady in 1980, include a sense of emotional numbness, reexperiencing of the traumatic event, nervousness, depression, nightmares, difficulty in developing close relationships, insomnia and survivor guilt.

As defined by most psychiatrists involved with Vietnam veterans, post-traumatic stress is a normal reaction that results from witnessing the violence and destruction of war. However, post-traumatic stress *disorder* signifies a disrupted recovery process, in which the combat veteran experiences abnormal difficulty in coming to terms with the event or events responsible for the symptoms.

Some have argued that a disproportionate number of Vietnam combat veterans suffer from symptoms of the disorder. Among the reasons cited for this are the failure of American society to absolve Vietnam veterans for their participation in a losing cause and the particularly grueling nature of guerrilla warfare, in which troops must be constantly on guard, whether engaged in battle or not. Myra MacPherson, in her book about the

Vietnam generation today, *Long Time Passing*, asserts that between 500,000 and 700,000 veterans suffer from some symptoms of the disorder. An estimated 10 percent of these suffer from the disorder itself.

Similar in many ways to shell shock and battle fatigue (terms associated with World War I and World War II respectively), the causes and exact nature of the disorder remain a matter of controversy.

Suggestions for further reading: *Long Time Passing: Vietnam and the Haunted Generation* by Myra MacPherson (New York: Doubleday, 1984).

POW/MIA

One of the lingering issues of the Vietnam war concerns accounting for those American service members held as prisoners of war (POWs) by the North Vietnamese and those still missing in action (MIAs). As of February 1985 there were some 2,483 Americans, including 42 civilians, unaccounted for in Vietnam, Laos and Cambodia during the war.

Between February and April 1973 the Hanoi

This photo, released by the North Vietnamese News Agency in Hanoi, shows American pilots being paraded through the streets of Hanoi. (AP/Wide World Photos.)

government released 591 American prisoners. An additional 68 Americans, stranded in Vietnam after April 1975, left during the following years. As of February 1985 the Vietnamese have returned 96 sets of remains. The most recent repatriation of remains from Vietnam, in July 1984, involved those of eight individuals, six of whom have been identified as U.S. military personnel.

Of the 2,483 total, nearly 600 are missing in Laos. In August 1978 the Lao government returned two sets of American remains, and in July 1985 13 additional sets of remains.

Political and military conditions in Cambodia have precluded accounting for Americans lost there. However, it is known that some U.S. personnel now listed as unaccounted for were captured in Cambodia.

There have been a number of reports from sources who claim they have personally seen captives whom they believe to be or were told were Americans. The U.S. government has investigated these reports and has thus far been unable to substantiate any of them. Further, U.S. representatives have held a series of meetings with members of the Foreign Ministry of Vietnam to work out a program for accelerating the search for Americans still missing in action. But so far, the Vietnamese continue to exploit the POW/MIA issue for their own political purposes by using American remains as bargaining chips for U.S. diplomatic concessions.

Although North Vietnam signed the Geneva Convention of 1949 on the treatment of POWs, they murdered, tortured and otherwise deliberately misused and abused American captives to force them to "confess" to war crimes. With the help of American collaborators the North Vietnamese also exploited American POWs for propaganda purposes, parading them before reporters and foreign visitors and even going so far as to portray them on their postage stamps.

Further information on POW/MIA issues can be obtained from Anne Mills Griffith, Executive Director, National League of Families of American POWs and MIAs in Southeast Asia, 1605 K Street N.W., Washington, D.C. 20006.

Suggestions for further reading: *Prisoner at War: The Survival of Commander Richard A. Stratton,* by Scott Blakey (Garden City: Doubleday, 1978); *Escape from Laos,* by Dieter Dengler (San Rafael: Presidio Press, 1979); *When Hell Was in Session,* by Jeremiah A. Denton (New York: Reader's Digest Press, 1976); *P.O.W.,* by Richard Garrett (London: David & Charles, 1981); *POW: A Definitive History of the American Prisoner of War Experience in Vietnam, 1964–1973* (New York: Reader's Digest Press, 1976); *Code of Honor,* by John A. Dramesi (New York: Norton, 1975); *The Passing of the Night: My Seven Years as a Prisoner of the North Vietnamese,* by Robinson Risner (New York: Random House, 1974); *Five Years to Freedom,* by James N. Rowe (Boston: Little, Brown, 1971); *In Love & War,* by Jim and Sybil Stockdale (New York: Harper & Row, 1984); *America in Vietnam,* by Guenter Lewy (New York: Oxford University Press, 1978); *POW-MIA Fact Book* (Washington, D.C.: Department of Defense, 1985); "Lost or Merely Forgotten?" by

This North Vietnamese stamp depicts an American POW guarded by a woman soldier.

Paul A. Gigot, in *National Review,* August 17, 1979; "The Myth of the Lost POWs," by James Rosenthal, in *The New Republic,* July 1, 1985.

PRESIDENTIAL UNIT CITATION

First authorized in World War II, the Presidential Unit Citation is awarded to units that have displayed such gallantry, determination and espirit de corps in accomplishing their mission under extremely difficult and hazardous conditions as to set them apart and above other units participating in the same campaign. The degree of heroism required is the same as that which would warrant award of a Distinguished Service Cross, Navy Cross or Air Force Cross to an individual.

The U.S. Army, Navy and Air Force Presidential Unit Citations, although sharing the same requirements for award, are each distinct awards. The Army and Air Force share the same award emblems, which are different from that of the Navy and Marine Corps. These emblems can be worn permanently by those personnel assigned to the unit at the time of award.

PRESIDENT OF THE UNITED STATES

Article II, Section 2 of the Constitution of the United States provides that "the President shall be Commander-in-Chief of the Army and Navy of the United States. . . ." From the first U.S. military deaths in 1959 until the end of the war in 1975, this position changed hands four times. In 1959 Dwight D. Eisenhower was President of the United States. He was succeeded by John F. Kennedy in January 1961. When President Kennedy was assassinated in November 1963, he was succeeded by Vice-President Lyndon B. Johnson, who in November 1964 was elected President. When President Johnson chose not to stand for reelection in 1968, Richard M. Nixon was elected to the presidency. Reelected in 1972, President Nixon resigned from office in August 1974 and was succeeded by Vice-President Gerald R. Ford.

In comparison to the five U.S. Presidents, Ho Chi Minh ruled North Vietnam from 1954 until his death in September 1969, when he was succeeded by Le Duan.

See also COMMAND AND CONTROL; EISENHOWER, DWIGHT D.; FORD, GERALD R.; JOHNSON, LYNDON B.; KENNEDY, JOHN F.; NIXON, RICHARD M.

PRG (PROVISIONAL REVOLUTIONARY GOVERNMENT OF SOUTH VIETNAM)

See VIET CONG.

PROTECTIVE REACTION STRIKES

See LAVELLE, JOHN D.

PROVINCES

South Vietnam was administratively divided into 44 provinces and 11 autonomous cities (Hué, Da Nang, Qui Nhon, Nha Trang, Cam Ranh, Da Lat, Vung Tau, My Tho, Can Tho, Rach Gia and the capital city of Saigon). These provinces in turn were divided into districts, villages and hamlets.

Four administrative regions, which were identical with the country's four military corps areas, were superimposed over the provinces.

See also I, II, III, IV CORPS TACTICAL ZONES.

PSYCHOLOGICAL OPERATIONS

Beginning in October 1965, elements of the U.S. Seventh Psychological Operations (PSYOPS) Group in Okinawa provided psychological operations support—loudspeaker broadcasts, propaganda leaflet printing, radio and television broadcasts, mobile radio monitoring, and research and analysis aimed at weakening the communists' morale and encouraging desertion.

In December 1967 the Fourth PSYOPS Group was organized with headquarters at Tan Son Nhut, in the suburbs of Saigon, and charged with providing psychological operations advice and support to the South Vietnamese Army.

The Sixth PSYOPS Battalion arrived in Vietnam in February 1966 from Fort Bragg, North Carolina to provide PSYOPS support in III Corps. The Seventh PSYOPS Battalion was organized in Vietnam in December 1967 to provide PSYOPS support in I Corps. At the same time the Eighth and 10th PSYOPS Battalions were formed to provide PSYOPS support in II and IV Corps respectively.

In addition to these PSYOPS units, the Second, 29th and 41st Civil Affairs Companies from Fort Gordon, Georgia, were sent to Vietnam in

```
                    DEPARTMENT OF THE ARMY
            HEADQUARTERS 1ST INFANTRY DIVISION
            OFFICE OF THE COMMANDING GENERAL


AVDB-CG                                  22 March 1967

SUBJECT:  Unsoldierly Conduct of Officers of Cong
          Truong 9


TO:       Commanding General
          Cong Truong 9
          HT 86500 YK


Dear General:

     This is to advise you that during the battle at
Ap Bau Bang on 20 March the Regimental Commander of
Q763 and his Battalion Commanders disgraced themselves
by performing in an unsoldierly manner.

     During this battle with elements of this Division
and attached units your officers failed to accomplish
their mission and left the battlefield covered with
dead and wounded from their units.

     We have buried your dead and taken care of your
wounded from this battle.

                              Sincerely,


                              J. H. HAY
                              Major General, USA
                              Commanding
```

An English language version of a propaganda leaflet distributed by the U.S. Army.

1965–1966 to provide civil affairs support in I, II and III Corps respectively.

By December 1971 all of these units had been withdrawn from Vietnam.

Suggestions for further reading: *Vietnam Order of Battle,* by Shelby L. Stanton (Washington, D.C.: U.S. News Books, 1981).

PUBLIC OPINION

In August 1965, at the time of the Southeast Asia Resolution known as the Gulf of Tonkin Resolution, 61 percent of the American people were in favor of U.S. involvement in Vietnam and only 24 percent were opposed to that involvement. The majority of Americans supported the

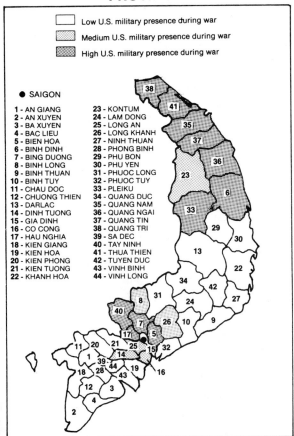

PROVINCES

Low U.S. military presence during war

Medium U.S. military presence during war

High U.S. military presence during war

● SAIGON

1 - AN GIANG	**23** - KONTUM
2 - AN XUYEN	**24** - LAM DONG
3 - BA XUYEN	**25** - LONG AN
4 - BAC LIEU	**26** - LONG KHANH
5 - BIEN HOA	**27** - NINH THUAN
6 - BINH DINH	**28** - PHONG DINH
7 - BING DUONG	**29** - PHU BON
8 - BINH LONG	**30** - PHU YEN
9 - BINH THUAN	**31** - PHUOC LONG
10 - BINH TUY	**32** - PHUOC TUY
11 - CHAU DOC	**33** - PLEIKU
12 - CHUONG THIEN	**34** - QUANG DUC
13 - DARLAC	**35** - QUANG NAM
14 - DINH TUONG	**36** - QUANG NGAI
15 - GIA DINH	**37** - QUANG TIN
16 - CO CONG	**38** - QUANG TRI
17 - HAU NGHIA	**39** - SA DEC
18 - KIEN GIANG	**40** - TAY NINH
19 - KIEN HOA	**41** - THUA THIEN
20 - KIEN PHONG	**42** - TUYEN DUC
21 - KIEN TUONG	**43** - VINH BINH
22 - KHANH HOA	**44** - VINH LONG

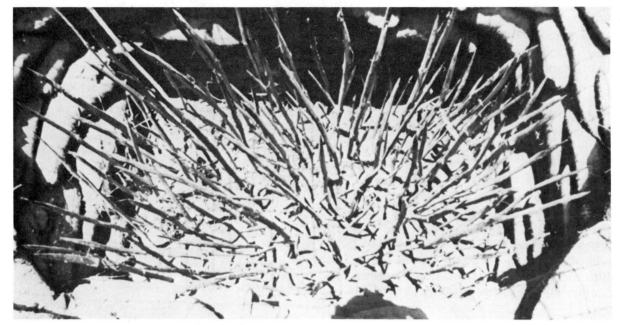

Pungi stakes. (Courtesy U.S. Army Military History Institute.)

war until October 1967, when a poll revealed that 44 percent of the American people backed the war while 46 percent believed sending troops to Vietnam had been a mistake. These figures temporarily reversed during the Tet Offensive of 1968, when Americans rallied again behind the war effort in the face of that crisis, but soon thereafter the majority of Americans opposed the war.

By the time President Nixon was in office, about one-third of the American populace still supported the war while over half opposed it. While Nixon was able to maintain public support for his handling of the war—especially his troop withdrawals and firm reaction to North Vietnamese and Viet Cong pressure—public reaction against the war itself remained relatively stable until the end of the war.

After the war the concensus in America was that sending troops to Vietnam had been a mistake. And yet most Americans also believed that once those troops had been committed, the United States should have done all within its power to achieve victory. According to a Veterans Administration survey in 1980, 82 percent of former U.S. soldiers involved in heavy combat in Vietnam believe that the war was lost because they were not allowed to win.

The role of public opinion in shaping the outcome of the Vietnam war continues to be a topic of great interest and debate.

See also ANTIWAR MOVEMENT.

Suggestions for further reading: *War, Presidents and Public Opinion,* by John E. Mueller (New York: John Wiley, 1973); *Vietnam: A History,* by Stanley Karnow (New York: Viking, 1983); "The Passing of the Class of 1941," by John P. Roche, *National Review,* October 19, 1984.

PUFF

Nickname for U.S. Air Force fixed-wing gunships, "Puff" was derived from the song "Puff the Magic Dragon," since a gunship firing at night looked like a dragon spitting fire.

See also GUNSHIPS.

PUNGI STAKES

Sharpened bamboo stakes used as booby traps, *pungi* stakes accounted for 2 percent of U.S. combat wounds in Vietnam.

See also CASUALTIES. *See* illustration at BOOBY TRAPS.

PURPLE HEART

The oldest U.S. military decoration, the Purple Heart Medal was first authorized by General George Washington during the Revolutionary War. It was revived in 1932 for award in the name of the President of the United States to any member of the armed forces or any civilian national of the United States who, while serving under competent authority in any capacity with one of the U.S. armed services, was wounded, killed or died after being wounded in action against the enemy or as a result of an act of any such enemy or as the result of an act of any hostile foreign force.

Not more than one award is made for more than one wound or injury received at the same instant or from the same missile, force, explosion or agent. A "wound" is defined as an injury to any part of the body from an outside force or agent sustained under one or more of the conditions listed above. A wound for which the award is made must have required treatment by a medical officer, and records of medical treatment for wounds or injuries received in action as described above must be a matter of official record. Subsequent awards are denoted by an oak leaf (a star for the Navy and Marine Corps) worn on the ribbon.

The Purple Heart.

QUANG TRI, BATTLE OF

Quang Tri was the capital of Quang Tri Province, the northernmost province of South Vietnam. Located in I Corps, the province was bounded on the north by the DMZ and on the west by Laos, through which ran the Ho Chi Minh Trail, North Vietnam's main north-south supply line. In 1972 Quang Tri was the site of a major battle during the Eastertide Offensive by the North Vietnamese Army (NVA).

On March 30, 1972, under cover of an artillery barrage, the NVA 304th and 308th Divisions, supported by two regiments of tanks, attacked across the DMZ. Facing this assault was the newly organized Third Infantry Division of the South Vietnamese Army (ARVN). While some members of this division fought well, others panicked in the face of the NVA attack. Just as the inexperienced U.S. 106th Infantry Division had panicked during the Battle of the Bulge in 1944 and two of its regiments had surrendered to the enemy, so the ARVN Third Division's 56th Regiment surrendered to the North Vietnamese. By the end of April, some six NVA divisions had been committed and the entire province of Quang Tri was in communist hands.

In May the ARVN First Infantry Division, Airborne Division and Marine Division began to counterattack. With massive support from U.S. fighter-bombers and B-52 strategic bombers, they finally recaptured Quang Tri City in September 17, 1972.

See also EASTERTIDE OFFENSIVE.

Suggestions for further reading: *Battles and Campaigns in Vietnam 1954–1984,* by Tom Carhart (New York: Crown Publishers, 1984); *South Vietnam on Trial,* by David Fulghum and Terrence Maitland (Boston: Boston Publishing Co., 1984); *The Easter Offensive—Vietnam 1972,* by Gerald H. Turley (Novato, Calif.: Presidio Press, 1984).

QUEEN'S COBRAS

Nickname of a Royal Thai Army elite infantry regiment deployed to Vietnam in September 1967. Located at Bear Cat, south of Bien Hoa, in III Corps with elements of the U.S. Ninth Infantry Division, it was replaced in August 1968 by elements of the Royal Thai Army Expeditionary Division.

See also FREE WORLD MILITARY FORCES, THAILAND.

Suggestions for further reading: *Vietnam Order of Battle,* by Shelby L. Stanton (Washington, D.C.: U.S. News Books, 1981); *Allied Participation in Vietnam,* by Stanley Robert Larsen and James Lawton Collins, Jr. (Washington, D.C.: U.S. Government Printing Office, 1975).

QUI NHON

A port located in Binh Dinh Province in II Corps, Qui Nhon was developed into a major supply base. Beginning in August 1965, the U.S. Army's First Logistical Command established a support command at Qui Nhon. The command included a transportation terminal, a supply depot, a POL (petroleum, oil and lubricants) depot and an ammunition dump to provide combat service support to the 95,000 U.S. and allied troops in northern II Corps.

Security for the port was provided by South Korea's Capital Division, which was headquartered in Qui Nhon. These facilities were turned over to South Vietnam in April 1972.

Qui Nhon fell to the North Vietnamese in March 1975, when II Corps collapsed in the face of the final offensive.

See also II CORPS, CAM RANH BAY.

Suggestions for further reading: *Vietnam Order of Battle,* by Shelby L. Stanton (Washington, D.C.: U.S. News & World Report Books, 1981).

RANCH HAND OPERATION

See AGENT ORANGE.

R & R

R & R was the abbreviation for rest and recreation, which was a program to give U.S. servicemen a respite from combat during their one-year tour of duty in Vietnam. R & R sites in South Vietnam existed at Vung Tau and China Beach. R & R away from Vietnam was permitted in Hawaii, Bangkok, Tokyo, Australia, Hong Kong, Manila, Penang, Taipei, Kuala Lampur and Singapore.

RANGERS

Until U.S. Long Range Reconnaissance Patrol (LRRP) units were redesignated ranger companies in 1969 (Companies C through I and K through P, 75th Infantry [Ranger]), ranger units, which had been deactivated after the Korean War, did not exist in the U.S. Army.

Ranger-qualified individuals—graduates of the U.S. Army's Ranger School at Fort Benning, Georgia—served throughout Vietnam with U.S. units and as advisers to South Vietnamese units, including ranger battalions.

Since after 1954 MAAG-Vietnam (U.S. Military Assistance Advisory Group Vietnam) set out to build the South Vietnamese Army (ARVN) in the image of the U.S. Army, no provision was made for ranger units. Without MAAG approval, in mid-1959 the ARVN activated 65 "Special Action" companies by taking one company from each of its four-company infantry battalions. By June 1960 the ARVN convinced the MAAG of the effectiveness of these units, and the MAAG agreed to fund and support the creation of specially trained ARVN ranger battalions. A ranger training center was established at Duc My and U.S. ranger-trained advisers were attached to these units.

Used as a reaction force both by the ARVN Joint General Staff (JGS) and by the four ARVN Corps, the rangers proved to be most effective on the battlefield. By 1968 there were 20 ARVN ranger battalions. In 1970, as U.S. Special Forces were beginning to withdraw, the JGS approved the conversion of the best of the Special Forces CIDG (Civilian Irregular Defense Group) units to ARVN ranger border defense battalions. Some 14,534 CIDG forces were formed into 37 ranger battalions. Now with 57 battalions, seven ranger group control headquarters were established. One such group took part in the South Vietnamese Army's Lam Son 719 raid into Laos in 1971 and saw particularly hard fighting there.

In January 1974 ARVN Ranger Command was reorganized into 15 ranger groups, with three ranger battalions each. Four groups (the 11th, 12th, 14th and 15th) were assigned to I Corps, seven groups (Fourth, Sixth, 21st, 22nd, 23rd, 24th and 25th) to II Corps, three groups (31st, 32nd and 33rd) to III Corps and the Seventh Group to JGS reserve at Long Binh, near Saigon. Because the threat in IV Corps had diminished, the nine ranger battalions there were deactivated and their personnel were reassigned within Ranger Command. Stationed primarily in forward defense bases along the Cambodian-Laotian border, each corps kept one ranger group in reserve as a reaction force. During the Final Offensive in 1975, these ranger groups, like the rest of the South Vietnamese Army, were overwhelmed by the North Vietnamese Army blitzkrieg.

See also LRRP (LONG RANGE RECONNAISSANCE PATROL).

Suggestions for further reading: *Vietnam From Ceasefire to Capitulation*, by William E. LeGro (Washington, D.C.: U.S. Government Printing Office, 1981); *Territorial Forces*, by Ngo Quang Truong (Washington, D.C.: Center for Military History, 1981); *The RVNAF*, by Dong Van Khuyen (Washington, D.C.: Center for Military History, 1980).

REEDUCATION CAMPS

A euphemism for concentration camps or gulags, "reeducation camps" were established by the North Vietnamese immediately after their conquest of the south. According to journalist Stanley Karnow, who visited Vietnam in 1981, the communists initially imprisoned 400,000 South Vietnamese civil servants and Army officers as well as doctors, lawyers, teachers, journalists and other intellectuals, including some Viet Cong veterans.

Estimates are that some 250,000 died in these camps, and as late as 1985, ten years after the war, some 6,000 to 8,000 political prisoners are still being held. A proposal to release them to the United States failed when the North Vietnamese imposed an unacceptable precondition that the U.S. guarantee that these prisoners would be prevented from speaking out about conditions in the concentration camps after their arrival in the United States.

See also BOAT PEOPLE, REFUGEES.

Suggestions for further reading: *After Saigon Fell*, by Nguyen Long (Berkeley: University of

California Press, 1981); *The Will of Heaven,* by Nguyen Ngoc Ngan (New York: Dutton, 1981); *Violations of Human Rights in the Socialist Republic of Vietnam,* by Ginette Sagan and Stephen Denney (Palo Alto: Aurora Foundation, 1983); *Vietnam: A History,* by Stanley Karnow (New York: Viking, 1983); *Death in the Rice Fields,* by Peter Scholl-Latour (New York: St. Martin's Press, 1985); *The Vietnam Gulag,* by Doan Van Toai (New York: Simon & Schuster, forthcoming 1986).

REFUGEES

Refugees were not only a constant in the Vietnam War, they were also a prelude and a postlude to that conflict. In 1954, upon the division of Vietnam, almost 1 million refugees fled from North Vietnam and resettled in the south. During the war approximately 1 million more refugees fled from Viet Cong terror in the countryside and from the North Vietnamese invasions into the border areas and resettled in South Vietnam's coastal cities. In 1967 it was estimated that about one-eighth of the South Vietnamese population was composed of recently displaced persons. In the final days of Vietnam, refugees fleeing from advancing North Vietnamese troops clogged roads and made military maneuvers almost impossible.

Since the fall of South Vietnam, more than 1 million people have risked their lives to escape from the country, most by sea. Since April 1975 more than 700,000 Indochinese refugees have been integrated into American society and since 1980 an additional 30,000 Vietnamese have been resettled in the United States.

See also BOAT PEOPLE, REEDUCATION CAMPS.

Suggestions for further reading: *Vietnam: A History,* by Stanley Karnow (New York: Viking, 1983). *The Refused,* by Barry Winn (New York: Simon & Schuster, 1981).

REGIMENT

A regiment, once one of the U.S. Army's basic organizational elements, is now used only for armored cavalry units (*see* BRIGADE). In Vietnam the only Army regiment was the 11th Armored Cavalry Regiment, which consisted of three squadrons of armored cavalry and an air cavalry troop.

In the U.S. Marine Corps the regiment, normally consisting of three infantry battalions, remains one of the basic organizational elements. During the Vietnam war eight U.S. Marine Corps regiments were deployed to Vietnam—the First, Fifth and Seventh Marine Regiments of the First Marine Division; the Third, Fourth and Ninth Marine Regiments of the Third Marine Division; and the 26th and 27th Marine Regiments detached from the Fifth Marine Division, which were deployed to reinforce the First Marine Division. In addition, the Marine Corps also deployed two artillery regiments—the 11th and 12th Marine Regiments—to Vietnam.

The regiment was also a basic organization element of both the South Vietnamese and North Vietnamese armies as well as Viet Cong main force units.

See also BRIGADE; DIVISION; 11TH ARMORED CAVALRY REGIMENT; MARINE CORPS, U.S.; NVA (NORTH VIETNAMESE ARMY); ORGANIZATION FOR COMBAT; SVNAF (SOUTH VIETNAMESE ARMED FORCES); VIET CONG.

Suggestions for further reading: *Vietnam Order of Battle,* by Shelby L. Stanton (U.S. News & World Report Books, 1981).

REGIONAL FORCES

See TERRITORIAL FORCES.

RESERVE FORCES

Although there was no general call-up of reserve forces (U.S. Army and Air Force National Guard and Army, Navy, Air Force and Marine Corps reserves), some such units and individuals did serve in Vietnam.

See also MOBILIZATION.

REVOLUTIONARY DEVELOPMENT

Part of the South Vietnamese government (GVN) pacification program, "revolutionary development" was officially defined by the MACV (U.S. Military Assistance Command Vietnam) in November 1967:

> Revolutionary development, the leading edge of pacification, is the formalized government of Vietnam program, under the sponsorship of the Ministry of Revolutionary Development, in specified hamlets generally within revolutionary development campaign areas. It includes the local security for these hamlets and the political, economic, and social activities at that level.

In 1966 the GVN developed the concept of revolutionary development (also known as rural development) cadres. Inspired by the Viet Cong's "action militia," the cadres were the ideological representative of the GVN and served as a direct link between the government and the people. After instruction at a Revolutionary Development Training Center at Vung Tau, the cadres were organized into 59-man groups and assigned to work in hamlets selected for pacification and development. Each group had a security section and a development section, with cadres responsible for education and culture, land reform, cooperatives, hygiene, sanitation, animal husbandry, cottage industries and public works construction. The cadres lived permanently in the hamlets to which they were assigned, and organized self-defense forces (later termed Popular Forces [PF]) among the people.

At their peak in 1969, 50,000 revolutionary development cadres were operating throughout the country. Their original 59-man groups had been reduced to 30-man groups in order to expand their coverage, and these revolutionary cadre groups were assigned to 1,400 villages across the country. Although they were the most effective of the counterinsurgency and pacification forces, as a result of U.S. aid cuts, the program began to decline in 1970, and in 1971 the revolutionary development cadres were disbanded.

See also PACIFICATION.

Suggestions for further reading: *Territorial Forces,* by Ngo Quang Truong (Washington, D.C.: U.S. Center of Military History, 1981); *Pacification,* by Tran Dinh Tho (Washington, D.C.: Center of Military History, 1980).

REVOLUTIONARY WAR

Revolutionary war, by definition, is a war in which the insurgents seek final victory by their efforts alone, as opposed to guerrilla war, in which insurgents are an adjunct to regular armed forces. Based on Mao Tse-tung's successful revolution in China and the Viet Minh's successful struggle against France, it was advanced as the model for the Viet Cong in the 1960s and 1970s. With their failure to spark a "great national uprising" during the Tet Offensive of 1968 and their virtual destruction in the counteroffensive by American and South Vietnamese Forces, any possibility that the Viet Cong could be a revolutionary force evaporated. From 1968 to the end of the war in 1975, they became a guerrilla force under the control and domination of the North Vietnamese Army (NVA), with the task of assisting NVA forces by harassing and wearing down the United States and South Vietnam. Successful in that effort, they facilitated the NVA 1975 blitzkrieg. After the victory, however, they were shunted aside and northern, not southern, communists now retain all power.

See also GUERRILLA WAR, NVA (NORTH VIETNAMESE ARMY), VIET CONG.

Suggestions for further reading: *Vietnam: A History,* by Stanley Karnow (New York: Viking, 1983); *On Strategy: A Critical Analysis of the Vietnam War,* by Harry G. Summers, Jr. (Novato, Calif.: Presidio Press, 1982).

RHEAULT AFFAIR

A cause célèbre in mid-1969, the Rheault affair had do with the imprisonment of Colonel Robert Rheault, the Commander of the U.S. Fifth Special Forces Group in Vietnam, and six of his officers on charges of premeditated murder in the summary execution of a Vietnamese national, namely

Thai Khac Chuyen, who worked as an agent in Special Forces Detachment B-57. Chuyen was identified as the double agent who had jeopardized Project GAMMA personnel and compromised a vital intelligence project. A pretrial investigation was conducted, but when the CIA refused to release highly classified information about the operations in which Detachment B-57 had been involved, the case was dismissed for reasons of national security on September 29, 1969. Colonel Rheault subsequently retired from the Army.

See also ATROCITIES.

Suggestions for further reading: *These Gallant Men on Trial in Vietnam*, by John Stevens Berry (Novato, Calif.: Presidio Press, 1984); *Inside the Green Berets: The First Thirty Years*, by Charles M. Simpson III (Novato, Calif.: Presidio Press, 1983); *The Green Berets at War*, by Shelby L. Stanton (Novato, Calif.: Presidio Press, 1985).

RIVERINE ASSAULT FORCE (TASK FORCE 117)

The U.S. Navy component of the Mobile Riverine Force, the Riverine Assault Force (Task Force 117) was activated on February 28, 1967. Organized eventually into four river assault squadrons, each 400-man squadron was further divided into river assault divisions. Each squadron contained a powerful fleet of five monitors armored with bar-and-plate armor and equipped with 50-caliber 40-mm and 20-mm gun mounts, 40-mm grenade launchers and an 81-mm mortar. The squadron also contained armored troop carriers mounting 50-caliber machine guns, rapid-fire grenade launchers, 20-mm cannons and, in some cases, installed flamethrowers. The vessels also carried helicopter landing platforms.

The task force maintained a mobile riverine base, from which two or three Army infantry battalions and one riverine assault squadron operated. The float base contained self-propelled and nonself-propelled barracks ships, LSTs (landing ships, tank), a landing craft repair ship, harbor tugs and a net-laying ship.

See also MOBILE RIVERINE FORCE, NINTH INFANTRY DIVISION.

Suggestions for further reading: *A Short History of the United States Navy and the Southeast Asia Conflict 1950–1975*, by Edward J. Marolda and G. Wesley Pryce, III (Washington, D.C.: Washington Naval Historical Center, 1984); *On Watch*, by Elmo R. Zumwalt, Jr. (New York: Quadrangle, 1976); *Riverine Operations 1966–1969*, by William B. Fulton (Washington, D.C.: U.S. Government Printing Office, 1973); *Riverine Warfare, the U.S. Navy's Operations on Inland Waterways* (Washington, D.C.: U.S. Government Printing Office, 1968).

RIVERINE FORCE

See MOBILE RIVERINE FORCE.

RIVER PATROL FORCE (TASK FORCE 116)

On December 18, 1965 River Patrol Force (Task Force 116) was organized by the U.S. Navy to direct naval forces engaged in Operation Game Warden, which was designed to deny the North Vietnamese and Viet Cong use of the 3,000 nautical miles of rivers, canals and smaller streams in South Vietnam, including the Mekong Delta and other inland waterways. Consisting of a number of river divisions, each controlling two 10-boat sections, Task Force 116 employed several aircraft and small boats. The River Patrol Force operated from LSTs (landing ships, tank) that had been designed to provide floating base facilities. The patrol began as a fleet of 28-foot fiberglass River Patrol Boats (PBRs), each manned by a crew of four, equipped with radars and radios and armed with a twin-mount 50-caliber machine gun forward, a 30-caliber machine gun aft and a rapid-fire 40-mm grenade launcher. These fiberglass boats were later replaced by aluminum boats with a speed of up to 29 knots. The task force also used experimental patrol air-cushioned vehicles in the Mekong Delta and the Da Nang area. Although able to move at great speeds over shallow marshy areas, these air-cushioned vehicles proved too noisy and too mechanically sophisticated for the riverine war in Vietnam. Another key element in the Task Force was air support, initially provided by Army helicopters. On April 1, 1967, the Navy activated Helicopter Attack (light) Squadron 3 at Vung Tau to provide aerial fire support, observation and medical evacuation. SEAL (Navy commando) teams also operated with the River Patrol Force to conduct night-and-day ambushes, hit-and-run raids, reconnaissance patrols, salvage dives and special intelligence operations. The minesweepers of Mine Division 112 were also used to prevent Viet Cong mining of the shipping channels.

In addition to other awards won by members of the River Patrol Force, two sailors of Task Force 116 were awarded the Medal of Honor for conspicuous bravery aboard river patrol boats.

See also GAME WARDEN; COASTAL SURVEILLANCE FORCE; NAVY, U.S.; RIVERINE ASSAULT FORCE.

Suggestions for further reading: *A Short History of the United States Navy and the Southeast Asia Conflict 1950–1975*, by Edward J. Marolda and G. Wesley Pryce, III (Washington, D.C.: Washington Naval Historical Center, 1984); *On Watch* by Elmo R. Zumwalt, Jr. (New York: Quadrangle, 1976); *Riverine Warfare: The Navy's Operations on Inland Waterways* (Washington, D.C.: U.S. Government Printing Office, 1968); *Riverine Operations 1966–1969* by William B. Fulton (Washington, D.C.: U.S. Government Printing Office, 1973). *The Brown Water Navy: The River and Coastal War in Indo-China and Vietnam 1948–1972* by Victor Croizat (Poole, UK: Blandford Press, 1984).

ROCKETS

During the Vietnam war the U.S. Army employed aerial rocket artillery (later known as aerial field artillery) in support of ground operations. The Second Battalion, 20th Artillery and Fourth Battalion, 77th Artillery were equipped with UH-1 helicopters armed with a weapons system that could fire 48 2.75-inch rockets each. In early 1968 these were replaced by AH-1 Cobra helicopters, which could carry a larger payload of 76 rockets. The U.S. Navy deployed several IFSs (in-shore fire support ships) and LSMRs (landing ships medium, rocket). These ships carried rocket launchers able to propell 380 5-inch rockets a minute.

While for the U.S. artillery rockets were anciliary to its regular field artillery, for the North Vietnamese and Viet Cong rockets were the primary heavy artillery weapons in the early days of the war. Three types of free-flight rockets were used—107-mm, 122-mm and 140-mm rockets. These rockets could be easily transported and fired from simple fork rests. Although much less accurate than artillery, they were effective against fixed positions, such as base camps and fire bases. The North Vietnamese and Viet Cong also used rockets extensively as terror weapons against the cities of South Vietnam. Although rockets continued to be used throughout the war (they were used, for example, in the initial assault on Tan Son Nhut Air Base on the morning of April 29, 1975), after 1967 they were increasingly supplemented by regular North Vietnamese field artillery.

See also ARTILLERY, MORTARS.

Suggestions for further reading: *The Vietnam Experience: Tools of War*, by Edgar C. Doleman, Jr. (Boston: Boston Publishing Co., 1984); *A Short History of the United States Navy and the Southeast Asian Conflict 1950–1975*, by Edward J. Marolda and G. Wesley Pryce, III (Washington: Naval Historical Center, 1984); *Field Artillery*, by David Ewing Ott (Washington, D.C.: U.S. Government Printing Office, 1975).

ROLLING THUNDER OPERATION

Code name for U.S. air operations over North Vietnam, Operation Rolling Thunder began in March 1965 and involved Air Force and Marine aircraft flying from bases in South Vietnam and Thailand and Navy aircraft flying from carriers in the South China Sea. The operation was designed to interdict North Vietnamese transportation routes in the southern part of North Vietnam and thereby slow infiltration of personnel and supplies into South Vietnam. In July 1966 Rolling Thunder was expanded to include North Vietnamese ammunition dumps and oil storage facilities, and in the spring of 1967 it was further expanded to

U.S. Air Force F-105s on the way to North Vietnam.

include power plants, factories, and airfields in the Hanoi-Haiphong area. The campaign was cut back in April 1968 by a partial bombing halt and ended on November 1, 1968.

Operation Rolling Thunder was closely controlled by the White House and at times targets were personally selected by President Johnson. From 1965 to 1968 some 643,000 tons of bombs were dropped on North Vietnamese targets at a cost of 922 aircraft lost to North Vietnamese action.

See also LINEBACKER OPERATIONS.

Suggestions for further reading: *Airpower in Three Wars,* by William W. Momyer (Washington, D.C.: U.S. Government Printing Office, 1978); *The United States Air Force in Southeast Asia 1961–1973,* edited by Carl Berger (Washington, D.C.: U.S. Government Printing Office, 1977); *Thunder from Above,* by John Morrocco (Boston: Boston Publishing Co., 1984); *Battles and Campaigns in Vietnam,* by Tom Carhart (New York: Crown Publishers, 1984); *The Tale of Two Bridges* and *The Battle for the Skies over North Vietnam,* edited by A. J. C. Lavalle (Washington, D.C.: U.S. Government Printing Office, 1976).

ROME PLOWS

Designed for jungle clearing operations, especially to clear out ambush sites along supply routes, the Rome plow was a large tractor with a specially configured dozer-type blade developed specifically for heavy-duty land-clearing operations, civilian and military, by the Rome Caterpillar Company of Rome, Georgia. The blade was more curved than the usual bulldozer blade and had a protruding, sharply honed lower edge. The lower edge curved out on one side to form a spike, used to split trees too large to cut with the blade alone, but the blade itself could slice through a tree of three feet in diameter. Bars were added to the top of the blade to force trees away from the tractor, and a safety feature—a "headache bar"—was installed over the operator's position to protect him from falling debris. Some Rome plows were also modified to include light armor for the operator.

Suggestions for further reading: *Tactical and Matériel Innovations,* by John H. Hay, Jr. (Washington, D.C.: U.S. Government Printing Office, 1974).

ROSTOW, WALT W(HITMAN) (1916–   )

Born on October 7, 1916 in New York City, Rostow graduated from Yale University in 1936. As a Rhodes Scholar, he studied at Oxford University from 1936 to 1938 before returning to Yale, where he received his PhD in 1940. During World War II Rostow served with the Office of Strategic Services. After service with the State Department in 1945–46, he became Professor of Economic History at the Massachusetts Institute of Technology in 1950.

Part of the Kennedy Administration "brain trust," Rostow served as Deputy National Security Adviser under McGeorge Bundy until November 1961, when he was appointed Counselor to the State Department and Chairman of its Policy Planning Council. In April 1966 Rostow succeeded Bundy as National Security Adviser to President Johnson and continued in that capacity until January 1969, when he left government service.

In the early 1960s Rostow advocated a strong U.S. diplomatic and military role in Vietnam and Laos to combat communist insurgencies. As Chairman of the Policy Planning Council, he prepared what came to be called the Rostow "thesis," his perspectives on Vietnam-type situations which maintained that externally supported insurgencies could be stopped only by escalating military measures against the external source of support. These measures would show that continued support of the insurgency would result in unacceptably heavy losses. Based on this approach, Rostow recommended in early 1964 that the United States take action to force North Vietnam to abide by the Geneva Accords, which prohibited foreign troops in Laos or South Vietnam. In November he stated it was necessary to apply limited but consistent military pressure on the North Vietnamese to force them to cease their support of the Viet Cong.

Rostow became increasingly identified with the administration's Vietnam policy and he defended it publicly, particularly after becoming National Security Adviser in April 1966. A month later he recommended systematic and continued bombing of North Vietnam's petroleum facilities. In 1967 Rostow moderated his commitment to bombing by seemingly supporting a proposal to limit bombing raids to the southern panhandle of North Vietnam, although he maintained that the bombing of the Hanoi-Haiphong area had to be left as an option. When Secretary of Defense Robert McNamara proposed a bombing halt in November, however, Rostow opposed it and maintained his opposition until Johnson announced on March 31, 1968 a policy of de-escalation that included a partial bombing halt as an inducement to negotiations.

See also JOHNSON, LYNDON B.; MCNAMARA, ROBERT S.

Suggestions for further reading: *The Best and the Brightest,* by David Halberstam (New York: Random House, 1972); *The Diffusion of Power: An Essay in Recent History,* by Walt Rostow (New York: Macmillan, 1972).

RPG (ROCKET-PROPELLED GRENADE)

A North Vietnamese Army and Viet Cong antitank weapon, the RPG (also known as the B-40) was a Soviet-supplied *Panzerfaust*-type weapon that fired a 82-mm rocket-propelled grenade (*see* illustration). The RPG-2 had a range of about 200 yards and its shaped-charge projectile could penetrate up to 7 inches of armor. The later model RPG-7 had almost twice the range and penetration.

To overcome this weapon, armor units used an "RPG screen," consisting of a stand-off constructed of regular cyclone fencing. This screen caused the RPG to detonate prematurely, thereby losing its shaped-charge penetrating power.

Suggestions for further reading: *Tactical and Matériel Innovations,* by John H. Hay, Jr. (Washington, D.C.: U.S. Government Printing Office, 1974); *The Vietnam Experience: Tools of War* by Edgar C. Doleman, Jr. (Boston: Boston Publishing Co., 1984).

RUBIN, JERRY (1938–   )

Born on July 14, 1938 in Cincinnati, Ohio,

A G.I. examines a captured RPG. (Courtesy Shelby L. Stanton.)

Rubin received a B.A. from the University of Cincinnati in 1961. Three years later he gravitated toward the radical movement in Berkeley and became active in the Free Speech Movement there.

In 1965 Rubin was a leading figure in the organization of a two-day teach-in at Berkeley, during which some 12,000 students and faculty heard such speakers as Norman Mailer, Benjamin Spock and Norman Thomas denounce the war in Vietnam. Out of the teach-in came the Vietnam Day Committee (VDC), which became one of the largest and most active antiwar organizations in the country. As a leader of the VDC, Rubin acquired a reputation as a skilled organizer with a flair for gaining media attention. In August the VDC staged several unsuccessful, but well-publicized, attempts to stop troop trains carrying Vietnam-bound soldiers.

In 1967 Rubin moved to New York, where he fell in with a drug-oriented circle and befriended Abbie Hoffman. Together they were prominent

organizers of the march on the Pentagon in October. Rubin declared the march of several thousand a victory. "We had symbolically destroyed the Pentagon . . . by throwing blood on it, pissing on it, dancing on it, painting 'Che Lives' on it." Rubin was convinced that the antiwar movement was at root a generational conflict of youth in search of fun and excitement against their elders.

In January 1968 Rubin, Hoffman and Paul Krassner formed the Yippies, or Youth International Party, a politically oriented counterculture group. During the summer Rubin and his fellow Yippies planned a massive festival of life in Chicago to contrast with what they interpreted as a festival of death at the Democratic National Convention in that city. On August 23 the Yippies opened their festival by nominating a pig for President, and two days later they clashed with the police in Lincoln Park. The following evening, at about the same time the Democratic convention formally opened, an even larger confrontation took place between police and demonstrators, resulting in numerous injuries to both sides.

Rubin was one of a group of demonstrators indicted by a federal grand jury in Chicago in connection with the 1968 disorders. The Chicago Seven, as they came to be known, were tried on charges of conspiracy to riot. Rubin and four others were convicted, but in 1972 the verdicts were overturned by an appeals court. In 1976 Rubin asserted in *Growing (Up) at 37* that both he and Hoffman had in fact gone to Chicago to disrupt the convention and the normal life of the city.

See also ANTIWAR MOVEMENT; CHICAGO SEVEN; DEMOCRATIC NATIONAL CONVENTION; HOFFMAN, ABBIE.

Suggestions for further reading: *Do It* (New York: Simon & Schuster, 1970) and *Growing (Up) at 37* (New York: M. Evans, 1976), by Jerry Rubin.

RUNG SAT

Rung Sat was the name given to the mud and mangrove swamp delta of the Saigon and Dong Nai Rivers. Viet Cong sapper units operating from this area placed water mines in the shipping channels to interdict the flow of supplies upriver to the port of Saigon.

See also MOBILE RIVERINE FORCE, SAPPER. *See* map at III CORPS TACTICAL ZONE.

Suggestions for further reading: *Riverine Operations 1966–1969,* by William B. Fulton, (Washington, D.C.: U.S. Government Printing Office, 1973).

RUSK (DAVID) DEAN (1909–   )

Born on February 9, 1909 in Cherokee Country, Georgia, Rusk graduated from Davidson College in 1931 and later studied at Oxford as a Rhodes Scholar. As a U.S. Army infantry officer, Rusk served in the China-India-Burma Theater as Operations Officer to General Joseph Stilwell. In 1946 Rusk joined the State Department. He was appointed Assistant Secretary of State for Far Eastern Affairs at the beginning of the Korean war. In 1952 he left the State Department to head the Rockefeller Foundation.

In December 1960 President-elect Kennedy selected Rusk as his Secretary of State. Rusk attempted to limit the role of the State Department in Vietnam, believing that American involvement there should be primarily military. But as the U.S. advisory role expanded and as the United States became increasingly concerned with South Vietnamese President Ngo Dinh Diem's ability to carry out internal reforms, Rusk played a more active role.

In August 1963 top U.S. foreign policy advisers began to reevaluate American support for Diem. Rusk, sensing Diem's isolation from the people of South Vietnam and his inability or unwillingness to stop the government's repression of Buddhists, advised that a change of government might be necessary. Prepared by State Department officials, the initial instructions sent to Ambassador Henry Cabot Lodge reflected Rusk's position. Lodge was told Diem must be given every chance to rid himself of elements hostile to reform, but that if he remained obdurate, the United States must "face the possibility that Diem himself cannot be preserved." Lodge was also instructed to inform

military leaders, who had been planning to overthrow Diem, that the United States would not attempt to thwart a coup. Rusk's role in the complicated decision making that preceded a coup on November 1 is not clear, as he preferred to let his subordinates, including Lodge, Averell Harriman and Roger Hilsman, expound the need for change in South Vietnam.

Rusk's influence on Vietnam policy increased markedly after Lyndon Johnson assumed the presidency. He helped Johnson make important decisions on escalation of the conflict. During 1964 and 1965 Rusk opposed attempts to negotiate a settlement, arguing that with the Viet Cong controlling more than half of South Vietnam, the United States could not bargain from a position of strength. Until military pressure on Hanoi tilted the balance of power in favor of the Saigon government, Rusk asserted, the North Vietnamese would have little incentive to negotiate. Rusk opposed the bombing halt of December 1965–January 1966 for similar reasons.

In addition to serving as a key adviser to the President, Rusk emerged as a chief public defender of administration policy. In February 1966 he appeared at televised hearings of the Senate Foreign Relations Committee, chaired by Senator William Fulbright, to explain administration policy on Vietnam. Rusk sought to refute Fulbright's charge that the conflict was a civil war in which the United States had no strategic interest by describing what he believed to be a long-term pattern of communist Chinese aggression. In an October 1967 press conference, he justified the U.S. presence in Southeast Asia as necessary to protect the region from the future threat of "a billion Chinese . . . armed with nuclear weapons."

When the military requested an additional 200,000 troops after the Tet Offensive of February 1968, Rusk recommended that the President approve the increase. However, after a bipartisan panel of statesmen recommended disengagement from the war because of its detrimental effects on the American economy and society, Johnson announced a policy of de-escalation and his desire to enter into negotiations with the North Vietnamese. Hanoi accepted Johnson's offer with the provision that initial meetings deal only with the conditions required for a total bombing halt. Rusk appears to have felt that such talks were not in the best interests of the United States. When the talks began in Paris in May 1968, Rusk played little part in them.

Rusk saw the conflict in Southeast Asia as an attempt by a militant Chinese government to expand its influence throughout Asia by means of "wars of liberation." Consequently, he argued, the United States was not in Vietnam simply because of commitments but because of the need to show that such expansion was doomed to failure. Although Rusk asserted that victory in Vietnam was necessary for American security, he did not define the war primarily as a battle for a strategic area but rather emphasized that it was a "psychological struggle for the conquest of minds and souls." The loss of Vietnam, he said, would mean "a drastic loss of confidence in the will and capacity of the free world to oppose aggression."

Rusk left office in January 1969.

See also DIEM, NGO DINH; FULBRIGHT, J. WILLIAM; HARRIMAN, AVERELL; HILSMAN, ROGER; LODGE, HENRY CABOT; KENNEDY, JOHN F.; JOHNSON, LYNDON B.; SENIOR ADVISORY GROUP; WARS OF LIBERATION.

Suggestions for further reading: *The Best and the Brightest*, by David Halberstam (New York: Random House, 1972); *The Limits of Intervention*, by Townsend Hoopes (New York: David MacKay Co., 1969).

RVNAF (REPUBLIC OF VIETNAM ARMED FORCES)

See SVNAF (SOUTH VIETNAMESE ARMED FORCES).

RVN (REPUBLIC OF VIETNAM) CIVIL ACTIONS MEDAL

See SOUTH VIETNAM CIVIL ACTIONS MEDAL.

RVN (REPUBLIC OF VIETNAM) GALLANTRY CROSS

See SOUTH VIETNAM GALLANTRY CROSS.

SAIGON

The capital of South Vietnam, Saigon was Vietnam's largest city, with an official population of over 1.5 million. During the war the population was in fact much greater because of the large influx of refugees. The city's French architecture and Westernized culture reflected the fact that it was formerly the capital of the French colony of Cochinchina. Saigon and its environs were in what was called the Capital Military Region, the Gia Dinh Province in the III Corps area.

It was the seat of the South Vietnamese government and the location of Headquarters MACV (U.S. Military Assistance Command Vietnam) and many other U.S. units. Saigon Support Command, for example, at its peak had some 33,000 personnel assigned to support approximately 235,000 U.S. and allied troops.

Saigon was also South Vietnam's largest port. Located 45 miles upriver from the South China Sea, it had major docking facilities for oceangoing ships and extensive storage areas. Its international airport, Tan Son Nhut, was also a major military air base.

On April 30, 1975 Saigon fell to a North Vietnamese Army blitzkrieg and is now officially known as Ho Chi Minh City.

See also LONG BINH, TAN SON NHUT, III CORP TAC-TICAL ZONE.

Suggestions for further reading: *Peace with Honor?* by Stuart Herrington (Novato, Calif.: Presidio Press, 1983) *Last Flight from Saigon,* by Thomas G. Tobin, Arthur E. Laehr and John F. Halgenberg, edited by A. J. C. Lavelle (Washington, D.C.: U.S. Government Printing Office, 1978); *The Vietnam Experience: The Fall,* by Clark Dougan and David Fulghum (Boston: Boston Publishing Co., 1985); *The Fall of Saigon,* by David Butler (New York: Simon & Schuster, 1985); *Decent Interval,* by Frank Snepp (New York: Random House, 1977); *55 Days: The Fall of South Vietnam,* by Alan Dawson (Englewood Cliffs, N.J.: Prentice-Hall, 1977); *The Last Day,* by John Pilger (New York: Vintage, 1976).

THE SAIGON- BIEN HOA- LONG BINH AREA

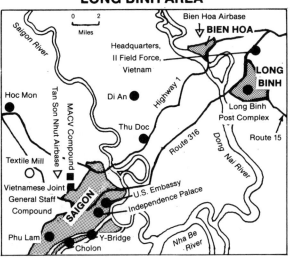

SALISBURY, HARRISON E(VANS) (1908–   )

Born on November 14, 1908 in Minneapolis, Minnesota, Salisbury worked for United Press from 1930 to 1948. The following year, he joined the *New York Times* and spent the next five years in Moscow as bureau chief, winning the 1955 Pulitzer Prize for international reporting. In 1964 he became Assistant Managing Editor of the *Times.*

In the mid-1960s Salisbury made repeated efforts to travel to North Vietnam, which few American reporters had visited since the escalation of U.S. military activity in Southeast Asia. In early December 1966 a series of bombing raids on Hanoi began, culminating in heavy attacks on December 13 and 14. The North Vietnamese government charged that American planes had bombed nonmilitary targets and inflicted heavy civilian casualties. On December 15 Salisbury received a cable from Hanoi granting him a visa, and he immediately left for North Vietnam.

On December 25 Salisbury reported, "Contrary to the impression given by United States communiques, on-the-spot inspection indicates that American bombing has been inflicting considerable civilian casualties in Hanoi and its environs for some time past. . . ." The following day, in response to Salisbury's report, officials of the Johnson Administration said that although U.S. policy was to attack only military targets, American pilots had in fact accidentally struck civilian areas. On December 27 Salisbury reported that Nam Dinh, 50 miles southeast of Hanoi, had been repeatedly bombed since June 28, resulting in a large number of civilian casualties. "Whatever the explanation" he wrote, "one can see that United States planes are dropping an enormous weight of explosives on purely civilian targets." Salisbury's dispatches indicated that in spite of the intensive bombing, the North Vietnamese leadership appeared willing to fight a prolonged war if necessary.

The *Times* reports sparked an intense debate over the bombing. President Johnson said at a December 31 press conference that he regretted "every single casualty" in both North and South Vietnam and reasserted that the raids were aimed solely at military targets, with all efforts taken to avoid civilian casualties. Salisbury's dispatches were attacked by both government officials and other newspapers for failing to specify the sources of information for casualties and bombing damage. The *Washington Post* reported that the casualty figures Salisbury cited for Nam Dinh were similar to those appearing in a North Vietnamese pamphlet. Clifton Daniel, managing editor of the *Times,* responded that this was not surprising since "they both came from the same source—the North Vietnamese government."

For his reporting from North Vietnam, the

Pulitzer Prize journalism jury recommended Salisbury be awarded the international reporting prize, but the advisory board rejected the recommendation by a vote of 5 to 4.

See also ANTIWAR MOVEMENT; MCNAMARA, ROBERT S.

Suggestions for further reading: *Behind the Lines: Hanoi, December 23, 1966–January 7, 1967,* by Harrison E. Salisbury, and *Vietnam Reconsidered: Lessons from a War,* edited by Harrison E. Salisbury (New York: Harper & Row, 1967 and 1984).

SAM (SURFACE-TO-AIR MISSILE)

U.S. Army and Marine Corps units deployed air defense battalions armed with Hawk surface-to-air missiles to Vietnam, but because the U.S. Air Force had air control over the entire country, they were not needed and were eventually withdrawn.

The Soviet Union supplied the North Vietnamese Army (NVA) with SA-2 surface-to-air missiles (SAMs), which were employed extensively by North Vietnamese air defense units. Similar to the U.S. NIKE, the SAM-2 had a range and altitude of about 19 nautical miles and 85,000 feet.

Described as looking like a telephone pole in flight, the SAM-2 was fired from a fixed launcher; its 2½ ton missile had a speed up to Mach 2.5. In 1965 North Vietnam fired 194 SAMs, downing 11 U.S. aircraft; in 1966, 1,966 SAMs brought down 31 planes; in 1967, 3,202 SAMs brought down 96 planes; from January to March 1968 (when the bombing halt began), 322 SAMs brought down three planes. During the Linebacker Operations in 1972 the NVA fired 4,244 SAMs and brought down 49 planes. Thanks to U.S. electronic countermeasures, SAM effectiveness declined from 5.7 percent in 1966 to 1.15 percent in 1972.

Another Soviet-supplied SAM was the handheld shoulder-fired SA-7 Strella, first introduced on the battlefield in 1972 during the North Vietnamese Eastertide Offensive. The U.S. Air Force and South Vietnamese Air Force lost 16 planes to SA-7 missiles at Quang Tri alone.

See also AIR DEFENSE.

Suggestions for further reading: *Airpower in Three Wars,* by William W. Momyer (Washington, D.C.: U.S. Government Printing Office, 1978); *The Vietnam Experience: Thunder from Above,* and *Rain of Fire* by John Morrocco, (Boston: Boston Publishing Co., 1984 and 1985).

SAN ANTONIO FORMULA

In September 1967 President Johnson, in a speech in San Antonio, Texas promised to halt the bombing of North Vietnam indefinitely if North Vietnam agreed to begin peace negotiations promptly and not to "take advantage" of the cessation in bombing by sending men and matériel south. The "San Antonio Formula" had been drafted by Assistant Secretary of Defense for International Affairs Paul Warnke, Deputy Secretary of Defense Paul Nitze and Secretary of Defense Robert McNamara and had been offered privately to North Vietnam in August 1967. It marked a significant change in what the United States required to end the bombing. Prior to this communication, the United States had offered to

A SAM site in North Vietnam. (Courtesy U.S. Air Force.)

end the bombing only if North Vietnam would stop its infiltration of the south. The San Antonio formula did not require a specific guarantee from Hanoi that infiltration would cease. The only condition was that the United States reserved the right to act if it concluded that the North Vietnamese were taking advantage of the bombing halt. The proposal was rejected by North Vietnam in October.

See also JOHNSON, LYNDON B; MCNAMARA, ROBERT S.; NITZE, PAUL H.; WARNKE, PAUL.

SANCTUARIES

The problem of sanctuaries—areas where enemy troops could retreat and be safe from attack—first surfaced during the Korean war, when President Truman forbade air strikes on the staging and supply areas of Chinese communist forces in Manchuria, north of the Yalu River. The Chinese argued (falsely) that their forces in Korea were "volunteers" and that they themselves were not at war. The United States went along with this subterfuge to avoid provoking a wider conflict.

In the early years of the Vietnam war the supply depots and rail lines across the border from North Vietnam in Laos and Cambodia were off limits to U.S. air strikes, again because of a desire not to provoke a war with China. Because to the very end of the war the North Vietnamese Army (NVA) denied that they had forces in the south or in Cambodia or Laos, the so-called "neutrality" of Laos and Cambodia at first gave the North Vietnamese Army (NVA) the opportunity to build supply routes (i.e., the Ho Chi Minh Trail), bases and arms depots in these safe areas. In April 1965 the United States began to launch air strikes against such areas in the southern panhandle of Laos, although ground attacks to sever these routes were never approved. In March 1969 the United States launched air strikes against the North Vietnamese base camps in Cambodia (the "secret bombing" of Cambodia) and from April to June 1970 launched a united ground attack "incursion") to root out sanctuaries in Cambodia.

See also CAMBODIA, HO CHI MINH TRAIL, MENU OPERATION; NEUTRALITY, STEEL TIGER, TIGER HOUND.

SAPPER

In the Middle Ages, a sapper was a soldier who dug a narrow trench, or sap, to undermine a castle wall or other fortification. In the Vietnam war sappers were special assault forces (usually expendable Viet Cong local guerrillas) who mined roads and waterways, emplaced booby traps and led enemy attacks by clearing paths through minefields and breaching defensive fortifications.

In the 1968 assault on Hué, for example, it was local Viet Cong sapper units who paved the way for the attack by the North Vietnamese Army's Fourth and Sixth Infantry Regiments.

By January 1973 the North Vietnamese Army and the Viet Cong had some four sapper regiments and 35 separate sapper battalions plus the 1,500-man DMZ Sapper Group and the 500-man 126th Naval Sapper Group.

SEABEES

Beginning in 1963, U.S. Navy SEABEE technical assistance teams were deployed to Vietnam for civic action support. With the help of local villagers, they constructed airstrips, bridges, small dams, roads, refugee housing, schools as well as fortifications for the Army Special Forces.

Aside from these technical assistance teams, the 30th Naval Construction Regiment was activated in May 1965 at Da Nang in I Corps and subsequently came under the control of the Third Naval Construction Brigade. In August 1967 the 32nd Navy Construction Regiment was organized to control construction in the Hué-Phu Bai area. From the first 600-man battalion in 1965, the SEABEE force grew to over 10,000 in 1968, with five construction battalions at Da Nang, two at Chu Lai, two at Phu Bai, two at Quang Tri and one at Dong Ha, plus other locations throughout Vietnam.

Often working under enemy fire, the SEABEEs constructed helicopter pads, runways, port facilities, roads, bridges, fortifications, fuel and ammunition storage areas and other such facilities in support of combat operations. The first Navy Medal of Honor awarded during the Vietnam war was won by a SEABEE during an attack on his

Insignia of the SEABEEs.

work site in June 1965. From 1965 to 1968, 57 SEABEEs were killed in action and hundreds more were wounded.

See also NAVY, U.S.

Suggestions for further reading: *A Short History of the United States Navy and the Southeast Asian Conflict 1950–1975,* by Edward J. Marolda and G. Wesley Pryce, III (Washington, D.C.: Naval Historical Center, 1984); *Southeast Asia: Building the Bases: The History of Construction in Southeast Asia,* by Richard Tregakis (Washington, D.C.: U.S. Government Printing Office, 1975); *Base Development in South Vietnam 1965–1970,* by Carroll H. Dunn (Washington, D.C.: U.S. Government Printing Office, 1972).

SEA DRAGON

A U.S. Navy operation to interdict North Vietnamese supply lines in conjunction with the Rolling Thunder air campaign, Sea Dragon began in October 1966. Cruisers, destroyers and—for one month—the battleship *New Jersey* ranged the North Vietnamese coast, at times as far north as the 20th parallel. Operating in pairs with two to four American and Australian destroyers and one cruiser, they used carrier-based spotter planes to find and identify targets. They bombarded infiltration routes, sunk supply craft and shelled enemy coastal batteries and radar sites. Nineteen ships operating with Sea Dragon were struck by enemy counterbattery fire but none were sunk.

Operation Sea Dragon was terminated when President Johnson announced a bombing halt in October 1968.

See also NAVAL GUNFIRE SUPPORT.

Suggestions for further reading: *A Short History of the United States Navy and the Southeast Asian Conflict 1950–1975,* by Edward J. Marolda and G. Wesley Pryce, III (Washington, D.C.: Naval Historical Center, 1984).

SEAL FORCES

An acronym for *Sea-Air-Land,* SEALs were U.S. Navy commando-type forces especially skilled at infiltrating enemy territory by sea in small boats or as frogmen, by air from helicopters or by parachute, and by land in ranger-type patrols. Gathering intelligence and breeching or emplacing underwater and beach obstacles, SEAL units in Vietnam operated with the River Patrol Forces and also were attached to the MACV-SOG (U.S. Military Assistance Command Vietnam-Studies and Observation Group) for highly secret intelligence operations.

See also RIVER PATROL FORCE, SOG (STUDIES AND OBSERVATION GROUP).

Suggestions for further reading: *A Short History of the United States Navy and the Southeast Asian Conflict 1950–1975,* by Edward J. Marolda and G. Wesley Pryce, III (Washington, D.C.: Naval Historical Center, 1984).

SEALORDS

An acronym for *Southeast Asia Lake, Ocean, River, and Delta Strategy,* SEALORDS was a concerted U.S. Navy-South Vietnamese Navy operation conducted in conjunction with the U.S. Ninth Infantry Division's Riverine Forces, the South Vietnamese Army and the South Vietnamese

Marine Corps ground forces. Its aim was to cut enemy supply lines from Cambodia and disrupt enemy base areas in the Mekong Delta and in other waterways.

Designated Task Force 194, SEALORDS was controlled by COMNAVFORV (Commander of U.S. Naval Forces Vietnam). Beginning in October 1968, it combined 586 vessels of the Coastal Surveillance Force (Task Force 115), the River Patrol Force (Task Force 116) and the Mobile Riverine Assault Force (Task Force 117) with 655 South Vietnamese Navy vessels.

The operation emplaced patrol "barriers," including electronics sensors, along the waterways paralleling the Cambodian border and was gradually extended along the coast and into the inland waterways; by the time the first phase was completed in January 1969, an uninterrupted waterway interdiction barrier existed from Tay Ninh northwest of Saigon to the Gulf of Siam.

SEALORDS operations were also conducted on the Cua Dai and Hoi An Rivers in Quang Nam Province in I Corps, on the Saigon River as far north as Dau Tieng in the Michelin Rubber Plantation in III Corps and on Ca Mau Peninsula waterways in IV Corps. During the Cambodian "incursion" in May 1970, a SEALORDS task force sailed up the Mekong River, and South Vietnamese Navy forces reached the Cambodian capital of Phnom Penh. In April 1971 the U.S. Navy's major role in SEALORDS ceased and the operation became a South Vietnamese Navy responsibility.

See also MOBILE RIVERINE FORCE.

Suggestions for further reading: *A Short History of the United States Navy and the Southeast Asian Conflict 1950–1975,* by Edward J. Marolda and G. Wesley Pryce, III (Washington, D.C.: Naval Historical Center, 1984); *Riverine Operations 1966–1969* by William B. Fulton (Washington, D.C.: U.S. Government Printing Office, 1973).

SEARCH-AND-DESTROY

An operational term adopted by the MACV (U.S. Military Assistance Command Vietnam) in

A SEALORDS river patrol conducted by U.S. Navy ships.

1964 to describe operations designed to find, fix in place and destroy enemy forces and their base areas and supply caches. Originally intended to delineate one of the basic missions performed by South Vietnamese military forces, the term became widely used by U.S. forces later in the war. Public repugnance toward the brutality implied by the term in addition to vivid media accounts of destruction of Vietnamese villages helped undermine support for the war.

See also CLEAR-AND-HOLD; STRATEGY, U.S.

Suggestions for further reading: *Report on the War in Vietnam*, by U. S. G. Sharpe and William C. Westmoreland (Washington, D.C.: U.S. Government Printing Office, 1968); *Tactical and Matériel Innovations*, by John H. Hay, Jr. (Washington, D.C.: U.S. Government Printing Office, 1974).

SEARCH-AND-RESCUE

Both the U.S. Air Force and the Navy developed extensive search-and-rescue (SAR) techniques to locate and rescue downed aircrews.

For carrier pilots the Navy stationed two destroyers at a northern SAR station (20° N, 107° E) and another two at a southern SAR station (19° N, 106° E) in the Gulf of Tonkin. One specially equipped UH-2 Seasprite helicopter was onboard at each location. Another four SH-3 Sea King helicopters were onboard carriers nearby at Yankee Station, and during major air operations they orbited over the two SAR sites. From June 6, 1964 to November 1, 1968, 458 of the 912 Navy aircrews downed over North Vietnam, Laos or at sea were recovered; Navy SAR forces suffered 26 casualties, and 33 aircraft were lost.

Air Force SAR operations began in 1962, when a six-man detachment was deployed to Vietnam from the Pacific Air Rescue Service. Lacking planes or equipment, they worked with Army and Marine helicopter units to rescue downed aircrews, but the shortage of such devices as hoist cables long enough to penetrate through the jungle hampered SAR attempts.

In January 1966 the Third Aerospace Rescue and Recovery Group was formed at Tan Son Nhut Air Base near Saigon to serve as the primary rescue agency in Southeast Asia. The group sta-tioned its 37th Aerospace Recovery and Rescue Squadron at Da Nang in I Corps, the 38th at Tan Son Nhut and the 39th at Tuy Hoa in II Corps. Later a fourth squadron, the 40th, was formed at Udorn, Thailand.

Rescue attempts were usually controlled by a Search-and-Rescue Task Force (SARTAF), which included two rescue helicopters as well as several A-1 fighters to search the area for downed crewmen. Once crewmen were located, the fighters would provide close air support to keep enemy troops at bay while helicopters went in to pick up the airmen on the ground. After November 1965 HH-3E "Jolly Green Giant" helicopters were the primary rescue aircraft. With 240 feet of cable, they could penetrate the densest jungle canopy, and extra fuel tanks allowed them to remain in an area for an extended period of time.

In 1966 the amphibian HC-130 Hercules added to SAR capabilities. Among other things the HC-130 could refuel helicopters in flight, adding to their loiter time. In 1967 the HH-53B "Super Jolly Green Giant" became available. It was the largest, fastest, most powerful heavy-lift helicopter the Air Force had, and eventually it was fitted with sophisticated navigation systems, electronic countermeasures to foil enemy radar and a night recovery system with low-light-level television and infrared lights. Air Force SAR operations recovered 3,883 personnel between 1964 and 1973. They included 926 Army, 680 Navy and 1,201 Air Force personnel as well as 555 allied military personnel and 521 civilians and other personnel. The price was 71 SAR personnel killed and 45 aircraft lost.

For SAR operations beyond the reach of Navy or Air Force capabilities, the MACV-SOG (U.S. Military Assistance Command Vietnam-Studies and Observation Group), a highly secret special operations unit, also assisted in rescue of downed aircrews.

See also SOG (STUDIES AND OBSERVATION GROUP).

Suggestions for further reading: *Search and Rescue in Southeast Asia 1961–1975*, by Earl H. Tilford, Jr. (Washington, D.C.: U.S. Government Printing Office, 1980); *A Short History of the United States Navy and the Southeast Asian Conflict 1950–1975* by Edward J. Marolda and G. Wesley Pryce, II (Washington, D.C.: U.S. Naval Historical Center

1984); *The United States Air Force in Southeast Asia 1961–1973,* edited by Carl Berger (Washington, D.C.: U.S. Government Printing Office, 1977). For an account of an actual SAR operation, see *Bat–21,* by William C. Anderson (New York: Bantam Books, 1983).

SEATO (SOUTH EAST ASIA TREATY ORGANIZATION)

Conceived by Secretary of State John Foster Dulles as a kind of Southeast Asian NATO (North Atlantic Treaty Organization), SEATO was founded in 1954. It included the United States, Britain, France, Australia, New Zealand, Pakistan, Thailand and the Philippines. A separate protocol extended SEATO's protection to nonmember states South Vietnam, Laos and Cambodia.

For the United States the purpose of SEATO was to provide a framework for building stable states to contain communist expansion. While Australia, New Zealand, Thailand and the Philippines assisted U.S. efforts in South Vietnam by dispatching of combat forces, other SEATO nations did not share American concerns.

Because of these major political differences, SEATO was relatively ineffective and was disbanded in 1977.

Suggestions for further reading: *American National Security: Policy and Process,* by Amos A. Jordan and William J. Taylor, Jr. (Baltimore: Johns Hopkins University Press, 1981). For an earlier assessment, see "The Asian Balance of Power: A Comparison with European Precedence," by Coral Bell, *Adelphi Papers No. 44* (London: The International Institute for Strategic Studies, February 1968).

SECOND CORPS TACTICAL ZONE

See II (i.e., TWO) CORPS TACTICAL ZONE.

SECOND FIELD FORCE VIETNAM

See II (i.e., TWO) FIELD FORCE VIETNAM.

SECRETARY OF DEFENSE

Under the President of the United States, who is also Commander-in-Chief, the Secretary of Defense exercises direction, authority and control over the Department of Defense, which includes the Army, Navy, Marine Corps, Air Force, the Joint Chiefs of Staff and the worldwide "unified commands," known as "theaters of operations" in World War II. Within the Pentagon it is this civilian Secretary, not the uniformed members of the Joint Chiefs of Staff, who actually commands America's fighting forces. During the Vietnam war the chain of command ran from the President to the Secretary of Defense and then through the Joint Chiefs of Staff to the CINCPAC (Commander-in-Chief of the Pacific Command) in Honolulu, Hawaii, the "theater commander" responsible for strategic direction of the Vietnam war.

The leadership of the Department of Defense changed frequently during the course of the Vietnam war. In December 1959 Thomas S. Gates, Jr. replaced Neil H. McElroy as Secretary of Defense to President Eisenhower. With the election of President Kennedy, Gates was replaced by Robert S. McNamara, who also served under President Johnson until he was replaced by Clark M. Clifford in March 1968. In 1969, with the election of President Nixon, Melvin R. Laird became Secretary of Defense. He was replaced in January 1973 by Elliot L. Richardson, who was succeeded in July 1973 by James R. Schlesinger. Schlesinger continued in this post under President Ford until after the war in Vietnam ended.

By comparison with these seven U.S. Secretaries of Defense, General Vo Nguyen Giap served as the North Vietnamese Minister of Defense through the entire course of the Vietnam war.

See also CLIFFORD, CLARK; COMMAND AND CONTROL; LAIRD, MELVIN R.; MCNAMARA, ROBERT S.

Suggestions for further reading: *The Secretary of Defense,* by Douglas Kinnard (Lexington, University of Kentucky Press, 1980).

SECRETARY OF STATE

The Secretary of State advises the President of

the United States on the formulation and execution of foreign policy with the primary objective of promoting the long-range security and well-being of the United States. During the Vietnam war, from 1959 to 1975, this post had the most continuity of any of the executive departments involved in the war. Following the resignation of John Foster Dulles, who was Secretary of State from January 1953 to April 1959, Christian A. Herter served as Secretary of State to President Eisenhower from April 1959 to January 1961. Dean Rusk served as Secretary of State from 1961 until 1969 under Presidents Kennedy and Johnson. He was succeeded by William P. Rogers, who served as Secretary of State during the first administration of President Nixon. In September 1973 Rogers was replaced by Henry A. Kissinger, who served Presidents Nixon and Ford.

See also DULLES, JOHN FOSTER; KISSINGER, HENRY A.; RUSK, DEAN.

Suggestions for further reading: *The Vietnam Trauma in American Foreign Policy, 1945–1975,* by Paul L. Kattenburg (New Brunswick, N.J.: Transaction Books, 1980).

SENIOR ADVISORY GROUP

A group of senior policy advisers who met with President Johnson, at Secretary of Defense Clark Clifford's request, in March 1968 to reevaluate America's policy in Vietnam.

According to Stanley Karnow in *Vietnam: A History,* the group consisted of Dean Acheson, Secretary of State under President Truman, Arthur Goldberg, the Ambassador to the United Nations at the time, "George Ball, McGeorge Bundy, Henry Cabot Lodge, and Abe Fortas, all veterans of past Vietnam debates, as well as newcomers to the subject like [former Secretary of the Treasury] Douglas Dillon . . . [presidential adviser] John J. McCloy, and Robert Murphy, a seasoned diplomat. The conclave also included Maxwell Taylor and two other retired Generals, Omar Bradley and Matthew Ridgway. . . . [Dean] Rusk, [Walt W.] Rostow, and [Chairman of the Joint Chiefs of Staff General Earle] Wheeler were there along with Clifford."

Only five months earlier many of the advisers

assembled had endorsed Johnson's Vietnam policies. But after being briefed by three specialists and discussing the policy options, the concensus was that the United States should disengage itself from the war. The basic reasons for this conclusion were that the South Vietnamese government and Army would take perhaps five years to reform, and that the erosion of domestic support for the war in the United States made it imprudent to further escalate the conflict. On March 31, 1968 Johnson announced that U.S. air strikes would be limited to the area south of the 20th parallel, thereby sparing most of North Vietnam. He called upon North Vietnam to "respond favorably to this new step toward peace." At the close of the speech Johnson shocked the nation by announcing that he would not seek the nomination of the Democratic Party for President. Johnson would later admit in his memoirs that his thinking on the war had been altered significantly by the Senior Advisory Group's recommendations.

See also ANTIWAR MOVEMENT; BALL, GEORGE W.; BUNDY, MCGEORGE; CLIFFORD, CLARK M.; GOLDBERG, ARTHUR J.; LODGE, HENRY C.; JOHNSON, LYNDON B.; ROSTOW, WALT W.; RUSK, DEAN; TAYLOR, MAXWELL D.; WHEELER, EARLE.

Suggestions for further reading: *Vietnam: A History,* by Stanley Karnow (New York: Viking, 1983); *The Vantage Point: Perspective of the Presidency 1963–1969,* by Lyndon Baines Johnson (New York: Popular Library, 1971).

SEVEN MOUNTAINS

A mountain stronghold in western Chau Doc Province near the Cambodian border, IV Corps, the Seven Mountains served as a fortified bastion for both Viet Cong and North Vietnamese Army Units. The U.S. Army Special Forces fought two major battles here, one at Nui Coto in 1969 and one at Nui Khet in 1970. These operations only temporarily cleared the cave-infested, boulder-strewn mountain fortresses, although high losses were taken by the Viet Cong and North Vietnamese in the assaults.

See also map of IV CORPS TACTICAL ZONE.

Suggestions for further reading: *The Green Berets*

at War, by Shelby Stanton (Novato, Calif.: Presidio Press, 1985).

SEVENTH AIR FORCE

Headquartered at Tan Son Nhut Air Base in the suburbs of Saigon, the Seventh Air Force was responsible for the conduct of the U.S. air war in South Vietnam. Under the operational control of COMUSMACV (Commander of the U.S. Military Assistance Command Vietnam), the commanding general of the Seventh Air Force was also the Deputy COMUSMACV for Air.

Organized on April 1, 1966 to replace the Second Air Division, which previously controlled U.S. Air operations in South Vietnam, the Seventh Air Force at its height in 1969 had many elements under its direct command. Fighter-bomber units included the Third Tactical Fighter Wing at Bien Hoa Air Base (III Corps), the 12th Tactical Fighter Wing at Cam Ranh Bay (II Corps), the 35th Tactical Fighter Wing at Phan Rang (II Corps) and the 366th Tactical Fighter Wing at Da Nang (I Corps).

Another subordinate element, the 834th Air Division, controlled tactical airlift throughout the country. Additional major units included a tactical reconnaissance wing, two special operations wings and a number of supporting groups. The MACV (U.S. Military Assistance Command Vietnam) Air Force Advisory Group was also under Seventh Air Force control.

Under CINCPAC (Commander-in-Chief of the Pacific Command) in Honolulu, Seventh Air Force and 13th Air Force at Clark Air Base in the Philippines shared a joint deputy commander, stationed at Udorn in Thailand, who controlled the three tactical fighter wings flying combat operations over North Vietnam and Laos. During the course of the Vietnam war, command of the Seventh Air Force changed seven times:

Commander	Assumed Command
Lt. Gen. Joseph H. Moore	April 1966
Gen. William W. Momyer	July 1966
Gen. George S. Brown	August 1968
Gen. Lucius D. Clay, Jr.	September 1970
Gen. John D. Lavelle	August 1971
Gen. John W. Vogt, Jr.	April 1972
Lt. Gen. Timothy F. O'Keefe	October 1973

See also CLOSE AIR SUPPORT, 834TH AIR DIVISION, FAC (FORWARD AIR CONTROLLER), FIGHTERS AND FIGHTER-BOMBERS, FIRST MARINE AIR WING, MILITARY AIRLIFT COMMAND, STRATEGIC AIR COMMAND, TACTICAL AIR COMMAND, TACTICAL AIRLIFT.

Suggestions for further reading: *The United States Air Force in Southeast Asia 1961–1973,* edited by Carl Berger (Washington, D.C.: U.S. Government Printing Office, 1977).

SEVENTH FLEET

Home-ported in Yokuska, Japan but with its headquarters afloat, the Seventh Fleet was responsible for U.S. Navy operations in the western Pacific. Subordinate to CINCPACFLT (Commander-in-Chief of the Pacific Fleet)—in turn subordinate to CINCPAC (Commander-in-Chief of the Pacific Command) in Honolulu—the Seventh Fleet deployed sizable task forces for combat operations in Southeast Asia. Task Force 77 was the fleet's attack carrier striking force, charged with aerial interdiction of enemy supply lines in North Vietnam and Laos and close air support in South Vietnam (*see* AIRCRAFT CARRIERS). Task Force 76 was the fleet's amphibious force (*see* AMPHIBIOUS FORCES).

Task Force 73 was the fleet's mobile logistic support force, charged with keeping the up to 100 ships of the deployed fleet refueled and resupplied, through underway replenishment, with ammunition, petroleum products, food, repairs and repair parts as well as communications, towing, salvage, port, postal and medical services. Among its vessels were the hospital ships *Repose* and *Sanctuary,* each of which had modern medical equipment and a staff of 24 doctors, 29 nurses and 250 medical corpsmen. Positioned off the coast of I Corps within 30 miles of the battlefield, the ships saved thousands of lives.

Task Group 70.8 was a Seventh Fleet cruiser-destroyer group charged with naval gunfire support and shore bombardment (*see* NAVAL GUNFIRE SUPPORT, SEA DRAGON).

From the time of the Tonkin Gulf incident until

The U.S.S. *Oriskany*, shown here cruising in the Gulf of Tonkin, was part of the Seventh Fleet. (Courtesy U.S. Navy.)

the end of the Vietnam war, command of the Seventh Fleet changed eight times:

Commander	Assumed Command
Vice Admiral Roy L. Johnson	June 1964
Vice Admiral Paul P. Blackburn, Jr.	Mar. 1965
Rear Admiral Joseph W. Williams, acting	Oct. 1965
Vice Admiral John J. Hyland	Dec. 1965
Vice Admiral William F. Bringle	Nov. 1967
Vice Admiral Maurice F. Weisner	Mar. 1970
Vice Admiral William P. Mack	June 1971
Vice Admiral James L. Holloway, III	May 1972

See also NAVY, U.S.; AIRCRAFT CARRIERS; AMPHIB-IOUS FORCES; NAVAL GUNFIRE SUPPORT.

Suggestions for further reading: *A Short History of the United States Navy and the Southeast Asian Conflict 1950–1975,* by Edward J. Marolda and G. Wesley Pryce, III (Washington, D.C.: Naval Historical Center, 1984).

SHARP, U. S. GRANT (1906–   )

Born on April 2, 1906 in Chinook, Montana, Sharp graduated from the U.S. Naval Academy in 1927. He commanded the minesweeper *Hogan* and the destroyer *Boyd* during World War II.

Appointed CINCPACFLT (Commander-in-

Ulysses S. Grant Sharp. (Courtesy U.S. Navy.)

Chief of the Pacific Fleet) on September 30, 1963, he controlled the Seventh Fleet's air operations over North Vietnam and Laos and surface operations in the western Pacific. On June 30, 1964 he was promoted to CINCPAC (Commander-in-Chief of the Pacific Command) and as such was responsible for overseeing the U.S. buildup in Vietnam and for executing American strategy in the theater of war. He held that post during the height of the U.S. involvement, including the Tet Offensive of 1968, and the allied reaction to it. On July 31, 1968 Admiral Sharp relinquished his command and retired from active duty.

See also PACOM (PACIFIC COMMAND).

Suggestions for further reading: *Strategy for Defeat*, by U. S. Grant Sharp, (Novato, Calif.: Presidio Press, 1978).

SHINING BRASS

Shining Brass was the code name given to U.S. Army Special Forces cross-border reconnaissance missions and raids into Laos under the MACV-SOG (U.S. Military Assistance Command Vietnam-Studies and Observation Group). Shining Brass started sending teams into Laos in the fall of 1965, and it was renamed Prairie Fire in 1968 and Phu Dung (pronounced "Foo Young") in the spring of 1971. The Army Special Forces also entered Laos on these missions from Thailand, when the weather prevented them from entering from Vietnam.

Suggestions for further reading: *The Green Berets at War*, by Shelby L. Stanton (Novato, Calif.: Presidio Press, 1985).

SIHANOUK, NORODOM (1922–)

Born on October 31, 1922 into the royal family of Cambodia, Prince Sihanouk was educated in French schools in Indochina and in Paris before being elected by the Royal Council to the Cambodian throne in 1941. When Japan occupied Indochina during World War II, Sihanouk was kept a virtual prisoner. After the post-World War II

French reoccupation, Sihanouk proclaimed a limited monarchy and elections in 1947 made him head of state. Two years later Cambodia became one of the three "associated states" of Indochina, and at the Geneva Conference in 1954 it won total independence.

When war broke out in Vietnam in 1959, Sihanouk bent with the wind. In 1956 he announced Cambodia would follow a neutralist policy. When it appeared the North Vietnamese would be victorious, he allowed them to use the port of Sihanoukville (Kompong Som) to bring in war supplies and to rent Cambodian trucks to haul the supplies to their base areas along the Vietnamese border. By the late 1960s when North Vietnam appeared to be losing, he intimated that he would not object if these base areas were attacked.

In March 1969 the secret bombing of Cambodia began. In reaction the North Vietnamese began supplying the poorly armed Cambodian Communist Party—the Khmer Rouge. While Sihanouk was traveling abroad, unrest within the country subsequently led to a seizure of power by Cambodian General Lon Nol on March 18, 1970.

Sihanouk has lived in China and North Korea and now works for Cambodian independence from North Vietnamese control.

See also CAMBODIA.

Suggestions for further reading: *Without Honor: Defeat in Vietnam and Cambodia*, by Arnold R. Isaacs (Baltimore: Johns Hopkins Press, 1983); *Vietnam: A History*, by Stanley Karnow (New York: Viking, 1983).

SILVER STAR MEDAL

First authorized in World War I, the Silver Star Medal, America's third highest award for bravery, is awarded in the name of the President of the United States for gallantry in action against the enemy. The required gallantry, while of a lesser degree than that required for the award of the Medal of Honor or the Distinguished Service Cross, Navy Cross or Air Force Cross, nevertheless has to have been performed with marked distinction. Subsequent awards are denoted by an oak leaf (a star for the Navy and Marine Corps) worn on the ribbon.

SKYCRANE

The CH-54 Skycrane helicopter was capable of lifting and transporting heavy equipment of up to ten tons in weight. This large helicopter was unusual because it had no cargo compartment. The Army Skycrane used a hoist mechanism to lift its cargo, which it sling-loaded from beneath the aircraft.

SOG (STUDIES AND OBSERVATION GROUP)

The MACV-SOG (U.S. Military Assistance Command Vietnam–Studies and Observation Group) was a joint service (U.S. Army-Navy-Air Force-Marine Corps) unconventional warfare task force engaged in highly secret operations throughout Southeast Asia.

The task force had about 2,000 U.S. personnel assigned. They included Special Forces-qualified Army personnel, Air Force 90th Special Operations Wing personnel, Navy SEAL personnel and

The Silver Star.

A CH-54 Skycrane hauling a section of a small bridge. (Courtesy Army News Features.)

Marine Corps force recon personnel. There were three control headquarters: Command and Control Central at Kontum in northern II Corps, Command and Control North at Da Nang in I Corps and Command and Control South at Ban Me Thuot in southern II Corps.

Suggestions for further reading: further details can be found in Shelby L. Stanton's *Vietnam Order of Battle* (Washington, D.C.: U.S. News & World Report Books, 1981) and *Green Berets at War* (Novato, Calif.: Presidio Press, 1985). For a fictionalized account of a SOG-type operation, see *Springer,* by Ward Just (Boston: Little, Brown, 1974).

SON TAY RAID

On November 21, 1970 a joint U.S. Army-Air Force raid was conducted on the Son Tay prison compound 20 miles northwest of Hanoi to rescue American prisoners of war (POWs) believed held there. Following the plans of Air Force Brigadier General Leroy J. Manner and Army Colonel Arthur D. Simons, the raiders flew some 400 miles from bases in Thailand in HH-53 "Jolly Green Giant" helicopters, with A-1E Skyraiders and specially equipped C-130 Es in support. While Air Force and Navy fighter-bombers launched diversionary air strikes nearby, the raiders landed, only to find the POWs had been moved to another location. The raiders killed some 25 North Vietnamese Army defenders, then returned to safety.

Suggestions for further reading: *The Raid,* by Benjamin Schemmer (New York: Harper & Row, 1976).

SORTIES

In military aviation terms, a sortie is one trip for cargo planes and helicopters or one attack by a single military aircraft for attack helicopters, fighters, fighter-bombers, gunships and strategic bombers. Thus 10 sorties could be 10 aircraft making one trip or one aircraft shuttling back and forth from its home base making 10 trips, or any combination equaling 10.

SOUTHEAST ASIA RESOLUTION

See TONKIN GULF RESOLUTION.

SOUTHEAST ASIA TREATY ORGANIZATION

See SEATO.

SOUTH VIETNAM

See PART I, THE SETTING.

SOUTH VIETNAM CIVIL ACTIONS MEDAL UNIT CITATION BADGE

The Civil Actions Medal was awarded by the South Vietnamese (Republic of Vietnam) government to U.S. individuals and to U.S. units for meritorious service. As a unit award, it can be worn by personnel assigned to the unit at the time of the award.

SOUTH VIETNAMESE ARMED FORCES

See SVNAF (SOUTH VIETNAMESE ARMED FORCES).

SOUTH VIETNAMESE NATIONAL POLICE

See NATIONAL POLICE, SOUTH VIETNAMESE.

SOUTH VIETNAM GALLANTRY CROSS UNIT CITATION BADGE

The Unit citation of the Gallantry Cross was

awarded by the South Vietnamese (Republic of Vietnam) government for valorous combat achievement. It was awarded in four degrees, as follows: (1) with Palm—to a unit which is cited before the armed forces; (2) with Gold Star—to a unit which is cited before a corps; (3) with Silver Star—to a unit which is cited before a division; and (4) with Bronze Star—to a unit which is cited before a regiment/brigade.

These emblems can be worn permanently by those personnel assigned to the unit at the time of the award.

SOVIET UNION

The Soviet Union is the only major power that could claim to be the strategic winner of the Vietnam war. An early supporter of the North Vietnamese, it was the major supplier of their hardware for the war. For example, the North Vietnamese fired almost 10,000 SA-2 SAMs (surface-to-air missiles) at U.S. aircraft from 1965 to 1972, and each of those 2½ ton missiles was supplied by the Soviet Union. The same was true of the T-54 Soviet medium tanks and the 130-mm field guns, the SA-7 Strela antiaircraft missiles and other sophisticated equipment the North Vietnamese used in abundance in their 1972 and 1975 offensives.

As a result of their wartime assistance to the North Vietnamese, the Soviets now have a naval base at Cam Ranh Bay, which allows them to monitor U.S. naval and air operations in the region and to extend their naval reach from home bases in the Soviet Far East through Southeast Asia to the Indian Ocean and the Persian Gulf.

As recently as 1983 the Soviet combined military and economic aid to Vietnam ran up to $4 million a day; at the same time the Soviets have been able to establish a military presence on China's southern flank and to demonstrate to other parties that the once-remote USSR is now a military force to be reckoned with throughout every corner of Asia.

Suggestions for further reading: *America in Vietnam,* by Guenter Lewy (New York: Oxford University Press, 1978); *White House Years,* by Henry Kissinger (Boston: Little, Brown & Co.,

1979); *Vietnam: A History,* by Stanley Karnow (New York: Viking, 1983); *The Soviet Role in Asia,* by William A. Brown (Washington, D.C.: Current Policy No. 521, U.S. Department of State, October 16, 1983).

SPECIAL FORCES

Drawing their heritage from the U.S.-Canadian First Special Service Force (the "Devil's Brigade") of World War II fame, the Army Special Forces were formed in 1952. Originally, the Special Forces were designed to organize guerrilla bands behind enemy lines and conduct other unconventional warfare operations. President Kennedy, impressed by the Special Forces in 1961, authorized them to wear distinctive green berets. Kennedy was responsible for the development of the Special Forces into a major counterinsurgency force.

The Army Special Forces first appeared in South Vietnam during 1957, and thereafter the First, Fifth and Seventh Special Forces Groups sent an increasing number of temporary-duty teams into the country. Their main task was organizing Montagnards and various paramilitary forces into the CIDG (Civilian Irregular Defense Group) program, but the massive move to establish a chain of fortified camps along the border was not accomplished until the Fifth Special Forces Group arrived for permanent duty in Vietnam during October 1964.

At peak strength the Army Special Forces controlled more than 42,000 CIDG and Regional Force/Popular Force personnel throughout South Vietnam. These were divided into the normal camp CIDG companies and mobile strike forces. During 1966 the Special Forces raised a few mobile guerrilla forces, which were not truly guerrillas but actually mobile strike forces that conducted extended search operations in Viet Cong base areas. The Army Special Forces' primary mission was advising the Vietnamese Special Forces (the Luc Luong Dac Biet, or LLDB), which were technically in charge of CIDG efforts. However, Special Forces also provided some special and strategic reconnaissance units for

MACV-SOG (U.S. Military Assistance Command Vietnam-Studies and Observation Group), MACV and field force commanders.

Although the Fifth Special Forces Group (with five C-detachments, or battalion-sized increments) was the major Special Forces organization in Southeast Asia, it is important to remember that the First Special Forces Group on Okinawa provided teams for Vietnam duty throughout the war, especially before and after the Fifth Special Forces Group served. The Seventh Special Forces Group in the United States also participated. The large 46th Special Forces Company, which contained two C-detachments, in Thailand fielded teams to Vietnam, Laos and Cambodia.

During their stay in Vietnam the Special Forces participated in 12 major campaigns. For bravery on the battlefield one member of the Seventh Special Forces Group earned a Medal of Honor and three won the Distinguished Service Cross; six members of the First Special Forces Group earned the Distinguished Service Cross; eight members of the Fifth Special Forces Group earned the Medal of Honor and 66 won the Distinguished Service Cross; and eight Special Forces personnel with MACV-SOG and other classified components earned the Medal of Honor and 13 the Distinguished Service Cross. The number of Silver Star Medals, Bronze Star Medals and other awards earned by Special Forces personnel has never been completely tabulated, in large measure because of security complications. In addition to these individual awards, Special Forces elements won numerous unit awards.

See also CIDG (CIVILIAN IRREGULAR DEFENSE GROUP), DELTA, FIFTH SPECIAL FORCES, MONTAGNARDS, SOG (STUDIES AND OBSERVATION GROUP).

Suggestions for further reading: *The Green Berets at War*, by Shelby L. Stanton (Novato, Calif.: Presidio Press, 1985); *Vietnam Order of Battle*, by Shelby L. Stanton (Washington, D.C.: US News & World Report Books, 1981), which has the most detailed breakout of Special Forces organization available; *US Army Special Forces 1961–1971*, by Francis J. Kelly (Washington, D.C.: US Government Printing Office, 1973); *Inside the Green Berets: The First Thirty Years*, by Charles M. Simpson, III (Novato, Calif.: Presidio Press, 1983).

SPOCK, BENJAMIN (McLAINE) (1903–)

Born on May 2, 1903 in New Haven, Connecticut, Spock obtained an M.D. from Columbia University. He practiced in New York and in 1946 wrote *The Common Sense Book of Baby and Child Care*, which by 1969 was the all-time best-seller by an American author.

During the Johnson Administration Spock was an ubiquitous figure at antiwar demonstrations. He participated in an April 1967 antiwar march planned by the Spring Mobilization Committee to End the War in Vietnam. Spock, Rev. Martin Luther King, Jr. and entertainer Harry Belafonte led an estimated 300,000 people on a march to the United Nations headquarters in New York City, the largest antiwar demonstration to date. Spock was one of the original signers of *A Call to Resist Illegitimate Authority*, published in September, which supported draft resistance and the refusal by servicemen to obey "illegal and immoral orders." In October he was one of a group that handed over hundreds of draft cards to the Justice Department.

In 1968 Spock, Yale University Chaplain William Sloane Coffin, Jr. and two others were convicted of counseling resistance to and evasion of the draft, but the convictions were overturned the following year. In November 1969 he joined a Washington, D.C. antiwar demonstration of more than 250,000 people, sponsored by the New Mobilization Committee, which Spock and others had created on July 4. Speaking for the group after the "incursion" into Cambodia in May 1970, Spock told a news conference that "the government is committing titanic violence in Vietnam and Cambodia." He was arrested May 3 during a rally near the White House sponsored by the Fellowship of Reconciliation and other religious groups. Nevertheless, he continued undaunted in his antiwar activities, often cooperating with radical groups whose views on personal morality and social and economic reform were far more extreme than his. Spock was among some 7,000 demonstrators arrested in May 1971 during an antiwar protest in Washington aimed at closing down the capital by means of traffic obstructions.

On November 27, a new left-wing antiwar movement, the People's Party, nominated Spock as its candidate for President in the 1972 presidential elections.

See also ANTIWAR MOVEMENT.

Suggestions for further reading: *Doctor Spock: Biography of a Conservative Radical* by Lynn Z. Bloom: Bobbs, (Indianapolis and New York 1972).

SPOOKY

See GUNSHIPS.

SPRING OFFENSIVE

See EASTERTIDE OFFENSIVE.

SQUAD

In the U.S. Army and Marine Corps—as in most other military organizations—a squad is the basic fighting element. Normally part of a platoon, a squad is commanded by a sergeant and usually consists of two fire teams of four men each. In an armor unit, the tank and its crew and, in an artillery unit, the howitzer or gun and its crew are the equivalent of a squad.

See also ORGANIZATION FOR COMBAT.

SQUADRON

In the U.S. Army, a squadron is the title used to designate a battalion-sized unit of cavalry. Commanded by a lieutenant colonel, it normally consists of three or more troops. Some squadrons are an integral part of an infantry division; others are independent. The strength of an independent squadron is approximately 1,000 officers and men; approximately 800 officers and men are assigned to a divisional squadron.

In the U.S. Air Force and in Naval and Marine air units, a squadron is a basic organizational element. Commanded by a lieutenant colonel (commander in the Navy), it consists of several

flights of approximately five aircraft each.

See also FLIGHT, WING.

SRV (SOCIALIST REPUBLIC OF VIETNAM)

The Socialist Republic of Vietnam (SRV) was formed on July 2, 1976 combining what had been the Democratic Republic of Vietnam (North Vietnam) and the Republic of Vietnam (South Vietnam). With its capital in Hanoi, it had a population in mid-1983 estimated at 57,610,000 and it covered an area of 127,330 square miles (larger than Virginia, North Carolina and South Carolina combined).

After reunification, the provinces were realigned (*see* illustration) and elections were held in April 1981 for a new National Assembly. Actual power, however, still resides in the Politburo of the Vietnamese Communist Party. Few, if any, members of the Southern Viet Cong exert much influence on government policy, which is dominated by northerners.

The SRV continues to maintain one of the largest military establishments in the world. Its 1 million-man army is organized into 16 corps, one armored division, 56 infantry divisions and 10 marine brigades; three divisions are stationed in Laos and 12 divisions are stationed in Cambodia. Arms and equipment include 2,500 light and medium tanks, more than 900 artillery guns and howitzers and other modern equipment. Its navy includes six frigates and about 1,300 other vessels. Its 15,000-man air force has 290 combat aircraft and 40 armed helicopters.

The SRV continues to hold an admitted 10,000 political prisoners in gulags and maintains repressive controls on what was South Vietnam. It wages a continuing war with Khmer Rouge insurgents in Vietnamese-occupied Cambodia and has sporadic armed border disputes with China.

Suggestions for further reading: *Background Notes: Vietnam* (Washington, D.C.: Bureau of Public Affairs, Department of State/U.S. Government Printing Office, May 1984); *The Military Balance 1984-1985* (London: International Institute for Strategic Studies, September 1984).

NORTH VIETNAM

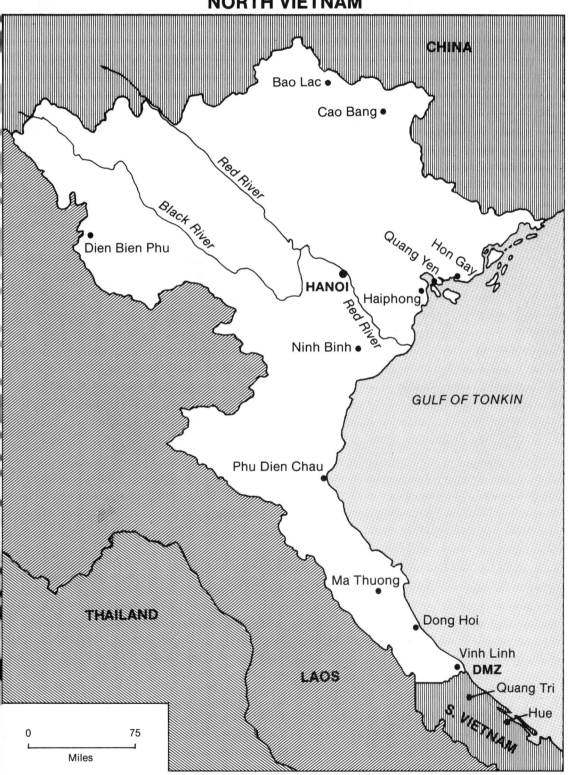

STATE DEPARTMENT

During the war in Vietnam the U.S. Department of State and its subordinate agencies—the U.S. Information Agency (USIA) and the U.S. Agency for International Development (USAID)—played a significant role. Not only did they maintain an embassy in Saigon and counselor offices in Bien Hoa, Can Tho and Nha Trang, they also helped staff the CORDS (Civil Operations and Revolutionary Development Support) program down to the province and district level.

During the war in Vietnam 36 State Department Foreign Service officers lost their lives, as did 37 members of the Agency for International Development.

See also CORDS (CIVIL OPERATIONS AND REVOLUTIONARY DEVELOPMENT SUPPORT), SECRETARY OF STATE.

STEEL TIGER

A complement to the Rolling Thunder air campaign to interdict the North Vietnamese transportation system and infiltration routes into South Vietnam, Operation Steel Tiger was the designation for U.S. air operations over the northern portion of the Laotian panhandle south to Route 9 west of the DMZ aimed at interdicting the Ho Chi Minh Trail. Beginning on April 3, 1965 the operation involved Navy aircraft from carriers in the South China Sea, Marine and Air Force aircraft from bases in South Vietnam and Thailand and eventually B-52 strategic bombers. The most effective aircraft, however, were fixed-wing gunships, such as the AC-47, AC-119 and AC-130. In 1968 this campaign was extended to cover the entire Ho Chi Minh Trail.

See also COMMANDO HUNT, GUNSHIPS, HO CHI MINH TRAIL, LAOS, TIGER HOUND.

Suggestions for further reading: *Airpower in Three Wars,* by William W. Momyer (Washington, D.C.: U.S. Government Printing Office, 1978); *The United States Air Force in Southeast Asia,* edited by Carl Berger (Washington, D.C.: U.S. Government Printing Office, 1977); *Thunder from Above,* by John Morrocco (Boston: Boston Publishing Co.,

1984); *Battles and Campaigns in Vietnam,* by Tom Carhart (New York: Crown Publishers, 1984).

STENNIS, JOHN C(ORNELIUS) (1901-)

Born on August 3, 1901 in Kemper County, Mississippi, Stennis graduated from Mississippi State College in 1923 and received a law degree from the University of Virginia in 1928. He became a circuit judge in 1937 and 10 years later succeeded Theodore Bilbo in the U.S. Senate.

In domestic affairs, Stennis was a conservative Democrat who opposed most social welfare programs and supported military appropriations requests. Wary of foreign entanglements, he was skeptical about the propriety of U.S. involvement in Southeast Asia. Nevertheless he felt that once the United States had committed itself, it could not shrink from that commitment, and he supported the Johnson Administration's war effort in Vietnam. In early 1966 he said, "Great Society programs should be relegated to the rear . . . secondary to the war," and he favored attacking the enemy as often as necessary to avoid a long bloody war of 10 to 15 years. An influential member of the Armed Services Committee who became its Chairman in 1969, Stennis favored maximum use of air power against the North Vietnamese and the Viet Cong to achieve a prompt victory and he believed that direction of the war effort should be left to the military.

Despite his support for the war, Stennis was concerned that it was rapidly draining the armed forces' stock of supplies, and he expressed the fear that the Vietnam war might establish a precedent for U.S. entry into future conflicts without congressional approval. Consequently, although he strongly backed President Nixon's Southeast Asia policy, Stennis worked to curb the President's war-making power. In 1971 he introduced a resolution that would have curbed the power of the President to commit the nation to war without the consent of Congress. With Senator Jacob Javits he was a co-sponsor of the War Powers Act.

See also WAR POWERS ACT.

STRATEGIC AIR COMMAND

The Strategic Air Command (SAC), the U.S. manned bomber and land-based missile nuclear strike force, is a specified command reporting directly to the Secretary of Defense. Thus before SAC B-52 strategic bombers could be used in Vietnam, approval had to be obtained from Washington. At times, approval was retained by the White House, and even though approval was later delegated to lower levels, the final authority was always in Washington.

SAC had earlier deployed the Third Air Division to Guam as a control headquarters. As B-52 activity increased, the Third Air Division was replaced by the Eighth Air Force in July 1970 and provisional air division headquarters were formed on Guam and in Thailand.

When B-52 strikes in South Vietnam began on June 18, 1965, all originally were flown by the 4133rd Bombardment Wing based on Guam. In April 1967 the 4258th Strategic Wing (later designated the 307th Strategic Wing) began flying missions from its base at U-Tapao, Thailand and in February 1968 the 4242nd Strategic Wing at Kadena Air Base on Okinawa was also committed.

Insignia of the Strategic Air Command.

SAC air operations over Vietnam ended on January 23, 1973, over Laos on April 17, 1973 and over Cambodia on August 15, 1973. From June 1965 to August 1973 SAC flew 126,615 B-52 sorties, 55 percent of them against targets in South Vietnam, 27 percent against targets in Laos, 12 percent against targets in Cambodia and 6 percent against targets in North Vietnam. In these actions, 29 B-52 bombers were lost, 17 to hostile action.

See also ARC LIGHT, BARREL ROLL, BOMBER AIRCRAFT, LINEBACKER OPERATIONS, MENU OPERATION, STEEL TIGER.

Suggestions for further reading: *The United States Air Force in Southeast Asia 1961–1973*, edited by Carl Berger (Washington, D.C.: U.S. Government Printing Office, 1977).

STRATEGIC DEFENSIVE

Warfare is conducted simultaneously on two broad levels—strategic and tactical. The *strategic* level refers to what you are trying to accomplish through the use of force. The *tactical* concerns how you do it.

In strategic defense the objective is to resist enemy aggression and repel attack, and thus it is a negative form of war. While it can lead to stalemate on the battlefield, it cannot be decisive in and of itself. The end result sought must be accomplished by other means, such as diplomatic or economic pressure. The strategic defensive is not necessarily passive, for at the tactical level offensive action, such as counterattacks, may be taken to destroy or disrupt enemy forces.

In the Korean war and in the Vietnam war, the national policy of containment of communist aggression, rather than rollback or liberation, dictated that the United States pursue a military *defensive* strategy. In both cases the battlefield was eventually stalemated and in both cases the final decision—the 1953 Korean Armistice and the 1973 Paris Accords—were achieved through diplomatic action.

In both wars U.S. national policy also tended to dictate the strategy of America's allies. Both

South Korea and South Vietnam were denied the military capability to attack north.

See also STRATEGIC OFFENSIVE.

Suggestions for further reading: *On Strategy: A Critical Analysis of the Vietnam War*, by Harry G. Summers, Jr. (Novato, Calif.: Presidio Press, 1982).

STRATEGIC HAMLETS

An outgrowth of an earlier *South Vietnamese agroville* program in 1959 to gather people in areas threatened by guerrilla attack into centralized locations, the strategic hamlet program was announced as national policy by South Vietnamese President Ngo Dinh Diem in March 1962.

Based on the British counterinsurgency program in Malaya, the concept was to turn each Vietnamese hamlet into a defense fortification. Although much time and money was put into the program, it had several basic weaknesses. First was the animosity of farmers forcibly displaced from their land. Second was the inadequacy of physical security, for by massing their forces, the Viet Cong were able to defeat the hamlets one at a time. Finally there was the mismanagement of the program by the Saigon government.

After the assassination of the program's sponsor and chief supporter, President Ngo Dinh Diem, in November 1963, the program fell into disfavor and was finally abandoned.

See also LAND REFORM; HILSMAN, ROGER; PACIFICATION; THOMPSON, ROBERT.

Suggestions for further reading: *Territorial Forces*, by Ngo Quang Truong (Washington, D.C.: Center of Military History, 1981); *Fire in the Lake: The Vietnamese and the Americans in Vietnam*, by Frances FitzGerald (Boston: Little, Brown, 1972); *Vietnam: A History*, by Stanley Karnow (New York: Viking, 1983); *Pacification*, by Tran Dinh Tho (Washington, D.C.: Center of Military History, 1980); *A Viet Cong Memoir*, by Truong Nhu Tang (New York: Harcourt Brace Jovanovich, 1985).

A strategic hamlet in Phu Bon Province, South Vietnam. (Courtesy Shelby L. Stanton.)

STRATEGIC OFFENSIVE

The strategic offensive aims to take the fight to the enemy, destroy his armed forces, seize his capital, occupy his territory and break his will to resist. It is a positive form of war since it forces the enemy to react, and it can produce decisive results, though on the strategic offensive, it may be necessary at times to assume the tactical defensive to rest, regroup or wait for a better time.

During the Vietnam war, the North Vietnamese Army was on the strategic offensive. Beginning in 1959 it focused single-mindedly on its ultimate objective—the conquest of South Vietnam. Although U.S. and South Vietnamese Army military actions several times temporarily forced it to assume a tactical defensive posture, the North Vietnamese Army went back on the tactical offensive at the first opportunity.

In the spring of 1975, with U.S. forces withdrawn, U.S. aid curtailed and U.S. will evaporated, the North Vietnamese launched a cross-border blitzkrieg to destroy the South Vietnamese Army, seize Saigon, occupy South Vietnam and break the South Vietnamese will to resist.

See also STRATEGIC DEFENSIVE.

Suggestions for further reading: *On Strategy: A Critical Analysis of the Vietnam War,* by Harry G. Summers, Jr. (Novato, Calif.: Presidio Press, 1982).

STRATEGY

Strategy is the use of means to achieve ends. It thus has three discreet elements. First is the determination of the end result. Among nation states this result is always a political object, that is, wresting something of value from the enemy or causing the enemy to desist in his efforts to wrest something from oneself. The destruction of an enemy's armed forces, for example, is of value only if it breaks the enemy's will to resist or his will to persist in his aggressive action. Thus in disputes among nations, there is no such thing as a "military solution," for military objectives are selected only for their value in influencing (or, as

in the case in World War II, destroying) the enemy's will.

Military forces are only one of the several means for achieving that end result. Their use to attain battlefield victories are best described as "tactics," not "strategies," for battlefield victories only have meaning if they assist in attaining a desired political end. Other means include diplomatic efforts, economic pressures and such psychological efforts as the influencing of public opinion.

The third element is the essence of strategy. It involves the very complex and difficult art of determining precisely how these various means can be used to accomplish the desired ends. It is impossible to comprehend the Vietnam war without a basic understanding of this concept.

See also STRATEGY, NORTH VIETNAMESE; STRATEGY, U.S.

Suggestions for further reading: *On War,* by Carl von Clausewitz, edited and translated by Michael Howard and Peter Paret (Princeton University Press, 1976); *On Strategy: A Critical Analysis of the Vietnam War,* by Harry G. Summers, Jr. (Novato, Calif.: Presidio Press, 1982).

STRATEGY, NORTH VIETNAMESE

North Vietnamese strategy during the Vietnam war was both simple and effective. Their ultimate aim—the conquest of South Vietnam and the imposition of their political will over the entire country—was kept constantly in view, and throughout the war they never wavered from those political aims despite the enormous costs these objectives entailed.

The means used included both the forces of their regular army as well as the forces of the Viet Cong guerrillas in the south. According to Douglas Pike, Director of the East Asia Institute, University of California at Berkeley, North Vietnam's overall strategy of *dau tranh* ("struggle movement") consisted of two elements—*dau tranh vu trang* ("armed struggle") and *dau tranh chinh tri* ("political struggle")—used in concert to achieve its overall objectives (*see* ARMED STRUGGLE and POLITICAL STRUGGLE).

Pike divides the war into four historical periods. The first was the revolutionary guerrilla war period, which began at the start of the Vietnam war in 1959 with the North Vietnamese decision to conquer South Vietnam by force and continued until February 1965, when the United States made the decision to intervene in the war with ground and air power. During this period the primary effort was "political struggle" by the Viet Cong guerrillas and their North Vietnamese cadres. It was so successful in undermining the South Vietnamese government that the United States was forced either to intervene or see its South Vietnamese ally go down in defeat.

With the American intervention in 1965, North Vietnamese strategy shifted to "armed struggle" and the decision was made to confront American military power head-on. In military terms this was a disastrous mistake, for the North Vietnamese and Viet Cong were defeated at every turn. This phase of the war terminated with the Tet Offensive of 1968, which, although a military debacle for the North Vietnamese, had an ultimately decisive effect on American will to persist in the war.

The third phase of the war, from July 1968 to April 1972, again placed major reliance on "political struggle," but now a "political struggle" was waged largely by North Vietnamese cadres rather than by the Viet Cong, who had been decimated during the 1968 Tet Offensive. This phase terminated with a return to "armed struggle" during the Eastertide Offensive of 1972, another debacle for the North Vietnamese Army.

From April 1972, and especially after the "peace treaty" in January 1973, the emphasis was again on "political struggle." This final phase terminated unexpectedly for the North Vietnamese in the spring of 1975 when their limited return to "armed struggle" had unanticipated successes, leading to their decision to launch a multidivisional, crossborder blitzkrieg that overwhelmed the South Vietnamese Army and led to the collapse of South Vietnam.

The interrelationship of "armed struggle" and "political struggle" (or in Western terms, the coordinated application of diplomatic, economic and, especially, psychological power along with military power) was dramatically illustrated by

this North Vietnamese strategy. Their decision to confront American military power head-on had disastrous battlefield effects, for from 1965 until 1972, the North Vietnamese and Viet Cong were defeated in every major military battle. Yet their "political struggle" during this same period, especially their "actions among the enemy"—involving the manipulation of public perceptions in the United States—was strategically decisive in undermining the American will to persist in the war. With the United States thus removed from active combat, the North Vietnamese then concentrated their efforts on "armed struggle" to strike the decisive blow against South Vietnam.

See also STRATEGY, U.S.; VIET CONG.

Suggestions for further reading: *History of the Vietnamese Communist Party*, by Douglas Pike (Stanford: Hoover Institute, 1978); *On Strategy: A Critical Analysis of the Vietnam War*, by Harry G. Summers, Jr. (Novato, Calif.: Presidio Press, 1982).

STRATEGY, U.S.

For American armed forces, military strategy is defined as "the art and science of employing the armed forces of a nation to secure the objectives of national policy by the application of force, or the threat of force." By this textbook definition, the U.S. military strategy in Vietnam was a failure because its strategic decision makers, civilian and military alike, came up with the wrong answer to what master military theoretician Karl von Clausewitz called "the first of all strategic questions and the most comprehensive." Establishing "the kind of war on which they are embarking; neither mistaking it for, nor trying to turn it into something that is alien to its nature," he wrote, "is the first, the supreme, the most far-reaching act of judgment that the statesman and commander have to make."

It is not surprising that this maxim was overlooked, since American strategies for Vietnam were not based on classic theories and doctrines of war, which many believed antiquated and irrelevant in the nuclear age. Rather, they were based on post-World War II academic limited-war theories that viewed military operations as diplomatic signaling rather than war-fighting devices and on the new and fashionable doctrines of counterinsurgency. These theories and doctrines became the frame of reference for the American conduct of the war, and, in so doing, served as a kind of Procrustean bed.

The effect was a failure to distinguish the First Indochina War between France and Vietnam from the Second Indochina War between North Vietnam and South Vietnam. This, in turn, led to a further failure to distinguish between the military actions appropriate for a colonial power like France in Indochina or Great Britain in Malaysia and the actions appropriate to the United States, a coalition partner in support of an ally (South Vietnam) faced with both an internal insurgency and an external threat. The result was overinvolvement in South Vietnamese internal affairs and failure to develop military strategies to implement the national policy of containment of communist expansion—specifically the containment of North Vietnamese expansion into South Vietnam by force of arms.

Ironically, in view of the way the war in Vietnam ultimately ended—i.e., through the 1975 North Vietnamese Army cross-border multidivisional blitzkrieg—initial American military strategies for Vietnam were designed to prevent just such an eventuality. In the period from 1954 to 1960, U.S. military assistance concentrated on preparing the South Vietnamese Army for a conventional delaying action against what was regarded as the most serious threat: a conventional, Korean-style North Vietnamese Army attack across the DMZ. The U.S. response to such an attack would include the early seizure of air and port facilities and the phased deployment of American ground combat units, first to block the North Vietnamese invasion and then to launch a joint airborne, amphibious and ground counterattack into North Vietnam to reunify Vietnam under South Vietnamese leadership.

All this came to an end in 1961, when counterinsurgency, not counterattack, became the watchword. This strategic doctrine had the support of the newly elected President, John F. Kennedy, who saw it as the counter to Soviet "wars of national liberation." The President sent a letter to the Army, directing compliance with this new doctrine; the Army Chief of Staff, Gen. George Decker (who had resisted the emphasis on guerrilla war), was replaced; and it was made known that "promotions of high-ranking officers would depend on their demonstration of experience in the counter-guerrilla or sublimited war theory." In August 1962 the National Security Council directed that plans of action be drawn up "consistent with the doctrine of counterinsurgency." In accordance with these plans, U.S. military assistance to Vietnam shifted from the external enemy to counterinsurgency, and from 335 U.S. military advisers in 1954, adviser strength grew to about 3,150 by April 1962. This emphasis continued under President Johnson, and in 1964 the MACV (U.S. Military Assistance Command Vietnam) adopted a series of terms to describe the basic missions performed by the Vietnamese military forces in support of this counterinsurgency effort. These ranged in intensity from "search-and-destroy operations," designed to find, fix, fight and destroy enemy forces, to "clearing operations," designed to drive large enemy forces out of populated areas, to "security operations," designed to protect pacification teams. The frame of reference that was to continue throughout the war had been set.

It was this frame of reference, as well as the faulty notions of the limited-war theorists, that shaped the United States' response after the reports of North Vietnamese attacks on two U.S. destroyers in the Gulf of Tonkin in August 1964. At first it was hoped that North Vietnamese aggression could be halted by selective application of U.S. air power against North Vietnam—the Rolling Thunder campaign—to "signal" U.S. resolve. Instead of being deterred, however, the North Vietnamese intensified the war to the point where by 1965 it appeared that the South Vietnamese would not able to hold without the assistance of U.S. forces. Instead of a massive commitment of U.S. combat power to overwhelm the enemy, American forces were committed piecemeal in what was dubbed "the strategy of slow-squeeze." As General Maxwell Taylor put it, the United States was not trying to "defeat" North Vietnam, only "to cause them to mend their ways." Initially U.S. ground combat forces were committed to protect air bases and supply facilities, but when this did not prove sufficient, the American forces were committed to direct combat. Their mission was spelled out in the MACV (U.S. Military Assistance Command Vietnam) campaign plan, which consisted of three phases:

Phase One: Commit those American and allied forces necessary "to halt the losing trend" by the end of 1965.

Phase Two: "During the first half of 1966," take the offensive with American and allied forces in "high priority areas" to destroy enemy forces and reinstitute pacification programs.

Phase Three: If the enemy persisted, he might be defeated and his forces and base areas destroyed during a period of a year to a year and a half following Phase Two.

Phase One was essentially accomplished in November 1965, when the U.S. First Cavalry Division (Air Mobile) routed three North Vietnamese regular army regiments that had launched an attack in the Central Highlands in an attempt to cut South Vietnam in two. Their attack should have provided a warning that North Vietnamese regular forces, not the internal insurgents, were the primary threat to South Vietnamese independence. But because of the faulty strategic frame of reference, this fact was not apparent. As U.S. military forces continued to build up in South Vietnam, they were concentrated on counterinsurgency operations and only an economy of force (i.e., the minimum force necessary) was used to contain North Vietnamese infiltration.

The American military was not completely happy with this strategy. In 1965 the Joint Chiefs of Staff had proposed isolating the battlefield by a Korean war-style defensive line across the 17th parallel and through Laos to physically bar North Vietnamese infiltration, and similar plans were proposed by the American field commander, General William C. Westmoreland, in 1967 and again in 1968. Evidently because they did not fit the counterinsurgency framework, such strategic alternatives were consigned to limbo, neither approved nor rejected by the Secretary of Defense or the President.

With the "strategy" of counterinsurgency, a whole set of statistical indicators were devised to measure progress. These included evaluations

based on complex social science criteria and, perhaps most damaging of all, statements of progress in terms of "body count." Although such statistical measurements were in accordance with the economic systems analysis approach to warfare favored by members of the U.S. Defense Department, they ultimately proved counterproductive. A decade after the end of U.S. combat involvement, controversy continues over these statistical indicators. Even at the time, the grisly measurement of "success" in terms of people killed inflamed U.S. public opinion and undercut support for the war. This support was further undercut by the very nature of search-and-destroy operations, which were perceived by the American public as deliberately laying waste to civilian property and the land.

Thus already weakened, American public support was irretrievably undermined by the Viet Cong Tet Offensive of 1968. This massive attack on the major cities of South Vietnam came as a shock both to the American people and to their political leadership. It led to President Johnson's decision not to stand for reelection, an end to the further commitment of U.S. military power and increasing congressional restrictions on U.S. combat operations. This was especially ironic, for as former Viet Cong leaders themselves now admit, their cadres were virtually destroyed by the American and South Vietnamese Tet counteroffensive. The Tet Offensive was, in actuality, the death knell of the guerrilla movement. From 1968 until the final collapse in 1975, the war was waged not by Viet Cong guerrillas, but by North Vietnamese regular forces. In his account of how the war was eventually won, the North Vietnamese field commander, General Van Tien Dung, barely mentions the role of guerrilla forces.

Although the U.S. commitment continued under President Nixon for another five years and although it would be seven years until South Vietnam ultimately collapsed, in strategic terms the United States lost the war in the spring of 1968. The Viet Cong Tet Offensive was a *strategic* defeat because it demonstrated conclusively the absence of a coherent U.S. strategy. "No one starts a war," Clausewitz had written 150 years earlier, "or rather no one in his senses ought to do so, without first being clear in his mind what he intends to achieve by that war and how he intends to conduct it." Confused by limited-war theories and doctrines of counterinsurgency, the United States had overlooked this commonsense advice. In his 1974 examination of the cause of the American failure, Brigadier General Douglas Kinnard (now Chief of U.S. Army Military History) found that "almost 70 percent of the Army generals who managed the war were uncertain of its objectives." General Kinnard went on to say that this "mirrors a deep-seated strategic failure: the inability of policymakers to frame tangible, obtainable goals."

General Kinnard's observations were validated by former Secretary of Defense Clark Clifford, who took office in the wake of the Tet Offensive. When he questioned his senior officials, Clifford found to his dismay that none of them could tell him what constituted victory. Even more disheartening, he found that the United States "had no military plan to win the war." Because of the Procrustean logic of counterinsurgency, the United States failed to recognize, until it was too late, that they were embarked on a *war* and not an exercise in social engineering. In retrospect, it is apparent that their defeat was not so much a failure of military strategy as it was a lack of a military strategy worthy of the name.

See also CLIFFORD, CLARK; JOHNSON, LYNDON B.; KENNEDY, JOHN F.; MCNAMARA, ROBERT S.; RUSK, DEAN; STRATEGY, NORTH VIETNAMESE; TAYLOR, MAXWELL D.

Suggestions for further reading: *On Strategy: A Critical Analysis of the Vietnam War,* by Harry G. Summers, Jr. (Novato, Calif.: Presidio Press, 1982); *The 25-Year War: America's Military Role in Vietnam,* by Bruce Palmer, Jr. (Lexington: University of Kentucky Press, 1984); *The War Managers,* by Douglas Kinnard (Hanover, N.H.: University Press of New England, 1977).

STUDIES AND OBSERVATION GROUP

See SOG (STUDIES AND OBSERVATION GROUP).

SVNAF (SOUTH VIETNAMESE ARMED FORCES)

Formed as the Vietnamese National Army on July 2, 1949, the South Vietnamese armed forces (SVNAF), formally known as the Republic of Vietnam Armed Forces (RVNAF), came into being when South Vietnam, or the Republic of Vietnam (RVN), was established on October 26, 1955. With U.S. military aid and under the guidance of the first MAAG-Vietnam (U.S. Military Assistance Advisory Group Vietnam) and later the MACV (U.S. Military Advisory Group Vietnam), the SVNAF grew into a large and modern fighting force. The SVNAF comprised five components, all under the overall command of the SVNAF Joint General Staff. They included the South Vietnamese Army (ARVN), Air Force (VNAF), Marine Corps (VNMC), Navy (VNN) and irregular homeguards of the Territorial Forces: the so-called Regional Forces (RF) and Popular Forces (PF).

By the time of the U.S. withdrawal in January 1973, the SVNAF had 1.1 million men under arms. The Army consisted of four corps (I, II, III and IV) organized into 12 divisions—the First, Second, Third, Fifth, Seventh, Ninth, 18th, 21st, 22nd, 23rd, 25th and Airborne Division—and other nondivisional units, for a total of 105 battalions of light infantry, nine airborne infantry battalions, 21 ranger battalions and 33 border defense battalions. Artillery included 44 battalions of 105-mm and 15 of 155-mm howitzers, four 175-mm gun battalions, four air defense artillery battalions and 176 separate 105-mm howitzer sections with the Regional and Popular Forces. Armored cavalry included 11 divisional cavalry squadrons, seven separate cavalry squadrons and three tank battalions, with M-48 tanks. In addition to these regular units in the irregular home guard, there were 1,810 Regional Force companies and 8,186 Popular Force platoons in the Territorial Forces.

The Air Force in 1973 consisted of 16 squadrons of propeller-driven A1 fighter-bombers, F-5 jet fighters and A-37 jet fighter-bombers, 17 squadrons of UH-1 Huey helicopters, four CH-47 Chinook squadrons, three transport squadrons of C-7 Caribous and two of C-130 Hercules, plus 13 reconnaissance, liaison and special mission squadrons. With over 2,000 aircraft it was the fourth largest air force in the world.

The Navy had grown to a force of 42,000 personnel with 1,500 ships and craft, including submarine chasers, former U.S. Coast Guard cutters, swift boats, picket boats, minesweepers, small oilers and the like.

After April 1965 a separate service, the South Vietnamese Marine Corps (VNMC) was organized into a division, with the 147th, 258th and 369th Marine Brigades and a total of nine Marine battalions.

Territorial Forces—the Regional Forces and Popular Forces—were scattered throughout the entire country. Armed only with light weapons, their mission was local security and they were neither trained nor equipped to hold off a conventional attack by regular forces.

The SVNAF, like the armed forces of all nations, had capable units as well as units that did not measure up to the stress of combat. The South Vietnamese Army Third Division, for example, was criticized for breaking at the Battle of Quang Tri in 1972, but it was the exception, not the rule. The U.S. 106th Infantry Division (like the South Vietnamese Third Division, never tested in battle) collapsed during the 1944 Battle of the Bulge and two of its regiments surrendered to the enemy, but neither the U.S. Army nor the South Vietnamese Army should be judged by such isolated failures. On the other end of the spectrum, the South Vietnamese Army 18th Division destroyed three North Vietnamese Army (NVA) divisions during the Battle of Xuan Loc in April 1975 before it was finally overwhelmed. South Vietnamese Army forces took three times the number of U.S. casualties every day of the war.

The best analogy to the collapse of the South Vietnamese Army in 1975 is the collapse of the French Army in 1940. The 1940 French Army was also well equipped, and was also undone by corrupt and defeatist political leaders, poor leadership and faulty battlefield tactics designed by its senior military commanders, and by roads so clogged with civilian refugees that it was impossible to maneuver and regroup. Finally, both the French and the South Vietnamese armies were done in by a brilliantly planned and superbly executed blitzkrieg that was well supported by tanks and artillery.

Two hundred twenty thousand three hundred fifty-seven of South Vietnam's soldiers, sailors, airmen and marines were killed in action and 570,600 wounded in action in the defense of their country before the Final Offensive of the North Vietnamese Army even began.

See also ADVISORY GROUP; AIRBORNE FORCES; AN LOC, BATTLE OF; EASTERTIDE OFFENSIVE; FINAL OFFENSIVE; I, II, III, IV CORPS TACTICAL ZONES; JOINT GENERAL STAFF; KONTUM; LAM SON 719; MAAG-VIETNAM; MACV (U.S. MILITARY ASSISTANCE COMMAND VIETNAM); QUANG TRI, BATTLE OF; RANGERS; TERRITORIAL FORCES; XUAN LOC, BATTLE OF.

Suggestions for further reading: For the South Vietnamese Army and Air Force, see *The RVNAF*, Dong Van Khuyen (Washington, D.C.: U.S. Government Printing Office, 1980) and *The United States Air Force in Southeast Asia 1961–1973*, edited by Carl Berger (Washington, D.C.: U.S. Government Printing Office, 1977); for the South Vietnamese Navy, see *A Short History of the United States Navy and the Southeast Asian Conflict 1956–1975*, by Edward J. Marolda and G. Wesley Pryce, III (Washington, D.C.: U.S. Naval Historical Center, 1984); for Regional Forces and Popular Forces, see *Territorial Forces*, by Ngo Quang Truong (Washington, D.C.: U.S. Government Printing Office, 1981); for final collapse, see *Vietnam from Ceasefire to Capitulation* by William E. LeGro (Washington, D.C.: U.S. Government Printing Office, 1981); *Reflections of the Vietnam War*, by Cao Van Vien and Dong Van Khuyen (Washington, D.C.: U.S. Government Printing Office, 1980); *The Final Collapse*, by Cao Van Vien (Washington, D.C.: U.S. Government Printing Office, 1983); *Our Endless War*, by Tran Van Don (Novato, Calif.: Presidio Press, 1978); *The Vietnamese Air Force, 1951–1975: An Analysis of its Role in Combat*, by William W. Momyer, edited by Charles McDonald and A. J. C. Lavelle (Washington, D.C.: U.S. Government Printing Office, 1976).

SYMINGTON, (WILLIAM) STUART (1901–   )

Born on June 26, 1901 in Amherst, Massachusetts, Symington attended Yale University after serving in World War I.

During the Truman Administration, Symington held important posts in federal agencies and from 1946 to 1950 served as Secretary of the Air Force. A Democrat, he was elected to the Senate in 1952. He continually fought for higher defense spending, particularly for the Air Force.

Although he had initially supported the war in Vietnam, Symington spoke out against U.S. involvement in that country in 1967. His change in position was influenced both by his experience on the Senate Foreign Relations Committee, to which he had been assigned in 1961, and by his sympathy for the Air Force and its personnel. Viewing Vietnam in terms of America's global commitments, Symington became convinced that the war was not vital for U.S. security and that the cost of the war effort was endangering the American economy.

As a result of several trips to Vietnam, he had also learned of the growing discontent among American pilots who felt constricted by the Johnson Administration's target limits and believed that the government was willing to sacrifice American lives to prevent North Vietnamese civilian casualties. Symington maintained that if pilots were going to be forced to fight a limited war, it would be better to pull out of Vietnam than to sacrifice their lives. In October 1967 he therefore urged a unilateral cease-fire aimed at initiating peace negotiations. His position on both the Foreign Relations Committee and the Armed Services Committee made him a powerful advocate of de-escalation and withdrawal in Congress.

During the Nixon Administration, Symington spoke out against the extension of the Vietnam war into Cambodia and Laos, supporting the Cooper-Church and McGovern-Hatfield Amendments. In March 1975 Symington opposed military aid to the faltering Cambodian government of Lon Nol while supporting additional food and medical help for the Cambodians.

In 1976 Symington chose not to seek reelection. *See also* ANTIWAR MOVEMENT.

TACTICAL AIR COMMAND

Unlike the U.S. Air Force's Military Airlift Command and Strategic Air Command, the Tactical Air Command (TAC) does not keep its units and aircraft under its own operational control but places them under the operating control of the command actually fighting the war.

In the Vietnam war TAC units were placed under the operational control of CINCPAC (Commander-in-Chief of the Pacific Command), who further placed them under control of the PACAF (Pacific Air Forces) and the MACV (U.S. Military Assistance Command Vietnam). Under the PACAF were such units as the 13th Air Force in the Philippines and the 315th Air Division at Tachikawa, Japan, which controlled several C-130 Hercules airlift wings. Under the MACV was the Seventh Air Force, including the 834th Air Division, which controlled several C-123 Provider and C-7 Caribou airlift wings, and some six TAC fighter wings plus reconnaissance and other TAC units.

See also FIGHTERS AND FIGHTER-BOMBERS, SEVENTH AIR FORCE, TACTICAL AIRLIFT.

Suggestions for further reading: *The United States Air Force in Southeast Asia 1961–1973,* edited by Carl Berger (Washington, D.C.: U.S. Government Printing Office, 1977).

TACTICAL AIRLIFT

Tactical airlift during the Vietnam war began

early with C-47 "Gooney Bird" twin-propeller aircraft. These and other World War II- and Korean war-vintage planes were gradually replaced by C-123 twin-propeller Provider aircraft and by the larger four-engine C-130 Hercules transports. The C-123 and C-130, together with the C-7 Caribou, became the tactical airlift backbone.

These fixed-wing transports lifted multibattalion task forces to forward airheads and resupplied them with fuel, ammunition and other necessities. They not only brought units into combat, but on several occasions they also brought them out under enemy fire. Casualty evacuation within Vietnam was another tactical airlift responsibility, as was air dropping of supplies to isolated units where airstrips were not available.

Between 1962 and 1973 Air Force tactical airlift delivered more than 7 million tons of passengers and cargo (compared with 750,000 tons in the Korean war). Often operating under enemy fire, 53 C-130s, 53 C-123s (including one defoliant sprayer) and 20 C-7s were lost. Sixty of these losses were caused by enemy action, the rest by mechanical and other operational causes. Among other awards received by airlifters, the Medal of Honor for conspicuous bravery in Vietnam was awarded to a C-123 pilot.

See also CARIBOU AIRCRAFT, 834TH AIR DIVISION, MILITARY AIRLIFT COMMAND, SEVENTH AIR FORCE.

Suggestions for further reading: *The U.S. Air Force in Southeast Asia 1961–1973*, edited by Carl Berger (Washington, D.C.: U.S. Government Printing Office, 1977); *The U.S. Air Force in Southeast Asia: Tactical Airlift*, by Ray L. Bowers (Washington, D.C.: U.S. Government Printing Office, 1983).

TACTICS

The favorite Viet Cong and North Vietnamese tactic in Vietnam was *cong don da vien* ("attack the outpost to smash the reinforcements"). With no fixed battle lines, North Vietnamese Army (NVA) and Viet Cong (VC) units would lay siege to an isolated outpost. Then they would prepare ambush positions along the route that reinforcements had to travel. This tactic had worked well for the Viet

Minh in their war against the French (1946–54) and for the NVA and VC against the South Vietnamese Army until 1965. And it was precisely how the Battle of the Ia Drang in November 1965—where U.S. troops first met the NVA in battle—began. But the NVA and VC were to find that American use of helicopters to bypass these ambush sites rendered their tactic ineffective.

A major development in American tactics was this use of helicopters to move troops into battle positions (*see* AIRMOBILE OPERATIONS). Another major change dictated by the nature of the terrain was in the classic infantry use of fire and maneuver. Traditionally, firepower (i.e., artillery and close air support) is used to fix the enemy in position and maneuvering infantry squads and platoons then destroy it by attacks on its flanks and rear. In Vietnam this tactic had to be reversed. Just as the hedgerows did in Normandy in World War II, the jungles of Vietnam limited visibility and provided a major advantage to the defender. Whole units could be in an enemy killing zone without even knowing it and be annihilated in a matter of seconds. To cope with this, there evolved the tactic of finding these enemy forces with infantry and then calling in massive artillery strikes and close air support to destroy them. These tactics included "cloverleafs," in which squads were dispatched in three directions from a central base in order to locate enemy positions, and "checkerboard," in which small units were placed into an area in a checkerboard pattern in order to locate enemy defensive positions.

Suggestions for further reading: *Tactical and Matériel Innovations*, by John H. Hay, Jr., (Washington, D.C.: U.S. Government Printing Office, 1974).

TAIWAN

Although officially not a participant in the war in Vietnam, the Republic of China, or Taiwan, did play an important part in the conflict there. The Republic of China offered to send combat troops to fight in Vietnam, but U.S. sensitivity to the reaction of the People's Republic of China and to the probable adverse reaction of the South Vietnamese themselves barred such direct involvement. In October 1964 the Republic of China furnished an advisory team, including political warfare advisers and medical personnel. Total advisory strength varied from 20 to 30 personnel. In addition, some Republic of China LSTs (landing ships tank) were provided to assist in coastal shipping.

The Taiwanese also provided substantial economic and technical assistance to South Vietnam.

U.S. Army, Navy and Air Force bases and supply and repair facilities on Taiwan supported the war in Vietnam. As a result of President Nixon's opening to mainland China in 1971, the United States pledged to reduce and eventually eliminate all U.S. military facilities on Taiwan, and on December 15, 1978, the United States severed formal diplomatic ties with the Republic of China. The United States now maintains the unofficial American Institute on Taiwan; the Republic of China has established the Coordination Council for North American Affairs in Washington, D.C.

Suggestions for further reading: *Vietnam Studies: Allied Participation in Vietnam*, by Stanley Robert Larsen and James Lawton Collins, Jr. (Washington, D.C.: Department of the Army, 1975).

TAN SON NHUT

The major air base and commercial airport in South Vietnam, Tan Son Nhut was located on the outskirts of Saigon.

In October 1962 the U.S. Air Force Second Air Division was established at Tan Son Nhut to control USAF air operations in South Vietnam. As the U.S. armed forces presence in Vietnam increased, the Second Air Division was replaced in April 1966 by Headquarters Seventh Air Force, which remained at Tan Son Nhut until the final withdrawal of American forces in March 1973. Also stationed at Tan Son Nhut during the 1962–73 period were the 834th Air Division, 460th Tactical Reconnaissance Wing, Third Aero Rescue and Recovery Group, 315th Troop Carrier Group, 505th Tactical Control Group and 1965th Communications Group. Tan Son Nhut was also the headquarters for the South Vietnamese Air Force and many of its squadrons were based here.

A headquarters complex to house the MACV (U.S. Military Assistance Command Vietnam), known as "Pentagon East," was constructed there, and when U.S. forces withdrew in 1973, it became the headquarters for the Defense Attaché Office (DAO). In addition, Tan Son Nhut Air Base served as the headquarters for the International Commission of Control and Supervision—Canada (later Indonesia), Iran, Poland and Hungary—and the North Vietnamese and Viet Cong delegations to the Four Party Joint Military Team (FPJMT), established by the 1973 Paris Accords, had their own compound on the base.

Bombed by captured South Vietnamese A-37 fighter-bombers on April 28, 1975, Tan Son Nhut came under North Vietnamese rocket and artillery fire the next day. A U.S. Air Force C-130 on the ground was destroyed and the airfield was closed to fixed-wing traffic. Shrapnel from one of the 122-mm rockets killed two U.S. Marine security guards, the last American servicemen killed in action in Vietnam. Later that day in Operation Frequent Wind, the U.S. Seventh Fleet evacuated some 5,000 Americans and Vietnamese refugees from landing zones in the DAO compound at Tan Son Nhut.

Pentagon East had already been wired with explosives by a U.S. Marine demolition team, and after the evacuation was completed, at 11:40 PM on April 29, 1975, Pentagon East (like the U.S. commitment it symbolized) went up in a cloud of smoke.

See also MACV (U.S. MILITARY ASSISTANCE COMMAND VIETNAM); FREQUENT WIND OPERATION; FOUR POINT JOINT MILITARY TEAM; DEFENSE ATTACHE OFFICE; SEVENTH AIR FORCE.

Suggestions for further reading: *Peace with Honor?* by Stuart A. Herrington, (Novato, Calif.: Presidio Press, 1983); *Last Flight from Saigon*, by Thomas G. Tobin, et al, edited by A. J. C. Lavalle (Washington, D.C.: U.S. Government Printing Office, 1978).

TAYLOR, MAXWELL D(AVENPORT) (1901–1987)

Born on August 26, 1901 in Keytesville, Missouri, Taylor graduated from the U.S. Military Academy in 1922. During World War II, after campaigns in North Africa and Sicily with the 82nd Airborne Division, Taylor commanded the 101st Airborne Division, parachuting into the Normandy beachhead. He was subsequently wounded in the Market Garden airborne operation in Holland.

After World War II General Taylor was appointed Superintendent of the U.S. Military Academy. In February 1953 he assumed command of the Eighth Army in Korea and participated in the bitter fighting that preceded the July 1953 armistice there, becoming Commander-in-Chief of the Far East Command in April 1955. In June, he was appointed Army Chief of Staff.

Opposed to the total reliance on nuclear weapons for America's defenses that prevailed at the time, General Taylor advocated building up conventional (nonnuclear) forces as an alternative to nuclear war, though his attempts to persuade the budget-minded Eisenhower Administration, which saw nuclear weapons as a "cheap" way to provide national security, met with only limited success. General Taylor retired from active duty on July 1, 1959.

His 1959 book, *The Uncertain Trumpet,* which detailed his proposals for a more flexible response, brought Taylor to the attention of Senator John F. Kennedy and some of Taylor's arguments were used in Kennedy's successful 1960 presidential campaign. On July 1, 1961 Taylor, who would become one of Kennedy's most influential advisers, was named Military Representative to the President, a post reportedly established because President Kennedy had lost faith in the military advice he was getting from the Joint Chiefs of Staff. Returning from a special mission to South Vietnam in November, Taylor recommended sending more military aid and advisers to Vietnam and pressing President Ngo Dinh Diem to carry out reforms. In a report kept secret at the time Taylor also advised dispatching 8,000 combat troops to South Vietnam as a sign of U.S. commitment and as a reserve emergency force. Kennedy decided not to send combat troops but approved the other recommendations.

In 1962 General Taylor was recalled to active duty and named Chairman of the Joint Chiefs of

Maxwell D. Taylor. (Courtesy U.S. Army Military History Institute.)

Staff. After President Kennedy's assassination President Johnson appointed Taylor Ambassador to South Vietnam in July 1964. As Ambassador, he pressed for the return of civilian rule after the military coup that overthrew Diem in 1963. In July 1965 General Taylor relinquished that post and served as a Special Consultant to President Johnson. As a member of the Senior Advisory Group convened in March 1968 to advise the President on the course of the war, Taylor was opposed to the policy of disengagement recommended by a majority of the group. In 1969 he returned to private life.

General Taylor was known within the military circle as both an intellectual and an innovator. During World War II he won fame with the new and innovative concept of airborne operations. As Army Chief of Staff in the late 1950s, Taylor restructured the Army for the "atomic" battlefield. The so-called pentomic division was created during his term in office, but it was abandoned soon thereafter as unworkable. His fears that the Army would be dismissed as irrelevant in the nuclear age (and there were some air power pro ponents who suggested just that) led him to continue to seek new and innovative roles for that service. Thus President Kennedy's fascination with counterinsurgency doctrine in the early 1960s fell on fertile ground.

The result was that General Taylor misjudged the true nature of the Vietnam war. Testifying before the Senate in 1966, he said that the United States was not trying to "defeat" North Vietnam, only "to cause them to mend their ways." Taylor likened the concept of defeating the enemy to "Appomattox or something of that sort." But "Appomattox or something of that sort" was exactly what the North Vietnamese had in mind.

See also COUNTERINSURGENCY; JOHNSON, LYNDON B.; KENNEDY, JOHN F.; SENIOR ADVISORY GROUP; STRATEGY, U.S.; WESTMORELAND, WILLIAM C.; WHEELER, EARLE G.

Suggestions for further reading: *The Uncertain Trumpet*, by Maxwell D. Taylor (New York: Harper's, 1959); *Swords and Plowshares*, by Maxwell D. Taylor (New York: Norton, 1972); *The Best and the Brightest*, by David Halberstam (New York: Random House, 1972); *The 25-Year War: America's Military Role in Vietnam*, by Bruce Palmer, Jr. (Lexington: University of Kentucky Press, 1984).

TELEVISION

A unique feature of the Vietnam war was its coverage by television, which replaced the newsreels of earlier wars. Television brought the war into American living rooms. According to a 1976 study by Professor George Bailey of the University of Wisconsin, during the height of American involvement from 1965 to 1970, there were some 184 hours of television coverage of Vietnam war news—roughly three minutes per network per day. Nearly half of the stories were about either ground or air combat.

This television coverage has sparked much criticism; some even going so far as to claim that television lost the Vietnam war. Although not taking that extreme view, former MACV commander General William C. Westmoreland has charged that "television's unique requirements contributed to a distorted view of the war," for given television's very nature, "the news had to be compressed and visually dramatic, and as a result the war that Americans saw was almost exclusively violent, miserable, or controversial." In a survey of general officers who served in Vietnam, Douglas Kinnard found that some 52 percent believed that television coverage was "not a good thing, since there was a tendency to go for the sensational, which was counterproductive to the war."

Critics of television coverage have charged that if the battles at Antietam had been televised, the American people would have abandoned the Civil War; that if the bloodshed at the Normandy beachhead had been televised, America would have given up on World War II. But such complaints miss the point. Television is extremely effective in portraying the "price" of a war. But price has meaning only in relationship to "value." In the Civil War and World War II the "value" had been established as the very preservation of the nation; thus the "price" that the American people were willing to pay was extremely high. In the Vietnam war the government had deliberately failed to stir up the passions of the American people and thus established the "value" of the war. Indeed, in 1985, ten years after the war ended, there is still considerable controversy over the objectives—and hence the "value"—of the Vietnam war. It should therefore not be surprising that the "price" soon became exorbitant. It was the lack of an objective—the lack of an established "value"—not television reporting, that ultimately undermined American public support for the war.

A more telling criticism of television is that its coverage is restricted to the film footage available. On the U.S. side, almost total coverage was permitted and footage was available on American and South Vietnamese mistakes as well as their successes. On the enemy's side, however, the media were instruments of the state and the only coverage permitted was propaganda footage that portrayed the North Vietnamese and Viet Cong in a favorable light. This structural imbalance is apparent in most television "histories" of the Vietnam war.

See also ANTIWAR MOVEMENT, CENSORSHIP, MEDIA.

Suggestions for further reading: "Television

War: Trends in Network Coverage of Vietnam 1965-1970," by George Bailey, in *Journal of Broadcasting* Spring 1976; "Comments on the Influence of Television on Public Opinion," by Lawrence W. Lichty, in *Vietnam as History,* edited by Peter Braestrup (Washington, D.C.: University Press of America, 1984); "Rough Justice on a Saigon Street: A Gatekeeper Study of NBC's Tet Execution Film," by George A. Bailey and Lawrence W. Lichty, in *Journalism Quarterly,* vol. 49, no. 2, Summer 1972; "Interpretive Reporting of the Vietnam War by Anchormen," by George Bailey, in *Journalism Quarterly,* vol. 53, no. 2, summer 1976; *Living Room War,* by Michael Arlen (New York: Viking, 1969); *The Camera at War,* by Jorge Lewinski (New York: Simon & Schuster, 1978).

TERRITORIAL FORCES

In the South Vietnamese Army, Territorial Forces were roughly akin to the American militia in colonial times. Recruited locally, they fell into two broad groups—Regional Forces (RF) and Popular Forces (PF)—known to Americans as "Ruff-Puff."

In the beginning the RF manned the country-wide outpost system and defended critical points, such as bridges and ferries. There were some 9,000 such fixed positions, half in the Mekong Delta. The PF were used to protect their home villages and hamlets from Viet Cong attack. Originally called the Civil Guard and the Self-Defense Corps, they were integrated into the South Vietnamese Army in 1964, as RF and PF were placed under the command of the Joint General Staff.

From 1965 to 1969, when U.S. units engaged Viet Cong and North Vietnamese Army (NVA) main forces—battalions and regiments—the South Vietnamese Army was able to provide local security. When U.S. units began to withdraw in 1969 and the South Vietnamese Army began to take on enemy main forces, RF and PF forces took on new importance. For the first time, they were deployed outside their home areas and were sometimes attached to South Vietnamese Army units.

During the 1968–1972 period, when U.S. units were being withdrawn and the South Vietnamese Army assumed primary responsibility for the war (including turning back the enemy's Eastertide Offensive), the South Vietnamese Army lost 36,982 soldiers killed in action, but during that same period, the RF and PF lost 69,291 personnel. By 1973 Territorial Forces had grown to 1,810 RF companies and 8,186 PF platoons. Charged primarily with local defense, and too lightly armed and equipped to withstand attack by regular North Vietnamese Army (NVA) units supported by tanks and artillery, they were overwhelmed in the 1975 North Vietnamese blitzkrieg.

See also PACIFICATION, SVNAF (SOUTH VIETNAMESE ARMED FORCES).

Suggestions for further reading: *Territorial Forces,* by Ngo Quang Truong (Washington, D.C.: Center of Military History, 1981); *Pacification,* by Tran Dinh Tho (Washington, D.C.: Center of Military History, 1980).

TET OFFENSIVE

"Tet" is a traditional Vietnamese holiday. It celebrates the beginning of the lunar new year and in Vietnam incorporates the festivities Westerners associate with both Christmas and New Year. It had been customary during the Vietnam war to observe a cease-fire during the Tet holidays and 1968 was no exception; in fact the National Liberation Front (North Vietnam's front organization for the Viet Cong) had publicly called for scrupulous observance of the Tet cease-fire.

While intelligence reports had been received that the North Vietnamese Army (NVA) and Viet Cong might take advantage of the holiday to launch an attack, there was no feeling that a major offensive was imminent.

On January 30, 1968 the Tet holiday began, but shortly after midnight several cities in I Corps and II Corps were attacked and by noon on January 30 all U.S. units were placed on maximum alert. At 3:00 AM on January 31 the North Vietnamese and Viet Cong launched what has become known as the Tet Offensive. Simultaneous attacks were made on Hué and other major cities, towns and military bases throughout Vietnam. One assault team got within the walls of the U.S. embassy in

American military police kneel behind a wall as they fight for control of the U.S. embassy compound. In the foreground are two U.S. soldiers who were killed in earlier fighting. In spite of the dramatic attack on the U.S. embassy compound, the Tet Offensive proved to be a tactical defeat for the North Vietnamese. (AP/Wide World Photos.)

Saigon before they were destroyed. Television footage of this attack received widespread attention in the United States. Initial media reports stated that U.S. and South Vietnamese Army forces had been surprised and defeated.

But it was not the United States that was defeated on the battlefield. It was the North Vietnamese Army and especially the Viet Cong. Their "general offensive and general uprising" had been a tactical disaster. Not only had their military forces been resoundingly defeated, but their ideological illusion that the South Vietnamese people would flock to their banner during the "general uprising" proved false. From Tet 1968 on, the NVA realized it would not be able to attain its political objective with guerrilla forces and increasingly the war became an affair for the regular forces of the NVA.

But if the United States had won tactically, it suffered a fatal strategic blow. False expectations had been raised at home that the war was virtually won. Public opinion had turned against the war in October 1967 and the events of Tet confirmed that disenchantment. The Tet Offensive cost the government and the military the confidence of the American people. Not only did the American public turn further against the war, but the Commander-in-Chief, President Johnson seemed psychologically defeated by the Tet Offensive. Challenged within his own party for renomination and with public support slipping away, he thereafter publicly announced that he would not seek reelection.

Although the war would continue for another seven years, the war for the support of the American people was lost on January 30, 1968. From that point on, the problem was not how to win the war but how to disengage.

See also ANTIWAR MOVEMENT; HUE, BATTLE OF; JOHNSON, LYNDON B.; KHE SANH, BATTLE OF; PUBLIC OPINION.

Suggestions for further reading: The landmark

work on the Tet Offensive is *Tet! The Turning Point of the Vietnam War,* by Don Oberdorfer (New York: Da Capo, 1983). For reporting of the Tet Offensive, see *Big Story,* by Peter Braestrup (New Haven: Yale University Press, 1983).

THAILAND

The Kingdom of Thailand assisted the United States and South Vietnam during the Vietnam war by providing both military bases and combat forces.

During the height of the Vietnam war, U.S. Army forces in Thailand included the Ninth Logistical Command, 44th Engineer Group and 40th Military Police Battalion at Korat, the 29th Signal Group at Bangkok and the 46th Special Forces Company. U.S. Air Force units included the Eighth Tactical Fighter Wing at the Royal Thai Air Force Base at U Bon, the 432nd Tactical Reconnaissance Wing at U Dorn, the 307th Strategic Wing at U Tapao, the 633rd Special Operations Wing and 56th Air Commando wing at Nakhon Phanom, the 355th and 366th Tactical Fighter Wings at Takhli, and the 388th Tactical Fighter Wing and 553rd Reconnaissance Wing at Korat. U.S. Marine Corps Marine Air Group 15 was also stationed at Nam Phong in 1972.

At the height of the war Thailand contributed some 11,568 combat troops to Vietnam. First to arrive were the Queen's Cobras—the Royal Thai Army volunteer regiment—which arrived in Vietnam in the fall of 1967 and was stationed at Bearcat, near Bien Hoa. They were replaced by the Royal Thai Army Volunteer Force in July 1968, which included the Black Panther Division, composed of two brigades of infantry, three battalions of 105-mm field artillery and an armored cavalry unit. In addition, the Royal Thai Air Force contributed C-47s and C-123s to what they called their Victory Flight.

The Royal Thai Army and the Border Patrol Police also faced a continual menace from the Communist Terrorist (CT) organizations along Thailand's northeastern Laotian border and lower Malaysian frontier. Although it is not widely known, several U.S. servicemen—mostly Army Special Forces—were killed during the period 1967–73 in the anti-CT campaign. The CT forces also conducted a number of raids on U.S. Air Force bases, notably at Udorn and Utapao, causing American casualties. The dead bodies of these CT sappers almost invariably turned out to be North Vietnamese.

In 1971, as part of the general draw-down of forces in Vietnam, Royal Thai forces were gradually withdrawn, and by April 1972 only a token force remained.

Suggestions for further reading: *Allied Participation in Vietnam* by Stanley Robert Larsen and James Lawton Collins, Jr. (Washington, D.C.: U.S. Government Printing Office, 1975).

THIEU, NGUYEN VAN (1923–)

Born on April 5, 1923 near Phan Rang in Ninh Thuan Province in the French protectorate of Annam, Thieu graduated from the Vietnamese National Military Academy in 1949. Commissioned in the infantry, he distinguished himself in actions against the Viet Minh. When the South Vietnamese Army was established in 1959, Thieu was appointed Commander of its 21st Infantry Division. He also served as Commandant of the National Military Academy.

After graduating from the U.S. Command and General Staff College at Fort Leavenworth, Kansas in 1957, Colonel Thieu commanded the South Vietnamese Army First Infantry Division from 1960 to 1962, when he was appointed to command the Fifth Infantry Division near Saigon. During the coup that overthrew President Ngo Dinh Diem in November 1963, Colonel Thieu led one of his regiments in an attack on the barracks of the presidential bodyguard. Promoted to Brigadier General, Thieu was appointed Commander of IV Corps. To end the near anarchy that followed the assassination of President Diem, General Thieu took part in a coup by Air Vice Marshal Nguyen Cao Ky in December 1964. A civilian government was installed and Thieu, now a Major General, became part of a 25-man Armed Forces Council. In June 1965 another coup resulted in a 10-man military National Leadership Committee, which elected General Thieu as Chairman and Chief of State and Air Marshal Ky as Premier. When

President Nguyen Van Thieu gives farmers in Soc Trang deeds to the land they till. (Courtesy U.S. Army Military History Institute.)

elections were held in 1967 the situation was reversed. Thieu was elected President and Ky Vice-President. Ky chose not to run against Thieu in 1971 and Thieu was reelected to the presidency, although charges of a rigged election surfaced.

Pressured by the United States to agree to the Paris Accords in 1973, which left the North Vietnamese Army (NVA) in control of large segments of the country, President Thieu's position was further undermined when the U.S. Congress cut promised military aid and especially when, after an open NVA attack on Binh Long Province in November 1974, President Ford failed to honor US guarantees to uphold the terms of the Paris Accords. With four NVA corps closing in on Saigon and all hope of outside assistance gone, President Thieu resigned and on April 25, 1975 he flew to Taiwan. He now resides in Great Britain.

See also FINAL OFFENSIVE.

Suggestions for further reading: *Without Honor: Defeat in Vietnam and Cambodia,* by Arnold R. Isaacs (Baltimore: Johns Hopkins Press, 1983); *Vietnam: A History,* by Stanley Karnow (New York: Viking, 1983).

THIRD CORPS TACTICAL ZONE

See III (i.e., THREE) CORPS TACTICAL ZONE.

III CORPS TACTICAL ZONE

With headquarters at Bien Hoa, South Vietnam's III Corps was responsible for the approaches to and the defense of Saigon, the republic's capital. Major assigned units included the South Vietnamese Army's Fifth, 18th (formerly the 10th) and 25th Divisions.

The North Vietnamese Army (NVA) saw Saigon as the ultimate objective of its conquest. Using the Ho Chi Minh Trail to establish base areas in Cambodia to the west, as well as in the Iron Triangle and War Zones C and D to the north, the NVA plan was to keep Saigon under a state of siege so that South Vietnamese forces could not be diverted to meet attacks elsewhere in South Vietnam.

Recognizing the strategic importance of III Corps, in March 1966 II Field Force Vietnam was deployed to the area to provide combat assistance to III Corps and to control U.S. combat operations. It established headquarters at Bien Hoa, constructed major logistical facilities at nearby Long Binh and expanded port facilities at Saigon. The jet-capable airfield at Bien Hoa was the home base for the U.S. Air Force's Third Tactical Fighter Wing and extensive Air Force operations were based at Tan Son Nhut in the suburbs of Saigon.

To guard the approaches to Saigon, the U.S. 173rd Airborne Brigade was deployed to Bien Hoa Air Base in May 1965, followed by the U.S. First Infantry Division in October 1965, the 25th Infantry Division in March 1966, the 11th Armored Cavalry Regiment in September 1966, and the Ninth Infantry Division and 199th Light Infantry Brigade in December 1966.

Major U.S. combat operations were conducted in III Corps, especially in the long-time Viet Cong base areas in Hau Ngia Province, in the Iron Triangle and in War Zones C and D. During the Tet Offensive of 1968, Viet Cong and North Vietnamese Army (NVA) attempts to capture Saigon were repulsed, and in March 1970 the U.S.-South Vietnamese "incursion" into Cambodia was launched from III Corps.

In October 1967 the 173rd Airborne Brigade was deployed to II Corps. In May 1969, however, the First Cavalry Division (Airmobile) deployed from II Corps to III Corps. As the U.S. draw-down began, the initial unit to depart was the Ninth Infantry Division, which departed Vietnam in August 1969. It was followed by the First Infantry Division in April 1970, the 199th Light Infantry Brigade in October 1970 and the 25th Infantry Division, minus its Second Brigade, in December 1970. In March 1971 the 11th Armored Cavalry Division, minus its Second Squadron, was withdrawn from Vietnam followed by the Second Brigade, 25th Infantry Division and the First Cavalry Division (Airmobile), minus its Third Brigade, in April 1971. In April 1972 the Second Squadron, 11th Armored Cavalry Regiment was withdrawn from Vietnam, and the last major U.S. ground combat unit in Vietnam, the Third Brigade, First Cavalry Division (Airmobile) was withdrawn in June 1972. Meanwhile, II Field Force Vietnam had been disbanded on May 2, 1971.

With the majority of American units withdrawn, the North Vietnamese launched their Eastertide Offensive in March 1972, striking at Quang Tri in I Corps, Kontum in II Corps and An

III CORPS AND CAPITAL SPECIAL ZONE

GIA DINH
RUNG SAT SPECIAL ZONE

Loc in III Corps. Some 65 air miles north of Saigon, An Loc was attacked by three divisions beginning on April 5, 1972. The assault continued for 95 days. Although driven back, the South Vietnamese Army's Fifth Infantry Division, supported by U.S. Air Force tactical fighter-bombers and B-52 strategic bombers, held its positions, and on July 11, 1972 the North Vietnamese withdrew to their base areas in Cambodia.

At the time of the Paris Accords in January 1973, the NVA had 24,600 troops in III Corps, including its Seventh, Ninth and 95C Infantry Divisions, six separate infantry regiments plus two armor battalions and six battalions of artillery. Reinforcements were close at hand from the nearby Ho Chi Minh Trail. On December 13, 1974 the NVA made the preliminary move that would lead to the Final Offensive in 1975. Preceded by a massive artillery barrage, its tank-supported Third and Seventh Divisions launched an attack on the province of Phuoc Long and on January 6, 1975 captured the first provincial capital in South Vietnam since the cease-fire two years before. When the United States did not react as promised to this flagrant violation of the Paris Accords, the North Vietnamese knew that the time had come for their Final Offensive to conquer South Vietnam.

After the fall of II Corps in March 1975, the North Vietnamese Army concentrated its entire force on III Corps. After a heroic battle at Xuan Loc from March 17 to April 15, 1975, South Vietnamese defenses were pushed in by this blitzkrieg, and on April 30, 1975 Saigon was surrendered. Before the fall the South Vietnamese Air Force flew some 132 aircraft—including 26 F-5 and 27 A-37 jet fighter-bombers—to U Tapao Royal Thai Air Force Base in Thailand and the Commanding General of the Fifth Infantry Division committed suicide rather than surrender.

See also AN LOC, BATTLE OF; BIEN HOA; EASTERTIDE OFFENSIVE; 11TH ARMORED CALVALRY REGIMENT; FINAL OFFENSIVE; FIRST INFANTRY DIVISION; HO CHI MINH TRAIL; IRON TRIANGLE; LONG BINH; NINTH INFANTRY DIVISION; 199TH LIGHT INFANTRY BRIGADE; 173RD AIRBORNE BRIGADE; SAIGON; TAN SON NHUT; TET OFFENSIVE; 25TH INFANTRY DIVISION; II FIELD FORCE VIETNAM; WAR ZONES C AND D; XUAN LOC, BATTLE OF.

Suggestions for further reading: *Vietnam Order*

of Battle, by Shelby L. Stanton (Washington, D.C.: U.S. News & World Report Books, 1981); *Vietnam from Ceasefire to Capitulation,* by William E. LeGro (Washington, D.C.: U.S. Government Printing Office, 1981).

III MARINE AMPHIBIOUS FORCE

A U.S. Marine amphibious force (MAF) normally consists of a Marine division, a Marine aircraft wing and necessary combat support forces (engineers, communications units and the like), but in Vietnam the III MAF came to be more akin to an Army corps-level headquarters with control of several Marine and Army divisions and for a time the Army's XXIV Corps. Formed on May 6, 1965, with headquarters at Da Nang, the III MAF's missions grew to include development and defense of the coastal bases of Da Nang, Phu Bai and Chu Lai, support of combat operations conducted by South Vietnam's Armed Forces I Corps, conduct of offensive actions against the Viet Cong and the North Vietnamese Army and support of pacification.

At its peak in 1968, the III MAF included the First and Third Marine Divisions, two Marine regimental landing teams, the First Marine Air Wing and the Army XXIV Corps, which included the Americal Division, the First Cavalry Division (Airmobile), the 101st Airborne Division (Airmobile) and the 1st Brigade (Mechanized), Fifth Infantry Division. With 85,755 Marines the III MAF had more troops than were ashore at Iwo Jima or Okinawa in World War II.

As U.S. forces withdrew, the III MAF relinquished overall responsibility for U.S. operations in I Corps to the U.S. Army's XXIV Corps in March 1970, and in April 1971 the III MAF departed Vietnam for Okinawa, where it remains headquartered today.

From 1961 to 1972 the III MAF lost 12,938 Marines killed in action, and 88,633 wounded in action. These 101,571 casualties were more than the 86,940 casualties the entire Marine Corps suffered in World War II. Fifty-seven III MAF Marines were awarded the Medal of Honor in addition to the other awards won by the III MAF.

During the course of the Vietnam war, command of the III Marine Amphibious Force changed seven times:

Commanders	Assumed Command
Maj. Gen. William R. Collins	May 1965
Maj. Gen. Lewis W. Walt	June 1965
Maj. Gen. Keith B. McCutcheon	February 1966
Lt. Gen. Lewis W. Walt	March 1966
Lt. Gen. Robert E. Cushman, Jr.	June 1967
Lt. Gen. Herman Nickerson, Jr.	March 1969
Lt. Gen. Keith B. McCutcheon	March 1970
Lt. Gen. Donn J. Robertson	December 1970

See also FIRST MARINE DIVISION; FIRST MARINE AIRCRAFT WING; I CORPS TACTICAL ZONE; KHE SANH, BATTLE OF; MARINE CORPS, U.S.; THIRD MARINE DIVISION; XXIV CORPS.

Suggestions for further reading: "Marine Corps Operations in Vietnam 1965–66, 1967, 1968, 1969–72," by Brigadier General Edwin H. Simmons, in *The Marines in Vietnam* (Washington, D.C.: U.S. Government Printing Office, 1974); *Semper Fidelis: The History of the United States Marine Corps,* by Allan R. Millett (New York: Macmillan, 1980); *Strange War, Strange Strategy,* by Lewis W. Walt (New York: Funk & Wagnall, 1976); *First to Fight: An Inside View of the U.S. Marine Corps,* by Victor H. Krulak (Annapolis: U.S. Naval Institute Press, 1984); *Vietnam Order of Battle,* by Shelby L. Stanton (Washington, D.C.: U.S. News & World Report Books, 1981); *U.S. Marines in Vietnam: The Advisory and Combat Assistance Era 1954–1964,* by Robert H. Whitlow (Washington, D.C.: U.S. Government Printing Office, 1977); *U.S. Marines in Vietnam: The Landing and the Buildup 1965,* by Jack Shulimson and Charles M. Johnson (Washington, D.C.: U.S. Government Printing Office, 1978); *U.S. Marines in Vietnam: An Expanding War 1966,* by Jack Shulimson (Washington, D.C.: U.S. Government Printing Office, 1982). For a fictionalized account of Marine Corps operations in Vietnam, see Vietnam Marine Corps veteran James Webb's *Fields of Fire* (Englewood Cliffs, N.J.: Prentice-Hall, 1978).

THIRD MARINE DIVISION

The Third Marine Division was first organized in 1942 and took part in the amphibious assaults on Bougainville and Guam and in the hard fighting on Iwo Jima during World War II. Deployed again to the Far East in 1953, it was stationed on Okinawa when the Vietnam war began.

In March 1965 forward elements of the Third Marine Division landed at Da Nang in I Corps to secure the air base there. By May 1965 the division itself was fully deployed. Initially assigned the defense of Quang Nam Province, including the vital ports and air base at Da Nang, in October 1966 it turned over these responsibilities to the recently arrived First Marine Division and moved north, taking responsibility for the defense of I Corps' northernmost provinces, Quang Tri and Thua Tien. Deployed along the DMZ, it established a series of fire support bases—Khe Sanh, the Rockpile, Ca Lu, Camp Carrol, Cam Lo, Cua Viet and Gio Linh—and conducted many combat operations in that area, including operations in the DMZ itself and the successful defense of Khe Sanh in 1968. At peak strength, it consisted of four regiments of infantry: the Third Marines, the Fourth Marines, the Ninth Marines and 26th Marines (attached from the Fifth Marine Division at Camp Pendleton, California). The division artillery, the 12th Marine Regiment at one time in 1967 had 11 battalions of 105-mm, 155-mm and 8-inch howitzers (including three Army battal-

ions) under its operational control. Other combat elements included the Third Tank Battalion (with M-48 tanks), the Third Antitank Battalion (with multibarreled 106-mm recoilless rifle ONTOs), the Third Amphibious Tractor Battalion, the Third Reconnaissance Battalion and the Third Force Recon Company. Returning to their home base on Okinawa in the fall of 1969, elements of the Third Marine Division embarked with the Seventh Fleet to assist in the evacuation of Phnom Penh and of Da Nang and Saigon in 1975, as well as the rescue of the *Mayaguez* later than same year.

Twenty-nine members of the Third Marine Division (including Marines from the attached 26th Marine Regiment) won the Medal of Honor for conspicuous bravery in Vietnam, as did one Navy medical corpsman serving with the division, in addition to other awards. For gallantry in action in Vietnam, the Third Marine Division was awarded the Presidential Unit Citation and the Vietnamese Cross of Gallantry with Palm. The Third Marine Division has an active veterans' association. Further information can be obtained from Colonel Edward F. Danowitz, USMC (Retired), Third Marine Division Association, 324 Hermitage Drive, Altamonte Springs, Florida 32701.

See also DMZ; KHE SANH, BATTLE OF; III MARINE AMPHIBIOUS FORCE.

Suggestions for further reading: *The 3d Marine Division and Its Regiments* (Washington, D.C.: Historical and Museums Division, USMC, 1983); "Marine Corps Operations in Vietnam 1965–66, 1967, 1968, 1969–72," by Edwin H. Simmons, in *The Marines in Vietnam* (Washington, D.C.: U.S. Government Printing Office, 1974); *Semper Fidelis: The History of the United States Marine Corps,* by Allan R. Millett (New York: Macmillan, 1980); *First to Fight: An Inside View of the U.S. Marine Corps,* by Victor H. Krulak (Annapolis: U.S. Naval Institute Press, 1984); *Vietnam Order of Battle,* by Shelby L. Stanton (Washington, D.C.: U.S. News & World Report Books, 1981). An account of Third Marine Division combat actions can be found in *The Rise and Fall of an American Army,* by Shelby L. Stanton (Novato, Calif.: Presidio Press, 1985). *U.S. Marines in Vietnam: The Advisory and Combat Assistance Era 1954–1964,* by Robert H. Whitlow (Washington, D.C.: U.S. Government Printing Office, 1977);

Insignia of the Third Marine Division.

U.S. Marines in Vietnam: The Landing and the Buildup 1965, by Jack Shulimson and Charles M. Johnson (Washington, D.C.: U.S. Government Printing Office, 1978); *U.S. Marines in Vietnam: An Expanding War 1966*, by Jack Shulimson (Washington, D.C.: U.S. Government Printing Office, 1982). For combat actions at Khe Sanh, see citations at entry on Khe Sanh. For a fictionalized account of Marine Corps operations in Vietnam, see Vietnam Marine Corps veteran James Webb's *Fields of Fire* (Englewood Cliffs, N.J.: Prentice-Hall, 1978).

THO, LE DUC (1912?–)

Born in about 1912 in the French protectorate of Tonkin in northern Vietnam, Le Duc Tho was a founding member of the Indochina Communist Party. He was North Vietnam's principal negotiator in the Paris peace negotiations, which ended with the January 1973 Agreement on Ending the War and Restoring Peace in Vietnam. Awarded the Nobel Peace Prize with Henry Kissinger in 1973, Le Duc Tho, knowing that North Vietnam was then finalizing plans for the conquest of South Vietnam, refused to accept the award.

See also PARIS ACCORDS, PEACE TALKS.

Suggestions for further reading: *Vietnam: A History*, by Stanley Karnow (New York: Viking, 1983).

THOMPSON, ROBERT (1916–)

Born on April 16, 1916, Sir Robert Thompson served in the Malayan Civil Service prior to World War II. After service in the Royal Air Force from 1939 to 1945, he returned to Malaya during the insurgency there, becoming Deputy Secretary of Defense for the Federation of Malaya in 1957 and Secretary for Defense from 1959 to 1961.

Head of the British Advisory mission to Vietnam from 1961 to 1965, he was very influential in his attempts to have the "lessons" of the successful British counterinsurgency effort in Malaya applied to Vietnam, especially the strategic hamlet program.

While his advice made some sense for the South Vietnamese government, Thompson's views were too eagerly accepted by Americans who failed to see that, in addition to other major differences, in Malaya during the insurgency the British had been the government, whereas in Vietnam the United States was *not* the government and had to work through South Vietnam. Further, the Malaya model did not provide for the regular forces of the North Vietnamese Army (NVA). In the end it was the NVA, not the Viet Cong insurgents, that proved to be decisive.

See also COALITION WARFARE, CAP (COMBINED ACTION PLATOONS), COUNTERINSURGENCY, HEARTS AND MINDS, STRATEGIC HAMLETS.

Suggestions for further reading: *Defeating Communist Insurgency* (New York: Praeger, 1966), *No Exit From Vietnam* (New York: McKay, 1970), *Revolutionary War in World Strategy 1945–1949* (New York: Taplinger, 1970), and *Peace Is Not at Hand* (New York: McKay, 1974), by Sir Robert Thompson.

THUY, XUAN (1912–1985)

Formerly North Vietnam's Foreign Minister, Xuan Thuy headed the official North Vietnamese delegation to the Paris Peace Talks from May 1968 until the signing of the cease-fire agreement in January 1973. Thuy, acting as Le Duc Tho's chief deputy, negotiated periodically with Henry Kissinger. He died in Hanoi on June 18, 1985.

See also KISSINGER, HENRY A.; PEACE TALKS; THO, LE DUC.

TIGER DIVISION

Nickname of South Korea's Capital Division, deployed to Vietnam in September 1966 (*see* KOREA).

TIGER HOUND

The name for air operations to interdict the Ho Chi Minh Trail in the lower portion of the Laotian panhandle from Route 9 west of the DMZ south to the Cambodian border. Operation Tiger Hound was controlled by COMUSMACV (Commander of the U.S. Military Assistance Command Vietnam) in Saigon and was part of Pacific Command's Operation Steel Tiger. Beginning in December 1965, it involved Navy aircraft from carriers in the South China Sea, Air Force and Marine aircraft flying from bases in South Vietnam and in Thailand and eventually B-52 strategic bombers. The most effective aircraft, however, were fixed-wing gunships such as the AC-47, AC-119, and the AC-130. After 1968 these operations were known as Commando Hunts and the term "Tiger Hound" was abandoned.

See also COMMANDO HUNT, GUNSHIPS, HO CHI MINH TRAIL, LAOS, STEEL TIGER.

Suggestions for further reading: *Airpower in Three Wars,* by General William W. Momyer (Washington, D.C.: U.S. Government Printing Office, 1978); *The United States Air Force in Southeast Asia,* edited by Carl Berger (Washington, D.C.: U.S. Government Printing Office, 1977); *The Vietnam Experience: Thunder From Above,* by John Morrocco (Boston: Boston Publishing Co., 1984); *Battles and Campaigns in Vietnam* by Tom Carhart (New York: Crown Publishers, 1984).

TONKIN GULF INCIDENT

See TONKIN GULF RESOLUTION.

TONKIN GULF RESOLUTION

On August 2, 1964 the U.S. destroyer *Maddox*—on patrol in international waters in the Gulf of Tonkin off the coast of North Vietnam—was attacked by North Vietnamese torpedo boats. The attack was repulsed. On August 4 the *Maddox,* joined by the destroyer *Turner Joy,* again reported an attack by North Vietnamese torpedo boats.

Using these incidents as a *casus bellum,* President Johnson asked Congress for a resolution empowering him to "take all necessary measures to repel an armed attack against the forces of the United States and to prevent further aggression." On August 7 the so-called Gulf of Tonkin Resolution (officially the Southeast Asia Resolution) passed the Senate by a vote of 88 to 2 and the House by a unanimous voice vote of 416 to 0.

The resolution was followed by a Viet Cong shelling of Bien Hoa Air Base on November 1, 1964, by a terrorist bombing of the Brinks officer billets in Saigon on December 24, 1964, and by attacks on American barracks at Pleiku on February 7, 1965 and on American barracks at Qui Nhon on February 10, 1965. Unlike the Gulf of Tonkin attack, Americans were killed in all these attacks. Thus later evidence that the second raid in the Gulf of Tonkin on August 4, 1964 probably never occurred and was the result of skittish and excited sonar operators is immaterial. The causes of war were already present.

Some have claimed that the Congress was misled by the Gulf of Tonkin Resolution and did not intend to grant the President a *de facto* declaration of war. On March 1, 1966, long after the bombing of North Vietnam had begun and American ground combat forces had been committed to battle, Senator Wayne Morse introduced an amendment to repeal this resolution. This amendment was defeated in the Senate by a vote of 92 to 5.

Later, on August 18, 1967, President Johnson repudiated the Gulf of Tonkin Resolution as the legal basis for the war in Vietnam and fell back on his authority granted by Article II of the Constitution as Commander-in-Chief of the Armed Forces. The Gulf of Tonkin Resolution was terminated by Congress in May 1970, but U.S. combat involvement in Vietnam continued until the Paris Accords in January 1973.

See also FULBRIGHT, J. WILLIAM; GRUENING, ERNEST; MORSE, WAYNE.

Suggestions for further reading: 91st Congress, 2nd Session, Committee on Foreign Relations, U.S. Senate, *Termination of Middle East and South Asia Resolutions;* Report to Accompany Senate Concurrent Resolution 64, May 15, 1970 (Washington, D.C.: U.S. Government Printing Office, 1970); *In Love and War,* by Jim and Sybil Stockdale (New York: Harper & Row, 1984); *Tonkin Gulf,* by Eugene C. Windchy (Garden City, N.Y.: Doubleday, 1971); *Vietnam: A History,* by Stanley Karnow (New York: Viking, 1983).

TON SON NHUT

See TAN SON NHUT.

TOWER, JOHN G(OODWIN) (1925-   )

Tower was born on September 29, 1925 in Houston, Texas. He enlisted in the Army in 1942 and after his discharge earned a B.A. in 1948 from Southwestern University.

In 1961 Tower, a Republican, narrowly won a special election to fill Lyndon B. Johnson's vacated U.S. Senate seat. He favored a militantly anti-communist foreign policy and was an adamant supporter of America's Vietnam war effort. In March 1967 Senate Majority Leader Mike Mansfield offered an amendment to a war appropriations bill urging international negotiations as a means of resolving the Vietnam conflict. Tower denounced the proposal, asserting that "if there is any way to strengthen the will of our opponents, it is to attach to an authorization of an appropriation to take care of our forces in the field another plaintive plea for peace."

A prominent conservative spokesman, Tower enthusiastically backed President Nixon's Vietnam war policy and voted against all attempts to limit U.S. involvement. Extremely critical of the antiwar movement, he characterized Democratic presidential nominee George McGovern in 1972 as "Hanoi's choice for the President." The following year he lobbied in the Senate to sustain Nixon's veto of Senator Jacob Javits' War Powers Act, which severely restricted the President's right to commit troops abroad.

Tower retired from the Senate when his term expired in 1985.

TRAN VAN TRA

See TRA, TRAN VAN.

TRA VAN DON

See DON, TRA VAN.

TRA, TRAN VAN (1918-   )

Born in 1918 in the French protectorate of Annam (central Vietnam), Tra joined the Indochina Communist Party in 1940. Imprisoned by the French for revolutionary activities from 1940 to 1943, he held high military and political posts in the Viet Minh during the 1946–54 war with the French.

After study in China and the Soviet Union in 1954, he was appointed Commander of the North Vietnamese Army (NVA) 330th Division in 1958 and then made Major General. Promoted to Lieutenant General in 1961, he was at the same time appointed Chairman of the Central Military Committee, Central Office of South Vietnam (COSVN).

As Deputy Commander of COSVN, he coordinated the Viet Cong guerrilla movement against South Vietnam. After the fall of Saigon, he challenged NVA General Van Tien Dung's account of Dung's conventional force blitzkrieg during the Final Offensive (*Great Spring Victory*) and sought to emphasize the role of guerrilla forces. He was reportedly purged for criticizing General Dung who is currently Minister of Defense.

Suggestions for further reading: *Vietnam: A History,* by Stanley Karnow (New York: Viking, 1983); *Ending the 30 Years War* (Ket Thuc Cuoc Chien Tranh 30 Nam), by Tran Van Tra (Ho Chi Minh City: Literature Publishing House, 1982). For an analysis of Tra's book, see "Communist Offensive Strategy and the Defense of South Vietnam," by Hung P. Nguyen, in *Parameters: Journal of the U.S. Army War College,* Winter 1984.

Tran Van Tra. (Courtesy U.S. Army Military History Institute.)

TROOP

In the U.S. Army, a troop is a company-sized element of cavalry. Commanded by a captain, it consists of two or more platoons. Although a troop is normally a part of a cavalry squadron, a number of separate cavalry troops were deployed to Vietnam. These included reconnaissance, armored cavalry and air cavalry troops.

See also ORGANIZATION FOR COMBAT.

Suggestions for further reading: *Vietnam Order of Battle,* by Shelby L. Stanton (U.S. News & World Report Books, 1981).

TRUMAN, HARRY S (1884–1972)

Truman was born on May 8, 1884, in Lamar, Missouri. During World War I he served with the American Expeditionary Force in France as Commander of a field artillery battery in the Vosges, Meuse-Argonne and St.-Mihiel campaigns. Elected to the U.S. Senate in 1939, he was selected as President Roosevelt's running mate in 1944 and succeeded to the presidency on April 12, 1945 upon Roosevelt's death, becoming the 33rd President of the United States. In 1948 he was elected in his own right.

During his second term he took several actions that later affected the Vietnam war. When North Korea attacked South Korea in June 1950, President Truman saw it as part of a worldwide move to extend "monolithic communism" by force of arms. On June 27, 1950 President Truman ordered American troops into Korea and also sent the Seventh Fleet into the Taiwan straits to prevent an attack by communist China on Taiwan, increased aid to President Magsaysay in the Philippines—who was battling communist insurgency—and directed "acceleration in the furnishing of military assistance to the forces of France and the Associated States in Indochina [i.e., Cambodia, Laos and Vietnam] and the dispatch of a military mission to provide close working relations with those forces." This military mission was called the U.S. Military Assistance Advisory Group-Indochina (MAAG-Indochina), established in Saigon on September 17, 1950. Thus President Truman set in motion events that 15 years later culminated in America's involvement in the Vietnam war.

Not only did Truman begin America's military involvement in Vietnam, he also had a profound impact on the way the war was fought. When communist Chinese forces intervened in the Korean war in the fall of 1950, President Truman—concerned about widening the war with monolithic communism and precipitating a Soviet attack on war-torn Western Europe—changed U.S. wartime military strategy for the first time from the strategic offensive to the strategic defensive and specifically prohibited military action against Chinese assembly areas and supply depots across the North Korean border in Manchuria. The strategic defensive was the strategy the United States would again employ in Vietnam, where American and South Vietnamese forces were prohibited from interdicting North Vietnamese supply lines and base areas in South China and (for too long) in Laos and Cambodia.

See also CONTAINMENT; DULLES, JOHN FOSTER; KENNAN, GEORGE F.; MAAG-VIETNAM (U.S. MILITARY ASSISTANCE ADVISORY GROUP-VIETNAM); SANCTUARIES; STRATEGIC DEFENSIVE.

Suggestion for further reading: *On Strategy: A Critical Analysis of the Vietnam War,* by Harry G. Summers, Jr. (Novato, Calif.: Presidio Press, 1982).

TUNNEL WARFARE

A remarkable feature of the Vietnam war was the Viet Cong's use of underground tunnels to serve as assembly areas, storage depots and hospitals. This was especially true in the area north and northwest of Saigon astride the Song Sai Gon ("Saigon River"). The so-called Iron Triangle on the river's eastern banks and the district of Cu Chi on its western banks was honeycombed with tunnels, which were used as base areas for attacking Saigon.

Originally dug as hiding places for the Viet Minh in their 1946–54 war with the French, the 30 miles of tunnels during that war had grown to some 125 miles by 1965.

In an attempt to combat the Viet Cong's use of these tunnels, the US military used volunteers to enter the tunnels and flush out the guerrillas. Self-styled "tunnel rats," these soldiers performed particularly arduous duties. Never completely successful in eliminating all of the tunnels, these structures survived the war and some are now maintained by the Socialist Republic of Vietnam as monuments to the war.

See also BEN SUC.

Suggestions for further reading: *The Tunnels of Cu Chi,* by Tom Mangold and John Penycate (New York: Random House, 1985); *Vietnam Studies: Tactical and Matériel Innovations,* by John H. Hay, Jr. (Washington: U.S. Government Printing Office, 1974).

20TH ENGINEER BRIGADE

Formed at Fort Bragg, North Carolina in May 1967, the 20th Engineer Brigade arrived in Vietnam in August 1967. It was stationed at Bien Hoa, III Corps, where it was responsible for engineer support to II Field Force Vietnam and for engineer activities in III and IV Corps. Under its operational control were the 34th Engineer Group (Construction), with eight engineer battalions, and the 79th Engineer Group (Construction) with 11 battalions, as well as several separate engineer battalions and companies. As U.S. forces withdrew from Vietnam, the 20th Engineer Brigade left in September 1971.

Suggestions for further reading: *Vietnam Order of Battle,* by Shelby L. Stanton (Washington, D.C.: U.S. News & World Report Books, 1981).

25TH INFANTRY DIVISION

Organized in October 1941 from elements of the old Hawaiian Division (made famous in James Jones' novel *From Here to Eternity*), the 25th Infantry Division received its baptism of fire on December 7, 1941, during the Japanese attack on Pearl Harbor. Given the nickname the "Tropic Lightning," the division took part in combat operations on Guadalcanal, the northern Solomons and Luzon and served as part of the Army of occupation of Japan. When the Korean war broke out in June 1950, the 25th Infantry Division was once again committed to combat, taking part in the defense of the Pusan perimeter and the drive into North Korea. In 1954, after more than 12 years' absence, it returned to its home state, Hawaii.

In January 1966 the division's Third Brigade (consisting of the First Battalion, 14th Infantry; the First and Second Battalions, 35th Infantry; the Second Battalion, Ninth Artillery; and the First Battalion, 69th Armor) arrived in Vietnam for combat operations in the Central Highlands of II Corps. Later attached to the Fourth Infantry Division, the brigade continued to serve in II Corps until August 1967, when the brigade headquarters (less its battalions) reverted to division control. In the meantime the remainder of the division closed in Vietnam in March 1966 for combat operations in III Corps. Attached to the division were elements of the Third Brigade, Fourth Infantry Division (consisting of the Second Battalion, 12th Infantry; the Second and Third Battalions, 22nd Infantry; Second Battalion, 77th Artillery; Second Battalion, 34th Armor). This Brigade served with the division until August 1967, when, less its battalions, it reverted to Fourth Infantry Division control. In addition to the units enumerated, the 25th Infantry Division consisted of four battalions of light infantry (the Fourth Battalion, Ninth Infantry; the Second Bat-

Insignia of the 20th Engineer Brigade.

talion, 14th Infantry; and the First and Second Battalions, 22nd Infantry) and two battalions of mechanized infantry (the First Battalion, Fifth Infantry and the Fourth Battalion, 23rd Infantry). Other combat elements included an armored reconnaissance unit (the Third Squadron, Fourth Cavalry); and in addition to the artillery battalions listed, three battalions—the First Battalion, Eighth Artillery; the Seventh Battalion, 11th Artillery; and the Sixth Battalion, 77th Artillery—of 105-mm howitzers and the Third Battalion, 13th Artillery with 155-mm howitzers.

The northwestern approaches to Saigon and the border regions between Vietnam and Cambodia in III Corps were the major battlefields for the 25th Infantry Division in Vietnam. It took part in Operation Junction City, the Tet counteroffensive of 1968 and the Cambodian "incursion" in 1970. Leaving behind its Second Brigade, which was later inactivated in April 1971, the 25th Infantry Division returned to Hawaii in 1970 and remains stationed at Schofield Barracks.

The 25th Infantry Division was awarded the Vietnamese Civil Action Medal and the Vietnamese Cross of Gallantry with Palm. During the fighting in Vietnam, the division suffered 34,484 soldiers killed or wounded in action, almost twice as many as its 5,432 casualties in World War II and its 13,685 casualties in the Korean war combined.

The 25th Infantry Division maintains a museum at Schofield Barracks, Hawaii, which has exhibits and material on the division's Vietnam experience. From the beginning of its involvement in Vietnam, the 25th Infantry Division Association maintained close ties with its Vietnam veterans. It has periodic reunions of "Tropic Lightning" veterans, and in 1982 sponsored its own "National Salute to Vietnam Veterans" during its convention in Washington, D.C. Further information can be obtained from Mr. Joseph S. Grasso, 25th Infantry Division Association, 31 Beech Road, Great Neck, New York 11023.

See also CAMBODIA, FOURTH INFANTRY DIVISION, III CORPS TACTICAL ZONE.

Suggestions for further reading: *Vietnam Studies· Cedar Falls-Junction City*, by Bernard W. Rogers (Washington, D.C.: U.S. Government Printing Office, 1974); *Vietnam Order of Battle*, by Shelby L. Stanton (Washington, D.C.: U.S. News & World Report Books, 1981). An account of the division's combat operations, including selected small unit actions, is contained in Shelby L. Stanton's *The Rise and Fall of an American Army* (Novato, Calif.: Presidio Press, 1985).

XXIV CORPS

Activated in Hawaii in 1944, the XXIV Corps of the U.S. Army first saw combat on Leyte in the Philippines in October 1944 and later took part in the battles on Okinawa in the closing days of World War II. Moved to Korea at the end of the war to disarm Japanese troops south of the 38th parallel, the XXIV Corps remained in Korea until it was deactivated in 1949.

On August 15, 1968, the XXIV Corps was reactivated with headquarters at Phu Bai in I Corps, replacing a provisional control headquarters that had been formed in the wake of the North

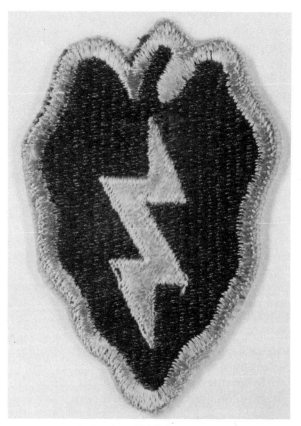

Insignia of the 25th Infantry Division.

Vietnamese Army (NVA) Tet Offensive earlier that year. Major subordinate units at one time or another included the American Division, the First Cavalry Division (Airmobile), the 101st Airborne Division (Airmobile), the First Brigade (Mechanized), the Fifth Infantry Division and the Third Brigade, 82nd Airborne Division. XXIV Corps artillery included the 108th Artillery Group, with three battalions of mixed self-propelled 175-mm guns and 8-inch howitzers, one self-propelled 155-mm howitzer battalion, one self-propelled 105-mm howitzer battalion and one towed 105-mm howitzer battalion.

Originally subordinate to the III Marine Amphibious Force (III MAF), which had the majority of forces in I Corps, on March 9, 1970 (after the withdrawal of the Third Marine Division) the roles were reversed and the III MAF was subordinated to the XXIV Corps, which relocated its headquarters to Da Nang and assumed responsibility for support and assistance to the South Vietnamese Army in I Corps. As U.S. force levels continued to decline, the XXIV Corps was deactivated on June 30, 1972.

During the course of the Vietnam war, command of XXIV Corps was held by:

Commanders	Assumed Command
Lt. General William B. Rosson	February 1968
Lt. General Richard G. Stilwell	July 1968
Lt. General Melvin Zais	June 1968
Lt. General James W. Sutherland, Jr.	June 1970
Lt. General Welborn G. Dolvin	June 1971

Suggestions for further reading: *Vietnam Order of Battle*, by Shelby L. Stanton (Washington, D.C.: U.S. News & World Report Books, 1981).

23RD INFANTRY DIVISION

See AMERICAN DIVISION.

II CORPS TACTICAL ZONE

With headquarters at Pleiku, South Vietnam's II Corps was reponsible for the defense of the central portion of the country. Major units assigned to the area included the South Vietnamese Army's 22nd and 23rd Divisions.

The North Vietnamese Army (NVA) saw the Central Highlands of II Corps as the key to the conquest of South Vietnam. Using the Ho Chi Minh Trail to establish base areas in "neutral" Cambodia to the west of II Corps, their plan was to attack eastward to the sea, cutting South Vietnam in two. To thwart this buildup, U.S. Special Forces teams established almost 60 CIDG (Civilian Irregular Defense Group) camps in II Corps, drawing their manpower from the many Montagnard tribes that lived in the Highlands.

Recognizing the strategic importance of II Corps, in August 1965 Task Force Alpha (later I Field Force Vietnam) was deployed to the area to provide combat assistance to II Corps and to control U.S. combat operations there. With headquarters at Nha Trang (also the headquarters for U.S. Special Forces, later to become the Fifth Special Forces Group), major port facilities were constructed at Cam Ranh Bay, Vung Ro (near Tuy Hoa), Phan Rang, Qui Nhon and at Nha Trang itself to bring in arms and supplies. Jet-capable airfields for U.S. Air Force units were also constructed at Cam Ranh Bay for the 12th Tactical Fighter Wing and 483rd Tactical Airlift Wing, at Phu Cat for the 37th Tactical Fighter Wing, at Tuy Hoa for the 31st Tactical Fighter Wing, and at Phan Rang for the 35th Tactical Fighter Wing, 14th Air Commando Wing and 315th Tactical Airlift Wing.

The first U.S. ground combat unit to deploy to II Corps was the First Cavalry Division (Airmobile) in September 1965, followed by the Third Brigade, 25th Infantry Division in December 1965; the First Brigade, 101st Airborne Division in October 1965; and the Fourth Infantry Division in September 1966. When the First Brigade, 101st Airmobile Division rejoined its parent division for operations in I Corps in November 1967, it was replaced by the 173rd Airborne Brigade. In the meantime South Korea had deployed its Capital Division to II Corps in September 1965, followed by its Ninth Division in September 1966.

Soon after its arrival in Vietnam, the First Cavalry Division was committed to the Western Highlands to check North Vietnamese thrust at Pleiku, and in November 1965 fought in the Battle of the Ia Drang valley, the first major clash between U.S. forces and North Vietnamese regu-

II CORPS

artillery, into II Corps to seize the provincial capital of Kontum, while another North Vietnamese division conducted raids in the coastal plans to tie South Vietnamese forces down. Overrunning outposts at Dak To, the North Vietnamese were stopped at Kontum by South Vietnam's 23rd Division, supported by U.S. air strikes, including B-52 bombing, and helicopter-mounted TOW antitank missiles. After their offensive proved a disaster, the North Vietnamese signed the Paris Accords in January 1973 and two months later the last of the allied forces, the South Korean Capital and White Horse Divisions, left Vietnam.

At the time of the peace agreement in January 1973, the North Vietnamese had 25,550 troops in II Corps, including their Third, 10th and 320th Divisions. But reinforcements were close at hand from the nearby Ho Chi Minh Trail. On March 10, 1975 they began their Final Offensive with a three-division attack on Ban Me Thout, repeating the tactic that had been foiled almost 10 years earlier by the First Cavalry Division at the Ia Drang. With his forces overextended, South Vietnam's President Nguyen Van Thieu on March 14 ordered the abandonment of the Central Highlands and a retreat to coastal enclaves. The most difficult of military maneuvers, this withdrawal under enemy pressure soon turned into a rout. On March 31, North Vietnam's 320th Division reached Tuy Hoa on the coast of the South China Sea. II Corps was no longer under the control of South Vietnam. For his part in the collapse of II Corps, General Pham Van Phu, the Corps Commander, was placed under house arrest by President Thieu in April 1975. After evacuating his family on April 30, General Phu committed suicide.

See also EASTERTIDE OFFENSIVE; FINAL OFFENSIVE; FIRST CAVALRY DIVISION; FOURTH INFANTRY DIVISION; HO CHI MINH TRAIL; IA DRANG, BATTLE OF; I FIELD FORCE VIETNAM; KOREA, SOUTH; MONTAGNARDS; 173RD AIRBORNE BRIGADE.

Suggestions for further reading: *Vietnam Order of Battle,* by Shelby L. Stanton (Washington, D.C.: U.S. News & World Report Books, 1981); *Vietnam from Ceasefire to Capitulation,* by William E. LeGro (Washington, D.C.: U.S. Government Printing Office, 1981); *The Fall of Saigon,* by David Butler (New York: Simon & Schuster, 1985).

lars. The U.S. Fourth Infantry Division (which absorbed the Third Brigade, 25th Infantry Division) was also committed to the Western Highlands to check North Vietnamese infiltration and established base camps at Pleiku and Kontum. The South Korean Capital and Ninth Divisions established security along the coast at Cam Ranh and Qui Nhon while the 173rd Airborne Brigade, after a stiff fight at Dak To north of Kontum in November 1967, went into action in the Bon Son area.

In November 1969 the First Cavalry Division redeployed to III Corps. As the U.S. draw-down began, the Fourth Infantry Division departed Vietnam in December 1970. I Field Force Vietnam was disestablished in April 1971 and the last U.S. ground combat unit, the 173rd Airborne Brigade, departed in August 1971.

With the Americans gone, the North Vietnamese launched their Eastertide Offensive, on March 30, 1972, striking at Quang Tri in I Corps and An Loc in III Corps, and on April 12, 1972 North Vietnam initiated a two-division attack from Cambodia, supported by tanks and heavy

II FIELD FORCE VIETNAM

Organized at the U.S. Army's Fort Hood, Texas, with cadres from the First and Second Armored Divisions and III Corps, II Field Force Vietnam was airlifted to Vietnam in March 1966 to provide combat assistance to South Vietnam's III and IV Corps and to control U.S. military operations on the approaches to Saigon and in the Mekong Delta. In addition, it commanded the 1971 U.S.-South Vietnamese "incursion" into Cambodia.

With headquarters at Bien Hoa, II Field Force Vietnam was a corps-level headquarters and exercised control over II Field Force artillery's 23rd Artillery Group and 54th Artillery Group. It was the largest Army combat command in Vietnam; attached to it at one time or another for special combat operations were the First Infantry Division, the First Cavalry Division (Airmobile), the Ninth Infantry Division, the 25th Infantry Division, the 101st Airborne Division (Airmobile), the Third Brigade, the 82nd Airborne Division, the 173rd Airborne Brigade and the 11th Armored Cavalry Regiment.

During the course of the Vietnam war, command of II Field Force Vietnam was held by:

Commanders	Assumed Command
Maj. Gen. Jonathan O. Seaman	March 1966
Lt. Gen. Bruce Palmer, Jr.	March 1967
Lt. Gen. Frederick C. Weyand	July 1967
Lt. Gen. Walter T. Kerwin, Jr.	August 1968
Lt. Gen. Julian J. Ewell	April 1969
Lt. Gen. Michael S. Davison	April 1970

As part of the U.S. military draw-down, II Field Force Vietnam was disbanded on May 2, 1971.

See also CAMBODIA; FIELD FORCES; IV CORPS TACTICAL ZONE; III CORPS TACTICAL ZONE.

Suggestions for further reading: *Vietnam Order of Battle*, by Shelby L. Stanton (Washington, D.C.: U.S. News & World Report Books, 1981).

TUY HOA

Together with the nearby port of Vung Ro, Tuy Hoa was a major U.S. installation located on the coast of the South China Sea in Phu Yen Province, II Corps. From December 1966 to October 1970 it was the home base of the U.S. Air Force 31st Tactical Fighter Wing. Security at Tuy Hoa was provided by South Korea's 28th Regiment, Ninth (White Horse) Infantry Division.

See also II CORPS TACTICAL ZONE.

U BON AIR BASE

See THAILAND.

U DORN AIR BASE

See THAILAND.

U MINH FOREST

A mangrove swamp area extending along the coast of the Gulf of Siam in An Xuyen Province, IV Corps, the U Minh Forest was a Viet Cong base area.

See map at IV CORPS TACTICAL ZONE.

Suggestions for further reading: *Riverine Operations 1966–1969*, by William B. Fulton (Washington, D.C.: U.S. Government Printing Office, 1973).

UNIT AWARDS

See MERITORIOUS UNIT AWARDS; NAVY UNIT COM-

MENDATION; PRESIDENTIAL UNIT CITATION; SOUTH VIETNAM CIVIL ACTIONS MEDAL UNIT CITATION; SOUTH VIETNAM GALLANTRY CROSS UNIT CITATION; VALOROUS UNIT AWARD.

USARV (U.S. ARMY VIETNAM)

Organized in July 1965 with headquarters in Saigon (later Long Binh), USARV (United States Army Vietnam) grew out of a support detachment furnished by the Ryukyus Command in Okinawa in October 1961 to oversee the logistics buildup in Vietnam, later renamed the U.S. Army Support Group Vietnam. COMUSMACV (the Commander of the U.S. Military Assistance Command Vietnam) was also ostensibly the USARV commander, but in reality the Deputy Commander of the MACV ran USARV on a day-to-day basis.

USARV was *not* what its name implied—a field Army headquarters overseeing Army combat operations. As an administrative and logistical headquarters, it was more akin to what would have been called a "Theater Army" or a "communications zone" in World War II.

In 1972 USARV was redesignated USARV/ MACV Support Command, with five Regional Assistance Commands throughout the country. USARV/MACV Support Command went out of existence in March 1973 after the signing of the Paris Accords.

See also 18TH MILITARY POLICE BRIGADE, FIRST AVIATION BRIGADE, FIRST LOGISTICAL COMMAND, FIRST SIGNAL BRIGADE, 44TH MEDICAL BRIGADE.

Suggestions for further reading: *Command and Control in Vietnam 1950–1969*, by George S. Eckhardt (Washington, D.C.: U.S. Government Printing Office, 1974). USARV was a large and complex organization; the best source is *Vietnam Order of Battle*, by Shelby L. Stanton (Washington, D.C.: U.S. News & World Report Books, 1981). See also Bruce Palmer, Jr.'s *The 25-Year War: America's Military Role in Vietnam* (Lexington: University of Kentucky Press, 1984).

USSR

See SOVIET UNION.

U TAPAO AIR BASE

See THAILAND.

VALOROUS UNIT AWARD

First authorized during the Vietnam war, the Valorous Unit Award is awarded by the U.S. Army to units of the armed forces of the United States for extraordinary heroism in action against the enemy. The Valorous Unit Award requires a lesser degree of gallantry, determination and esprit de corps than that required for the Presidential Unit Citation. Nevertheless, the unit must have performed with marked distinction under difficult and hazardous conditions in accomplishing its mission so as to set it apart from the other units participating in the same conflict. The degree of heroism required is the same as that which would warrant award of the Silver Star to an individual. The award emblem can be worn permanently by personnel assigned to the unit at the time of award.

See also NAVY UNIT COMMENDATION.

VAN TIEN DUNG

See DUNG, VAN TIEN.

"V" DEVICE

To denote an award for heroism for those U.S. decorations that can be awarded for either bravery or meritorious service—i.e., the Bronze Star Medal, the Air Medal and the Commendation Medals—a metallic "V" device is worn on the medal ribbon.

VETERANS

Of the 9,087,000 U.S. military personnel who served on active duty during the Vietnam era—from August 5, 1964 to May 7, 1975—8,744,000 were on active duty during the period of direct U.S. involvement in the war from August 5, 1964 to January 27, 1973. Of these personnel, 3,403,100 served in the Southeast Asia Theater (Vietnam, Laos, Cambodia, flight crews based in Thailand and sailors in the South China Sea). Of the 2,594,000 personnel who served within the borders of South Vietnam, from 40 percent to 60 percent were at least exposed to enemy attack on a fairly regular basis. Only about 20 percent, however, actually served in infantry, armor or artillery units that regularly pursued and engaged the enemy in combat.

The average age of the Vietnam serviceman was 19, compared with 26 for World War II, but 79 percent of those who served in Vietnam had a high school education, compared with only 45 percent for World War II. 97 percent of Vietnam-era veterans received an honorable discharge.

In 1973 some 15 percent of Vietnam veterans identifed themselves with the antiwar movement. Membership in the Vietnam Veterans Against the War—which admitted college students and professors as well as veterans—peaked at about 7,000 members. Some 90 percent of those who saw heavy combat have said they were proud to have served their country, and about 66 percent of Vietnam veterans say the would serve again if called upon. More than 90 percent of Vietnam-era

veterans are employed, and some 80 percent report that they have made a successful transition to civilian society. Yet unemployment among those who served in Vietnam remains higher than the norm, and other problems, including alcoholism and drug addiction, continue to affect some Vietnam veterans. The Veterans Administration as well as state and local agencies have instituted programs specifically aimed at helping Vietnam veterans, and the various veterans organizations provide information on benefits and assistance in dealing with these agencies. While in the decade after the war there was much reported alienation among Vietnam veterans who believed their sacrifices were not appreciated, the dedication of the Vietnam Memorial in Washington, D.C. and the retrospection surrounding the 10th anniversary of the fall of Saigon in 1985 appears to have healed many of these wounds.

See also AGENT ORANGE; BLACKS IN THE U.S. MILITARY; DRAFT; POST-TRAUMATIC STRESS DISORDER; VIETNAM VETERANS LEADERSHIP PROGRAM; VIETNAM VETERANS MEMORIAL.

Suggestions for further reading: *Long Time Passing: Vietnam and the Haunted Generation*, by Myra MacPherson (Garden City: Doubleday, 1984); *America in Vietnam*, by Guenter Lewy (New York: Oxford University Press, 1978); *Touched with Fire: The Future of the Vietnam Generation*, by John Wheeler (New York: Franklin Watts, 1984); *The Wounded Generation: America After Vietnam*, edited by A. D. Horne (Englewood Cliffs, N.J.: Prentice Hall, 1981).

Among sources of information available to Vietnam veterans, one of the most useful is the *Vietnam War Newsletter*, published since 1979 by Vietnam veteran Tom Hebert. The newsletter contains excerpts of articles pertaining to Vietnam veterans, information on organizational reunions and reviews of new books on Vietnam. Affiliated with the newsletter is the *Vietnam Bookstore*, which has the most comprehensive listing of Vietnam war literature available anywhere. Further information can be obtained from the *Vietnam War Newsletter*, P.O. Box 122, Collinsville, Connecticut 26022.

VIET CONG

Viet Cong was a derogatory term for Vietnamese communists in the south. At the end of the War between the French and the Viet Minh (1946–54) 90,000 Viet Minh troops in what was to become South Vietnam were to be repatriated to the north. But the Viet Minh left behind an estimated 5,000 to 10,000 soldiers as a fifth column in the south. Instructed by Hanoi to lie low until 1959, they were then activated by the North Vietnamese Politburo to begin a guerrilla war in the south in an attempt to subvert and overthrow the standing government. Viet Cong forces included "main force" units organized into companies and battalions (and later into regiments and divisions) and after 1964 reinforced by North Vietnamese regular Army units. There was also what was called the Viet Cong infrastructure, or VCI, which consisted of a party secretary, a finance and supply unit, and information and cultural, social welfare, and proselyting sections to gain recruits both from the civilian population and the South Vietnamese military. Search-and-destroy operations by both U.S. and South Vietnamese units were designed to neutralize the Viet Cong and North Vietnamese Army main force units while clear-and-hold operations, and after 1968 the Phoenix program, were designed to root out the VCI with interdependent operations.

The Viet Cong were effectively destroyed by the Tet Offensive of 1968, when believing their propaganda that such an attack would provoke a "general uprising," Viet Cong led an assault on cities throughout South Vietnam. Thereafter the Viet Cong remnants were cadred and controlled by North Vietnamese regulars.

See also PACIFICATION; PHOENIX PROGRAM; TET OFFENSIVE.

Suggestions for further reading: The leading American authority on the Viet Cong is Douglas Pike, who now heads the Indochina Resource Center at the University of California at Berkeley. Among his works are *Viet Cong: The Organization and Techniques of the National Liberation Front of South Vietnam* (Cambridge: MIT Press, 1966); *History of the Vietnamese Communist Party* (Stanford: Hoover Institution Press, 1978); and *The Viet Cong Strategy of Terror* (Saigon: U.S. Information Agency, 1970). A recent book by one of the founders of the National Liberation Front is *A Viet Cong Memoir*, by Truong Nhu Tang, (with David Chanoff and Doan Van Toai) (New York: Harcourt Brace Jovanovich, 1985). For VCI infrastructure, see *Infrastructure and the Marxist Power Seizure: An Analysis of the Communist Models of Revolution*, by Andrew P. O'Meara, Jr. (New York: Vantage Press, 1973) and Appendix B, *Territorial Forces*, by Ngo Quang Truong (Washington, D.C.: Center for Military History, 1981); *Vietnam: A History*, by Stanley Karnow (New York: Viking, 1983).

Viet Cong soldiers. Black pajamas and sandles were part of the standard Viet Cong garb. (Courtesy U.S. Army Military History Institute.)

VIET MINH

Contraction of "Vietnam Doc Lap Dong Minh" (League for Vietnamese Independence), the Viet Minh was founded at the Eighth Plenum of the Indochina Communist Party in 1941. It was the overall title of the Vietnamese—nationalists as well as communists—who fought the French from 1946 to 1954.

See also PART I, THE SETTING; HO CHI MINH.

VIETNAM

See PART I, THE SETTING; SVNAF (SOUTH VIETNAMESE ARMED FORCES); NVA (NORTH VIETNAMESE ARMY).

VIETNAMIZATION

The word itself coined by Secretary of Defense Melvin Laird, "Vietnamization" was officially initiated by President Nixon on June 8, 1969.

Vietnamization was an integral part of President Nixon's strategy to bring the Vietnam war to a close. Essentially, it consisted of a gradual turnover of the war from the U.S. military to South Vietnamese Armed Forces and a buildup of South Vietnam's war supplies. As South Vietnam assumed responsibility for the war, U.S. combat forces were gradually withdrawn.

See also NIXON, RICHARD M.; WITHDRAWAL OF U.S. FORCES.

Suggestions for further reading: *Vietnamization and the Cease-Fire* by Nguyen Duy Hinh (Washington, D.C.: Center of Military History, 1980); *No More Vietnams* by Richard Nixon (New York: Arbor House, 1985).

VIETNAM, NORTH

See (SRV) SOCIALIST REPUBLIC OF VIETNAM.

VIETNAM SERVICE AWARDS

South Vietnam awarded its own decorations and service medals to both U.S. units and to service members to recognize their service in Vietnam. The Republic of Vietnam Gallantry Cross and Republic of Vietnam Civil Actions Medal were awarded to many of the units that served in Vietnam (see RVN Civil Actions Medal, RVN Gallantry Cross). The Gallantry Cross, Navy Gallantry Cross, Air Gallantry Cross, Armed Forces Honor Medal, Civil Actions Medal and Special Service Medal were also awarded to U.S. service personnel for individual acts of heroism or distinguished service. With the approval of the U.S. government, these medals can be worn by personnel so honored.

In addition, all members of the U.S. Armed Forces who served in Vietnam were awarded the Republic of Vietnam Campaign Medal by the South Vietnamese government.

See also CAMPAIGN MEDALS.

VIETNAM, SOUTH

See Part I, THE SETTING.

VIETNAM VETERANS LEADERSHIP PROGRAM

Established by President Reagan on November 10, 1981, the Vietnam Veterans Leadership Program (VVLP) was a federal initiative administered by ACTION, the national volunteer agency. The program encouraged successful Vietnam veterans to volunteer their time, effort and creative leadership to help solve the problems still faced by some of their fellow veterans.

Some 50 VVLP chapters have been established across the United States. All are developed and implemented by Vietnam veterans and approximately half the chairmen and project directors hold at least one Purple Heart for wounds received in action.

Federally assisted until 1984, the VVLP program is now self-sustaining and based on local community support.

See also VETERANS.

VIETNAM VETERANS MEMORIAL

The Vietnam Veterans Memorial in Washington, D.C. was the dream of Vietnam veteran Jan Skruggs, whose Vietnam Veterans Memorial Fund collected 7 million dollars and conducted a design contest for the memorial. It was won by a 21-year-old architecture student at Yale, Maya Ying Lin, in 1981. Her design consisted of a 594-foot chevron-shaped wall of polished black granite cut into a hillside, with the names of servicemen and women killed or missing in Vietnam engraved into the surface. Dedicated in 1982, the memorial was the object of some controversy because many veterans felt that its stark modernistic design failed to properly commemorate the sacrifice of the men and women who fought and died in Vietnam.

The Vietnam Veterans Memorial (lower right) in Washington, D.C., shown during dedication ceremonies in 1982. (AP/Wide World Photos.)

In an effort to accommodate those who felt this way, a more traditional statue of four fighting men was placed near the wall. That statue, by sculptor Frederick E. Hart, was dedicated on Memorial Day, 1984.

The wall, the most visited memorial in Washington in 1984, now contains the names of 58,022 service members who died or are missing in action in Vietnam.

VNAF (REPUBLIC OF VIETNAM AIR FORCE)

See SVNAF (SOUTH VIETNAMESE ARMED FORCES).

VNMC (REPUBLIC OF VIETNAM MARINE CORPS)

See SVNAF (SOUTH VIETNAMESE ARMED FORCES).

VNN (REPUBLIC OF VIETNAM NAVY)

See SVNAF (SOUTH VIETNAMESE ARMED FORCES).

VOGT, JOHN W., JR. (1920–   )

Born on March 19, 1920 in Elizabeth, New Jersey, Vogt enlisted in the U.S. Army Air Corps in 1941 and won his commission and pilot's wings in 1942. During World War II he served as a fighter pilot with both the 63rd Fighter Squadron and 360th Fighter Squadron during two European combat tours.

From 1965 to 1968 General Vogt served as Deputy for Plans and Operations in PACAF (Pacific Air Force) in Honolulu, participating in the planning and direction of the air campaign against North Vietnam. In 1972 Vogt was appointed Commander of the Seventh Air Force in Vietnam (and concurrently Deputy Commander of the MACV [U.S. Military Assistance Command Vietnam]).

General Vogt commanded the massive U.S. air response to the North Vietnamese Eastertide

Offensive of 1972, a response that was critical in turning back that invasion. He also presided over the draw-down of U.S. forces in Vietnam and the ~~final withdrawal in March 1973 after the signing~~

VO NGUYEN GIAP

See GIAP, VO NGUYEN

VUNG TAU

Vung Tau was a port in Phuc Tuy Province, III Corps. It served as an anchorage and as a support area for the Mobile Riverine Force.

See also MOBILE RIVERINE FORCE. *See* MAP AT III CORPS TACTICAL ZONE.

Lewis W. Walt. (Courtesy U.S. Marine Corps.)

that command, which included serving as Chief of Naval Forces Vietnam as well as being Senior Adviser to and Coordinator of South Vietnam's I Corps, responsible for the security of the northern portion of Vietnam. After supervising the I Corps area buildup from 1965 to 1967, General Walt returned to the United States and later served as Assistant Commandant of the Marine Corps. On February 1, 1971 he retired from active duty.

Suggestions for further reading: *Strange War, Strange Strategy,* by Lewis W. Walt (New York: Funk & Wagnalls, 1976).

WAR CORRESPONDENTS

See MEDIA.

WAR CRIMES

See ATROCITIES.

WARNKE, PAUL C(ULLITON) (1920–   )

Following his graduation from Yale in 1941, Warnke, who was born on January 31, 1920 in Webster, Massachusetts, joined the U.S. Coast Guard Reserve, serving until 1946. Two years later he received his law degree from Columbia.

Warnke became General Counsel for the Defense Department in August 1966 and in June 1967 he was appointed Assistant Secretary of Defense for International Security Affairs. Two months later he helped Secretary of Defense Robert S. McNamara draft the "San Antonio Formula." The conciliatory proposal, sent privately to Hanoi, stated that the United States was "willing immediately to stop all aerial and naval bombardment of North Vietnam when [this will lead] promptly to productive discussions." In October North Vietnam emphatically rejected the plan as "sheer deception."

During the first months of 1968 Warnke stepped up his efforts to reduce the level of U.S. military activity in Vietnam. Following the Tet Offensive of January and February, he served as a member of a special committee, convened by the President to examine the military's request for over 200,000 additional troops. In meetings at the beginning of March headed by incoming Secretary of Defense Clark Clifford, Warnke opposed a troop increase and questioned the military's interpretation of the communist offensive as an act of desperation or an attempt to precipitate a popular uprising against the government of South Vietnam. He thought that the offensive was designed to show American citizens that the United States was not winning the war and could not win without undermining its foreign and domestic interests. His opinion was that the United States should not attempt to win a military victory but should use only the degree of force necessary to achieve a compromise political settlement. He therefore objected to further troop increases and suggested instead a strategy designed to protect population centers rather than extend areas of control. The committee rejected Warnke's recommendation and backed the military's request.

On March 12 Warnke wrote a memorandum to Clifford suggesting that Hanoi had recently given indications that it now accepted the provisions of the San Antonio Formula. In light of this, he recommended that the United States begin a policy of de-escalation as a sign of good faith. Warnke's advice in the committee meetings and in his correspondence with Clifford had an important influence on the Secretary of Defense, who in turn played a large role in convincing President Johnson of the need for de-escalation. Johnson announced this policy on March 31.

Warnke resigned his defense post in February 1969 to become a partner in a Washington law firm.

See also AD HOC TASK FORCE ON VIETNAM; CLIFFORD, CLARK; MCNAMARA, ROBERT S.; SAN ANTONIO FORMULA.

WAR POWERS ACT

In November 1973 Congress, over the veto of President Nixon, passed the War Powers Resolution. It requires the President to consult with Congress before military forces are committed. Military involvement can continue for 60 days, and for another 30 days thereafter if the President certifies in writing that the safety of the force so requires, but unless Congress specifically authorizes it by a declaration of war, resolution or legislation, the involvement cannot be continued beyond 90 days.

Some have challenged the constitutionality of this legislation as an infringement on the powers granted by Article II of the Constitution to the President as Commander-in-Chief, but as of 1985 this challenge has not been put to a legal test.

See also DECLARATION OF WAR; JAVITS, JACOB.

Suggestions for further reading: *Who Makes War: The President versus Congress*, Jacob K. Javits (New York: Morrow, 1973); *The War Powers Resolution*, 94th Congress, 2nd Session, Committee on International Relations, U.S. House of Representatives (Washington, D.C.: U.S. Government Printing Office, 1975).

WARS OF NATIONAL LIBERATION

Announced by Soviet Premier Nikita Khrushchev in January 1961, "wars of national liberation" were a Soviet ploy to use surrogate forces to advance their objectives without risking a direct confrontation with the United States.

Vietnam was seen as a test case for this Soviet encouragement of unconventional forces to undermine and eventually conquer American allies. Forgetting that a war of national liberation was first and foremost a *war* in which all the old rules still applied (as the North Vietnamese Army was to prove most conclusively), the United States relied on doctrines of counterinsurgency as the appropriate response.

But in the end Vietnam was won by a conventional cross-border invasion by some 20 North Vietnamese Army divisions, more akin to the Nazi blitzkrieg that swept across France in 1940, rather than by war of national liberation.

See also COUNTERINSURGENCY, PEOPLES' WARS.

Suggestions for further reading: *On Strategy: A*

Critical Analysis of the Vietnam War, by Harry G. Summers, Jr. (Novato, Calif.: Presidio Press, 1982).

WAR ZONES C AND D

Dating from before American involvement in Vietnam, War Zones C and D were inexact terms used to describe major Viet Cong guerrilla areas located to the north of Saigon.

War Zone C was bordered by Cambodia on the west, which gave guerrillas there access to North Vietnamese supply base areas in "neutral" Cambodia. It included the northern half of Tay Ninh Province, the western half of Binh Long Province, and the northwestern quarter of Binh Duong Province in III Corps. Several major U.S. combat operations were conducted in this area, including one of the largest, Operation Junction City, in 1967.

War Zone D was located to the east of War Zone C and included the northwestern portion of Binh Duong Province, a northeastern portion of Bien Hoa Province, the southern portion of Phuoc Long Province and the northern portion of Long Khanh Province in III Corps; it stretched to the northeast II Corps-III Corps boundary. A U.S. infantry brigade base was established at Phuoc Vinh in the center of War Zone D to interdict enemy activity.

See also III CORPS TACTICAL ZONE.

Suggestions for further reading: *Cedar Falls-Junction City: A Turning Point*, by Bernard William Rogers (Washington, D.C.: U.S. Government Printing Office, 1974).

WESTMORELAND, WILLIAM C(HILDS) (1914-   )

Westmoreland was born in Spartanburg County, South Carolina on March 26, 1914. He graduated from the U.S. Military Academy in 1936. During World War II Westmoreland, then a Lieutenant Colonel, commanded a field artillery battalion during the North African and Sicily campaigns and later was Chief of Staff of the Ninth

Infantry Division during the invasion of Europe. After serving as an instructor at both the Command and General Staff College and Army War College, Colonel Westmoreland fought in the Korean war as commander of the 187th Airborne Infantry Regimental Combat Team. After his return to the United States and promotion to General, he commanded the 101st Airborne Division and later served as Superintendent of the U.S. Military Academy. When Secretary of Defense Robert S. McNamara selected him as Commander of the MACV (U.S. Military Assistance Command Vietnam), General Westmoreland was in command of America's rapid reaction force, the XVIII Airborne Corps.

Serving briefly as the Deputy Commander, General Westmoreland assumed command of the MACV on June 20, 1964. His initial task was to provide military advice and assistance to the government of South Vietnam. Less than 60 days later, however, with the Gulf of Tonkin Incident, General Westmoreland assumed the added responsibility of commanding America's armed forces in combat in Vietnam.

One of the Vietnam war's most controversial figures, General Westmoreland was given many honors when the fighting was going well, but when the war turned sour, many Americans saw him as a cause of U.S. problems in Vietnam. Negative feeling about Westmoreland grew particularly strong following the Tet Offensive of 1968, when he and General Earle Wheeler requested a large number of additional troops for deployment to Vietnam.

It is grossly misleading to think of General Westmoreland as the counterpart of the North Vietnamese Commander, General Vo Nguyen Giap. General Giap was a Deputy Premier in the North Vietnamese government, a member of the Politburo, the Minister of Defense and the Commander-in-Chief of the army of North Vietnam. On the American side, such roles and responsibilities were divided among National Security Adviser Walt Rostow; General Maxwell D. Taylor, the President's personal military adviser; Secretary of Defense Robert McNamara (and later Clark Clifford); Chairman of the Joint Chiefs of Staff General Earle Wheeler; and the strategic commander for the Vietnam war, Admi-

William C. Westmoreland. (Courtesy U.S. Army Military History Institute.)

ral U.S. Grant Sharp, the Commander-in-Chief of the Pacific Command (CINCPAC) in Honolulu. Although these individuals exercised strategic control over military operations in Vietnam, they were thousands of miles away from the war. General Westmoreland was only the commander of forces in the field, and even within Vietnam his authority was restricted. CINCPAC in Honolulu exercised much of the control over U.S. Navy and Air Force Units and South Vietnamese Armed Forces were under their own national control.

Seen in his true role as the tactical commander, General Westmoreland's service in Vietnam takes on a new light. When he took command of the MACV in June 1964, South Vietnam was under intense pressure from the Viet Cong guerrillas and the country was in imminent danger of collapse. When he left in the summer of 1968 to assume duties as Army Chief of Staff in Washington, the guerrillas were by their own admission a spent force, and from 1968 on, the war was increasingly waged not by Viet Cong guerrillas but by regular forces of the North Vietnamese Army. As the British strategist Brigadier Shelford Bidwell has remarked, however, the strategic price of these tactical successes, heavily dependent as they were on "fire power of crushing intensity," was "American society in turmoil." In other words, the use of heavy firepower, effective though it was in combating the guerrillas in the south, alienated the American public because of its immense destructive power.

Perhaps General Westmoreland's greatest service to his country, and undoubtedly the one most painful to him, was taking much of the blame and absorbing much of the burden of American civilian and military frustration over the Vietnam war. Unfair as it may be to him, the result of such draining off of animosity was that no stab-in-the-back syndrome ever developed in America as had developed in Germany after World War I, in France after Algeria or in Portugal after Angola. Although U.S. troops were still fighting in Vietnam when he retired from active duty in 1972, and although three years would elapse before the war finally came to an end with the 1975 North Vietnamese Army cross-border blitzkreig, General Westmoreland remains closely identified with America's defeat in Vietnam.

In January 1982, in a documentary called "The Uncounted Enemy: A Vietnam Deception," CBS portrayed Westmoreland as manipulating intelligence data, particularly enemy troop strength figures in Vietnam. CBS correspondent Mike Wallace told viewers that CBS would present "evidence of what we have come to believe was a conscious effort—indeed a conspiracy at the highest levels of American military intelligence—to suppress and alter critical intelligence on the enemy in the year leading up to the Tet offensive." Westmoreland sued CBS for libel and the case went to trial in the fall of 1984. The trial lasted 18 weeks and came to a surprise end on February 18, 1985 with an out-of-court settlement in which no money changed hands. The statement, which Westmoreland called an apology, said that CBS "never intended to assert, and does not believe, that Gen. Westmoreland was unpatriotic or disloyal in performing his duties as he saw them." But it added that Westmoreland

recognized the rights of journalists "to present perspectives contrary to his own" on the Vietnam war. For its part, CBS claimed that "we continue to stand by the broadcast. . . ."

Testimony during the trial made it fairly apparent that some manipulation of figures had been carried out, although the exact nature of and explanation for that manipulation remains unclear. CIA and U.S. Army figures on troop strength and on infiltration of North Vietnamese troops differed on many occasions throughout the conflict. In a war without front lines, determining the numerical strength of the enemy was anything but an exact science, and since troop strength was a politically sensitive figure, it is hardly surprising that the figures released by military intelligence were altered to take these factors into account.

The Westmoreland trial made headlines not only because of the legal issues it addressed concerning libel suits filed by public figures, but also because it brought to the fore many of the arguments that raged during the war, including the right of the American public to accurate military information, even if that information is sensitive enough to have an impact upon the capacity of the military to fulfill its objectives.

See also IA DRANG, BATTLE OF; JOHNSON, LYNDON B.; KHE SANH, BATTLE OF; MEDIA; SEARCH-AND-DESTROY; STRATEGY, U.S.; TET OFFENSIVE

Suggestions for Further Reading: *A Soldier Reports,* by William C. Westmoreland (Garden City: Doubleday, 1976); *The Best and the Brightest,* by David Halberstam (New York: Random House, 1972); *The 25-Year War: America's Military Role in Vietnam,* by Bruce Palmer, Jr. (Lexington: University of Kentucky Press, 1984); *A Matter of Honor,* by Don Kowet (New York: Macmillan, 1984).

WEYAND, FREDERICK C(ARLTON) (1916–   )

Born on September 15, 1916 at Arbuckle, California, Weyand graduated from the University of California at Berkeley in 1939. Originally commissioned in the Coast Artillery Corps, he served as an intelligence officer in the China-Burma-

India Theater in World War II. Transferring to the infantry in 1948, he won the Silver Star Medal for gallantry in action as a combat infantryman during the war in Korea.

In March 1966 General Weyand took the 25th Infantry Division into combat in Vietnam. After 12 months of battlefield activity with his division in western III Corps, he was selected to command the corps-level II Field Force Vietnam. During the Tet Offensive in 1968 his forces were instrumental in turning back the Viet Cong attack on Saigon. Departing Vietnam in August 1968, he later served as the Military Adviser to the U.S. Peace Delegation in Paris from March 1969 to June 1970.

In September 1970 General Weyand returned to Vietnam to serve as Deputy Commander of the MACV (U.S. Military Assistance Command Vietnam) and in June 1972 succeeded General Creighton Abrams as COMUSMACV (Commander of the U.S. Military Assistance Command Vietnam). Faced with the difficult and dangerous task of winding down the U.S. military presence in Vietnam, he was fated to be the last MACV commander. When the Paris Accords were signed in January 1973, General Weyand withdrew the last U.S. military forces.

Soon thereafter Weyand was named Army Vice Chief of Staff. Upon the death of Army Chief of Staff General Creighton Abrams on September 4, 1974, General Weyand assumed that office. Sent to Vietnam in April 1975 by President Gerald Ford to assess the military situation there, General Weyand was unable to dissuade America's political leaders from abandoning its ally in its most dire time of need.

General Weyand took the Army through its most difficult days. Carrying out the programs General Abrams had set in motion to build a post-Vietnam Army, he also set the course for an objective analysis of the Vietnam war within the Army so as to improve its ability to serve the American people. General Weyand retired from active duty in September 1976.

Suggestions for further reading: "Vietnam Myths and American Military Realities," by Fred C. Weyand in *Commanders Call*, July/August 1976; "Serving the People: The Basic Case for the U.S. Army," by Fred C. Weyand in *Commanders Call*, May/June 1976; "Serving the People: The Need for Military Power," by Fred C. Weyand in *Military Review*, December 1976.

Fred C. Weyand. (Courtesy U.S. Army Military History Institute.)

WHEELER, EARLE G(ILMORE) (1908–1975)

Born on January 13, 1908 in Washington, D.C., Wheeler graduated from the U.S. Military Academy in 1932. Although commissioned in the infantry, Wheeler had no combat experience in either World War II or Korea. Rising to prominence in the Army as an administrator, he became a protégé of General Maxwell D. Taylor.

When President Kennedy recalled General Taylor to active duty as Chairman of the Joint Chiefs of Staff in 1962, General Wheeler was named Army Chief of Staff. A former mathematics professor at the Military Academy, General Wheeler, according to accounts, "gained a reputation for playing the Pentagon's game under Mr. McNamara's rules." Thus, when General Taylor was nominated as Ambassador to South Vietnam in 1964, General Wheeler replaced him as Chairman of the Joint Chiefs of Staff.

As the senior military officer in the United States from 1964 to 1970—from the beginning of the commitment of U.S. combat forces to the start of their final withdrawal—General Wheeler was responsible for providing military advice to the President on the strategy and conduct of the Vietnam war. He was also a member of the Senior Advisory Group, which was so influential in President Johnson's decision to de-escalate the war in 1968.

General Wheeler retired from active duty in 1970. He died on December 18, 1975.

See also SENIOR ADVISORY GROUP.

Suggestions for further reading: *The Best and the Brightest,* by David Halberstam (New York: Random House, 1972); *The 25-Year War: America's Military Role in Vietnam,* by Bruce Palmer, Jr. (Lexington: University of Kentucky Press, 1984); *The Unmaking of a President: Lyndon Johnson and Vietnam,* by Herbert Schandler (Princeton: Princeton University Press, 1977).

WHITE HORSE DIVISION

Nickname of South Korea's Ninth Infantry Division, deployed to Vietnam in September 1965 (*see* KOREA).

WHITE STAR MOBILE TRAINING TEAM

Designation of a U.S. Special Forces training team introduced into Laos in July 1959, the mission of the White Star Mobile Training Team was to establish a sound basic training system for the Laotian army. With an initial strength of 107 personnel, these Special Forces teams rotated between Laos and their home bases in the United States and Okinawa. In 1960 their mission was extended to provide aid and assistance to the Hmoung tribesmen in the Laotian mountains. With the Geneva Accords in 1962, these Special

Forces teams, now grown to some 512 personnel, were withdrawn, and by the late summer of 1962, the White Star program ended.

See also LAOS, SPECIAL FORCES.

Suggestions for Further Reading: *The End of Nowhere: American Policy Toward Laos Since 1954,* by Charles A. Stevenson (Boston: Beacon Press, 1973); "White Star in Laos: A Study in Miscalculation," by Rod Paschall (unpublished manuscript, U.S. Army Military History Institute, Carlisle Barracks, Pa., June 1985); *The Green Berets At War,* by Shelby L. Stanton (Novato, Calif.: Presidio Press, 1985).

WILD WEASEL

Nickname for a U.S. Air Force aircraft (usually an F-105) stocked with special electronic countermeasures (ECM) equipment that could pick up SAM (surface-to-air missile) locations, and armed with air-to-ground missiles that could home-in on SAM radar beams.

Wild Weasels were one of the many methods used to attempt to counter North Vietnamese antiaircraft missile defense. Other methods included using evasive flying techniques, dropping chaff (i.e., strips of metal foil) to confuse radar systems and employing ECM aircraft to block out enemy radar.

See also SAM (SURFACE-TO-AIR MISSILE).

Suggestions for further reading: *Airpower in Three Wars,* by William W. Momyer, (Washington, D.C.: U.S. Government Printing Office, 1978).

WING

During the Vietnam war the wing was a major organizational element of the U.S. Air Force and Navy. Commanded by a colonel, a typical Air Force fighter wing consisted of a headquarters, a supply squadron, an engineering squadron, a medical unit and three fighter squadrons of about 25 aircraft each. Naval air was organized into a carrier air wing based on board each aircraft carrier. Commanded by a Navy captain, each air wing contained about 75 aircraft. A typical carrier air wing consisted of two fighter squadrons, four attack squadrons and reconnaissance and early-warning detachments.

In the Marine Corps, a wing is a much larger unit. Commanded by a major general, it includes as many as 500 operational aircraft, helicopters as well as fighters and fighter-bombers. A Marine aircraft wing (MAW) is divided into groups under the command of a colonel, thus a Marine aircraft group is equivalent to a Navy or Air Force "wing."

See also FLIGHT, SQUADRON.

WITHDRAWAL OF U.S. FORCES

One of the most difficult military operations is a withdrawal while in enemy contact. The danger is that as units move out of position and as force levels decrease, the enemy may take advantage of such lack of balance and turn the withdrawal into a rout. It is made even more difficult when the pace of withdrawal is dictated not by battlefield conditions but by domestic political pressure.

Ordered by President Nixon and Secretary of Defense Melvin Laird to withdraw U.S. military forces from Vietnam, then COMUSMACV (Commander of the U.S. Military Forces Vietnam) General Creighton Abrams devised a "glide path" to gradually draw down U.S. forces. The withdrawal was broken into 14 increments. The time frame for Increment I was July 1, 1969–August 13, 1969, and for Increment XIV September 1, 1972–November 30, 1972. The Marines were generally withdrawn in Increments I through VI, as were five Army infantry divisions. The rest were phased out gradually, with the last ground combat battalion, the Third Battalion, 21st Infantry departing on August 23, 1972.

The controversial Cambodian "incursion" from April 30 and June 30, 1970 has been justified as an integral part of this withdrawal plan, designed to throw the North Vietnamese Army (NVA) off balance so it could not interfere with the drawdown. But the North Vietnamese did not interfere. Instead, they waited until there were only about two U.S. ground combat brigades left in Vietnam—the Third Brigade, First Cavalry Division (Airmobile); and the 196th Light Infantry Brigade—and then launched their Eastertide Offensive on March 30, 1972. Committing almost their entire regular army, supported by heavy artillery and T-54 Soviet-supplied tanks, they launched multi-division attacks at Quang Tri in I Corps, Kontum in II Corps and An Loc in III Corps. North Vietnam evidently believed that with U.S. units withdrawn, South Vietnam would collapse.

But after initial reverses, the South Vietnamese Army held. Supported by U.S. fighters, fighter-bombers, B-52 strategic bombers, and naval gunfire, South Vietnam counterattacked, and by September 1972 the North Vietnamese Army fell back, half its heavy equipment lost with over 100,000 casualties. With all U.S. combat units withdrawn from Vietnam by August 1972, security for the residual U.S. force was provided by the South Vietnamese until the final U.S. withdrawal in March 1973.

Suggestions for further reading: A table showing U.S. Army withdrawal increments is contained in Appendix A, *Vietnam Order of Battle,* by Shelby L. Stanton (Washington, D.C.: U.S. News & World Report Books, 1981). Marine withdrawal increments are contained in "Marine Corps Operations in Vietnam 1969–1972," by Edwin H. Simmons, in *The Marines in Vietnam 1954–1973* (Washington, D.C.: U.S. Government Printing Office, 1974). Air Force withdrawals are shown in Appendix 1, *The United States Air Force in Vietnam 1961–1973,* edited by Carl Berger (Washington, D.C.: U.S. Government Printing Office, 1977). Navy withdrawal is discussed in *A Short History of the United States Navy and the Southeast Asian Conflict 1950–1975,* by Edward J. Marolda and G. Wesley Pryce, III (Washington, D.C.: Naval Historical Center, 1984).

WOMEN IN THE U.S. MILITARY

Formally incorporated in the armed forces at the beginning of the century, over 1 million women have served in the military, including service in both World Wars, the Korean war and the war in Vietnam. Although statistics are not exact, it is estimated that some 261,000 women served in the military during the Vietnam era, and over 7,500 actually served in Vietnam, including 5,000 women in the Army in Vietnam, almost 2,000 in the Air Force, 500 in the Navy and 27 in the

Major (now Brigadier General) Evelyn P. Foote with Vietnamese children in a village near Chu Lai.

Marine Corps. Eight military women—seven Army nurses and one Air Force nurse—died in Vietnam, including one killed in action, Lieutenant Sharon A. Lanz, Army Nurse Corps, who was mortally wounded during a rocket attack on Chu Lai on June 8, 1969. The majority of American military women in Vietnam served in the Nurse Corps and in other medical fields, but they also served in administrative positions, as trainers and advisers to South Vietnamese Women's Army Corps as well as in combat related positions, such as photo interpreters with Military Intelligence units.

In addition to American women in the military, other American women served in Vietnam as part of the American embassy and the U.S. military civilian work force, including foreign service officers, administrative personnel, librarians, and Red Cross and USO volunteers. Among the last American deaths in Vietnam were 37 female civilian employees killed in the crash of an Air Force evacuation transport on April 4, 1975.

Suggestions for further reading: *Women Veterans: America's Forgotten Heroines,* by June A. Willenz (New York: Continuum, 1984); *Women in the Military,* by Jeanne Holm (Novato, Calif.: Presidio Press, 1982); *Data on Vietnam Era Veterans* (Washington, D.C.: Veterans Administration, 1983).

XUAN LOC, BATTLE OF

Xuan Loc, the capital of Long Khanh Province in III Corps, 40 miles northeast of Saigon, was defended by the South Vietnamese Army's 18th Infantry Division. During the North Vietnamese Army's (NVA) Final Offensive, Xuan Loc came under attack on March 17, 1975 by its Sixth and Seventh Divisions. Their attack was repulsed, but on April 9, 1975 the North Vietnamese 341st Division joined the attack. After an artillery bombardment of some 4,000 rounds and supported by Soviet-supplied medium tanks, they again struck the South Vietnamese defenses at Xuan Loc. But again, the 18th Infantry Division held. On April 15, 1975 the North Vietnamese reinforced the Sixth, Seventh and 341st Divisions with their 325 Division and began moving their 10th and 304th Divisions into position.

Under constant attack by four NVA divisions, the South Vietnamese Army's 18th Division finally gave ground on April 17, 1975. The 18th had held for almost a month and had virtually destroyed three NVA divisions, but its valiant stand was to be the last major battle of the Vietnam war.

See also FINAL OFFENSIVE.

Suggestions for further reading: *Vietnam from Cease-Fire to Capitulation*, by William E. LeGro (Washington, D.C.: U.S. Government Printing Office, 1981).

XUAN THUY

See THUY, XUAN.

YANKEE STATION

Name for a fixed point off the Vietnamese coast in the South China Sea, located at 17°30′N 108°30′E. It was used as an operating area by the U.S. Navy's Seventh Fleet Attack Carrier Striking Force (Task Force 77).

See also AIRCRAFT CARRIERS, DIXIE STATION, SEVENTH FLEET.

Suggestions for further reading: *A Short History of the United States Navy and the Southeast Asian Conflict 1950-1975*, by Edward J. Marolda and G. Wesley Pryce, III (Washington, D.C.: Naval Historical Center, 1984).

Z

ZUMWALT, ELMO R(USSELL), JR. (1920–   )

Born on November 29, 1920 in San Francisco, California, Zumwalt graduated from the U.S. Naval Academy in 1942. During World War II he served on destroyers in the Pacific Theater.

On September 30, 1968 Admiral Zumwalt was appointed COMNAVFORV (Commander of U.S. Navy Forces Vietnam) and as such was responsible for naval operations including the Coastal Surveillance Force, the River Patrol Force and the Riverine Assault Force, as well as the Naval Advisory Group to the South Vietnamese Navy, the SEABEEs of the Third Naval Construction Brigade and other activities that included Coast Guard Activities, Vietnam. While COMNAVFORV, Admiral Zumwalt organized a concerted U.S. and South Vietnamese Navy operation to cut enemy supply lines from Cambodia. Titled Operation Sealords, this effort succeeded in establishing patrol barriers that severely restricted enemy infiltration.

Named Chief of Naval Operations, Admiral Zumwalt departed Vietnam in May 1970 and assumed his new office on July 1, 1970. He retired from active duty on July 1, 1974. His son, Elmo R. Zumwalt, III, a Navy officer who commanded a swift boat unit of the Coastal Surveillance Force in Vietnam, is believed to be suffering from the aftereffects of Agent Orange, which, as COMNAVFORV, Admiral Zumwalt ordered used as a

Elmo R. Zumwalt. (Courtesy U.S. Navy.)

defoliant to reduce enemy ambush positions along coastal waterways.

See also AGENT ORANGE, CHIEF OF NAVAL OPERATIONS, NAVAL FORCES VIETNAM.

Suggestions for further reading: *On Watch: A Memoir,* by Elmo R. Zumwalt, Jr. (New York: Quadrangle, 1976).

selective bibliography

SELECTIVE BIBLIOGRAPHY

As a practical matter, almost any bibliography on Vietnam must be selective, for there are literally thousands of books and articles on America's involvement in Vietnam. Richard Dean Burrs and Milton Leitenberg's *The Wars in Vietnam, Cambodia and Laos 1945–1982: A Bibliographic Guide* (Santa Barbara: ABC-Cleo Information Services, 1984), for example, has over 6,000 entries to 1982 alone.

The works listed in this bibliography are primarily those recommended as *Suggestions for further reading* in the almanac itself. For that reason the bibliography is more diversified than ones normally found on the Vietnam war, for, where possible, dissenting viewpoints were deliberately included. For example, a listing on a personality might include his own works as well as those of his critics.

Another feature of this bibliography is the inclusion of the official histories and monographs published by the Centers of Military, Naval, Air Force and Marine Corps History. These works, many by first-hand participants in the events described, add a valuable dimension to an understanding of the war.

This bibliography does not purport to contain the last word on the Vietnam war. If past wars are any guide, many fine books remain to be written, for usually at least 10 years must pass before objective and even-handed accounts of a war begin to appear. While individual books listed below may be neither objective nor evenhanded (especially true of those written in the late 1960s and early 1970s when passions ran high), it is hoped that the reader will find that the bibliography as a whole meets precisely the standards of objectivity and evenhandedness.

Albright, John, John A. Cash, and Allan W. Sandstrum. *Seven Firefights in Vietnam*. Washington, D.C.: U.S. Government Printing Office, 1970.

Alexander, Charles C. *Holding the Line: The Eisenhower Era 1952–1961*. America Since World War II Series. Bloomington: Indiana University Press, 1975.

Ambrose, Stephen E. *Eisenhower, Volume Two: President and Elder Statesman 1952–1969*. New York: Simon & Schuster, 1984.

America's Medal of Honor Recipients. Golden Valley, Minn.: Highland Publishers, 1980.

Anderson, Charles B. *The Grunts*. Novato, Calif.: Presidio Press, 1976.

Anderson, William C. *Bat-21*. New York: Bantam Books, 1983.

Anson, Robert Sam. *McGovern: A Biography*. New York: Holt, Rinehart & Winston, 1972.

Arlen, Michael. *Living Room War*. New York: Viking, 1969.

Bailey, George A. "Interpretive Reporting of the Vietnam War by Anchormen." *Journalism Quarterly* 53, no. 2 (Summer 1976).

———. "Television War: Trends in Network Coverage of Vietnam 1965–1970." *Journal of Broadcasting* (Spring 1976).

Bailey, George A., and Lawrence W. Lichty. "Rough Justice on a Saigon Street: A Gatekeeper Study of NBC's Tet Execution Film," *Journalism Quarterly* 49, no. 2 (Summer 1972).

Ball, George W. *Diplomacy for a Crowded World*. Atlantic-Little, Brown, 1976.

Ballard, Jack S. *The United States Air Force in Southeast Asia: Fixed Wing Gunships*. Washington, D.C.: U.S. Government Printing Office, 1982.

Baldwin, Hanson W. *Strategy for Tomorrow*. New York: Harper & Row, 1970.

Barnouw, Erik. *The Image Empire*. A History of Broadcasting in the United States. New York: Oxford University Press, 1970.

Baskir, Lawrence M., and William A. Strauss. *Chance and Circumstance: The Draft, the War, and the Vietnam Generation*. New York: Knopf, 1978.

Beech, Keyes. *Not Without the Americans*. Garden City, N.Y.: Doubleday, 1971.

Bell, Coral. "The Asian Balance of Power: A Comparison with European Precedence." In *Adelphi Papers No. 44*. London: The International Institute for Strategic Studies, 1968.

Bell, J. Bower. *The Myth of the Guerrilla: Revolutionary Theory and Malpractice*. New York: Knopf, 1971.

Bender, David L., ed. *The Vietnam War: Opposing Viewpoints*. St. Paul: Greenhaven Press, 1984.

Berger, Carl, ed. *The United States Air Force in Southeast Asia 1961–1973*. Washington, D.C.: U.S. Government Printing Office, 1977.

Berry, John Stevens. *These Gallant Men on Trial in Vietnam*. Novato, Calif.: Presidio Press, 1984.

Betts, Richard K. *Soldiers, Statesmen and Cold War Crises*. Boston: Harvard University Press, 1977.

Binkin, Martin, et al. *Blacks in the Military*. Washington, D.C.: Brookings Institution, 1982.

Blakey, Scott. *Prisoner at War: The Survival of Commander Richard A. Stratton*. Garden City, N.Y.: Anchor Press/Doubleday, 1978.

Blaufarb, Douglas S. *The Counterinsurgency Era: U.S. Doctrine and Performance 1950 to Present*. New York: Free Press, 1977.

Bloom, Lynn Z. *Doctor Spock: Biography of a Conservative Radical*. Indianapolis and New York. Bobbs, 1972.

Bonds, Ray, ed. *The Vietnam War: The Illustrated*

History of the Conflict in Southeast Asia. New York: Crown Publishers, 1983.

Bouscaren, Anthony T., ed. *All Quiet on the Eastern Front.* Old Greenwich, Conn.: Devin-Adair, 1977.

Bowers, Ray L. *The U.S. Air Force in Southeast Asia: Tactical Airlift.* Washington, D.C.: U.S. Government Printing Office, 1983.

Boyne, Walter J. *Phantom in Combat.* Annapolis: Naval Institute Press, 1985.

Braestrup, Peter. *Battle Lines: Report of the Twentieth Century Fund Task Force on the Military and the Media.* New York: Priority Press, 1985.

——— . *Big Story: How the American Press and Television Reported and Interpreted the Crisis of Tet 1968 in Vietnam and Washington.* New Haven: Yale University Press, 1983.

——— , ed. *Vietnam As History.* Washington, D.C.: University Press of America, 1984.

Broughton, Jack. *THUD Ridge.* New York: Lippincott, 1969.

Brown, William A. *The Soviet Role in Asia.* Current Policy no. 521. Washington, D.C.: U.S. Department of State, October 16, 1983.

Bryant, C. D. B. "The Veterans' Ordeal." Review of *Waiting for an Army to Die: The Tragedy of Agent Orange,* by Fred A. Wilcox. *The New Republic,* June 27, 1983.

Buckingham, William A. *Operation Ranch Hand: The United States Air Force and Herbicides in Southeast Asia, 1961–1971.* Washington, D.C.: U.S. Government Printing Office, 1982.

Bunting, Josiah. *The Lionheads.* New York: Braziller, 1972.

Burbage, Paul, et al. *The Battle for the Skies Over North Vietnam, 1964–1972.* Washington, D.C.: U.S. Government Printing Office, 1976.

Burrs, Richard Dean, and Milton Leitenberg. *The Wars in Vietnam, Cambodia, and Laos, 1945–1982: A Bibliographic Guide.* Santa Barbara: ABC-Cleo Information Services, 1984.

Butler, David. *The Fall of Saigon.* New York: Simon & Schuster, 1985.

——— . "Nguyen Van Hao's Missing Visa." *National Review,* March 23, 1984.

Buttinger, Joseph. *The Smaller Dragon: A Political History of Vietnam.* New York: Praeger, 1958.

——— . *Vietnam: A Dragon Embattled.* New York: Praeger, 1967.

——— . *Vietnam: A Political History.* New York: Praeger, 1968.

——— . *Vietnam: The Unforgettable Tragedy.* New York: Horizon, 1977.

Cady, John. *The Roots of French Imperialism in Indochina.* Ithaca: Cornell University Press, 1954.

Carhart, Tom. *Battles and Campaigns in Vietnam.* New York: Crown, 1984.

Cash, John A. "Fight at Ia Drang, 14–16 November 1965." In *Seven Firefights in Vietnam,* by John Albright, et al. Washington, D.C.: U.S. Government Printing Office, 1970.

Chai, Winberg, ed. *Essential Works of Chinese Communism.* New York: Pica Press, 1970.

Chen, King C. *Vietnam and China 1938–1954.* Princeton: Princeton University Press, 1969.

Chester, Lewis, Godfrey Hodgson, and Bruce Page. *An American Melodrama.* New York: Viking, 1969.

Clark, Doug. "The Loneliness and Pain of Canadian Veterans of the Vietnam War" *Toronto Globe and Mail* (9 July 1984).

Clausewitz, Carl von. *On War.* Translated by Michael Howard and Peter Paret. Princeton: Princeton University Press, 1976.

Clavell, James, ed. *The Art of War,* by Sun Tzu. New York: Delacorte Press, 1983.

Cohen, Eliot A. *Citizens and Soldiers: The Dilemmas of Military Service.* Ithaca: Cornell University Press, 1985.

Cohen, Steven. "Homefront USA." In *Vietnam Anthology and Guide to a Television History.* New York: Knopf, 1983.

Colby, William, and Peter Forbath. *Honorable Men: My Life in the CIA.* New York: Simon & Schuster, 1978.

Collins, James Lawton, Jr. *The Development and Training of the South Vietnamese Army 1950–1972.* Washington, D.C.: U.S. Government Printing Office, 1975.

Collins, John M. *U.S. Defense Planning: A Critique.* Boulder: Westview Press, 1982.

Cooke, James E., ed. *The Federalist.* Middletown: Wesleyan University Press, 1961.

Corson, William R. *The Betrayal.* New York: Ace Books, 1968.

Cortright, David. *Soldiers in Revolt.* Garden City, N.Y.: Doubleday, 1976.

Croizat, Victor. *The Brown Water Navy: The River and Coastal War in Indo-China and Vietnam, 1948–1972.* Poole, U.K.: Blandford Press, 1984.

Dawson, Alan. *55 Days: The Fall of South Vietnam.* Englewood Cliffs, N.J.: Prentice-Hall, 1977.

Dellinger, Dave. *Revolutionary Non-violence.* New York: Doubleday, 1970.

Del Vecchio, John. *The 13th Valley.* New York: Bantam, 1982.

Dengler, Dieter. *Escape from Laos.* Novato, Calif.: Presidio Press, 1979.

Denton, Jeremiah A. *When Hell Was in Session.* New York: Reader's Digest Press, 1976.

Destler, I. M., Leslie H. Gelb, and Anthony Lake. *Our Own Worst Enemy.* New York: Simon & Schuster, 1984.

Dillard, Walter Scott. *Sixty Days to Peace.* Washington, D.C.: U.S. Government Printing Office, 1982.

Doleman, Edgar C., Jr. *Tools of War.* The Vietnam Experience. Boston: Boston Publishing Co., 1984.

Don, Tran Van. *Our Endless War: Inside Vietnam.* Novato, Calif.: Presidio Press, 1978.

Donovan, John C. *The Cold Warriors: A Policy–Making Elite.* Lexington: D.C. Heath, 1974.

Dougan, Clark, and David Fulghum. *The Fall of the South.* The Vietnam Experience. Boston: Boston Publishing Co., 1985.

Dougan, Clark, and Samuel Lipsman. *A Nation Divided.* The Vietnam Experience. Boston: Boston Publishing Co., 1984.

Dougan, Clark, and Steven Weiss. *1968.* The Vietnam Experience. Boston: Boston Publishing Company, 1984.

Doyle, Edward, and Samuel Lipsman. *Setting the Stage.* The Vietnam Experience. Boston: Boston Publishing Co., 1981.

Doyle, Edward, Samuel Lipsman and Stephen Weiss. *Passing the Torch.* The Vietnam Experience. Boston: Boston Publishing Co., 1981.

Downs, Frederick. *The Killing Zone: My Life in the Vietnam War.* New York: Norton, 1978.

Dramesi, John A. *Code of Honor.* New York: Norton, 1975.

Drendel, Lou. *Air War over Southeast Asia.* Carrollton, Tex.: Squadron/Signal Publications, 1984.

———. *B-52 Strato Fortress in Action.* Carrollton, Tex.: Squadron/Signal Publications, 1984.

———. *Huey.* Carrollton, Tex.: Squadron/Signal Publications, 1983.

Dung, Van Tien. *Our Great Spring Victory.* Translated by Foreign Broadcast Service, FBIS Supplement 38, June 7, 1976; FBIS Supplement 42, July 7, 1976.

Dunn, Carroll H. *Base Development in South Vietnam 1965–1970.* Washington, D.C.: U.S. Government Printing Office, 1972.

Dunstan, Simon. *Vietnam Tracks: Armor in Battle 1945–75.* Novato, Calif.: Presidio Press, 1982.

Eastman, James N., Jr., Walter Hanak, and Lawrence J. Paszek, eds. *Aces and Aerial Victories—The United States Air Force in Southeast Asia 1965–1973.* Washington, D.C.: U.S. Government Printing Office, 1976.

Eckhardt, George S. *Command and Control 1950–1969.* Washington, D.C.: U.S. Government Printing Office, 1974.

Eisele, Albert. *Almost to the Presidency: A Biography of Two American Politicians.* Blue Earth, Minn.: Piper Co., 1972.

Elegant, Robert. "How to Lose a War." *Encounter,* August 1981.

Ellsberg, Daniel. *Papers on the War.* New York: Pocket Books, 1972.

Enthoven, Alain C., and K. Wayne Smith. *How Much is Enough: Shaping the Defense Program 1961–1969.* New York: Harper & Row, 1971.

Ezell, Edward Clinton. *The Great Rifle Controversy.* Harrisburg: Stackpole, 1984.

Fall, Bernard. *Hell in a Very Small Place: The Siege of Dien Bien Phu.* Philadelphia: Lippincott, 1966.

———. *Street Without Joy: Insurgency in Vietnam, 1946–1963.* Harrisburg: Stackpole Books, 1961.

———. *The Two Vietnams: A Political and Military Analysis.* New York: Praeger, 1967.

———. *The Viet Minh Regime.* Ithaca: Cornell University Press, 1956.

————, ed. *Ho Chi Minh on Revolution*. New York: Signet, 1968.

Fenn, Charles. *Ho Chi Minh: A Biographical Introduction*. New York: Charles Scribner's Sons, 1973.

First Air Cavalry Division in Vietnam. New York: W. M. Lads Publishing Co., 1967.

The First Air Cavalry Division: Vietnam, August 1965 to December 1969. Tokyo: Dia Nippon Printing Co., 1970.

The First Marine Division and Its Regiments. Washington, D.C.: History and Museums Division, USMC, 1981.

FitzGerald, Frances. *Fire in the Lake: The Vietnamese and the Americans in Vietnam*. Boston: Little, Brown, 1972.

Franck, Thomas M., and Edward Weisband. *Foreign Policy by Congress*. New York: Oxford University Press, 1980.

Fulbright, J. William. *The Arrogance of Power*. New York: Random House, 1967.

————. *The Crippled Giant*. New York: Random House, 1972.

Fulghum, David, and Terrence Maitland. *South Vietnam on Trial*. The Vietnam Experience. Boston: Boston Publishing Co., 1984.

Fulton, William B. *Riverine Operations 1966–1969*. Washington, D.C.: U.S. Government Printing Office, 1973.

Futrell, Robert F. *The United States Air Force: The Advisory Years, 1961 to 1965*. Washington, D.C.: U.S. Government Printing Office, 1981.

Garland, Albert N., ed. *Infantry in Vietnam: Small Unit Actions in the Early Days 1965–66*. Nashville: Battery Press, 1982.

————. *A Distant Challenge: The U.S. Infantryman in Vietnam 1967–1972*. Nashville: Battery Press, 1983.

Garrett, Richard. *P.O.W.* London: David & Charles, 1981.

Gershen, Martin. *Destroy or Die: The True Story of My Lai*. New Rochelle: Arlington House, 1971.

Giap, Vo Nguyen. *Dien Bien Phu*. Hanoi: Foreign Language Publishing House, 1962.

————. *Big Victory, Big Task*. New York: Praeger, 1967.

————. *Unforgettable Days*. Hanoi: Foreign Language Publishing House, 1978.

Gigot, Paul A. "Lost or Merely Forgotten?" *National Review*, August 17, 1979.

Glasser, Ronald J. *365 Days*. New York: Braziller, 1971.

Goff, Stanley, and Robert Sandfors. *Brothers: Black Soldiers in the Nam*. Novato, Calif.: Presidio Press, 1982.

Goldman, Peter, and Tony Fuller. *Charlie Company: What Vietnam Did to Us*. New York: Morrow, 1983.

Goodman, Allan E. *The Lost Peace: America's Search for a Negotiated Settlement of the Vietnam War*. Stanford: Hoover Institution Press, 1978.

Halberstam, David. *The Best and the Brightest*. New York: Random House, 1972.

————. *Ho*. New York: Random House, 1971.

————. *The Making of a Quagmire*. New York: Random House, 1965.

————. *One Very Hot Day*. New York: Warner Books, 1984.

————. *The Powers That Be*. New York: Knopf, 1979.

————. *The Unfinished Odyssey of Robert Kennedy*. New York: Random House, 1968.

Hammer, Richard. *The Court Martial of Lieutenant Calley*. New York: Coward, McCann & Geoghegan, 1971.

Hannah, Norman B. "Vietnam, Now We Know." In *All Quiet on the Eastern Front*. Edited by Anthony T. Bouscaren, Old Greenwich, Conn.: Devin-Adair, 1977.

Harriman, Averell, and Elie Abel. *Special Envoy to Churchill and Stalin, 1941–1946*. New York: Random House, 1975.

Hay, John H., Jr. *Tactical and Matériel Innovations*. Washington, D.C.: U.S. Government Printing Office, 1975.

Heiser, Joseph M., Jr. *Logistic Support*. Washington, D.C.: U.S. Government Printing Office, 1974.

Herr, Michael. *Dispatches*. New York: Knopf, 1977.

Herrington, Stuart A. *Peace with Honor?* Novato, Calif.: Presidio Press, 1983.

————. *Silence Was a Weapon: The Vietnam War in th Villages*. Novato, Calif.: Presidio Press, 1982.

Hersh, Seymour. *Cover-up.* New York: Random House, 1972.

———. *The Price of Power: Kissinger in the Nixon White House.* New York: Summit Books, 1983.

Higgins, Marguerite. *Our Vietnam Nightmare.* New York: Harper & Row, 1965.

Hilgartner, Peter L. "Amphibious Doctrine in Vietnam." In *The Marines in Vietnam 1954–1973.* Washington, D.C.: U.S. Government Printing Office, 1974.

Hilsman, Roger. *To Move a Nation: The Politics of Foreign Policy in the Administration of John F. Kennedy.* Garden City, N.Y.: Doubleday, 1967.

Hinh, Nguyen Duy. *Lam Son 719.* Washington, D.C.: U.S. Government Printing Office, 1981.

———. *Vietnamization and the Cease-Fire.* Washington, D.C.: Center of Military History, 1980.

Holm, Jeanne. *Women in the Military.* Novato, Calif.: Presidio Press, 1982.

Hooper, Edwin B. *Mobility, Support, Endurance: A Story of Naval Operational Logistics in the Vietnam War, 1965–1968.* Washington, D.C.: Naval History Division, U.S. Government Printing Office, 1972.

Hooper, Edwin B., Dean C. Allard, and Oscar P. Fitzgerald. *The United States Navy and the Vietnam Conflict: The Setting of the Stage to 1959.* Washington, D.C.: U.S. Government Printing Office, 1976.

Hoopes, Townsend. *The Devil and John Foster Dulles.* Boston: Atlantic-Little, Brown, 1973.

———. *The Limits of Intervention.* New York: David MacKay Co., 1969.

Horne, A. D., ed. *The Wounded Generation: America After Vietnam.* Englewood Cliffs, N.J.: Prentice Hall, 1981.

Horner, D. M., ed. *The Commanders: Australian Military Leadership in the Twentieth Century.* Boston: George Allen & Unwin, 1984.

Hosmer, Stephen T., et al. *The Fall of South Vietnam: Statements by Vietnamese Military and Civilian Leaders.* Santa Monica: Rand, 1978.

Hubbell, John G. et al. *POW.* New York: Reader's Digest Press, 1976.

Isaacs, Arnold R. *Without Honor: Defeat in Vietnam*
and Cambodia. Baltimore: Johns Hopkins Press, 1983.

Javits, Jacob K. *Who Makes War: The President Versus Congress.* New York: Morrow, 1973.

Johnson, Chalmers. *Autopsy on People's War.* Berkeley: University of California Press, 1973.

Johnson, Haynes, and Bernard Gwertzman. *Fulbright: The Dissenter.* Garden City, N.Y.: Doubleday & Co., 1968.

Johnson, James Turner. *Just War Tradition and the Restraint of War.* Princeton: Princeton University Press, 1981.

Johnson, Lyndon Baines. *The Vantage Point: Perspective of the Presidency 1963–1969.* New York: Popular Library, 1971.

Jordan, Amos A., and William J. Taylor, Jr. *American National Security: Policy and Process.* Baltimore: Johns Hopkins University Press, 1981.

Just, Ward. *Springer.* Boston: Little, Brown, 1974.

Kalb, Marvin, and Elie Abel. *Roots of Involvement: The U.S. in Asia 1784–1971.* New York: Norton, 1971.

Karnow, Stanley. *Vietnam: A History.* New York: Viking, 1983.

Kattenburg, Paul L. *The Vietnam Trauma in American Foreign Policy 1945–1975.* New Brunswick: Transaction, 1980.

Kearns, Doris. *Lyndon Johnson and the American Dream.* New York: Harper & Row, 1976.

Kelly, Francis J. *U.S. Army Special Forces 1961–1971.* Washington, D.C.: U.S. Government Printing Office, 1973.

Khuyen, Dong Van. *The RVNAF.* Washington, D.C.: U.S. Government Printing Office, 1980.

King, Martin Luther, Jr. *Where Do We Go from Here: Chaos or Community?* New York: Bantam, 1967.

King, Peter, ed. *Australia's Vietnam.* Boston: George Allen & Unwin, 1983.

Kinnard, Douglas. *The Secretary of Defense.* Louisville: University of Kentucky Press, 1980.

———. *The War Managers.* Hanover, N.H.: University Press of New England, 1977.

Kissinger, Henry. *White House Years.* Boston: Little, Brown, 1979.

————. *Years of Upheaval.* Boston: Little, Brown, 1982.

Komer, Robert W. *Bureaucracy Does Its Thing: Institutional Constraints on US-GVN Performance.* Santa Monica: Rand Corp., 1972.

Korb, Lawrence J. *The Joint Chiefs of Staff: The First Twenty-five Years.* Bloomington: Indiana University Press, 1976.

Kowet, Don. *A Matter of Honor.* New York: Macmillan, 1984.

Krulak, Victor H. *First to Fight: An Inside View of the U.S. Marine Corps.* Annapolis: U.S. Naval Institute Press, 1984.

Ky, Nguyen Cao. *Twenty Years and Twenty Days.* New York: Stein & Day, 1976.

Lacouture, Jean. *Ho Chi Minh: A Political Biography.* Translated by Peter Wiles. New York: Random House, 1968.

Lansdale, Edward Geary. *In the Midst of Wars: An American's Mission to Southeast Asia.* New York: Harper & Row, 1972.

Larsen, Stanley Robert, and James Lawton Collins, Jr. *Allied Participation in Vietnam.* Washington, D.C.: U.S. Government Printing Office, 1975.

Lavalle, A. J. C., ed. *Airpower and the 1972 Spring Invasion.* Washington, D.C.: U.S. Government Printing Office, 1976.

————, ed. *The Battle for the Skies Over North Vietnam.* Washington, D.C.: U.S. Government Printing Office, 1976.

————, ed. *Last Flight from Saigon,* by Thomas G. Tobin, Arthur E. Laehr, and John F. Hilgenberg. Washington, D.C.: U.S. Government Printing Office, 1978.

————, ed. *The Tale of Two Bridges.* Washington, D.C.: U.S Government Printing Office, 1976.

LeGro, William E. *Vietnam from Cease-Fire to Capitulation.* Washington, D.C.: U.S. Government Printing Office, 1981.

Lewinski, Jorge. *The Camera at War.* New York: Simon & Schuster, 1978.

Lewis, David. *King: A Critical Biography.* New York: Praeger, 1970.

Lewy, Guenter. *America in Vietnam.* New York: Oxford University Press, 1978.

Lichty, Lawrence W. "Comments on the Influence of Television on Public Opinion." In *Vietnam as History,* edited by Peter Braestrup. Washington, D.C.: University Press of America, 1984.

Long, Hoang Ngoc. *Strategy and Tactics.* Washington, D.C.: U.S. Government Printing Office, 1980.

Long, Ngo Vinh. *Before the Revolution: The Vietnamese Peasants Under the French.* Cambridge: MIT Press, 1973.

Long, Nguyen. *After Saigon Fell.* Berkeley: University of California Press, 1981.

Lowry, Timothy S. *And Brave Men, Too.* New York: Crown, 1985.

Luttwak, Edward N. *The Pentagon and the Art of War.* New York: Simon & Schuster, 1985.

Maclear, Michael. *The Ten Thousand Day War: Vietnam 1945–1975.* New York: St. Martin's Press, 1981.

MacPherson, Myra. *Long Time Passing: Vietnam and the Haunted Generation.* New York: Doubleday, 1984.

Mangold, Tom, and John Penycate. *The Tunnels of Cu Chi.* New York: Random House, 1985.

The Marines in Vietnam 1954–1973. Washington, D.C.: History and Museums Division, USMC, 1974.

Marolda, Edward J. and G. Wesley Pryce, III. *A Short History of the United States Navy and the Southeast Asian Conflict 1950–1975.* Washington, D.C.: Naval Historical Center, 1984.

Marr, David G. *Vietnamese Anticolonialism 1885–1925.* Berkeley: University of California Press, 1981.

Marshall, S. L. A. *Ambush: The Battle of Dau Tieng, Also Called The Battle of Dong Ming Chau, War Zone C, Operation Attleboro, and Other Deadfalls in South Vietnam.* New York: Cowles, 1969.

————. *Battles in the Monsoon: Campaigning in the Central Highland, South Vietnam, Summer 1966.* New York: Morrow, 1966.

————. *Bird: The Christmastide Battle.* New York: Cowles, 1968.

————. *The Fields of Bamboo: Dong Tre, Trung Luong,*

and Hoa Hoi: Three Battles Just Beyond the China Sea. New York: Dial, 1971.

———. *West to Cambodia.* New York: Cowles, 1968.

Mason, Robert. *Chicken Hawk.* New York: Viking/Penguin, 1983.

McCarthy, Eugene. *The Year of the People.* New York, Doubleday, 1969.

McDonald, Charles, and A. J. C. Lavalle, eds. *The Vietnamese Air Force 1951–1975: An Analysis of Its Role in Combat,* by William W. Momyer. Washington, D.C.: U.S. Government Printing Office, 1976.

McGovern, James R. *Black Eagle: General Daniel "Chappie" James, Jr., USAF.* University: University of Alabama Press, 1985.

Meconis, Charles A. *With Clumsy Grace: The American Catholic Left 1961–1975.* New York: Seabury-Continuum, 1979.

Mersky, Peter, and Norman Polmar. *The Naval Air War in Vietnam: 1965–1975.* Annapolis: The Nautical and Aviation Publishing Co. of America, 1981.

Mertel, Kenneth D. *Year of the Horse—Vietnam: First Air Cavalry in the Highlands.* New York: Exposition Press, 1968.

The Military Balance 1963–1964. London: International Institute for Strategic Studies, 1963.

The Military Balance 1974–1975. London: International Institute for Strategic Studies, 1974.

Miller, Kenneth E. *Tiger, The LURP Dog.* Boston: Little, Brown, 1983.

Millett, Allan. *Semper Fidelis: The History of the United States Marine Corps.* New York: Macmillan, 1980.

Mills, Nick. *Combat Photographer.* The Vietnam Experience. Boston: Boston Publishing Co., 1983.

Minh, Ho Chi. *Prison Diary.* Hanoi: Foreign Language Publishing House, 1966.

———. *Selected Works,* Vols. 1–4. Hanoi: Foreign Language Publishing House, 1966–67.

Momyer, William W. *Airpower in Three Wars.* Washington, D.C.: U.S. Government Printing Office, 1978.

Morris, Richard B., and Graham W. Irwin, eds. *Harper Encyclopedia of the Modern World.* New York: Harper & Row, 1970.

Morris, Stephen. "Vietnam's Vietnam." *The Atlantic,* January 1985.

Morrocco, John. *Rain of Fire: Air War 1969–1973.* The Vietnam Experience. Boston: Boston Publishing Co., 1984.

Morrocco, John. *Thunder From Above: Air War 1941–1968.* The Vietnam Experience. Boston: Boston Publishing Co., 1985.

Mueller, John E. "Reflections on the Vietnam Antiwar Movement and on the Curious Calm at the War's End." In *Vietnam As History,* edited by Peter Braestrup. Washington, D.C.: University Press of America, 1984.

———. "The Search for the 'Breaking Point' in Vietnam: The Statistics of a Deadly Quarrel." *International Studies Quarterly* 4, no. 4 (December 1980).

———. *War, Presidents, and Public Opinion.* New York: John Wiley, 1973.

Mus, Paul. *Viêt-Nam: Sociologie d'une guerre.* Paris: Editions du Seuil, 1950.

Mus, Paul, and John T. McAlister, Jr. *The Vietnamese and Their Revolution.* New York: Harper & Row, 1970.

Naval Facilities Engineering Command. *Southeast Asia: Building the Bases The History of Construction in Southeast Asia.* Washington, D.C.: U.S. Government Printing Office, 1975.

Neel, Spurgeon. *Medical Support of the U.S. Army in Vietnam 1965–1970.* Washington, D.C.: U.S. Government Printing Office, 1973.

Ngan, Nguyen Ngoc. *The Will of Heaven.* New York: Dutton, 1981.

Nguyen, Hung P. "Communist Offensive Strategy and the Defense of South Vietnam." *Parameters: Journal of the U.S. Army War College* (Winter 1984).

Nicoli, Robert V. "Fire Support Base Development." In *The Marines in Vietnam 1954–1973.* Washington, D.C.: U.S. Government Printing Office, 1974.

Nixon, Richard M. *No More Vietnams.* New York: Arbor House, 1985.

———. *RN: The Memoirs of Richard Nixon.* New York: Grosset & Dunlop, 1978.

Nolan, Keith W. *Battle for Hue: Tet 1968.* Novato, Calif.: Presidio Press, 1983.

O'Ballance, Edgar. *The Indochina War 1945–1954: A Study in Guerrilla Warfare.* London: Faber & Faber, 1964.

Oberdorfer, Don. *TET: The Turning Point of the Vietnam War.* New York: Da Capo, 1983.

O'Brien, William V. *The Conduct of Just and Limited War.* New York: Praeger, 1981.

O'Meara, Andrew P. *Infrastructure and the Marxist Power Seizure: An Analysis of the Communist Model of Revolution.* New York: Vantage Press, 1973.

O'Neill, Robert J. *General Giap: Politician and Strategist.* New York: Praeger, 1969.

Ott, David Ewing. *Field Artillery 1954–1973.* Washington, D.C.: U.S. Government Printing Office, 1975.

Owens, Mackubin T. "Vietnam and Just War Tradition." *This World,* Winter 1984.

Palmer, Bruce, Jr. *The 25-Year War: America's Military Role in Vietnam.* Lexington: University of Kentucky Press, 1984.

Palmer, Dave R. *Summons of the Trumpet: U.S.-Vietnam in Perspective.* New York: Ballantine, 1984.

Palmer, Gregory. *The McNamara Strategy and the Vietnam War: Program Budgeting in the Pentagon 1960–1968.* Westport, Conn.: Greenwood Press, 1978.

Parker, William D. *U.S. Marine Corps Civil Affairs in I Corps, Republic of Vietnam, April 1966–April 1967.* Washington, D.C.: Historical Division, USMC, 1970.

Paschall, Rod. "White Star in Laos: A Study in Miscalculation." Manuscript. Carlisle Barracks, Pa.: U.S. Army Military History Institute, 1985.

Patti, Archimedes L. A. *Why Vietnam? Prelude to America's Albatross.* Berkeley: University of California Press, 1980.

Pearson, Willard. *The War in the Northern Provinces 1966–1968.* Washington, D.C.: U.S. Government Printing Office, 1975.

Peers, W. R. *The My Lai Inquiry.* New York: Norton, 1979.

Pentagon Papers. Gravel edition. Boston: Beacon Press, 1971.

Pentagon Papers. New York Times edition. Toronto: Bantam Books, 1970.

Pettit, Clyde Edwin. *The Experts.* Secaucus: Lyle Stuart, 1975.

Pilger, John. *The Last Day.* New York: Vintage, 1976.

Pike, Douglas. *History of the Vietnamese Communist Party.* Palo Alto: Hoover Institution, 1978.

———. *Viet Cong: The Organization and Techniques of the National Liberation Front of South Vietnam.* Cambridge: MIT Press, 1966.

———. *The Viet Cong Strategy of Terror.* Saigon: U.S. Information Agency, 1970.

Pisor, Robert. *The End of the Line: The Siege of Khe Sanh.* New York: Norton, 1982.

Ploger, Robert R. *U.S. Army Engineers 1965–1970.* Washington, D.C.: U.S. Government Printing Office, 1974.

Podhoretz, Norman. *Why We Were in Vietnam.* New York: Simon & Schuster, 1982.

Ponchaud, Francois. *Cambodia: Year Zero.* Translated by Nancy Amphous. New York: Holt, Rinehart & Winston, 1978.

Popkin, Samuel L. "Pacification: Politics and the Village." *Asian Survey,* August 1970.

———. *The Rational Peasant: The Political Economy of Rural Society in Vietnam.* Berkeley: University of California Press, 1979.

POW: A Definitive History of the American Prisoner of War Experience in Vietnam 1964–1973. New York: Reader's Digest Press, 1976.

POW-MIA Fact Book. Washington, D.C.: Department of Defense, February 1985.

Powers, Thomas. *The War at Home: Vietnam and the American People.* New York: Grossman, 1973.

Prados, John. *The Sky Would Fall: Operation Vulture; The U.S. Bombing Mission in Indochina, 1954.* New York: Dial, 1983.

Prugh, George S. *Law at War: Vietnam 1964–1973.* Washington, D.C.: U.S. Government Printing Office, 1975.

Pruessen, Ronald W. *John Foster Dulles: The Road to Peace.* New York: The Free Press, 1982.

Quigley, Thomas E., ed. *American Catholics and Vietnam.* Grand Rapids: Eerdman's, 1968.

Reeves, R. "Fallibility and the Fourth Estate." *Esquire,* February, 1978.

Ridgway, Matthew B. *Soldier: The Memoirs of Matthew B. Ridgway.* New York: Harper & Bros., 1956.

Rienzi, Thomas M. *Communications-Electronics 1962–1970.* Washington, D.C.: U.S. Government Printing Office, 1972.

Risner, Robinson. *The Passing of the Night: My Seven Years as a Prisoner of the North Vietnamese.* New York: Random House, 1974.

Riverine Warfare: The U.S. Navy's Operations on Inland Waterways. Washington, D.C.: U.S. Government Printing Office, 1968.

Robbins, Christopher. *Air America.* New York: G. P. Putnam's Sons, 1979.

Roche, John P. *Sentenced to Life: Reflections on Politics, Education, and Law.* New York: Macmillan, 1974.

Rogers, Bernard William. *Cedar Falls-Junction City: A Turning Point.* Washington, D.C.: U.S. Government Printing Office, 1974.

Rosen, Stephen Peter. "Vietnam and the American Theory of Limited War." *International Security* 7, no. 2. (Fall 1982).

Rosenthal, James. "The Myth of the Last POWs." *The New Republic,* July 1, 1985.

Rowe, James N. *Five Years to Freedom.* Boston: Little, Brown, 1971.

Roy, Jules. *The Battle of Dien Bien Phu.* Translated by Robert Baldick. New York: Harper & Row, 1965; Carroll & Graff, 1984.

Rubin, Jerry. *Do It!* New York: Simon & Schuster, 1970.

———. *Growing (Up) at 37.* New York: M. Evans, 1976.

Rust, William J. and the editors of U.S. News Books. *Kennedy in Vietnam.* New York: Charles Scribner's Sons, 1985.

Sack, John. *Lieutenant Calley: His Own Story.* New York: Viking, 1971.

Sagan, Ginette, and Stephen Denney. *Violations of Human Rights in the Socialist Republic of Vietnam.* Palo Alto: Aurora Foundation, 1983.

Salinger, Pierre. *With Kennedy.* Garden City, N.Y.: Doubleday, 1966.

Salisbury, Harrison E., ed. *Vietnam Reconsidered: Lessons from a War.* New York: Harper & Row, 1984.

Sananikone, Gudone. *The Royal Lao Government and U.S. Army Advice and Support.* Washington, D.C.: U.S. Government Printing Office, 1981.

Santoli, Al. *Everything We Had.* New York: Random House, 1981.

———. *To Bear Any Burden: The Vietnam War and Its Aftermath in the Words of Americans and Southeast Asians.* New York: Dutton, 1985.

Schandler, Herbert Y. *The Unmaking of a President: Lyndon Johnson and Vietnam.* Princeton: Princeton University Press, 1977.

Schell, Jonathan. *The Village of Ben Suc.* New York: Knopf, 1967.

Schlemmer, Benjamin. *The Raid.* New York: Harper & Row, 1976.

Schlesinger, Arthur, Jr. *A Thousand Days: John F. Kennedy in the White House.* Boston: Houghton Mifflin, 1965.

———. *Robert Kennedy and His Times.* Boston: Houghton Mifflin, 1976.

Scholl-Latour, Peter. *Death in the Rice Fields: An Eyewitness Account of Vietnam's Three Wars 1945–1979.* New York: St. Martin's Press, 1985.

Sharp, U. S. G. *Strategy for Defeat: Vietnam in Retrospect.* Novato, Calif.: Presidio Press, 1978.

Sharp, U. S. G., and William C. Westmoreland. *Report on the War in Vietnam.* Washington, D.C.: U.S. Government Printing Office, 1968.

Shawcross, William. *Sideshow: Kissinger, Nixon, and the Destruction of Cambodia.* New York: Simon & Schuster, 1979.

Shore, Moyers S. II. *The Battle for Khe Sanh.* Washington, D.C.: Historical Branch, USMC, 1969.

Shulimson, Jack. *U.S. Marines in Vietnam: An Expanding War 1966.* Washington, D.C.: U.S. Government Printing Office, 1982.

Shulimson, Jack, and Charles M. Johnson. *U.S. Marines in Vietnam: The Landing and the Buildup 1965.* Washington, D.C.: U.S. Government Printing Office, 1978.

Simmons, Edwin H. "Marine Corps Operations in Vietnam: 1965–66, 1967, 1968, 1969–72." In *The Marines in Vietnam 1954–1973.* Washington, D.C.: U.S. Government Printing Office, 1974.

Simpson, Charles M., III. *Inside the Green Berets: The.*

First Thirty Years. Novato, Calif.: Presidio Press, 1983.

Smith, Harvey H., et al. *Area Handbook for North Vietnam.* Washington, D.C.: U.S. Government Printing Office, 1967.

———. *Area Handbook for South Vietnam.* Washington, D.C.: U.S. Government Printing Office, 1967.

Smith, R. B. *An International History of the Vietnam War: Revolution Versus Containment 1955–61.* New York: St. Martin's Press, 1983.

Snepp, Frank. *Decent Interval.* New York: Random House, 1977.

Spector, Ronald H. *Researching the Vietnam Experience.* Washington, D.C.: U.S. Army Center of Military History, 1984.

———. *United States Army in Vietnam: Advice and Support: The Early Years 1941–1960.* Washington, D.C.: U.S. Government Printing Office, 1983.

Stanton, Shelby L. *Green Berets at War.* Novato, Calif.: Presidio Press, 1985.

———. *The Rise and Fall of an American Army: U.S. Ground Forces in Vietnam 1965–1973.* Novato, Calif.: Presidio Press, 1985.

———. *Vietnam Order of Battle.* Washington, D.C.: U.S. News Books, 1981.

Starry, Donn A. *Mounted Combat in Vietnam.* Washington, D.C.: U.S. Government Printing Office, 1979.

Steele, Ronald. *Walter Lippmann and the American Century.* New York: Random House, 1980.

Stevenson, Charles A. *The End of Nowhere: American Policy Toward Laos Since 1954.* Boston: Beacon Press, 1973.

Stockdale, Jim, and Sybil Stockdale. *In Love and War: The Story of a Family's Ordeal and Sacrifice During the Vietnam Years.* New York: Harper & Row, 1984.

Stolfi, Russell H. *U.S. Marine Corps Civil Action Efforts in Vietnam, March 1965–March 1966.* Washington, D.C.: Historical Branch, USMC, 1968.

Stuckey, John D., and Joseph H. Pistorius. *Mobilization of the Army National Guard and Army Reserve: Historical Perspective and the Vietnam War.* Carlisle Barracks, Pa.: U.S. Army War College, 1984.

Summers, Harry G., Jr. "The Bitter Triumph of Ia Drang." *American Heritage,* February 1984.

———. "How We Lost." *The New Republic,* April 29, 1985.

———. "Politics and Culture in Southeast Asia." *Military Review,* June 1970.

———. "Vietnam Reconsidered." *The New Republic,* July 12, 1982.

———. "Tet: 15 Years After." *The New Republic,* February 7, 1983.

———. *On Strategy: A Critical Analysis of the Vietnam War.* Novato, Calif.: Presidio Press, 1982.

Surrey, David S. *Choice of Conscience: Vietnam Era Military and Draft Resisters in Canada.* New York: Praeger, 1982.

Sutsakhan, Sak. *The Khmer Republic at War and the Final Collapse.* Washington, D.C.: Indochina Monograph, U.S. Army Center of Military History, 1980.

Szulc, Tad. *The Illusion of Peace: Foreign Policy in the Nixon Years.* New York: Viking, 1978.

Tang, Truong Nhu with David Chanoff and Doan Van Toai. *A Viet Cong Memoir.* Washington, D.C.: Harcourt Brace Jovanovich, 1985.

Taylor, Keith Weller. *The Birth of Vietnam.* Berkeley: University of California Press, 1983.

Taylor, Maxwell D. *Swords and Plowshares.* New York: Norton, 1972.

———. *The Uncertain Trumpet.* New York: Harper's, 1959.

Terry, Wallace. *Bloods: An Oral History of the Vietnam War by Black Veterans.* New York: Random House, 1984.

The Third Marine Division and Its Regiments. Washington, D.C.: Historical and Museums Division, USMC, 1983.

Tho, Tran Dinh. *The Cambodian Incursion.* Washington, D.C.: Indochina Monograph, U.S. Army Center of Military History, 1979.

———. *Pacification.* Washington, D.C.: Indochina Monograph, U.S. Army Center of Military History, 1979.

Thompson, Robert. *Defeating Communist Insurgency.* New York: Praeger, 1966.

———. *No Exit From Vietnam.* New York: McKay, 1970.

———. *Peace Is Not at Hand.* New York: McKay, 1974.

———. *Revolutionary War In World Strategy 1945–1949.* New York: Taplinger, 1970.

Tilford, Earl H., Jr. *Search and Rescue in Southeast Asia 1961–1975.* Washington, D.C.: U.S. Government Printing Office, 1980.

Taoi, Doan Van and David Chanoff. *The Vietnam Gulag.* New York: Simon & Schuster, 1986.

Tolson, John J. *Airmobility 1961–1971.* Vietnam Studies. Washington, D.C.: U.S. Government Printing Office, 1973.

Tra, Tran Van. *Ending the 30 Years War.* Ho Chi Minh City: Literature Publishing House, 1982.

Tregakis, Richard. *Southeast Asia: Building the Bases; The History of Construction in Southeast Asia.* Washington, D.C.: U.S. Government Printing Office, 1975.

Triotti, John. *Phantom Over Vietnam: Fighter Pilot, USMC.* Novato, Calif.: Presidio Press, 1984.

Truong, Ngo Quang. *The Easter Offensive of 1972.* Washington, D.C.: U.S. Government Printing Office, 1980.

———. *Territorial Forces.* Washington, D.C.: Center for Military History, 1981.

The Truth about Vietnam-China Relations over the Last Thirty Years. Hanoi: Ministry of Foreign Affairs, 1979.

Tulich, Eugene. *The United States Coast Guard in Southeast Asia During the Vietnam Conflict.* Washington, D.C.: United States Coast Guard Historical Monograph Program, 1975.

Turley, G. H. *The Easter Offensive: Vietnam 1972.* Novato, Calif.: Presidio Press, 1985.

Turner, Kathleen J. *Lyndon Johnson's Dual War: Vietnam and the Press.* Chicago: University of Chicago Press, 1985.

U.S. Department of State. Bureau of Public Affairs. *Background Notes: Vietnam.* Washington, D.C.: U.S. Government Printing Office, 1984.

U.S. House of Representatives. Committee on International Relations. *The War Powers Resolution.* 94th Congress, 2nd Session. Washington, D.C.: U.S. Government Printing Office, 1975.

U.S. Joint Logistics Review Board. *Logistic Support in the Vietnam Era: A Report.* Washington, D.C.: U.S. Department of Defense, 1970.

U.S. Senate. Committee on Armed Services. *Report on Airlift and Sealift to South Vietnam.* 90th Congress, 1st Session. Washington, D.C.: U.S. Government Printing Office, 1967.

U.S. Senate. Committee on Foreign Relations. *Termination of Middle East and South Asia Resolutions,* Report to Accompany Senate Concurrent Resolution 64. 91st Congress, 2nd Session. Washington, D.C.: U.S. Government Printing Office, 1970.

Vien, Cao Van. *The Final Collapse.* Washington, D.C.: U.S. Government Printing Office, 1983.

———. *The U.S. Adviser.* Washington, D.C.: U.S. Government Printing Office, 1980.

Vien, Cao Van, and Dong Van Khuyen. *Reflections of the Vietnam War.* Washington, D.C.: U.S. Government Printing Office, 1980.

Vietnam: 10 Years Later. Fort Benjamin Harrison: Defense Information School, 1984.

Vongsavanh, Solitchay. *RLA Military Operations and Activities in the Laotian Panhandle.* Washington, D.C.: U.S. Government Printing Office, 1981.

Wain, Barry. *The Refused.* New York: Simon & Schuster, 1981.

Walt, Lewis W. *Strange War, Strange Strategy.* New York: Funk & Wagnall, 1976.

Walzer, Michael. *Just and Unjust Wars: A Moral Argument with Historical Illustrations.* New York: Basic Books, 1977.

Warner, Denis. *The Last Confucian.* New York: Macmillan, 1963.

Webb, James. *Fields of Fire.* Englewood Cliffs, N.J.: Prentice-Hall, 1978.

Webb, Kate. *On the Other Side: 23 Days with the Viet Cong.* New York: Quadrangle, 1972.

West, Francis J. *Small Unit Action in Vietnam, Summer 1966.* Washington, D.C.: U.S. Government Printing Office, 1967.

———. *The Village.* New York: Harper & Row, 1972.

Westmoreland, William C. *A Soldier Reports.* Garden City, N.Y.: Doubleday, 1976.

Weyand, Fred C. "Serving the People: The Basic Case for the U.S. Army." *Commander's Call,* May/June 1976.

————. "Serving the People: The Need for Military Power." *Military Review,* December 1976.

————. "Vietnam Myths and American Military Realities." *Commander's Call,* July/August 1976.

Wheeler, John. *Touched with Fire: The Future of the Vietnam Generation.* New York: Franklin Watts, 1984.

Whitlow, Robert H. *U.S. Marines in Vietnam: The Advisory and Combat Assistance Era, 1954–1964.* Washington, D.C.: U.S. Government Printing Office, 1977.

Wilcox, Fred A. *Waiting for an Army to Die: The Tragedy of Agent Orange.* New York: Random House, 1983.

Willenz, June A. *Women Veterans: America's Forgotten Heroines.* New York: Continuum, 1984.

Williams, William Appleman, et al, eds. *America in Vietnam: A Documentary History.* Garden City, N.Y.: Anchor Press/Doubleday, 1985.

Wills, Garry. *The Kennedy Imprisonment: A Meditation on Power.* Boston: Little, Brown & Co., 1982.

Windchy, Eugene C. *Tonkin Gulf.* Garden City, N.Y.: Doubleday, 1971.

Zaroulis, Nancy, and Gerald Sullivan. *Who Spoke Up? American Protest Against the War in Vietnam 1963–1975.* Garden City, N.Y.: Doubleday, 1984.

Zumwalt, Elmo R., Jr. *On Watch.* New York: Quadrangle, 1976.

index

A

Abel, Elie, 245

Abrams, Creighton W., Jr., 47, 56, 58, 63, 117, 185, 362

Accelerated Pacification Program. *See* Phoenix Program

Ace, 63-64, 74

Acheson, Dean, 211, 310

Ad Hoc Task Force on Vietnam, 46, 64, 123, 210-211, 267

Advisory effort, U.S., 64-66, 325

Aerial evacuation, 66, 148, 150, 249

Aerial warfare. *See* Ace; Barrel Roll operations; Bolo; Bombing; types of planes

Agent Orange, 39, 66-68, 74

Air America, 68

Airborne forces, 69-70
  See Parachutes; Pathfinders

Air cavalry, 70

Air Controller. *See* FAC (Forward Air Controller)

Aircraft
  Caribou, 110, 162
  1st Marine Wing, 165-166
  U.S. losses, 74
  See also Bombers; Fighters and fighter-bombers; Gunships; Helicopters; Sorties

Aircraft carriers, 70-71

Air cushion vehicles, 71
  See also River Patrol Force

Air defense, 71-72

Air force, North Vietnamese. *See* Air defense; fighters and fighter bombers

Air force, South Vietnamese. *See* fighters and fighter bombers; SVNAF (South Vietnamese Armed Forces)

Air Force, U.S., 73-74
  casualties, 74
  divisions, 143
  organizational units, 168
  1st Aviation Brigade, 162
  3rd Tactical Fighter Wing, 36, 97
  7th Air Force, 37, 74, 143, 166
  8th Tactical Fighter Wing, 99
  12th Tactical Fighter Wing, 108
  14th Air Commando Wing, 37
  31st Tactical Fighter Wing, 40
  35th Tactical Fighter Wing, 37
  164th Aviation Group, 169
  173rd Airborne, 54
  315th Air Commando Wing, 37
  366th Tactical Wing, 37
  460th Tactical Wing, 37
  483rd Tactical Air Wing, 39, 108
  834th Air Division, 39, 143
  See also Chief of Staff, U.S. Air Force; Organization for Combat

Air Force Cross, 72-73, 137

Airfields, U.S. *See* Base camps, U.S., names

Airlift, tactical. *See* Tactical airlift

Airlift Control Center (ALCC), 150

Airlifts
  homeless children, 59
  military command, 248-249
  tactical, 239-240

E

G

H

I

J

K

L

Q

R

T

W

X

Y

Z